A Bibliography of Police Administration, Public Safety and Criminology
TO JULY 1, 1965

A Bibliography of Police Administration, Public Safety and Criminology

TO JULY 1, 1965

By

PROFESSOR WILLIAM H. HEWITT, B.S., M.A.

Chairman, Department of Police Science
State University of New York
Farmingdale, L.I., New York

With a Foreword by

OSCAR H. IBELE, Jr., Ph.D.

Professor of Political Science
Kent State University
Kent, Ohio

CHARLES   C   THOMAS   ·   PUBLISHER
Springfield   ·   Illinois   ·   U.S.A.

Published and Distributed Throughout the World by

CHARLES C THOMAS • PUBLISHER

BANNERHOUSE HOUSE

301-327 East Lawrence Avenue, Springfield, Illinois, U.S.A.

NATCHEZ PLANTATION HOUSE

735 North Atlantic Boulevard, Fort Lauderdale, Florida, U.S.A.

With THOMAS BOOKS *careful attention is given to all details of manufacturing and design. It is the Publisher's desire to present books that are satisfactory as to their physical qualities and artistic possibilities and appropriate for their particular use.* THOMAS BOOKS *will be true to those laws of quality that assure a good name and good will.*

Printed in the United States of America
N-10

To all those serious students of contemporary police administration and public safety who strive so hard to achieve the ideal in American police administration—a professional police service for the American people.

FOREWORD

We have in this work what I believe to be the first serious attempt to fill a void in the field of police administration—the absence of a comprehensive bibliography. The publisher is to be congratulated for his recognition of this need, and the author is to be commended for his painstaking and thorough analysis of sources, and for his splendid achievement in providing a useful instrument for further research in the area. This is a comprehensive bibliography covering police administration, criminology, criminal law and police science.

The author seems well qualified to undertake this study, having had a background of academic studies in police administration and political science, teaching on the collegiate level, and considerable experience in police work. He has numerous publications to his credit, and is in demand as a consultant to police organizations. His bibliography is the first attempt in the sphere of criminal justice to aid students, researchers, police administrators and laymen in their search for relevant information.

Fortunately, the material included does not confine itself to the United States, but is international and comparative in scope, offering sources and ideas from the rich experience of a variety of nations which function under diverse philosophies and institutions. Completely and systematically alphabetized, and including approximately 11,000 listings, the book is organized according to functions: detective, patrol, traffic, personnel and training, administration, technical services and corrections. There is an extensive section on public administration and juvenile delinquency which does not appear in any other published works. I believe the author has used good judgment in avoiding selectivity in favor of an all-inclusive coverage.

This book should be a part of all police training academy libraries, and should be found on the shelves of libraries of colleges and universities where police administration degrees are conferred. In addition, it deserves a place in the libraries of police departments of the larger cities in the United States and other English speaking nations. It would certainly seem to be an essential part of the book collection of every student of police administration.

OSCAR H. IBELE, JR., PH.D.
Professor of Political Science
Kent State University
Kent, Ohio

ACKNOWLEDGMENTS

A reference text of this kind, a first to serve the law enforcement and public safety community, owes much thanks to many. However, the author desires to express his special appreciation to many authors who furnished their own entire bibliography collection; to many individuals who supplied reference lists of materials from their own personal files; and to the many scholars and academicians for providing encouragement and guidance during the production of this text, for without their help this reference document could not have been realized. A special debt of thanks is due Dr. Oscar H. Ibele, Jr., Professor of Political Science, Kent State University, for his special guidance, counsel, and for supplying the Foreword to this document. Last, and not least, a special thanks is due my wife, Barbara, for typing the entire manuscript.

W.H.H.

HOW TO USE THIS REFERENCE TEXT

The author has arranged this text in complete alphabetical format to enhance its use. Police departments, in the United States, are organized according to functions, that is, corrections, detective operations, patrol, traffic, etc. Therefore, the chapters are in alphabetical order by function. The subheadings within each chapter are also in alphabetical order, again to ease the use of this document. In addition, all articles and authors within each chapter, and subheading, are completely alphabetized. In other words, *the entire text is completely alphabetized.* One need only know the chapter, and/or subheading, to find his desired reference material rapidly. Where an article should have been crossed-referenced into another chapter, and/or subheading, because of subject matter, it has been accomplished. There are a total of nine chapters, sixty-four subheadings and over 11,000 entries.

Appendix I contains a complete alphabetical listing, by abbreviated initials, of all journals and periodicals used in the many entries throughout the text. Appendix II contains an alphabetical listing of all publishers, and addresses, that appear in this text. It is the author's desire to assist the researcher in securing the desired material with dispatch.

If anyone possesses a bibliography list or has any knowledge of published, or unpublished, materials which do not appear in this volume, the author would appreciate receiving this information. This will aid in preparing future supplements to this volume.

CONTENTS

A Bibliography of Police Administration, Public Safety and Criminology
TO JULY 1, 1965

Chapter One

CORRECTIONAL ADMINISTRATION

PROBATION, PAROLE AND PENOLOGY

Abrahamsen, David: Evolution of the Treatment of Criminals, in D. H. Hoch (ed.), *Failures in Psychiatric Treatment.* New York, Grune and Stratton, 1948.

Adams, W. Thomas, and Barker, Jordon H.: The Social Structure of a Correctional Insituation, JCLC&PS, Vol.49, No.5 (1958-59), 417.

Advisory Council of Judges of the National Probation and Parole Association: *Guides for Sentencing.* New York, The Association, 1957.

Air Transport of Prisoners, TPC, Vol.31 (Nov., 1964), 10.

Akers, Elmer R.: A Prison Trade School—Students and Training, JCLC&PS, Vol.35, No.5 (Jan.-Feb., 1945), 311.

Alexander, Myrl E.: *Jail Administration.* Springfield, Thomas, 1957.

Allen, Francis A.: Criminal Justice, Legal Values and the Rehabilitative Ideal, JCLC&PS (Sept.-Oct., 1959).

Allen, Robert M.: Problems of Parole, JCLC&PS, Vol.38, No.1 (Mar.-Apr., 1947-48), 7-13.

Alt, Herschel: The Training School and Residential Treatment, FP, Vol.16 (Mar., 1952), 32-35.

American Academy of Political and Social Science: *Crime and the American Penal System.* Washington, D.C., The Academy, 1962.

American Correctional Association: *Manual of Correctional Standards.* New York, American Correctional Association, 1959.

American Law Institute: *Model Penal Code, Proposed Official Draft.* Philadelphia, The American Law Institute, 1962.

American Prison Association: Committee on Classification and Casework, *Handbook on the Inmate's Relationship with Persons from Outside the Adult Correctional Institution.* New York, The Association, 1953.

————: Committee on Personnel Standards and Training, *In-Service Training Standards for Prison Custodial Officers.* New York, The Association, 1953.

————: Committee on Riots, *A Statement Concerning Causes, Preventive Measures, and Methods of Controlling Prison Riots and Disturbances.* New York, The Association, 1953.

————: Committee to Revise the 1946 Manual of Suggested Standards for a State Correctional System, *A Manual of Correctional Standards.* New York, the Association, 1954.

————: *Handbook on Classification in Correctional Institutions.* New York, The Association, 1947.

————: *Handbook on Pre-release Preparation in Correctional Institutions.* New York, The Association, 1950.

————: *Library Manual for Correctional Institutions.* New York, The Association, 1950.

————: *Prison Riots and Disturbances.* New York, The Association, 1953.

————: *Proceedings of the Annual Congress of Correction of the American Prison Association.* New York, The Association, published annually.

Arnold, Wm. R.: A Functional Explanation of Recidivism, JCLC&PS, Vol.56, No.2 (June, 1965), 212-220.

Baker, J. E.: Inmate Self-Government, JCLC&PS, Vol.55, No.1 (Mar., 1964). 39.

Barker, Gordon H., and Adams, W. Thomas: The Social Structure of a Correctional Institution, JCLC&PS, Vol.49 (1959), 417-422.

Barnes, Alfred J.: A Follow-up Study of Minnesota Reformatory Inmates, JCLC&PS, Vol. 43, No.5 (Jan.-Feb., 1953), 622.

Barnes, Harry E.: *A Concise Plan for the Organization of a State Department of Correction.* Institute of Local Government, Pennsylvania State College, College Park, 1945.

————: Transportation of Criminals, ESS, Vol. 15,   90.

Bass, Bernard M., and Dobbins, D. A.: Effects of Unemployment on White and Negro Prison Admissions in Louisiana, JCLC&PS, Vol.48, No.5 (Jan.-Feb., 1958), 522.

Bates, Sanford: The Establishment and Early Years of the Federal Probation System, FP, Vol.14 (June, 1950), 16-21.

————: One World in Penology, JCL&C, Vol.38, No.6. (Mar.-Apr., 1947-48), 565-575.

Bateson, Charles: *The Convict Ships, 1787-1868.* Glasgow, Brown & Ferguson, 1959.

Bell, Marjorie (ed.): *Cooperation in Crime Control.* 1944 Yearbook. New York, National Probation Association, 1945.

————: *Parole in Principle and Practice.* New York, National Probation Association, 1957.

Bennett, James V.: Correctional Problems the Courts Can Help Solve, C&D, No.7 (Jan., 1961), 1-8.

————: Delaware Abolishes Capital Punishment, ABAJ, Vol.44 (Nov., 1958), 1053-1054.

————: Prison Population Increase, TPC (Feb., 1961), 35.

————: Progress Report on Jails, PW, No.7 (Mar., 1945), 9-11.

————: The Story of McNeil Island Penitentiary and a Correctional Program Dedicated to Preparation for Release, *Police,* Vol.4, No.5 (May-June, 1960), 23-28.

Biscailuz, E.: Los Angeles County Jail Units, Proceedings of the American Prison Association, 1947, 58-60.

Bixby, F. Lovell, and McCorkle, Lloyd W.: Applying the Principles of Group Therapy in Correctional Institutions, FP, Vol.14, No.1 (Mar., 1950), 36-40.

————: Guided Group Interaction in Correctional Work, ASR, Vol. 16 (Aug., 1951), 455-459.

Black, James V.: Pilot Sentencing Institute, *Correction,* Vol.50, No.4 (1959-60), 358.

Blackinston, Don T.: Previous Criminal Records and the Indeterminate Sentence in Cook County, CJ, No.76 (Sept., 1948).

Blake, Marilyn A.: Probation Is Not Casework, FP, Vol.12 (June, 1948), 54-57.

Bogen, David: Large Scale Detention, *Probation* (Feb., 1945), 65-68, 86-90.

Boolsen, Frank M.: *Jail Practices and Procedures.* Sacramento, California State Dept. of Education, 1954.

Bridges, Francis R., Jr.: Probation and Parole Are Effective, POLICE, Vol.9, No.2 (Nov.-Dec., 1964), 40-45.

Brown, Paul R.: The Advantage of Segregating Inmates, Agitators and Trouble Makers, PW, Vol.12 (Sept.-Oct., 1950), 14-16, 21.

Bruce, Andrew A.: A Travesty of Justice, *Proceedings of the American Prison Association,* 1946.

Caldwell, E. R.: *Redhannah, Delaware's Whipping Post.* Philadelphia, University of Pennsylvania Press, 1947.

Caldwell, Morris G.: Group Dynamics in the Prison Community, JCLC&PS, Vol.46 (1955-56), 648-657.

————: Review of a New Type of Probation Study Made in Alabama, FP, Vol.15, No.2 (June, 1951), 3-11.

California Laws Relating to Youthful Offenders —Including the Youth Authority Act and of the Juvenile Court Law. Sacramento, prepared by California Youth Authority (Sept., 1953).

California State Board of Corrections: *Minimum Jail Standards: Including Standards for Feeding, Clothing and Bedding.* Sacramento, Calif. State Board of Corrections, 1952.

California State Board of Corrections and Special Crime Study Commissions: *Source for the Study of the Administration of Criminal Justice.* Sacramento, Calif. State Board of Corrections, Apr., 1949.

California State Department of Corrections: Advisory Committee on Institutional Recreation, *Preliminary Report: Recreation in the Department of Corrections.* Sacramento, Calif. State Dept. of Corrections, Mar., 1950. (Mimeo.)

————: *An Introduction to Classification and Treatment in State Correctional Service.* Sacramento, Correctional Employees Training Manual, No.3, Calif. State Dept. of Corrections, 1953.

————: *Biennial Report 1959-1960, Department of Corrections.* Sacramento, Dept. of Corrections, Adult Authority Board of Corrections, Board of Trustees, 1961.

————: *California Correction—Parole Program: A Review.* Sacramento, Calif. State Dept. of Corrections, 1962.

————: *California Prisoners, 1960: Summary Statistics of Prisoners and Parolees.* Sacramento, Research Division, Administrative Statistics Section, 1961.

————: *Custodial Procedures in State Correctional Service.* Sacramento, Correctional Employees Training Manual, No.2, Calif. State Dept. of Corrections, 1952.

————: *Supervision Techniques in State Correctional Service.* Sacramento, Employees Training Manual, No.4, Calif. State Dept. of Corrections.

California State Department of Education, Bureau of Industrial Education: *Jail Practice and Procedure.* Sacramento, Dept. of Education.

————: *Powers and Duties of the Sheriff and other County Officers.* Sacramento, Dept. of Education.

————: *Transportation of Prisoners.* Sacramento, Dept. of Education, 1949.

————: *Prisoner Transportation Manual Describing Methods of Transporting Persons*

Under Restraint. Sacramento, Dept. of Education, 1951.

California State Recreation Commission: *Plan for Development of Recreation in the California Correctional Institutions.* Sacramento, Calif. State Recreation Commission, 1951.

Campbell, James M.: Let's Talk About Food, PW, Vol.15 (Sept.-Oct., 1953), 22-23.

Campion, Donald: The State Police and the Death Penalty, *Canadian Joint Committee on Capital and Corporal Punishment,* 1955.

Camus, Albert: *Reflections on the Guillotine.* Michigan City, Fridtjof-Karla, 1959.

Canizio, Frank: *A Man Against Fate.* New York, Permabooks, 1958.

Cantine, H., and Ranier, D. (ed.): *Prison Etiquette.* Bearsville, N.Y., Retort Press, 1950.

Cartwright, Dorwin: Achieving Change in People: Some Applications of Group Dynamics Theory, HR, Vol.4 (1951), 381-392.

————: *The Modern Jail: Design, Equipment and Operation.* Keene, Texas, Continental Press, 1958.

Cass, Edward A.: Jails for Profit, PW, Vol.7, No.3 (Sept., 1945).

Cavan, Ruth S., and Zemans, Eugene: Marital Relationships of Prisoners, JCL&C, Vol.49 (May-June, 1958), 133-39.

Chandler, Henry P.: Latter-Day Procedures in the Sentencing and Treatment of Offenders in the Federal Courts, FP, Vol.16 (Mar., 1952), 3-12.

Chappell, Richard: Federal Probation Service: Its Growth and Progress, FP, Vol.11 (Dec., 1947), 29-34.

Chase, Robert L.: Community's Responsibility to the Jail, PW, Vol.12 (July-Aug., 1950), 3-5.

Chenault, Price: *Diagnostic and Remedial Teaching in Correctional Institutions.* Albany, New York Dept. of Correction, 1945.

————: Education, in Paul Tappan (ed.), *Contemporary Correction.* New York, McGraw-Hill, 1951.

————: Treatment Techniques in Correctional Institutions, *Proceedings of the American Prison Association,* 1947.

Chessman, Caryl: *Cell 2455—Death Row.* New York, Prentice-Hall, 1954.

A Chronology of Corrections, The Last Half Century in the United States, NPPAJ, Vol.3 (1957), 413-468.

Cicuourel, Aaron V.: The Prison: Studies in Institutional Organization and Change, JCLC&PS, Vol.53, No.2 (June-Aug., 1962), 243.

Civil Service Assembly: *Placement and Probation in the Public Service.* Chicago, Publication No. CS23, Civil Service Commission, 1946.

Clarke, Eric K.: Group Therapy in Rehabilitation, FP, Vol.16 (Dec., 1952), 28-32.

Clemmer, Donald: A Beginning in Social Education in Correctional Institutions, FP, Vol.13 (Mar., 1949), 32-35.

————: *The Prison Community.* New York, Rinehart, 1958.

Cleveland, Ralph L.: What Price Honor Farms, POLICE, Vol.3, No.2 (Nov.-Dec., 1958), 19-21.

Clinard, Marshall B.: The Group Approach to Social Reintegration, ASR, Vol.14 (Apr., 1949), 257-262.

Coe, Rodney M.: Characteristics of Well Adjusted and Poorly Adjusted Inmates, JCLC&PS, Vol.52, No.2 (July-Aug., 1961), 178.

————: Relationships of Scores and Education to Adjustment, JCLC&PS, Vol.50, No.5 (Jan.-Feb., 1960), 460.

Construction and Design of Correctional Institutions. A Report, Washington, D.C., U.S. Bureau of Prisons, 1949.

Contest Winners: The Voice of the Convict, HARPER'S, Vol.228, No.1367 (Apr., 1964), 164-170.

Coogan, Father John Edward, S.J.: The Myth Mind in an Engineer's World, FP, Vol.16, No.1 (Mar., 1952), 26-30.

Corsin, Raymond: The Method of Psychodrama in Prison, GP, Vol.3 (Mar., 1951), 321-326.

————: Non-directive Vocational Counseling of Prison Inmates, JCP, Vol.3 (1947), 96-100 (discussion of the value of non-directive vocational counseling in prisons).

————: A Note Towards an Experimental Penology, PW, Vol.7 (Sept., 1945), 12.

Coulter, Charles W., and Korpi, Orvo E.: Rehabilitation Programs in American Prisons and Correctional Institutions, JCL&C, Vol.44, No.5 (Jan.-Feb., 1953), 611-615.

Cressey, Donald R. (ed.): *The Prison: Studies in Institutional Organization and Change.* New York, Holt, Rinehart & Winston, 1961.

Crihfield, B. E.: The Interstate Parole and Probation Compact, FP, Vol.17 (June, 1953), 3-7.

Curran, F. J.: Group Treatment in Rehabilitation of Offenders, *Proceedings of the American Prison Association,* 1945.

Dann, Robert H.: Capital Punishment in Oregon, THE ANNALS, Vol.284 (Nov., 1952), 110-114.

Davis, David B.: The Movement to Abolish Capital Punishment, 1787-1861, AHR, Vol.63 (Oct., 1957), 23-46.

Deets, Lee Emerson: Changes in Capital Punishment Policy Since 1939, JCL&C, Vol. 38, No.6 (Mar.-Apr., 1947-48), 584-594.

DeFord, Miriam Allen: *Stone Walls.* New York, Chilton, 1962.

Derrick, C.: Segregation, Self-government and State Control, *Proceedings of the American Prison Association,* 1947.

Dession, George H.: Justice After Conviction, CBJ, Vol.25 (Sept., 1951), 215-235.

DeStephens, William P.: Initial Failures in Rehabilitation Among 16,965 Ohio State Reformatory Inmates, JCL&C, Vol.44, No.5 (Jan.-Feb., 1954), 596-603.

Deutschberger, P.: Case Work Failure and the Psychology of Restriction, PROBATION, Vol.24 (Mar.-Apr., 1946), 103-108.

Diana, Lewis: What Is Probation? JCLC&PS, Vol.51 (July-Aug., 1960), 189-200.

Dobbins, D. A., and Bass, Bernard M.: Effects of Unemployment on White and Negro Prison Admissions in Louisiana, JCLC&PS, Vol.48, No.5 (Jan.-Feb., 1958), 522.

Dolson, Hildegarde: A Most Embarrassing Prisoner, HARPER'S, Vol.228, No.1367 (Apr., 1964), 176-179.

Donigan, Robert L.: Why Bail in Traffic Cases; An Indigent Defendant, TDR (May, 1965), 4-7.

Downey, Richard N.: The Selection of Prison Guards, JCLC&PS, Vol.49, No.3 (1958-59), 234.

Dressler, David: *Parole Chief.* New York, Viking Press, 1951.

————: *Practice and Theory of Probation and Parole.* New York, Columbia University Press, 1959.

————: *Probation and Parole Practice.* New York, Columbia University Press, 1951.

Drzazga, John: Capital Punishment, L&O, Vol.9 (Dec., 1961).

Duffy, Warden Clinton T.: *The San Quentin Story.* Garden City, Doubleday, 1950.

East, E. R.: Is Reformation Possible in Prison Today? JCL&C, Vol.38, No.2 (Mar.-Apr., 1947-48), 128-131.

East, W. R.: The Legal Aspects of Psychiatry, Crime and Punishment, JMS, Vol.92 (Oct., 1946), 682-712.

Eaton, Joseph W.: Prison Reform in California, POLICE, Vol.8, No.1 (Sept.-Oct., 1963), 6-8.

Ehrmann, Herbert B.: The Death Penalty and the Administration of Justice, THE ANNALS, Vol.284 (Nov., 1952), 73-84.

Elliott, Mabel A.: *Coercion in Penal Treatment.* Ithaca, Pacifist Research Bureau, 1947.

Ellis, W. J.: New Jersey's Program for Training Prison and Reformatory Officers. *Proceedings of the American Prison Association,* 1945.

England, Ralph W.: *Prison Labour.* New York, U.N Dept. of Economic & Social Affairs, 1955.

Englash, Albert: Creative Restitution, JCLC&PS, Vol.48, No.6 (Mar.-Apr., 1958), 619.

Eriksson, Thorsten: Postwar Prison Reform in Sweden, THE ANNALS, Vol.293 (May, 1954), 152-162.

Estes, Marion M., and New, James S.: Some Observations on Prison Psychoses, JMAG, Vol.37 (Jan., 1948), 2-5.

The Ex-G.I. in Federal Prison, *Proceedings of the American Prison Association,* 1953.

Federal Bureau of Prisons, United States Department of Justice: *Annual Reports on Federal Prisons.* Leavenworth, Kan., United States Penitentiary.

————: *Handbook of Correctional Institution Design and Construction.* Washington, D.C., Federal Bureau of Prisons, 1949.

————: *Manual of Jail Management.* Washington, D.C., Federal Bureau of Prisons, Apr., 1948.

————: *National Prisoner Statistics.* Washington, D.C., Federal Bureau of Prisons.

————: *Recent Prison Construction 1950-1960.* Washington, D.C., Federal Bureau of Prisons, 1960.

Federal Offenders. Annual bulletin published by Bureau of Prisons, U.S. Dept. of Justice, Washington, D.C.

Federal Prisons: 1950, 1952, 1953, and 1954. A report prepared by the U.S. Dept. of Justice, Washington, D.C., 1951, 1953, 1954, 1955.

Fenton, Norman: Adult Education in the California Prison System, CJCP, Vol.3 (Jan., 1947), 96-100.

————: *The Prisoner's Family.* Palo Alto, Pacific Books, 1959.

————: The Relationship of the Reception Center to the Correctional Program. *Proceedings of the American Prison Association,* 1947.

Flack, Katherine E.: Advantages in Nutrition, PW, Vol.15 (July-Aug., 1953), 20-21, 24.

Floch, Maurice: Are Prisons Outdated, JCLC&PS, Vol.47, No.4 (Nov.-Dec., 1956), 444.

————: A Social-Psychological Analysis of Prison Riots, JCLC&PS, Vol.47, No.1 (May-June, 1956), 51.

Flynn, Frank: Employment and Labor, in Paul Tappan (ed.), *Contemporary Correction.* New York, McGraw-Hill, 1951.

————: The Federal Government and the Prison Labor Problem in the States, SSR, Vol.24 (Mar. and June, 1950), 19-40, 213-236.

Fox, Lionel W.: *The English Prison and Borstal Systems.* London, England, Routledge & Kegan Paul, Ltd., 1952.

———: *Prison Management Under War Conditions,* JCL&C, Vol.36, No.3 (1945-46), 184.

Fox, Vernon: Analysis of Prison Disciplinary Problems, JCLC&PS, Vol.49, No.6 (1958-59), 608.

———: Citizens Groups and Penal Progress, JCLC&PS, Vol.48, No.5 (Jan.-Feb., 1958), 517.

———: Classification in a Minimum Security Institution, JCL&C, Vol.39, No.4 (Mar.-Apr., 1948-49), 471-485.

———: Probation and Parole, CORRECTION, Vol.50, No.1 (1959-60), 52.

———: Probation and Parole: Theory Versus Practice, JCLC&PS, Vol.50, No.1 (May-June, 1959), 52.

Freedman, Harry L.: Comments on Recent Guidance Center Trends, JCL&C, Vol.36, No.5 (1945-46), 326.

Fricke: *Sentence and Probation, the Imposition of Penalties upon Convicted Criminals.* Los Angeles, Legal Bookstore, 1960.

Friedman, Edwin I.: Institutional Life—A Program of Social Education, PW, Vol.11 (July, 1949), 14-17.

Frym, Marcel: The Treatment of Recidivists: JCLC&PS, Vol.47, No.1 (May-June 1956), 1.

Fuller, Justin K.: Prison Feeding: Significant Factors, PW, Vol.12 (Nov.-Dec., 1950), 7-9.

Garmire, Bernard L.: Selection and Probation, TPY, 1962.

Geis, Gilbert: Chronicles of San Quentin: The Biography of a Prison, JCLC&PS, Vol.53, No.2 (June-Aug., 1962), 241.

Giardini, G. I.: *Manual of Parole Procedures and Supervision.* Harrisburg, Pa., Commonwealth of Pennsylvania, 1951.

———: *The Parole Process.* Springfield, Thomas, 1959.

Giarrusso, Joseph I.: The Role of Penal Procedure, TPY, 1962.

Gilbert, G. M.: Crime and Punishment: An Exploratory Comparison of Public Criminal and Penological Attitudes, MH, Vol.42 (Oct., 1948), 550-557.

Gill, Howard B.: Correctional Philosophy and Architecture, JCLC&PS, Vol.53, No.3 (Sept.-Nov., 1962), 312.

———: Correction's Sacred Cows, JCLC&PS, Vol.50, No.1 (May-June, 1959), 53; POLICE, Vol.9, No.4 (Mar.-Apr., 1965), 44-50.

Gillin, John Lewis: *Criminology and Penology,* 3rd ed. New York, Appleton-Century-Crofts, 1945.

———: Executive Clemency in Wisconsin, JCLC&PS, Vol.42 (1951-52), 755.

———: *The Wisconsin Prisoner.* Madison, University of Wisconsin Press, 1946.

Glaser, Daniel: *The Effectiveness of a Prison and Parole system.* New York, Bobbs-Merrill, 1964.

———: Testing Correctional Decisions, JCLC&PS, Vol.45 (1954), 679-684.

Glover, Elizabeth R.: *Probation and Re-education.* London, Routledge, 1949.

Glueck, Sheldon: Beccaria and Criminal Justice, HLSB, Vol.16, No.3 (Jan., 1965), 3-5.

———: *Crime and Correction.* Cambridge, Addison-Wesley, 1952.

———: *Is a Pre-sentence Examination of the Offender Advisable?* Report to the 12th International Penal and Penitentiary Congress, The Hague, 1950.

———: Pre-sentence Examination of Offenders to Aid in Choosing a Method of Treatment. The Hague, JCL&C, Vol.41 (1950), 717.

———: Probation and Social Agencies, ULR, Vol.8, No.3 (1963).

———: *Special Commission on the Laws Relating to the Sentencing, Treatment and Release of Prisoners in the Penal Institutions.* Cambridge, The Commonwealth of Mass., Report of the special commission under Chapt. 59, Resolves of 1951, and Chapt. 102, Resolves of 1952.

———: *Special Commission on the Laws Relating to the Sentencing, Treatment and Release of Prisoners in the Penal Institutions.* Boston, Wright & Potter, 1953. Report of the unpaid special commission relative to prisoners, appointed under Chapt. 59, Resolves of 1951.

———: Twelfth International Penal and Penitentiary Congress (The Hague) and Second International Congress of Criminology (Paris), AJPSY, Vol.107 (1951), 551.

Goodman, Leo A.: Generalizing the Problem of Prediction, ASR, Vol.17 (Oct., 1952), 609-612.

Gordon, Walter A.: The Adult Authority and Individual Treatment, *Proceedings of the American Prison Association,* 1945.

———: Parole Relating to the Classification Process, FOCUS, Vol.27 (Sept., 1948), 129-32.

Graham, Mary Ruth: *These Came Back.* University, University of Alabama Press, 1946.

Great Britain, Royal Commission on Capital Punishment, 1949-1953: *Report.* (Command 8932), 1953.

Grosser, George (ed.): *Theoretical Studies in the Social Organization of the Prison.* New

York, Social Science Research Council, 1960.

Grunhut, Max: *Penal Reform.* Oxford, Oxford University Press, 1948.

Hakeem, Michael: Glueck Method of Parole Prediction Applied to 1,861 Cases of Burglars, JCL&C, Vol.36, No.2 (1945-46), 87.

————: Prediction of Parole Outcome from Summaries of Case Histories, JCLC&PS, Vol.52, No.2 (July-Aug., 1961), 145.

————: Product of Criminality, FP, Vol.9 (July, 1945), 31-38.

Halpren, Irving W.: Probation Is Planned Treatment, FP, Vol.11 (Jan., 1947), 38-41.

Hardman, Dale G., and Margaret, P.: Three Postulates in Institutional Care, NPPAJ, Vol.4 (1956), 22-27.

Hartung, Frank E.: *On Capital Punishment.* Detroit, Wayne University Department of Sociology and Anthropology, 1951.

————: Trends in the Use of Capital Punishment, THE ANNALS, Vol.284 (Nov., 1952), 8-19.

Haskett, Martin R.: Role Training as Preparation for Release from a Correctional Institute, CORRECTION, Vol.50, No.5 (1959-60), 441.

Haynes, Fred E.: Sociological Study of the Prison Community, JCL&C, Vol.39, No.4 (Mar.-Apr., 1948-49), 432-41.

Health and Welfare Federation of Allegheny County, Bureau of Social Research: *The Mentally Ill in Jail,* Pittsburgh, 1953.

Hermon, Z.: The Penitentiary Aspects of the Problem of Sex Offenders in Israel, JCLC&PS, Vol.53, No.1 (Mar.-Apr., 1962), 62.

Herre, Ralph S.: *The History of the Auburn Prison from the Beginning to about 1867.* Unpublished Dissertation, University Park, Pennsylvania State Univ., 1950.

Hill, Robert M.: State Administration of Adult Probation, JCLC&PS, Vol.42 (Mar.-Apr., 1952), 707-28.

Hiller, Francis H., and Reed, Hugh P.: *The Probation and Parole Service of the Wisconsin Department of Public Welfare.* New York, National Probation and Parole Assoc., 1948. (Survey of conditions in a state parole system.)

Hoefer, Frederick: The Nazi Penal System II, The . . . , JCL&C, Vol.36, No.1 (1945-46), 30.

Hooper, Columbos B.: The Conjugal Visit at Mississippi State Penitentiary, JCLC&PS, Vol.53, No.3 (Sept.-Nov., 1962), 340.

Howard, D. L.: *John Howard: Prison Reformer.* London, Johnson, 1958.

Howe, Paul E.: Nutritional Accounting, PW, Vol.12 (Mar.-Apr., 1950), 20-21, 26.

————: Nutritional Accounting—An Administrative Service, PW, Vol.15 (May-June, 1953), 14, 26-27.

Hulin, Charles L., and Maher, Brendan A.: Changes in Attitudes Toward Law Concomitant with Imprisonment, JCLC&PS, Vol.50, No.3 (Sept.-Oct., 1959), 245.

Illing, Hans A.: Special Treatment Program, JCLC&PS, Vol.49, No.5 (1958-59), 423.

————: The "Visitor" and His Role of Transference in Group Therapy, JCLC&PS, Vol.44, No.6 (Mar.-Apr., 1954), 753-58.

Informants, Probationer and Parolee, TPC, Vol.31 (July, 1964), 49.

Inmate Manual. *Multnomah County Correctional Institution.* Portland, Multnomah County Jail, 1963.

Jails and the Positive Approach, PW, Vol.12 (Jan.-Feb., 1950), 18.

Jeffery, C. Ray: Criminology and Penology, JCLC&PS, Vol.51, No.1 (Mar.-Apr., 1960-61), 82.

Jenkins, R. L.: The Constructive Use of Punishment, MH, Vol.29 (Oct., 1945), 561-74.

Jenkinson, C. V.: How Can Prison Industries Contribute to the Preparation of Inmates for Release? *Proceedings of the American Prison Association,* 1948.

Johnson, Elmer Hubert: *Crime, Correction and Society.* Homewood, Dorsey Press, 1964.

————: The Parole Supervisor in the Role of Stranger, JCLC&PS, Vol.50, No.1 (May-June, 1959), 38.

————: Sociology of Confinement: Assimilation and the Prison "Rat," JCLC&PS (Jan.-Feb., 1961), 528-533.

Johnston, James A.: *Alcatraz Island Prison.* New York, Scribners, 1949.

Jones, Howard: *Crime and the Penal System.* London, University Tutorial Press, 1956.

Kane, Francis F.: Houses of Detention for Untried Prisoners, PW, Vol.12 (Jan., 1950), 3-4.

Karpman, Benjamin: Sex Life in Prison, JCL&C, Vol.38, No.5 (Mar.-Apr., 1947-48), 475-486.

Kay, Barbara A.: Female Prisoners; Their Concepts of Self, POLICE, Vol.7, No.2 (Nov.-Dec., 1962), 39-41.

————, and Vedder, Clyde B.: Parole: A Reentry Process, POLICE, Vol.7, No.5 (May-June, 1963), 32-34.

Kendall, G. M.: The New York State Reception Center, FP, Vol.12 (Sept., 1948), 42-47.

————: General and Social Education in Correctional Treatment, *Proceedings of the American Prison Association,* 1946.

Kerner, Otto: Correctional Services in Illinois, POLICE, Vol.7, No.3 (Jan.-Feb., 1963), 13-15.

Kevorkian, Jack: Capital Punishment or Capital Gain, CORRECTION, Vol.50, No.1 (1959-60), 50.

Killinger, George C.: Parole and Other Release Procedures in Tappan, Paul (ed.), *Contemporary Correction.* New York, McGraw-Hill, 1951.

Kirby, Bernard C.: Parole Prediction Using Multiple Correlation, AJS, Vol.59 (May, 1954), 539-551.

Klare, Hugh J.: *Anatomy of Prison.* Baltimore, Penguin Books, 1960.

Knopka, Gisela: The Group Worker's Role in an Institution for Juvenile Delinquents, FP, Vol.15 (June, 1951), 15-23.

Kobrin, Solomon: Theoretical Studies in Social Organization of the Prison, JCLC&PS, Vol.51, No.4 (Mar.-Apr., 1960-61), 454.

Korn, Richard R., and McCorkle, Lloyd W.: *Criminology and Penology.* New York, Henry Holt, 1959.

Kornitsky, Lillian: How to Censor Mail in Women's Correctional Institutions, PW, Vol.12 (Mar.-Apr., 1950), 13, 25.

Laulicht, Jerome: Problems of Statistical Research: Recidivism and Its Correlates, JCLC&PS, Vol.54, No.2 (1963), 163.

Laurence, John: *A History of Capital Punishment.* New York, Citadel, 1960.

Layfield, M. H.: Penology, JCLC&PS, Vol.47 (1956-57).

Leonard, Charles W.: Relationship of the Correctional Institution to Community Agencies from the Viewpoint of the Institution, JCE, Vol.2 (1950), 121-27.

Leonard, V. A.: 100th Birthday of the Prison Association of New York, JCL&C, Vol.35, No.5 (Jan.-Feb., 1945), 328.

———: Prison Journal 100 Years Old, JCL&C, Vol.35, No.6 (Mar.-Apr., 1945), 399.

———: Recommendations of the New York Prison Association, JCL&C, Vol.35, No.6 (Mar.-Apr., 1945), 395.

Lester, E. W.: Parole Treatment and Surveillance which Should Dominate? *National Probation and Parole Association Yearbook,* 1952.

Levin, Stanley H.: Post Convictional Remedies in Illinois, JCL&C, Vol.40, No.5 (Jan.-Feb., 1950), 606.

Lewis, Edward B., Peizer, Sheldon B., and

Scallon, Robert W.: Correctional Rehabilitation as a Function or Interpersonal Relations, JCLC&PS, Vol.46 (1955-56), 632-39.

Lincke, Jack: Gardena's Electronic Lock-up, POLICE, Vol.9, No.1 (Sept.-Oct., 1964), 88-90.

Linder, Robert M.: *Stone Walls and Men.* New York, Odyssey Press, 1946.

Long, Jean: Job Placements for Overtime Inmates, *National Probation and Parole Association Yearbook,* 1952.

Long, Harvey L.: Pre-release Preparation of Parolees, FOCUS (Sept., 1952), 1-4.

Los Angeles (City) Police Department, Jail Division: *Main Jail Rules.* Los Angeles, The Dept., 1952.

Los Angeles (County) Sheriff's Department, Jail Division: *Officers Manual: Instructions and Duties.* Los Angeles, Sheriff's Dept., 1952.

Loveland, Frank: Classification in the Prison System, in Paul Tappan (ed.), *Contemporary Correction.* New York, McGraw-Hill, 1951.

Lowe, Duane H.: Rehabilitation Programs for County Jails, POLICE, Vol.7, No.1 (Sept.-Oct., 1962), 75-77.

Lundberg, D. E.: Methods of Selecting Prison Personnel, JCL&C, Vol.38, No.1 (Mar.-Apr., 1947-48), 14-39.

Lunden, Walter A.: Death Penalty Delays, POLICE, Vol.7, No.6 (July-Aug., 1963), 18-22.

———: Social Innovations in Prisons, POLICE, Vol.1, No.6 (July-Aug., 1957), 57-61.

Luszki, Walter A.: Beating the Underground Molers, JCLC&PS, Vol.48, No.1 (May-June, 1952), 103.

Lykke, A. F.: Of Steel Bars and Acid Tests, POLICE, Vol.2, No.4 (Mar.-Apr., 1958), 28-81.

———: Training and Placement Opportunities for Federal Prisoners, POLICE, Vol.2, No.2 (Nov.-Dec., 1957), 26-30.

McCleery, Richard H.: *Policy Change in Prison Management.* East Lansing, Michigan State University, 1957.

McCorkle, Lloyd: Group Therapy, in Paul W. Tappin (ed.), *Contemporary Correction.* New York, McGraw-Hill, 1951.

———: Group Therapy in the Treatment of Offenders, FP, Vol.16, No.4 (Dec., 1952), 22-27.

———, and Elias, Albert: Group Therapy in Correctional Institutions, FP, Vol.24, No.2 (June, 1960), 57-63.

McGee, Richard A.: The Administration of

Justice: The Correctional Process, NPPAJ, Vol.5 (July, 1959), 225-39.

Maestro, M. T.: *Voltaire and Beccaria as Reformers of the Criminal Law.* New York, Columbia University Press, 1942.

Maher, Brendon A.: Changes in Attitude Toward Law Concomitant with Imprisonment. CORRECTION, Vol.50, No.3 (1959-60), 245.

Manella, Frand L.: Aftercare Programs, NPPPAJ, Vol.4 (1958), 74-80.

Mannheim, Hermann: *Criminal Justice and Social Reconstruction.* New York, Oxford University Press, 1946.

Martin, John Bartlow: *Break Down the Walls.* New York, Ballantine Books, 1954.

Mattick, Hans W.: Some Latent Functions of Imprisonment, JCLC&PS, Vol.50, No.3 (Sept.-Oct., 1959), 237.

Meacham, W. S.: Conditions of Probation and Parole: Do They Help or Hinder? NPPAY, 1947.

Meeker, Ben S.: The Federal Probation Service Training Center, FP, Vol.15 (Dec., 1951), 51-54.

————: Probation Is Case Work, FP, Vol.12 (June, 1948), 51-54.

Methods and Reasons for Jail Escapes, PW, Vol.12 (May-June, 1950), 7-10, 29.

Meyer, Charles H. Z.: A Half Century of Probation and Parole, JCLC&PS, Vol.42, No.6 (Mar.-Apr., 1952), 707-28.

————: Jails: Care and Treatment of Misdemeant Prisoners in the United States, JCL&C, Vol.35, No.5 (Jan.-Feb., 1945), 335.

Monachesi, E. D.: A Comparison of Predicted with Actual Results of Probation, ASR, Vol.10 (Feb., 1945), 26-31.

Moore, Frank B.: How to Avoid the Poor Approach to Inmates, PW, Vol.11 (July-Aug., 1949), 22, 24-25, 29.

Moran, F. A.: The Origin of Parole, NPPAY, 1945.

Morris, N.: *The Habitual Criminal.* Cambridge, Harvard University Press, 1951.

Morrison, Neil W.: How to Search the Person of an Inmate, PW, Vol.10 (Mar.-Apr., 1948), 8-10.

National Conference on Parole: *Parole in Principle and Practice: a Manual and Report.* New York, Ntl. Probation and Parole Association, 1957.

National Council on Crime and Delinquency: Standards and Guides for Adult Probation. New York, Ntl. Council on Crime and Delinquency, 1962.

National Probation Association: Guides for Juvenile Court Judges, 1957. New York, The Association, 1957.

————: Guides for Sentencing. New York, The Association, 1957.

————: PROBATION, five issues yearly.

————: *Standard Probation and Parole Act.* New York, The Association, 1955.

————: *Standards and Guides for the Detention of Children and Youth.* New York, The Association, 1956.

————: *Standards for Selection of Probation and Parole Officers.* New York, The Association, 1945.

————: *Yearbooks.* 1790 Broadway, New York, New York, published annually.

National Parole Board, TPC, Vol.30 (Jan., 1963), 32.

Newell, Gordon: Remarkable Innovations Characterize New Washington State Corrections Center, POLICE, Vol.9, No.4 (Mar.-Apr., 1965), 37-39.

Newman, Charles L.: Re-establishment of the Adult Probation and Parolee in the Family and in the Community, POLICE, Vol.4, No.3 (Jan.-Feb., 1960), 11-15.

Newman, Donald J.: Research Interviewing in Prison, JCLC&PS, Vol.49, No.2 (1958-59), 127.

Norman, Sherwood: *The Design and Construction of Detention Homes for the Juvenile Court.* New York, National Probation Association, 1947.

Odell, Charles E.: Job Adjustment for Probationers and Parolees, FP, Vol.15 (June, 1951), 12-15.

The Offender Re-enters the Community, PJ, Vol.25 (1945), Entire Issue.

Ohio Department of Mental Hygiene and Correction Division of Business Admin. Bureau of Research and Statistics: *1959 Ohio Judicial Criminal Statistics.* Columbus, Heer Printing, n.d.

Ohlin, Lloyd E.: The Routinization of Correctional Change, JCLC&PS, Vol.45 (1954-55), 400-11.

————: *Selection for Parole.* New York, Russell Sage Foundation, 1951.

Pantun, James H.: Use of the MMPI as an Index to Successful Parole, JCLC&PS, Vol.53, No.4 (Dec., 1962), 484.

Parole Supervision: A Case Analysis, FP, Vol.15 (June, 1951), 36-42.

Peizer, Sheldon B.: What Do Prisons Do Anyway? POLICE, Vol.6, No.2 (Nov.-Dec., 1961), 6-10.

Pirkey, Jane Sedgwick: *Food Service.* New York, American Prison Association, 1952. (Preliminary draft for revised manual for suggested standards for state correctional system.)

Playfair, Giles: Without Bars: Some Bold (and Some Timorous) Experiments, HARPER'S, Vol.228, No.1367 (Apr., 1964), 171-75.

Ploscowe, Morris: A Legal Phantasy: The Parole Commission Law, JCL&C, Vol.39, No.6 (Mar.-Apr., 1948-49), 714-21.

Poindexter, W. R.: Mental Illness in a State Penitentiary, JCLC&PS, Vol.45 (1954-55), 559-64.

Powelson, Harvey, and Reinharp, Bendix: Psychiatry in Prison, PSYCHIATRY, Vol.14 (Feb., 1951), 13-86.

Prins, Herschel: The Probation Officer, JCLC&PS, Vol.49, No.6 (1958-59), 557.

Probation Is Casework, FP, Vol.12 (June, 1948), 51-54.

Putney, Gladys J.: Origins of the Reformatory, JCLC&PS, Vol.53, No.4 (Dec., 1962), 437.

Rafferty, Frank: Men in State Prison, CORRECTION, Vol.50, No.6 (1959-60), 551.

Ragen, Joseph E., and Finston, Charles: *Inside the World's Toughest Prison.* Springfield, Thomas, 1962.

Raney, Hubert R.: Fraternizing with Inmates, PW, Vol.11 (May-June, 1949), 16, 18-19.

Rasmussen, Donald: Prisoners Opinion about Parole Personnel, FOCUS, Vol.27 (Mar., 1948), 44-48.

Reckless, Walter C.: Training the Correctional Worker, in Paul Tappan (ed.), *Contemporary Correction.* New York, McGraw-Hill, 1951.

Redmount, Robert S.: Basic Consideration Regarding Penal Policy, JCLC&PS, Vol.49, No.5 (1958-59), 426.

Reiwald, Paul: *Society and Its Criminals.* New York, International Universities Press, 1950.

Robinson, Louis N.: The Perennial Jail Problem, JCL&C, Vol.35, No.6 (Mar.-Apr., 1945), 369.

——: Pioneering in Penology, JCL&C, Vol.35, No.6 (Mar.-Apr., 1945), 402.

Roebuck, Julion, and Zelhart, Paul: The Problem of Educating the Correctional Practitioner, JCLC&PS, Vol.56, No.1 (Mar., 1965), 45-53.

Rozyck, J. J.: *Early Recidivism among First Offenders.* Washington, The Catholic Univ. of America, 1948.

Rubin, Sol: The Intermediate Sentence—Success or Failure, FOCUS, Vol.28 (Mar., 1949), 47-52.

——: Sentencing and Correctional Treatment Under the Law Institute's Model Penal Code, ABAJ, Vol.46 (Sept., 1960), 994-998.

——, & Weihofen, Henry; Edwards, George and Rosenzweig, Simon: *The Law of Criminal Correction.* St. Paul, West, 1963.

Rubin, Theodore Issac: *In the Life.* New York, Ballantine Books, 1961.

Rumney, Jay, and Murphy, J. P.: *Probation and Social Adjustment.* New Brunswick, Rutgers University Press, 1952.

Runyon, Tom: *In for Life.* New York, Norton, 1953.

Sale, J. T.: Prison Food and the Inmates' Viewpoint, PW, Vol.14 (Sept.-Oct., 1952), 20, 22-23, 33.

Savits, Leonard D.: Study in Capital Punishment, JCLC&PS, Vol.49, No.4 (1958-59), 338.

Schmidt, G.: Levels of Intelligence in Prison Inmates, AJMD, Vol.51 (July, 1946), 63-66.

Schnur, Alfred C.: The Educational Treatment of Prisoners and Recidivism, AJS, Vol.54 (Sept., 1948), 142-47.

——: Prediction in Probation and Parole, *Proceedings of the American Prison Association,* 1948.

——: Pre-service Training, JCLC&PS, Vol.50, No.1 (May-June, 1959), 27.

——: Prison Conduct and Recidivism, JCL&C, Vol.40, No.1 (May-June, 1949), 36.

Schrag, Clarence: Leadership Among Prison Inmates, ARS, Vol.19 (Feb., 1954), 37-42.

Schuessler, Karl F.: The Deterrent Influence of the Death Penalty, THE ANNALS, Vol.284 (Nov., 1952), 54-62.

——: Parole Prediction: Its History and Status, JCL&C, Vol.45 (Nov.-Dec., 1954), 425-431.

Schwaner, George W., Jr.: The Illinois Sentence and Parole Act, CJ, No.77 (Jan., 1950), 27-28.

Schwartz, Louis B. (ed.): Crime and the American Penal System, THE ANNALS, Vol.339 (Jan., 1962).

——: The Model Penal Code: An Invitation to Law Reform, ABAJ (May, 1963).

Schwartz, Rudolph. Prediction of Parole in Prison, FP, Vol.11 (Apr., 1947), 37-41.

Scott, George Ryley: *The History of Capital Punishment.* London, Torchstream, 1950.

Scudder, K. J.: *Prisoners Are People.* Garden City, Doubleday, 1952.

Sedgwick, Jane: Feeding and Morale, PW, Vol.11 (July-Aug., 1949) 18, 20, 31.

——: Menu Review, PW, Vol.11 (Sept.-Oct., 1949), 21-22.

——: Special Diets and Diet Therapy in Prison Hospitals, PW, Vol.10 (July-Aug., 1948), 10-14.

——: Standards for Kitchen and Dining Equipment Care, PW, Vol.10 (July-Aug., 1948), 10-14.

Sellin, Thorsten: Adult Probation and the Conditional Sentence: JCLC&PS, Vol.49, No.6 (1958-59), 553.

————: The Death Penalty and Police Safety, *Canadian Joint Committee on Capital and Corporal Punishment*, 1955.

————: A Note on the Capital Executions in the United States, BJD, Vol.1 (July, 1950), 6-14.

———— (ed.): Prisons in Transformation, THE ANNALS, Vol.293 (May, 1954).

————: Two Myths in the History of Capital Punishment, CORRECTION, Vol.50, No.2 (1959-60), 114.

Shaw, George Bernard: *The Crime of Imprisonment.* New York, Philosophical Library, 1946.

Shelly, Ernest L. V., and Toch, Hans H.: The Perception of Violence as an Indicator of Adjustment in Institutional Offenders, JCLC&PS, Vol.53, No.4 (Dec., 1962), 463.

Shulman, H. M.: What Is Wrong with American Prisons and Jails, JCL&C, Vol.45 (1954-55), 662-667.

Size, Mary: *Prisons I Have Known.* London, Allen & Urwin, 1957.

Skidmore, Rex A.: An American Prison School in the Eighteenth Century, JCLC&PS, Vol.46 (1955-56), 211-13.

————: Penological Pioneering in the Walnut Street Jail, 1789-1799, JCL&C, Vol.39, No.2 (Mar.-Apr., 1948-49), 167-181.

Sklar, Ronald B.: Law and Practice in Probation and Parole Revocation Hearings, JCLC&PS, Vol.55, No.2 (June, 1964), 175.

Skousen, W. Cleon: Is Your Jail a Jinx? L&O, Vol.12 (June, 1964).

————: Law Enforcement Looks at Capital Punishment, L&O, Vol.10, No.7 (July, 1962), 20.

Smith, Alexander B., and Bassin, Alexander: Research in a Probation Department, C&D, Vol.8 (Jan., 1962), 46-51.

Smith, F. S., et al.: Some Notes on Jail Escapes, PW, Vol.10 (Mar.-Apr., 1948), 3-5, 25.

Smith, O. W.: *Penal Code of the State of California,* Los Angeles, n.d.

Smith, Ralph Lee: Research Behind Bars, NEW YORK TIMES MAG. (Dec., 1960).

Social Science Research Council: *Theoretical Studies in Social Organization of the Prison.* New York, Social Science Research Council, 1960.

Sokol, Jack: A Pioneer Approach in the Treatment of Offenders, JCLC&PS, Vol.45 (1954-55), 279-90.

Spencer, John C.: The Use of Corrective Training in the Treatment of the Persistent Offender in England, JCL&C, Vol.34, No.1 (May-June, 1953), 40-48.

Stahl, June Wooliver: Caged or Cured: Classification and Treatment of California Felons

at the California Medical Facility, JCLC&PS, Vol.56, No.2 (June, 1965), 174-89.

State of California: *California Penal Code.* Sacramento, State Printing Office.

Stern, Leon T.: Jails: Yesterday and Today, PJ, Vol.25 (July, 1945), 88-89.

Sternberg, David: Synan House—A Consideration of Its Implications for American Correction, JCLC&PS, Vol.54, No.4 (1963), 447.

Sykes, G. M.: The Corruption of Authority and Rehabilitation, SF (Mar., 1956), 257-62.

————: The Dilemma of Penal Reform, HJ, Vol.10 (1960), 194-200.

————: *The Society of Captives.* Princeton, Princeton University Press, 1958.

Tappan, Paul W.: *Contemporary Correction.* New York, McGraw-Hill, 1951.

————: *Crime, Justice and Correction.* New York, McGraw-Hill, 1960.

————: Habitual Offenders Laws in United States, FP, Vol.13 (Mar., 1949), 28-31.

————: Objectives in Methods in Correction in Paul W. Tappan, *Contemporary Correction.* New York, McGraw-Hill, 1951.

Teeters, Negley K.: *The Cradle of the Penitentiary.* Philadelphia, Pennsylvania Prison Society, 1955.

————: Does the Prison Reform Criminals, JCL&C, Vol.35, No.6 (Mar.-Apr., 1945), 408.

————: Early Days of the Maine State Prison at Thomaston, JCL&C, Vol.38, No.2 (Mar.-Apr., 1947-48), 104-118.

————: How Effective Is Classification in Prisons, JCL&C, Vol.35, No.6 (Mar.-Apr., 1945), 411.

————: The International Penal and Penitentiary Congress (1910) and the Indeterminate Sentence, JCL&C, Vol.39, No.5 (Mar.-Apr., 1948-49), 618-29.

————: The Loss of Civil Rights and Their Reinstatement, PJ, Vol.25 (July, 1945), 77-87.

————: Should Confirmed Criminals Be Paroled? JCL&C, Vol.35, No.6 (Mar.-Apr., 1945), 412.

————: To What Degree Can We Practice Self-Government in Prison? JCL&C, Vol.35, No.6 (Mar.-Apr., 1945), 412.

————: What Will Happen to Prison After the War? JCL&C, Vol.35, No.6 (Mar.-Apr., 1945), 410.

————: Without Prisons What Shall We Do With Criminals? JCL&C, Vol.35, No.6 (Mar.-Apr., 1945), 409.

————, & Shearer, John D.: *The Prison at Philadelphia: Cherry Hill.* New York, Columbia, University Press, 1957.

Teets, Harley: Photography Valuable Tool at San Quentin Prison, POLICE, Vol.1, No.5 (May-June, 1957), 24-27.

————, and Young, W. M.: San Quentin's Court

Plan and Procedure, PW, Vol.15 (Sept.-Oct., 1952), 13-16.

Terry, James G.: *Ten Year Report*—1949-59. Santa Rita Rehabilitation Clinic, Alameda County (Calif.) Sheriff's Dept., 1960.

Terry, Luther L.: Federal Prisoners Volunteer, POLICE, Vol.8, No.2 (Nov.-Dec., 1963), 14-15.

Terry, William D.: *Jail Practice and Procedure.* Sacramento, California State Dept. of Education, 1947.

Thorson, Anton L.: How to Promote the Institutional Sanitation Program, PW, Vol.11 (Jan.-Feb., 1949), 21-22, 29.

Toby, Jackson: Is Punishment Necessary, JCLC&PS, Vol.55, No.3 (Sept., 1964), 332.

Train, George J.: Unrest in the Penitentiary, JCL&C, Vol.44, No.3 (Sept.-Oct., 1953), 277-95.

Tully, Joseph: How to Transport Prisoners, PW, Vol.10 (July-Aug., 1948), 20-33.

Turner, James D.: *Differential Punishment in a Bi-Racial Community.* Unpublished Master's Thesis, Bloomington, Indiana University, 1948.

United Nations: *Capital Punishment.* Dept. of Economic and Social Affairs, New York, United Nations, 1962.

————: *Parole and Aftercare.* Dept. of Economic and Social Affairs, New York, United Nations, 1954.

U.S. Bureau of the Census: *Annual Reports on Prisoners in State and Federal Prisons and Reformatories.* Washington, D.C., Government Printing Office, Published annually since 1926.

U.S. Bureau of Prisons: *Federal Prisons—1959.* El Reno, Oklahoma, U.S. Reformatory, 1960.

————: *Feeding Jail Procedures.* Correspondence Course for Jailers, Lesson No. 3. Washington, D.C., Government Printing Office, n.d.

————: *Jail Security.* Correspondence Course for Jailers, Lesson No.2. Washington, D.C., Government Printing Office, n.d.

————: *The Jailer's Public Responsibility and Relationships.* Correspondence Course for Jailers, Lesson No.10. Washington, D.C., Government Printing Office, n.d.

————: *Let's Look at the Jailer's Job.* Correspondence Course for Jailers, Lesson No.1. Washington, D.C., Government Printing Office, n.d.

————: *Manual of Jail Management.* Washington, D.C., Government Printing Office, 1948.

————: *Medical and Health Services.* Correspondence Course for Jailers, Lesson No.6. Washington, D.C., Government Printing Office, n.d.

————: *Plant and Equipment.* Correspondence

Course for Jailers, Lesson No.9. Washington, D.C., Government Printing Office, n.d.

————: *Receiving Prisoners.* Correspondence Course for Jailers, Lesson No.5. Washington, D.C., Government Printing Office, n.d.

————: *Sanitation, Housekeeping and Safety.* Corespondence Course for Jailers, Lesson No.4. Washington, D.C., Government Printing Office, n.d.

————: *Supervision of Prisoners.* Correspondence Course for Jailers, Lesson No.7. Washington, D.C., Government Printing Office, n.d.

————: *Unusual Prisoners in the Jail.* Correspondence Course for Jailers, Lesson No.8. Washington, D.C., Government Printing Office, n.d.

U.S. Federal Security Agency, National Advisory Policy Committee on Social Protection: *Recommendations on Standards for Detention of Juveniles and Adults.* Washington, D.C., Government Printing Office, 1945.

Vedder, Clyde B.: Counter Forces in Prison Inmate Theory, JCLC&PS, Vol.45 (1954-55), 455-46.

————, **& Kay, Barbara A.:** Probation: Humanitarian Justice, POLICE, Vol.8, No.1 (Sept.-Oct., 1963), 59-64.

Vine, Margaret Wilson: The Selection of Offenders for Probation, JCLC&PS, Vol.51, No.3 (Mar.-Apr., 1960-61), 340.

Wagner, Allen H.: *Probation: A Selected Bibliography on the Individualized Treatment of the Offender.* New York, Russell Sage Foundation, 1948.

Wallack, Walter M.: The Difference Between Traditional and Modern Penology, JCL&C, No.35, No.5 (Jan.-Feb., 1945), 341.

————: Instructing Penal Personnel, JCL&C, Vol.35, No.5 (Jan.-Feb., 1945), 338.

————: Medium and Maximum of Security Confinement, JCL&C, Vol.35, No.5 (Jan.-Feb., 1945), 339.

————: Prisoners' Attitudes Toward Judicial Procedure, JCL&C, Vol.35, No.5 (Jan.-Feb., 1945), 340.

————: Public Feeling Toward Penal Practice, JCL&C, Vol.35, No.5 (Jan.-Feb., 1945), 337.

————: Purpose and Essentials of Classification of Prisoners, JCL&C, Vol.35, No.5 (Jan.-Feb., 1945), 339.

————: Religion and the Chaplain in Correctional Treatment, JCL&C, Vol.35, No.5 (Jan.-Feb., 1945), 342.

————: Some Suggestions for Basic Reforms in Prison Industries for Improved Production and Vocational Training, *Proceedings of the American Prison Association,* 1947.

————: What System of Education Should Be

Adopted in Prison? JCL&C, Vol.35, No.5 (Jan.-Feb., 1945), 338.

Wallinga, Jack V.: The Probation Officer's Role in Psychiatric Cases, JCLC&PS, Vol.50, No.4 (Nov.-Dec., 1959), 364.

Weaver, Le Roy, and Owens, C. D.: Social Education Program at Elmira Reformatory, JCE, Vol.2 (1950), 81-93.

Weber, George H.: Explorations in the Similarites, Differences, and Conflicts between Probation, Parole, and Institutions, JCLC&PS, Vol.48 (1958), 580-89.

Webster, Stanley A.: Personality and Intelligence of Convicts in West Virginia, JCLC&PS, Vol.45 (1954-55), 176-79.

Wechsler, Herbert: Sentencing, Correction and the Model Penal Code, UPLR, Vol.109 (Feb., 1961), 465-93.

Weeks, H. Ashley: Preliminary Evaluation of the Highfields Project, ASR, Vol.18 (June, 1953), 280-87.

Weisheit, Heinz R.: What Has Psychiatry to Offer in Correctional Work? PW, Vol.12 (Sept.-Oct., 1950), 23-29.

When Criminals Are Set Free too Soon. U.S. NEWS & WORLD REPORT (May 17, 1965), 21 (an interview with J. Edgar Hoover).

Whittier, Horrace B.: A Follow-up Study of Minnesota Reformatory Inmates, JCL&C, Vol.43, No.5 (Jan.-Feb., 1953), 622.

Wilson, Donald Powell: *My Six Convicts.* New York, Pocket Books, 1956.

Wilson, Joseph G.: *Are Prisons Necessary?* Philadelphia, Dorrance, 1950.

Wingersky, Melvin F.: Report of the Royal Commission on Capital Punishment (1949-53): A Review, JCL&C, Vol.34, No.6 (Mar.-Apr., 1954), 695-715.

Wolfgang, Marvin E.: Quantitative Analysis of Adjustment to the Prison Community, JCLC&PS, Vol.51, No.6 (Mar.-Apr., 1961), 607.

Wood, Arthur Lewis: The Alternatives to the Death Penalty, THE ANNALS, Vol.284 (Nov., 1952), 63-72.

Woughter, C. C.: Vocational Education and the Prisoner, IAVE, Vol.40 (Sept., 1951), 279-281.

Wright, Roberts J.: The Jail and Misdemeant Institutions in Paul W. Tappan, *Contemporary Correction.* New York, McGraw-Hill, 1951.

Yahraes, Herbert: *Epilepsy—The Ghost Is Out of the Closet.* Public Affairs Pamphlet No.98. New York, Public Affairs Committee, 1947.

Young, Pauline V.: *Social Treatment in Probation and Delinquency.* New York, McGraw-Hill, 1952.

Zalesnik, Abraham (An Ex-convict): Dishonest Employees—the Inmate's Mule, CR (Mar.-Apr., 1963), 19-21.

Zemans, Eugene: Marital Relationships of Prisoners, JCLC&PS, Vol.49, No.1 (1958-59), 50.

Ziskind, Lovis: Social Work and the Correctional Field, FP, Vol.14 (Mar., 1950), 46-49.

Zuckerman, Stanley B.: A Follow-up of Minnesota Reformatory Inmates, JCL&C, Vol.43, No.5 (Jan.-Feb., 1953), 622.

Chapter Two

DETECTIVE BUREAU ADMINISTRATION AND CRIMINAL INVESTIGATION*

ABORTION

Bates, Jerome: The Abortion Mill: An Institutional Analysis, JCLC&PS, Vol.45 (July-Aug., 1954).

————, & **Zawodski, Edward S.:** *Criminal Abortions.* Springfield, Thomas, 1964.

Bauer, F. C.: Sterilization and Abortion, RMSJUAM, Vol.11, No.1 (Winter, 1962-63), 26-31.

Devereux, George: *A Study of Abortion in Primitive Societies.* New York, Julian Press, 1954.

Donner, James: *Women in Trouble.* Derby, Monarch, 1959.

Dr. X, as told to Lucy Freeman: *The Abortionist.* New York, Doubleday, 1962.

Fisher, Russell S.: Criminal Abortion, JCLC&PS, Vol.42 (July-Aug., 1951).

Gebhard, Paul H., Pomeroy, Wardell B., Martin, Clyde E., and Christenson, Cornelia V.: *Pregnancy, Birth and Abortion.* New York, Harper-Hoeber, 1958.

Hahm, Pyong C., and Jan, Byong J.: The Criminality of Abortion in Korea, JCLC&PS, Vol.56, No.1 (Mar., 1965), 18-26.

Hogan, Frank: *Report of the District Attorney, County of New York,* 1946-48. New York, 1948.

Kinsey, Alfred C.: In Mary S. Calderone (ed.), *Abortion in the United States.* New York, Hoeber, 1958.

Martin, John Barthlow: Abortion, SATURDAY EVENING POST (May 20, 1961).

Packer, Herbert L., and Gampell, Ralph J.: Therapeutic Abortion: A Problem in Law and Medicine, STAN.LR, Vol.11 (May, 1959), 418-19.

Pommerenke, W. T.: Abortion in Japan, O&GS, Vol.10 (1955).

Rosen, Harold (ed.): *Therapeutic Abortion.* New York, Julian, 1954.

Schur, Edwin M.: Abortion and the Social System, SP, Vol.3 (Oct., 1955), 94-99.

Tietze, Christopher: Report on a Series of Illegal Abortions Induced by Physicians, Mair, George F. (ed.), *Studies in Population.* Princeton, Princeton University Press, 1949.

ARSON

Adames, Donald L.: The Extraction and Identification of Small Amounts of Accelerants from Arson Evidence, PCLC&PS, Vol.47, No.5 (Jan.-Feb., 1957), 593.

Adams, John Q.: Searching the Fire Scene, POLICE, Vol.9, No.1 (Sept.-Oct., 1964), 15-59.

Adelson, Lester: Role of the Pathologists in Arson Investigations, JCLC&PS, Vol.45 (1954-55), 760-68.

————: Spontaneous Human Combustion and Preternatural Combustibility, JCLC&PS, Vol.42 (1951-52), 793.

Alletto, William C.: MO System of Investigation and Reporting Arson, L&O, Vol.11, No.10 (Oct., 1963).

Armour, Claude A.: Report of the Arson Committee, TPY, 1964.

————: Report of the Arson Committee, TPY, 1965, 194-99.

Arson Investigation Chart, TPC, Vol.31 (May, 1964), 44.

Arson Investigation to Determine the Fire Cause, JCLC&PS, Vol.46 (1955-56), 428.

Bagot, Michal H.: Civil Recourse in Fire Losses, JCLC&PS, Vol.45 (1954-55), 491-98.

---

* This chapter includes: Abortion, Arson, Assault, Auto Theft, Burglary, Embezzlement, Forgery, Fraud, Homosexuality, Interrogation, Investigation, Juvenile Delinquency and Youth Bureau, Kidnaping, Murder-Homicide, Pornography, Robbery, Sex Offenses, Theft, and Vagrancy. The Crime Laboratory and all its functions follows the section on Vagrancy.

Battle, Brendon P., and Weston, Paul B.: *Arson—A Handbook of Detection and Investigation.* New York, Arco, 1959.

Bennett, Charles L.: Mobilizing Community Support, POLICE, Vol.6, No.3 (Jan.-Feb., 1962), 62-64.

Bennett, Glenn D.: The Arson Investigator and Technical Aids, JCLC&PS, Vol.49, No.2 (1958-59), 172.

——: The Detroit Arson Squad, POLICE, Vol.4, No.4 (Mar.-Apr., 1960), 38-42.

——: Physical Evidence in Arson Cases, JCL&C, Vol.34, No.5 (Jan.-Feb., 1954), 652-60.

Berdan, George W.: Investigation of Wildland Fires, POLICE, Vol.7, No.6 (July-Aug., 1963), 45-52.

Brackett, J. W., Jr.: Separation of Flammable Material of Petroleum Origin from Evidence Submitted in Cases Involving Fires and Suspected Arson, JCLC&PS, Vol.46 (1955-56), 554-61.

Braun, William C.: Legal Aspects of Arson, JCLC&PS, Vol.43, No.1 (May-June, 1952), 53.

——: Report of the Committee on Arson, TPY, 1960.

Burd, David Q.: Detection of Traces of Combustible Fluids in Arson Cases, JCLC&PS, Vol.51, No.2 (Mar.-Apr., 1960-61), 263.

Chemistry of Fire, JCLC&PS, Vol.46 (1955-56), 909.

Childers, James C.: The Juvenile Fire-setter, TPY, 1961.

Cobb, S. S.: At the Fire Scene, POLICE, Vol.5, No.4 (Mar.-Apr., 1961), 28-31.

Cohn, Herman H.: Convicting the Arsonist, JCL&C, Vol.38, No.3 (Mar.-Apr., 1947-48), 286-303.

Davis, Joseph H.: Pathological Techniques in Fire Investigation, POLICE, Vol.8, No.5 (May-June, 1964), 81-82.

Deaths During Fires, JCLC&PS, Vol.46 (1955-56), 147.

Doud, Donald, and Hilton, Ordway: The Document Examiner Aids the Arson Investigator, JCLC&PS, Vol.46 (1955-56), 404-07.

Econ, Dan: Physical Evidence in Arson Investigations, POLICE, Vol.5, No.5 (May-June, 1961), 54-62.

Feeheley, Thomas: Suggestions for Improving Arson Investigations, JCLC&PS, Vol.47, No.3 (Sept.-Oct., 1956), 357.

Felony—Murder Rule Applied in Arson Cases, JCLC&PS, Vol.46 (1955-56), 239.

Fisher, Russel S.: How the Pathologist Can Aid the Arson Investigator, JCLC&PS, Vol.43, No.2 (July-Aug., 1952), 237.

Flynn, John L.: Porro of the Corpus Delicti in Arson Cases, JCLC&PS, Vol.45 (1954-55), 185-91.

Fox, Vernon: The Behavioral Criminologist in Arson Investigation, POLICE, Vol.7, No.3 (Jan.-Feb., 1963), 68-71.

Glassman, Mitchell: The Applicability of the Mail Fraud Statute to Arson Cases, POLICE, Vol.8, No.4 (Mar.-Apr., 1964), 17-19.

Hendrickson, Dar: Determining the Origin and Cause of Fire, POLICE, Vol.8, No.3 (Jan.-Feb., 1964), 32-36.

Hopper, William H.: Arson's Corpus Delicti, JCLC&PS, Vol.47, No.1 (May-June, 1956), 118.

——: Burning Time-candles, POLICE, Vol.8, No.6 (July-Aug., 1964), 14-16.

——: Circumstantial Aspects of Arson, JCLC&PS, Vol.46 (1955-56), 129-134.

——: Elements Necessary for an Arson Conviction, POLICE, Vol.1, No.1 (Sept.-Oct., 1956), 14-19.

Hoyek, Camille Faris: Observations on the Prevention of Arson, JCLC&PS, Vol.42 (1951-52), 694.

Johnson, Allen: Fingerprints of Fire, POLICE, Vol.6, No.5 (May-June, 1962), 55-60.

Johnson, Madeline: Interviewing the Youthful Arson Suspect, L&O, Vol.10, No.2 (Feb., 1962), 30.

Kennedy, John: Investigating Arson Incentives, JCLC&PS, Vol.47, No.6 (Mar.-Apr., 1957), 709.

——: Photography In Arson Investigation, JCLC&PS, Vol.46 (1955-56), 726-36.

Kettering, Paul T.: Magnesium Bombs in Arson, L&O, Vol.7 (June, 1964), 76-77.

Lee, Kuan-Lou: Arson Investigation in Selected American Cities, JCLC&PS, Vol.42 (1951-52), 250.

Lewis, Nolan D. C., and Yarnell, Helen: *Pathological Firesetting (Pyromania).* New York, Nervous & Mental Disease Monographs, 1951.

Lockwood, Joseph E.: Arson and Sabotage, JCLC&PS, Vol.45 (1954-55), 340-48.

Martin, W. L.: Application of Legal Authority in Arson Investigation, JCLC&PS, Vol.42 (1951-52), 468.

Morgan, Charles S.: Preventing Arson, JCL&C, Vol.34, No.2 (July-Aug., 1953), 258-61.

Morgan, James W.: As The Court Sees It, POLICE, Vol.6, No.6 (July-Aug., 1962), 51-53.

Morris, Donald W.: Preparation of a Case for Court, POLICE, Vol.7, No.2 (Nov.-Dec., 1962), 46-50.

National Automobile Theft Bureau, Chicago: Automobile Fire Investigation, POLICE, Vol.3, No.2 (Nov.-Dec., 1958), 16-18.

Nicks, D. L.: The Camera Looks At Arson, POLICE, Vol.4, No.3 (Jan.-Feb., 1960), 75-77.

Nugent, Howard W.: Surveillance in the Investigation of Arson and Other Felonies, POLICE, Vol.9, No.4 (Mar.-Apr., 1965), 39-42.

O'Neal, Wyatt G.: Interrogation in Arson Investigations, POLICE, Vol.6, No.2 (Nov.-Dec., 1961), 35-38.

Priar: L. L.: Clues and Leads in Arson Investigation, POLICE, Vol.5, No.1 (Sept.-Oct., 1960), 52-28, 64.

Reineri, Louis, Jr.: International Association of Arson Investigators Physical Evidence in Auto Investigation, POLICE, Vol.4, No.1 (Nov.-Dec., 1959), 25-29.

Rethoret, H.: *Fire Investigations.* Toronto, Recording & Statistical Corp., 1945.

Rosie, D. M.: Gas Chromatography: A New Tool in Arson Investigation, POLICE, Vol.6, No.4 (Mar.-Apr., 1962), 48-51.

Rossiter, William D.: Investigation of Fires Resulting in Death, POLICE, Vol.4, No.5 (May-June, 1960), 39-42; Vol.4, No.6 (July-Aug., 1960), 31-33.

Salzenstein, Marvin A.: Spontaneous Combustion, POLICE, Vol.6, No.5 (May-June, 1962), 52-54.

———, **Reffner, Marvin A., and Reffner, John A.:** Modern Laboratory Methods in Arson Investigation, POLICE, Vol.9, No.5 (May-June, 1965), 48.

Sattenfield, Val Beyer: Criteria for Detection and Control of Arsonists, JCL&C, Vol.34, No.4 (Nov.-Dec., 1953), 417-27.

Schmideberg, Melittg: Pathological Firesetters, JCL&C, Vol.34, No.1 (May-June, 1953), 30-39.

Schuck, J. P.: Rural Investigation of Arson, POLICE, Vol.5, No.6 (July-Aug., 1961), 28-33.

Shaver, Paul A.: Arson, TPY (1963).

———: Arson: Juvenile Set Fires, TPY (1962).

———: The Motive in Arson Cases, TPY (1961).

———: Report of the Arson Committee, TPY (1963).

Shifflett, Glen A.: Investigating Automobile Fire Cases, JCLC&PS, Vol.49, No.3 (1958-59), 276.

Silvarman, Allen B. I.: Security Techniques at the Scene of a Fire, POLICE, Vol.9, No.5 (May-June, 1965), 62.

Smith, Miles B.: The Investigator Arrives at the Fire Scene, POLICE, Vol.7, No.4 (Mar.-Apr., 1963), 59-65.

Staff, Western Division, National Automobile Theft Bureau: Automobile Fire Investigation, POLICE, Vol.3, No.3 (Jan.-Feb., 1959), 6-11; Vol.3, No.4 (Mar.-Apr., 1959), 7-12; Vol.3, No.5 (May-June, 1959), 9-14.

Stevens, Samuel L.: Evidence of Arson and Its Legal Aspects, JCL&C, Vol.34, No.6 (Mar.-Apr., 1954), 817-826.

———: Physical Evidence in Arson Investigation, POLICE, Vol.6, No.1 (Sept.-Oct., 1961), 52-55.

Stoffel, Joseph F.: Determining the Cause of An Explosion, POLICE, Vol.7, No.3 (Jan.-Feb., 1963), 64-67.

Straeter, Raymond L.: Insurance Motive Fire, JCLC&PS, Vol.46 (1955-56), 277-80.

Stuerwald, John E.: International Association of Arson Investigators, POLICE, Vol.4, No.1 (Sept.-Oct., 1959), 46-51.

Sullivan, Joseph A.: Some Legal Aspects of Arson, POLICE, Vol.7, No.1 (Sept.-Oct., 1962), 32-36.

Training—Arson Investigator's Seminar, TPC, Vol.30 (Apr., 1963), 33.

Wakefield, E. A.: Rural Arson Problems, JCLC&PS, Vol.45 (1954-55), 613-20.

Walker, Glenroy M.: Recognition, Collection and Preservation of Evidence in Arson Cases, POLICE, Vol.5, No.2 (Nov.-Dec., 1960), 61-63; Vol.5, No.3 (Jan.-Feb., 1961), 60-61.

Watson, Herbert C.: The Pyromaniac, TPY (1961).

———: Report of the Arson Committee, TPY (1956), (1957), (1958), (1959), (1961), (1962).

Wedekind, Richard: Manual for the Identification of Automobiles, A Valuable Tool for the Arson Investigator, POLICE, Vol.7, No.5 (May-June, 1963, 25-27.

ASSAULT

Peterson, Richard A., O'Neal, Patricia, and Pittman, David J.: Stabilities in Deviance: A Study of Assaultive & Non-assaultive Offenders, JCLC&PS, Vol.53, No.1 (May-June, 1962), 44.

Purcell, Phillip: Assault, TPY (1962).

Smith, Justin C.: Investigation of Fatal Gunshot Wounds, Cleveland, Law-Medicine Center, Western Reserve Univ., 1963.

Waller, James I.: Re-definition of Aggravated Assault, TPY (1961).

AUTO THEFT

Daniel, John F.: Report of the Committee on Automobile Theft, TPY (1957).

Davis, William J.: Automobile Fires—Their Relation to Automobile Thefts, POLICE, Vol.7, No.5 (May-June, 1963), 24.

———: Auto Theft, TPY (1962).

Escapes from Submerged Vehicles, TPC, Vol. 30 (May, 1963), 38.

Fritts, G. S.: *Auto Theft Investigations.* Washington, D.C., I.A.C.P., 1965.

King, Ray M.: The Trend to Reduce Automobile Theft, POLICE, Vol.9, No.5 (May-June, 1965), 58.

Lane, Marvin G.: The Juvenile Auto Thief, TPY (1961).

Lawrence, Leonard G.: Auto Theft Prevention Through Citizen Education—Workshop, TPY (1965), 174-76.

———: Report of the Auto Theft Committee, TPY (1963), (1964), and (1965).

Mullen, John F.: Processing Auto Theft Data, TPC, Vol.29, No.5 (May, 1962), 4.

Nelson, A. T., and Smith, Howard E.: *Car Clouting, the Crime, the Criminal and the Police,* Springfield, Thomas, 1958.

———, & ———: A Major Police Problem—Theft from Vehicle, POLICE, Vol.3, No.1 (Sept.-Oct., 1958), 7-14.

New York City Police Department: *Auto Larcenies,* N.Y.C.P.D., 1954.

Otlewis, George A.: Report of the Committee on Automobile Theft, TPY (1956).

Richards, Karl M.: Automobile Manufacturers Association Report, TPY (1963).

———: Thwarting the Auto Thief, TPY (1957).

Rocco, Daniel, and Snack, Edward: Notes on the Stolen Car Problem, L&O, Vol.9 (Nov., 1961).

Rowe, Wayne F.: The Stolen Car and the Traffic Officer, POLICE, Vol.4, No.4 (Mar.-Apr., 1960), 68-73.

Savitz, Leonard D.: Automobile Theft, JCLC&PS (July-Aug., 1959), 132-43.

Scanlon, Charles P.: Notes on Stolen Cars, L&O, Vol.8, No.8 (1960).

Schepses, Erwin: The Young Car Thief, JCLC&PS, Vol.50, No.6 (Mar.-Apr., 1960), 569.

Sweeney, Frank A.: Report of Automobile Theft Committee, TPY (1958, 1959, 1960, 1961 and 1962).

Toothman, E. M.: Barriers to Auto Theft, TPC, Vol.31 (Aug., 1964), 48.

Truett, John T.: Notes on Auto Theft, L&O, Vol.11, No.6 (June, 1963).

Wattenbert, William E., and Balistrieri, James: Automobile Theft: A "Favored Group" Delinquency, AJS, Vol.57 (May, 1952), 575-79.

Wedekind, Richard: Automobile Theft, the Thirteen Million Dollar Parasite, JCLC&PS, Vol.48 (1957), 443-46.

Welch, Neil J.: Auto Theft: A Law Enforcement Problem, TPY (1961).

BURGLARY

Black, Jack: A Burglar Looks at Laws and Codes, HARPER'S, Vol.160, 306-313.

California Department of Education, Bureau of Trade and Industrial Education: *Burglary—Commercial,* Sacramento, 1949.

———: *Burglary—Residence.* Sacramento, 1949.

———: *Burglary—Safes.* Sacramento, 1949.

Cochran, Murray O.: Police Science Traps Lone Wolf Burglar, L&O, Vol.12 (July, 1964).

Girard, Paul J.: Burglary Trends and Protection, JCLC&PS, Vol.50, No.5 (Jan.-Feb., 1960), 511.

Holcomb, Richard: *Armed Robbery.* Iowa City, Bureau of Public Affairs, State University of Iowa, 1951.

———: *Protection Against Burglary.* Iowa City, University of Iowa Press, 1953.

Lawrence, Leonard G.: Burglary, TPY (1962).

Michael, H. B.: Modern Burglary and Robbery Protection Methods, in *Scientific Evidence and Scientific Crime Detection.* Buffalo, Hein, 1964. Vol.2:1.

Wilson, Herbert Emerson: *I Stole $16,000,000.* New York, Signet, 1956.

EMBEZZLEMENT

Aubert, Vilhelm: White Collar Crime and Social Structure, AJS, Vol.58 (Nov., 1952), 263-71.

Caldwell, Robert G.: A Re-examination of the Concept of White-collar Crime, FP, Vol.22, No.1 (Mar., 1958), 30-36.

Cort, David: The Embezzler, TN, Vol.188 (Apr. 18, 1959), 339-42.

Cressey, Donald R.: Embezzlement: Robbery by Trust, SEC.W., Vol.2, No.3 (May, 1965), 16.

———: *Other People's Money: A Study of the*

Social Psychology of Embezzlement. Glencoe, Free Press, 1953.

Davis, John R.: The Combating of Theft from Within . . . What Is the Answer? POLICE, Vol.9, No.2 (Nov.-Dec., 1964), 46-47.

Embezzlers: The Trusted Thieves, FORTUNE, Vol.56 (Nov., 1957), 142-44.

Emerson, Thomas I.: Review of White Collar Crime, YLJ, Vol.59 (Feb., 1950), 581-85.

Hartung, Frank E.: White-collar Crime: Its Significance for Theory and Practice, FP, Vol.17, No.2 (June, 1953), 31-36.

————: White Collar Offenses in the Wholesale Meat Industry in Detroit, AJS, Vol.56 (July, 1950), 25-32.

Hewitt, William H.: Combating the White Col-lar Criminal, L&O, Vol.11, No.2 (Feb., 1963).

Jaspan, Norman, and Black, Hillel: *The Thief in the White Collar.* Philadelphia, Lippin-cott, 1960.

Neal, H. E.: Wanted: Facts in Fake Securities Cases, TPC, Vol.31 (Jan., 1964), 40.

Newman, Donald J.: White-collar Crime, L&CP, Vol.23 (Autumn, 1958), 735-53.

Quinney, Earl R.: The Study of White Collar Crime: Toward a Reorientation in Theory and Research, JCLC&PS, Vol.55, No.2 (June, 1964), 208.

Sutherland, Edwin H.: Is White Collar Crime a Crime? ASR, Vol.10 (Apr., 1945), 132-39.

————: *White Collar Crime.* New York, Dryden Press, 1949.

FORGERY

Beary, E. R.: Worthless Check Bulletin Pays Off, L&O, Vol.10, No.9 (Sept., 1962), 14.

Black, David A.: Forged Signatures More Skill-fully Written than the True Signature, JCLC&PS, Vol.53, No.1 (Mar.-May, 1962), 109.

————: Fraudulent Check Notations, JCLC&PS, Vol.54, No.2 (1963), 220.

Black, James V.: Forgery Above a Genuine Signature, JCLC&PS, Vol.50, No.6 (1959-60).

Christiano, Conrad, and Van Buren, John: The Great "Miracle Ink" Swindle. READER'S DIGEST (Feb., 1957).

Conway, James V. P.: *Evidential Documents.* Springfield, Thomas, 1959.

Cuelenaere, Al: Secret Communications—A Bib-liography of Secret Writing and Cryptog-raphy, JCLC&PS, Vol.50, No.3 (Sept.-Oct., 1959), 307.

Fricke, Charles W.: The Successful Trial of Forgery Cases, POLICE, Vol.2, No.4 (Mar.-Apr., 1958), 48-50.

Harris, John J.: Disguised Handwriting, JCL&C, Vol.43, No.5 (Jan.-Feb., 1953), 685.

————: How Much Do People Write Alike, JCLC&PS, Vol.49 (Mar.-Apr., 1958-59), 647.

Hilton, Ordway: Can the Forger Be Identified From His Handwriting? JCLC&PS, Vol.43, No.4 (Nov.-Dec., 1952), 547.

————: Forged Wills Revealed by Scientific Ex-amination of Documents, MLQ, Vol.6 (1952), 560-67.

————: A Further Look at Writing Standards, *Proceedings of the First International Meet-ings in Questioned Documents.* London (Apr., 1963).

————: Handwriting and the Mentally Ill, JFS, Vol.7, No.1 (1962), 131-39.

————: Handwriting and Typewriting Identifi-cation, *Encyclopedia Americana*, 1948.

————: Handwriting Comparison Clears the Innocent Suspect, CLR, Vol.3, No.1 (Au-tumn, 1956), 63-75.

————: Identification of the Make of Type-writer, ICPR, No.51 (1951), 287-93.

————: Identification of the Work from an IBM Electric Typewriter, JFS, Vol.7, No.3 (July, 1962), 286-302.

————: I'm on Trial and Need a Handwriting Expert, C&C, Vol.68, No.1 (Jan.-Feb., 1963), 24-31.

————: Influence of Serious Illness on Handwrit-ing Identification, POST.M., Vol.19, No.2 (Feb., 1956), A-36-A-48.

————: The Need for Accurate Findings and Effective Testimony as a Basis for Progres-sive Appellate Decisions, JFS, Vol.4, No.3 (1959), 347-50.

————: Neu Aspekte zu den Vergleichs—Schrift Problem, KRIMINALISTIK, Vol.12 (Dec., 1963), 586-591.

————: Photographic Methods for Deciphering Erased Pencil Writing, ICPR, No.85 (Feb., 1955), 47-50.

————: Photographing Documents, PP, Vol.78 (Mar., 1951), 39-41; Vol.78 (Apr., 1951), 37-39; (May, 1951), 39-40.

————: The Preparation and Signing of Legal Documents, CONN.LR, Vol.29, No.3 (Sept., 1955), 218-28.

————: Pre-trial Preparation in a Questioned Document Case, TLR, Vol.27 (1953), 473-77.

————: Problems in the Identification of Pro-portional Spacing Typewriting, JFS, Vol.3, No.3 (July, 1958), 263-87.

————: Procuring Handwriting Specimens During Cross-examination, CONN.BJ., Vol.28, No.2 (June, 1954), 168-72.

———: Proper Evaluation of Dissimilarities in Handwriting, CPR, No.105 (Feb., 1957), 48-51.

———: Relationship of Mathematical Probability to Handwriting, *Royal Canadian Mounted Police Seminar,* No.5, Oct. 27-Nov. 1, 1958, 121-28.

———: The Role of the Document Section in the Academy, *American Academy of Forensic Sciences Newsletter,* July, 1964.

———: Science and the Scientific Examination of Signatures, TLR, Vol.24 (1950), 304-10.

———: *Scientific Examination of Questioned Documents.* Chicago, Callaghan, 1956.

———: Some Basic Rules for the Identification of Handwriting, MS&L, Vol.3, No.3 (Apr., 1963), 107-17.

———: Traced Forgeries and Infrared Photography, ICPR, No.159 (June-July, 1963), 195-97.

———: The Typewriter Testifies, TTLG, Vol.2, No.3 (Aug., 1958).

———, **Purtell, David J., Ashton, Harry M.,** and **Brooks, C. D.:** Seminar on Testimony, JFS, Vol.2, No.2 (Apr., 1957), 177-85.

———, & **Sellers, Clark:** Code of Ethics Adopted by Questioned Document Examiners, ABAJ, Vol.40, No.8 (Aug., 1954), 690-91.

———, & **Stein, Elbridge W.:** Ball Point Pens: Questions Raised by Examiners of Signa-

tures and Documents, ABAJ, Vol.34 (1948), 373-76.

———, & **Turner, Ralph:** Documents, in *Forensic Science and Laboratory Techniques.* Springfield, Thomas, 1949.

Humphreys, Ray: Purging the Paper Hangers, L&O, Vol.7 (Apr., 1959).

Lemert, Edwin M.: An Isolation and Closure Theory of Naive Check Forgery, JCL&C, Vol.47 (Sept.-Oct., 1953), 296-307.

Metzger, George: The Philadelphia Plan, L&O, Vol.7 (July, 1959).

Morada, R. J.: *Variations in Genuine Writing as an Identification Factor in the Detection of Forgery.* Washington, IACP, 1955.

Purtell, David J.: The Identification of Checkwriters, JCLC&PS, Vol.45 (1954-55), 229-35.

Sellers, Clark: Albert S. Osborn, JCL&C, Vol.38, No.1 (Mar.-Apr., 1947-48), 75-58.

———: Assisted and Guided Signatures, JCLC&PS, Vol.53, No.2 (June-Aug., 1962), 245.

———: Document Examination Abroad, JCLC&PS, Vol.51, No.6 (Mar.-Apr., 1960-61), 663.

Sternitzsky, Julius L.: *Forgery and Fictitious Checks.* Springfield, Thomas, 1955.

———: Suggestions to Officers on Forgery Investigation, POLICE, Vol.1, No.6 (July-Aug., 1957), 31-35.

Totten, James C.: Phoney Check Artists Make Crime Pay—Almost, L&O, Vol.8, No.8 (1960).

FRAUD

Arm, Walter: *Pay-off.* New York, Appleton-Century-Crofts, 1951.

Barash, James T.: Compensation and the Crime of Pigeon Dropping, J.CRIM.PSY., Vol.18 (Oct., 1951), 92-94.

Bloom, Murray Teigh: *Money of Their Own.* New York, Ballantine Books, 1960.

California Department of Education, Bureau of Trade and Industrial Education: *Bunco.* Sacramento, 1949.

———: *Corporate Security Frauds.* Sacramento, 1949.

Irey, E. L., and **Slocum, W. H.:** *The Tax Dodgers.* New York, Greenbert, 1948.

Jarman, Rufus: How the Spanish-prisoner Swindle Works, SATURDAY EVENING POST, Vol.225 (Nov. 8, 1952), 29.

Persuading the Taxpayer It Doesn't Pay to Cheat. BUSINESS WEEK (Aug. 1, 1959), 50-51.

Schur, Edwin M.: Sociological Analysis of Confidence Swindling, JCLC&PS, Vol.48 (Sept.-Oct., 1957), 296-304.

HOMOSEXUALITY

Ayer, A. J.: Homosexuals and the Law, NS (June 25, 1960).

Bailey, Derrick S.: *Homosexuality and the Western Christian Tradition.* London, Longmans, 1955.

——— **(ed.):** *Sexual Offenders and Social Punishment.* London, Church of England Moral Welfare Council, 1956.

Baldwin, James: *Another Country.* New York, Dial Press, 1962.

Becker, Howard S.: *Outsiders: Studies in the Sociology of Deviance.* New York, Free Press, 1963.

Bieber, Irving, *et al.:* *Homosexuality: A Psychoanalytic Study.* New York, Basic Books, 1962.

Caprio, Frank S.: *Female Homosexuality.* New York, Grove Press, 1962.

Cory, Donald W.: *The Homosexual in America: a Subjective Approach,* 2nd Ed. New York, Castle Books, 1960.

———, & Le Roy, John P.: *The Homosexual and His Society: A View From Within.* New York, Citadel Press, 1963.

DeBeauvoir, Simone: *The Second Sex.* New York, Knopf, 1952.

Dotty, Robert C.: Growth of Overt Homosexuality Provokes Wide Concern, THE NEW YORK TIMES, WESTERN EDITION (Dec. 27, 1963), p.7.

Ellis, Albert: *The American Sexual Tragedy.* New York, Grove Press, 1962.

Ford, Clellan, and Beach, Frank: *Patterns of Sexual Behavior.* New York, Ace Books, 1951.

Goffman, Erving: *Stigma: Notes on the Management of Spoiled Identity.* Englewood Cliffs: Prentice-Hall, 1963.

Great Britain, Committee on Homosexual Offences and Prostitution: *Report.* (Command 247, 1957), His Majesty's Stationery Office, London.

Greenspan, Herbert, and Campbell, John D.: The Homosexual as a Personality Type, AJPSY, Vol.101 (Mar., 1945), 682-89.

Hart, H. L. A.: *Law, Liberty and Morality.* Stanford, Stanford University Press, 1963.

Helmer, William J.: New York's Middle-class Homosexuals, HARPER'S (Mar., 1963).

Her Majesty's Stationery Office: *Committee on Homosexual Offences and Prostitution.* A Report Published in 1957. London, Her Majesty's Stationery Office.

Hooker, Evelyn: Homosexuality in E. and W. Genne (eds.), *Foundation for Christian Family Policy.* New York, National Council of Churches, 1961.

Kinsey, Alfred C., Pomeroy, W. B., and Martin, C. E.: *Sexual Behavior in the Human Male.* Philadelphia, Saunders, 1948.

Lindner, Robert: Homosexuality and the Contemporary Scene, in *Must You Conform?* New York, Grove Press, 1961.

Needham, Merrill A., and Schur, Edwin M.: Student Punitiveness Toward Sexual Deviation, M&FL, Vol.25 (May, 1963), 227-28.

Leznoff, Maurice, and Westley, William A.: The Homosexual Community, SP, Vol.3 (Apr., 1956).

Lynd, Helen Merrell: *On Shame and the Search for Identity.* New York, Science Editions, 1958.

Perlman, David: Study of Sex Offenders: Research Into a Vast Area of Ignorance, SAN FRANCISCO CHRONICLE (Dec. 11, 1963).

Ploscowe, Morris: *Sex and the Law,* Rev. Ed. New York, Ace Books, 1962.

Private Consensual Homosexual Behavior: The Crime and Its Enforcement, YLJ, Vol.70 (Mar., 1961), 623-35.

Rechy, John: *City of Night.* New York, Grove Press, 1963.

Rees, J. T., and Usill, H. V. (eds.): *They Stand Apart.* New York, Macmillan, 1955.

Reiss, Albert J., Jr.: Sex Offenses: The Marginal Status of the Adolescent, L&CP, Vol.25 (Spring, 1960).

———: The Social Integration of Queers and Peers, SP, Vol.9 (Fall, 1961).

Rolph, C. H.: The Problem for the Police, NS (June 25, 1960).

Rose, Arnold, and Press, E. E.: Does the Punishment Fit the Crime? A Study in Social Valuation, AJS, Vol.61 (Nov., 1955), 247-59.

Ruitenbeek, Hendrik M. (ed.): *The Problem of Homosexuality In Modern Society.* New York, Dutton, 1963.

St. John-Stevas, Norman: *Life, Death and the Law.* Bloomington, Indiana Univ. Press, 1961.

Stearn, Jess: *The Sixth Man.* New York, Macfadden, 1961.

Westwood, Gordon: *Society and the Homosexual.* New York, Dutton, 1953 (for an interesting discussion of different "levels" of homosexual life in England).

Wheeler, Stanton: Sex Offenses: A Sociological Critique, L&CP, Vol.25 (Spring, 1960), 262.

Wildeblood, Peter: *Against the Law.* London, Penguin Books, 1955.

Williams, J. E. Hall: Sex Offenses: The British Experience, L&CP, Vol.25 (Spring, 1960), 334-60.

Wolf, D., and Francher, E. (eds.): *The Village Voice Reader.* New York, Grove Press, 1963.

INTERROGATION

Admissibility of Tape Recorded Confession, JCLC&PS, Vol.46 (1955-56), 420.

Arthur, Richard O.: Interrogation for Investigators, L&O, Vol.7 (Mar., 1959).

Bristow, Allen: *Field Interrogation.* Springfield, Thomas, 1963.

Brown, Lawrence E.: Police Interrogation Dilemma, POLICE, Vol.8, No.3 (Jan.-Feb., 1964), 75-77.

Caputo, Rudolph R.: The Confession, POLICE, Vol.9, No.5 (May-June, 1965), 85.

Cohen, J. Arnold: The Integrated Control Question Technique, POLICE, Vol.6, No.1 (Sept.-Oct., 1961), 56-58.

Dienstein, William: The Importance of Words in Questioning Techniques, POLICE, Vol.1, No.4 (Mar.-Apr., 1957), 47-51.

Earhart, Robert S.: A Critical Analysis of Investigator—Criminal Informant Relationships in Law Enforcement, Unpublished Master's Thesis, School of Police, Admin., Michigan State University, East Lansing, 1964.

Eichelberger, Robert S.: Sincerity of Purpose, POLICE, Vol.4, No.3 (Jan.-Feb., 1960), 52-60.

Epstein, David M.: Advance Notice of Alibi, JCLC&PS, Vol.55, No.1 (Mar., 1964), 29.

Geis, Gilbert: In Scopolamine Veritas, JCLC&PS, Vol.50, No.4 (1959-60), 347.

Holmes, Warren: Interrogation, SEC.W., Vol.1, No.2 (Sept.-Oct., 1964), 10-15.

Hornady, William T.: The Effects of Authority Factors in Interrogations, JCLC&PS, Vol.55, No.3 (Sept., 1964), 420.

Indau, Fred E.: Legal Pitfalls to Avoid in Criminal Interrogations, JCLC&PS, Vol.40, No.2 (July-Aug., 1949), 211.

————: Police Interrogation—A Practical Necessity, JCLC&PS, Vol.52, No.1 (May-June, 1961), 16.

————: *Self-incrimination.* Springfield, Thomas.

————, & **Reid, John E.:** *Criminal Interrogation and Confession.* Baltimore, Williams & Wilkins, 1962.

————, & ————: *Lie Detection and Criminal Interrogation.* Baltimore, Williams & Wilkins, 1953.

Kidd, Worth R.: *Police Interrogation.* New York, Basuino, 1948.

Levy, Sheldon S.: Hypnosis and Legal Immutability, JCLC&PS, Vol.46 (1955-56), 333-46.

Lyng, J. F. X.: Interrogation, L&O, Vol.12 (Sept., 1964).

McDonald, Hugh: Interrogation: Remarks of, TPY, 1964.

Muehlberger, C. W.: Interrogation Under Drug Influence, The So-Called "Truth Serum" Technique, JCLC&PS, Vol.42 (1951-52), 513.

Mulbar, Harold: *Interrogation,* Springfield, Thomas.

Right to De Novo Determination of Physical Coercion of Confession, JCLC&PS, Vol.46 (1955-56), 532.

Ross, J. L., et al.: *Elements of Interrogation.* Sacramento, Calif. State Dept. of Education, 1963.

Schultz, Leroy G.: Interviewing the Sex Offender's Victim. JCLC&PS, Vol.50, No.5 (Jan.-Feb., 1960), 448.

Silence after Being Accused Not Admission of Guilt, JCLC&PS, Vol.46 (1955-56), 152.

Tocchio, O. J.: Lie Detection Under Hypnosis, POLICE, Vol.8, No.1 (Sept.-Oct., 1963), 9-11.

Ward, Francis M.: In-custody Interrogations, TPC, Vol.32, No.3 (Mar., 1965), 52-59.

Weisbert, Bernard: Police Interrogation of Arrested Persons: A Skeptical View, JCLC&PS, Vol.52, No.1 (May-June, 1961), 21.

Wellman, Francis: *The Art of Cross Examination.* Garden City, Garden City Publishers, 1959.

Wood, Alan C.: The Information Room, L&O, Vol.8, No.9 (1960).

INVESTIGATION

Aldrich, John M.: The Permanent Record of Gemstone Identification, JCLC&PS, Vol.42 (1951-52), 114.

Allen, A. L.: *Personal Descriptions.* Toronto, Carswell Co.

Arm, Walter: Case for the Police, TPC (Apr., 1961), 5.

Aubry, Arthur S.: The Collection of Evidence, POLICE, Vol.7, No.4 (Mar.-Apr., 1963), 40-43.

————: Ethics for Investigation, JCLC&PS, Vol.53, No.2 (July-Aug., 1962), 269.

Bliss, Edward N.: Defense Detective, JCLC&PS, Vol.47, No.2 (July-Aug., 1956), 264.

————: *Defense Investigation.* Springfield, Thomas, 1965.

Boolsen, Frank M., et al.: *Basic Criminal Investigation.* Sacramento, California Peace Officers' Training Series No. 70, California State Dept. of Education, 1956.

————: *Elements of Police Investigation.* Sacra-

mento, California Peace Officers' Training Series No.25, California State Dept. of Education.

Brittain, Robert P.: Tatooed Letters and Identification, JCL&C, Vol.40, No.6 (Mar.-Apr., 1950), 787.

Busch, Francis X.: *Casebook of the Curious and True.* New York, Charter Books, 1962.

California Dept. of Justice, Division of Criminal Law and Enforcement, Bureau of Criminal Identification and Investigation: *Modus Operandi and Report Writing.* Sacramento, 1952.

California State Peace Officers' Training Series: *Elements of Police Investigation.* Sacramento, California Dept. of Education, 1964.

Campbell, Norman R.: *Foundations of Science.* New York, Dover, 1957.

Caputo, Rudolph R.: Notes on Eye-witness Identification, L&O, Vol.8, No.12 (1960).

Civil and Criminal Identification and Investi-

gations. Chicago, Institute of Applied Science.

Civil Service Employees Not Allowed to Enjoin Commission, JCLC&PS, Vol.46 (1955-56), 287.

Collins, Robert L.: Improved Crime Scene Investigation, JCLC&PS, Vol.52, No.4 (Nov.-Dec., 1961), 469.

Conrad, Edwin C.: The Electroencephalograph (EEG) As Evidence of Criminal Responsibility, JCLC&PS, Vol.50, No.4 (Nov.-Dec., 1959), 405.

Coon, Thomas F.: Government Security and Investigations, POLICE, Vol.8, No.4 (Mar.-Apr., 1964), 69-72.

———: Miscellaneous Files, POLICE, Vol.7, No.6 (July-Aug., 1963), 42-44.

Curry, Jesse E.: Criminal Investigations, TPY, 1963.

Daloia, Robert J.: The Truth and the Investigator, L&O, Vol.7 (Sept., 1964).

Dieckmann, Edward A.: Trained Seals in a Squirrel Cage, POLICE, Vol.5, No.5 (May-June, 1961), 12-14.

Dienstein, William: *Techniques for the Crime Investigator.* Springfield, Thomas, 1963.

Dinneen, Joseph F.: *The Alternate Case: A Documentary Novel.* Boston, Little, Brown, 1958.

Dondero, John: The Identification Man, TPC (June, 1961), 22.

Dunlap, Al: Science vs. Practical Common Sense in Crime Detection, SCIENTIFIC EVIDENCE AND SCIENTIFIC CRIME DETECTION, Vol.2:4. Buffalo, Hain, 1964.

Dutra, Frank R.: Medicolegal Aspects of Conflagrations, JCL&C, Vol.39, No.6 (Mar.-Apr., 1948), 771-78.

Eiseman, James S.: *Elements of Investigation Techniques.* Bloomington, McNight & McNight, 1949.

Fagan, Edward F.: The Problem of Silence, POLICE, Vol.3, No.2 (Nov.-Dec., 1958), 34-37.

The First Class in Scientific Crime Detection Held in Chicago: SE&SCD, Vol.2, No.2, 1964.

Fisher, Jacob: *The Art of Detection.* New York, Sterling, 1953.

Fitzgerald, Maurice J.: *Handbook of Criminal Investigation.* New York, Arco, 1959.

Frike, Charles W., Revised by Kolbrek, LeRoy M.: *Criminal Investigation.* 6th Ed. Los Angeles, Legal Book Store, 1962.

Gerber, Samuel R., and Schroeder, Oliver, Jr.: *Crime Investigation and Interrogation.* Cincinnati, Anderson, 1962.

Goddard, Calvin: Full Course in Methods of Scientific Crime Detection, SE&SCD, Vol.2, No.4 (1964).

———: The Valentine Day Massacre: A Study in Ammunition Tracing, SE&SCD, Vol.1, No.1, 1964.

Godown, Linton: How to Recognize Type Faces, JCLC&PS, Vol.51, No.2 (Mar.-Apr., 1960-61), 282.

Gorphe, F.: Showing Prisoners to Witnesses for Identification, SE&SCD, Vol.1, No.1, 1964.

Grant, C. E.: *Information: Sources and Uses of Investigators.* Sacramento, Bureau of Industrial Education, 1963.

Harper, C. R.: Aircraft Accident Investigation, TPC, Vol.31 (Nov., 1963), 36.

Harris, Raymond I.: Accessory After the Fact—The Officer on the Scene, POLICE, Vol.8, No.6 (July-Aug., 1963), 6-13.

Harney, Malachi, and Cross, John C.: *The Informer in Law Enforcement.* Springfield, Thomas, 1959.

Heffron, Floyd N.: *Evidence for the Patrolman.* Springfield, Thomas, 1958.

Hicks, Sam: Tracking—A Vanishing Heritage, POLICE, Vol.4, No.5 (May-June, 1960), 43-46.

Homphreys, Ray: Ferreting Out the Fade Aways, L&O, Vol.7 (Dec., 1959).

Howe, Ronald M., *et al.:* *Criminal Investigation,* 4th Ed. London, Sweet & Maxwell, 1950.

Hunter, T. P.: History of the Bureau of Criminal Identification and Investigation, unpublished paper. Sacramento, Dept. of Justice, State of Calif., n.d.

Hutchinson, W. J.: Plans and Sketches, SE&SCD, Vol.3, No.2, 1964.

The I.A.I. Convention, SE&SCD, Vol.2, No.4, 1964.

Iannarelli, Alfred Victor: *The Iannarelli System of Ear Identification.* Brooklyn, Foundation Press, 1964.

Inbau, Fred E.: Techniques, TPY, 1963.

———, **& Reid, John E.:** *Lie Detection and Criminal Investigation.* Baltimore, Williams & Wilkins, 1953.

John Foley Murder, SE&SCD, Vol.1, No.1 (1964).

John Korman Case, SE&SCD, Vol.1, No.3 (1964).

Jones, Leland V.: *Scientific Investigation and Physical Evidence: a Handbook for Investigators.* Springfield, Thomas, 1959.

Kasman, Saul: Human Nature for Investigators, JCL&C, Vol.44, No.6 (Mar.-Apr., 1954), 737-45.

Keating, William J., and Carter, Richard: *The*

Man Who Rocked the Boat. New York, Harper & Bros., 1956.

Kenehan, Richard F.: Converting Words into Pictures, POLICE, Vol.5, No.1 (Sept.-Oct., 1960), 19-22.

Kennedy, John: Some Practical Suggestions for the Taking of Criminal Confessions, JCLC&PS, Vol.48, No.6 (Mar.-Apr., 1958), 660.

Kerbach, M.: Felonious Shooting—One or Two Persons Involved, SE&SCD, Vol.3, No.2 (1964).

Kessler & Weston: *Detection of Murder.* New York, Greenberg, 1953.

Kirk, Paul L.: *Crime Investigation.* New York, Interscience Publishers, 1960.

Lorence, Earl F.: Undercover Investigation: Management's Periscope, SEC.W., Vol.2, No.4 (June, 1965), 24.

McArthur, Jack: Crime Scene Sketching: A Simple Procedure, POLICE, Vol.8, No.5 (May-June, 1964), 39-42.

McCann, M. G.: *The Police and the Confidential Informant: an Outline for the Development and Management of Police—Informant Relationships.* Washington, IACP, 1957.

McClellan, John L.: *Crime Without Punishment.* New York, Duell, Sloane & Pearce, 1962.

McDonell, R. E.: Cooperative Information Sharing Programs for Law Enforcement, TPC, Vol.31 (July, 1964), 22.

McIntyre, Donald M., Jr., Tiffany, Lawrence P., and Rotenberg, Daniel L.: *Detection of Crime.* Boston, Little, Brown & Co., 1965.

Madigan, F. I.: More, Not Less, Information Exchange, TPC, Vol.31 (Nov., 1964), 37.

Merkeley, Donald: *The Investigation of Death.* Springfield, Thomas, 1957.

Miloslavic, Edward L.: Uncommon Criminal Methods of Infanticide, JCLC&PS, Vol.42 (1951-52), 414.

Moir, John B., and Wattenberg, William W.: A Phenomenon in Search of a Cause, JCLC&PS, Vol.48, No.1 (May-June, 1957), 54.

A New Police Investigative Tool, Townsend Engineered Products Incorporated, POLICE, Vol.4, No.3 (Jan.-Feb., 1960), 16-17.

O'Flaherty, Liam: *The Informer.* New York, Signet, 1961.

O'Hara, Charles: *Fundamentals of Criminal Investigation.* Springfield, Thomas, 1963.

Osterburg, James W.: Crime Scene Search, L&O, Vol.7 (Mar., 1964).

———: Selection of Criminal Investigators in Law Enforcement Agencies, JCLC&PS, Vol.53, No.2 (June-Aug., 1962), 264.

———: Significant Concepts in Scientific Criminal Investigation, L&O, Vol.7 (July, 1964).

Pei, Mario: What Did He Say? POLICE, Vol.4, No.1 (Sept.-Oct., 1959), 54-58.

Pena, Manuel S.: *Criminal Investigation.* Los Angeles, East Los Angeles College, 1962.

Peper, John P., Boolsen, Frank M., and Grant, Charles E.: *Elements of Police Investigation.* Sacramento, 1950.

Piedelievre, R.: Case "C.," SE&SCD, Vol.2, No.6 (1964).

Pouliot, J. E.: How Is Your Identification? L&O, Vol.7 (Feb., 1964).

Price, Carroll S.: Sources of Information, POLICE, Vol.4, No.4 (Mar.-Apr., 1960), 47-51.

Rizer, Conrad K.: A Women Falls on a Stairway, JCLC&PS, Vol.52, No.1 (May-June, 1961), 134.

Schulz, George: The Criminal Investigation Bureau of Land Lower Saxony, JCLC&PS, Vol.46 (1955-56), 722-25.

Scientific Evidence and Scientific Crime Detection, Vols.1-3, Buffalo, Wm. S. Hein & Co., 1964.

Shaw, William: Facsimile, L&O, Vol.11, No.3 (Mar., 1963).

Smith, Emory: The Fallibility of Eyewitness Testimony, SE&SCD, Vol.1, No.5 (1964).

Soderman, Harry, and O'Connell, John J.: *Modern Criminal Investigation.* Revised by Charles E. O'Hara. New York, Funk & Wagnalls Co., 1962.

The Southwestern Law Enforcement Institute: *Criminal Investigation.* Springfield, Thomas, 1962.

Svensson, A., and Wendel, O.: *Crime Detection.* New York, Elsevier Pub., 1955.

Third International Congress of Criminal Police, SE&SCD, Vol.1, No.6 (1964).

Toler, B.: Case History of an Invention, TPC, Vol.30 (Aug., 1963), 47.

Ullrich, Gustave: The Role of Firearms in Investigations, POLICE, Vol.8, No.1 (Sept.-Oct., 1963), 80-81.

U.S. War Department: *Criminal Investigation.* Field Manual FM 19-20. Washington: Government Printing Office, 1951.

Wels, Kirk: Investigation for Defense as Well as Prosecution. POLICE, Vol.6, No.5 (May-June, 1962), 21.

Wiard, Seth: The Preparation and Presentation of Expert Testimony, SE&SCD, Vol.2, No.2 (1964).

Wickersham Report on Police: SE&SCD, Vol.2, No.4 (1964).

Williams, John F.: Physical Evidence in Hit and

Run Traffic Deaths, JCLC&PS, Vol.50, No.1 (May-June, 1959), 80.

————: Trace Evidence, JCLC&PS, Vol.49, No.3 (1958-59), 285.

Wood, J. Fordyce: The Loeb-Leopold Case, SE&SCD, Vol.1, No.4 (1964).

Woodall, Benjamin: Testimony and Witness Errors in Major Trials, POLICE, Vol.4, No.6 (July-Aug., 1960), 34-36.

Wyatt, Mildre: Technology in Law Enforcement, L&O, Vol.10, No.11 (Nov., 1962), 51.

JUVENILE DELINQUENCY
AND
YOUTH BUREAU

Adams, William T.: Comparison of the Delinquencies of Boys and Girls, JCLC&PS, Vol.53, No.4 (Dec., 1962), 470.

Aichhorn, August: *Wayward Youth.* New York, Meridian, 1958.

Aldrich, Alexander: The Police Role in the Social Investigation, LAR, Vol.57 (Fall, 1959), 14-19.

Alexander, Paul W.: What's This About Punishing Parents? FP (Mar., 1948), 23-29.

Allaman, Richard: Human Relations at the Detention Home, FP, Vol.16 (Dec., 1952), 38-41.

————: Managing Misbehavior at the Detention Home, FP, Vol.17 (Mar., 1953), 27-32.

————: True or False? Some Questions About Your Detention Homes. FOCUS (May, 1948), 69-75.

American Academy of Political and Social Science: Juvenile Delinquency, THE ANNALS, Vol.261 (Jan., 1949), 1-178.

————: Prevention of Juvenile Delinquency, *The Annals* (Mar., 1959).

American Law Institute: *Youth Correction Authority Act.* Philadelphia, The American Law Institute, 1940.

American Psychiatric Association: *Guide to Planning for Training Schools for Delinquent Children, with Particular Reference to Clinical Facilities.* Washington, D.C., A report prepared by the American Psychiatric Association, Subcommittee on Standards for Training Schools, 1952.

Amos, William E., and Manella, Raymond L.: *Readings in the Administration of Institutions for Delinquent Youth.* Springfield, Thomas, 1965.

Applegate, Melbourne S.: *Helping Boys in Trouble: the Layman in Child Guidance.* New York, Association Press, 1950.

Assault the Battered Child Syndrome, TPC, Vol.30 (Jan., 1963), 32.

Ausubel, David P.: *Theory and Problems of Adolescent Development.* New York, Grune and Stratton, 1954.

Axelrad, Sidney: Negro and White Institutionalized Delinquents, AJS, Vol.57 (May, 1952), 569-574.

Bach, George R.: Father-fantasies and Father-typing in Father-separated Children, CD, Vol.17 (1946), 63-80.

Baker, Gordon H.: Comparison of the Delinquencies of Boys and Girls, JCLC&PS, Vol.53, No.4 (Dec., 1962), 470.

Ball, Harry V.: Delinquency and Opportunity: A Theory of Delinquent Gangs, JCLC&PS, Vol.52, No.1 (May-June, 1961), 99.

Ball, John C.: Delinquent and Non-delinquent Attitudes Toward the Prevalence of Stealing, JCLC&PS, Vol.48, No.3 (Sept.-Oct., 1957), 259.

Balogh, Joseph K.: Juvenile Delinquency Proneness—A Study of Predictive Factors Involved in Delinquent Phenomena, JCLC&PS, Vol.45, No.6 (Mar.-Apr., 1958), 615.

————, & Rumage, Charles J.: *Juvenile Delinquency Proneness, a Study of the Kvaraceus Scale,* Annals of American Sociology, Public Affairs Press, Washington, D.C., 1956.

Bander, Edward, J.: Problems of Area Jurisdiction in Juvenile Court, JCLC&PS, Vol.45 (1954-55), 668-674.

Barker, Gordon H.: Juvenile Delinquency and Housing in a Small City, JCLC&PS, Vol.45 (1954-55), 442-44.

————: Parent Organizational Affiliation and Juvenile Delinquency, JCL&C, Vol.44, No.2 (July-Aug., 1953), 204-07.

Barron, M. L.: Juvenile Delinquency and American Values, ASR, Vol.16, No.2 (Apr., 1951).

————: *The Juvenile in Delinquent Society.* New York, Knopf, 1956.

Bartlett, Bill: The House that PAL Rebuilt, L&O, Vol.2 (Feb., 1959).

Bates, William, Robins, Lee N., and O'Neal, Patricia: *Prisons and the Problem Child.* Address given at the Midwest Sociological Society, 1960. Dittoed, Department of Psychiatry and Neurology, Washington Univ., School of Medicine, St. Louis, Missouri.

Baur, E. Jackson, and McCluggage, Marston M.: Drinking Patterns of Kansas High School Students, SP, Vol.5 (Spring, 1958), 317-26.

Beck, Bertram M.: *Five States: a Study of the Youth Authority Program as Promulgated* by the American Law Institute. Philadelphia, American Law Institute, 1951.

Beely, Arthur L.: A Socio-psychological Theory of Crime and Delinquency: A Contribution of Etiology, JCLC&PS, Vol.45 (1945-55), 391-99.

Beemsterboer, Matthew J.: The Juvenile Court—Benevolence in the Star Chamber, JCLC&PS, Vol.50, No.5 (Jan.-Feb., 1960), 464.

Bennett, Lawrence A.: Perpetuation of Delinquency Through Language Usage, JCLC&PS, Vol.50, No.1 (May-June, 1959), 34.

Berkowitz, Bernard: The Juvenile Police Officer, POLICE, Vol.11, No.1 (Sept.-Oct., 1957), 37-38; FOCUS, Vol.31 (1952), 129-34.

Berlin, Louis: Adolescent Recidivism, NPPAJ, Vol.4 (1958), 275-77.

Bernabeu, Edrita P.: Underlying Ego Mechanisms in Delinquency, PQ, Vol.27 (1958), 383-96.

Bernard, William: *Jailbait—The Story of Juvenile Delinquency.* New York, Greenberg, 1949.

Bernstein, Saul: *Youth on the Streets: Work with Alienated Youth Groups.* New York, Association Press, 1964.

Bernstein, Walter: The Cherubs Are Rumbling, NY (Sept. 21, 1957), 120-47.

Bettleheim, Bruno: *Love Is Not Enough.* Glencoe, Free Press, 1950.

————: The Special School for Emotionally Disturbed Children, in Nelson B. Henry (ed.), *Juvenile Delinquency and the Schools.* Chicago, University of Chicago Press, 1948.

————: *Truants from Life, the Rehabilitation of Emotionally Disturbed Children.* Glencoe, Free Press, 1955.

Betz, Elizabeth A.: Release from Training School, New York, *1950 Yearbook, National Probation & Parole Assoc.*, 1950.

Binford, Jesse F.: The Schools and the Delinquency Problem, JCLC&PS, Vol.43, No.5 (Jan.-Feb., 1953), 574.

Birkness, Valborg, and Johnson, Harry C.: A Comparative Study of Delinquent and Nondelinquent Adolescents, JER, Vol.42 (Apr., 1949), 551-72.

Bloch, Herbert A.: Juvenile Delinquency: Myth or Threat? JCLC&PS, Vol.49 (Nov.-Dec., 1958), 303-309.

————: The Juvenile Gang: A Cultural Reflex. THE ANNALS, Vol.347 (May, 1963), 20.

————, & Flynn, Frank T.: *Delinquency: The Juvenile Offender in America Today.* New York, Random House, 1956.

————, & Niederhoffer, Arthur: *The Gang: a Study in Adolescent Behavior.* New York, Philosophical Library, 1958.

Blue, John T.: The Relationship of Juvenile Delinquency, Race, and Economic Status, JNE, Vol.17 (Fall, 1948), 469-77.

Boeder, Alexander H.: The Youth Program of Whitefish Bay, Wisconsin, L&O, Vol.2 (May, 1959).

Bohlke, Robert H.: Social Mobility, Stratification Inconsistency and Middle Class Delinquency, SP, Vol.8 (1961), 351-63.

Bordua, David J.: Measuring Delinquency: A Study of Probation Department Referrals, JCLC&PS, Vol.53, No.2 (June-Aug., 1962), 242.

————: *Sociological Theories and Their Implications for Juvenile Delinquency.* Washington, D.C., Dept. of Health, Education & Welfare, 1960.

Borys, John M., Mackay, James, and Collins, Alice: Reactions of Delinquents to Secure Custody, POLICE, Vol.3, No.5 (May-June, 1959), 20-24; Vol.3, No.6 (July-Aug., 1959), 56-60.

Boswell, Charles H.: The Role of Citizens Advisory Council in a Juvenile Court Program, *Advances in Understanding the Offender*, 1950 Yearbook, National Probation and Parole Assoc., New York, 1951.

Bovet, Lucien: *Psychiatric Aspects of Juvenile Delinquency.* Geneva, World Health Organization, 1951.

Bowen, Croswell: *They Went Wrong.* New York, McGraw-Hill, 1954.

Bower, Eli M.: How Can Schools Recognize Early Symptoms of Maladjustment in Children and Youth? FP, Vol.16 (June, 1952), 3-7.

Bowers, Swithun: The Application of School Work in the Correctional Field, NPPAJ, Vol.5 (1959), 16-20.

Braisted, John M., Jr.: Television and the Juvenile, TPY, 1960.

Brannon, W. T.: Yellow Kid in *Weil—Con Man.* New York, Ziff-Davis, 1948.

Breed, Allen F.: California Youth Authority Forestry Camp Program, FP, Vol.17 (June, 1953), 37-43.

Brennan, James J.: Police and Delinquent Youth, JCJC&PS, Vol.46 (1955-56), 886-91.

————: Public Relations in Police Work with Delinquents, POLICE, Vol.9, No.4 (Mar.-Apr., 1965), 14-17.

Brewer, Edgar W.: *Detention Planning.* Washington, D.C., Children's Bureau, Pub., No.381, 1967.

Brietenbach, Eugene H.: Pathways of Delinquency, JSBC, Vol.31 (1956), 18-27.

Briggs, Peter F., and Wirt, Robert D.: The Efficacy of Ten of the Gluecks' Predictors,

JCLC&PS, Vol.50, No.5 (Jan.-Feb., 1960), 478.

Bright Shadows in Bronzetown. Chicago, The Area Project, 160, N. LaSalle St.

Bromage, Kenneth G., and Ball, Harry V.: A Study of Juvenile "Battery" Cases, AKD, Vol.28 (Spring, 1958), 18-24.

Brown, Roscoe C., Jr., and Dodson, Dan W.: The Effectiveness of a Boys Club in Reducing Delinquency, THE ANNALS, Vol.322 (1949), 47-52.

Brown, Wenzel: *Teen-age Mafia.* Greenwich, Fawcett, 1959.

———: *Teen-age Terror.* Greenwich, Fawcett, 1959.

Brucker, Herbert: The Right to Know about Juvenile Delinquency, FP, Vol.23 (Dec., 1959), 20-22.

Buckland, R. C.: Delinquency—What Are We Dealing With? L&O, Vol.2 (June, 1959).

Burgess, Ernest W.: Can Potential Delinquents Be Identified Scientifically? *Twenty-fourth Annual Governor's Conference on Youth and Community Service,* Springfield, Illinois Youth Commission, Springfield, 1955.

———: The Economic Factor in Juvenile Delinquency, JCLC&PS, Vol.43 (May-June, 1952), 29-42.

Burt, Cyril: *The Young Delinquent,* 4th & Rev. Ed., Bickley, Kent. London, Univ. of London Press, 1945.

Cabot, P. S.: *Juvenile Delinquency.* An Annotated Bibliography. New York, Wilson, 1946.

Caldwell, Morris G.: The Control of Postwar Delinquency, FP, Washington, D.C., Administrative Office of the United States Court (Oct.-Dec., 1945).

———: Personality Trends in the Youthful Male Offender, JCLC&PS, Vol.49, No.5 (1958-59), 405.

Caldwell, Robert G.: The Juvenile Court: Its Development and Some Major Problems, JCLC&PS, Vol.51, No.5 (Mar.-Apr., 1960-61), 493.

California Department of Education, Bureau of Trade and Industrial Education. *Juvenile Delinquency Control.* Sacramento, 1949.

California Juvenile Court Law. (Pamphlet) Los Angeles, Legal Book Store, 1965.

California State Department of Youth Authority: *California Laws Relating to Youthful Offenders, Including the Youth Authority Act and Juvenile Court Law.* Sacramento, 1961.

———: *The California Youth Authority Program.* Sacramento, 1961.

———: *A Guide for Juvenile Control by Law Enforcement Agencies.* Sacramento, 1951.

California Youth Authority, Program and Progress, 1943-48. Sacramento, Calif. Youth Authority, 1949.

California Youth Authority Quarterly. Published quarterly, Room 401, State Office Building, No.1, Sacramento, California.

Capes, Robert P.: New York State's Blueprint for Delinquency Prevention, FP, Vol.18 (June, 1954), 45-50.

Caravello, S. J.: The Drop-out Problem, HSJ, Vol.41 (1959), 335-40.

Carr, Lowell J.: *Delinquency Control.* New York, Harper & Bros, 1950.

Casey, Barbara: Delinquent Parents Anonymous, FOCUS, Vol.32 (1953), 178-82.

Caven, Ruth: Concepts of Tolerance and Contraculture as Applied to Delinquency, Presidential Address, Midwest Sociological Society, April 28, 1961; SQ, Vol.2 (1961), 243-58.

———: *Juvenile Delinquency.* Philadelphia, Lippincott, 1962.

Cavenaugh, John R.: The Comics War, JCL&C, Vol.40 (May, 1949), 28-35.

Cedarleaf, J. L.: The Chaplain's Role with Delinquent Boys in an Institution, FP, Vol.18 (Mar., 1954), 40-45.

Chalfant, Milo W.: Motivating the Adolescent Driver for Responsible Driving, POLICE, Vol.9, No.4 (Mar.-Apr., 1965), 64-68.

Chein, Isidor: Narcotics Use Among Juveniles, SW, Vol.1 (Apr., 1956), 50-60.

———: Studies on Narcotics Use Among Juveniles, Paper presented at Meeting of the National Research Council, Research Center for Human Relations, New York, New York University, Sept., 1955.

———, & **Rosenfeld, Eva.:** Juvenile Heroin Users in New York City, L&CP, Vol.22 (Winter, 1957), 52-68.

Chess, Abraham P.: Curfew for Juveniles? POLICE, Vol.4, No.5 (May-June, 1960), 13-18; Vol.4, No.6 (July-Aug., 1960), 60-64.

Chessman, Caryl: *The Kid Was a Killer.* Greenwich, Fawcett, 1960.

Children and Youth at the Midcentury: Fact Finding Report. A Digest prepared by the Midcentury White House Conference on Children and Youth, Washington, D.C., 1950.

Children Served by Public Welfare Agencies and Institutions, 1945. A report prepared by the Federal Security Agency Children's Bureau Pub., No.3, Washington, D.C., 1947.

Children's Bureau, U.S. Dept. of Health, Education and Welfare: *Training Personnel* *for Work with Juvenile Delinquents.* Washington, D.C., Social Security Admin., 1954.

Chudd, William V., and Donnelly, Agnes A.: Characteristics of the Investigative Process in a Children's Court, SC, Vol.40 (1959), 262-68.

Chwast, Jacob: Perceived Parental Attitudes and Predelinquency, JCLC&PS, Vol.49, No.2 (1958-59), 116.

————: Police Methods for Handling Delinquent Youth, JCLC&PS, Vol.46 (1955-56), 255-58.

Cicero, Sal J.: Effect of Police Training on Juvenile Recidivism, POLICE, Vol.8, No.2 (Nov.-Dec., 1963), 63-67.

Citizen's Committee on Children of New York: *Police and Children.* New York, The Committee, 1951.

Clark, Walter Houston: Sex Differences and Motions in the Urge to Destroy, JSP, Vol.36 (1952), 167-77.

Clayson, M. David: Juvenile Recidivism, JCLC&PS, Vol.51, No.1 (Mar.-Apr., 1960-61), 77.

————: Juvenile Recidivism—A Reassessment, JCLC&PS, Vol.52, No.3 (Sept.-Oct., 1961), 302.

Clinard, Marshall B.: *Sociology of Deviant Behavior.* New York, Rinehart, 1957.

————, & Wade, Andrew L.: Toward the Delineation of Vandalism as a Sub-type in Juvenile Delinquency, JCLC&PS, Vol.48 (1958), 493-99.

Close, Kathryn: Jail Is no Place for a Child. SURVEY (Mar., 1950), 138-43.

Cloward, Richard A., and Ohlin, Lloyd E.: *Delinquency and Opportunity: a Theory of Delinquent Gangs.* Glencoe, Free Press, 1960.

————, & ————: *New Perspectives on Juvenile Delinquency.* New York, New York School of Social Work, 1959.

Cohen, Albert K.: *Delinquent Boys: the Culture of the Gang.* Glencoe, Free Press, 1955.

————: *Juvenile Delinquency and the Social Structure.* Boston, Ph.D. Dissertation, Harvard Univ., 1951.

————, & Short, James F., Jr.: Research in Delinquent Subcultures, JSI, Vol.14, No.5 (1958), 20-37.

Cohen, Eli E., and Rosenbau, Lila: Will Relaxing Child Labor Laws Help Prevent Delinquency? FP, Vol.23 (Mar., 1959), 44-47.

Cohen, Frank J.: The Child in the Detention Home Program, FP (Jan.-Mar., 1946), 36-41.

Collins, Arthur T., and Poole, Vera E.: *These Our Children.* London, Victor Golblanez, Ltd., 1950.

Comic Books and Juvenile Delinquency, *Interim Report of the Subcommittee to Investigate Juvenile Delinquency.* Washington, D.C., a report prepared by the Committee on the Judiciary, S.Res. 89 and S.Res. 190, 1955.

Committee on the Judiciary, U.S. Senate, 83rd Congress: Subcommittee to Investigate Juvenile Delinquency, *Juvenile Delinquency (Comic Books),* Washington, D.C., U.S. Govt. Printing Office, 1954.

Conant, J. B.: *Slums and Suburbs.* New York, McGraw-Hill, 1961.

Cooper, Robert L.: Racial Antagonism as a Factor in Delinquency, NP and YEARBOOK, NPPA (1946).

Corbett, Gerald R.: The Juvenile and the Community, TPY (1958).

Corcoran, Robert P.: Police Officer Views Juvenile Delinquency, L&O, Vol.9 (Oct., 1961).

Corsini, Raymond J., and Rosenberg, Bina: Mechanisms of Group Psychotherapy: Processes and Dynamics, JA&SP, Vol.51 (1955), 406-411.

Costa, Rudy: Visit to Big League Baseball, A, L&O, Vol.8, No.3 (1960).

Costello, John B.: Institutions for Juvenile Delinquents, THE ANNALS, Vol.261 (1949), 166-178.

Coulter, Charles W.: Family Disorganization as a Causal Factor in Delinquency and Crime, FP, Vol.12 (Sept., 1948), 13-17.

County Institutes Handling Juveniles, TPC, Vol.30 (Jan., 1963), 32.

Cox, Rachel: The School Counselor's Contribution to Prevention of Delinquency, FP, Vol.14 (Mar., 1950), 23-28.

Craig, Maude M.: Six Years of a Validation Experiment on the Glueck Social Factor Prediction Table of Juvenile Delinquency, JCLC&PS, Vol.50, No.1 (1959-60), 49.

Crime—and Delinquency Publications Available, TPC, Vol.31 (Aug., 1964), 53.

Crosby, LeRoy: What the Church Can Do About Juvenile Delinquency, TPY (1958).

Crossley, Evan: Group Training for Predelinquents, Delinquents and Their Parents, FP, Vol.22 (June, 1958), 25-30.

Curfew as a Measure for the Control of Juvenile Delinquency. Washington, D.C., IACP, 1965.

Dia, Bingham: Some Problems of Personality Development Among Negro Children, in Kluckhohn, Clyde, Murray, Henry A., and Schneider, David M. (eds.): *Personality in Nature Society and Culture.* New York, Knopf, 1955.

Davidson, Harold E.: The Chaplaincy in the

Juvenile Institution, NPPAJ, Vol.6 (1960), 69-74.

Davis, Allison: *Social Class Influences Upon Learning.* Cambridge, Harvard University Press, 1948.

Davis, F. James: The Iowa Juvenile Court Judge, JCLC&PS, Vol.42 (1951-52), 338.

Davis, Fred: The Real Bohemia: A Sociological & Psychological Study of the "Beat," JCLC&PS, Vol.53, No.2 (June-Aug., 1962), 233.

Dealing with the Conflict Gang in New York City. New York, Interim Report No.14, Juvenile Delinquency Evaluation Project of the City of New York, The City College, 1961.

Deardorff, Neva: Central Registration of Delinquents, PROBATION, Vol.23 (June, 1945), 141-48.

Deland, P. S.: Battling Crime Comics to Protect Youth, FP, Vol.19 (Sept. 1955), 26-30.

———: Crime News Encourages Delinquency and Crime, FP, Vol.11 (Apr., 1947), 3-6.

Delany, Lloyd, Chwst, Jacob, and Harari, Carmi: Experimental Techniques in Group Psychotherapy with Delinquents, JCLC&PS, Vol.52, No.2 (July-Aug., 1961), 156.

Delinquency Control Institute, TPC, Vol.31 (June, 1964), 43.

Delinquency Control Institute: *Delinquency Prevention and Control.* Los Angeles, Univ. of Southern Calif., 1946. (Six volumes under various titles on this subject, mimeographed.)

Delinquency Prediction, a Progress Report, 1952-1956, an Experiment in the Validation of the Glueck Prediction Scale. New York, New York City Youth Board, 1957.

DeMers, Donald O.: *Outline of Juvenile Delinquency Control.* Sacramento: Calif. State Dept. of Education, Bureau of Trade and Industrial Education, 1949.

Derning, Don: Let's Check Our Perspective, TPY (1964).

Deutsch, Albert: *Our Rejected Children.* Boston, Little, Brown, 1950.

Diana, Lewis: Is Casework in Probation Necessary? FOCUS, Vol.34 (1955), 1-8.

———: The Rights of Juvenile Delinquents, JCLC&PS, Vol.47, No.5 (Jan.-Feb., 1957), 561.

Dienstein, William: Delinquency Control Techniques as Influenced by Beliefs and Attitudes of Police Personnel, POLICE, Vol.5, No.1 (Sept.-Oct., 1960), 23-26.

———: Inter-professional Differences in Beliefs About the Etiology of Juvenile Delinquency,

JCLC&PS, Vol.51, No.1 (Mar.-Apr., 1960-61), 79.

Dinello, Frank A.: Teen-agers Need Guidance, L&O, Vol.7 (Dec., 1959).

Dintz, Simon, Reckless, Walter C., and Kay, Barbara: A Self Gradient Among Potential Delinquents, JCLC&PS, Vol.49 (1958), 230-33.

———, & Murray, Ellen: The "Good" Boy in a High Delinquency Area, JCLC&PS, Vol.48, No.1 (May-June, 1957), 18.

Dirksen, Cletus: *Economic Factors of Delinquency.* Milwaukee, Bruce Pub., Co., 1948.

Dobbs, Harrison Allen: The Classroom Teacher and Delinquency Prevention, ESJ, Vol.50 (Mar., 1950), 376-83.

Dollard, John, Miller, Neal E., Doob, Leonard W., Mowrer, O. H., and Sears, Robert: *Frustration and Aggression.* New Haven, Yale Univ. Press, 1945.

Dominic, S. M.: Religion and the Juvenile Delinquent, ACSR, Vol.15 (1954), 256-64.

Doniger, Simon: The Psychiatric Treatment of a Juvenile Delinquent, NC, Vol.6 (Oct., 1947), 424-35.

Down, Jack: Juvenile Office Must Be Someone Special, L&O, Vol.8, No.1 (1960).

Drake, Francis M.: A Juvenile Officer at Work, L&O, Vol.12 (Aug., 1964).

Drake, St. Clair, and Cayton, Horace R.: *Black Metropolis: A Study of Negro Life in a Northern City.* New York, Harcourt, Brace, 1945.

Drug Addiction Among Young Persons in Chicago. Chicago, A Report of a Study Conducted by the Illinois Institute for Juvenile Research and the Chicago Area Project, 1953.

Dub, Leonard M.: Institutional Treatment of Juvenile Delinquents, AJPSY Vol.103 (May, 1947), 818-22.

Dumpson, James R.: An Approach to Anti-Social Street Gangs, FP, Vol.13 (Dec., 1949), 22-29.

Duvall, Evelyn Millis: *Family Development.* Philadelphia, Lippincott, 1957.

Edelston, H.: *The Earliest Stages of Delinquency.* Edinburgh, Livingstone, 1952.

Educational Level in the Public Child Welfare Program, 1953. Washington, D.C., A report prepared by the U.S. Children's Bureau, Statistical Series, No.26, 1955.

The Effectiveness of Delinquency Prevention Programs. Washington, D.C., Children's Bureau, 1954.

Eisner, E. A.: Relationship Found by a Sexually Delinquent Adolescent Girl, AJO, Vol.15 (1945), 301-08.

Eissler, K. R., and Federn, Paul (eds.): *Search-*

lights on Delinquency. New York, International Universities Press, 1949.

Ellington, John R.: *Protecting Our Children from Criminal Careers*. Englewood Cliffs, Prentice-Hall, 1948.

Ellsworth, L. L.: A Grain of Faith, L&O, Vol.8, No.4 (1960), 38.

Engel, K. E.: What Makes a Juvenile Delinquent? TPC, Vol.31 (June, 1964), 40.

England, Ralph W., Jr.: A Theory of Middle Class Juvenile Delinquency, JCLC&PS, Vol.50 (1960), 535-40.

Erikson, Erik H.: *Childhood and Society*. New York, Norton, 1950.

Evans, Nell: A Clown Sells Safety to Children, L&O, Vol.7 (Aug., 1959).

Fagerstrom, Dorothy: PAL Leaders Discuss Problems, L&O, Vol.8, No.3 (1960).

————: PAL on Parade, L&O, Vol.8, No.7 (1960).

————: Stand Up and Be Heard, L&O, Vol.8, No.5 (1960), 41.

Ferdinand, Theodore N.: An Evaluation of Milieu Therapy & Vocational Training as Methods for the Rehabilitation of Youthful Offenders, JCLC&PS, Vol.53, No.1 (Mar.-Apr., 1962), 49.

Ferguson, Thomas: *The Young Delinquent in His Social Setting*. London, A Glasgow Study, Published for the Nuffield Foundation by Oxford University Press, 1952.

Feuss, Charles D. and Goldman, Douglas: The Function of a Psychiatrist in a Juvenile Court, POLICE, Vol.8, No.4 (Mar.-Apr., 1964), 33-35.

Fine, Benjamin: *1,000,000 Deliquents*. New York, Signet, 1957.

Finestone, Harold: Cats, Kicks & the Color, SP, Vol.5 (July, 1957), 3-13.

————: *A Proposed Framework for the Analysis of Juvenile Delinquency*. Presented at meeting of American Sociological Society, August, 1958.

Fleisher, B. M.: The Effect of Unemployment on Juvenile Delinquency, JPE (Dec., 1963).

For Every Child a Healthy Personality. Washington, D.C., A report prepared by the U.S. Midcentury White House Conference on Children and Youth, 1950.

Fording, A. H.: Juvenile Delinquency and Youth Crime, Workshop, TPY (1964).

Frank, Anne: *The Diary of a Young Girl*. New York, Pocket Books, 1953.

Franklin, Adele: The All-day Neighborhood Schools, THE ANNALS, Vol.322 (1959), 62-66.

Freeman, Ira Henry: *Out of the Burning, the Story of Frenchy, a Boy Gang Leader*. New York, Crown Publishers, 1960.

Friedlander, Kate: *The Psycho-analytical Approach to Juvenile Delinquency*. New York, International Univ. Press, 1947.

Friedlander, Walter A.: *Introduction to Social Welfare*. New York, Prentice-Hall, 1955.

From School to Work. Washington, D.C., U.S. Dept. of Labor, Bureau of Labor Statistics, 1960.

Frum, Harold S.: Adult Criminal Offenses Trends Following Juvenile Delinquency, JCLC&PS, Vol.49 (1958), 29-49.

Furman, Sylvan S. (ed.): *Reaching the Unreached*. New York, New York City Youth Board, 1952.

Galvin, James: Some Dynamics of Delinquent Girls, JN&MD, Vol.123 (1956), 292-95.

Gandy, John M.: Preventive Work with Streetcorner Groups, Chicago, Hyde Park Youth Project, AAPSS, Vol.32 (1959), 107-16.

Gardner, George E.: The Community and the Aggressive Child. The Aggressive Destructive Impulses in the Sex Offender. MH, Vol.34 (1950), 44-63.

————: The Institution as Therapist, TC (Jan., 1952), 70-72.

————: Publicity and the Juvenile Delinquent, FP, Vol. 23 (Dec., 1959), 23-25.

————: Separation of the Parents and the Emotional Life of the Child, MH, Vol.40 (1956), 53-64.

Geertsma, Robert H.: Group Therapy with Juvenile Probationers and Their Parents, FP, Vol.24 (Mar., 1960), 45-52.

Geis, Gilbert: Juvenile Delinquency: Its Nature and Control, JCLC&PS, Vol.51, No.4 (Mar.-Apr., 1960-61), 453.

————: Juvenile Justice: Great Britain and California, C&D, Vol.7 (Apr., 1961), 111-20.

————: Publicity and Juvenile Court Proceedings, NPPAJ, Vol.4 (Oct., 1958), 333-55.

————: Publicity and Juvenile Court Proceedings, RMLR, Vol.30 (Feb., 1958), 1-26.

————, & **Costner, Herbert:** Matching Probation Officer and Delinquent, NPPAJ, Vol.2 (Jan., 1956), 58-62.

George, Gus: Juvenile Delinquency, A Problem for the Entire Department, TPY (1954).

Gerald, Donald L., and Kornetsky, Conan; Adolescent Opiate Addiction: A Study of Control and Addict Subjects, PQ, Vol.29 (1955), 457-86.

————, & ————: A Social and Psychiatric Study of Adolescent Opiate Addicts, PQ, Vol.28 (1954), 113.

Gerstle, Mark Lewis: The California Youth Authority Psychiatric Treatment Program, Its Historical Significance and Philosophy, CM, Vol.92 (Apr., 1960), 277-79.

———, & **Ames, Louis Bates:** *Youth, the Years from Ten to Sixteen.* New York, Harper & Bros., 1956.

———, & **Ilg, Francis L.:** *The Child from Five to Ten.* New York, Harper & Bros., 1946.

Giesecke, W. K.: An Accounting Plan for Juvenile Probation, JCLC&PS, Vol.43, No.6 (Mar.-Apr., 1953), 705.

Gladstone, Irving Arthur: Spare the Rod and Spoil the Parent, FP, Vol.19 (June, 1955), 37-41.

Glane, Sam: Juvenile Gangs in East Side Los Angeles, FOCUS, Vol.29 (1950), 136-41.

Gleason, John M.: The Role of the Boys' Clubs, TPY (1958).

Glick, Selma J.: Spotting Potential Delinquents in School, EC, Vol.20 (May, 1954), 342-46.

Glover, Edward: Delinquency Work in Great Britain: JCLC&PS, Vol.46 (1955-56), 172-77.

———: On the Desirability of Isolating a "Functional" (Psychosomatic) Group of Delinquent Disorders. BJD, Vol.1 (1950), also in *On the Early Development of Mind,* London, Imago, 1956.

Glueck, Eleanor T.: Body Build in the Prediction of Delinquency, JCLC&PS, Vol.48, No.6 (Mar.-Apr., 1958), 577.

———: Early Detection of Future Delinquents, JCLC&PS, Vol.47, No.2 (July-Aug., 1956), 174.

———: Efforts to Identify Delinquents, FP, Vol.24 (1960), 49.

———: Identifying Juvenile Delinquents and Neurotics, MH, Vol.10 (1956), 24-43.

———: Predictive Juvenile Delinquency, SURVEY, Vol.88 (1952), 206-09.; BJD, Vol.2 1952), 275-86.

———: Predictive Techniques in the Management of Juvenile Delinquency; Part II, The Workability of Predictive Techniques. Trans. by T. Miyamoto and H. Abe. HORITSU NO HIROBA (THE LAW FORUM) Vol.13 (1960), 39-43.

———: A Preview of *Family Environment and Delinquency,* prepared for the Sixth International Congress on Mental Health, Paris, Sept., 1961; IJSP, Vol.8 (1962); IAC, Vol.2 (1962).

———: Role of the Family in the Etiology of Delinquency, ACJ, Vol.7 (1960), 63.

———: Spotting Potential Delinquents: Can It Be Done? FP, Vol.20 (1956), 7-13.

———: Status of Glueck Prediction Studies, JCLC&PS, Vol.47, No.1 (May-June, 1956), 18.

———: Techniques of the Research, L'ENFRANCE DELINQUANTE (1950), 278-91.

———: Toward Further Improving the Identification of Delinquents, JCLC&PS, Vol.54, No.2 (1963).

———: Toward Improving the Identification of Delinquents. Address delivered before the American Society of Criminology, Denver, Colorado, Dec., 1961; JCLC&PS, Vol.53, No.2 (June-Aug., 1962), 164.

———: *The Workability of Predictive Techniques, Part II, Predictive Techniques in the Prevention and Treatment of Delinquency.* Address at Conference of National Council of Juvenile Court Judges, Boston, Mass., June 19, 1956.

———: *The Workability of Predictive Techniques, Part II, Predictive Techniques in the Prevention and Treatment of Delinquency. Salute to American Youth.* Boston Conference National Council of Juvenile Court Judges, National Juvenile Court Foundation, Pittsburgh, Penn., 1956.

———: Foreword to *Reaching the Fighting*

Glueck, Sheldon: Foreword to *Reaching the Fighting Gang.* New York, The New York City Youth Board, 1960.

———: Home, the School and Delinquency, HER, Vol.23 (1953), 17-32.

———: The Meaning and Management of Delinquency; Part I, Crime Causation; Theory and Fact. Trans. by Katsuhiko Nishimura. HORITSU JIHO (THE LAW TIMES JOURNAL), Vol.32 (1960), 111-25, Tokyo.

———: The Meaning and Management of Delinquency; Part II, Methods of Coping with Delinquency and Crime, Trans. by Katsuhiko Nishimura, HORITSU JIHO (THE LAW TIMES JOURNAL), Vol.32 (1960), 81-93, Tokyo.

———: *The Nature of Predictive Techniques: Part I, Predictive Techniques in the Prevention and Treatment of Delinquency.* Address at Conference of National Council of Juvenile Court Judges, Boston, Mass., June 19, 1956.

———: *The Nature of Predictive Techniques: Part I, Predictive Techniques in the Prevention and Treatment of Delinquency, Salute to American Youth.* Boston Conference, National Council of Juvenile Court Judges, National Juvenile Court Foundation, Pittsburgh, Penn., 1956.

———: Predictive Techniques in the Management of Juvenile Delinquency: Part I, The Nature of Predictive Techniques. Trans. by T. Miyamoto and H. Abe. HORITSU NO HIROBA (THE LAW FORUM) Vol.13 (1960), 34-39. Tokyo.

——— (ed.): *The Problem of Delinquency.* Boston, Houghton Mifflin, 1959.

————: Purpose and Design of a Multi-discipline Study of the Causes of Juvenile Delinquency, L'ENFRANCE DELINQUANTE (1950), 262-77.

————: *Social Work in a Troubled World*. Address at New York School of Social Work, November 4, 1949.

————: Some Unfinished Business' In the Management of Juvenile Delinquency, SLR, Vol.15, No.4 (Summer, 1964), 628-59.

————: Ten Years of Unraveling Juvenile Delinquency, JCLC&PS, Vol.51, No.3 (Mar.-Apr., 1960-61), 283.

————: What Makes a Bad Boy? HAB, Vol.53 (1950), 167.

Glueck, Sheldon and Eleanor: *After-conduct of Discharged Offenders*. London, Macmillan, 1945.

————: *A Preview of Physique and Delinquency*. London, prepared for Plenary Session, Third International Congress of Criminology, 1955.

————: *Basic Researches into the Causes, Management and Prevention of Juvenile Delinquency Being Carried On at the Harvard Law School*. Spring, 1960.

————: *Delinquents in the Making: Paths to Prevention*. New York, Harper, 1952.

————: Family Environment and Delinquency in the Perspective of Etiologic Research, IAC (1963), 211-18.

————: *Physique and Delinquency*, New York, Harper & Bros., 1956; MH (July, 1957), 449.

————: Plans for Further Unraveling Juvenile Delinquency, JCL&C; Vol.41 (1951), 759.

————: *Predicting Delinquency and Crime*. Cambridge, Harvard University Press, 1960.

————: *Predictive Techniques in the Prevention and Treatment of Delinquency*. Boston Conference of National Council of Juvenile Court Judges, Boston, Mass., 1956.

————: Reflections on Basic Research in Juvenile Delinquency, WMH, Vol.12 (1960), 6.

————: *Research Project into the Causes, Treatment and Prevention of Juvenile Delinquency, Progress Report,* 1955-56. Cambridge, Harvard Univ. Law School, 1956.

————: *Unraveling Juvenile Delinquency*. New York, The Commonwealth Fund, 1950.

————: Why Young People "Go Bad," USN&WR, Vol.58, No.17 (1965), 56-62.

————: Working and Delinquency, MH, Vol.41 (1957), 327-52.

Gold, Leo: Toward an Understanding of Adolescent Drug Addiction, FP, Vol.22 (Sept., 1958), 42-48.

Goldberg, Harriet L., and Sheridan, William H.: *Family Courts—an Urgent Need*. Washington, D.C., Children's Bureau Report No.6, U.S. Govt. Printing Office, 1960.

Goldsmith, Arnold L.: Oliver Wendell Holmes: Father and Son, JCLC&PS, Vol.48, No.4 (Nov.-Dec., 1957), 394.

Grayson, Horace V.: Program for Non-delinquents, TPC, Vol.29, No.5 (May, 1962), 14.

————: Recognizing the Non-delinquents, TPY (1963). Greenblatt, Bernard: *Staff and Training for Juvenile Law Enforcement Urban Police Departments*. Washington, D.C. U.S. Government Printing Office, 1960.

Gross, Fred: *Detention and Prosecution of Children*. Chicago, Central Howard Assoc., 1946.

Grunwald, Hanna: Group Counseling in Combating Delinquency, FP, Vol.22 (Dec., 1958), 32-36.

Guide for Cooperation Between School Officials and Police. Harrisburg, Commonwealth of Penn., Dept. of Public Instruction, 1962.

Guides for Juvenile Court Judges. New York, National Probation Association, 1957.

Hackett, D. L.: Federal Anti-delinquency Program, TPC, Vol.29, No.9 (Sept., 1962), 10.

Hager, Don J.: Religion, Delinquency and Society, SW, Vol.14 (July, 1957), 16-21.

Hall, J. R.: Youth Bureau and Community Councils Decrease Juvenile Delinquency, L&O, Vol.8, No.2, 1960.

Hand, Jack: An Abbreviated Form of the Wechsler Intelligence Scale for Children, JCLC&PS, Vol.51, No.1 (Mar.-Apr., 1960-61), 81.

Handlin, Oscar: *The Newcomers, Negroes and Puerto Ricans in a Changing Metropolis*. Cambridge, Harvard Univ. Press, 1959.

Hardman, Dale G.: The Function of the Probation Officer, FP, Vol.24 (Sept., 1960), 3-10.

Hardt, R. H.: *A Delinquency of Syracuse and Onondaga County*, New York, 1957-58. Youth Development Center, Syracuse Univ., Syracuse, New York, 1960.

Harris, D. B., and Tseng, Sing Chu: Children's Attitudes Toward Peers and Parents as Revealed by Sentence Completion, CD, Vol.28 (1957), 401-11.

Harris, Raymond I.: L.A.D.S. POLICE, Vol.9, No.5 (May-June, 1965), 22.

Hathaway, Starke R., and Monachesi, Elio D.: *Analyzing and Predicting Juvenile Delinquency with the MMPI*. Minneapolis, Univ. of Minnesota, 1953.

————, & ————: The Personalities of Predelinquent Boys, JCLC&PS, Vol.48, No.2 (July-Aug., 1957), 149.

———, ———, & **Young, Lawrence A.**: Delinquency Rates and Personality, JCLC&PS, Vol.50, No.5 (Jan.-Feb., 1960), 433.

Havighurst, Robert J.: *Human Development and Education.* New York, Longman's Green, 1953.

———, & **Stiles, Lindley J.**: National Policy for Alienated Youth, PDK, Vol. 42 (1961), 283-91.

Haydon, E. M.: Re-education and Delinquency, JSI, Vol.1 (Winter, 1945), 23-32.

———: Thoughts About Juvenile Courts, FP, Vol.13 (Sept., 1949), 16-19.

Helfer, Harold: The Plebe Police, L&O, Vol.7 (Apr., 1959).

Helping Children in Trouble. Washington, D.C., U.S. Children's Bureau Publication No.320, U.S. Govt. Printing Office, 1947.

Hengerer, Gertrude M.: Organizing Probation Service, *Reappraising Crime Treatment*, NPAY (1953).

Henry, Nelson B. (ed.): *Juvenile Delinquency and the School.* Chicago, National Society for the Study of Education Yearbook No.47, Part I, University of Chicago Press, 1948.

Hentig, Hans Von: The First Generation and a Half: Notes on the Delinquency of Native Whites of Mixed Parentage, ASR, Vol.10 (Dec., 1945), 792-98.

Herman, Stephen M.: Scope and Purpose of Juvenile Court Jurisdiction, JCLC&PS, Vol.48 (1958), 590-606.

Hertel, Norman: Metro Youth Services, TPC, Vol.29, No.1 (Jan., 1962), 24.

———: The Strategic Position, L&O, Vol.9 (Sept., 1961).

Herzog, Elizabeth: *Identifying Potential Delinquents,* Washington, D.C., Children's Bureau Report No.5, U.S. Govt. Printing Office, 1960.

Heschel, Abraham J.: The Call of the Hour, L&O, Vol.8, No.5 (1960).

Hewitt, Lester E., and **Jenkins, Richard L.**: *Fundamental Patterns of Maladjustment: The Dynamics of Their Origin.* Springfield, State Printer, 1946.

Hibbard, Melvin R.: Delinquency and Curfew, L&O, Vol.8, No.1 (1960).

———: The Juvenile Officer, L&O, Vol.8, No.3 (1960).

Hibbard, Roy: Prevention Standards (Delinquency Control), TPC (Aug., 1961), 40.

Higgins, Lois L.: Training and Performance Standards, Delinquency Control, TPC (Aug., 1961), 41.

———: The Golden Anniversary White House Conference on Children and Youth, PO-

LICE, Vol.5, No.2 (Nov.-Dec., 1960), 29-32.

Hildebrand, James A.: Why Runaways Leave Home, JCLC&PS, Vol.54, No.2 (1963), 211.

Hill, Arthur S., Miller, Leonard M., and **Gabbard, Hazel F.**: Schools Face the Delinquency Problem, TB, Vol.37, No.198 (Dec., 1953), 181-221.

Hillman, Arthur: *Community Organization and Planning.* New York, Macmillan, 1950.

Hilton, Joseph: *Angels in the Gutter.* Greenwich, Fawcett, 1959.

Holcomb, R. L.: Crime and Kids, JCLC&PS, Vol.51, No.1 (Mar.-Apr., 1960-61), 126.

———: Police Work with Juveniles, JCLC&PS, Vol.51, No.1 (Mar.-Apr., 1960-61), 125.

———: Race Tensions and the Police, JCLC&PS, Vol.53, No.3 (Sept.-Nov., 1962), 398.

Holladay, E. F.: Techniques in Handling Juveniles, POLICE, Vol.8, No.1 (Sept.-Oct., 1963), 56-59.

Hollingshead, A. de B.: *Elmtown's Youth: The Impact of Social Classes on Adolescents.* New York, Wiley, 1949.

———, & **Redlich, Fredrick C.**: *Social Class and Mental Illness.* New York, Wiley, 1958.

Holton, Karl: California Youth Authority Eight Years of Action, JCLC&PS, Vol.41 (1950), 1-23.

———: California Youth Authority, *Proceedings of the American Prison Association*, 1947.

Holyes, J. Arthur: *Treatment of the Young Delinquent.* London, Epworth, 1952.

Hoover, J. Edgar: Editorial in the FBILB, Vol.26 (Feb., 1957), reprinted under the title The Mollycoddling Charge, NPPAJ, Vol.36 (May, 1957), 1-3, 8.

Hopper, Edward P.: Putting Neighborhoods on Probation, FP, Vol.19 (Sept., 1955), 38-43.

Housing and Community Development, M&FL, Vol.17 (1955), entire issue.

Houston Council of Social Agencies: *Houston Children and the Police,* Houston, Texas, 1946.

Howe, Hubert Shattuck: *Narcotics and Youth.* West Orange, Brook Foundation, 1953.

Hunt, Elizabeth V.: Foster Care for Delinquent Girls, CHILDREN (Sept.-Oct., 1962).

Illing, Hans A.: Das Verbrechen, Vol. I: Der Kriminelle Mensch im Krabftesdial von Zeit und Raum, JCLC&PS, Vol.53, No.1 (Mar.-May, 1962), 80.

———: The Social Welfare Forum, JCLC&PS, Vol.53, No.2 (June-Aug., 1962), 237.

Illinois Institute for Juvenile Research and the Chicago Area Project: *Drug Addiction Among Young Persons in Chicago.* Chicago, 1953 (Mimeographed).

Ingram, Christine P.: *Educational Training in Schools for Delinquent Youth.* Washington, D.C., U.S. Office of Education, Bulletin, No.5, 1945.

Institutions Serving Delinquent Children, Guides and Goals. Washington, D.C., Children's Bureau Publication No.360, U.S. Government Printing Office, 1957.

Jaffe, Lester D.: Delinquency Proneness and Family Anomie, JCLC&PS, Vol.54, No.2 (1963), 146.

Jameson, Samuel H.: Community's Role in Training for Delinquency, L&O, Vol.7 (Mar., 1964).

————: The Policeman's Non-official Role in Combating Gangs and Vandalism, POLICE, Vol.1, No.5 (May-June, 1957), 45-49.

Jeffery, C. Ray: War and Delinquency, JCLC&PS, Vol.51, No.5 (Mar.-Apr., 1960-61), 551.

————: *Breaking the Patterns of Defeat.* Philadelphia, Lippincott, 1954.

Jennings, H.: *Leadership and Isolation,* Rev. Ed. New York, Longmans, Green, 1950.

Jepsen, Jorgen: Drug Addiction—Crime or Disease, JCLC&PS, Vol.53, No.1 (Mar.,-May, 1962), 76.

Jeter, Helen: *State Agencies and Juvenile Delinquency.* Washington, D.C., Children's Bureau Report No.12, U.S. Govt. Printing Office, 1960.

Johnson, Adelaide M.: Sanctions for Superego Lacunae of Adolescents in K. R. Eissler (ed.), *Searchlights on Delinquency.* New York, International Univ. Press, 1948.

Johnson, Arne R.: Recent Developments in the Law of Probation, JCLC&PC, Vol.53, No.2 (June-Aug., 1962), 194.

Johnson, Madeline: Interviewing Youth, L&O, Vol.7 (July, 1959).

Johnson, Robert M. L.: Young Adults in Action, L&O, Vol.7 (May, 1949).

Jones, Stacy V.: The Cougars, Life with a Brooklyn Gang, HARPER'S (Nov., 1954), 35-43.

Juergensmeyer, Irving K.: Education for Delinquency Prevention, POLICE, Vol.3, No.4 (Mar.-Apr., 1959), 19-23; Vol.3, No.5 (May-June, 1959), 24-28.

The Juvenile Court as a Child Care Institution, FP, Vol.16 (June, 1952), 8-12.

Juvenile Court Statistics, 1946-1949. Washington, D.C., A Report prepared by the Federal Security Agency, Children's Bureau Statistical Series Publ. No.8, U.S. Govt. Printing Office, 1951.

Juvenile Court Statistics, 1950-52. Washington,

D.C., A Report prepared by the U.S. Dept. of Health, Education and Welfare, Children's Bureau Statistical Series Pub. No.18, U.S. Govt. Printing Office, 1954.

Juvenile Court Statistics 1953. Washington, D.C., A Report prepared by the U.S. Dept. of Health, Education and Welfare, Children's Bureau Statistical Series Pub. No.28, U.S. Govt. Printing Office, 1955.

Juvenile Delinquency (Comic Books). Washington, D.C., A Report prepared by the U.S. Senate, Hearings before the Subcommittee to Investigate Juvenile Delinquency, Committee on the Judiciary, 83rd Congress, 2nd Session, S. Res., 190, U.S. Govt. Printing Office, 1954.

Juvenile Delinquency among Negroes, JNE, Vol.28 (Summer, 1959), entire issue.

Juvenile Delinquency and Youth Crime—the Police Role. Washington, D.C., IACP, 1964.

Juvenile Delinquency Control Act. Washington, D.C., Hearings before the special subcommittee on Education of the Committee on Education and Labor, House of Representatives, 87th Congress, 1st Session, U.S. Govt. Printing Office, 1961.

Juvenile Assault by Parents, TPC, Vol.30 (Jan., 1963), 32.

Kahn, Alfred J.: *A Court for Children, a Study of the New York Children's Court.* New York, Columbia University Press, 1953.

————: *For Children in Trouble.* New York, Citizen's Committee for Children of New York City, Inc., 1957.

————: *Crisis in the New York City Police Program for Youth.* New York, Citizen's Committee for Children of New York City, Inc., 1957.

————: The Functions of Police and Children's Courts, *The Community and the Correctional Process.* New York, NPPAY (1951).

————: Function of Youth Police in an Integrated Community Plan for Helping Children in Trouble, JES, Vol.24 (May, 1951).

————: *Police and Children.* New York, Citizen's Committee on Children of New York City, 1951.

Kanum, Clara: Delinquency and the Validating Scales of the Minnesota Multiphasic Personality Inventory, DELINQUENCY, Vol.50, No.6 (1959-60), 525.

————, & **Monachesi, Elio D.:** Delinquency and the Validating Scales of the Minnesota Multiphasic Personality Inventory, JCLC&PS, Vol.50, No.6 (Mar.-Apr., 1960), 525.

Kaplan, B. R., and Lodge, Sidney: The Police

and the Schools, TPC, Vol.32, No.6 (June, 1965), 24.

Kawin, Irene: Family Dissention as a Factor in Delinquency, NPPAY (1946).

Kay, Barbara: A Self Gradient Among Potential Delinquents, JCLC&PS, Vol.49, No.3 (1958-59), 230.

Keith-Lucas, Alan: The Role of the House-parent in the Training School, NPPAJ, Vol.4 (1958), 156-60.

Kellar, Gladys I.: Court Foster Home Program, NPPAJ, Vol.4 (1958), 57-65.

Keniston, Kenneth: Entangling Juvenile Delinquency, COMMENTARY, Vol.29 (1960).

Kennedy, Foster, Hoffman, Harry, and Haines, William H.: Psychiatric Study of William Heirens, JCL&C, Vol.38 (1947), 311-41.

Kenney, John P., and Pursuit, Dan G.: *Police Work with Juveniles.* Springfield, Thomas, 1965 **(must reading).**

Kerpon, Nick E.: Juvenile Problems, L&O, Vol.7 (Oct., 1959).

Kinch, John W.: Continuities in the Study of Delinquent Types, JCLC&PS, Vol.53, No.3 (Sept.-Nov., 1962), 323.

King, Charles W.: Community Factors in Juvenile Delinquency, S&SR (Sept.-Oct, 1954).

Kinsey, Alfred C., Pomeroy, Wardell B., and Martin, Clyde E.: *Sexual Behavior in the Human Male.* Philadelphia, Saunders, 1955.

Kirkendall, Lester A.: Circumstances Associated with Teenage Boys Use of Prostitution, M&FL, Vol.22 (1960), 145-49.

Kitsuse, John I.: New Perspectives for Research on Juvenile Delinquency, JCLC&PS, Vol.51, No.6 (Mar.-Apr., 1960-61), 645.

Kneisel, Stephan H.: Detention Home Programming, Reappraising Crime Treatment, NPPAY (1953), New York.

Knudson, Theodore B.: Training Program for Juvenile Offenders, JCLC&PS, Vol.45 (1954-55), 633-42.

Kobrin, Solomon: The Chicago Area Project— A 25 Year Assessment, THE ANNALS, Vol.322 (1959), 19-29.

————: The Conflict of Values in Delinquency Areas, ASR, Vol.16 (Oct., 1951), 653-61.

Kogan, Bernard: Probation Camps, FP, Vol.22 (Sept., 1958), 34-40.

Kogan, Herman: Dope and Chicago's Children, THE CHICAGO SUN TIMES, 1950.

Kohler, Mary Conway: The Courts for Handling Youth, NPPAJ, Vol.2 (1956), 123-41.

Konopka, Gisela: *Therapeutic Group Work with Children.* Minneapolis, Univ. of Minnesota Press, 1949.

Kramer, Samuel Noah: A Father and His Perverse Son, NPPAJ, Vol.3 (1957), 169-73.

Krueger, Gladys M.: *Survey of Probation Officers,* 1959. Washington, D.C., Children's Bureau Report No.15, U.S. Govt. Printing Office, 1960.

Kuharich, Anthony S.: What Can We Do About Juvenile Delinquency? POLICE, Vol.3, No.1 (Sept.-Oct., 1958), 34-36; Vol.3, No.2 (Nov.-Dec., 1958), 58-59.

Kurtz, Russell H.: *Social Work Year Book.* New York, Russell Sage Foundation, 1947.

Kvaraceus, Wm. C.: *The Community and the Delinquent.* New York, World Book Co., 1954.

————: Forecasting Juvenile Delinquency, JE, Vol.138 (Apr., 1956), 1-43.

————: *Juvenile Delinquency and the Courts.* New York, World Book Co., 1945.

————: *Juvenile Delinquency and the School.* New York World Book Co., 1955.

————, **& Miller, Walter B.:** *Delinquent Behavior: Culture and the Individual.* Washington, D.C., National Education Association of the U.S., U.S. Govt., Printing Office, 1959.

————, **& Ulrich, William E.:** *Delinquent Behavior: Principles and Practices.* Washington, D.C., National Education Association of the U.S., U.S. Govt. Printing Office, 1959.

Lander, B.: *Towards an Understanding of Juvenile Delinquency.* New York, Columbia Univ. Press, 1954.

Landis, Paul H.: *Social Policies in the Making.* New York, Heaty, 1947.

Lawder, Lee E.: Patterns of Youth, L&O, Vol.8, No.6 (1960).

Lawton, S. U., and Archer, Jules: *Sexual Conduct of the Teen-ager.* New York, Berkley Publishing, 1959.

Lee, Robert: The Church and the Problem of Delinquency, RE, Vol.52 (1957), 125-29.

————, **Wilner, Daniel M., Rosenfield, Eva, Gerard, Donald L., and Chein, Isidor:** Heroin Use and Street Gangs, JCLC&PS, Vol.48, No.4 (Nov.-Dec., 1957), 399.

Lejins, Peter: Is the Youth Authority Idea Really Paying Off? *Proceedings of the National Conference of Juvenile Agencies,* 1951.

Lentz, John M.: Rural Urban Differentials and Juvenile Delinquency, JCLC&PS, Vol.47, No.3 (Sept.-Oct., 1956), 331.

Leonard, V. A.: Research Project Into the Causes and Treatment of Juvenile Delinquency, JCL&C, Vol.35, No.6 (Mar.-Apr., 1945), 394.

————: The State and Delinquency, JCL&C, Vol.35, No.6 (Mar.-Apr., 1945), 397.

Levin, J. L.: *How Cities Control Juvenile De-*

linquency. Chicago, American Municipal Assoc., 1957.

Levy, Sheldon S.: Criminal Liability for the Punishment of Children: An Evaluation of Means and Ends, JCLC&PS, Vol.43, No.6 (Mar.-Apr., 1953), 719.

Lewin, K.: *Resolving Social Conflicts*. New York, Harper & Bros, 1948.

Liccione, John V.: The Changing Family Relationships of Adolescent Girls, JA&SP, Vol.51 (1955), 421-26.

Linn, Edward: Wiltwyck: Home of the Wild Ones. READER'S DIGEST, Vol.72 (Feb., 1958), 192-96.

Lippman, Hyman S.: Difficulties Encountered in the Psychiatric Treatment of Chronic Juvenile Delinquents in K. R. Essler, and Paul Federn (eds.), *Searchlights on Delinquency*. New York, International Univ., Press, 1949.

———: The Role of the Probation Officer in the Treatment of Delinquency in Children, FP, Vol.12 (June, 1948), 36-39.

Lipton, Lawrence: *The Holy Barbarians*. New York, Messner, 1959.

Liu, Daniel S. C.: Juvenile Delinquency: Workshop, TPY (1963).

LoCicero, Sal J.: Effect of Police Training on Juvenile Recidivism, POLICE, Vol.8, No.3 (Jan.-Feb., 1964), 58-62.

Loeb, Martin B.: Implications of Status Differential for Personal and Social Development, HER, Vol.23, No.3 (Summer, 1953), 168-74.

Loevinger, G.: The Court and the Child, FOCUS, Vol.28 (May, 1949), 65-69.

Lohman, Joseph D.: Manpower Is Not Enough. L&O, Vol.7 (Jan., 1959).

Lopez-Rey, Manuel: Juvenile Delinquency, Maladjustment and Maturity, JCLC&PS, Vol.51, No.1 (Mar.-Apr., 1960-61), 34.

———: Police and Juvenile Delinquency, L&O, Vol.9 (Aug., 1961).

Los Angeles County Sheriff's Department: *Manual of Juvenile Procedures*. Los Angeles, Los Angeles County Sheriff's Department, 1965.

Los Angeles Police Department: *Youth and Narcotics* (Rev. Ed.). Los Angeles, Los Angeles Police Dept., 1953.

Louwage, F. E.: Delinquency in Europe After World War II, JCLC&PS, Vol.42 (1951-52), 53.

Ludwig, Fredrick J.: *Youth and the Law*. Brooklyn, The Foundation Press, 1955.

Lundberg, George A., Schrag, Clarence C., and Larsen, Otto N.: *Sociology*. New York, Harper & Bros, 1954.

Lunden, Walter A.: Juvenile Delinquency in Japan. Prewar and Postwar Years, JCL&C, Vol.44 (Nov.-Dec., 1953), 428-32.

Lynn, D. B.: A Note on Sex Differences in the Development of Masculine and Feminine Identification, PR, Vol.66 (1959), 126-35.

McCandless, Boyd R., and McDavid, John W.: Psychological Theory Research and Juvenile Delinquency, JCLC&PS, Vol.8, No.1 (Mar.-May, 1962), 1.

McCann, Richard V.: Juvenile Delinquency and the Church's Opportunity, RE, Vol.50 (1955), 88-92.

———: The Self-image and Delinquency: Some Implications for Religion, FP, Vol.20 (Sept., 1956), 14-23.

McCord, William M.: A Comparative Study of Delinquents and Non-delinquents, JCLC&PS, Vol.51, No.6 (Mar.-Apr., 1960-61), 643.

———: Legal and Criminal Psychology, JCLC&PS, Vol.53, No.1 (Mar.-May, 1962), 78.

———, & **Joan**: *Origins of Crime a New Evaluation of the Cambridge-Sommerville Youth Study*. New York, Columbia Univ. Press, 1959.

———, & ———: Two Approaches to the Cure of Delinquents, JCL&C, Vol.44, No.4 (Nov.-Dec., 1953), 442-67.

McCorkle, Lloyd W., Elias, Albert, and Bixby, F. Lowell: *The Highfields Story: A Unique Experiment in the Treatment of Juvenile Delinquency*. New York, Holt & Co., 1957.

McMillen, Wayne: *Community Organization for Social Welfare*. Chicago, Univ. of Chicago Press, 1945.

McMullan, David A.: Juvenile Court and Rules of Detention, TPY (1963).

McMurray, George: Youth and Work Project, L&O, Vol.11, No.11 (Nov., 1963).

McNichols, Albert: Comprehensive Youth Safety Program, L&O, Vol.9 (May, 1961).

MacCormick, A. H., and Dooling, J. H.: Keeping Children Out of Jails: It Can Be Done, FP, Vol.13 (Sept., 1949), 40-45.

MacMillan, W. L., Jr.: The Scent of Danger, TPC, Vol.30, No.5 (May, 1963), 42.

MacNair, A. Stanley: Delinquency—What Can We Do About It? L&O, Vol.7 (Sept., 1959).

MacNamara, Donald E. J.: Ten Premises Concerning Juvenile Delinquency, POLICE, Vol.8, No.3 (Jan.-Feb., 1964), 71-74.

Mays, John B.: A Study of a Delinquent Community, BJD, Vol.3 (July, 1952), 5-19.

Maisel, Albert Q.: America's Forgotten Children, WHC (Jan., 1947).

Maloney, E. F.: Arresting the Juvenile, L&O, Vol.8 (1960).

————: Learning to Understand the Juvenile, L&O, Vol.9 (Apr., 1961).

Manella, Frank L.: Curfew Laws, NPPAJ, Vol.4 (1958), 161-68.

Martin, John Bartlow. An Abbreviated Form of the Wechsler Intelligence Scale for Children, JCLC&PS, Vol.51, No.1 (Mar.-Apr., 1960-61), 81.

————: End of a Boy's Life, McCALL'S MAGAZINE, Vol.75, 25.

————: *My Life in Crime.* New York, Harper & Bros, 1952.

Martin, John M.: A County-wide Delinquency Recording System, JCLC&PS, Vol.47, No.6 (Mar.-Apr., 1957), 682.

————: Some Characteristics of Vandals, DELINQUENCY, Vol.50, No.6 (1959-60), 477.

Matza, David: Review of Delinquency and Opportunity, AJS, Vol.46 (May, 1961), 631-33.

Mayer, Frederick: *Our Troubled Youth.* New York, Bantam, 1960.

Melchionne, Theresa M.: The Bridge Between, L&O, Vol.9 (July, 1961).

————: Delinquency Control Programs, L&O, Vol.12 (Apr.-June, 1964).

Merrill, Maud A.: *Problems of Child Delinquency.* New York, Houghton Mifflin, 1947.

Merton, R. K.: *Social Theory and Social Structure.* Glencoe, Free Press, 1957.

Meyer, Charles H. Z.: Delinquency and the Community in Wartime, JCL&C, Vol.35, No.6 (Mar.-Apr., 1945), 406.

————: Street Corner Society: The Social Structure of an Italian Slum, JCL&C, Vol.35, No.6 (Mar.-Apr., 1945), 404.

Michael, Carmen Miller: Follow-up Studies of Introverted Children, III, Relative Incidence of Criminal Behavior, JCLC&PS, Vol.47 (1956), 414-22.

Michelson, Bettie E.: Vandalism in Our Schools, IE, Vol.44 (1956), 294.

Miller, Michael M.: Psychodrama in the Treatment Program of a Juvenile Court, DELINQUENCY, Vol.50, No.5 (1959-60), 453.

Miller, Walter B.: The Impact of a Community Group Work Program on Delinquent Corner Groups, SSR, Vol.31 (Dec., 1957), 390-406.

————: Implications of Urban Lower-class Culture for Social Work, SSR, Vol.33 (Sept., 1959), 219-236.

————: Lower Class Culture as a Generating Milieu of Gang Delinquency, JSI, Vol.14 (Apr., 1959).

————: Preventive Work with Street Corner Groups: Boston Delinquency Project, AAAPSS, Vol.322 (1959), 97-106.

Millikin, Rhoda J.: The Police and Children in Trouble, FP, Vol.19 (Mar., 1955), 24-27.

Milner, John G.: Working with Juvenile Gang Members, CYAQ.

Minor, Entitled to Assistance of Counsel, JCLC&PS, Vol.46 (1955-56), 851.

Monachesi, Elio D.: Personality Characteristics of Institutionalized and Non-Institutionalized Male Delinquents, JCL&C, Vol.41 (July-Aug., 1950), 167-79.

————, & **Hathaway, Starke R.:** The Personalities of Pre-Delinquent Boys, JCLC&PS, Vol.48, No.2 (July-Aug., 1957), 149.

Monahan, Thomas P.: Broken Homes by Age of Delinquent Children, JSP, Vol.51 (1960), 387-97.

————: Family Status and the Delinquent Child: A Reappraisal and Some New Findings, SF, Vol.35 (1957), 250-58.

————: The Trend in Broken Homes Among Delinquent Children, M&FL, Vol.19 (1957), 362-65.

Moore, Paul J.: Religious Role in Preventing and Treating Crime and Delinquency, C&D, Vol.6 (1960), 376-79.

More Than Meets the Eye: The Shaping of Public Opinion, NPPAJ, Vol.36 (1957), 5-6.

Morris, Charles V.: Worldwide Concern with Crime, FP, Vol.24 (Dec., 1960), 21-30.

Mueller, Gerhard O. W.: Stafrecht-Allemeiner Teil (Criminal Law—General Part), JCLC&PS, Vol.53, No.2 (June-Aug., 1962), 238.

Murphy, Charles F.: A Seal of Approval for Comic Books, FP, Vol.19 (June, 1955), 19-20.

Murphy, Fred J., Shirley, Mary M., and Witmer, Helen L.: The Incidence of Hidden Delinquency, AJO, Vol.16 (1946), 686-96.

————, ————, & ————: The Incidence of Hidden Delinquency, AJO, Vol.16 (Oct., 1946), 586-96.

Murray, Ellen M.: Space Age Delinquency, POLICE, Vol.9, No.2 (Nov.-Dec., 1964), 22-24.

Murray, Henry A., and Kluckhohn, Clyde: Outline of a Conception of Personality, in Clyde Kluckhohn, Henry A. Murray, and David M. Schneider (eds.), *Personality in Nature, Society and Culture.* New York, Knopf, 1955.

Murray, Robert V.: Report of the Juvenile Delinquency Committee, TPY (1956).

Myers, C. K.: *Light the Dark Streets.* Greenwich, Seabury, 1957.

Myren, Richard A.: New Frontier in Juvenile Delinquency and Youth Crime Control, POLICE, Vol.7, No.5 (May-June, 1963), 20-23.

Naar, Ray: Referral of Juvenile Delinquents: A Guidepost for Social Workers and Probation

Officers, JCLC&PS, Vol.53, No.1 (Mar.-May, 1962), 62.

National Bridge Camp for Boys. Washington, D.C.: Bureau of Prisons, Department of Justice, U.S. Govt. Printing Office, 1959.

National Council on Crime and Delinquency: *Standards and Guides for the Detention of Children and Youth*. New York, National Council on Crime and Delinquency, 1961.

National Police Conference on PAL and Youth Activities, L&O, Vol.9 (Sept., 1961).

National Probation and Parole Association: *Standard Juvenile Court Act*, 6th Ed. New York, National Probation and Parole Association, 1959.

National Society for the Study of Education: *Juvenile Delinquency and the Schools*. Chicago, Univ. of Chicago Press, 1948.

Neumeyer, Martin H.: Delinquency Trends in Wartime, S&SR, Vol.29 (Mar.-Apr., 1945), 262-75.

————: *Juvenile Delinquency in Modern Society*. New York, Nostrand, 1953.

————, & **Esther S.:** *Leisure and Recreation*. New York, Barnes, 1949.

New Directions in Delinquency Prevention, 1947-57. New York, New York City Youth Board, n.d.

New Goals for Juvenile Detention: CYAQ (Summer, 1951) and FP, Vol.13 (Dec., 1949), 29-33.

New York (City) Board of Education: *What Secondary Schools Can Do About Narcotics Addiction*. New York, Bulletin, No.3 Board of Ed., 1957.

New York (City) Police Department: *Use of Narcotics by Children and Adolescents*. New York City Police Dept., 1951.

New York City Youth Board: *Reaching the Fighting Gang*. New York, N.Y. City Youth Board, 1960.

New York State Youth Commission: *Reducing Juvenile Delinquency: What New York State Schools Can Do*. Albany, The Commission, 1952.

Nolan, James B.: Police and Youth, JCLC&PS, Vol.43, No.3 (Sept.-Oct., 1952), 339.

Norman, Sherwood: *The Design and Construction of Detention Homes for the Juvenile Court*. New York, NPPA, 1947.

————: Detention Intake, *Crime Prevention Through Treatment*, NPPAY (1952).

————: *Detention Practice*. New York, National Probation and Parole Association, 1960.

————: Juvenile Detention, NPPAJ, Vol.3 (1957), 392-403.

————: New Goals for Juvenile Detention, FP, Vol.13 (Dec., 1949), 29-35.

————, & **Helen:** *Detention for the Juvenile Court*. New York, National Probation Association, 1946.

————, & **Costella, John B.:** Juvenile Detention and Training Institutions, in *Contemporary Correction*. New York, McGraw-Hill, 1951.

Nunberg, Henry: Problems in the Structure of the Juvenile Court, JCLC&PS, Vol.48, No.5 (Jan.-Feb., 1958), 500.

Nutt, Alice Scott: Juvenile and Domestic Relations Court, SWY (1947).

————: The Responsibility of the Juvenile Courts and the Public Welfare Agency, NPPAY (1947).

Nye, F. Ivan: Child Adjustment in Broken and in Unhappy Unbroken Homes, M&FL, Vol.19 (1957), 356-361.

————: Employment Status of Mothers and Adjustment of Adolescent Children, M&FL, Vol.21 (1959), 240-44.

————: *Family Relationships and Delinquent Behavior*. New York, Wiley, 1958.

————: Unrecorded Juvenile Delinquency, JCLC&PS, Vol.49, No.4 (1958-59), 296.

Nyquist, Ola: How Sweden Handles Its Juvenile and Youth Offenders, FP, Vol.20 (Mar., 1956), 36-42.

O'Connell, Harold P.: Panel on Juvenile Delinquency: Tender Years, Tough Criminals, TPY (1957).

O'Connor, George W.: Juvenile Delinquency: A Policy Statement, TPY (1963).

————: Police Opinion Study, Juvenile Delinquency Questionnaires, TPC, Vol.31 (Jan., 1964), 20.

————: Procedure and Evidence in the Juvenile Court, TPC, Vol.30 (Jan., 1963), 32.

————, & **Watson, Nelson A.:** *Juvenile Delinquency and Youth Crime: the Police Role*. Washington, D.C., IACP, 1964.

O'Hara, Gerald P.: Why Detain Juveniles? POLICE, Vol.8, No.5 (May-June, 1964), 76-78.

O'Neal, Patricia: The Relation of Childhood Behavior Problems to Adult Psychiatric Status, AJPSY, Vol.114 (1958), 961-69.

————, & **Robins, Lee N.:** Childhood Patterns Predictive of Adult Schizophrenia: A Thirty-year Follow-up Study, AJP, Vol.115 (1959), 385-91.

O'Neal, Patricia, Schaefer, Jeanette, Bergmann, John, and Robins, Lee N.: A Psychiatric Evaluation of Adults Who Had Sexual Problems as Children: A Thirty-year Follow-up Study, HO, Vol.19 (Spring, 1960), 32-39.

Ohlin, Lloyd E., and Lawrence, William C.: Social Interaction Among Clients as a Treatment Problem, SW, Vol.4 (Apr., 1959), 3-13.

Olejar, John: Are Juvenile Arrests Necessary? L&O, Vol.7 (June, 1959).

Orrison, Sally M.: Justice and the Juvenile, TPC (1958).

Palmieri, Henry J.: Private Institutions, NPPAJ, Vol.4 (1958), 51-56.

Papanek, Ernest: The Training School: Its Program and Leadership, FP, Vol.17 (June, 1953), 16-27.

Parents and Delinquency. A report prepared by the U.S. Dept. of Health, Education and Welfare, Children's Bureau, Washington D.C., U.S. Govt. Printing Office, 1954.

Parsons, Malcolm B.: The Administration of Police Juvenile Services in the Metropolitan Regions of the United States, JCLC&PS, Vol.54, No.1 (1963), 114.

Parsons, Talcott: Certain Primary Sources and Patterns of Aggression in the Social Structure of the Western World, PSYCHIATRY, Vol.10 (1947), 167-81.

Peck, H. B., and Bellsmith, V.: *Treatment of the Delinquent Adolescent: Group and Individual Therapy with Parent and Child.* New York, Family Service Assoc. of America, 1954.

Perlman, I. Richard: Delinquency Prevention: The Size of the Problem, THE ANNALS, Vol.322 (1959), 1-9.

———: The Meaning of Juvenile Delinquency Statistics, FP, Vol.13, No.3 (Sept., 1949), 63-67.

Phillips, Orie L.: The Federal Youth Corrections Act, FP, Vol.15, No.1 (Mar., 1951), 3-11.

Pierce, L. W.: New York City's Delinquency Control and Community Prevention Program, TPC, Vol.29, No.10 (Oct., 1962), 10.

Pierce, Stanley: Sertoma Junior Rifle Club, L&O, Vol.7 (Nov., 1959).

Pizzuto, C. S.: Police Responsibility in the Detention of Juveniles, TPC, Vol.30 (May, 1963), 10.

Pleune, F. Gordon: Effects of State Training School Programs on Juvenile Delinquents, FP, Vol.21 (Mar., 1957), 24-32.

The Police Department. Juvenile Delinquency Evaluation Project of the City of New York. New York, City College, 1957.

Police Services for Juveniles. Washington, D.C., Children's Bureau Publication No.344, U.S. Govt. Printing Office, 1954.

Police Training Practices Related to Juvenile Delinquency, TPC, Vol.30 (Jan., 1963), 29.

Polier, Justine Wise: *Back to What Woodshed?* New York, Public Affairs Pamphlet No.232, Public Affairs Committee, 1956.

———: The Woodshed Is No Answer, FP, Vol.29 (Sept., 1956), 3-6.

Porterfield, Austin L.: *Youth in Trouble.* Fort Worth, The Leo Potishman Foundation, Texas Christian Univ., 1946.

Pound, Roscoe: The Juvenile Court and the Law, NPPAY (1945).

———: The Place of the Family Court in the Judicial System, NPPAJ, Vol.5 (1959), 161-71.

Powdermaker, Hortense: The Channeling of Negro Aggression by the Culture Process, in Clyde Kukhohn, Henry A. Murray, and David M. Schneider (eds.), *Personality in Nature, Society and Culture.* New York, Knopf, 1955.

Powers, Edwin: An Experiment in the Prevention of Delinquency, THE ANNALS, Vol.261 (Jan., 1949), 77-88.

Powers, Edwin: Schools' Responsibility for the Early Detection of Delinquency-prone Children, HEP, Vol.19 (Spring, 1949), 80-86.

———, & **Witmer, Helen:** *An Experiment in the Prevention of Delinquency: The Cambridge-Somerville Youth Study.* New York, Columbia University Press, 1951.

Prigmore, Charles S.: An Analysis of Rater Reliability on Glueck Scale for the Prediction of Juvenile Delinquency, JCLC&PS, Vol.54, No.1 (1963), 30.

Printzlien, Conrad P.: Deferred Prosecution for Juvenile Offenders, FP, Vol.12 (Mar., 1948), 17-22.

Public Training Schools for Delinquent Children, May, 1955. Washington, D.C., A Directory Prepared by the U.S. Dept. of Health, Education and Welfare, Children's Bureau, U.S. Govt. Printing Office, 1955.

Pursuit, Dan G., and Kenney, John P.: *Police Work with Juveniles.* 3rd Ed. Springfield, Thomas, 1965.

Rahm, Harold J., and Weber, J. Robert: *Office in the Alley,* Austin, Report on a project with gang youngsters, Hogg Foundation for Mental Health, 1958.

Ramseier, Irvin, and Giesecke, W. K.: An Accounting Plan for Juvenile Probation, JCLC&PS, Vol.43, No.1 (Mar., 1953), 705.

Rappaport, Maxie F.: The Possibility of Help for the Child Returning from a State Training School, in Sheldon Glueck (ed.), *The Problem of Delinquency.* Boston, Houghton Mifflin, 1959.

Reaching the Fighting Gang. New York, New York City Youth Board, 1960.

Reading and Delinquency, NPPAJ, Vol.1 (1955), 1-30 (seven articles).

Reckless, Walter C.: A Self Gradient Among Potential Delinquents, JCLC&PS, Vol.49, No.3 (1958-59), 230.

———: Significant Trends in the Treatment of Crime and Delinquency, FP, Vol.13 (Mar., 1949), 6-11.

———, Sinitz, Simon, and Kay, Barbara: The "Good" Boy in a High Delinquency Area, JCLC&PS, Vol.48 (1959), 18-25.

———, ———, and ———: The Self-component in Potential Delinquency & Potential Non-delinquency, AJR, Vol.22 (1957), 566-570.

———, ———, & Murray, Ellen: Self Concept as an Insulator against Delinquency, ASR, Vol.21 (1956), 744-46.

Recommended Standards for Services for Delinquent Children. Washington, D.C., a report prepared by the U.S. Department of Health, Education and Welfare, Children's Bureau, U.S. Govt. Printing Office, 1953.

Redl, Fritz: The Psychology of Gang Formation and the Treatment of Juvenile Delinquency, in *The Psycholanalytic Study of the Child,* Vol.I. New York, International Univ. Press, 1956.

———, & Wineman, D.: *The Aggressive Child.* Glencoe, Free Press, 1957.

———, & ———: *Children Who Hate.* Glencoe, Free Press, 1951.

———, & ———: *Controls from Within.* Glencoe, Free Press, 1952.

Reed, Ellery F.: How Effective Are Group-work Agencies in Preventing Delinquency? FOCUS, Vol.28 (1949), 170-76.

Reifen, David: Protection of Children Involved in Sexual Offences, JCLC&PS, Vol.49, No.3 (1958-59), 222.

Reinemann, John Otto: The Expansion of the Juvenile Court Idea, FP, Vol.13 (Sept., 1949), 34-40.

———: Juvenile Delinquency in Philadelphia and Economic Trends, TULQ, Vol.20 (Apr., 1947), 576-83.

———: Our Responsibility Toward Wayward Youth in War-torn Europe and Asia, JCL&C, Vol.35, No.6 (Mar.-Apr., 1945), 375.

———: Probation and the Juvenile Delinquent, THE ANNALS, Vol.261 (1949), 109-19.

———: Probation and the Juvenile Delinquent, THE ANNALS, Vol.261 (1949), 109-29.

———: The Truant Before the Court, FP, Vol.12 (Sept., 1948), 8-12.

Reinhardt, James M.: The Delinquent and the Value, POLICE, Vol.1, No.1 (Sept.-Oct., 1956), 51-54.

Reiss, Albert J., Jr.: Delinquency as the Failure of Personal and Social Controls, ASR, Vol.16 (Apr., 1951), 196-208.

———: Sex Offenses: the Marginal Status of the Adolescent L&CP (Spring, 1960), 310-333.

———: Social Correlates of Psychological Types of Delinquency, ASR, Vol.17 (1952), 710-718.

———: *Unraveling Juvenile Delinquency,* An Appraisal of the Research Methods, ASJ, Vol.57 (1951), 115-20.

———, & Rhodes, Albert L.: The Distribution of Juvenile Delinquency in the Social Structure, ASR, Vol.26 (Oct., 1961), 720-732.

Reizen, Paul: Family Casework with Boys Under Court Jurisdiction, SC, Vol.37 (1955), 208-14.

Report of the Governor's Special Study Commission on Juvenile Justice, Part II. Sacramento, California, 1960.

Report on Institutional Treatment of Delinquent Juveniles. A report prepared by the National Conference on Prevention and Control of Juvenile Delinquency. Washington, D.C., 1947.

Report on Juvenile Court Administration. A report prepared by the National Conference on Prevention and Control of Juvenile Delinquency, Washington, D.C., 1947.

Report on Juvenile Detention. A report prepared by the National Conference on Prevention and Control of Juvenile Delinquency. Washington, D.C., 1947.

Report on Role of Police. National Conference on Prevention and Control of Delinquency. Washington, D.C., 1947.

Research Bureau, Council of Social Agencies: *Social Statistics: the Houston Delinquent in His Community Setting,* Vol.II, No.1, Houston, 1945.

Retention in High Schools in Large Cities. Washington, D.C., Bulletin No. 15, U.S. Dept. of Health, Education and Welfare, U.S. Office of Education, 1957.

Ritchie, Oscar W.: Thoughts Upon and Impact Study of an Industrial School for Male Delinquents, CORRECTION, Vol.520, No.5 (1959-60), 462.

Rittwagen, Marjorie: *Sins of Their Fathers.* New York, Pyramid Books, 1959.

Roalfe, William R.: John Henry Wigmore Scholar and Reformer, JCLC&PS, Vol.53, No.3 (Sept.-Nov., 1962), 277.

Robert, Guy, L.: *How the Church Can Help Where Delinquency Begins.* New York, Knox Press, 1957.

Roberts, John L.: Factors Associated with Truancy, P&GJ, Vol.34 (1956), 431-36.

Robertson, R. Vance: The Role of a Juvenile Evaluation Center in the Treatment of Delinquency, POLICE, Vol.7, No.2 (Nov.-Dec., 1962), 42-45.

Robins, Lee N.: The Marital History of Former Problem Children, SP, Vol.5 (1948), 347-58.

———: Mental Illness and the Runaway: A Thirty-year Follow-up Study. HO, Vol.16, No.4, 11-15, n.d.

———, & O'Neal, Patricia: The Adult Prognosis for Runaway Children, AJO, Vol.29 (1959), 752-61.

———, Bates, William, and O'Neal, Patricia: Adult Drinking Patterns of Former Problem Children, Dittoed, Dept. of Psychiatry and Neurology, Washington Univ., School of Medicine, St. Louis, Missouri.

Robinson, D. M.: *Chance to Belong.* New York, Woman's Press, 1949.

Robinson, Elizabeth W.: Let's Build Them Better. NASSP, Vol.40 (1956), 119-24.

Robinson, Sophia M.: *Juvenile Delinquency, Its Nature and Control.* New York, Holt, 1960.

Rogers, F. H.: *Street Gangs in Toronto.* Toronto, Ryerson Press, 1945.

Rose, Arnold M., and Weber, George H.: Changes in Attitudes Among Delinquent Boys Committed to Open and Closed Institutions, JCLC&PS, Vol.52, No.2 (July-Aug., 1961), 166.

Rose, Arnold M., and Weber, George: Predicting the Population in Institutions for Delinquent Children and Youth, JCLC&PS, Vol.50, No.2 (July-Aug., 1959), 124.

Rosenfeld, Eva: Social Research and Social Action in Prevention of Juvenile Delinquency, SP, Vol.4 (1956), 138-48.

Rosehneim, Margaret K. (ed.): *Justice for the Child.* New York, Free Press, 1962.

Rosenthal, Leslie: Group Therapy with Problem Children and Their Parents, FP, Vol.17 (Dec., 1953), 27-34.

Roser, Mark C.: The Schools and the Delinquency Problem, JCLC&PS, Vol.43, No.5 (Jan.-Feb., 1953), 576.

Ross, Mabel: Emotional Aspects of Juvenile Delinquency, FP, Vol.15 (Sept., 1951), 12-14.

Roucek, Joseph S. (ed.): *Juvenile Delinquency.* New York, Philosophical Library, 1958.

Rubin, Sol: Changing Youth Correction Authority Concepts, FOCUS, Vol.29, No.3 (May, 1950), 77-82.

———: *Crime and Juvenile Delinquency: a Rational Approach to Penal Problems,* Rev. Ed. New York, Oceana, 1961.

———: The Legal Character of Juvenile Delinquency, THE ANNALS, Vol.261 (Jan., 1949), 1-8.

———: Protecting the Child in Juvenile Court, JCLC&PS, Vol.43 (Nov.-Dec., 1952), 425-40.

———: Unraveling Juvenile Delinquency, Illusions in a Research Project Using Matched Pairs, AJS, Vol.57 (1951), 107-14.

Rubinstein, Marion: The Two Percent Reduction, L&O, Vol.9 (Feb., 1961).

Russell, Bernard: *Current Training Needs in the Field of Juvenile Delinquency.* Washington, D.C., Children's Bureau Publication No.8, U.S. Govt. Printing Office, 1960.

Rutters, Mickey L.: Pennsylvania Officers Attend a Juvenile Study, L&O, Vol.9 (Dec., 1961).

Salisbury, Harrison E.: *The Shook-up Generation.* Greenwich, Fawcett Pub., 1959.

Samuels, Gertrude: Visit to a "600 School," NEW YORK TIMES MAGAZINE (Mar., 1958), 12, 57-58.

Sandelier, Tony: PAL Program, Hollywood, Florida, L&O, Vol.7 (Nov., 1964).

Sauber, Mignon: *Personnel in Public Child Welfare Programs:* 1953. Washington, D.C., a report prepared for the U.S. Dept. of Health, Education and Welfare, Children's Bureau Statistical Series Pub., No.20, 1954.

Sauignano, Joseph P.: Citizenship Training Program for Juveniles, L&O, Vol.9 (Dec., 1961).

Savitz, Leonard D.: Juvenile Delinquency in American Society, JCLC&PS, Vol.53, No.1 (Mar.-May, 1962), 81.

Scarpitti, Frank R., Murray, Ellen, Dinitz, Simon, and Reckless: The "Good" Boy in a High Delinquency Area: Four Years Later, ASR, Vol.25 (1960), 555-58.

Schepses, Erwin: The Academic School Experiment of the Training School Student, FP, Vol.19 (June, 1955), 47-51.

Schilder, Clark L.: Juvenile Offenders Should Be Fingerprinted, FP (Jan.-Mar., 1947), 44-48.

Schneidewing, Frederic F.: The Police and Delinquency Control, POLICE, Vol.1, No.6 (July-Aug., 1957), 20-23.

Schnidelberg, Melitta: Child Murderers, JCLC&PS, Vol.49 (1959), 569-70.

Schoeppe, Aileen: Sex Differences in Adolescent Socialization, JSP, Vol.38 (1953), 175-85.

Schofield, William E.: The New Look in Police Work with Juveniles, TPY (1958).

School and Delinquency, C&D, Vol.7 (July, 1961), entire issue.

Schram, Gustav L.: Philosophy of the Juvenile

Court, THE ANNALS, Vol.261 (1949), 101-08.

Schreiber, Paul: *How Effective Are Services for the Treatment of Delinquents.* Washington, D.C., Children's Bureau Report No.9, U.S. Govt. Printing Office, 1960.

Schrotel, Stanley R.: Developing Leadership for Delinquency Control, TPC (Aug., 1961), 5.

Schwartz, Edward E.: A Community Experiment in the Measurement of Delinquency, NPPAY (1945), 157-82.

_____: Statistics on Juvenile Delinquency in the United States, THE ANNALS, Vol.261 (Jan., 1949), 9-20.

Schwitzgebel: *Street-corner Research: an Experimental Approach to the Juvenile Delinquent.* Cambridge, Harvard Univ. Press, 1964.

Scott, Clifford L.: Criminality and the Kid Next Door, POLICE, Vol.5, No.2 (Nov.-Dec., 1960), 72-75.

Secretariat, United Nations: *New Forms of Juvenile Delinquency: Their Origin, Prevention and Treatment.* New York, United Nations, 1960.

Seliger, Robert V., Lukas, Edwin J., and Linder, Robert M. (eds.): *Contemporary Criminal Hygiene.* Baltimore, Oakridge Press, 1946.

Sellin, Thorsten (ed.): Juvenile Delinquency, THE ANNALS, Vol.261 (Jan., 1949).

_____: Sweden's Substitute for the Juvenile Court, THE ANNALS, Vol.261 (1949), 137-49.

Selvidge, Jean: The Police Juvenile Bureau's Job. NPPAJ, Vol.3 (1957), 39-47.

Senate Judiciary Committee: *Hearings, Subcommittee to Investigate Juvenile Delinquency.* Washington, D.C. A report prepared by the Senate Judiciary Committee (June 5, Oct. 19 & 20, 1954), 1955.

Service for Children and Youth: Improvement and Demonstration Grants. Harrisburg, Commonwealth of Penn., Dept. of Public Welfare, Office for Children and Youth, 1964.

Shawson, John: *The Delinquent Boy.* Boston, Badger, 1926.

Sheldon, William H.: *The Varieties of Temperament.* New York, Harper and Bros., 1949.

_____, Hartl, Emil M., and McDermott, Eugene: *Varieties of Delinquent Youth.* New York, Harper & Bros., 1949.

Shiereman, Charles H.: *The Hype Park Youth Project, May, 1955-May, 1958.* Chicago, Welfare Council of Metropolitan Chicago, n.d.

Short, James F.: A Report on the Incidence of Criminal Behavior, Arrests, and Convictions

in Selected Groups, *Research Studies of the State College of Washington,* 22:110-118, June, 1954.

_____: Reported Behavior as a Criterion of Deviant Behavior, SP, 5:207-213, Winter, 1957-58.

_____: Scaling Delinquent Behavior, ASR, 22:326-331, 1957.

_____, & Nye, F. Ivan: Extent of Unrecorded Juvenile Delinquency; Tentative Conclusions, JCLC&PS, 49:296-302, 1958.

Shower, Gazen: The Scouting Story, TPY, Washington: I.A.C.P., 1958.

Shulman, Harry M.: *The Detention of Youth Awaiting Court Action.* New York, National Probation and Parole Assn., 1958.

_____: The Family and Juvenile Delinquency, THE ANNALS, 261:21-31, January, 1949.

_____: Intelligence and Delinquency, JCL&C, Vol.XLI (Mar.-Apr., 1951), 763-781.

Silving, Helen: The Criminal Law of Mental Incapacity, JCLC&PS, Vol.LIII, No.2 (June-Aug., 1962), 129.

Sisney, Vernon V.: Psychological Motivation of Juveniles, POLICE, Vol.V, No.2 (Nov.-Dec., 1960), 24-25.

Skousen, W. Cleon: Meet a Gentleman Bronco!, L&O, Vol.13, No.4 (Apr., 1965), 22-26.

Slavson, S. R.: Social Reeducation in an Institutional Setting, NP&PAY, 1950, 50-64.

Smith, Bruce: *The New York City Police Survey.* New York, Institute of Public Administration, 1952.

Smith, B. K., & Loughmiller, C.: *The Worth of a Boy.* Austin, Hogg Foundation for Mental Health, 1958.

Smith, P. M.: The School as a Factor, Chapter 7 in Joseph S. Roucek (ed.), *Juvenile Delinquency.* New York: Philosophical Library, 1958.

Snyder, Dr. Harry A.: Some Characteristics of the Juvenile Delinquent, POLICE, Vol.V, No.6 (July-Aug., 1961), 51-53.

Social Class Structure and American Education, HER, 23 (Summer, 1953) and 23 (Fall, 1953), entire issues.

Social Statistics. A report prepared by the U.S. Department of Labor, Children's Bureau, Washington, D.C., 1945.

Social Statistics, II, the Child. A report prepared by the U.S. Department of Labor, Children's Bureau, Washington, D.C., 1946.

Solomon, Ben: The Anatomy of Vandalism, POLICE, Vol.VI, No.6 (July-Aug., 1962), 26-29.

_____: The Juvenile Court Age, POLICE, Vol.VI, No.3 (Jan.-Feb., 1962), 17-18.

_____: Vandalism—What Can We Do About It?

POLICE, Vol.VII, No.I (Sept.-Oct., 1962), 71-74.

———:Why We Have Not Solved the Delinquency Problem, FP, 17:11-19, December, 1953.

Some Aspects of Authority, C&D, 6, July, 1960, entire issue.

Some Facts About Juvenile Delinquency. A report prepared by the U.S. Department of Health, Education and Welfare, Children's Bureau, Publication No. 340, Washington, D.C., 1953.

Some Facts About Public State Training Schools for Juvenile Delinquents. Children's Bureau Statistical Series, No.33. Washington: U.S. Government Printing Office, 1956.

Sorrentino, Anthony: The Chicago Area Project After Twenty-five Years, FP, 23 (June, 1959), 40-45.

Southern California, University of: *Delinquency Prevention Techniques.* Los Angeles, Delinquency Control Institute, University of Southern California, 1947.

Southwestern Law Enforcement Institute, The: *Institute on Juvenile Delinquency.* Springfield, Charles C Thomas, 1962.

Southwestern Law Enforcement Institute, The: *Law Enforcement and the Juvenile Offender.* Springfield, Charles C Thomas, 1963.

Special Police Departments for the Prevention of Juvenile Delinquency. A report submitted by the International Criminal Police Organization, Interpol, General Secretariat, Paris, to the Second United Nations Congress for the Prevention of Crime and the Treatment of Delinquents, London, Aug., 1960.

Spence, Ralph B.: *Reducing Juvenile Delinquency.* Albany, New York State Youth Commission, 1955.

Stahl, Warren E.: Juvenile Card Referral System, L&O, Vol.XII (June, 1964).

Standard Family Court Act. New York, National Probation and Parole Assn., 1959; also printed in NP&PAJ, 5 (1959), 99-160.

Standard Juvenile Court Act. 6th ed. New York, National Probation and Parole Assn., 1959.

Standards and Guides for the Detention of Children and Youth. New York, National Probation and Parole Assn., 1958.

Standards for Specialized Courts Dealing with Children. Washington: U.S. Government Printing Office, 1954.

State of California: *California Youth Authority. California State Juvenile Officers' Assn., First Annual Conference, Long Beach, California.* Sacramento, State Printing Office, April, 1950 (multilithed).

Statistics on Public Institutions for Delinquent Children, 1958. Children's Bureau Statistical Series, No.59. Washington, Children's Bureau, 1960.

Stoke, Stuart M.: An Inquiry into the Concept of Identification, JGP, 76:163-189, 1950.

Stone, L. Joseph, and Church, Joseph: *Childhood and Adolescence: a Psychology of the Growing Person.* New York, Random House, 1957.

Storm, Bill: The PAL's Homecoming Class, L&O, Vol.8, No.2, 1960.

Stranahan, Marion, and Schwartzman, Cecil: An Experiment in Reaching Asocial Adolescents Through Group Therapy, THE ANNALS, 322 (1959), 117-125.

Stroup, Herbert H.: *Community Welfare Organization.* New York, Harper and Brothers, 1952.

———: *Social Work: an Introduction to the Field.* New York, American Book Co., 1960.

Studt, E.: The Nature of Hard-to-reach Groups, *Children,* Vol.4, No.6 (Nov.-Dec., 1957).

———, **and Russell, Bernard:** *Staff Training for Personnel in Institutions for Juvenile Delinquents.* Children's Bureau Publication No.364. Washington, U.S. Government Printing Office, 1958.

Stullken, Edward H.: Chicago's Special School for Social Adjustment, FP, Vol.20 (Mar., 1956), 31-36.

———: Misconceptions About Juvenile Delinquency, JCLC&PS, Vol.46 (1955-56), 833-842.

———: The Schools and the Delinquency Problem, JCLC&PS, Vol.43 (1953), 563-577.

Sussman, Frederick B.: *Law of Juvenile Delinquency.* New York Oceana Publications, 1959.

Swanson, Lynn D.: Delinquency, Police and the Family, TPY (I.A.C.P.), 1964.

Sykes, G. M., and Matsa, David: Techniques of Neutralization: A Theory of Delinquency, ASR, Vol.22 (1957), 664-670.

Taber, Robert C.: The Potential Role of the School Counselor in Delinquency Prevention and Treatment, FP, Vol.13 (Sept., 1949), 52-56.

Tait, C. D. Jr., and Hodges, E. Jr.: Delinquency Prevention: A Review and a Proposal, POLICE, Vol.8, No.4 (Mar.-Apr., 1964), 36-39.

Talese, Gay: A Youth Looks at Gangs, THE NEW YORK TIMES, Oct. 2, 1959.

Tamm, Quinn: Parent-Police Partnership Can Help Our Youngsters, TPC, Vol.XXX (July, 1963), 7.

——: Parents Should Police Too, TPC, Vol.XXX (Oct., 1963), 7.

Tappan, Paul W.: The Adolescent in Court, JCL&C, Vol.37 (1946), 216-230.

——: Children and Youth in the Criminal Court, THE ANNALS, Vol.261 (1949), 128-136.

——: *Comparative Survey of Juvenile Delinquency,* Part I, North America. New York: United Nations Department of Economics and Social Affairs, 1958.

——: *Delinquent Girls in Court.* New York, Columbia University Press, 1947.

——: *Juvenile Delinquency.* New York, Mc-Graw-Hill Book Co., 1949.

——: Treatment Without Trial, SF, Vol.24 (1946), 306-311.

——: Young Adults Under the Youth Authority, JCLC&PS, Vol.47, No.6 (Mar.-Apr., 1957), 629.

Teacher Opinion on Pupil Behavior, 1955-56, RBNEA, Vol.34, (Apr., 1956), 51-107.

Teeters, Negley K., and Reinemann, John Otto: *The Challenge of Delinquency.* New York, Prentice-Hall, 1950.

Tesseneer, R. A., and Tesseneer, L. M.: Review of the Literature on School Dropouts, PNASSP, Vol.42 (May, 1958), 141-53.

Thimm, Joseph L.: The Juvenile Court and Restitution, C&D, Vol.6 (1960), 276-86.

Thomas, Brother Aquinas, F.S.C.: Why the Violent Generation? PMR, Vol.2, No.10 June, 1965), 5-15.

Thomas, Charles P.: Youth—Our Primary "Target," TPY (1957).

Thompson, George N.: *The Psychopathic Delinquent and Criminal.* Springfield, Thomas, 1953.

Thompson, Richard E.: A Validation of the Glueck Social Prediction Scale for Proneness to Delinquency, JCLC&PS, Vol.43 (1952), 453-70.

——: Further Validation of the Glueck Social Prediction Table for Identifying Potential Delinquents, JCLC&PS, Vol.45, No.2 (July-Aug., 1957), 175.

Tolman, Ruth S., and Wales, Ralph: *Juvenile Detention in California: Current Practice and Recommendations.* Los Angeles, Calif. Advisory Committee on Detention Home Problems, 1946.

Training for Probation and Parole Work, NPPAJ, Vol.2 (July, 1956), entire issue.

Training Personnel for Work with Juvenile Delinquents. Washington, D.C., Children's Bureau Pub. No.348, U.S. Govt. Printing Office, 1954.

Training Practices Related to Juvenile Delinquency, TPC, Vol.30 (Jan. 1963), 29.

Training Schools for Delinquent Children. Washington, D.C., American Psychiatric Association, 1952.

Trice, Harrison, M., and Pittman, David J.: Social Organization and Alcoholism: A Review of Significant Research Since 1940, SP, Vol.5 (Spring, 1958), 294-307.

Turner, Stanley H.: Some Methods for Estimating Uncleared Juvenile Offenses, JCLC&PS, Vol.56, No.1 (Mar., 1965), 54-58.

Twain, David C.: Juvenile Recidivism, JCLC&PS, Vol.51, No.1 (Mar.-Apr., 1960-61), 77.

United States Children's Bureau: *Juvenile Court Statistics.* Washington, D.C., Govt. Printing Office.

——: *Police Services for Juveniles.* Washington, D.C., U.S. Govt. Printing Office, 1954.

——: *Report to the Congress on Juvenile Delinquency.* Washington, D.C., U.S. Govt. Printing Office, 1960.

——: *Social Statistics,* supplement of THE CHILD, Juvenile Court Statistics. Washington, D.C., Federal Security Agency, 1965.

U.S. Congress, Senate, Committee on the Judiciary: *Juvenile Delinquency.* Washington, D.C., Report No. 130, 85th Congress, 1st Session, U.S. Govt. Printing Office, 1957.

U.S. Dept. of Health, Education and Welfare, Supt. of Documents: *Police Services for Juveniles.* Washington, D.C., U.S. Govt. Printing Office, 1954.

——, **Children's Bureau:** *Recommended Standards for Services for Delinquent Children.* Washington, D.C., U.S. Govt. Printing Office, 1953.

U.S. Senate: *Interim Report of the Committee on the Judiciary.* Washington, D.C., a report prepared by the Subcommittee to Investigate Juvenile Delinquency, U.S. Senate, 83rd Congress, 1st Session, Report No.1064, U.S. Govt. Printing Office, Mar. 15, 1954.

——: *Interim Report of the Committee on the Judiciary.* Washington, D.C., a report prepared by a Subcommittee to Investigate Juvenile Delinquency, U.S. Senate, 84th Congress, 1st Session, Report No.61, U.S. Govt. Printing Office, Mar. 14, 1955.

University of Southern California: *Progress Report of the Delinquency Control Institute.* Los Angeles, Univ. of Southern California Press, 1949.

Ullman, Charles A.: Identification of Maladjusted School Children (Comparison of Three Methods of Screening), *Public Health Monograph.* Washington, D.C., No.7, U.S. Govt. Printing Office, 1952.

Vandalism, FP, Vol.18 (Mar., 1954), eight brief articles.

Vedder, Clyde B. (ed.): *The Juvenile Offender.* New York, Random House, 1954.

Voight, Lloyd L.: Need for a Community Program for Troubled or Maladjusted Children, POLICE, Vol.4, No.2 (Nov.-Dec., 1959), 58-61; Vol.4, No.4 (Mar.-Apr., 1960), 65-67.

Von Hentg, Hans: The Delinquency of the American Indian, JCL&C, Vol.36, No.2 (1945-46), 75.

Voss, George B.: The Predictive Efficiency of the Glueck Social Prediction Table, JCLC&PS, Vol.54, No.4 (1963), 421.

Wakefield, Dan: Gang That Went Good, HARPER'S, Vol.216 (June, 1948), 36-43.

Walker, Glenn J.: Group Counseling in Juvenile Probation, FP, Vol.23 (Dec., 1959), 31-38.

Wallerstein, James S., and Wyle, Clement J.: Our Law-abiding Law Breakers, PROBATION (Mar.-Apr., 1947).

Watson, N. A.: Analysis & Self-criticism in Juvenile Work, TPC, Vol.31 (June, 1964), 22.

———: Police Profiles Revealed by Juvenile Delinquency Studies, TPC, Vol.30 (Oct., 1963), 16.

———: Police Work With Children: A Review, TPC, Vol.30 (Sept., 1963), 36.

Watterberg, William: Boys Who Get in Trouble, JE, Vol.131 (1948), 117-18.

———: Church Attendance and Juvenile Delinquency, S&SR, Vol.34 (Jan., 1950), 195-202.

———: Differences Between Girl and Boy "Repeaters," JEP, Vol.47 (1956), 137-46.

———: Factors Associated with Repeating Among Preadolescent "Delinquents," JCP, Vol.84 (1954), 189-96.

———: Girl Repeaters, NPPAJ, Vol.3 (1957), 48-53.

———: Juvenile Repeaters from Two Viewpoints, ASR, Vol.18 (1953), 631-35.

———: Normal Rebellion—or Real Delinquency, CS, Vol.34 (Fall, 1957), 15-20.

———: Recidivism Among Girls, JA&SP, Vol.50 (1955), 405-06.

———: Ten-year-old Boys in Trouble, CD, Vol.28 (1957), 43-46.

———, & Balistrieri, J. J.: Automobile Theft: A "Favored Group" Delinquency, AJS, Vol.57 (1952), 575-79.

———, & ———: Gang Membership and Juvenile Misconduct, ASR, Vol.15 (Dec., 1950), 744-52.

———, & Mair, John B.: A Study of Teenagers Arrested for Drunkenness, QJSA, Vol.17 (1956), 426-36.

———, & Quiroz, Frank: Follow-up Study of Ten-year-old Boys with Police Records, JCP, Vol.17 (1953), 309-13.

———, & Saunders, Frank: Sex Differences Among Juvenile Offenders, S&SR, Vol.39 (1954), 24-31.

Webb, Robert & Muriel: *The Churches and Juvenile Delinquency.* New York, Associated Press, 1957.

———, & ———: How the Churches Can Help in the Prevention and Treatment of Juvenile Delinquency, FP, Vol.21 (Dec., 1957), 22-25.

Weber, George H.: The Boy Scout Program as a Group Approach in Institutional Delinquency Treatment, FP, Vol.19 (Sept., 1955), 47-54.

———: *Camps for Delinquent Boys, a Guide to Planning.* Washington, D.C., Children's Bureau Publication, No.385, U.S. Government Printing Office, 1960.

Weeks, H. A.: *Youthful Offenders at Highfields.* Ann Arbor, Univ. of Michigan Press, 1958.

Weiner, Arthur K.: Cracking the Hard Core Area, TPC, Vol.32, No.1 (Jan., 1965), 27-31.

Welfare Council of Metropolitan Los Angeles: *Recreation for Everybody.* Los Angeles, Welfare Council, 1945.

Wertham, Fredric: *Seduction of the Innocent.* New York, Rinehart & Co., 1953.

What's Happening to Delinquent Children in Your Town? Washington, D.C., prepared by the U.S. Dept. of Health, Education and Welfare, No.342, 1953.

What's This About Punishing Parents? FP (Mar., 1948), 23-29.

Wheelock, Walter: Death by Detonation, L&O, Vol.7 (Feb., 1959).

Whelan, R. W.: Experiment in Predicting Delinquency, JCLC&PS (1954), 432-41.

———: New York City's Approach to the Delinquency Problem, FP, Vol.17 (Dec., 1953), 19-25.

Why Young People "Go Bad," USN&WR, Vol.108, No.17 (Apr., 26, 1965), 56-62 (an exclusive interview with Dr. Sheldon Glueck).

Williams H.: Foster Homes for Juvenile Delinquents, FP, Vol.13 (Sept., 1949), 46-51.

Wilner, Daniel M., Rosenfeld, Eva, Lee, Robert S., Gerard, Donald L., and Chein, Isidor: Heroin Use and Street Gangs, JCLC&PS, Vol.48 (1957), 399-409.

Wilson, Edwin B.: Symposium on Unraveling Juvenile Delinquency, HLR, Vol.64 (1951), 1039-41.

Winters, John E.: Awareness of Crime and Youth Problems, L&O, Vol.7 (Apr., 1964).

———: *Crime and Kids,* Springfield, Thomas, 1959.

———: The Role of the Police in the Prevention and Control of Delinquency, FP, Vol.21 (June, 1957), 3-8.

Wisconsin, Univ. of: *Guides for Cooperation—School and Law Enforcement.* Washington, IACP, 1965.

Witmer, Helen L.: *Parents and Delinquency: Report of a Conference.* Washington, D.C., Children's Bureau, U.S. Govt. Printing Office, 1954.

———— (ed.): Prevention of Juvenile Delinquency, THE ANNALS, Vol.322 (1959), entire issue.

————, & Kotinsky, R. (eds.): *New Perspectives for Research on Juvenile Delinquency.* Washington, D.C., Children's Bureau, U.S. Govt. Printing Office, 1956.

————, & Tufts, Edith: *The Effectiveness of Delinquency Prevention Programs.* Washington, D.C., U.S. Dept. of Health, Education & Welfare, Children's Bureau Pub. No.350, U.S. Govt. Printing Office, 1954.

Wittman, Gerald P.: Community Partners in Delinquency Control, L&O, Vol.7 (July, 1959).

Witty, Paul: Comics, Television and Our Children, TH, Vol.33 (Feb., 1955), 18-21.

Wogahan, Lester E., Sommer, Edith, & Lawsen, Lawrence: An Experiment in Group Placement of Juvenile Parolees, NPPAJ, Vol.4 (1958), 66-73.

Wolfbein, Seymour L.: Transition from School to Work: A Study of the School Leaver, P&GJ, Vol.38 (1959), 98-105.

Wolke, Michael S.: Comprehensive Program for Working With Youth, L&O, Vol.8, No.1 (1960).

————: Police Need Training in Problems of Youth, L&O, Vol.7 (Oct., 1959).

World Health Organization: *Trends in Juvenile Delinquency.* Geneva, Public Health Papers No.5, T.C.N. Gibbens, United Nations, 1961.

Wyegala, Victor B.: Juvenile Offenders Should Not Be Fingerprinted, FP (Jan.-Mar., 1947), 44-48.

Yablonsky, Lewis: The Delinquent Gang as a Near-group, SP, Vol.7 (Fall, 1959), 108-117.

————: The Violent Gang, THE ANNALS, Vol.347 (May, 1963), 168.

————: The Role of Law & Social Science in the Juvenile Court, JCLC&PS, Vol.53, No.4 (Dec., 1962), 426.

Yinger, J. Milton: Contraculture and Subculture, ASR, Vol.25 (1960), 625-35.

Young, Pauline V.: *Social Treatment in Probation and Delinquency.* New York, McGraw-Hill, 1952.

Zald, Mayer N.: The Correctional Institution for Juvenile Offenders: An Analysis of Organizational "Character," SP, Vol.8 (1960), 57-67.

Zimmering, Paul, Toolon, James, Solrin, Renate, and Wortis, Bernard: Heroin Addiction in Adolescent Boys, JN&MD, Vol.114 (1951), 19-34.

KIDNAPING

Radin, Edward D.: *12 Against Crime.* New York, G. P. Putnam's 1950.

State of New Jersey vs. Bruno Richard Hauptmann. Trial Transcripts.

State of New Jersey vs. John Hughes Curtis.

Trial Transcript.

United States vs. Gaston B. Means and Norman T. Whitaker. Trial Transcript.

Waller, George: *Kidnap.* New York, Dial Press, 1961.

MURDER—HOMICIDE

Arons, Harry: Hypnosis Clears Two Murder Suspects, POLICE, Vol.7, No.6 (July-Aug., 1962), 19-22.

Bensing, Robert C., and Schroeder, Oliver, Jr.: *Homicide in an Urban Community.* Springfield, Thomas, 1960.

Blinn, Keith W.: First Degree Murder, a Workable Definition, JCL&C, Vol.40, No.6 (Mar.-Apr., 1950), 729.

Bloch, Herbert A.: *Research Report on Homicides, Attempted Homicides and Crimes of Violence.* Int'l. Cooperation Administration, U.S. Operations Mission to Ceylon, 1960.

Bohannan, Paul (ed.): *African Homicide and Suicide.* Princeton, Princeton Univ. Press, 1960.

Bok, Curtis: *Star Wormwood.* New York, Medallion, 1960.

Bullock, Henry A.: Urban Homicide in Theory and Fact, JCLC&PS, Vol.45 (Jan.-Feb., 1955), 565-573.

Cohen, Louis H.: *Murder, Madness and the Law.* New York, Signet, 1954.

Decrease in Homicide Rate, Metropolitan Life Insurance Co., *Statistical Bulletin*, Vol.39 (Sept., 1958), 8-10.

DeSaram, G. S. W., Webster, G., and Kathirga-mathaby, N.: Post Mortem Temperature and Time of Death, JCLC&PS, Vol.46 (1955-56), 562-577.

Dieckmann, Sr.: Handbook for Investigating Homicide, L&O, Vol.8, Nos.1-2 (1960).

Donovan, Robert J.: *The Assassins.* New York, Popular, 1955.

Durkheim, Emile: *Suicide.* Glencoe, Free Press, 1951.

Ford, Richard: Critical Times in Murder Investigation, JCLC&PS, Vol.43, No.5 (Jan.-Feb., 1953), 672.

———: Motor Vehicular Suicides, JCLC&PS, Vol.54, No.3 (1963), 357.

Freeman, Lucy: *Catch Me Before I Kill More.* New York, Pocket Books, 1956.

Gibbens, T. C.: Sane and Insane Homicide, JCLC&PS, Vol.49, No.2 (1958-59), 110.

Gillin, John L.: Murder as a Sociological Phenomenon, THE ANNALS, Vol.284 (Nov., 1952), 20-25.

Grunhut, Max: Murder and the Death Penalty in England, THE ANNALS, Vol.284 (Nov., 1952).

Guttmacher, Manfred S.: *The Mind of the Murderer.* New York, Farrar, 1960.

Handler, Joel F.: Background Evidence in Murder Cases, JCLC&PS, Vol.51, No.3 (Mar.-Apr., 1960-61), 317.

Harlan, Howard: Five Hundred Homicides, JCL&C, Vol.40, No.6 (Mar.-Apr., 1950), 736.

Helpern, Milton: The Postmortem Examination in Cases of Suspected Homicide, JCL&C, Vol.36, No.6 (1945-46), 485.

Henry, Andrew F., and Short, James F.: *Suicide and Homicide.* Glencoe, Free Press, 1954.

Holmes, Paul: *The Sheppard Murder Case.* New York, Bantam, 1962.

Howes, Royce: Beating Homicide Rap, TPC (Mar., 1961), 24.

Hutter, Ernie: *The Chillingworth Murder Case.* Derby, Monarch, 1963.

Illing, Hans A.: The Mold of Murder: A Psychiatric Study of Homicide, JCLC&PS, Vol.53, No.3 (Sept.-Nov., 1962), 362.

Jesse, F. Tennyson: *Murder and Its Motives.* London, Harrar, 1952.

Kempner, Robert M. W.: Murder by Government, JCL&C, Vol.38, No.3 (Mar.,-Apr., 1947-48), 235-38.

Kessler, William F., and Weston, Paul B.: *Detection of Murder.* New York, Arco, 1959.

MacDonald, John M.: *The Murderer and His Victim.* Springfield, Thomas, 1961.

Merkeley, Donald K.: *The Investigation of Death.* Springfield, Thomas, 1957.

Moseley, A. L.: Motor Vehicular Suicides, JCLC&PS, Vol.54, No.3 (1963), 357.

Palmer, Stuart: A Case Study of Fifty-one New England Murderers, POLICE, Vol.7, No.6 (July-Aug., 1963), 65-67.

———: Frustration and Murder, JCLC&PS, Vol.50, No.3 (1959-60), 276.

———: *A Study of Murder.* New York, Crowell, 1960.

Peck, David W.: *The Greer Case.* New York, Simon & Schuster, 1955.

Poddlsky, Edward: Mind of the Murder, JCLC&PS, Vol.45 (1954-55), 48-50.

Race, George J., and Nickey, William M., Jr.: Identification of Bodies Including Skeletal Remains and Determination of the Time of Death, POLICE, Vol.6, No.6 (July-Aug., 1962), 6-10.

Ravkind, William M.: Justifiable Homicide in Texas, SLJ, Vol.13 (Fall, 1959), 508-524.

Rawson, Tabor: *I Want to Live.* New York, Signet, 1958.

Reik, T.: *The Unknown Murderer.* New York, Prentice-Hall, 1945.

Reinhardt, James M.: The "Gentle" Sex Murder —A Special Problem of Investigation, POLICE, Vol.1, No.4 (Mar.-Apr., 1957), 12-14.

———: *The Murderous Trial of Charles Starkweather.* Springfield, Thomas, 1960.

Rice, Craig (ed.): *Los Angeles Murders.* New York, Duell, 1947.

Sellin, Thorsten (ed.): Murder and the Penalty of Death, THE ANNALS, Vol. 284 (Nov., 1952).

Skousen, W. Cleon: Specter of a Political Assassin, L&O, Vol.9, No.12 (Dec., 1963).

Snyder, LeMoyne, et al.: *Homicide Investigation: Practical Information for Coroners, Police Officers and other Investigators.* Springfield, Thomas, 1959.

Straus, Jacqueline H., and Straus, Murray A.: Suicide, Homicide and Social Structure in Ceylon, AJS, Vol. 48 (Mar., 1953), 461-69.

Traver, Robert: *Anatomy of a Murder.* New York, St. Martin's Press, 1958.

Turner, Ralph F.: Homicide Investigation Techniques, JCLC&PS, Vol.53, No.3 (Sept.-Nov., 1962), 397.

Unraveling the Mystery of the Assassination of John F. Kennedy: The Official Story, USN&WR (Oct., 5, 1964), 35-97.

Verkko, Veli: *Homicides and Suicides in Finland.* Copenhagen, G.E.C. Gads, 1951.

VonHentig, Hans: Pre-murderous Kindness and

Post-murder Grief, JCLC&PS, Vol.48, No.4 (Nov.-Dec., 1957), 369.

Walker, Bill: *The Case of Barbara Graham.* New York, Ballantine, 1961.

Wilson, Colin, and Pitman, Pat: *Encyclopedia of Murder.* New York, Putnam's, 1961.

Wilson, Robert A.: *Homicide Investigation Techniques.* Springfield, Thomas, 1961.

Wolfgang, Marvin E.: *Patterns in Criminal Homicide.* Philadelphia, Univ. of Pennsylvania, 1958.

PORNOGRAPHY

Beman, Lamar: *Selected Articles and Censorship of the Theater and Motion Pictures.* New York, Wilson, 1951.

Blanshard, Paul: *The Right to Read—The Battle Against Censorship.* Boston, Beacon Press, 1955.

Bromberg, Benjamin: Five Tests for Obscenity, CBR, Vol.41, No.416 (1960).

Eliasberg, W. G.: Art: Immoral and Immortal, JCLC&PS, Vol.45 (1954-55), 274-78.

Ernst, Morris L., and Schwartz, Alan U.: *Censorship the Search for the Obscene.* New York, Macmillan, 1964.

Fagerstrom, Dorothy: Pornography—A Moral Disease, L&O, Vol.7 (Oct., 1964).

Fostes, Henry H., Jr.: The Comstock Load, JCLC&PS, Vol.48, No.3 (Sept.-Oct., 1957), 245.

Gardiner, Harold C.: Moral Principles Towards a Definition of the Obscene, L&CP, Vol.20, No.560 (1955).

Higgins, Lois L.: Obscenity, Pornography & Delinquency, L&O, Vol.8, No.2 (1960).

——: Pornography and Our Moral Climate, L&O, Vol.7 (Mar., 1964).

Kilpatrick, James Jackson: *The Smut Peddlers.* New York, Avon, 1960.

King, Daniel P.: A Proposal for an Obscenity Ordinance, POLICE, Vol.8, No.6 (July-Aug., 1964), 41-43.

Kuh, Richard H.: Obscenity Prosecution Problems and Legislative Suggestions, POLICE, Vol.9, No.5 (May-June, 1965), 42.

Lockhart, William B., and McClure, Robert C.: Censorship of Obscenity: The Developing Constitutional Standards, MLR, Vol.45, No.5 (1961).

——, & ——: Literature, the Law of Obscenity and the Constitution, Vol.38, No.295, MLR (1954).

McKeon, Richard, Merton, Robert K., and Gellhorn, Walter: *Freedom to Read.* New York, Bowhev, 1957.

Montague, Henry B.: Pornography, TPY (1963).

Murphy, Terrence J.: *Censorship: Government and Obscenity.* Baltimore, Helicon, 1963.

O'Connor, Frank D.: Pornography, TPY (1960).

Skousen, W. Cleon: Obscene Literature—What Can the Police Do About It? L&O, Vol.9 (Aug., 1961).

Paul, James N., and Schwartz, Murray: *Federal Censorship: Obscenity in the Mail.* New York, Free Press, 1961.

States Act Against Lewd Literature, JCLC&PS, Vol.46 (1955-56), 688.

Zeichner, Irving B.: Obscene Publications, L&O, Vol.11, No.2 (Feb., 1963).

——: Objectional Publications, L&O, Vol.11, No.5 (May, 1963).

ROBBERY

Bank Robbers, BANKING, Vol.51 (June, 1959), 42-43.

Block, Eugene B.: *Great Train Robberies of the West.* New York, Coward-McCann, 1959.

The Boom in Bank Robbery, FORTUNE, Vol.61 (Jan., 1960), 115-17.

California Dept. of Education, Bureau of Trade and Industrial Education: *Robbery.* Sacramento, 1949.

DeBaun, Everett: The Heist: The Theory and Practice of Armed Robbery, HARPER'S, Vol.200 (Feb., 1950), 69-77.

Dibble, R. F.: Jesse James, SE&SCD, Vol.2, No.3 (1964).

Gordons, The: *Experiment in Terror.* New York, Bantam, 1962.

Gosling, John, and Craig, Dennis: *The Great Train Robbery.* New York, Bobbs-Merrill, 1965.

Holcomb, Richard L.: *Armed Robbery.* Iowa City, University of Iowa Press, 1949.

Lawder, Lee E.: Robbery With a Match, L&O, Vol.8, No.1 (1960).

Radzinowicz, Leon, and McClintock, F. H.: Robbery in London, ECONOMIST, Vol.197 (Nov., 26, 1960), 860-61.

Titus, Charles M.: Armed Robbery, SW, Vol.1, No.1 (July-Aug., 1964), 22-26.

SEX OFFENSES

Adams, Frank H.: *Basic Criminal Psychiatry with Emphasis on Sex Crimes.* Sacramento, Dept. of Education, Peace Officers' Training, 1950.

Albert, Ellis: Interrogation of Sex Offenders, JCLC&PS, Vol.45 (1954-55), 41-47.

Amend Illinois Criminal Sexual Psychopathic Persons Act, JCLC&PS, Vol.46 (1955-56), 682.

American Social Hygiene Assoc., Inc.: *Problems of Sexual Behavior.* New York, American Social Hygiene Assoc., Inc., 1948.

Ball, John C.: Early Sexual Behavior of Lower Class Delinquent Girls, JCLC&PS, Vol.51, No.2 (Mar.-Apr., 1960-61), 209.

Bergman, Werner: The Sexual Psychopath, JCLC&PS, Vol.43, No.5 (Jan.-Feb., 1953), 593.

Blackwelder, Helen McLarin: *Tell Girls Why.* Atlanta, Turner E. Smith, 1947.

Bowling, R. W.: The Sex Offender and the Law, FP, Vol.14 (Sept., 1950), 11-16.

Braude, Jacob M.: The Sex Offender and the Court, FP, Vol.14 (Sept., 1950), 17-22.

Brown, Julia S.: A Comparative Study of Deviations From Sexual Mores, ASR, Vol.17 (Apr., 1952), 135-46.

Brown, William P.: Training to Meet the Sex Criminal Seminar, TPY (1963).

California Dept. of Education Bureau of Industrial Education: *Basic Criminal Psychiatry with Emphasis on Sex Crimes.* Sacramento, Peace Officers' Training, prepared by Freedman H. Adams and George Tarjan, n.d.

California Legislature, Assembly, Judiciary Subcommittee on Sex Research: *California Sexual Deviation Study.* Sacramento, Dept. of Mental Hygiene, 1953.

California Legislature, Interm Committee on Judicial System and Judicial Process: *Preliminary Report of the Subcommittee on Sex Crimes.* Sacramento, 1949.

Cantor, Donald J.: Deviation and the Criminal Law, JCLC&PS, Vol.55, No.4 (Dec., 1964), 441.

Carpenter, Lester J.: The Roving Sex Offender, TPY (1964).

Cason, Hulsey: A Case of Sexual Psychopathy, JCLIN.PSY. Vol.8 (July-Oct., 1947), 785-800.

Criminal Sexual Psychopathic Act in Indiana, JCLC&PS, Vol.46 (1955-56), 853.

de River, J. Paul: *The Sexual Criminal.* Springfield, Thomas, 1950, 1956.

Dickel, Herman A.: The Sexual Psychopath, JCLC&PS, Vol.43, No.5 (Jan.-Feb., 1953), 595.

Drummond, Isabel: *The Sex Paradox.* New York, Putnam, 1952.

Dubowski, Kurt M.: The Sexual Psychopath, JCLC&PS, Vol.43, No.5 (Jan.-Feb., 1953), 598.

Dunham, H. Warren: *Crucial Issues in the Treatment and Control of Sexual Deviation in the Community.* Lansing, Michigan, Dept. of Mental Health, 1951.

Ellis, Albert, and Brancale, Ralph: *The Psychology of Sex Offenders.* Springfield, Thomas, 1956.

Fairly, Kenneth W.: The M. C. Parker Rape Case, POLICE, Vol.8, No.2 (Nov.-Dec., 1963), 78-82.

Fisher, Edward C., and Reinhardt, James W.: The Sexual Psychopath and the Law, JCL&C, Vol.39, No.6 (Mar.-Apr., 1948-49), 734-43.

Ford, Clellan, and Beach, Frank A.: *Patterns of Sexual Behavior.* New York, Harper, 1951.

Generaces, C. D. S.: The Sexual Psychopath, JCLC&PS, Vol.43, No.5, (Jan.-Feb., 1953), 594.

Guttmacher, Manfred S.: *Sex Offenses: The Problem, Causes, and Prevention.* New York, Norton, 1951.

——, **& Weihofen, Henry:** Sex Offenders, JCLC&PS, Vol.43, No.2 (July-Aug., 1952), 153.

Haines, William H., and Hoffman, Harry R.: Commitments Under the Sexual Psychopath Law in the Criminal Court of Cook County, Illinois, AJPSY, Vol.105 (Dec., 1948), 420-25.

Hayakawa, S. I.: Sexual Fantasy and the 1957 Car, Vol.14 (Spring, 1957), 163-68.

Henry, George W.: *Sex Variants.* New York, Harper & Bros., 1949.

Hirning, L. Clovis: The Sex Offender in Custody, R. M. Lindner, and R. V. Seliger (eds.), *Handbook of Correctional Psychology.* New York, Philosophical Lib., 1947.

Holcomb, R. L.: Sex Crimes, JCLC&PS, Vol.51, No.4 (Mar.-Apr., 1960-61), 492.

Hughes, Graham: The Crime of Incest, JCLC&PS, Vol.55, No.3 (Sept., 1964), 322.

Humphreys, Ray: Catching the Masked Cupids, L&O, Vol.8, No.5 (1960).

Karpman, Benjamin: Considerations of Bearing

Upon the Problem of Sex Offenders, JCL&C, Vol.43, No.1 (May-June, 1952), 13.

Kaepman, Benjamin: Psychosis as a Defense Against Yielding to Perversive (Paraphiliae) Sexual Crimes, JCL&C, Vol. 44, No.1 (May-June), 1953.

————: Psychosomatic Neurosis as a Barrier Against Craved but Prohibited Sexual Drives, JCL&C, Vol.44, No.6 (Mar.-Apr., 1954), 746-52.

————: *The Sexual Offender and His Offenses.* New York, Julian, 1954.

————: The Sexual Psychopath, JCL&C, Vol.42 (1951-52), 184.

Kinsey, Alfred C., et al.: *Sexual Behavior in the Human Female.* Philadelphia, Saunders, 1955.

LeMaire, Louis: Danish Experience Regarding Castration of Sexual Offenders, JCLC&PS, Vol.47 (Sept.-Oct., 1956), 294-310.

Loewenberg: The Sexual Psychopath, JCLC&PS, Vol.43, No.5 (Jan.-Feb., 1953), 607.

Logan, Nell: Early Sexual Behavior of Lower-class Delinquent Girls, JCLC&PS, Vol.51, No.2 (Mar.-Apr., 1960-61), 209.

McLaughlin, Victor V.: Police Study of the Sex Offender, TPY (1963).

————: The Sex Offender, TPC, Vol.29, No.12 (Dec., 1962), 26.

Mihm, Ferd Paul: A Re-examination of the Validity of Our Sex Psychopath Statutes in the Light of Recent Appeal Cases and Experiences, JCL&C, Vol.45, No.6 (Mar.-Apr., 1954), 716-36.

Minow, Newton: Illinois Proposal to Confine Sexually Dangerous Persons, JCL&C, Vol.40, No.2 (July-Aug., 1949), 186.

Mussachio, F. A.: The Sexual Psychopath, JCLC&PS, Vol.43, No.5 (Jan.-Feb., 1953), 592.

Ploscowe, Morris: *Sex and the Law.* New York, Prentice-Hall, 1951.

Prall, Robert H.: Sex Crime Laws Fail, POLICE, Vol.2, No.4 (Mar.-Apr., 1958), 32-34.

Radzinowicz, Leon: *Sex Offences.* London, Macmillan, 1957.

Reinhardt, James M.: The Sex Killer—A Special

Problem of Investigation, POLICE, Vol.5, No.3 (Jan.-Feb., 1951), 10-13.

————: *Sex Perversions and Sex Crimes.* Springfield, Thomas, 1957.

————, & Fisher, Edward C.: The Sexual Psychopath and the Law, JCL&C, Vol.39, No.6 (Mar.-Apr., 1948-49), 734-43.

Rickles, Nathan K.: *Exhibitionism.* Philadelphia, Lippincott, 1950.

Roth, Nathan: Factors in the Motivation of Sexual Offenders, JCLC&PS, Vol.42 (1951-52), 630.

Scatterfield, Val B.: The Education of a Metropolitan Police Department Respecting Sex Molestation, JCLC&PS, Vol.42 (1951-52), 403.

Schultz, Leroy G.: Interviewing the Sex Offenders Victim, JCLC&PS, Vol.50, No.5 (1959-60), 448.

Sex Offenses, L&CP, Vol.25 (Spring, 1960), entire issue.

Sherwin, Robert V.: *Sex and Statuatory Law.* New York, Oceana, 1949.

Shoenfield, Allen: *The Sexual Criminal.* Detroit, DETROIT NEWS, 1950.

Skousen, W. Cleon: "Sex Deviates"—A Review of a New Film, L&O, Vol.11, No.11 (Nov., 1963).

————: Sex Racketeers, L&O, Vol.11, No.12 (Dec., 1963).

————: What Can the Police Do About Them, L&O, Vol.9 (June, 1961).

Smith, Charles E.: The Homosexual Federal Offender: A Study of 100 Cases, JCL&C, Vol.44, No.5 (Jan.-Feb., 1954), 582-591.

Swanson, Alan H.: Sexual Psychopath Statutes: Summary and Analysis, JCLC&PS, Vol.51, No.2 (Mar.-Apr., 1960-61), 215.

Tappan, Paul W.: Sentences for Sex Criminals, JCLC&PS, Vol.42 (1951-52), 332.

————: Sex Offender Laws and Their Administration, FP, Vol.14 (Sept., 1950), 32-37.

Taylor, F. H.: Observations on Some Cases of Exhibitionism, JSH, Vol.35 (Nov., 1949), 354-68.

Wittels, David G.: What Can We Do About Sex Crimes? SATURDAY EVENING POST, Vol.221 (Dec. 11, 1948).

THEFT

Chandler, Frank W.: *The Literature of Roguery,* 2 Vols. New York, Franklin, 1958.

Clinard, Marshall B.: *The Black Market.* New York, Rinehart, 1952.

Cressey, Donald R.: *Other People's Money.* Glencoe, Free Press, 1953.

Gardner, George E.: The Primary and Second-

ary Gains in Stealing, NC, Vol.6 (Oct., 1947), 436-46.

Hall, Jerome: *Theft, Law and Society,* 2nd Ed. Indianapolis, Bobbs-Merrill, 1952.

Jackson, Karma Rae, and Clark, Shelby G.: Thefts Among College Students, P&GJ, Vol.36 (Apr., 1958), 557-62.

McKenzie, Donald: *Occupation: Thief.* Indianapolis, Bobbs-Merrill, 1955.

Maurer, David W.: The Technical Argot of the Pickpocket and Its Relation to the Culture Pattern, NARCOTICS (Dec., 1947).

Pouliot, Joseph E.: Diamonds in the Rough, L&O, Vol.11, No.4 (Apr., 1963).

Smigel, Erwin O.: Public Attitudes Toward Chiseling, ASR, Vol.18 (Feb., 1953), 59-67.

———: Public Attitudes Toward Stealing in Relation to the Size of the Victim Organization, ASR, Vol.21 (June, 1956), 320-27.

Zullinger, Hans: Unconscious Motives for Theft, BJD, Vol.1.

VAGRANCY

Douglass, William O.: Vagrancy and Arrest on Suspicion, YLJ, Vol.70 (Nov., 1960), 1-14.

Foote, Caleb: Vagrancy-type Law and Its Administration, UPLR, Vol.104 (Mar., 1956), 603-50.

Lacey, Forrest W.: Vagrancy and Other Crimes

of Personal Condition, HLR, Vol.66 (May, 1953), 1203-26.

Sherry, Arthur H.: Vagrants, Rogues and Vagabonds—Old Concepts in Need of Revision, CAL.LR, Vol.48 (Oct., 1960), 557-73.

CRIME LABORATORY*

Ballistics

Bigler, Edward G.: Identification by Means of Revolver Chamber Markings, JCLC&PS, Vol.55, No.1 (Mar., 1964), 155.

Breazeale and Knott: The Gonzales Test for Powder Residues, POLICE, Vol.6, No.3 (Jan.-Feb., 1962), 65.

Bristow, Allen P.: Which Cartridge for Police, JCLC&PS, Vol.53, No.2 (June-Aug., 1962), 249.

Burton, Joseph, Jr.: The Science of Ballistics: Judicial Applications, SE&SCD, Vol.2, No.3 (1964).

Class Similarity of Bullets as Evidence, SE&SCD, Vol.3, No.1 (1964).

Davis, John E.: Firearms Evidence—Replicas of Fired Bullets, JCLC&PS, Vol.51. No.6 (Mar.-Apr., 1960-61), 666.

Ellis, Harry D.: Split Bullet Wounds, POLICE, Vol.3, No.5 (May-June, 1959), 51-53.

Kempe, C. R., and Gibble, W. P.: The Effect of BHT in the Dermo-nitrate Test for Powder Residues, POLICE, Vol.6, No.5 (May-June, 1962), 74-75.

King, Daniel P.: Legal Aspects of Firearms Evidence, POLICE, Vol.6, No.6 (July-Aug., 1962), 45-46.

Kraft, B.: Apparatus Used in Forensic Ballistics, SE&SCD, Vol.2, No.5 (1964).

———: Critical Review of Forensic Ballistics, SE&SCD, Vol.2, No.1, & Vol.2, No.2 (1964).

Serhant, Joseph F.: The Admissibility of Ballistics in Evidence, SE&SCD, Vol.2, No.3 (1964).

Sloan, Chief Clyde: Duds May Cost a Life—Yours, L&O, Vol.12 (Sept., 1964).

Tangen, Ed.: The Schopflin Case, SE&SCD, Vol.2, No.6 (1964).

Tyrrell, John F.: Documentary Ballistics, SE&SCD, Vol.2, No.2 (1964).

Weight of Ballistic Expert's Testimony, SE&SCD, Vol.2, No.6 (1964).

Weston, Paul B.: Ricochets, POLICE, Vol.5, No.1 (Sept.-Oct., 1960), 32-33; Vol.4, No.5 (May-June, 1960), 29-30; No.6 (July-Aug., 1960), 58-59.

Wiard, Seth: Application of Ballistics in Legal Cases, SE&SCD, Vol.2, No.2 (1964).

———: Ballistics as Applied to Police Science, SE&SCD, Vol.1, No.6 (1964).

———: The Preliminary Identification of Fired Bullets, SE&SCD, Vol.3, No.1 (1964).

Explosives

Barrett, James R.: A Dangerous Incendiary Device, JCL&C, Vol.36, No.5 (1945-46), 388.

Brodie, T. G.: Handling Bombs & Explosives, TPC, Vol.29, No.9 (Sept., 1962), 16.

* This subsection includes: Ballistics, Explosives, Fingerprinting, Forensic Medicine, Photography, Polygraph, and Weapons, Handguns and Firearms I.D.

Fagerstrom, Dorothy: Danger—Bomb Squad at Work, L&O, Vol.10, No.11 (Nov., 1962), 62.

Lenz, Robert R.: Backyard Explosives, POLICE, Vol.9, No.2 (Nov.-Dec., 1964), 36-39.

———: *Explosives and Bomb Disposal Guide.* Springfield, Thomas, 1965.

Ronayne, John A.: Investigating Crimes Involving Explosions, POLICE, Vol.4, No.3 (Jan.-

Feb., 1960), 64-67; No.4 (Mar.-Apr., 1960), 11-16.

————: Package Bombs and Their Investigation, POLICE, Vol.4, No.1 (Sept.-Oct., 1959), 6-14.

Shirer, Chief Donald J.: Oxygen Warning, L&O, Vol.8, No.4 (1960), 25 & 62.

Stoffel, Joseph F.: Dynamics and Blasting Caps, POLICE, Vol.8, No.1 (Sept.-Oct., 1963), 23-25.

————: Explosive Disposal, TPC, Vol.31 (Mar., 1964), 34.

————: *Explosives and Homemade Bombs.* Springfield, Thomas, 1962.

————: Explosives and the Police Officer, PO-LICE, Vol.7, No.1 (Sept.-Oct., 1962), 6-10.

Zeichner, Irving B.: The Bombings, L&O, Vol.7 (Mar., 1959).

Fingerprinting

Akowicz, Henry G.: The Index to Guilt, L&O, Vol.8, No.4 (1960).

Baumann, William H.: Identifying A Victim of Drowning, L&O, Vol.7 (Mar., 1959).

Bluhm, R. J., and Lougheed, W. J.: *Results of Time, Temperature, and Humidity on Latent Fingerprints.* Flint, Flint, Mich. Police Dept., 1960.

Bonara, Matthew J.: The Bonora Method of Spraying for Prints, L&O, Vol.7 (Dec., 1959).

Bridges, B. C.: *Practical Fingerprinting.* New York, Funk, 1963.

California Dept. of Education, Bureau of Trade and Industrial Education: *Fingerprint Identification and Classification.* Sacramento, 1949.

Carlson, Charles E.: Fingerprints in Putty, L&O, Vol.8, No.9 (1960).

Cataldo, Louis: The Cataldo System, L&O, Vol.7 (Mar., 1959).

Cronkite, Dean W.: Identification Yesterday—Today—Tomorrow, L&O, Vol.7, Nov. 1959.

Davis, Charles A.: A Method of Obtaining Fingerprints for Identification by Histologic Section, JCLC&PS, Vol.48, No.4 (Nov.-Dec., 1957), 468.

Estery, Tim: New Methods Solves Fingerprint Record Problem, L&O, Vol.10, No.12 (Dec., 1962), 6.

Federal Bureau of Investigation. *Classification of Fingerprints.* Washington, D.C., U.S. Govt. Printing Office, 1945.

Field, Annita T.: *Fingerprint Handbook.* Springfield, Thomas, 1955.

Fingerprint and Identification Magazine. Published monthly by the Institute of Applied Science, 1920 Sunnyside Ave., Chicago 40, Illinois.

Fingerprint Identification. Washington, Federal Bureau of Investigation.

Fingerprints: Admissible as Evidence, SE&SCD, Vol.3, No.2 (1964).

Frappoli, Carlo L.: Nation-wide Fingerprinting for Disaster Victim Identification, L&O, Vol.11, No.5 (May, 1963).

Gootee, Francis L.: Simultaneous Impression Method of Fingerprint Classification, PO-LICE, Vol.4, No.6 (July-Aug., 1960), 10-13.

Hammond, Bertic S.: Fingerprints and the Ruxton Murders, JCLC&PS, Vol.43, No.6 (Mar.-Apr., 1953), 805.

Herrman, Louis: Finger Patterns, SE&SCD, Vol.2, No.4 (1964).

Hobart, Vernon B.: Precision Recording (Optical) of Fingerprints, L&O, Vol.8, No.12 (1960).

Hoover, J. Edgar: Criminal Identification, SE&SCD, Vol.2, No.1 (1964).

————: The National Division of Identification and Information, SE&SCD, Vol.2, No.3 (1964).

————: The Work of the Bureau of Identification, SE&SCD, Vol.2, No.2 (1964).

Jaycox, Thomas H.: Classification of the Single Fingerprint, SE&SCD, Vol.2, No.5 (1964).

Kimura, Y.: Electronic Fingerprinting, TPC, Vol.31 (Aug., 1964), 40.

King, Daniel P.: Post Mortem Fingerprinting, POLICE, Vol.7, No.1 (Sept.-Oct., 1962), 21-26.

Lauer, A., and Poll, H.: Tracing Paternity by Fingerprints, SE&SCD, Vol.1, No.1 (1964).

Leung, D.: New Method for Transferring Fingerprint Traces, SE&SCD, Vol.2, No.2 (1964).

MacDonnell, Herbert L.: The Use of Hydrogen Fluoride in the Development of Latent Fingerprints Found on Glass Surfaces, JCLC&PS, Vol.51, No.4 (Mar.-Apr., 1960-61), 465.

Mason, Dwain H.: Fingerprints in Putty, L&O, Vol.8, No.9 (1960).

Miller, Ted, Jr., and Hobbs, R. J., Jr.: Your Number Is Up, L&O, Vol.9 (Mar., 1961).

Moore, Rolland B.: Identification of Dead Bodies by Dentures, L&O, Vol.11, No.10 (Oct., 1963).

O'Neill, John J., as told to Dorothy Fagerstrom: Killing the Time-consuming Demon, L&O, Vol.11, No.7 (July, 1963), 16.

Oakland Police Department: *A Survey and Re-*

port on Latent Fingerprint Procedures. Oakland, Oakland Police Dept., 1961.

Palla, Rinaldo F., and Wiebe, Leonard F.: Development of Latent Fingerprints on Greasy Surfaces, JCL&C, Vol.39, No.5 (May-June, 1948-49), 681-84.

Ronayne, John A.: Unusual Latent Fingerprint Identifications, POLICE, Vol.6, No.4 (Mar.-Apr., 1962), 6-11.

Sannie, Charles: Alphonse Bertillon and Fingerprint Identification, FP&IM (Feb., 1951).

The Science of Fingerprint Identification, SE&SCD, Vol.2, No.4 (1964).

Scott, Walter R.: *Fingerprint Mechanics.* Springfield, Thomas, 1951.

Teeples, Earl: Make Your Own Iodine Fuming Gun: L&O, Vol.9 (Mar., 1961).

Van Der Meulen, Louis J.: False Fingerprints, JCLC&PS, Vol.46 (1955-56), 122-28.

Vehrkens, Kenneth J.: Just One Single Print, L&O, Vol.7 (Sept., 1959).

Walsh, Richard M.: Single Fingerprint File System, L&O, Vol.11, No.2 (Feb., 1963).

Watzek, Ferdinand: Criminalistic Technique in the Treatment of Finger and Palm-print Traces and Their Value as Circumstantial Evidence, SE&SCD, Vol.1, No.4; No.5; and No.6 (1964).

Wiebe, Leonard F., and Palla, Rinaldo F.: Development of Latent Fingerprints on Greasy Surfaces, JCL&C, Vol.39, No.5 (Mar.-Apr., 1948-49), 681-84.

Wigmore, John H.: Fingerprint Testimony, SE&SCD, Vol.2, No.3 (1964).

Forensic Medicine and Crime Laboratory

Adelson, Lester, and Sunshine, Irving: Fatal and Non-fatal Poisonings, JCL&C, Vol.43, No.1 (May-June, 1953), 116-24.

Amanita Toxin in Mushrooms, JCLC&PS, Vol.46 (1955-56).

Analysis of Lipstick, JCLC&PS, Vol.46 (1955-56), 595.

Arai, Shigeo: The Application of Electrolytic Polishing to Restore Obliterated Letters on Metal, JCLC&PS, Vol.43, No.6 (Mar.-Apr., 1953), 809.

Arther, Richard O.: The Investigator and the Crime Laboratory, L&O. This article appears monthly.

Bamford, Frank: *Poisons—Their Isolation and Identification.* Philadelphia, Blakiston, 1947.

Barron, David C.: Evaluation of Textile Fibers as Evidence, JCLC&PS, Vol.43, No.3 (Sept.-Oct., 1952), 382.

Beck, Ed, Dragel, Daniel T., and Principe, Andrew H.: Some Applications of Gas Chromatography to Forensic Chemistry, JCLC&PS, Vol.54, No.1 (1963), 96.

Beddoe, Harold L.: Problems of Identifying a Body, POLICE, Vol.3, No.3 (Jan.-Feb., 1959), 11-15.

Beeman, Joseph: The Effect of Temperature Variations on the Determination of Specific Gravity of Glass Fragments, JCL&C, Vol.36, No.4 (1945-46), 298.

Best, Charles H., and Taylor, Norman B.: *The Physiological Basis of Medical Practice.* Baltimore, Williams & Wilkins, 1950.

Biasatti, Alfred A.: A Comparison of Hatched Cuts on Wire, JCLC&PS, Vol.47, No.4 (Nov.-Dec., 1956), 497.

———: Plastic Replicas in Firearms and Tool

Mark Identification, JCLC&PS, Vol.47, No.1 (May-June, 1956), 110.

Black, David A.: Decipherment of Charred Documents, JCL&C, Vol.38, No.5 (Mar.-Apr., 1947-48), 542-46.

———: The Microscope in Document Examination, JCLC&PS, Vol.42 (1951-52), 810.

Blood Group Determination of Saliva Traces, JCLC&PS, Vol.46 (1955-56), 907.

Bloodstains: Expert Testimony Required, SE&SCD, Vol.3, No.1 (1964).

Bloodstains: Identification of Board as the One on Which Stains Were Found, SE&SCD, Vol.2, No.6 (1964).

Blood Tests Not Admissible to Show Possible Paternity, JCLC&PS, Vol.46 (1955-56), 81.

Brackett, J. W., Jr.: Chromatographic Identification of Organic Compounds; Use of Derivatives, JCLC&PS, Vol.54, No.2 (1963), 217.

———: Storage, Preservation and Handling of Toxicological Samples, JCL&C, Vol.44, No.6 (Mar.-Apr., 1954), 795-798.

———, & Bradford, Lowell: Comparison of Ink Writing on Documents by Means of Paper Chromatography, JCLC&PS, Vol.43, No.4 (Nov.-Dec., 1952), 530.

Bradford, Ralph: Handwriting Casebook No.6 and Notebook No.6, SW, Vol.2, No.3 (May, 1965), 44.

Bradley, Julio H.: Sequence of Pencil Strokes, JCLC&PS, Vol.54, No.2 (1963), 232.

Brewer, James G., and Burd, David Q.: Paint Comparison a Method for the Preparation of Cross Sections of Paint Chips, JCL&C, Vol.40, No.2 (July-Aug., 1949), 230.

Brockett, J. W., Jr.: The Acid Phosphatase Test

for Seminal Stains, JCLC&PS, Vol.47, No.6 (Mar.-Apr., 1957), 717.

Bromberg, Walter: The Medicolegal Dilemma; A Suggested Solution, JCLC&PS, Vol.42 (1951-52), 729.

Brown, Charlotte, and Kirk, Paul L.: An Improved Density Gradient Technique and Its Application to Paper and Cloth Ash, JCLC&PS, Vol.43, No.4 (Nov.-Dec., 1952), 540.

———, & ———: Horizontal Paper Chromatography in the Identification of Ball Point Pen Inks, JCLC&PS, Vol.45 (1954-55), 333-39.

———, & ———: Identification of Typewriter Ribbons, JCLC&PS, Vol.46 (1955-56), 882-85.

———, & ———: Paper Electrophoresis and the Identification of Writing Inks, JCLC&PS, Vol.45 (1954-55), 473-80.

Brown, Sanborn C., and Stein, Eldridge W.: Benjamin Thompson and the First Secret-ink Letter of the American Revolution, JCL&C, Vol.40, No.5 (Jan.-Feb., 1950), 627.

Brues, Alice M.: Identification of Skeletal Remains, JCLC&PS, Vol.48, No.5 (Jan.-Dec., 1958), 551.

Burd, David Q.: The Laboratory Section of the California State Bureau of Criminal Investigation and Identification, JCLC&PS, Vol.43, No.6 (Mar.-Apr., 1953), 829.

———, & Green, Roger S.: Tool Mark Comparisons in Criminal Investigations, JCL&C, Vol.39, No.3 (Mar.-Apr., 1948-49), 379-92.

Cady, Elwyn L., Jr.: The Law of Medical Practice, JCLC&PS, Vol.51, No.4 (Mar.-Apr., 1960-61), 454.

California Department of Education, Bureau of Trade and Industrial Education: *Laboratory Techniques in Criminal Investigation*. Sacramento, 1949.

Camp, W. J. R.: Functions of a Toxicologist, JCLC&PS, Vol.42 (1951-52), 270.

Car Submergence Tests, L&O, Vol.9 (Nov., 1961).

Cayet, Jean: A Method of Superimposed Photography Applied to Criminalistics, JCL&C, Vol.44, No.3 (Sept.-Oct., 1953), 379-92.

Cerney, J. V.: Does "Flatfoot" Always Mean Cop? POLICE, Vol.7, No.2 (Nov.-Dec., 1962), 11-12.

Chaille, Stanford Emerson: Origin and Progress of Medical Jurisprudence, 1776-1876, JCL&C, Vol.40, No.4 (Nov.-Dec., 1949), 397.

Chastain, J. D.: Blood and Blood Stains in Criminal Investigation, POLICE, Vol.3, No.1 (Sept.-Oct., 1958), 37-38.

———: Laboratory Toxicology and the Investigator, POLICE, Vol.3, No.3 (Jan.-Feb., 1959), 32-35.

Chavigny, Paul: Tracks of Vehicles, SE&SCD, Vol.1, No.2 (1964).

Chemical Tests Institute, TPC, Vol.31 (July, 1964), 48.

Chemical Test Laws, Recent Developments in, TPC, Vol.30 (Aug., 1963), 42.

Chinese Immigration Blood Tests, JCLC&PS, Vol.46 (1955-56), 742.

Cholak, J.: Analysis of Evidence with Special Emphasis on the Detection of Poisons, JCLC&PS, Vol.47, No.4 (Nov.-Dec., 1956), 482.

Chromatographic Fractionation of Roofing Asphalt, JCLC&PS, Vol.46 (1955-56), 286.

Clarke, Carl D.: *Molding and Casting*, 2nd Ed. Baltimore, Standard Arts Press, 1946.

Clayton, William R.: Separation of Blood Stains and other Soluble Materials by Capillary Action, JCLC&PS, Vol.42 (1951-52), 392.

Clinard, Marshal B.: Essays in Criminal Science, JCLC&PS, Vol.53, No.1 (Mar.-June, 1962), 74.

Coleman, A. H.: Journal of Forensic Sciences, NARCOTICS, Vol.3, No.4 (Oct., 1958).

Colorimetric Determinations of N-Phenyl-1-Naphthylamine in Oils, JCLC&PS, Vol.46 (1955-56), 596.

Conrad, Edwin C.: *Modern Trial Evidence*, Vol.I, Secs. 1-770. St. Paul, West Publishing Co., 1956.

Conway, James V. P.: *Evidential Documents*. Springfield, Thomas, 1959.

———: The Identification of Handwriting, JCLC&PS, Vol.45 (1954-55), 605-12.

———, Crown, David A., and Kirk, Paul L.: Differentiation of Blue Ballpoint Pen Inks, JCLC&PS, Vol.52, No.3 (Sept.-Oct., 1961), 338.

Cook, E. Fullerton, and Martin, Eric W.: *Remington's Practice of Pharmacy*. Easton, Pa., Mack, 1948.

Coon, John E.: Collection and Preservation of Evidence, TPY (1961).

Cooper, Robert, and Kirk, Paul L.: An Improved Technique for Sectioning Hair, JCL&C, Vol.44, No.1 (May-June, 1953), 124-27.

Corrington, Julian: *Adventures with the Microscope*. Rochester, Bausch Lomb Optical Co.

Cowan, Mary E., and Gerber, S. E.: Associated Evidence as a Means of Identification in Mass Disasters, JCL&C, Vol.44, No.3 (Sept.-Oct., 1953), 393-401.

Cowles, David L., and Dodge, James K.: A Method for Comparison of Tool Marks, JCL&C, Vol.39, No.2 (Mar.-Apr., 1948-49), 262-65.

Cramblett, Henry G.: The Uses of Poisoning by the Barbituates, JCLC&PS, Vol.43, No.3 (Sept.-Oct., 1952), 390.

Cramp, Arthur J.: The Bureau of Investigation of the American Medical Association, SE&SCD, Vol.2, No.1, 1964.

Cross, Earle: Test Bullet Recovery in Water, JCLC&PS, Vol.42 (1951-52), 259.

Curry, A. S.: The Application of Paper Chromatography to Forensic Chemistry, JCL&C, Vol.44, No.6 (Mar.-Apr., 1959), 787-794.

Davis, Charles A.: Detection of Carbon Monoxide Hemoglobin During Routine Blood Alcohol Analyses, JCL&C, Vol.48, No.5 (Jan.-Feb., 1958), 567.

———: Notes on Physical Evidence, JCLC&PS, Vol.50, No.3 (Sept.-Oct., 1959), 302.

———: Restoration of Eradicated Serial Numbers by an Inexpensive Electro-acid-etch Method, JCLC&PS, Vol.48, No.4 (Nov.-Dec., 1957), 459.

Davis, John E.: Barbiturate Differentiation by Chemical Microscopy, JCLC&PS, Vol.52, No.4 (Nov.-Dec., 1961), 459.

———: *An Introduction to Tool Marks, Firearms and the Striagraph.* Springfield, Thomas, 1958.

———: Refractive Index Determinations of Glass Fragments, JCLC&PS, Vol.47, No.3 (Sept.-Oct., 1956), 380.

———: The Striagraph: A New Police Science Instrument, POLICE, Vol.1, No.2 (Nov.-Dec., 1956), 26-29.

Derr, Douglas: *Forensic Medicine.* New York, Macmillan.

Determination of Carbon Monoxide in Blood by Microdiffusion Analysis, JCLC&PS, Vol.46 (1955-56), 597.

Determination of Cyanide, JCLC&PS, Vol.46 (1955-56), 147.

Determination of Mercury in Biological and Mineral Materials, JCLC&PS, Vol.46 (1955-56), 906.

Determination of Phenobarbital and Dephenyl Hydantoin in Blood, JCLC&PS, Vol.46 (1955-56), 596.

Development of Ethanol in Blood Samples and Human Organs, JCLC&PS, Vol.46 (1955-56), 596.

DeWitt, Clinton: *Privileged Communications Between Physician and Patient.* Springfield, Thomas, 1958.

Document Examination: Qualifications of Expert Witnesses, SE&SCD, Vol.3, No.1 (1964).

Dodge, James K., and Cowles, David L.: A Method of Comparison of Tool Marks, JCL&C, Vol.39, No.2 (Mar.-Apr., 1948-49), 262-68.

Dollar, A. Melville, and Kirk, Paul: Temperature Variations with Respect to the Specific Gravity of Glass Fragments (Comments on Donald F. McCall's Paper), JCL&C, Vol.39, No.5 (Mar.-Apr., 1948-49), 684.

Donigan, Robert: *Chemical Test and the Law.* Evanston, Traffic Institute, Northwestern Univ., 1958.

Doud, Donald: Charred Documents, Their Handling and Decipherment, JCLC&PS, Vol.43, No.6 (Mar.-Apr., 1953), 812.

———: Evidential Documents, JCLC&PS, Vol.51, No.3 (Mar.-Apr., 1960-61), 383.

———: The Identification of Handwriting and Cross Examination of Experts, JCLC&PS, Vol.53, No.4 (Dec., 1962), 535.

———: Investigation of Charred Documents, POLICE, Vol.8, No.5 (May-June, 1964), 17-21.

———: John F. Tyrrell: Pioneer Document Examiner, JCLC&PS, Vol.47, No.1 (May-June, 1965), 91.

———: Report on the Reconstruction of Two Time Payment Ledgers Damaged by Fire and Water, JCLC&PS, Vol.50, No.3 (Sept.-Oct., 1959), 291.

Dragel, Daniel T., Beck, Ed, and Principe, Andrew H.: Some Applications of Gas Chromatography to Forensic Chemistry, JCLC&PS, Vol.54, No.1 (1963), 96.

Dubowski, Kurt M.: Organization of Forensic Chemical Laboratories in Non-metropolitan Areas, JCLC&PS, Vol.51, No.5 (Mar.-Apr., 1960-61), 575.

———: Some Major Developments Related to Chemical Tests, POLICE, Vol.1, No.3 (Jan.-Feb., 1957), 31-32; Vol.2, No.2 (Nov.-Dec., 1957), 54-56.

Dutra, Frank R.: Carbon Monoxide Poisoning from the Exhaust Gases of Motor Vehicles, JCLC&PS, Vol.48, No.3 (Sept.-Oct., 1957), 333.

———: Physiological Principals of Carbon Monoxide Poisoning, JCLC&PS, Vol.54, No.4 (1963), 513.

———: Progress in Medicolegal Investigations of Gunshot Injuries, JCL&C, Vol.39, No.4 (Mar.-Apr., 1948-49), 524-32.

———: Simulated Spermatozoa, JCLC&PS, Vol.48, No.1 (May-June, 1957), 106.

Eliasberg, W.: Mind, Medicine and Man, JCL&C, Vol.35, No.5 (Jan.-Feb., 1945), 330.

Eliminating the Pseudo-expert, SE&SCD, Vol.1, No.2 (1964).

Elliot, Robert B.: The Value of Roentgenology

in the Identification of Mutilated and Burnt Bodies, JCLC&PS, Vol.43, No.5 (Jan.-Feb., 1953), 682.

Emmons, R. C.: The Identification of Gems and Precious Stones, SE&SCD, Vol.1, No.6 (1964).

Errata, TPC, Vol.31 (Mar., 1964), 47 & (Nov., 1964), 29.

Fagerstrom, Dorothy: The "Bristleless" Brush, L&O, Vol.9 (Oct., 1961).

Fahr, Sam: Courtroom Medicine, JCLC&PS, Vol.51, No.1 (Mar.-Apr., 1960-61), 126.

F.B.I. Laboratory, The. Washington, Federal Bureau of Investigation.

Fearon, Edwin H., and McMillan, William R.: Examination of Papers in Questioned Documents: Differentiation by Chemical Tests, JCL&C, Vol.38, No.3 (Mar.-Apr., 1947-48), 282-85.

Ferrari, Mario J.: Camden Police Mobile Crime Unit, POLICE, Vol.7, No.2 (Nov.-Dec., 1962), 72-73.

Firth, J. B.: A General Account of Micro-chemical Methods in Criminal Investigations, JCL&C, Vol.40, No.3 (Sept.-Oct., 1949), 381.

Fisher, Russel S.: The Results of Studies on the Determination of Ethyl Alcohol in Tissues, JCLC&PS, Vol.42 (1951-52), 399.

Fong, William: Identification of Minerals Other Than Soil by the Density Gradient Tube, JCLC&PS, Vol.42 (1951-52), 682.

Forbes, Gilbert: Some Observations on Occupational Markings, JCL&C, Vol.38, No.4 (Mar.-Apr., 1947-48), 423-36.

Gaines, Helen F.: *Cryptanalysis: a Study of Ciphers and Their Solution.* New York, Dover, 1956.

Garbarino, Joseph J.: The Identification of Barbiturates, Narcotics and Patented Specialties by X-ray. JCL&C, Vol.44, No.4 (Nov.-Dec., 1953), 525-30.

Gayet, Jean: Efforts at Disguise in Typewritten Documents, JCLC&PS, Vol.46 (1955-56), 867-78.

————: A Method of Superimposed Photography Applied to Criminalistics, JCL&C, Vol.44, No.3 (Sept.-Oct., 1953), 379-92.

Gilmore, Allan E.: Semi-micro Method for Flash Point Determination, JCLC&PS, Vol.49, No.4 (1958-59), 391.

Gilmore, Julius: When Was a Smoke Damaged Document Typewritten? JCLC&PS, Vol.49, No.4 (1958-59), 395.

Glaister, John: Medical Jurisprudence and Toxicology, INVESTIGATION (1957).

Glass, Parker A.: Visualization of Writing on Charred Paper, JCLC&PS, Vol.42 (1951-52), 112.

Goddefroy, E.: A Process of "Moulage" for Reproducing Marks Indicative of Forcible Entry and Moulding Those Left by Tools, SE&SCD, Vol.3, No.1 (1964).

Godown, Linton: A Note on Identifying Typewriting, JCLC&PS, Vol.53 (Mar.-May, 1959-60), 102.

————: New Non-destructive Document Testing Methods, JCLC&PS, Vol.55, No.2 (June, 1964), 280.

————: Sequence of Writings, JCLC&PS, Vol.54, No.1 (1963), 101.

Goin, Laurea J.: Details Reproduced by Metal Casting, JCLC&PS, Vol.43, No.2 (July-Aug., 1952), 250.

————, & Kirk, Paul L.: Application of Microchemical Techniques: Identity of Soil Samples, JCL&C, Vol.38, No.3 (Mar.-Apr., 1947-48), 267-81.

Gonzales, Thomas A., Morgan, Vance, Wilton, Helpburn, and Umberger, Charles J.: *Legal Medicine Pathology and Toxicology.* New York, Appleton-Century-Crofts, 1954.

Goodman, Herman: Medicolegal Uses of Filtered Ultra-violet or Black Light, SE&SCD, Vol.1, No.3 (1964).

Gradwohl, R. B. H.: Legal Medicine, INVESTIGATION (1954).

Greene, Roger S., and Burd, David Q.: Toolmark Comparisons in Criminal Investigations, JCL&C, Vol.39 (Mar.-Apr., 1948-49), 379-92.

Grodsky, Morris: Simplified Preliminary Blood Testing, An Improved Technique and a Comparative Study of Methods, JCLC&PS, Vol.42 (1951-52), 95.

Handwriting: Qualifications of An Expert, SE&SCD, Vol.3, No.1 (1964).

Handwriting: Weight of Expert Testimony, SE&SCD, Vol.3, No.1 (1964).

Haraguchi, Ichioku: Type Determination with Used Toothpicks and Cigarette Stubs, SE&SCD, Vol.1, No.4 (1964).

Harger, R. N.: Medicolegal Aspects of Chemical Tests of Alcoholic Intoxication: Comments on Dr. J. M. Rabinowitch's Paper, JCL&C, Vol.39, No.3 (Mar.-Apr., 1948-49), 402-11.

Harris, John L.: Typewriting—Original and Carbon Copies, JCLC&PS, Vol.50, No.2 (July-Aug., 1959), 211.

Harrison, Wilson R.: *Suspect Documents.* London, Sweet & Maxwell, Ltd., 1958.

Hartmann, Magy and Brown: *Inflammability and Explosibility of Metal Powders.* Washington, D.C., No.3722, U.S. Dept. of Interior, Bureau of Mines Report on Investigations.

Hazen, Claud B.: Measurement of Acid Phosphatase Activity to Identify Seminal Stains, JCLC&PS, Vol.46 (1955-56), 408-413.

Henderson and Haggard: *Noxious Gasses and the Principles of Respiration Influencing Their Action.* New York, Reinhold, n.d.

Henry, Thomas A.: *The Plant Alkalids.* Philadelphia, Blakiston, 1949.

Hilton, Ordway: The Academy's Role in the Future of Forensic Sciences, JFS, Vol.5, No.3 (1960), 281-86.

——: Characteristics of the Ball Point Pen and Its Influence on Handwriting Identification, JCLC&PS, Vol.47, No.5 (Jan.-Feb., 1957), 606.

——: Contrasting Defects of Forged and Genuine Signature, FP&IM (Oct., 1964), 3-6 & 11-14.

——: Cross-examination of a Handwriting Expert by Test Problem, RLR, Vol.13, No.2 (1958), 307-13.

——: Dating Typewriting by an Analysis of Variable Defects, JCLC&PS, Vol.51, No.3 (Mar.-Apr., 1960-61), 373.

——: Education and Qualifications of Examiners of Questioned Documents, JFS, Vol.1, No.3 (July, 1956), 35-42.

——: Elements of Effective Expert Testimony, JFS, Vol.2, No.1 (Jan., 1957), 74-79.

——: Employee Dishonesty: How the Document Examiner Can Help, PERSONNEL, Vol.36, No.2 (Mar.-Apr., 1959), 82-87.

——: An Evaluation of Chemical Methods for Restoring Erased Ink Writing, TPJ, England, Vol.29, No.4 (1956), 264-72.

——: The Examination of Questioned Documents, WRLR, Vol.6 (Fall, 54), 45-48.

——: Handwriting Identification vs. Eye Witness Identification, JCLC&PS, Vol.45 (1954-55), 207-12.

——: Identification of Typewriting—Problems Encountered with Shaded and Proportional Spacing Type Faces, JCLC&PS, Vol.48, No.2 (July-Aug. 1957), 219.

——: The Influence of Variation on Typewriting Identification, JCLC&PS, Vol.50, No.4 (Nov.-Dec., 1959), 420.

——: Pencil Erasures—Detection and Decipherment, JCLC&PS, Vol.54, No.3 (1963), 381.

——: Pitfalls in the Use of Ultraviolet Examinations to Differentiate Between Writing Papers, JCL&C, Vol.40, No.4 (Nov.-Dec., 1949), 476.

——: *Scientific Examination of Questioned Documents.* Chicago, Callaghan, 1956.

——: Test Plate for Proportional Spacing Typewriter Examination, JCLC&PS, Vol.47, No.2 (July-Aug., 1956), 257.

Hoff, Ebbe C.: Identification and Determination of Strychnine by Ultraviolet Spectrophotometry, JCLC&PS, Vol.43, No.2 (July-Aug., 1952), 246.

Holcomb, Richard L.: Scientific Investigation and Physical Evidence, JCLC&PS, Vol.53, No.2 (July-Aug., 1962), 275.

Hooker, Sanford B., and Boyd, William C.: The Chances of Establishing Non-paternity by Blood Grouping Tests, SE&SCD, Vol.1, No.2 (1964).

Houts, Marshall: *Courtroom Medicine.* Springfield, Thomas, 1957.

——: *From Evidence to Proof: a Searching Analysis of Methods to Establish Fact.* Springfield, Thomas, 1956.

IACP Endorses Medic Alert, TPC, Vol.31 (Jan., 1964), 34.

Inbau, Fred E.: The Perversion of Science in Criminal and Personnel Investigation, JCLC&PS, Vol.43, No.1 (May-June, 1952), 128.

——: Questioned Document Problems, JCL&C, Vol.35, No.6 (Mar.-Apr., 1945), 402.

Iyengar, N. K.: Acid Phosphatase Reaction as a Specific Test for the Identification of Seminal Stains, JCLC&PS, Vol.55, No.4 (Dec., 1964), 522.

Jacobs, Morris B.: *Analytical Chemistry of Industrial Poisons, Hazards and Solvents.* New York, Interscience, n.d.

Jauhari, Mohan: Determination of Firing Distance in Cases Involving Shooting Through Glass, JCLC&PS, Vol.54, No.3 (1963), 351.

Jones, Leland V.: The Role of Dust, Dirt and Debris in Criminal Investigation, POLICE, Vol.5, No.2 (Nov.-Dec., 1960), 14-16.

——: *Scientific Investigation and Physical Evidence.* Springfield, Thomas, 1959.

Kaye, Sidney: Collection and Preservation of Biological Materials and General Procedure for Toxicological Analysis, JCL&C, Vol.38, No.6 (Mar.-Apr., 1947-48), 670-676.

——: Identification of Seminal Stains, JCL&C, Vol.38, No.1 (Mar.-Apr., 1947-48), 79-83.

——, & Hoff, E. C.: Identification and Determination of Strychnine by Ultraviolet Spectrophotometry, JCLC&PS, Vol.43, No.2 (July-Aug., 1952), 246.

Kayssi, A. I.: A Simple Technique for the Precipitin Test, JCL&C, Vol.40, No.4 (Nov.-Dec., 1949), 523.

Keeler, Leonarde: A Method of Detecting Deception, SE&SCD, Vol.1, No.1 (1964).

Kempe, Carl R.: The Chloride Test as a Technique in the Investigation of Suspected Drownings, POLICE, Vol.4, No.6 (July-Aug., 1960), 6-9.

Kind, Stuart S.: The ABO Grouping of Blood Stains, JCLC&PS, Vol.53, No.3 (Sept.-Nov., 1962), 367.

———: Prevention of Haemolysis in Bloodstain Grouping, JCLC&PS, Vol.46 (1955-56), 905-06.

———: A Useful Application of the Agar Double-diffusion Technique in the Precipitin Test, JCLC&PS, Vol.50, No.5 (Jan.-Feb., 1960), 509.

King, Daniel: The Dermal Nitrate Test: Useful or Not? POLICE, Vol.7, No.6 (July-Aug., 1963), 60-62.

King, Earl Judson: *Micro-analysis in Medical Biochemistry.* New York, Grune and Stratton, 1947.

Kingston, C. R.: The Use of Statistics in Criminalistics, JCLC&PS, Vol.55, No.4 (Dec., 1964), 514.

Kirk, Paul L.: *Crime Investigation: Physical Evidence and the Police Laboratory.* New York, Interscience, 1953.

———: Microscopic Evidence—Its Use in the Investigation of Crime, JCL&C, Vol.40, No.3 (Sept.-Oct., 1949), 362.

———: The Ontogeny of Criminalistics, JCLC&PS, Vol.54, No.2 (1963), 235.

———: The Use of Statistics in Criminalistics, JCLC&PS, Vol.55, No.4 (Dec., 1964), 514.

———, & **Bradford, Lowell W.:** *The Crime Laboratory.* Springfield, Thomas, 1965.

———, **Brown, Charlotte,** and **Boyd, Connors A.:** Some Problems in Blood Testing and Grouping, JCLC&PS, Vol.45 (1954-55), 80-84.

———, and **Dollar, A. Melville:** Temperature Variations with Respect to the Specific Gravity of Glass Fragments (Comments on Donald F. McCall's Paper), JCL&C, Vol.39, No.5 (Mar.-Apr., 1948-49), 684.

———, and **Goin, Lauren J.:** Applications of Microchemical Techniques: Identity of Soil Samples, JCL&C, Vol.38, No.3 (Mar.-Apr., 1947-48), 267.

———, **Goin, Lauren J.,** and **McKee, William H.:** Human Hair Studies, JCLC&PS, Vol.43, No.2 (July-Aug., 1952), 263.

———, and **Kingston, Charles R.:** Present Status of Gas Liquid Chromatography in the Criminalistics Laboratory, JCLC&PS, Vol.56, No.2 (June, 1965), 247-56.

———, **Magagnose, Stanley,** and **Salisbury, Doris:** Casting of Hairs—Its Technique and Application to Species and Personal Identification, JCL&C, Vol.40, No.2 (July-Aug., 1949), 236.

———, and **Roche, G. W.:** Application of Microchemical Techniques: Differentiation of Similar Glass Fragments by Physical Properties, JCL&C, Vol.38, No.2 (Mar.-Apr., 1947-48), 168-171.

Kirwan, William E.: The Value of Medicolegal Autopsy to the Arson and Criminal Investigator, JCLC&PS, Vol.43, No.3 (Sept.-Oct., 1952), 396.

Kolmer, J. A., and **Boerner, F.:** Approved Laboratory Technic, NARCOTICS (1945).

Kytka, T.: Description of Methods by Which Secret Communications May Be Prepared—and of the Procedures Employed to Render Them Visible, SE&SCD, Vol.1, No.3 (1964).

Lachman, Ernest: X-ray Studies in Establishing Identity and Manner of Dealth, JCLC&PS, Vol.50, No.2 (July-Aug., 1959), 195.

Lacouture, Ronald A.: A Crime Lab on Wheels, L&O, Vol.9 (Nov., 1961).

Lacy, Lucile P.: Modern Printing Processes, JCLC&PS, Vol.47, No.6 (Mar.-Apr., 1957).

Ladd, M., and **Givson, R.:** *Medico-legal Aspects of the Blood Test to Determine Intoxication.* Evanston, Traffic Institute, Northwestern University.

Laudermilk, J. D.: Concerning Quicklime Burial, SE&SCD, Vol.3, No.1 (1964).

Laviano, P. Jerome, and **Newman, Bernard:** A Simplified and Accurate Procedure for the Determination of Ethyl Alcohol in Brain or Other Tissues, JCLC&PS, Vol.50, No.1 (May-June, 1959), 77.

Lee, Frances Glessner: Legal Medicine at Harvard University, JCLC&PS, Vol.42 (1951-52), 674.

Lee, W. J., and **Wolfer, D. A.:** Application of Magnetic Principles to the Restoration of Serial Numbers, JCLC&PS, Vol.50, No.5 (Jan.-Feb., 1960), 519.

Leffman, Henry: Chemistry as an Aid in the Detection of Crime, SE&SCD, Vol.2, No.5 (1964).

Levin, M.: The Medicolegal Autopsy and the Police, TPC, Vol.31 (Jan., 1964).

Lipman, Jerome, and **Turkel, Henry W.:** Unreliability of Dermal Nitrate Test for Gunpowder, JCLC&PS, Vol.46 (1955-56), 281-84.

Livingston, Orville B.: Bogus Check File Classified by Trademarks, JCL&C, Vol.39, No.6 (Mar.-Apr., 1948-49), 782-90.

———: Handwriting and Pen Printing System for Identifying Law Violators, JCLC&PS, Vol.49, No.5 (1958-59), 487.

Locard, Edmund: An Analysis of Dust Traces, SE&SCD, Vol.1, No.3; Vol.1, No.4; Vol.1, No.5 (1964).

Longia, H. S.: A Convenient and Rapid Method

for the Comparison of Soils, JCLC&PS, Vol.55, No.1 (Mar., 1964), 165.

Lucas, Alfred: *Forensic Chemistry and Scientific Crime Investigation.* New York, Longmans, 1949.

Lushbaugh, C. C., Rose, Jesse, and Wilson, Dean: A Practical Means for Routine Approximation of the Time of Recent Death, POLICE, Vol.5, No.1 (Sept.-Oct., 1960), 10-13.

McBay, Arthur J.: The Problems of the New Drugs in Poisoning Cases, POLICE, Vol.7, No.3 (Jan.-Feb., 1963), 26-29.

McCall, Donald F.: Temperature Variations with Respect to the Specific Gravity of Glass Fragments, JCL&C, Vol.39, No.1 (Mar.-Apr., 1948), 113-18.

McKee, William H., Goin, L. J., and Kirk, P. L.: Human Hair Studies, JCLC&PS, Vol.43, No.2 (July-Aug., 1952), 263.

McMillan, William R., and Fearon, Edwin H.: Examination of Papers in Questioned Documents: Differentiation by Chemical Tests, JCL&C, Vol.38, No.3 (Mar.-Apr., 1947-48), 282-85.

MacDonald, John M.: Truth Serum, JCLC&PS, Vol.46 (1955-56), 259-263.

MacDonell, Herbert L.: Characterisation of Fountain Pen Inks by Porous Glass Chromatography and Electrophoresis, JCLC&PS, Vol.53, No.4 (Dec., 1962), 507.

———: Iodine Fuming—New Apparatus, POLICE, Vol.3, No.4 (Mar.-Apr., 1959), 12-14.

Maise, Clemens R.: Organization of a Laundry Mark and Dry Cleaner's File, JCL&C, Vol.44, No.5 (Jan.-Feb., 1954), 671-83.

Major, Francis J.: Using Documents as Evidence, POLICE, Vol.6, No.3 (Jan.-Feb., 1962), 19-21.

Mathews, J. H.: A Measurement of Land Impressions on Fired Bullets, JCL&C, Vol.44, No.6 (Mar.-Apr., 1954), 799-809.

———: Metallographic Analysis in Crime Detection, SE&SCD, Vol.1, No.5 (1964).

———: The Murder of Blackie Atkins, SE&SCD, Vol.3, No.1 (1964).

Mathyer, Jacques: The Expert Examination of Signatures, JCLC&PS, Vol.52, No.1 (May-June, 1961), 122.

Matwejeff, S. N.: Criminal Investigation of Broken Window Panes, SE&SCD, Vol.2, No.2 (1964).

May, Luke S.: The Identification of Knives, Tools, and Instruments as a Positive Science, SE&SCD, Vol.1, No.3 (1964).

Mezger, O., Hasslacher, Fritz, and Frankle, Paul: Identification of Marks Made on Trees, SE&SCD, Vol.1, No.4 (1964).

Miloslavich, Edward L.: Forensic Pathologic and Criminalistic Analysis of Obscure Murder Cases, JCLC&PS, Vol.42 (1951-52), 689.

Mitchell, C. Ainsworth: Circumstantial Evidence from Hairs and Fibres, SE&SCD, Vol.1, No.6 (1964).

———: Science and the Detective, SE&SCD, Vol.3, No.2 (1964).

———, **and Hepworth, T. C.:** *Inks, Their Composition and Manufacture.* London, Griffin.

Modified Technique of Determining the ABO Group of Blood Stains, JCLC&PS, Vol.46 (1955-56), 909.

Moessens, Andre A.: Narcoanalysis in Law Enforcement, JCLC&PS, Vol.52, No.4 (Nov.-Dec., 1961), 453.

Muehberger, C. W.: Medicine, Science and the Law, JCLC&PS, Vol.53, No.2 (June-Aug., 1962), 240.

———: Medicolegal Aspects of Chemical Tests of Alcoholic Intoxication: Comments on Dr. J. M. Rabinwitch's Paper, JCL&C, Vol.39, No.3 (Mar.-Apr., 1948-49), 411.

Murdy, Ralph G.: The Informer in Law Enforcement, JCLC&PS, Vol.51, No.4 (Mar.-Apr., 1960-61), 490.

Naimark, George M.: Killer on the Loose in Your Town, POLICE, Vol.8, No.4 (Mar.-Apr., 1964), 73-74.

Nakamura, George R., and Shimoda, S. C.: Examination of Micro-quantity of Ball Point Inks from Documents by Thin-layer Chromatography, JCLC&PS, Vol.56, No.1 (Mar., 1965), 113-18.

Nelson, Donald F.: Illustrating the Fit of Glass Fragments, JCLC&PS, Vol.50, No.3 (Sept.-Oct., 1959), 312.

Nicol, Joseph D.: Application of Thermofax Copying Process to Obliteration Writing Problems, JCLC&PS, Vol.48, No.2 (July-Aug., 1957), 230.

———: Combustibility of Automobiles: Results of Total Burning, JCLC&PS, Vol.54, No.3 (1963), 366.

———: The Submission of Firearms Tests to Police Laboratories, JCL&C, Vol.39, No.1 (Mar.-Apr., 1948-49), 111-13.

O'Hara, Charles E., and Osterburg, James W.: *An Introduction to Criminalistics.* New York, Macmillan, 1956.

Osborn, Paul A.: Discussion of the Sequence of Fluid Ink Lines and Intersecting Paper Folds, Perforations, Tears and Cut Edges, JCLC&PS, Vol.55, No.3 (Sept., 1964), 412.

Osterburg, James W.: Suspected Blood Stains and Their Significance, L&O, Vol.12 (Dec., 1964).

Otlewis, George: Emergency Medical Identification, TPC (Aug., 1961), 8.

Outline of Teaching Program for a Course in Methods of Scientific Crime Detection, SE&SCD, Vol.12, No.1 (1964).

Overley, Lee, and Nicol, Joseph D.: Combustibility of Automobiles: Results of Total Burning, JCLC&PS, Vol.54, No.3 (1963), 366.

Ozmon, Nat. P.: Blood Test Results as Conclusive Proof of Non-paternity, JCL&C, Vol.44, No.4 (Nov.-Dec., 1953), 472-477.

Paessler, Robert T.: The Cessaro Case, SE&SCD, Vol.1, No.2 (1964).

Patty, Frank A.: *Industrial Hygiene and Toxicology*, 2 Vols. New York, Interscience, 1949.

Pavlovsky, V.: Use of Grenz Rays in the Crime Laboratory, JCL&C, Vol.40, No.1 (May-June, 1949), 90.

Peclet, Bernard, and Frachere, Pepin: The Scientific Aspect of the Guay Case, JCLC&PS, Vol.46 (1955-56), 272-76.

Piedelieve R.: Case C., SE&SCD, Vol.2, No.6 (1964).

Pines, Charles C.: The Story of Ink, SE&SCD, Vol.2, No.4 (1964).

Plda, Gabriel L.: Evaluation of Textile Fibers as Evidence, JCLC&PS, Vol.43, No.3 (Sept.-Oct., 1952), 382.

Polson, Cyril John: Carbon Monoxide Poisoning in the Home, JCL&C, Vol.44, No.4 (Nov.-Dec., 1953), 531-44.

Principe, Andrew M., Dragel, Daniel T., and Beck, Ed: Some Applications of Gas Chromatography to Forensic Chemistry, JCLC&PS, Vol.54, No.1 (1963), 96.

Principles of Precision Colorimetry, JCLC&PS, Vol.46 (1955-56), 595.

Purtell, David J.: Handwriting Standard Forms, JCLC&PS, Vol.54, No.4 (1963, 522.

———: The Identification of Paper Cutting Knives and Paper Cutters, JCL&C, Vol.44, No.2 (July-Aug., 1953), 262-68.

Rabinowitch, I. M.: Medicolegal Aspects of Chemical Tests of Alcoholic Intoxication, JCL&C, Vol.39, No.2 (Mar.-Apr., 1948-49), 225-53.

Radley, Jack A., and Grant, Julius: *Fluorescence Analysis in Ultra Violet Light*. London, Chapman & Hall, 1948.

Raju, P. S.: Acid Phosphatase Reaction as a Specific Test for the Identification of Seminal Stains, JCLC&PS, Vol.55, No.4 (Dec., 1964), 522.

Rape: Following the Development of a Venereal Disease, SE&SCD, Vol.3, No.1 (1964).

Rape: Test for Semen Admissible, SE&SCD, Vol.3, No.1 (1964).

Ray, Dean N.: Use of Nylon Spray as a Lifting Medium for Latent Impressions, JCLC&PS, Vol.51, No.6 (Mar.-Apr., 1960-61), 661.

Rehfuss, Martin Emil, Albrecht, F. Kenneth, and Price, Allison Howe: *A Course in Practical Therapeutics*. Baltimore, Williams & Wilkins, 1948.

Reinhardt, James M.: Psychographology in Handwriting Identification, POLICE, Vol.2, No.5 (May-June, 1958), 7-14.

Report of Committee on Medicolegal Problems of the American Medical Association, SE&SCD, Vol.2, No.3 (1964).

Report of Medicolegal Committee of American Bar Association, SE&SCD, Vol.1, No.4 (1964).

Rhodes, Henry T.: *Alphonse Bertillon, Father of Scientific Detection*. New York, Abelard-Schuman, 1956.

Richardson, James R.: *Modern Scientific Evidence*. Cincinnati, Anderson, 1961.

Ripple Soles Misleading, TPC, Vol.30 (Mar., 1963), 45.

Rizer, Conrad: Blood Drop Patterns, POLICE, Vol.4, No.3 (Jan.-Feb., 1960), 18-19.

Roche, G. W., and Kirk, Paul L.: Application of Microchemical Techniques: Differentiation of Similar Glass Fragments by Physical Properties, JCL&C, Vol.38, No.2 (Mar.-Apr., 1947-48), 168-171.

Roper, James E., and Robinson, Donald: Atomic Energy—Ace Detective, READER'S DIGEST (Sept., 1964), 122-26.

Rosenzweig, Saul: Unconscious Self-defense in an Uxoricide, JCLC&PS, Vol.46 (1955-56), 791-95.

St. John, J. L.: Modern Handwriting Analysis (Graphology), POLICE, Vol.3, No.2 (Nov.-Dec., 1958), 70-74.

Scanlon, Charles P.: Notes on Emergency Care for the Diabetic, L&O, Vol.8, No.4 (1960).

Schatz, W.: Dirt Scraped from Shoes, as a Means of Identification, SE&SCD, Vol.1, No.1 (1964).

Schneider, Albert: The Compound Microscope in Detective Work, SE&SCD, Vol.2, No.1 (1964).

Schroeder, Oliver, Jr.: Legal Aspects of Chemical Tests for Intoxication, L&O, Vol.8, No.2 (1960).

Schuldiner, J. A.: Analytical Chemistry, NARCOTICS, Vol.21 (Feb., 1949), 298.

Schwarzacher, D.: Determination of Age of Blood Stains, SE&SCD, Vol.1, No.4 (1964).

Scott, W. W.: Standard Methods of Chemical Analysis, NARCOTICS (1945).

Seale, E. L., Sr.: Non-examiner Investigators, TPC, Vol.29, No.8 (Aug., 1962), 24.

Sellers, James Clark: Science and Advancements in the Examination of Questioned Documents, SE&SCD, Vol.3, No.2 (1964).

Shartel, B., and Plant, M.: *Law of Medical Practice.* Springfield, Thomas, n.d.

Shaw, William: Case on Splitting Hairs, L&O, Vol.12 (May, 1964).

Simpson, Keith: *Forensic Medicine.* Baltimore, Williams & Wilkins, 1947.

Smith, Hobart M., and Boys, Floyd: Determination of Snakebite as Dangerous or Harmless, POLICE, Vol.7, No.4 (Mar.-Apr., 1963), 6-13.

Smith, Sidney: *Mostly Murder.* New York, Mc-Kay, 1960.

Smith, Stanley S.: Obtaining Document Standards for Comparison, JCL&C, Vol.40, No.1 (May-June, 1949), 105.

—— (ed.): *Taylor's Principles and Practice of Medical Jurisprudence.* London, Churchill, 1948.

Smith, Theodora: Determining Tendencies—the Second Half of a Classification for Handwriting, JCLC&PS, Vol.55, No.4 (Dec., 1964), 526.

Smith, Theodore L. H.: Six Basic Factors in Handwriting Classification, JCL&C, Vol.44, No.6 (Mar.-Apr., 1954), 582-91.

Soderman, Harry, and O'Connell, John J.: *Modern Criminal Investigation.* New York, Funk & Wagnalls, 1954.

Sollmann, Torald: *A Manual of Pharmacology and Its Application to Therapeutics and Toxicology.* Philadelphia, Saunders, 1948.

Souder, William: Composition Properties and Behavior of Ball Pens and Inks, JCLC&PS, Vol.45 (1954-55), 743-47.

Soule, Rolland L.: Reproduction of Foot and Tire Tracks by Plaster of Paris Casting, JCLC&PS, Vol.50, No.2 (July-Aug., 1959), 198.

Starkey, Norris J.: You Can Make Your Own Major Crime Kit, L&O, Vol.12 (July, 1964).

Stein, Elbridge W.: Handwriting Testimony in a Criminal Conviction and the Disbarment of a Lawyer, JCL&C, Vol.39, No.4 (Mar.-Apr., 1948-49), 519-524.

Sunshine, Irving: Practical Homicide Investigation, JCLC&PS, Vol.53, No.3 (Sept.-Nov., 1962), 397.

Sweet, George G.: The Dating of Typewriting, JCLC&PS, Vol.50, No.1 (May-June, 1959), 86.

Tappan, Paul W.: Medicolegal Concepts of Criminal Insanity, JCLC&PS, Vol.43, No.3 (Sept.-Oct., 1952), 333.

Tire Facility Service, TPC, Vol.30 (Oct., 1963), 32.

Tire Identification: Expert Testimony, SE&SCD, Vol.3, No.1 (1964).

Trovillo, Paul V.: Scientific Proof of Credibility,

POLICE, Vol.1, No.6 (July-Aug., 1957), 36-43.

Tuchmann, Barbara W.: *The Zimmermann Telegram.* New York, Viking, 1958.

Turner, Ralph F.: The First American Medicolegal Congress, JCL&C, Vol.39, No.1 (Mar.-Apr., 1948-49), 104-11.

——: *Forensic Science and Laboratory Technics.* Springfield, Thomas, 1953.

——: Organization and Standardization of Police Science Technics, JCL&C, Vol.39, No.5 (Mar.-Apr., 1948-49), 675-784.

Vasistha, S. C.: Three Chemical Tests for Comparing the Age of Paper, JCLC&PS, Vol.53, No.1 (Mar.-Apr., 1962), 120.

Walter, Herbert J.: Rex V. Mike Hack: Handwriting in a Murder Trial in Western Canada, SE&SCD, Vol.3, No.1 (1964).

Waters, Louis A.: Questioned Documents in Police Work, JCL&C, Vol.38, No.6 (Mar.-Apr., 1947-48), 649-53.

Watzek, F.: Searching for and Recording Circumstantial Evidence, SE&SCD, Vol.1, No.3 (1964).

Webster, G., and De Sarem, G. S. W.: Estimation of Age from Bone Development, JCLC&PS, Vol.45 (1954-55), 230-39.

Wescott, Alan P.: The Literature of Gunshot Injuries, SE&SCD, Vol.3, No.1 (1964).

Wiener, Alexander: *Blood Groups and Blood Transfusion.* Springfield, Thomas, 1945.

Williams, John F.: Examination of Paint Chips and Scrapings with the Spectrophotometer, JCL&C, Vol.44, No.5 (Jan.-Feb., 1954), 647-60.

——: Technical Laboratory of the Missouri State Highway Patrol, JCLC&PS, Vol.42 (1951-52), 679.

Williams, Richard T.: *Detoxication Mechanics.* N.Y., Wiley, 1949 (the Metabolism of Drugs & Allied Organic Compounds).

Wilson, E. Bright, Jr.: *An Introduction to Scientific Research.* New York, McGraw-Hill, 1952.

Wright, Keith: Simplified Preliminary Blood Testing (An Improved Technique and a Comparative Study of Methods), JCLC&PS, Vol.42 (1951-52), 95.

Zangemeister, W., and Krieger S.: Serological Research with the New Zeiss Graduated Photometer. Specific Reaction Between New-Born Infants and Their Parents, SE&SCD, Vol.1, No.4 (1964).

Zeichner, Irving B.: According to Law—Blood Test Bribe, L&O, Vol.10 (Jan., 1962), 39.

Zmuda, Charles W.: Identification of Crepe-sole Shoes, JCL&C, Vol.44, No.3 (Sept.-Oct., 1953), 374-78.

Photography

Barnes, David F.: *Infrared Luminescence of Minerals*. Washington, D.C., U.S. Govt. Printing Office, Survey Bulletin 1052C, 1958.

Batchelor, George R.: Picture of a Burglar, L&O, Vol.11, No.5 (May, 1962), 38.

Beeman, Joseph: Photoresistor Photographic Slave Units, JCLC&PS, Vol.49, No.5 (1958-59), 510.

Boone, Bob: Using Sound Movies in Police Work, L&O, Vol.8, No.3 (1960).

Boyd, William: Forensic Immunology, JCL&C, Vol.36, No.6 (1945-46), 455.

Brewer, Edward J.: Photography at Night, L&O, Vol.11, No.4 (Apr., 1963).

The Camera Column—Immediate Training by Photography, L&O, Vol.10, No.7 (July, 1962), 36.

Caputo, Rudolph R.: Notes on Undercover Photography, L&O, Vol.9 (Apr., 1961).

Carlson, Charles E.: Advice to Police Photographers, L&O, Vol.10, No.4 (Apr., 1962).

———: Your Camera Has Wings, L&O, Vol.9, No.10 (Oct., 1963).

Cecere, Anthony L.: Take Pictures Before Anything Is Moved, L&O, Vol.7 (Apr., 1959).

Clark, Walter: *Photography by Infared*. New York, Wiley, 1946.

Conrad, Edwin: Color Photography, an Instrumentality of Proof, JCLC&PS, Vol.49, No.3 (Sept.-Oct., 1957), 321.

Crawford, William: How to Improve Police Photography, L&O, Vol.10, No.4 (Apr., 1962), 16.

Criminal Evidence: Admission of Photographs, SE&SCD, Vol.3, No.1 (1964).

Crumb, Owen: Photography—The Investigator's Tool, L&O, Vol.12 (Apr., 1964).

Daidone, Peter: Color Pictures for Better Identification, L&O, Vol.13, No.5 (May, 1965), 6.

Dery, Dan: Instant Photography for Police, L&O, Vol.10, No.4 (Apr., 1962), 8.

Eastman Kodak Company: *Basic Police Photography*, 2nd Ed. Rochester, Eastman Kodak, 1964.

———: *Radiography in Modern Industry*. Rochester, Eastman Kodak, 1957.

Ebberts, Dan: Photographing Legal Evidence, L&O, Vol.9 (June, 1961).

Evans, Ralph M.: *An Introduction to Color*. New York, Wiley, 1948.

———: *Eye, Film & Camera in Color Photography*. New York, Wiley, 1959.

Fagerstrom, Dorothy: Police Photographers at Work, L&O, Vol.8, No.4, 1960.

Fellers, William S., Jr.: MO in Pictures, L&O, Vol.11, No.3 (Mar., 1963).

Forensic Dentistry, TPC, Vol.31 (Sept., 1964), 59.

Fuller, Leland: The Project-o-printer, L&O, Vol.10, No.10 (Nov., 1962), 62.

Gerber, S. R., Adelson, Lester, and Johnson, Lawrence: The Role of Photography in the Coroner's Office, POLICE, Vol.1, No.2 (Nov.-Dec., 1956), 19-25 (reprinted from *Medical Radiography and Photography*, Eastman Kodak Co., Rochester, N.Y.).

Goetz, Rachel: *Visual Aids for the Public Service*. Chicago, Public Administration Service, 1954.

Hall, William E. B.: A Proposal to Introduce Forensic Science in the University Curriculum, JCLC&PS, Vol.42 (1951-52), 549.

Horak, Charles J.: Color Photography in Police Work, L&O, Vol.9, No.12 (Dec., 1963).

How the Camera Catches Crooks, PS (June, 1962), 50-54.

Killick, Larry: Unsuspected Command Performance, L&O, Vol.7 (Apr., 1959).

King, Daniel P.: Admissibility of Photographic Evidence in Prosecution for Felonious Homicide, POLICE, Vol.7, No.5 (May-June, 1963), 17-19.

Kingslake, Rudolph: *Lenses in Photography*. New York, Barnes, 1963.

Kirsch, Robert: Color Identification Cards, L&O, Vol.10, No.4 (Apr., 1962), 5.

———: This Is What He Looked Like, L&O, Vol.10, No.9 (Sept., 1962), 60.

Klein, Alexander: Forensic Value of Teeth in Identification of Fire Victims, SE&SCD, Vol.1, No.3 (1964).

Krosnick, David A.: Movietone Goes to Court, SE&SCD, Vol.1, No.5 (1964).

Kruse, Benedict: Added Impetus to Police Photography Comes Through New Los Angeles Facilities, POLICE, Vol.2, No.3 (Jan.-Feb., 1958), 54-58.

Kuhn, Richard J.: Infared Examinations with an Electronic Image Converter, JCLC&PS, Vol.45 (1954-55), 486-90.

Kyler, Clare W.: Camera Surveillance of Sex Deviates, L&O, Vol.9, No.11 (Nov., 1963).

Lee, George E.: The Photographer and the Investigator, L&O, Vol.10, No.11 (Nov., 1962), 49.

———: Training Police Photographers, L&O, Vol.8, No.4 (1960).

Lawder, Lee E.: Police Training Films, L&O, Vol.10, No.4 (Apr., 1962), 22.

————: Public Relations and Your Camera, L&O, Vol.9 (Apr., 1961).

Leonard, V. A.: It's New (Complete Revision of Kodak Master Photoguide Includes All Data on Latest Films), POLICE, Vol.1, No.2 (Nov.-Dec., 1956), 57.

Levine, Philip: The Application of Blood Groups in Forensic Medicine, SE&SCD, Vol.3, No.2 (1964).

Logan, C. E.: A New Concept in Visual Identification, L&O, Vol.8, No.3 (1960).

McKee, William F.: Evidentiary Problems— Camera Surveillance of Sex Deviates, L&O, Vol.7 (Aug., 1964).

MacDonnell, Herbert L.: A Splendid Saver for Photographic Entrapment Devices, L&O, Vol.8, No.8 (1960).

————: Single Exposure Test Strip Method for Photomacrography, Photomicrography and Polaroid Photography, L&O, Vol.12, (Apr., 1964).

Martin, Milton R.: Police Photographer in Action, L&O, Vol.9 (Apr., 1961).

Mascelli, Joseph V.: *American Cinematographer Manual.* New York, Amphoto, 1960.

Mauk, Arthur A.: Police Photography Advances, L&O, Vol.10, No.10 (Oct., 1962), 54.

————: Progress in Photography, TPC, Vol.29, No.10 (Oct., 1962), 16.

Mikoda, Philip M.: Tips on Simplified Darkroom Procedures, L&O, Vol.11, No.4 (Apr., 1963).

Miller, Ralph: Electronic Flash in Law Enforcement Photography, L&O, Vol.11, No.4 (Apr., 1963).

Mitzdor, Dan: The Advantage of a Large Format Camera, L&O, Vol.10, No.8 (Aug., 1962), 14.

Moreton, David O.: The Camera Column, L&O, Appears Monthly.

————: The Foto Focuser, L&O, Vol.7 (Mar., 1959).

Morton, H. R.: Modus Operandi in Color, TPC, Vol.31 (Jan., 1964), 42.

Murray, Robert V.: Color Photography for Police, TPC, Vol.29, No.1 (Jan., 1962), 12.

New Films Give Latitude to Police Photographers, L&O, Vol.9 (Dec., 1961).

O'Hara, Charles E.: *Photography in Law Enforcement.* Rochester, Eastman Kodak Co., 1959.

Pacini, A. J.: The Ultra-violet Detective, SE&SCD, Vol.1, No.3 (1964).

————: Ultra-violet Spectographic Detection of Mercury, SE&SCD, Vol.1, No.4 (1964).

Pappele, John R.: Video Security System for Line Up, TPC, Vol.29, No.7 (July, 1962), 26.

Parlato, Louis P.: The Recording Eye, L&O, Vol.8, No.4 (1960).

Photography Used in Identifying Narcotic Traffickers, L&O, Vol.9 (Apr., 1961).

Ponemon, Richard D.: Now Darkness Helps Law Enforcement, L&O, Vol.7 (Mar., 1959).

Radley, J. A.: *Photography in Crime Detection.* London, Chapman and Hall, 1948.

Ross, Victor: Win Public Support with Audiovisual Techniques, L&O, Vol.9 (Aug., 1961).

Russell, Rusty: Color Photography at Low Cost, L&O, Vol.11, No.4 (1963).

Sanford, Jack G.: TV for Surveillance, L&O, Vol.12 (Dec., 1964).

Schernhorst, John N.: Forensic Photogrammetry, POLICE, Vol.9, No.2 (Nov.-Dec., 1964), 6-10.

Schoen, Arthur E.: Using Microfilm for Criminal Identification, L&O, Vol.11, No.7 (July, 1963).

Shaw, William: An Introduction to Infrared, L&O, Vol.9 (Apr., 1961).

Soule, Rolland L.: The Use of Visual Aids in Training Identification Officers, JCLC&PS, Vol.51, No.3 (Mar.-Apr., 1960-61), 363.

Sperling, Robert E.: Observe and Photograph, L&O, Vol.9, No.1 (Jan., 1963).

Swett, George G.: The Use of Individual Photographic Charts in Presenting Questioned Document Testimony, JCLC&PS, Vol.42 (1951-52), 826.

Tuttle, Harris B.: Color Photography in Law Enforcement, TPY (1958).

————: Color Photography in Police Science, L&O, Vol.8, No.4 (1960).

————: Criminal Detection Devices Employing Photography, POLICE, Vol.1, No.3 (Jan.-Feb., 1957), 7-11.

————: History of Photography in Law Enforcement, FP&IM Vol.43, No.4 (Sept., 1961), 3-28.

————: New Photo System for Nassau County, TPC (Apr., 1961), 6.

————: Photography, a How-to Program for the Police and Sheriff in Communities under 75,000, TPC, Vol.31 (Aug., 1964), 26.

————: Photography's Place in Law Enforcement Today, POLICE, Vol.1, No.1 (Sept.-Oct., 1956), 9-13.

————: Photography Plays Major Role in Arson Investigation, L&O, Vol.11, No.4 (Apr., 1963).

————: The Police Photographer in Court, L&O, Vol.13, No.4 (Apr., 1965), 8.

————: Where Do We Stand With Our Law Enforcement Photography? POLICE, Vol.2, No.4 (Mar.-Apr., 1958), 22-27.

Watson, James A.: Method of Lifting and Photographing for Evidence, JCLC&PS, Vol.49, No.1 (1958-59), 89.

Weaver, Gilbert A., and Bollinger, Elroy W.: *Visual Aids: Their Construction and Use.* New York, Van Norstrand, 1949.

Wesson, Jerry: Police Photography in Pittsburgh, Penn., L&O, Vol.13, No.4 (Apr., 1965), 10.

Wright, B. C.: Infrared Film in Photography, L&O, Vol.9 (Mar., 1961).

Zeichner, Irving B.: Photography of Autopsy, L&O, Vol.11, No.10 (Oct., 1963).

————: Photograph of Check and Defendant, L&O, Vol.9 (Aug., 1961).

Polygraph

Adams, Thomas F.: Field Preparation for the Polygraph, POLICE, Vol.9, No.4 (Mar.-Apr., 1965), 17-20.

————: Legal Aspects of the Polygraph, POLICE, Vol.6, No.2 (Nov.-Dec., 1961), 52-58.

Allmers, Herbert H., Jr.: Creating Proper Environment Improves Polygraph Examinations, L&O, Vol.12 (Dec., 1964).

————: Role of the Investigator in Preparing for a Polygraph Examination, L&O, Vol.12 (Mar., 1964).

Arnold, Edwin W.: Investigators Get Full Value from a Polygraph Examination, POLICE, Vol.6, No.4 (Mar.-Apr., 1962), 45-47.

————: Polygraph Tests Using an Interpreter, POLICE, Vol.5, No.4 (Mar.-Apr., 1961), 53-55.

Arther, Richard O.: Blood Pressure Rises on Relevant Questions in Lie Detection Sometimes an Indication of Innocence Not Guilt, JCLC&PS, Vol.46 (1955-56), 112-115.

————: Further Interpretations of Innocent Blood Pressure Rises in Polygraph Testing, JCLC&PS, Vol.47, No.2 (July-Aug., 1956), 260.

————: Investigator and the Crime Laboratory, L&O, Vol.9 (June, 1961).

————: The Polygraph's Enemies, L&O, Vol.12 (Nov., 1964).

————, & **Reid, John E.:** Behavior of Lie-detector Subjects, JCL&C, Vol.44, No.1 (May-June, 1953), 104-108.

————, & ————: Utilizing the Lie Detector Technique to Determine the Truth and Disputed Paternity Cases, JCLC&PS, Vol.45 (1954-55), 213-721.

Aubrey, Arthur, S.: Are We Using Lie Detection? POLICE, Vol.6, No.3 (Jan.-Feb., 1962), 40-42.

Backster, Cleve: Backster Chart Reliability Rating Method, L&O, Vol.11, No.1 (Jan., 1963).

————: Don't Trust the Lie Detector vs. Do Trust the Lie Detector, L&O, Vol.11, No.2 (Feb., 1963).

————: Do the Charts Speak for Themselves? L&O, Vol.11, No.6 (June, 1963).

————: The Grand Duchess of the Polygraph, L&O, Vol.12 (Jan. 1964).

————: Lie Detection Comes of Age, L&O, Vol.10, No.11 (Nov., 1963), 73.

————: Methods of Strengthening Our Polygraph Technique, POLICE, Vol.6, No.5 (May-June, 1962), 61-68.

————: Polygraph Professionalization Through Technique Standardization, L&O, Vol.11, No.4 (Apr., 1963).

————: Polygraph Technique Trouble Shooting, L&O, Vol.11, No.9 (Sept., 1963).

————: Technique Standardization, L&O, Vol.11, No.4 (Apr., 1963), 63.

————: Total Chart Minutes Concept, L&O, Vol.11, No.10 (Oct., 1963).

Baesen, Henry V., Chia-Mow Chung, and Chen-Ya Yang: A Lie Detector Experiment, JCL&C, Vol.39, No.4 (Mar.-Apr., 1948-49), 532-38.

Bates, Edward A.: Can A Small Department Afford to Use the Polygraph? POLICE, Vol.3, No.5 (May-June, 1959), 44-48.

Berry, Robert L., and Malinowski, Benjamin F.: Fort Gordon Lie Detector Course Updated, L&O, Vol.11, No.12 (Dec., 1963).

Bristow, Allen P.: Atmosphere in the Interrogation Room, POLICE, Vol.7, No.2 (Nov.-Dec., 1962), 59-62.

Brokaw, J. R., Heckel, R. H., Salzbert, H. C., and Wiggins, S. L.: Polygraphic Variations in Reactivity Between Delusional, Non-delusional, and Control Groups in a Crime Situation, JCLC&PS, Vol.53, No.3 (Sept.-Nov., 1962), 380.

Burack, Benjamin: A Critical Analysis of the Theory, Method and Limitations of the Lie Detector, JCLC&PS, Vol.46 (1955-56), 414-426.

Caputo, Rudolph R.: Danger of the "Interrogate as through Guilty" Practice, L&O, Vol.11, No.3 (Mar., 1963).

————: Question of "Inconclusives," L&O, Vol.11, No.7 (July, 1963).

Chandler, Lee: The Polygraph, SEC.W., Vol.1, No.1 (July-Aug., 1964), 30-32.

Cumley, William E.: Hypnosis and the Polygraph, POLICE, Vol.4, No.2 (Nov.-Dec., 1959), 39-40.

Curtis, J. S.: Stress vs. Empathy Interview Techniques, POLICE, Vol.3, No.2 (Nov.-Dec., 1958), 55-57; No.3 (Jan.-Feb., 1959), No.4 (Mar.-Apr., 1959), 46-50.

Davis, John Richelieu: The Use of the Polygraph in Private Industry, POLICE, Vol.5, No.1 (Sept.-Oct., 1960), 44-46.

Day, Frank D.: An Instructional Approach to Criminal Interrogation, POLICE, Vol.2, No.5 (May-June, 1958), 47-52.

Dienstein, William: The Importance of Words in Questioning Techniques, POLICE, Vol.1, No.4 (Mar.-Apr., 1957), 47-51.

————: Mortality and Lie Detection, POLICE, Vol.8, No.5 (May-June, 1964), 35-38.

————: The Rights of the Subject in Lie-Detector Interrogation, POLICE, Vol.1, No.2, (Nov.-Dec., 1956), 41-51.

Elam, Gerald: Polygraph an Aid to Recruiting, L&O, Vol.8, No.7 (1960).

Faulk, J. Frank, Jr.: South Carolina Polygraph Solves Four Murders, POLICE, Vol.2, No.4 (Mar.-Apr., 1958), 40.

Ferguson, John P.: The Polygraph Knockers, TPC, Vol.29, No.5 (May, 1962), 26.

Fisher, Jacob: *The Art of Detection.* New Brunswick, Rutgers University Press, 1947.

Floch, Maurice: Limitations of the Lie-detector, JCL&C, Vol.40, No.5 (Jan.-Feb., 1950), 651.

Frisby, B. R.: *The Semantics of the Irrelevant Question in Lie Detector Examination.* Washington, IACP, 1961.

Gately, Robert D.: Investigator's Role in a Successful Polygraph Examination, L&O, Vol.11, No.5 (May, 1963).

Gooch, Charles D.: An Inquiry into the Use of the Polygraph in Applicant Evaluation and Personnel Screening. Unpublished Master's Thesis, School of Police Admin. & Pub. Safety, Michigan State University, East Lansing, 1964.

Gootnick, Louis: *A Survey of Police Use of the Lie Director.* Master's Thesis, New York University, October, 1959.

Gugas, Cris: Better Policemen Through Better Screening, POLICE, Vol.6, No.6 (July-Aug., 1962), 54-58.

Hanscom, C. B.: NARCO Interrogation, POLICE, Vol.11, No.2 (Nov.-Dec., 1957), 44-50.

Harmon, George W.: The Anti-polygraph Smear, SEC.W., Vol.1, No.2 (Sept.-Oct., 1964), 26-28.

————, & Reid, John E.: The Selection and Phrasing of Lie Detection Test Questions, JCLC&PS, Vol.46 (1955-56), 578-82.

Harrelson, Leonard H.: The Prerequisites of a Qualified Examiner, POLICE, Vol.6, No.3 (Jan.-Feb., 1962), 57-61.

Holcomb, Richard: Ban the Polygraph? TPC (May, 1961), 41.

————: Use of Polygraph, TPC, Vol.29, No.1 (Jan., 1962), 46.

Holmes, Warren D.: Continuous vs. Discontinuous Polygraph Measurement of Blood Pressure, POLICE, Vol.4, No.2 (Nov.-Dec., 1959), 40-47.

Inbau, Fred E.: The First Polygraph, JCLC&PS, Vol.43, No.5 (Jan.-Feb., 1953), 679.

————: Lie Detector Test Limitations, TPY (1956).

————: Some Avoidable Lie Detector Mistakes, JCL&C, Vol.40, No.6 (Mar.-Apr., 1950), 791.

————, & Reid, John E.: *Lie Detection and Criminal Investigation.* Baltimore, Williams and Wilkins, 1953.

Inman, Richard W.: Businessman Give an Assist, L&O, Vol.7 (June, 1959).

Johnston, Orville: The Lie Detector Protects the Innocent, L&O, Vol.9 (Mar., 1961).

Klump, Carl S.: So You Want to Beat the Polygraph! SEC.W., Vol.2, No.4 (June, 1965), 30.

Lee, C. D.: *Instrumental Detection of Deception.* Springfield, Thomas, 1953.

Legislation—N.Y.—On Use of Lie Detector, TPC, Vol.31 (Apr., 1964), 22.

Leonard, V. A.: *Academy Lectures on Lie Detection,* Vols.1 & 2, Springfield, Thomas, 1958.

————: Indicated Research in the Field of Deception Detection, POLICE, Vol.11, No.1 (Sept.-Oct., 1957), 55-58.

Levin, L. M.: Lie Detector Can Lie! TPC, Vol.31 (Apr., 1964), 20.

McInerney, Charles A.: Routine Screening of Criminal Suspects by the Polygraph (Lie-detector) Technique, JCLC&PS, Vol.45 (1954-55), 736-42.

McLoughlin, Glen H.: The Lie Detector as an Aid in Arson and Criminal Investigation, JCLC&PS, Vol.43, No.5 (Jan.-Feb., 1953), 690.

Martin, Frederic C.: Use of the Polygraph in Disputed Paternity Cases, L&O, Vol.11, No.11 (Nov., 1963).

Moenssens, Andre A.: Lie Detection Under Hypnosis and the Law, POLICE, Vol.8, No.3 (Jan.-Feb., 1964), 67-69.

Myatt, M. W.: Polygraph Clears Victim of Mistaken Identity, POLICE, Vol.1, No.5 (May-June, 1957), 40-41.

————: The Polygraph in Homicide Investigation, POLICE, Vol.3, No.1 (Sept.-Oct., 1958), 46-50.

————: The Truth Wins Again, POLICE, Vol.2, No.4 (Mar.-Apr., 1958), 41-42.

Nichol, Fred W.: Polygraph as a Profession, POLICE, Vol.4, No.1 (Sept.-Oct., 1959), 61-64.

Oldham, C. C.: Polygraph Knockers? TPC, Vol.30 (Jan., 1963), 39.

————: Questions Practices in Use of Polygraph, TPC (Aug., 1961), 14.

Paull, F. S., Jr.: A $$$ Evaluation of the Polygraph, TPC, Vol.31 (Aug., 1964), 45.

Polygraph Can Help—If You Want It To, L&O, Vol.9 (Apr., 1961).

Price, Carroll S.: Interviews, Interrogations and Use of the Polygraph, POLICE, Vol.4, No.4 (Mar.-Apr., 1960), 52-55; No.5 (May-June, 1960), 32-35; No.6 (July-Aug., 1960), 50-53; Vol.5, No.1 (Sept.-Oct., 1960), 47-49; and No.2 (Nov.-Dec., 1960), 48-50.

————: An Instrumental Approach to Applicant Evaluation, POLICE, Vol.5, No.5 (May-June, 1961), 39-42.

Rainey, R. P., Jr.: Scientific Interrogation in Criminal Cases, POLICE, Vol.3, No.6 (July-Aug., 1959), 35-59.

Reid, John E.: Simulated Blood Pressure Responses in Lie-Detector Test and a Method for Their Detection, JCL&C, Vol.36, No.3 (1945-46), 201.

Riley, Paul T.: The Use of the Polygraph for Pre-employment Testing of Police Recruits, POLICE, Vol.5, No.6 (July-Aug., 1961), 42-43.

Skousen, W. Cleon: What About Polygraph Examinations for Police Personnel? L&O, Vol.9 (July, 1961).

Seale, E. L., Sr.: Orienting the Non-examiner Police Investigators, TPC, Vol.29, No.8 (Aug., 1962), 24-29.

Slavin, James M.: Use of the Polygraph Workshop, TPY (1963).

Spohn, Edward A.: The Army Trains Polygraph Examiners, POLICE, Vol.5, No.3 (Jan.-Feb., 1961), 40-44.

Steel, Robert D.: Polygraph and Interrogation, POLICE, Vol.1, No.3 (Jan.-Feb., 1957), 46-49.

————: Polygraph and Interrogation, a Tribute to Leonarde Keeler, 1903-1949, POLICE, Vol.2, No.6 (July-Aug., 1958), 40-45.

————: Who Is a Fit Polygraph Subject? POLICE, Vol.3, No.3 (Jan.-Feb., 1959), 64-68.

Tamm, Quinn (ed.): Polygraph Hearing Testimony Published, TPC, Vol.32, No.2 (Feb., 1965), 41.

Thirteenth Annual Law Institute of the University of Tennessee: The Polygraphic Truth Test Symposium, Knoxville, Tenn., Nov. 14, 1952.

Trovilla, Paul V.: Scientific Proof of Credibility POLICE, Vol.1, No.6 (July-Aug., 1957), 36-43; Vol.2, No.3 (Jan.-Feb., 1958), 36-49.

Watts, Dell R.: Education of Police Personnel to the Use of the Polygraph, POLICE, Vol.1, No.1 (Sept.-Oct., 1956), 23-28.

Wheeler, Dee E.: Pre-employment Polygraph Examination of Police Applicants, L&O, Vol.11, No.8 (Aug., 1963).

Winner, Lewis: Voice Behavior, L&O, Vol.7 (Aug., 1959).

Yankee, W. J., Schmidt, R. H., and Barber, W. E.: On the Selection of Candidates for Polygraph Training: Predicting Academic Success, POLICE, Vol.7, No.1 (Sept.-Oct., 1962), 48-50.

Yeschke, Charles L.: Ethics and the Polygraph Examiner, JCLC&PS, Vol.56, No.1 (Mar., 1965), 109-112.

Zweiful, Robert L.: Adaptation of the Opaque Projector to Lie Detector Tests, JCLC&PS, Vol.43, No.2 (July-Aug., 1952), 256.

Weapons, Handguns
and
Firearms Identification

Aldrich, Tom: Supervised Shooting Program for Teen-agers, L&O, Vol.7 (July, 1959).

Amber, John T. (ed.): *Gun Digest.* Chicago, The Gun Digest Co., 1965.

Baker, Newman F.: The Campbell Case, SE&SCD, Vol.3, No.1 (1964).

Berg, Stanton O.: Filing .22 Firing Pin Impressions, JCLC&PS, Vol.55, No.2 (June, 1964), 290.

Bigler, Edward G.: A Water Tank System of

Bullet Recovery, POLICE, Vol.6, No.1 (Sept.-Oct., 1961), 72-74.

Brown, Earle B.: *Basic Optics for the Sportsman.* New York, Stoeger, Arms Corp., 1949.

Camp, Raymond R.: *The Hunter's Encyclopedia.* Harrisburg, Stackpole, 1948.

Camp, William F.: Firearms Instruction for Civilians by Police Officers, L&O, Vol.12 (Aug., 1964).

Cerney, J. V.: Feet: Their Effect on Marksmanship, POLICE, Vol.6, No.6 (July-Aug., 1962), 38-39.

Chalkley, Mason T.: Why Fast Draw, L&O, Vol.12 (Apr., 1964).

Chapman, Samuel C., and Crockett, Thompson: Gunsight Dilemma: Police Firearms Policy, POLICE, Vol.7, No.4 (Mar.-Apr., 1963), 20-25.

Creshire, L. L.: The How-to of Hip Shooting, POLICE, Vol.4, No.4 (Mar.-Apr., 1960), 32-35.

Crossman, Edward G.: Some ??? Not in the Programme, SE&SCD, Vol.1, No.3 (1964).

Crowley, William F.: A New Weapon Against Confidence Games, JCLC&PS, Vol.50, No.3 (1959-60), 233.

Davis, John E.: *Introduction to Tool Marks, Firearms and The Straigraph.* Springfield, Thomas, 1958.

Drazga, John: Concealable Firearms Under New York Laws, POLICE, Vol.2., No.3 (Jan.-Feb., 1958), 95-105.

Einreinhof, Emery: A Small Arms Serial Numbers File, L&O, Vol.9 (Aug., 1961).

Exhumation of Deceased's Body for Purpose of Examing Bullet Wound, SE&SCD, Vol.2, No.6 (1964).

Frederick, Karl T.: Pistol Regulations: Its Principles and History, SE&SCD, Vol.2, No.5, & Vol.3, No.1 (1964).

Garrett, Norman J.: Computer Scores Pistol Shoot at Illinois Tollway, L&O, Vol.11, No.5 (May, 1963).

Gaylord, Chic: The Quick and the Dead, L&O, Vol.9 (Oct., 1961).

————: Riot Gun, L&O, Vol.11, No.2 (Feb., 1963).

General Admissibility of Firearms Identification Evidence, SE&SCD, Vol.3, No.2 (1964).

Goddard, Calvin: Books on Arms, Ammunition and Firearms Identification, SE&SCD, Vol.2, No.1 (1964).

————: Firearms as Evidence, SE&SCD, Vol.2, No.1 (1964).

————: The Pistol Bogey, SE&SCD, Vol.1, No.2 (1964).

————: Police Pistol Practice, SE&SCD, Vol.1, No.4, & Vol.1, No.5 (1964).

Hall, A. L.: The Missile and the Weapon, SE&SCD, Vol.2, No.4 (1964).

Hanna, Donald G.: Sidearms Belong . . . Where? L&O, Vol.12 (May, 1964).

Harvey, James E.: Shooting from the Hip . . . In Sub-miniature, L&O, Vol.11, No.6 (June, 1963).

Hatcher, Julian: *Notebook: a Standard Reference Book for Shooters, Gunsmiths, Ballis-*ticians, Historians Hunters, and Collectors. Harrisburg, Stackpole & Heck, 1947.

————, **Jury, Frank J., and Wellen, Jac:** *Firearms Investigation, Identification and Evidence.* Harrisburg, Stackpole & Heck, 1957.

————: *Textbook of Firearms, Investigation, Identification and Evidence.* Georgetown, Small Arms Tech. Publ., 1951.

Hess, John J.: Sidearms Belong at the Right, L&O, Vol.12 (July, 1964).

Holcomb, R. L.: Encyclopedia of Modern Firearms, JCLC&PS, Vol.51, No.6 (Mar.-Apr., 1960-61), 678.

————: Practical Demonstration of Police Weapons, L&O, Vol.7 (Nov., 1959).

Howe, Walter J.: Do You Really Know Guns, POLICE, Vol.1, No.4 (Mar.-Apr., 1957), 44-46.

————: Handling Revolvers, POLICE, Vol.1, No.4 (Mar.-Apr, 1957), 22-23.

————: *Professional Gunsmithing.* Plantersville, Small Arms Tech. Publ., 1946.

Hurley, John A.: Arming the Criminal, POLICE, Vol.3, No.2 (Nov.-Dec., 1958), 7-9.

Identification of Shotgun, Wads, and Shells by Coroner, SE&SCD, Vol.2, No.6 (1964).

Kraft, B.: A Central Registry for Forensic Firearms Identification, SE&SCD, Vol.2, No.3 (1964).

Keller, John E.: Introducing a Rookie to His Gun: L&O, Vol.9 (Oct., 1961).

————: New and Revolutionary Law Enforcement Weapon, L&O, Vol.11. No.10 (Oct., 1963).

Kirwan, Wm. E., and Hart, A. B.: Water-tank Bullet Recovery, POLICE, Vol.1, No.6 (July-Aug., 1957), 9-11.

Lawder, Lee E.: It's the Little Things That Make the Match, L&O, Vol.12 (June, 1964).

————: Let's Have a Match, L&O, Vol.9 (July, 1961).

————: Revolver Reloaders, L&O, Vol.12 (Feb., 1964).

————: Something New in a Police Combat Match, L&O, Vol.9 (Aug., 1961).

————: Visit to a Modern Indoor Range, L&O, Vol.9 (Mar., 1961).

Marco, Gary: Handloading for Economy, L&O, Vol.11, No.3 (Mar., 1963).

Martello, Francis L.: Before the Last Resort, POLICE, Vol.5, No.3 (Jan.-Feb., 1961), 22-23.

————: Before the Last Resort, POLICE, Vol.5, No. 3 (Mar.-Apr., 1961), 44-46.

Martin, Harrison P.: Sidearms Belong at the Left, L&O, Vol.12 (Mar., 1964).

Martin, T. F., and Priar, L. L.: Police Techniques in Gun Fights, JCLC&PS, Vol.46 (1955-56), 396-403.

Mathews, J. Howard: *Firearms Identification.* Madison, Univ. of Wisconsin Press, 1962 (2 Vols.).

———: The Measurement of Rifling Characteristics of Firearms, POLICE, Vol.1, No.6 (July-Aug., 1957), 15-19.

Matt, Robert A.: A University Plans a Shooting Match, L&O, Vol.7 (Apr., 1959).

———: Police Firearms Training Programs, POLICE, Vol.4, No.3 (Jan.-Feb., 1960), 72-74.

Mezger, Otto, Heess, Walter, and Hasslacher, Fritz: Determination of the Type of Pistol Employed from an Examination of Fired Bullets and Shells, SE&SCD, Vol.2, No.6; and Vol.3, No.2 (1964).

Pfeuffer, Dan: Sidearms Belong . . . Where? L&O, Vol.12 (May,1964).

Piedlievre, R., and Simonin, C.: Medicolegal Study of Residue in Barrel of Firearms, SE&SCD, Vol.1, No.3 (1964).

Police, and the Pistol, SE&SCD, Vol.1, No.4 (1964).

Prehle, Jack: Straight from the Shoulder, L&O, Appears in every issue.

Rastogi, R. P.: Identification of Shotguns by Fired Shell, JCLC&PS, Vol.55, No.4 (Dec., 1964), 529.

Roper, Walter: *Pistol and Revolver Shooting.* New York, Macmillan, 1945.

Rychetnik, Joe: Holdout for Your Life, L&O, Vol.11, No.1 (Nov., 1963).

Rymer, Fred R.: .22 Caliber Firing Pin Impression File, JCLC&PS, Vol.52, No.2 (July-Aug., 1961), 239.

Sasovetz, Thomas A.: The No Key Gun Lock, L&O, Vol.8, No.5 (1960).

Saul, John R.: The BCPC (Basic Combat Pistol Course), L&O, Vol.12 (Nov., 1964).

Sawyer, Charles W.: *Firearms in American History.* Boston, Cornhill Publishing Co.

Schira, Frank J.: Firearms Control in the United States, L&O, Vol.7 (June, 1959).

Sharma, B. R.: The Importance of Firing Pin Impressions in the Identification of Firearms, JCLC&PS, Vol.54, No.3 (1963), 378.

Sharpe, Philip B.: *Complete Guide to Handloading.* New York, Funk & Wagnalls, 1952.

———: *The Rifle in America.* New York, Funk & Wagnalls, 1947.

Simmons, Richard F.: *Wildcat Cartridges.* New York, Morrow, 1947.

Smith, Leslie L.: Zip Guns, POLICE, Vol.7, No.3 (Jan.-Feb., 1963), 10-12.

Smith, Sydney: Injuries from Firearms, SE&SCD, Vol.1, No.6 (1964).

Smith, Walter H. B.: *The Basic Manual of Military Small Arms.* Harrisburg, Military Service Publ., 1945.

———: *Pistols and Revolvers.* Harrisburg, Military Service Publ. 1948 (2 Vols.).

Stevenson, Jan A.: The Case for the .41, L&O, Vol.12 (Nov.-Dec., 1964).

Suskin, N.: Military Firearms Adopted by Criminals to Suit Their Purposes, SE&SCD, Vol.1, No.6 (1964).

Tangen, Ed: Spring Guns, SE&SCD, Vol.1, No.3 (1964).

U.S. Federal Bureau of Investigation: *Firearms Identification.* Washington.

Vickery, W. F.: *Advanced Gunsmithing.* Plantersville, Small Arms Tech., 1945.

Wallack, Bob: The Smith and Wesson .41, L&O, Vol.12 (Sept., 1964).

Westcott, Allan P.: The Literature of Gunshot Injuries, SE&SCD, Vol.3, No.1 (1964).

Weston, Paul B.: Basic Revolver Shooting, L&O, Vol.11, No.4, 7, & 10 (Apr., July, & Oct., 1964).

———: Bulls Eyes on Rodman's Neck, POLICE, Vol.6, No.4 (Mar.-Apr., 1962), 69-71.

———: Combat Shooting, POLICE, Vol.4, No.1 (Sept.-Oct., 1959), 39-43.

———: *Combat Shooting for the Police.* Springfield, Thomas, 1960.

———: College Level Firearms Training, POLICE, Vol.6, No.5 (May-June, 1962), 72-73.

———: Double Action Shooting, POLICE, Vol.3, No.3 (Jan.-Feb., 1959), 58-60.

———: Firearms Safety for Police Officer—A Discussion, POLICE, Vol.5, No.6 (July-Aug., 1961), 61-64.

———: Greater Fire-power for Police, POLICE, Vol.3, No.5 (May-June, 1959), 48-51.

———: Hide-out Holster Builder, POLICE, Vol.4, No.1 (Sept.-Oct., 1959), 39-43.

———: The .357 Magnum, POLICE, Vol.3, No.6 (July-Aug., 1959), 26-29.

———: Ricochets, POLICE, Vol.4, No.2 (Nov.-Dec., 1959), 34-37; Vol.5, No.3 (Jan.-Feb., 1961), 23-24; Vol.5, No.4 (Mar.-Apr., 1961), 47-48.

———: Slinging Lead at Less Cost, POLICE, Vol.7, No.1 (Sept.-Oct., 1962), 51-52.

———: Trigger Control Through Sighting and Aiming, POLICE, Vol.6, No.3 (Jan.-Feb., 1962), 66-68.

———: When to Shoot, POLICE, Vol.5, No.5 (May-June, 1961), 36-39.

Whelan, Townsend: *Small Arms Design and Ballistics.* Plantersville, Small Arms Publ., 1946 (2 Vols.).

Chapter Three

PATROL ADMINISTRATION*

PATROL

Adams, Thomas F.: Field Interrogations, PO-LICE, Vol.7, No.4 (Mar.-Apr., 1963), 26-29.

Arenburg, Gerald: Study of Police Officers' Line of Duty Deaths in the United States, L&O, Vol.8, No.12 (1960).

Auto 1-D: a Law Enforcement Aid. Lomita, Calif., Box 725, No Author.

Baumann, William H.: All Emergency Vehicle, TPC (Aug., 1961).

Bednarz, Edward J.: Policing the New York World's Fair, L&O, Vol.12 (Aug., 1964).

Beier, L. E.: Effects of Increased Patrol: A Research Report, TPY (1959).

Benjamin, Philip: The "Finest" on Horseback, POLICE, Vol.1, No.6 (July-Aug., 1957), 12-14.

Bishop, John L.: Turnpike Police Patrol, FBILEB (Feb., 1958).

Bradley, V.: Pacific Grove's Auxiliary Police Marine Unit, TPC, Vol.30 (Aug., 1963), 8.

Bradshaw, Beverly H.: Illuminated Map, L&O, Vol.11, No.7 (July, 1963).

Brannon, Bernard C.: One-man Car Patrol, TPY (1956).

————: One Man Patrol Cars Will Serve, TPC, Vol.22, No.2 (Dec., 1955).

————: Report on One-man Police Patrol Cars in Kansas City, Missouri, JCLC&PS, Vol.47, No.2 (July-Aug., 1956), 238.

Brinkman, O. F.: The Peoria Police Emergency Car, JCL&C, Vol.38, No.6 (Mar.-Apr., 1947-48), 677-79.

Bristow, Allen P.: *Field Interrogation.* Springfield, Thomas, 1964.

Brooker, Leo H.: Bicycle Patrol Highly Effective on Night Beats, FBILEB (June, 1960).

Brostron, Curtis: Concepts of Police Patrol & the Strategy & Tactics of Line Operations, POLICE, Vol.6, No.5 (May-June, 1962), 42-45.

————: Strategy and Tactics, POLICE (May-June, 1962).

Burling, Howard L.: Skin Diving in Police Work, L&O, Vol.8, No.8 (1960).

California, Dept. of Education, Bureau of Trade and Industrial Education: *Covering Roads*

for Wanted Cars and Fugitives. Sacramento, 1949.

————: *Descriptions of Persons and Portrait Parle.* Sacramento, 1949.

————: *Field Note Taking.* Sacramento, 1950.

Cannon, D. E.: Underwater Search, TPC, Vol.31 (Feb., 1964), 43.

Carroll, William: Police Transportation, L&O, Vol.9 (Nov., 1961).

————: What About Compact or Economy Cars for Police Work? L&O, Vol.7 (Dec., 1959).

Carroll, Patrick: Evaluating the One-man vs. Two-man Patrol Car, L&O, Vol.9 (Nov., 1961).

Cato, B. G.: Rescue via Radar, L&O, Vol.13, No.5 (May, 1965), 12.

Chapman, Samuel G.: *Patrol and Moving Traffic Enforcement.* Portland, Multnomah Co. Sheriff's Office, Portland, 1965.

————: *Police Patrol Readings.* Springfield, Thomas, 1964.

————, & **Mitchell, Robert F.:** 1-man Motor Patrol Training Manual, TPC, Vol.32, No.2 (Feb., 1965), 12-28.

Charles, William F.: Underwater Patrolmen, L&O, Vol.7 (July, 1959).

Chicago Police Department: *One-man Patrol Cars.* Chicago, Chicago Police Dept. A report prepared by the Chicago P.D., 1963.

Cincinnati Regional Crime Committee: *Cincinnati Police Beat Survey.* Chicago, American Public Welfare Assoc., 1963.

Clift, Raymond E.: The Objectives of Police Patrol, POLICE, Vol.3, No.3 (Jan.-Feb., 1959), 35-37.

Clowers, Norman L.: One and One-half Man Cars, POLICE, Vol.4, No.4 (Mar.-Apr., 1960), 78-79.

————: *Patrolman Patterns, Problems and Procedures.* Springfield, Thomas, 1962.

Connecticut State Police Air Patrol, TPC, Vol.30 (Oct., 1963), 14.

Cornelius, A., Jr.: High Speed Pursuit, TPC, Vol.31 (Nov., 1964), 40.

Cox, Dick: River Patrols in California, L&O, Vol.13, No.5 (May, 1965), 16.

Crawford, William: Field Interrogation, L&O, Vol.13, No.5 (May, 1965), 82.

---

* This Chapter includes Patrol Administration, Crime Prevention and Police Dogs.

Darragh, Charles: Beat-patrol, POLICE, Vol.3, No.4 (Mar.-Apr., 1959), 30-33.

Day, Frank D.: The Issue of One Man vs. Two Man Police Patrol Cars, JCLC&PS, Vol.46 (1955-56), 698-706.

Diamond, Harry: Operation Decoy, POLICE, Vol.7, No.4 (Mar.-Apr., 1963), 50-52.

Dobrovolny, Fred: Flying Squad for Small Departments, L&O, Vol.11, No.10 (Oct., 1963).

Dougherty, Edward E.: Pursuit Driving, POLICE, Vol.4, No.5 (May-June, 1960), 19-22; No.6 (July-Aug., 1960), 37-39.

————: *Safety in Police Pursuit Driving.* Springfield, Thomas, 1961.

Draznin, Yaffa: Watching the Waterways of the Windy City, L&O, Vol.13, No.5 (May, 1965), 8.

Droutzkog, Alexis: Advantages of the Helicopter in Law Enforcement, TPY (1952).

Duncan, Dale: Pursuit Driving, TPY (1964).

Dyment, Robert: A Case for the Foot Patrolman, L&O, Vol.8, No.7 (1960).

Eastman, George D.: The Flexible Unit—A Unique Striking Force, POLICE, Vol.4, No.6 (July-Aug., 1960), 14-17.

Elam, Gerald: A Copper in a Chopper, L&O, Vol.8, No.6 (1960).

Fagerstrom, Dorothy: Police Transportation Mobile Patrol Survey, 1963, L&O, Vol.11, No.11 (Nov., 1963).

A Former Denver Police Officer: What Makes a Policeman Go Wrong? DENVER POST, Oct. 8, 1961.

Frazier, Dick: High Speed Pursuit, TPC (May, 1961), 38.

Garden, A. Newhall: Marine Patrol to the Rescue, L&O, Vol.12 (May, 1964).

Germann, A. C.: Patrol Administration, JCLC&PS, Vol.53, No.1 (May-June, 1962), 126.

Gillmouthe, Rupert L.: The Use of Small Aircraft in Police Work, FBILEB (Mar., 1959).

Gilston, David H., and Podell, Lawrence: *The Practical Patrolman.* Springfield, Thomas, 1959.

Gourley, G. Douglas, and Bristow, Allen P.: *Patrol Administration.* Springfield, Thomas, 1961.

Governmental Research Institute: *One-man Police Patrol Car Operation.* Washington, Governmental Research Institute (Nov., 1955).

Graney, Edward J.: Do Modern Patrol Cars Do the Job? L&O, Vol.10, No.7 (July, 1962), 6.

Hallstead, William F.: Patrolling for Safety, L&O Vol.12 (Sept., 1964).

Hamilton Police Department: *One-man Car Procedure.* Hamilton, Ontario, Canada, Hamilton Police Dept., 1959. A Report prepared by the Hamilton Police Dept.

Hansson, C. F.: On-the-scene Preventive Tactics, TPC, Vol.30 (June, 1963), 44.

Harper, E. S.: Supplementing Patrol Plan, TPC, Vol.29, No.9 (Sept., 1962), 8.

Hastings, C. Marshall: Underwater Recovery Unit, Minneapolis Police Dept., L&O, Vol.11, No.2 (Feb., 1963).

Heffron, Floyd: *Descriptions of Persons and Portrait Parle.* Seventh Annual Calif. Technical Institute of Peace Officers' Training, Santa Rita, 1948.

————: *Evidence for the Patrolman.* Springfield, Thomas, 1954.

Hogan, John C.: The Manly Art of Observation and Deduction, JCLC&PS, Vol.55, No.1 (Mar., 1964), 157.

Holcomb, R. L.: Field Interrogation, JCLC&PS, Vol.51, No.4 (Mar.-Apr., 1960-61), 491.

————: *Police Patrol.* Springfield, Thomas, 1961.

————: *Police Patrol.* Iowa City, State Univ. of Iowa, Institute of Public Affairs, 1948, 34pp.

Holmgren, R. Bruce: Police Reserves? POLICE, Vol.5, No.3 (Jan.-Feb., 1961), 14-17; No.4 (Mar.-Apr., 1961), 32-34.

Holstrom, J. D.: *Police Beat Survey.* Police Dept., Berkeley, Calif., 1945.

Hrunek, Jack R.: One-man Squad Car in a Small Village, L&O, Vol.11, No.2 (Feb., 1963).

Jacobs, Will: Life Saving Techniques with Scuba Equipment, L&O, Vol.12 (May, 1964).

Jessup, Frank A.: Selective Enforcement Experience in Indiana, TPY (1956).

Jones, Emmet L.: Police Fire Emergency Rescue, TPC, Vol.32, No.1 (Jan., 1965), 8-9.

Jones, E. W.: Police Pursuit Driving, TPC, Vol.30 (1963), (Jan.), 14; (Feb.), 10; (Mar.), 26; (Apr.), 22.

Kearney, Paul W.: *I Drive the Turnpikes . . . and Survive.* New York, Ballantine Books, 1956.

Kinz, Wallace H.: Cleveland Puts Station Wagons in the Patrol Unit, L&O, Vol.12 (Nov., 1964).

Kirkwood, Robert H.: *Effect of Single and Multiple Patrols on Police Fatalities.* New York, Institute of Public Administration, July, 1950.

Klotzback, Walter E.: The Helicopter New York Police on Patrol, JCLC&PS, Vol.48, No.5 (Jan.-Feb., 1958), 547.

Kohler, Alfred C.: The Harbor Patrol—Guardians of the Water Ways, L&O, Vol.7 (June, 1959).

Landis, Eugene A., Jr.: Cruiser Meters for Accountability and Control, POLICE, Vol.9, No.4 (Mar.-Apr., 1965), 20-22.

Langford, Beryl, *et al.: Stopping Vehicles and Occupant Control.* Springfield, Thomas, 1960.

Lauer, A. R.: Driving Efficiency Requires Optimal Stimulation, POLICE, Vol.3, No.3 (Jan.-Feb., 1959), 37-40.

———: Making License Plates More Legible, POLICE, Vol.4, No.2 (Nov.-Dec., 1959), 65-71; No.3 (Jan.-Feb., 1960), 36-40.

———, & Swanson, C. O.: A Method of Determining a Safe Driving Speed at Night, POLICE, Vol.3, No.3 (Jan.-Feb., 1959), 60-64.

Lawder, Lee E.: Death on Two Wheels, L&O, Vol.6 (July, 1958).

———: Notes on Observation and Memory, L&O, Vol.8, No.10 (1960).

Leonard A. E.: Task Force for Better Police Service, TPC, Vol.31 (June, 1964), 12.

Leonard, Glenford S.: Tactical Police Unit, TPC, Vol.29, No.4 (Apr., 1962), 34.

Lyng, John F. X.: Eyewitness—Use Caution, L&O, Vol.11, No.12 (Dec., 1963).

McCain, E. K.: Police Dogs on Three Wheels, TPC (Aug., 1961), 18.

McCartney, A.: Personal Wireless for the Man on the Beat, TPJ (June, 1962).

MacNamara, Donal E., and Smith, Robert A.: *Bristol's Police Problems.* New York, Institute of Criminology, 1965.

Marshall, J. T.: Eastern States TW Net Now Fully Automatic, TPC, Vol.31 (May, 1963), 16.

Members of the Michigan Law Enforcement Blockade Committee: The Michigan Blockade System, FBILEB (Apr., 1961).

Meulen, L. J. van der: A System for Vehicle Rearlighting, POLICE, Vol.3, No.3 (Jan.-Feb., 1959), 40-42.

Millman, Ron: Mobilized Patrol for Private Police, L&O, Vol.8, No.7 (1960).

Morris, William H., and Jones, J. L.: State Police Aircraft Scores Again, POLICE, Vol.6, No.4 (Mar.-Apr., 1962), 12-13.

Morrison G. I.: A "Fluid Patrol Force" Concept, L&O, Vol.12 (Oct., 1964).

Mulcahy, L. J.: The Case for the Unmarked Police Car, TPC, Vol.29, No.7 (July, 1962), 12-14.

Murphy, Glen R., and Holladay, Roy E.: The Hundred System, POLICE, Vol.5, No.3 (Jan.-Feb., 1961), 26-30.

Murphy, Michael J.: Expands Radio Patrol, TPC, Vol.29 (Apr., 1962), 45.

Nelson, Alfred T., and Smith, Howard E.: *Car*

Clouting: the Crime, the Criminal and the Police. Springfield, Thomas, 1958.

New York City Police Dept.: *Operation 25.* New York, Police Dept., 1954.

Neyhart, Amos E.: Driver Attitudes, POLICE, Vol.4, No.2 (Nov.-Dec., 1959), 31-34.

Northwestern University Traffic Institute: *Patrol for Traffic Law Enforcement,* No.2426. Chicago, 1958.

———: *Pursuit in Traffic Law Enforcement.* No.2436. Chicago, 1958.

———: *Stopping and Approaching the Traffic Law Violator,* No.2368. Chicago, 1958.

Nugent, Howard W.: Surveillance, L&O, Vol.11, No.8 (Aug., 1963).

Osborn, Alex F.: *Applied Imagination.* New York, Scribner's, 1963, **Must reading.**

Patterson, Alex J.: *The Results of Team Policing in Salford.* Report of the Chief Constable on the Police Establishment for the year ended Dec. 31, 1951.

Payton, George L.: *Patrol Procedures.* Los Angeles, Legal Book Store, 1964.

Piercy, Donald William: Police Patrol Car, JCLC&PS, Vol.45 (1954-55), 748-759.

Porter, J. D.: Seattle's Underwater Police, POLICE, Vol.2, No.4 (Mar.-Apr., 1958), 13-16.

Richmond, Harry: The Davy Jones Beat, L&O, Vol.1 (July, 1959).

Robby, Lee W.: Medic Alert—An Aid to Officers in an Emergency, POLICE, Vol.9, No.4 (Mar.-Apr., 1965), 28-30.

Rogers, Thomas J.: *Review of Foot Patrol in Chicago.* Chicago, Police Planning Division, May, 1961.

Rouse, O. W.: and Melnicoe, William: *Beat Patrol and Observation.* Sacramento, California Peace Officers' Training Publication, No.65, Calif. State Dept. of Education, 1963.

Rudwick, Elliot M.: The Unequal Badge, JCLC&PS (July-Aug., 1960); JNE (Spring-Fall, 1961).

Runyan, Richard T., and Ostertag, F. Samuel: Field Interrogation of Pedestrians, POLICE, Vol.3, No.6 (July-Aug., 1959), 51-53.

———, & ———: The One-man Patrol Car, POLICE, Vol.2, No.6 (July-Aug., 1958), 7-8; Vol.3, No.1 (Sept.-Oct., 1958), 15-17; Vol.3 No.2 (Nov.-Dec., 1958), 9-11; Vol.3, No.4 (Mar.-Apr., 1959), 26-28; Vol.4, No.1 (Sept.-Oct., 1959), 29-31; Vol.4, No.2 (Nov.-Dec., 1959), 6-8.

———, & ———: One-man Patrol Car—Approaching a Stopped Automobile, POLICE, Vol.3, No.3 (Jan.-Feb., 1959), 15-18.

———, & ———: The One-man Patrol Car—Patrol Procedure When a Crime Is in Progress, POLICE, Vol.4, No.3 (Jan.-Feb., 1960), 60-61.

——, & ——: The One-man Patrol Car—Routine Operations Under Normal Conditions, POLICE, Vol.4, No.4 (Mar.-Apr., 1960), 17-18.

Scheidt, Edward: Police Pursuit and Its Impact on the Public and Police, TPY (1964).

Schwarz, John I.: *Police Roadblock Operations.* Springfield, Thomas, 1962.

Schwartz, Mortimer D.: The Manly Art of Observation and Deduction, JCLC&PS, Vol.55, No.1 (Mar., 1964), 157.

Scott, Edgar E.: Alertness in Handling Suspects Is Urged, POLICE, Vol.3, No.6 (July-Aug., 1959), 63-65.

Seares, R. S.: Operation House Watch, POLICE, Vol.1, No.6 (July-Aug., 1957), 54-56.

Shaw, B. M. W.: St. Louis Patrol Plan, TPC, Vol.29, No.9 (Sept., 1962), 8.

Sheehan, Robert, *et al.: Stopping Vehicles and Occupant Control.* Springfield, Thomas, 1960.

Skousen, W. Cleon: Building an Efficient Patrol Division, L&O, Vol.9, Nos.2 & 3 (Feb.-Mar., 1963).

——: Is the Solo Motorcycle a Sound Investment for Police Work? L&O, Vol.8, No.11 (1960).

Slayton, John E.: When "Man's Best Friend" Becomes a Problem, L&O, Vol.12 (Jan., 1964), 52.

Smith, H. M., Jr.: Virginia and Implied Consent, TPC, Vol.29, No.8 (Aug., 1962), 6-12.

Smith, R. D.: *Random Patrol.* Washington, IACP, 1960.

Steeber, Robert A.: Seen and Heard on Waterways, L&O, Vol.12 (May, 1964).

Story, F. W.: Multi-purpose Ambulances for Cleveland, TPC (Nov., 1961), 60.

Swartzpager, G. L.: Three-wheel Vehicles Aid Patrol and Traffic Duties, L&O, Vol.11, No.6 (June, 1963).

To Speed . . . or Not to Speed, L&O, Vol.9 (Jan., 1961).

Toothman, Edward M.: *Who Are the Police?* Oakland, Police Dept. Annual Report, 1960.

Traffic Institute of Northwestern University: *Pursuit in Traffic Law Enforcement,* Pub. No.2021. Chicago, 1958.

Truitt, John T.: Approaching a Motor Vehicle, L&O, Vol.10, No.1 (Jan., 1962).

Tutuska, John B.: Diving for Community Service—Diving Deputies, POLICE, Vol.7, No.2 (Nov.-Dec., 1962), 25-27.

U.S. Federal Bureau of Investigation: *Personal Descriptions Portrait Parle and Speaking Likeness.* Washington.

U.S. Work Progress Administration, Division of Women's and Professional Projects: *Distribution of Police Beats,* No.2. Washington, Public Administration Circular, Govt. Printing Office.

U.S. Treasury Department: *Pursuit Driving,* No.403. Washington, U.S. Govt. Printing Office, 1957.

Versnik, L. V.: *Feasibility of Pooling Patrol Vehicles.* Madison, prepared for Commissioner James L. Karns of the Wisconsin Motor Vehicle Dept., Wisconsin State Patrol, 1962.

Wall, Patrick, M.: *Eye-witness Identification in Criminal Cases.* Springfield, Thomas, 1965.

Walton, Frank E.: Selective Distribution of Police Patrol Force, JCLC&PS, Vol.49, No.2 (1958-59), 165.

Weatherall, Ernie: A Tough Police Beat, TPC (Mar., 1961), 34.

Whipperman, Robert F.: The ABC of Private Patrol, SEC.W., Vol.2, No.4 (June, 1965), 15.

Wilson, O. W.: One-man Patrol Cars, TPC, Vol.30 (May, 1963), 18.

——: Put the Cop Back on the Beat P.MGT (June, 1953).

Wisconsin—Merger for State-county Patrols, TPC, Vol.30 (Mar., 1963), 50.

Zeichner, Irving B.: According to Law—Emergency Call, L&O, Vol.9 (Mar., 1961).

CRIME PREVENTION

Ahern, Francis J.: Crime Prevention—Do It Yourself, TPY (1958).

——: Report of Committee on Crime Prevention, TPY (1958).

Allen, Edward J.: Do-it-yourself Crime Prevention, TPY (1958).

Andenaes, John: General Prevention—Illusion or Reality, JCLC&PS, Vol.43, No.2 (July-Aug., 1952), 176.

Anderson, Clinton H.: Crime Prevention by Education, TPY (1958).

Bray, William G.: Law and Order Versus Violence, POLICE, Vol.9, No.4 (Mar.-Apr., 1965), 82-84.

Brown, Thad F.: Crime Prevention and the Youthful Offender, TPY (1957).

Cahill, Thomas, J.: Crime Prevention—Fact or Fantasy? TPY (1960).

———: Prevention: Workshop, TPY (1962).

———: Report of Crime Prevention Committee, TPY (1960); (1961); (1962); (1963) & (1964).

Crihfield, B. E.: Crime Control and Uniformity of Criminal Laws, JCLC&PS, Vol.42 (1951-52), 571.

———, & **Wiltsee, Herbert:** Recent Developments in Inter-State Crime Control Legislation, JCLC&PS, Vol.45 (1954-55), 641-51.

DeMers, Donald O.: *Outline of Juvenile Delinquency Control.* Sacramento, Calif. State Dept. of Education, Bureau of Trade and Industrial Education, 1949.

Ellingston, John R.: *Protecting Our Children from Criminal Careers.* New York, Prentice-Hall, 1948.

Ellis, David C.: Crime Prevention by Closed-circuit Television, TPY (1962).

Fording, A. H.: Crime Prevention Problems Caused by Transients—College Students, TPY (1964).

———: Report of the Crime Prevention Committee, TPY (1965).

Garren, B. C.: Preventive Maintenance in Tulsa, TPC, Vol.30 (Sept., 1963), 40.

Gertsenzon, A. A.: The Community's Role in the Prevention and Study of Crime, SR, Vol.2 (Jan., 1961), 14-27.

Glueck, E.: Guideposts to Crime Prevention, FSH, Vol.17 (June, 1956).

———: Newer Ways of Crime Control, HER, Vol.9, 184-202.

Glueck, S.: Philosophy and Principles of Delinquency Prevention, Trans. by Shinichiro Michida, KYOTO LAW REVIEW, Vol.67 (1960), 1-23.

———, & **Glueck, E.:** Preventing Delinquency, NEWSWEEK, Vol.36, 56.

Grevemberg, Francis C.: Report of the Committee on Crime Prevention, TPY (1956).

Grinnell, Flint: The Better Business Bureau, SE&SCD, Vol.2, No.3 (1964).

Harper and Shaw: Crime Prevention with the Operative Deployment System, POLICE, Vol.6, No.3 (Jan.-Feb., 1962), 10-13.

Hergenhan, John C.: Crime Control: The Score —1955. TPY (1957).

Higgins, Lois L.: Crime Prevention Total Community Problem, L&O, Vol.9 (May, 1961).

———: The Femine Force in Crime Prevention, TPY (1958).

Higgins and Fitzpatrick: *Criminology and Crime Prevention.* Milwaukee, Bruce Publ.

Hogan, Fr. William E.: The Role of Religion in the Prevention of Crime and Delinquency, POLICE, Vol.1, No.4 (Mar.-Apr., 1957), 27-33.

Kelly, John C.: Report of Crime Prevention Committee, TPY (1957).

———: The Role of the Police in Crime Prevention, TPY (1957).

Lacey, Frederick R.: The Community and Crime Prevention, TPY (1957).

Leonard, V. A.: Changing Concepts in Crime Control, JCL&C, Vol.35, No.6 (Mar.-Apr., 1945), 398.

———: Whipping Post as an Instrument of Crime Control, JCL&C, Vol.35, No.6 (Mar.-Apr., 1945), 397.

Liu, Daniel: Crime Prevention, POLICE, Vol.2, No.5 (May-June, 1958), 15-19.

Lukas, E. J.: Crime Prevention; Who Prevents What? FP, Vol.12 (June, 1948), 19-23.

Lumbard, Eliot H.: Local and State Action Against Organized Crime, THE ANNALS, Vol.347 (May, 1963), 82.

Mattin, Matthew: Second U.N. Congress on the Prevention of Crime and the Treatment of Offenders, JCLC&PS, Vol.50, No.5 (Jan.-Feb., 1960), 479.

Murray, J. G.: Some Aspects of Fraud, Control and Investigation, JCLC&PS, Vol.49, No.1 (1958-59), 79.

National Conference on Prevention and Control of Juvenile Delinquency: *Report on Role of Police.* Washington, U.S. Govt. Printing Office, 1947.

Parker, W. H.: Is Total Prevention Attainable? TPY (1957).

Paul, Anthony R.: Crime Prevention—Where Do We Stand? TPY (1959).

Perlman, I. Richard: *Delinquency Prevention: the Size of the Problem.* Washington, Dept. of Health, Education & Welfare, 1960.

Peterson, Virgil W.: Facts and Fancies in Crime Prevention, JCL&C, Vol.38, No.5 (Mar.-Apr., 1947-48), 466-74.

Phillips, Bob M.: An Ounce of Prevention Is Worth a Pound of Crime, POLICE, Vol.9, No.5 (May-June, 1965), 27.

Pickpocketing: A Survey of the Crime and Its Control, UPLR, Vol.104 (Dec., 1955), 408-20.

Plavsic, Milan N.: Good Relations Necessary in Crime Prevention, TPY (1957).

Plascowe, Morris: New Approaches to the Control of Organized Crime, THE ANNALS, Vol.347 (May, 1963), 74.

Powers, Edwin, and Witmer, Helen: *An Experiment in the Prevention of Delinquency.* New York, Columbia Univ. Press, 1951.

Prevention and Treatment of Offenders, U.N. Congress, TPC, Vol.30 (Sept., 1963), 26.

Pursuit, Dan G.: A University and Law Enforcement Work Together in the Control of Juvenile Delinquency, JCL&C, Vol.38, No.4 (Mar.-Apr., 1947-48), 416-22.

Shenehon, Eleanor: Prevention and Repression of Prostitution in North America, IRCP, Vol.13 (Oct., 1958), 15-25.

Snow, Margaret: Woman's Role in Crime Control, TPY (1956).

Swanson, Lynn D.: Role of Delinquency Prevention, TPY (1962).

Templewood, Viscount: The Criminal Justice Bill: International Aspects of Prevention and Treatment, JCL&C, Vol.39, No.2 (Mar.-Apr., 1948-49), 135-93.

Thornton, Robert Y.: A State Mobilizes for Crime Prevention, TPC (May, 1961), 10.

Truett, John T.: Notes on Burglary Prevention, L&O, Vol.7 (Feb., 1959).

Turnbladh, Will C.: A New Force Enlisted to Fight Crime With Knowledge to Get Action Where It Counts, POLICE, Vol.1, No.5 (May-June, 1957), 50-54.

Taylor, Lawrence M.: Crime Prevention and Pilferage, POLICE, Vol.9, No.5 (May-June, 1965), 90; TPY (1965).

Tyler, Gus: An Interdisciplinary Attack on Organized Crime, THE ANNALS, Vol.347 May, 1963), 104.

Witmer, Helen L., and Tufts, Edith: *The Effectiveness of Delinquency Prevention Programs.* Washington, Children's Bureau Pub. No.350, U.S. Govt. Printing Office, 1954.

Wolkg, Michael S.: Prevention or Apprehension, L&O, Vol.8, No.11 (1960).

POLICE DOGS

Arundel, Reginald: *Training the Dog for Guard Work.* Richmond, Denlinger's, 1952.

Atlanta Police Dept.: *Annual Report,* 1959. Atlanta, Atlanta Police Dept., 1960.

Baltimore Police Dept.: K-9 Corps, *Report of the Police Commissioner for the City of Baltimore to His Excellency The Governor of Maryland for the Year 1965.* Baltimore, Police Dept. Printing Bureau, 1958.

———: K-9 Corps, *Report of the Police Commissioner for the City of Baltimore to His Excellency The Governor of Maryland for the Year 1957.* Baltimore, Police Dept. Printing Bureau, 1958.

———: K-9 Corps, *Report of the K-9 Corps.* Baltimore, Police Dept. Printing Bureau, 1957.

Barbaresi, Sara M.: *How to Raise and Train a German Shepherd.* New York, Sterling, 1957.

Begley, Frank: St. Louis Police Dogs, L&O, Vol.7 (May, 1959).

Birmingham Will Inaugurate Use of Dogs in Police Work, AMJ, Vol.17 (Dec., 1959), 34.

Brown, William F.: Dog, *Encyclopedia Americana* (1957), Vol.9, 222b.

California State Legislature: *Canine Police, a Progress Report of the Assembly Interim Committee on Governmental Efficiency and Economy on Using Dogs in Police Work.* Sacramento, Calif. State Legislature, 1960.

Chapman, Samuel G.: The Dog in Law Enforcement—A Brief Résumé, POLICE, Vol.4, No.5 (May-June, 1960), 52-56.

———: *Dogs in Police Work: a Summary of Experience in Great Britain and the United States.* Chicago, Public Administration Service, 1960.

———: The Literature of Police Dog Use, POLICE, Vol.6, No.2 (Nov.-Dec., 1961), 11-12.

———: Whether to Use Police Dogs, POLICE, Vol.6, No.1 (Sept.-Oct., 1961), 62-67.

Coon, Thomas F.: Watchdogs of the Waterfront, L&O, Vol.9, Feb., 1961.

Criminal Evidence: Tracking by Bloodhounds, SE&SCD, Vol.3, No.1 (1964).

Darwish, Abdel Karim: Dogs in Police Service, L&O, Vol.7 (Sept., 1959).

Dodge, Geraldine R., and Rine, Josephine A.: *The German Shepherd Dog in America.* New York, Orange Judd, 1956.

Dogs, *Encyclopedia Britannica* (1958), 7,496.

The Dog as a Guard, *The Modern Dog Encyclopedia.* New York, Stackpole & Heck, 1949.

Dog—Man Teams Prove Value to Metropolitan Police Department, MO.PJ, Vol.7 (Spring, 1960), 6-10.

Dog Patrol, SPRING 3100, Vol.25 (Mar., 1954), **15.**

Dogs on Park Patrol in Philadelphia, TAC, Vol.75 (Apr., 1960), 9.

Dogs as Policemen: New Answer to Crime, USNWR, Vol.47 (Dec. 28, 1959), 56-59.

Donahue, Vincent J.: Hound Dog Man, POLICE, Vol.6, No.4 (Mar.-Apr., 1962), 16-25.

Furnas, J. C.: Four-footed Cops, SATURDAY EVENING POST, Vol.229 (Sept. 22, 1956), 38-39, 76, 80.

Genus Canis—Prima Facie—When, Where and If to Use Police Dogs, TPC, Vol.27 (May, 1960), 4-8, 10, 12.

Great Britain, Home Office: *Working Party on Police Dogs.* London, June 20, 1957.

———: *Home Office Working Party on Police Dogs, Report (Northern Group) Visit to Germany, 7th to 14th October, 1956.* London, Oct. 26, 1956.

Handy, William F., Harrington, Marilyn, and Pittman, David J.: The K-9 Corps: The Use of Dogs in Police Work, JCLC&PS, Vol.52, No.3 (Sept.-Oct., 1961), 328.

Henry, Omer: Four-footed Patrolmen, FW (Nov. 8, 1959), 24-25.

Hepbron, James M.: Baltimore Police Dogs, TAC, Vol.72 (Oct. 1957), 173-75.

Holman, Arthur: *My Dog Rex.* New York, Funk, 1958.

Houston Police Dept.: K-9 *Corps, Houston Police Department.* Houston, Police Dept., 1960.

Kelly, Leo T.: The Canine (K-9) Corps of the Baltimore Police Dept., POLICE, Vol.4, No.2 (Nov.-Dec., 1959), 19-25.

Kuellquist, R. L., Sr.: The Small Department and the K-9 Corps, L&O, Vol.12 (Feb., 1964).

Lancashire County, Lancashire Constabulary: *A Brochure in Honour of the Visit of Her Majesty the Queen and H.R.H. The Duke of Edinburgh to The Headquarters, Lancashire Constabulary, Hutton, Preston.* (Apr. 13, 1955).

———: *Report on the Lancashire Constabulary Dog Section.* 1958.

Latham, Sid: Putting Teeth into the Law. TRUE, Vol.39 (Apr., 1958), 52-55.

Leedham, Charles: The Law on a Leash, DIC, Vol.49 (Sept., 1959), 19-20, 67.

Lewis, Alfred E.: Metropolitan Begins Dog Training Work, PAN, Vol.6 (Jan., 1960), 6.

Linehan, Edward J.: Dogs Work for Man, NGM, Vol.14 (Aug., 1958), 190-233.

London, Metropolitan Police District: *Metropolitan Police Orders* (Nov. 22, 1954), 887.

———: *Notes on the Use of Dogs in the Metropolitan Police Force.* Fall, 1957.

McCall, Donald F.: Dogs in Police Work, JCLC&PS, Vol.53, No.1 (Mar.-May, 1962), 127.

Mannix, Daniel P.: Tracked by Bloodhounds, SATURDAY EVENING POST, Vol.221 (Apr. 9, 1949), 36-37, 77-79.

Marders, Irvin E.: *How to Use Dogs Effectively in Modern Police Work.* Cocoa Beach, Police Science, 1960.

Maricopa County's Bloodhounds, FBILEB, Vol.17 (Sept., 1948), 4-7.

Mobile Patrol Dogs, L&O, Vol.9 (Nov., 1961).

Monahan, J.: Ben Gets His Man: Scotland Yard's Labrador Retriever, READER'S DIGEST, Vol.60 (Mar., 1952), 59-62.

More Cities Using Police Dogs, P.MGT, Vol.42 (Apr., 1960), 90.

Most, Konrad: *Training Dogs.* New York, Coward-McCann, 1955.

Newman, M. W.: St. Louis Police Dogs Make Criminals Whine the Blues, THE CHICAGO DAILY NEWS (Feb. 13, 1960).

Nott-Bower, Sir John: Development and Use of Police Dogs in London, FBILEB, Vol.24 (Sept., 1955), 6-12, 26-27.

O'Conner, J. C.: Man's Best Friend—For Police Anyway, WCM, Vol.36 (May, 1960), 26, 28.

Parks, James P., Jr.: More Cities Enlist Dogs to Help Police Nip Crime Rates Rise, THE WALL STREET JOURNAL, Midwest Edition (Jan. 28, 1960), 1.

Papashively, George and Helen: *Dogs and People.* New York, Lippincott, 1954.

Pennsylvania State Police: *Basic Principles of Dog Training.* Hershey, State Police Training School, 1958.

Purcell, Jim, Jr.: Our K-9 Corps in Portland, TPC, Vol.24 (Feb., 1957), 14-16.

Roehrick, Edward W.: Chicago Police Dept. Cainine Patrol Unit, POLICE, Vol.5, No.6 (July-Aug., 1961), 6-10.

Ross, Gordon E.: Dogs: The Patrolling Officer's Sixth Sense, SEC.W., Vol.2, No.3 (May, 1965), 12.

St. Louis Police Dept.: *A Report on the St. Louis Board of Police Commissioners on the Use of Dogs as an Aid to Police.* St. Louis, 1958.

Sandy, William F., Harrington, Marilyn, and Pittman, David J.: *The K-9 Corps: the Use of Dogs in Police Work.* A report prepared for the Social Science Institute, Washington Univ., and the St. Louis Metropolitan Police Dept., St. Louis, 1961.

Schurmacher, Emile, C.: Bloodhound—Most Misunderstood Dog, SCIENCE DIGEST, Vol.30 (Nov., 1951), 41-43.

Skousen, W. Cleon: Do's and Don'ts for a K-9 Corps, L&O, Vol.8, No.8 (1960).

Sloane, Charles F.: Dogs in War, Police Work and on Patrol, JCLC&PS, Vol.46 (1955-56), 385-395.

Smith, Charles P.: Pima County Sheriff's Office Acquires Police Dog . . . and Puts Him to Work, THE SHERIFF, Vol.12 (Oct., 1958), 45.

Stockton's Canine Corps Are Regulars Now, CPO, Vol.10 (Mar.-Apr., 1960), 7.

Stoneman, William H.: British Police Dogs Bite into Dark Park Crimes, CHICAGO DAILY NEWS (Feb. 9, 1960), 2.

Strumm, Johannes: Training and Using Police Dogs in Berlin, MPJ, Vol.20 (July, 1951), 2.

U.S. Conference of Mayors: *The Use of Dogs in Police Work.* Washington, D.C., Research Reports, U.S. Conference of Mayors, 1960.

U.S. Dept. of the Air Force: *United States Air*

Force Sentry Dog Manual. Washington, D.C., Dept. of the Air Force, 1956.

U.S. Dept. of the Army: *Dogs and National Defense.* Washington, Dept. of the Army, Office of the Quartermaster General, 1958, 59-63.

———: *Military Dog Training and Employment.* Washington, Headquarters, Dept. of the Army, 1960.

Vllamos, James: The Hounds of Baltimore, ODS, Vol.28 (Sept., 1959), 24-27, 44-46.

Whitby, J. E.: Four-footed Policemen, POLICE, Vol.7, No.5 (May-June, 1963), 68-70; COSMOPOLITAN, Vol.39 (Sept., 1965), 515-518.

White Alsatian in the Metropolitan Police, THE ILLUSTRATED LONDON NEWS, Vol.222 (Mar. 7, 1953), 373.

———: *Dog Psychology: The Basis of Dog Training.* Springfield, Thomas, 1964.

———: Dog Training the Easy Way, POLICE, Vol.9, No.5 (May-June, 1965), 9.

Wilson, O. W.: The British Police, JCLC&PS, Vol.40 (Jan.-Feb., 1950), 642.

Chapter Four

PERSONNEL AND TRAINING ADMINISTRATION

PERSONNEL*

Adkins, Dorothy C., et al.: *Construction and Analysis of Achievement Texts.* Washington, U.S. Civil Service Commission, 1947.

American Bar Association: *Report of the Committee on Labor Relations of Governmental Employees.* Chicago, 1955.

American Management Association: *Aptitude Testing, Training, and Employee Development, No.128.* New York, American Management Assoc., 1949.

———: *The Human Relations Job of Personnel Management.* Personnel Series No.132. New York, American Management Association, 1950.

———: *Individualized Executive Selection, Training and Follow-up,* Personnel Series No.89. New York, American Management Assoc., 1945.

———: *Personnel: Maintaining Two-way Communication—Company Experiences and Techniques.* New York, American Management Association, 1950.

———: *Rating and Training Executives and Employees,* Personnel Series No.100. New York, American Management Association, 1946.

American Society of Planning Officials: *Manual of Recommended Personnel Standards in Public Planning.* Chicago, The Society, 1949.

Anastasi, Anne: *Psychological Testing,* 2nd Ed. New York, Macmillan, 1961.

Andrews, R. C.: Recruitment Program, L&O, Vol.9 (Oct., 1961).

Andrews, Rex R.: Police Recruiting as Geared to Available Manpower, TPY (1959).

Annals of the American Academy of Political and Social Science. Philadelphia. Issued bimonthly.

Appleby, Paul: *Big Democracy.* New York, Knopf, 1954. (A "must" for all students of public administration.)

Arkin, Joseph: How Your Pension Is Taxed, L&O, Vol.9 (May, 1961).

Arthur, Richard O.: Why Does Police Work Attract So Many Failures? L&O, Vol.12 (Sept., 1964), 62.

---

* This Section includes: Police Personnel Administration and Police Women.

Baker, Alton Wesley: *Sources of Information on Personnel Management and Labor Relations.* Columbus, Bureau of Business Research, Ohio State Univ. Press, 1951.

Baker, Helen: *Retirement Procedures Under Compulsory and Flexible Retirement Policies.* Princeton, Research Report Series No.86, Princeton Univ., Industrial Relations Section, 1952.

Barry, A. J., Bernauer, E. M., and Mole, P. A.: The Energies of Police Officers, POLICE, Vol.7, No.5 (May-June, 1963), 39-45.

Batson, Eleanor R., et al.: *Municipal Personnel Administration.* Chicago, International City Managers' Assoc., 1960.

Batson, Robert J.: *Employee Evaluation: a Review of Current Methods and a Suggested New Approach,* Personnel Report No.571, Chicago, Public Personnel Assoc., 1957.

———: *Employee Turnover Statistics: Collection, Analysis, Use,* Personnel No.17. Chicago, Public Personnel Assoc., 1956.

Bean, Kenneth L.: *Construction of Educational and Personnel Tests.* New York, McGraw-Hill, 1953.

Becker, Joseph N.: *The Problem of Abuse in Unemployment Benefits.* New York, Columbia Univ. Press, 1953.

Bellows, Roger: *Psychology of Personnel in Business and Industry.* Englewood Cliffs, Prentice-Hall, 1961.

Belsley, G. Lyle: *Federal Personnel Management in Transition.* Chicago, Public Administration Clearing House, 1953.

Berkowitz, Leonard: *Aggression—a Social Psychological Analysis.* New York, McGraw-Hill, 1950.

Betlach, R. A.: Performance Evaluation, TPC, Vol.30 (Feb., 1963), 16.

Bittner, Reign: Developing an Employee Merit-rating Procedure, PERSONNEL, Vol.25 (Jan., 1949), 275-291.

Blum, R. H.: Case Identification in Psychiatric Epidemiology; Methods and Problems, MMFQ, Vol.40 (1962), 254-88.

———: Police Personnel Selection in Europe, POLICE, Vol.5, No.4 (Mar.-Apr., 1961), 39-41, 71-72; No.5 (May-June, 1961), 32-34; No.6 (July-Aug., 1961), 72-74.

———: *Police Selection.* Springfield, Thomas, 1964.

———, **Goggin, W., Whitmore, E. J., and Pomeroy, W. J.**: A Further Study of Deputy Sheriff Selection Procedures, POLICE, Vol.6 1962), 77-79.

———, ———, ———, & ———: A Study in Deputy Sheriff Selection Procedure, PO-LICE, Vol.6 (1961), 59-63.

Bohart, Paul H.: Tucson Uses New Police Personnel Selection Methods, FBILEB, Vol.28 (Sept., 1959), 8-12.

Boynton, Paul W.: *Selecting the New Employee: Techniques of Employment Procedure.* New York, Harper, 1949.

Brattin, Barbara: The Dismissal Pattern in the Public Service, PPR, Vol.8 (Oct., 1947), 211-15.

Brereton, George H.: California Studies Mandatory Minimum Police Personnel Standards, POLICE, Vol.11, No.1 (Sept.-Oct., 1957), 25-28.

Bristow, Allen P.: A Comparative Examination of Performance Rating Forms Used by Police Agencies, POLICE, Vol.5, No.3 (Jan.-Feb., 1961), 18-21.

———: Training in the Evaluation of Police Personnel, POLICE, Vol.5, No.2 (Nov.-Dec., 1960), 17-20.

Broaded, C. H.: *Essentials of Management for Supervisors.* New York, Harper, 1947.

Brown, Albert N.: Recruiting, TPY (1957).

Buel, William D.: Items Scales and Rater's, PA (Sept.-Oct., 1962), 15-20.

Bureaucracy in America, THE ANNALS (Mar., 1954).

Burnham, Paul S., and Palmer, Stuart H.: *Counseling in Personnel Work. A Bibliography: 1945-1949.* Chicago, Public Administration Service, 1951.

Buros, Oscar Krisen (ed.): *The Fifth Mental Measurements Yearbook.* Highland Park, Gryphon, 1959.

Busse, Frank A.: Selection, SM (May, 1959), 13-18.

Cahn, Francis T.: *Federal Employees in War and Peace.* Washington, Brookings Institution, 1949.

Calhoon, Richard P.: *Problems in Personnel Administration.* New York, Harper & Bros., 1949.

Carami, Charles A.: Find Out What Your People Really Think, NAT.B (Mar., 1961), 74-79.

Caroll, Gil: Retirement City for Policemen, L&O, Vol.7 (Jan., 1959).

Cartwright, D., and Zander, A.: *Group Dynamics.* Evanston, Row, Peterson, 1963.

Case, Harry L.: *Personnel Policy in a Public Agency: the TVA Experience.* New York, Harper, 1955.

Catalog of Personnel Tests for Police and Fire Departments. Chicago, Public Personnel Association, 1965.

Cattell, Raymond B.: *Descriptions and Measurement of Personality.* New York, World Book, 1946. (One of the first books on personality testing.)

Caughley, J. G.: Correctional Psychology for Law Enforcement Officers, JCLC&PS, Vol.49, No.2 (1958-59), 184.

Cerney, J. V.: Foot Disability—A Crime That Doesn't Pay, POLICE, Vol.7, No.6 (July-Aug., 1963), 78-79.

———: Poor Posture in Policemen Basic Problem in Arthritis, POLICE, Vol.8, No.2 (Nov.-Dec., 1963), 37-39.

———: Trouble Afoot in Crime Detail, POLICE, Vol.7, No.4 (Mar.-Apr., 1963), 18-19.

Chapman, Samuel C.: Workshop: Personnel Leadership Development, TPY (1964).

———: Your Widow Faces the Future, L&O, Vol.13, No.5 (May, 1965), 30.

Case, Harry L.: *Personnel Policy in a Public Agency.* New York, Harper, 1955.

Chenoweth, James H.: Situational Tests—A New Attempt at Assessing Police Candidates, JCLC&PS, Vol.52, No.2 (July-Aug., 1961), 232.

Christopherson, Richard: *Regulating Political Activities of Public Employees,* Personnel Report No.543. Chicago, Public Personnel Assoc., 1954.

Chruden, Herbert J., and Sherman, Arthur W., Jr.: *Personnel Management.* Cincinnati, Southwestern, 1959.

Chwast, Jacob: The Selection of Personnel for a Police Juvenile Service, JCLC&PS, Vol.51, No.3 (Mar.-Apr., 1960-61), 357.

Civil Service Assembly of the United States and Canada: *The Elements of a Comprehensive Personnel Program,* Pub. No.CS26. Chicago, 1947.

———: *Longevity Pay Plans.* Chicago, 1953.

———: *Medical Examination for Public Employees.* Chicago, 1954.

———: *Placement and Probation in the Public Service.* Chicago, 1946.

CIVIL SERVICE JOURNAL. Washington, 1960. (The new periodical organ of the U.S. Civil Service Commission. Published quarterly. Valuable for its official source material as well as professional articles.)

Clairman, A. H.: Psychological Tests in Executive Selection, *Selected References* (Published periodically by Princeton University,

Industrial Relations Section), 1959. A short annotated listing of top works on the subject.

Cogshall, Fred J.: Standards in the Selection of Police Instructors, JCL&C, Vol.39, No.1 (Mar.-Apr., 1948-49), 99-111.

Colarelli, Nick S.: A Method of Police Personnel Selection, JCLC&PS, Vol.55, No.2 (June, 1964), 287.

Commission of Inquiry on Public Service Personnel: *Better Government Personnel.* New York, the Report of the Commission, 1935.

Minutes of Evidence. Hearings in Washington, New York, Chicago, Minneapolis, St. Paul, Seattle, San Francisco, Los Angeles and Richmond.

A Bibliography of Civil Service and Personnel Administration. By Sarah Greer (Monograph 1).

Civil Service Abroad: Great Britain, Canada, France, Germany. By Leonard D. White, Charles H. Bland, Walter R. Sharp, and Fritz Morstein Marx (Monographs 2-5 in one volume).

Training Public Employees in Great Britain. By Harvey Walker (Monograph 6).

Problems of the American Public Service. (Monographs 7-11 in one volume).

"Responsible Government Service Under the American Constitution," by Carl J. Friedrich.

"Municipal Civil Service in the United States," by William C. Beyer.

"Employer and Employee in the Public Service," by Sterling D. Spero.

"Veteran Preference in the Public Service," by John F. Miller.

"Personnel Practices in Business and Governmental Organizations," by George A. Graham.

Government by Merit: an Analysis of the Problem of Government Personnel. By Lucius Wilmerding, Jr. (Monograph 12).

Commission on Organization of the Executive Branch of the Government: *Federal Personnel.* Washington, Task Force Report, Jan., 1949.

————: *Personnel Management: a Report to the Congress.* Washington, Feb., 1949.

————: *Personnel and Civil Service.* Washington, Feb., 1955.

————: *Task Force Report on Personnel and Civil Service.* Washington, Feb., 1955.

Coppock, Robert W., and Coppock, Barbara B.: *How to Recruit and Select Policemen and Firemen.* Chicago, Public Personnel Association, 1958.

Corson, John J.: *Executives for the Federal Service: a Program for Action in Time of Crisis.* New York, Columbia Univ. Press, 1952.

————: What Are the Special Problems of Obtaining Quality in Municipal Public Service? THE ANNALS (Aug., 1963), 51-60.

Cronbach, Lee J.: *Essential of Psychological Testing,* 2nd ed. New York, Harper, 1960.

Crowley, John C.: *Institutional Employee Maintenance.* Chicago, Public Administration Service, 1947.

————: Job Evaluation Methods in Salary Analysis, PPR, Vol.7 (Oct., 1946), 194-99.

Diagnostic Forced—Choice Personnel Evaluation. Columbus, Ohio State Highway Patrol.

Dickinson, Harold L.: Semantics: Its Application to Personnel Administration, PA (Jan., 1951), 8-14.

Dillman, Everett G.: Analyzing Police Recruitment and Retention Problems, POLICE, Vol.8, No.5 (May-June, 1964), 22-26.

Dooher, Joseph M., and Marquis: *Rating Employee and Supervisory Performance: a Manual of Merit Rating Techniques.* New York, American Management Assoc., 1950.

————, & **Marting, Elizabeth:** *Selection of Management Personnel.* New York, American Management Association, 1957.

Dotson, Arch: The Emerging Doctrine of Privilege in Public Employment, PAR (Spring, 1955).

Drake, Francis S.: *Manual of Employment Interviewing.* Research Report No.9, American Management Assoc., New York.

Dubois, P. H., and Watson, R. I.: The Selection of Patrolmen, JAP, Vol.34 (Feb., 1950), 90-95.

Dudek, Jack: Developments Affecting Police Personnel, TPY (1959).

Dudycha, G. J.: Rating and Testing Policemen, POLICE, Vol.1, No.1 (Sept.-Oct., 1956), 37-49.

Dunhill, Frank: *The Civil Service: Some Human Aspects.* London, Allen & Unwin, 1956.

Dyas, Robert V.: The Mental Miasma—A Police Personnel Problem, POLICE, Vol.3, No.6 (July-Aug., 1959), 65-70; Vol.4, No.1 (Sept.-Oct., 1959), 35-39.

Earl, David M.: Item Analysis in Public Personnel Testing, PPR, Vol.10 (Apr., 1949), 79-85.

East, Edmund R.: Classification Reception Center, JCL&C, Vol.36, No.4 (1945-46), 243.

Ells, Ralph W.: *The Basic Abilities System of Job Evaluation.* Wisconsin Commercial Reports, Vol.111, No.2, Madison University of Wisconsin, 1951.

Elsbree, Willard S., and Reutter, Edmund E.: *Staff Personnel in the Public Schools.* Englewood Cliffs, Prentice-Hall, 1954.

Erickson, C. E.: *The Counseling Interview.* New York, Prentice-Hall, 1950.

Evans, J. J., Jr.: *A Program for Personnel Administration.* New York, McGraw-Hill, 1954.

Fay, Lew, and Peterson, Gordon W.: *Medical Examinations for Public Employees.* Chicago, Civil Service Assembly, 1954.

Fenlason, Anne F.: *Essentials of Interviewing.* New York, Harper, 1952.

Fields, Harold: An Analysis of the Use of the Group Oral Interview, PERSONNEL, Vol.27 (May, 1951), 480-86.

Flanagan, John C.: Principles and Procedures in Evaluating Performance, PERSONNEL, Vol.28 (Mar., 1952), 373-86.

——, Adkins, Dorothy C., and Cadwell, Dorothy G. B.: *Major Developments in Examining Methods.* Chicago, Civil Service Assembly, 1950.

Fleetwood, Charles: Leadership Development in Business, TPY (1964).

Flippo, Edwin B.: *Principles of Personnel Management.* New York, McGraw-Hill, 1961.

Frost, Thomas M.: Selection Methods for Police Recruits, JCLC&PS, Vol.46 (May, 1955), 135-145.

Frym, Marcel J. D.: Character Underwriters, POLICE, Vol.1, No.5 (May-June, 1957), 28-31.

Gallati, Robert R. J.: Police Personnel Testing Experience, TPY (1959).

Garmire, Bernard L.: Personnel Leadership Development, TPY (1964).

——: Progress in Eroding Residence Requirements, TPC (Apr., 1961), 35.

Gaudet, Frederick J.: *Labor Turnover: Calculation and Cost.* Research Study No.39, New York, American Management Association, 1960.

Gehlmann, Frederick, Ferguson, L. W., and Scott, John F.: *Personality Tests—Uses and Limitations.* Personnel Report No.561, Chicago, Public Personnel Association, 1956.

Germann, A. C.: Hurdles to Professional Police Competence, POLICE, Vol.11, No.2 (Nov.-Dec., 1957), 51-53.

——: The Michigan Police Personnel Management Survey, POLICE, Vol.1, No.4 (Mar.-Apr., 1957), 34-36.

——: *Police Personnel Management.* Springfield, Thomas, 1958.

——: *Police Personnel Management, a Study and Critical Survey of Selected Michigan Municipal Police Agencies and Suggested Minimum Program.* Unpublished Doctoral Dissertation, U. of Southern Cal., Los Angeles, June, 1956.

——: The Strict Seniority System, POLICE, Vol.2, No.3 (Jan.-Feb., 1958), 19-21.

Ginsberg, Eli: Spot and Encourage Initiative, NAT.B (Apr., 1961), 74-78.

Goheen, Howard W., and Kavruck, Samuel: *Selected References on Test Construction, Mental Test Theory, and Statistics.* Washington, U.S. Civil Service Comm., 1950.

Gomberg, William: *A Labor Union Manual on Job Evaluation,* 2nd ed. Chicago, Roosevelt College, Labor Education Division, 1948.

Goode, Cecil E. (ed.): *The Federal Career Service: a Look Ahead.* Pamphlet No.8, Washington, Society for Personnel Administration, 1954.

——: Personnel Opinions, PPR (Apr., 1954), 95-96.

——: *Personnel Research Frontiers.* Chicago, Public Personnel Association, 1958.

Goodenough, Florence I.: *Mental Testing.* New York, Rinehart, 1949.

Gourley, G. Douglas: Recognition and Status for Rank and File Policemen, JCL&C, Vol.40, No.1 (May-June, 1959), 75.

——: State Standards for Local Police Recruitment and Training, JCLC&PS, Vol.53 (Dec., 1962), 522-25.

Gray, Robert D. (ed.): *Frontiers of Industrial Relations.* Pasadena, Calif. Institute of Technology, 1959.

Green, Edward B.: *Measurements of Human Behavior,* Rev. Ed. New York, Odyssey, 1952.

Greenwalt, Crawford H.: *The Uncommon Man.* New York, McGraw-Hill, 1959.

Gugas, Chris: A Scientifically Accurate Method of Personnel Screening, POLICE, Vol.6, No.2 (Nov.-Dec., 1961), 19-24.

Hagerty, Philip E.: *The Placement Interview.* Personnel Brief No.18, Public Personnel Association, Chicago.

——: Why Not Take the "Rating" out of Performance Rating? PPR, Vol.16 (Jan., 1955), 39-44.

Hall, Calvin C., and Lindzey, Gardner: *Theories of Personality.* New York, Wiley, 1957.

Hall, Milton, and Mallard, William P.: Making Employer—Employee Cooperation Practicable, PERSONNEL (Jan., 1946).

Halsey, George D.: *Handbook of Personnel Management.* New York, Harper, 1953.

——: *Selecting and Inducting Employees.* New York, Harper, 1951.

Hanman, Bert: *Physical Capabilities and Job Placement.* Stockholm, Nordisk, Rotogravyr, 1951.

Hart, Wilson R.: *Collective Bargaining in the Federal Civil Service.* New York, Harper, 1961.

Hawthorne, J. W.: Crisis in Recruitings, TPC, Vol.29 (May, 1962), 10.

Hersh, Charles M.: *College Seniors and Federal Employment.* Washington, American University, 1953.

Hewitt, William H.: *British Police Administration.* Springfield, Thomas, 1965.

Holcomb, Richard: *Selection of Police Officers.* Iowa City, University of Iowa Press, 1946.

Hoogenboom, Ari: *Outlawing the Spoils—a History of the Civil Service Reform Movement, 1865-1883.* Urbana, Univ. of Ill. Press, 1961.

Hoover, J. Edgar: Urges Help for Assaulted Officers, TPC (Dec., 1961), 20.

Hooper, F. E.: Personnel Rotation, TPC, Vol.31 (Feb., 1964), 8.

Hubbard, Henry: *The Elements of a Comprehensive Personnel Program.* Chicago, Civil Service Assn., 1947.

Hubers, Donald F.: Projective Technique in Personnel Selection, PERSONNEL JOURNAL (Dec., 1963), 563-69.

Institute for Training in Municipal Administration: *Municipal Personnel Administration.* Chicago, International City Managers' Assoc., 1947.

International City Managers' Association: *Municipal Year Book.* Chicago, Published Annually.

Jacobs, David L. G.: Employment Interviews, TDR, Vol.7 (July, 1959), 4.

Jenkins, James J., and Paterson, Donald G. (eds.): *Studies in Individual Differences.* New York, Appleton, 1961.

Jones, Helen L.: *Personnel Management.* Los Angeles, Hayness Foundation, 1952.

Jucius, Michael J.: *Personnel Management,* 4th ed. Homewood, Irwin, 1959.

Jurgensen, Clifford E., Lopez, Felix M., and Richards, Kenneth E.: *Employee Performance Appraisal Re-examined.* Personnel Report No.613. Chicago, Public Personnel Assoc., 1961.

Kahn, Robert L., and Cannell, Charles F.: *The Dynamics of Interviewing.* New York, Wiley, 1957.

Krammerer, Gladys: *Impact of Way on Federal Personnel Administration, 1939-1945.* Lexington, Univ. of Kentucky Press, 1951.

Kaplan, H. Eliot: Legal Aspects of Public Employee Relations, PPR, Vol.10 (Jan., 1949), 40-42.

Kates, S. L.: Rorschach Responses, Strong Blank Scales and Job Satisfaction among Police-men, JAP (1950). (Study of 25 New York City Policemen.)

Kelley, D. M.: Psychiatry in Police Recruitment, TPY (1955).

Kentucky Recruits Trooper Cadets, TPC, Vol.30 (Oct., 1963), 43.

Kephart, Newell C.: *The Employment Interview in Industry.* New York, McGraw-Hill, 1952.

Kilpatrick, F. P., Cummings, Milton C., Jr., and Jennings, M. Kent: *The Image of the Federal Service.* Washington, Brookings Institution, 1962.

Kimball, Raymond A.: The Civil Service Selection of Policemen in Denver, Colorado. JCL&C, Vol.37 (Nov.-Dec., 1946), 333-45.

Kindall, Alva F.: *Personnel Administration: Principles and Cases.* Homewood, Irwin, 1961.

Knowles, William: *Personnel Management: a Human Relations Approach.* New York, American, 1955.

Kyte, Aileen L.: Employee Motivation, CBBMR (Sept., 1963), 7-12.

Laird, Donald A.: *The Technique of Personnel Analysis.* New York, McGraw-Hill, 1945.

Lang, Theodore H.: Role of Central Personnel Agency in Police Personnel Problems, JCLC&PS, Vol.51, No.4 (Mar.-Apr., 1960-61), 471.

Lanham, E.: *Job Evaluation.* New York, McGraw-Hill, 1955.

Lawsche, C.: *Principles of Personnel Testing.* New York, McGraw-Hill, 1948.

Liebers, Arthur: *The Civil Service and Promotional Police Manual.* Yonkers, Alicat Bookshop Press, 1947.

Life Office Management Association Clerical Study Committee: *Clerical Salary Determination,* New York, 1948.

Lilenthal, David E.: Modern Tools for a Modern Job:. PA, Vol.7 (Apr., 1945), 1-5.

Lomax, Richard W.: Prestige Values in Public Employment in the United States and Canada, PA, Vol.12 (Jan., 1950), 12-18.

Los Angeles City Civil Service: *Medical Standards for Police and Fire Service.* Los Angeles, 1962. (Mimeographed.)

Lothian, Robert A.: Operation of a Police Merit System, THE ANNALS, Vol.291 (Jan., 1954), 97-106.

McCann, Forbes E.: *The Flexible Passing Point.* Chicago, Public Personnel Assoc., 1965.

———, **Cunningham, William A., and Holley, Clifford S.:** *Physical Condition Tests in the Selection of Public Employees.* Chicago, Public Personnel Assoc., 1965.

McCarthy, John P.: *Veteran's Preference in Pub-*

lic Employment. Unpublished thesis, Univ. of Chicago, Dec., 1947.

McConnell, Ira E.: An Application of Test Item Analysis, PPR, Vol.8 (Oct., 1947), 205-10.

McCrensky, Edward: Personnel Management— Soviet Style, PA (Sept.-Oct., 1960), 44-55.

Mahler, W. R.: *Twenty Years of Merit Rating, 1926-1946*. New York, Psychological Corp., 1947.

Maier, Norman R. F., and Danielson, Lee E.: An Evaluation of Two Approaches to Discipline in Industry, JAP (Oct., 1956), 319-23.

Mailick, Sidney: Public Service Prestige: Problem and Paradox, PPR, Vol.10 (July, 1949), 155-62.

Mandell, Milton M.: *The Employment Interview*. Research Study No.47, American Management Assoc., 1961.

————: *Employment Interviewing Personnel Methods*, Series No.5. Washington, D.C., U.S. Civil Service Comm. 1956.

Marryott, Frank J.: What of "Merit Rating Systems" and "Assigned Risk Plans"? POLICE, Vol.9, No.1 (Sept.-Oct., 1964), 91-95.

Massarik, Fred, Weschler, Irving, and Tannenbaum, Robert: Evaluating Efficiency Rating Systems Through Experiment, PA, Vol.14 (Jan., 1951), 42-47.

Matarazzo, Joseph D., *et al.*: Characteristics of Successful Policeman and Fire Applicants, JAP (Apr., 1964), 122-23.

Mee, John F.: *Personnel Handbook*. New York, Ronald, 1951.

Meyer, Hetbert H., and Worbois, Greydon M.: The Use of Tests in the Selection of Supervisors, POLICE, Vol.2, No.5 (May-June, 1958), 57-60.

Miller, J. Guy: We Pay Our Policemen $6,000 per Year, POLICE, Vol.7, No.6 (July-Aug., 1963), 63-64.

Mingle, George: Police Personnel Evaluation and Development, JCL&C, Vol.36, No.4 (1945-46), 277.

Misner, Gordon E.: Mobility and the Establishment of a Career System in Police Personnel Administration, JCLC&PS, Vol.54, No.4 (1963), 529.

Mitchell, Bernice Fry: *Recruiting Ideas That Get Results*. Chicago, Public Personnel Assoc., 1965.

Moore, Elon H.: *The Nature of Retirement*. New York, Macmillan, 1959.

Morman, Robert R., Hankey, Richard O., Kennedy, Phyliss, and Heywood, Harold L.: Predicting State Traffic Officer Performance with TVA Selection System Theoretical

Scoring Keys, POLICE, Vol.9, No.5 (May-June, 1965), 70.

Mosher, Frederick C.: Is Veteran Preference the Answer? PA (Jan., 1946).

————, & Sayer, Wallace S.: *An Agenda for Research in Public Personnel Administration*. Washington, National Planning Association, 1959.

Mosher, W. E., Kingsley, J. D., and Stahl, O. G.: *Public Personnel Administration*, 3rd Ed. New York, Harper, 1950.

Mullineaux, Jewel A.: An Evaluation of the Predictors Used to Select Patrolmen, PPR, Vol.16 (Apr., 1955), 84-86.

Municipal Finance Officers' Association: *Public Employee Retirement Administration*. Chicago, Municipal Finance Officers' Assoc., 1951.

————: *Retirement Plans for Public Employees*. Chicago, The Association, 1958.

Municipal Manpower Commission: Governmental Manpower for Tomorrow's Cities, THE ANNALS (Aug., 1963), 197-209.

Murray, Robert V.: Recruiting—A Balanced Formula, TPY (1957).

National Civil Service League: *Employee Organization in the Public Service*. New York, National Civil Service League, 1946.

————: *Report of the Committee on Veteran Preference*. New York, The League, 1945.

National Industrial Conference Board: *Personnel Administration in the Small Company*, Studies in Personnel Policy No.117, New York, 1951.

National Safety Council: *Industrial Safety and Health: a Bibliography*. Chicago, National Safety Council, 1945.

Nelson, Dalmas H.: Public Employees and the Right to Engage in Political Activity, *Vanderbilt Law Review* (Dec., 1955), 27-50; and Political Expression Under the Hatch Act and the Problem of Statutory Ambiguity, MIDWEST JOURNAL OF POLITICAL SCIENCE (Feb., 1958), 76-88.

Nigro, Felix: *Public Personnel Administration*. New York, Holt, 1959.

Northcott, C. H.: *Personnel Management: Its Scope and Practice*. London, Pitman, 1953.

O'Connor, G. W.: *Survey of Selection Methods*. Washington, IACP, 1962.

O'Keefe, Jack A.: Police Applicant Screening, TPY (1963).

Ocheltree, Keith: *Police Cadet Programs*. Chicago, Public Personnel Assoc., 1965.

Oglesby, T. W.: Use of Emotional Screening in the Selection of Police Applicants, PPR,

Vol.20 (1959), 191-96; POLICE, Vol.2, No.3 (Jan.-Feb., 1958), 49-53.

Otis, Jay L., and Leukart, Richard H.: *Job Evaluation: Basis for Sound Wage Administration*, 2nd Ed. New York, Prentice-Hall, 1954.

Ozmon, Nat P.: Policemen's Indemnification Statute, JCL&C, Vol.44, No. 3 (Sept.-Oct., 1953), 343-48.

Parson, Richard E.: Praise Reappraised, HBR (Sept.-Oct., 1963), 61-66.

Peacock, William G.: Police Selection and Training, PJ, Vol. 44 (Nov. 2, 1962), 4-14.

Peres, Sherwood H., and Chiaramonte R. M.: *Diagnostic Forced-Choice Personnel Evaluation*. A report prepared for the Ohio State Highway Patrol, Columbus, 1958.

Perkins, Rollin M.: *Police Examinations*. Brooklyn, Foundation Press, 1947.

Perry, John: When the Boss Interviews, PERSONNEL (July-Aug., 1960), 67-72.

PERSONNEL. Published bi-monthly by the American Management Association, 333 West 42nd Street, New York, N.Y.

PERSONNEL ADMINISTRATION. Published monthly, except July and August, by the Society for Personnel Administration, 5506 Connecticut Ave., N.W., Washington, D.C.

PERSONNEL ADMINISTRATION ABSTRACTS. Washington, D.C. A bi-monthly publication of brief abstracts of current books and periodical articles. Also includes selected cases and exhibits.

Personnel Opinions, PPR (Jan., 1961). (The topic is the question: "Is it desirable as a matter of broad public policy to facilitate mobility in the public service by enabling employees to transfer retirement credits from one retirement system to another?" Responses of educators and practitioners were all in the affirmative.)

Personnel Polices and Practices. New York, Prentice-Hall, 1956.

PERSONNEL PSYCHOLOGY. Washington, 1948 —a privately published quarterly which presents a very considerable contribution to the study of the application of psychology to work situations, Most of the articles are based on original research.

Pigors, Paul, and Myers, Charles A.: *Personnel Administration*, 4th Ed. New York, McGraw-Hill, 1961.

———, ———, & Malm, F. T. (eds.): *Readings in Personnel Administration*, 2nd Ed. New York, McGraw-Hill, 1959.

Pomeroy, Wesley A.: Supplementing Sworn Personnel as Seen by a Police Administrator.

Presentations before the Administrative Institute for Law Enforcement Officers, on Dec. 7, 1962, Peace Officers Assn., of Calif.

Powell, Norman J.: *Personnel Administration in Government*. Englewood Cliffs, Prentice-Hall, 1956.

President's Commission on Veterans' Pensions: *Veterans' Benefits in the United States: a Report to the President*. Washington, 1956.

Princeton Univ., Industrial Relations Section: The Shorter Work Week, *Selected References*, No.75 (May, 1957).

Probst, John B.: *Measuring and Rating Employees Value*. New York, Ronald Press, 1947.

Public Administration Service: *Counseling in Personnel Work: a Bibliography*. Chicago, Public Administration, 1951.

———: *Placement and Probation in the Public Service: Reports to the Assembly by the Committee on Placement in the Public Service and the Committee on Probation in the Public Service*. Chicago, 1946.

PUBLIC PERSONNEL REVIEW. The quarterly journal of the Civil Service Assembly of the United States and Canada, Room 456, 1313 East 60th Street, Chicago, Illinois.

Radcliffe, S. B.: Performance Evaluation and Inspection for Ohio State Troopers, TPC, Vol.30 (Feb., 1963), 36.

Rankin, James H.: Preventive Psychiatry in the Los Angeles Police Department, POLICE, Vol.1, No.6 (July-Aug., 1957), 24-29.

———: Psychiatric Screening of Police Recruits, PPR, Vol.20 (1959), 191-196.

Reiner, H.: Another View on Psychiatric Screening of Police Recruits, PPR, Vol.21 (1960), 41-55.

Reining, Henry, Jr.: *Cases of Public Personnel Administration*. Dubuque, Brown, 1949.

Robson, Wm. A. (ed.): *The Civil Service in Britian and France*. New York, Macmillan, 1956.

Routh, Thomas A.: A Concept of Motivation, PJ (June, 1963), 294-96, 301.

Rules and Regulations, Commission on Peace Officer Standards and Training, Oct. 23, 1960, and subsequent directives in compliance with Sections 13506 and 13510 of the *Penal Code of California*.

Rush, A. C.: Better Police Personnel Selection, TPC, Vol.30 (Sept., 1963), 18.

Rynearson, Edward H.: Obesity (The Overweight Problem), POLICE, Vol.1, No.1 (Sept.-Oct., 1956), 56-57.

Sollenberger, David R.: Controlling Gifts Acceptance, PA (July-Aug., 1963), 39-45, 64.

Sandell, Roland: Using Basic Human Drives to Get the Job Done, PJ (Nov., 1963), 508-511.

Santa Clara County: Medical Standards for Deputy Sheriff, Unpublished, 1956.

Sayre, Wallace S.: *Federal Government Service,* 2nd Ed. Englewood Cliffs, Prentice-Hall, 1965.

Schneckloth, Merle R.: Do Honest Employees React Dishonestly? CR (Calif.) (Mar.-Apr., 1963), 14-18.

Schrader, Albert: *Personnel Management: New Perspectives.* Bulletin No.29, Ann Arbor, Univ. of Michigan, School of Business Admin., 1961.

Schuler, Stanley: Use Gripes to Build Morale, NAT.B (Feb., 1961), 96-98.

Scott, Roberta: *The Group Oral Test in Selecting Public Employees.* Chicago, Civil Service Assembly, 1950.

Scott, Walter D., Clothier, Robert C., and Spriegel, William R.: *Personnel Management,* 6th Ed., New York, McGraw-Hill, 1961.

Siegel, Saul M.: A Method of Police Personnel Selection, JCLC&PS, Vol.55, No.2 (June, 1964), 387.

Skousen, W. Cleon: A Chief Surveys His Central Services, L&O, Vol.12 (May, 1964).

———: What About a Police Reserve Corps, L&O, Vol.9 (Sept., 1961).

Smith, Bruce J.: The Policeman's Hire, THE ANNALS, Vol.291 (Jan., 1954), 119-126.

Snibbe, Richard H.: A Personnel Relations Program for Police Departments, unpublished Master's Thesis, Dept. of Criminology, Fresno State College, 1963.

Sperhoff, B. J.: Scripts vs. Roleplaying, PJ (Jan., 1954), 305-06.

Spero, Sterling D.: *Government as Employer.* New York, Remsen, 1948.

Spiegelblatt, Henry: *Charter Provisions for Personnel Administration in Michigan Cities.* Ann Arbor, Bureau of Govt., Institution of Public Administration, Univ. of Mich. Press, 1955.

Stahl, O. Glenn: Perspective on Promotion Policy, PPR (July, 1954), 115-22.

———: *Public Personnel Administration,* 5th Ed. New York, Harper & Row, 1962.

———: Security of Tenure: Career or Sinecure, THE ANNALS (Mar., 1954), 45-56.

Stewart, Nathaniel: Keep Morale High, NAT.B (Mar., 1963), 70-78.

Stockford, Lee, and Bissell, H. W.: Factors Involved in Establishing a Merit Rating Scale, PERSONNEL, Vol.26 (Sept., 1949), 94-116.

Stone, C. Harold, and Kendall, William E.:

Effective Personnel Selection Procedures, 2nd Ed. Englewood Cliffs, Prentice-Hall, 1956.

Stottler, Richard H.: Police Personnel—A Beginning Without an End, TPY (1961).

Stover, Robert: The Minnesota Cost of Living Pay Plan, PPR, Vol.9 (July, 1948), 133-37.

Strauss, George, and Sayles, Lenord R.: *Personnel: the Human Problems of Management.* Englewood Cliffs, Prentice-Hall, 1960.

Stromsen, Karl E., and Dreese, Mitchell: Attitudes of NIPA Interns Towards a Career in the Federal Service, PAR (Autumn, 1950), 254-61.

Super, Donald E.: *Appraising Vocational Fitness.* New York, Harper, 1949.

Thorndike, R. L.: *Test and Measurement Techniques.* New York, Wiley, 1949.

———: *Personnel Selection.* New York, Wiley, 1949.

———, **and Hagen, Elizabeth:** *Ten Thousand Careers.* New York, Wiley, 1959.

Torgerson, Warren S.: *Theory and Methods of Scaling.* New York, Wiley, 1958.

Torpey, William G.: *Public Personnel Management.* New York, Van Nostrand, 1953.

Trull, Samuel G.: Strategies of Effective Interviewing, HBR (Jan.-Feb., 1964), 89-94.

U.S. Civil Service Commission: *A Bibliography of Public Personnel Administration Literature.* Washington, 1956—Supplements Nos.1-6, 1957-62. (A most detailed bibliography on the subject.)

———: *Biography of an Ideal,* prepared by Charles Cooke, Washington, 1958.

———: *Building Better Promotion Programs.* Personnel Management Series No.2, Washington, 1958.

———: *The Civil Service Recruiter.* (A periodical news sheet on recruiting developments and events in the federal service, not containing job information for the applicant but illustrating recruitment methods and success.)

———: *Evaluating Your Personnel Management.* Personnel Management Series No.6, Washington, Oct., 1954.

———: *Federal Employment Statistics Bulletin,* published monthly. A report on the location and turnover of federal manpower.

———: *Federal Personnel Manual.* Washington, D.C., Govt. Printing Office, 1951.

———: *The Government Personnel System.* Personnel Management Series No.4, Washington, D.C., 1960.

———: *History of Veteran Preference in Federal*

Employment, 1865-1955. Washington, U.S. Govt. Printing Office, 1955.

————: *The Older Worker in the Federal Service.* Washington, Govt. Printing Office, 1961.

————: *Pay Structure of the Federal Civil Service.* Washington, published annually.

————: *Position Classification.* Personnel Bibliography Series No.1, Washington, U.S. Govt. Printing Office, 1960.

————: *Rating Unassembled Examinations for Scientific, Professional, Technical, and Administrative Positions.* Federal Personnel Manual Supp., 337-76, Washington, Govt. Printing Office.

————: *Recognizing Employees Through Incentive Awards.* Washington, Govt. Printing Office, 1954.

————: *Recruitment for the Public Service.* Personnel Bibliography Series No.3, Washington, Govt. Printing Office, 1961.

————: *A Report on How People Are Recruited, Examined, and Appointed in the Competitive Civil Service.* Washington, Govt. Printing Office, 1959.

————: *The Role of the Civil Service Commission in Federal Employment,* Pamphlet No.52, Washington, Govt. Printing Office, 1955.

U.S. Congress: *Organization, Functions and Relative Costs of Personnel Offices.* House Rep. No.2198, 8th Congress, 2nd Session, Washington, 1948.

————: *Senate Committee on Retirement Policy for Federal Personnel.* Sen. Document No.89, 83rd Congress, 2nd Session, Washington, 1954.

U.S. Dept. of the Army: *Performance Ratings.* Washington, Govt. Printing Office, 1949.

U.S. Dept. of Health, Education, and Welfare: *Directory of State Merit Systems.* Washington, published annually.

————, **Division of State Merit Systems:** *Merit System Methods.* A monthly news sheet on state personnel practices.

————: *Problems of Mandatory and Variable Retirement Ages in State Employment.* Washington, U.S. Govt. Printing Office, 1954.

U.S. Dept. of Labor: *Manpower-Challenge of the 1960's.* Washington, U.S. Govt. Printing Office, 1960.

————, **Bureau of Labor Statistics:** *Wartime Employment, Production and Conditions of Work in Shipyards.* Bulletin No. 824, Washington, U.S. Govt. Printing Office, 1945.

U.S. Employment Service: *Industrial Job Evaluation Systems.* Washington, U.S. Govt. Printing Office, 1947.

U.S. Naval Institute: *Personnel Administration at the Executive Level.* Annapolis, U.S. Naval Institute, 1948.

U.S. Office of Strategic Services, Assessment Staff: *Assessment of Men: Selection of Personnel for OSS.* New York, Rinehart, 1948.

U.S. Public Health Service: *Employee Health Education Program.* Washington, Govt. Printing Office, 1945.

Van Riper, Paul P.: *History of the United States Civil Service.* Evanston, Row, Peterson, 1958.

Vernon, Philip E.: *The Measurement of Abilities,* Rev. Ed. London, Univ. of London, 1947.

Viteles, Morris B.: Psychological Methods in the Selection of Policemen in Europe, THE ANNALS, Vol.146 (1949), 160-65.

————: *Motivation and Morale in Industry.* New York, Norton, 1953.

Von Mol, L. J.: *Effective Procedures for Handling Employee Grievances.* Chicago, Civil Service Assembly, 1953.

Wahlen, Howard: Special Pay Status for Police, TPC, Vol.29, No.6 (June, 1962), 42.

Warner, W. Lloyd, Van Riper, Paul P., Martin, Norman H., and Collins, Orvis F.: Profiles of Government Executives, *Business Topics* (Michigan State Univ.) (Autumn, 1961), 13-24.

Warren, B. B. *et al.: Advances in Methods of Personnel Evaluation: Rating Management Jobs; Seniority vs. Merit: Testing.* New York, American Management Assoc., 1947.

Watkins, Gordon S., Dodd, Paul A., McNaughton, Wayne L., and Prason, Paul: *The Management of Personnel and Labor Relations,* 2nd Ed. New York, McGraw-Hill, 1950.

Webster, E. C.: Decision Making in Employment Interviews, PA, Vol.22 (1959), 15.

Wechsler, David: *The Range of Human Capacities,* 2nd Ed. Baltimore, Williams & Wilkins, 1952.

Weston, Paul B., and McCann, Harry P.: *Police Promotion Quizzer.* Springfield, Thomas, 1959.

White House Government on Scientists and Engineers for Federal Government Programs: *Survey of Attitudes of Scientists and Engineers in Government and Industry.* Washington, Government Printing Office, 1957.

White, Leonard D. (ed.): *The Federalists: The Jacksonians: The Republican Era.* New

York, Macmillan, 1958. (Unexcelled for historical insight.)

——: *Introduction to the Study of Public Administration.* 4th Ed. New York, Macmillan, 1955.

Whyte, William H., Jr.: *The Organization Man.* New York, Harper, 1956.

Williams, Edgar G.: *Cases and Problems in Personnel and Industrial Relations.* New York, Ronald, 1955.

Wilson, D. H.: The Function of Psychiatry in a Municipal Law Enforcement Agency, AJPSY, Vol.116 (1960), 870-72.

Wilson, O. W.: Address delivered before the International Association Chiefs of Police in Los Angeles, Calif., Sept., 1962.

——: Problems in Police Personnel Administration, JCLC&PS, Vol.43, No.6 (Mar.-Apr., 1953), 840.

——: Toward a Better Merit System, THE ANNALS, Vol.291 (Jan., 1954), 87-95.

Wood, Dorothy Adkins: *Test Construction.* Columbus, Merrill, 1960.

Yoder, Dale: *Personnel Management and Industrial Relations.* New York, Prentice-Hall, 1948.

——: *Personnel Principles and Policies—Modern Manpower Management.* New York, Prentice-Hall, 1952.

Zell, Anthony: A Further Inquiry into the Group Oral., PPR, Vol.14 (1953), 55-59.

Policewomen

Clifford, Alice E.: The Policewoman in Family Problems, TPY (1959).

Fagerstrom, Dorothy: Make the Most of Every Opportunity, L&O, Vol.8, No.11 (1960), 54.

——: Practical Handbag for Policewomen, L&O, Vol.12 (Feb., 1964).

Higgins, Lois: A Career in Law Enforcement for Women, POLICE, Vol.6, No.5 (May-June, 1962), 46-49.

——: Golden Anniversary of Women in Police Service, L&O, Vol.8, No.8 (1960).

——: The Policewoman, POLICE, Vol.3, No.2 (Nov.-Dec., 1958), 66-69.

——: *Policewoman's Manual.* Springfield, Thomas, 1961.

——: Policewoman's Seminar, TPC, Vol.29, No.1 (Jan., 1962), 33.

——: Women in Law Enforcement, L&O, Vol.10, No.8 (Aug., 1962), 18.

Leevy, J. Roy: The Role of the Police Matron, JCL&C, Vol.39, No.4 (Mar.-Apr., 1948-49), 538.

Melchionne, Theresa M.: Policewomen in the Investigative Function, TPY (1960).

Olson, Marilyn G.: Women in Police Work, TPY (1957).

Owens, James M.: Policewoman in the Line, POLICE, Vol.3, No.1 (Sept.-Oct., 1958), 21.

Salzbrenner, Dorothy: Military Policewomen, L&O, Vol.11, No.2 (Feb., 1963).

Shpritzer, Felicia: A Case for the Promotion of Policewomen in the City of New York, POLICE, Vol.5, No.6 (July-Aug., 1961), 57-60.

Tenney, Evabel: Women's Work in Law Enforcement, JCL&C, Vol.44, No.2 (July-Aug., 1952), 239-46.

U.S. Federal Security Agency, National Advisory Police Committee on Social Protection: *Techniques in Law Enforcement in the Use of Policewomen with Special Reference to Social Protection.* Washington, D.C., the Agency, 1945.

Williams, Carol M.: *The Organization and Practices of Policewomen's Divisions in the United States.* Detroit, National Training School of Public Service, 1946.

TRAINING*
Arrest, Search and Seizure

Alexander, Clarence: *The Law of Arrest.* Buffalo, Dennis & Co., 1949 (2 Vols.).

Allen, Francis A.: The Exclusionary Rule in the American Law of Search and Seizure, JCLC&PS, Vol.52, No.3 (May-June, 1961), 246.

---

* This section includes: Arrest, Search and Seizure; Civil Rights, Liberties and Human Relations; Courts; Criminal Law; Military Law; Riots and Training and Education.

Are We Handcuffing Our Police, reprint from article printed in LOS ANGELES EXAMINER, Sept. 27, 28, 29, and Oct., 1, 1959.

Arrest by Force Renders Confession Inadmissible, JCLC&PS, Vol.46 (1955-56), 600.

Arrest by State Officer Insufficient to Render Illegally Seized Evidence Inadmissible, JCLC&PS, Vol.46 (1955-56), 365.

Arrest-Search-Seizure—The Role of the Police in Protection of Human Rights, TPC, Vol.31 (May, 1964), 31.

Barnett, Elliot B., Tresolini, Rocco, and Taylor, Richard W.: Arrest With Warrant: Extent and Social Implications, JCLC&PS, Vol.46 (1955-56), 187-98.

Barth, Alan: *The Price of Liberty.* New York, Viking, 1961.

Blight of Our Nation's Capitol, USN&WR (Feb. 18, 1963), 37.

Brannon, B. C.: The Leash on Law Enforcement, TPC, Vol.31 (Mar., 1964), 38.

Brown, L. E.: The Escobedo Doctrine, L&O, Vol.13 (Apr., 1965), 80.

Burger, Warren E.: External Checks—Views of Jurist, TPY (1965).

California Dept. of Education, Bureau of Trade and Industrial Education: *Law of Arrest.* Sacramento, 1949.

California State Peace Officers' Training Series: *The Law of Arrest, Search & Seizure,* No.1. Sacramento, Calif. State Dept. of Ed., 1964.

Cantey, R. C.: *The Law of Search and Seizure.* Athens, Univ. of Georgia Press, 1957.

Civil Action for False Arrest and Imprisonment, JCLC&PS, Vol.46 (1955-56), 913.

Clark, Tom C.: We Seek Not Efficient Tyranny, But Effective Freedom, TPY (1965).

Cogan, John: *Law of Search and Seizure.* Cook County, Ill., States Attorney Office.

———: *Law of Search and Seizure.* Dobbs Ferry, Oceana, 1950.

Dax, Hubert E., and Tibbs, Brooke, *Arrest, Search and Seizure.* Milwaukee, Hammersmith, 1950.

Damages in Action for False Arrest and Imprisonment, JCLC&PS, Vol.46 (1955-56), 429.

Diamond, Harry (ed.): *Readings in Arrest, Search & Seizure.* Los Angeles, L.A. State College, Dept. of Police Science & Admin. (Paperback).

Dowling, Donald C.: Escobedo and Beyond: The Need for a Fourteenth Amendment Code of Criminal Procedure, JCLC&PS, Vol.56 (June, 1965), 143-57.

Flynn, John L.: The State Exclusionary Rule as a Deterrent Against Unreasonable Search and Seizure, JCLC&PS, Vol.45 (1954-55), 697-707.

Foote, Caleb: The Fourth Amendment: Obstacle or Necessity in the Law of Arrest? JCLC&PS, Vol.51, No.4 (Mar.-Apr., 1960-61), 402.

Galiher, Richard W.: Mallory Revisited, TPY (1959).

Gardner, Harold J.: Search & Seizure, POLICE, Vol.4 (Mar.-Apr., 1961), 60-61.

Garmire, Bernard L.: Report of the Committee on Arrest, Search & Seizure, TPY (1964).

Gasch, Oliver: The Mallory Decision and Law Enforcement, TPY (1961).

Gowran: How Supreme Court Ruling Puts Straightjacket on Police, CHICAGO TRIBUNE (Aug. 11, 1964), 27.

———: Tell How Acts of High Court Impede Police, CHICAGO TRIBUNE (Aug. 10, 1964), 9.

Guidelines for New York Police on Stop-and-frisk and Knock-knock Laws, TPC (Aug., 1964).

Gold, Lewis H.: *The Law of Search and Seizure.* A Report reprinted from VILLANOVA LAW REVIEW, Villanova Univ., 1962.

Heffron, F. N.: *Mechanics of Arrest.* Sacramento, Bureau of Industrial Education, 1964.

Hewitt, William H.: *Are the Courts Handcuffing the Police.* Speech given May 23, 1964, Shaker Heights, Ohio, before the Ohio Identification Officers Assn. (unpublished).

Hill, Warren P., and Watson, Daniel: Right of Federal Officer to Search and Seize without Warrant Confined to Instances of "Inherent Necessity," JCL&C, Vol.39, No.2 (Mar.-Apr., 1948-49), 208-225.

Hobbs, Leonard J.: *Police Manual of Arrests and Searches.* Toronto, Canada, Carswell.

Kaufman, Irving R.: The Uncertain Criminal Law, ATLANTIC MONTHLY (Jan., 1965), 61.

King, Daniel P.: Some Reflections on Investigative Detention, L&O, Vol.12 (Sept., 1964).

Krichamer, Arnold: Jurist's Viewpoint, TPY (1964).

Kolbiek & Porter: *Law of Arrest, Search and Seizure,* Los Angeles, Legal Book Store, 1965.

Kotin, Lawrence L.: The Carignan Case: A Study of the McNabb Rule, JCLC&PS, Vol.42 (1951-52), 351.

Kuh, Richard H.: Reflections on New York's "Stop-and-frisk" Law and Its Claimed Unconstitutionality, JCLC&PS, Vol.56, No.1 (Mar., 1965), 32-38.

———: New York's "Stop-and-frisk" Law, L&O, Vol.12 (Oct., 1964).

LaFave, Wayne R.: *Arrest.* Boston, Little, Brown, 1965.

Layton, John B.: The Impact of the Mallory Rule on Law Enforcement in the District of Columbia, TPY (1965).

Leagre, Richard M.: The Fourth Amendment and the Law of Arrest, JCLC&PS, Vol.54, No.4 (1963), 393.

Legislation—Stop & Frisk & Knock-knock Laws Issued by N.Y. State Council, TPC, Vol.31 (Aug., 1964), 39.

Leonard, Donald S.: Checks and Balances, TPY (1965).

Levering, Johnson, Cavan, Ruth S., and Zemans, Eugene S.: *Chicago Police Lockups*. Chicago, John Howard Assn., 1963.

Liability for Excessive Force Used in Making a Misdemeanor Arrest, JCLC&PS, Vol.46 (1955-56), 913.

Lichtenstein, Thomas: Attorney's Viewpoint, TPY (1964).

McArthur, Jack: Stop, Look, Listen and Search, POLICE, Vol.9, No.4 (Mar.-Apr., 1965), 6-10.

More, Harry W., Jr., and Fabian, F. M.: The McNabb-Mallory Rule and Law Enforcement, POLICE, Vol.9, No.1 (Sept.-Oct., 1964), 42-48.

Mueller, Gerard O. W.: The Law Relating to Police Interrogation Privileges and Limitations, JCLC&PS, Vol.52, No.1 (May-June, 1961), 2.

Northwestern University School of Law: Federal Search and Seizure Exclusionary Rule; Its Origin, Development, Present Status and Trend, JCLC&PS, Vol.45 (1954-55), 51-61.

Palmore, John S.: A Turn of the Screw, TPY (1965).

Parker, William H.: Birds Without Wings, TPY (1965).

Penn. Rules on Search and Seizure, TPC, Vol.30 (May, 1963), 40.

Priar, L. L., and Martin T. F.: Searching and Disarming Criminals, JCLC&PS, Vol.45 (1954-55), 481-85.

Remington, Frank J.: The Law Relating to On the Street Detention, Questioning and Frisking of Suspected Persons and Police Arrest Privileges in General, JCLC&PS, Vol.51, No.4 (Mar.-Apr., 1960-61), 388; (Nov.-Dec., 1960), 386-94.

Rights of Prisoners Extended Further, *Cleveland Plain Dealer* (Apr. 7, 1965), 1.

Rudensky, Morris: After the Stretch, HARPER'S, Vol.228, No.1367 (Apr., 1964), 180-82.

Runyan, Richard T., and Ostertag, F. Samuel: Searching and Arresting Felons, POLICE, Vol.3, No.5 (May-June, 1959), 6-9.

Ryan, Daniel P.: Prosecutor's Viewpoint, TPY (1964).

Scott, Edgar W.: The Mallory Decision and the Vanishing Rights of Crime Victims, POLICE, Vol.4, No.5 (May-June, 1960), 61-64.

Searches and Seizure, TPC, Vol.30 (May, 1963), 40.

Sherry, A. H.: *The Law of Arrest, Search & Seizure*. Sacramento, Bureau of Industrial Education, 1962.

Shoplifting and the Law of Arrest, YLJ, Vol.62, No.5.

Sobel, Nathan R.: *The Law of Search and Seizure*. Brooklyn, Kings County Criminal Bar Association, THE PLEADER, 1961.

Slaten, Lynn: Are We Handcuffing Our Police? Reprinted from LOS ANGELES EXAMINER (Oct., 1959).

Smith, Howard: *Arrest, Search and Seizure*. Springfield, Thomas, 1959.

Sondern, Frederic, Jr.: Take the Handcuffs Off Our Police, READER'S DIGEST (Sept., 1964), 64-68.

Sowle, Claude: Workshop: Arrest, Search and Seizure, TPY (1964).

Unnecessary Delay in Formally Charging Arrestee, JCLC&PS, Vol.46 (1955-56), 152.

Use of Vagrancy-Type Laws for Arrest and Detention of Suspicious Persons, YLJ, Vol.59 (June, 1950), 1351-64.

Vallow, Herbert Phillip: *Police Arrest and Search*. Springfield, Thomas, 1962.

Varon, Joseph A.: *Searches, Seizures, and Immunities*. Indianapolis, Bobbs-Merrill, 1961.

Walker, Daniel: Federal Protection Against State Searches and Seizures, JCL&C, Vol.39, No.3 (Mar.-Apr., 1948-49), 354-57.

Way, Frank H.: Sufficiency of Warrants Under the Fourth Amendment, JCLC&PS, Vol.49, No.6 (1958-59), 612.

Wayne, Gerald: The Case for Investigative Detention, L&O, Vol.12 (Jan., 1964).

Whittlesey, John S.: Authority of Highway Patrol to Stop and Search Motor Vehicles Without Warrant, JCL&C, Vol.38, No.3 (Mar.-Apr., 1947-48), 239-244.

Wilson, O. W.: Police Arrest Privileges in a Free Society: A Plea for Modernization, JCLC&PS, Vol.51, No.4 (Mar.-Apr., 1960-61), 395.

Zeichner, Irving B.: According to Law: Affidavit for Search, L&O, Vol.11, No.4 (Apr., 1963).

——: Affidavit for Search Warrant, L&O, Vol.11, No.2 (Feb., 1963).

——: Description in Search Warrant, Vol.9 (June, 1961).

——: Illegal Search, L&O, Vol.10, No.11 (Nov., 1963), 46.

——: Search & Seizure, L&O, Vol.9 (Aug. & Oct., 1961); Vol.13, No.4 (Apr., 1965), 42-43.

——: This Is the Law, L&O, Vol.9 (Aug., 1961).

Zemans, Eugene S.: *Held Without Bail, Physical Aspects of the Police Lockups in the City of Chicago*, 1947-48. Chicago, John Howard Assoc., 1949.

Civil Rights, Liberties
and Human Relations

Abrams, Charles: *Forbidden Neighbors: a Study of Prejudice in Housing.* New York, Harper & Bros., 1955.

Adams, Thomas F.: Police—Minority Group Relations, POLICE, Vol.7, No.6 (July-Aug., 1963), 35-37.

Allen, Alexander J.: What We in the Civil Rights Movement Expect of Public Administrators, *Administration and Race Relations,* Washington, D.C., American Society for Public Administration, 1965.

Allen, W. L.: Burdens and Liabilities of Citizenship Must Be Accepted as Well as the Privileges, TPC, Vol.30 (June, 1963), 24-26.

Allport, Gordon W.: *The Nature of Prejudice.* Garden City, Doubleday, 1958.

American Management Association: *Personnel: the Human Relations Job of Personnel Management.* New York, The Association, 1950.

Anderson, Harold H., and Anderson, Gladys, M. L.: *An Introduction to Projective Techniques and Other Devices for Understanding the Dynamics of Human Behavior.* New York, Prentice-Hall, Inc., 1951.

Andrews, Kenneth R.: *The Case Method of Teaching Human Relations and Administration.* Cambridge, Harvard, Univ. Press, 1951.

————: *Human Relations and Administration: the Case Methods of Teaching.* Cambridge, Harvard Univ. Press, 1953.

Anti-defamation League of B'Nai B'Rith: Police and Free Choice, TPC, Vol.32, No.2 (Feb., 1965), 8-9.

Association of the Bar of the City of New York: *Equal Justice for the Accused.* New York, Dodd, Mead, 1959.

————: *The Federal Loyalty-Security Program.* New York, Dodd, Mead, 1958.

Auerbach, F. L.: *Immigration Laws of the United States.* New York, Bobbs-Merrill, 1955.

Baker, Helen: *Centralization and Decentralization in Industrial Relations.* Princeton, Princeton Univ. Press, 1954.

Baker, Robert E.: Revived KKK Isn't Funny Anymore, WASHINGTON POST (July 5, 1964), E.1.

Bakke, E. Wright: *Bonds of Organization: an Appraisal of Corporate Human Relations.* New York, Harper & Bros., 1950.

Bamford, Paul W.: Procurement of Oarsmen for the French Galleys, 1660-1748, AHR, Vol.65 (Oct., 1959), 31-48.

Banton, M.: Social Integration and Police Authority, TPC, Vol.30 (Apr., 1963), 8.

Barker, Lucius J., and Barker, Twiley W., Jr.: *Freedoms, Courts, Politics: Studies in Civil Liberties.* Englewood Cliffs, Prentice-Hall, 1965.

Barrett, E. L., Jr.: *The Tenney Committee: Legislative Investigation of Subversive Activities in California.* Ithaca, Cornell Univ., 1951.

Barth, Alan: *Government by Investigations.* New York, Viking, 1955.

————: *The Loyalty of Free Men.* New York, Viking, 1951.

————: *The Price of Liberty.* New York, Viking, 1961.

————: *When Congress Investigates Loyalty and Security in a Democracy.* Washington, Public Affairs Committee, 1956.

Bates, Sanford: Review of Society of Captives, AJC, Vol.21 (May-June, 1954), 28.

Beaney, W. M.: *The Right to Counsel in American Courts.* Ann Arbor, U. of Michigan, 1955.

Becker, C. L., et al.: *Safeguarding Civil Liberty Today.* Ithaca, Cornell Univ., 1945.

Beisel, A. R.: *Control Over Illegal Enforcement of the Criminal Law: Role of the Supreme Court.* Boston, Boston Univ. Press, 1955.

Bell, Ralph: Families—America's Strength, L&O, Vol.11, No.1 (Jan., 1963).

Berger, M.: *Equality by Statute.* New York, Columbia, 1952.

Berns, W.: *Freedom, Virtue and the First Amendment.* Baton Rouge, Louisiana State Univ. Press, 1957.

Berry, Brewton: *Race Relations.* Boston, Houghton Mifflin Co., 1951.

Beth, Loren: *The American Theory of Church and State.* Gainesville, Fla., Univ. of Florida Press, 1958.

Bibby, C.: *Race Prejudice, and Education.* London, 1960.

Biddle, Francis: *The Fear of Freedom.* Garden City, Doubleday, 1951.

Blume, William W.: *American Civil Procedure.* Englewood Cliffs, Prentice-Hall, 1955.

Bok, C.: *Star Wormwood.* New York, Knopf, 1959.

Bontecou, E.: *The Federal Loyalty-Security Program.* Ithaca, Cornell, 1953.

Bouscaren, A. T.: *The Security Aspects of Im-*

migration Work. Milwaukee, Marquette Univ. Press, 1959.

Boyd, F. L.: Situations Were Settled Amicably, TPC, Vol.30 (June, 1963), 26-28.

Brookings Institution: *Suggested Standards for Determining Un-American Activities.* Washington, D.C., 1945.

Brostron, Curtis: Police Planning Operations and Techniques, TPC, Vol.30 (June, 1963), 38-40.

Brown, Albert N.: Human Behavior, TPC, Vol.29, No.5 (May, 1962), 22.

Brown, R. S., Jr.: *Loyalty and Security: Employment Tests in the United States.* New Haven, Yale Univ. Press, 1958.

Bruce, J. C.: *The Irony of our Immigration Policy.* New York, Random House, 1954.

Bucker, H.: *Freedom of Information.* New York, Macmillan, 1949.

Buckley, W. F., Jr.: *God and the Man at Yale.* Chicago, Regnery, 1951.

Bullock, Henry Allen: Significance of the Racial Factor in the Length of Prison Sentences, JCLC&PS, Vol.52, No.4 (Nov.-Dec., 1961), 411.

Buranelli, V. (ed.): *The Trial of Peter Zenger.* New York, New York Univ., 1957.

Bursk, Edward C. (ed.): *Human Relations for Management.* New York, Harper, 1958.

Busch, Henry M.: *Conference Methods in Industry: a Practical Handbook of Basic Theory of Group Thinking and Tested Applications to Industrial Situations.* New York, Harper, 1949.

Cabot, Hugh, and Kahl, Joseph A.: *Human Relations: Concepts and Cases in Concrete Social Science.* Cambridge, Harvard Univ. Press, 1953.

Cahill, Thomas J.: Inter-racial Programs, TPC, Vol.30 (Dec., 1963), 34.

————: A New Concept in Community Relations, FBILEB, Vol.32, No.12 (Dec., 1963), 3-6.

————: Seminar: Police Training for Interracial Problems, TPC, Vol.30, No.12 (Dec., 1963), 34-37.

Cahn, E.: *Can the Supreme Court Defend Civil Liberties.* New York, Sidney Hillman Fund, 1956.

————: *The Sense of Injustice.* New York, New York Univ. Press, 1949.

Caldwell, A. B.: The Civil Rights Law—Its Scope & Limitations, TPC, Vol.30 (Sept., 1964), 10.

————: Cooperation Between State and Federal Law Enforcement Officials in Civil Rights, POLICE, Vol.8, No.6 (July-Aug., 1964), 70-73.

————: Needed Areas of Cooperation—Federal and Local, TPC, Vol.30 (June, 1963), 34-37.

————: The Police and the Citizen—Individual Rights vs. Common Security, POLICE, Vol.7, No.2 (Nov.-Dec., 1962), 77-81.

Calhoun, Paul B.: Respect and Acceptance Cannot Be Decreed . . . These Must Be Earned, TPC, Vol.30 (June, 1963), 28-30.

California Department of Justice, Division of Criminal Law and Enforcement: *A Guide to Race Relations for Peace Officers.* Chicago, American Council on Race Relations, 1958.

Canlis, Michael: Civil Rights, TPC, Vol.30 (Dec., 1963), 29.

————: The Police Position, TPC, Vol.30, No.12 (Dec., 1963), 29-31.

————: Workshop: Civil Rights, TPY (1964).

Carl, Earl L.: Reflections on the Sit-ins, CLQ, Vol.46, No.444 (Spring, 1961).

Carr, R. K.: *Federal Protection of Civil Rights: Quest for a Sword.* Ithaca, Cornell Univ. Press, 1947.

————: *The House Committee on Un-American Activities, 1945-50.* Ithaca, Cornell Univ. Press, 1952.

Cartwright, Dorwin, and Yander, Alvin: *Group Dynamics: Research and Theory.* Evanston, Row, Peterson, 1953.

Caughey, J.: *Their Majesties the Mob.* Chicago, Univ. of Chicago Press, 1960.

Chafee, Zecaria: *The Blessings of Liberty.* Philadelphia, Lippincott, 1956.

————: *Free Speech in the United States.* Cambridge, Harvard Univ. Press, 1954.

————: *How Human Rights Got Into the Constitution.* Boston, Boston Univ. Press, 1952.

Chalmere, David M.: *Hooded Americanism.* Garden City, Doubleday, 1965. **(Must reading.)**

Chambers, W.: *Witness.* New York, Random House, 1956.

Chapman, Samuel G.: Views of a "Social Nature" on Police Problems in Social Change, TPY (1965).

Chase, Stuart: *The Proper Study of Mankind.* New York, Harper, 1948.

————: *Roads to Agreement.* New York, Harper, 1951.

Childs, Richard S.: *Civic Victories.* New York, The National Municipal League, 1952.

Civil Rights Act of 1964, TPC, Vol.31 (Sept., 1964), 8.

The Civil Rights Act of 1964: Its Implications for Law Enforcement, TPC, Vol.31 (Sept., 1964), 8-44.

Civil Rights: The White House Meeting, NEWSWEEK (Aug., 1964), 15.

Clark, Donald E.: Minority Group Rights and the Police, TPC, Vol.32, No.3 (Mar., 1965), 43-45.

Clark, Pearl Franklin: *Challenge of the American Know-how.* New York, Harper & Bros., 1948.

Cleeton, Glen U.: *Making Work Human.* Yellow Springs, Ohio, Antioch, 1949.

Clowers, Norman L.: Prejudice and Discrimination in Law Enforcement, POLICE, Vol.8, No.2 (Nov.-Dec., 1963), 50-54.

Cogley, John (ed.): *Religion in America.* New York, Meridian Books, 1958.

Cogshall, Fred J.: Are We Buying the Trojan Horse? Need for Police Respect of Constitutional Rights, JCL&C, Vol.40, No.2 (July-Aug., 1949), 242.

Coles, Robert: The Question of Negro Crime, HARPER'S, Vol.228, No.1367 (Apr., 1964), 134-39.

Collins, LeRoy: The Federal Community Relations Service, TPC, Vol.31 (Sept., 1964), 18-21.

Commager, Henry S.: *Freedom, Loyalty, Dissent.* New York, Oxford Univ. Press, 1954.

Cook, T. I.: *Democratic Rights Versus Communist Activity.* New York, Doubleday, 1954.

Cousin, R. E., et al.: *South Carolinans Speak: a Moderate Approach to Race Relations.* Columbia, Univ. of South Carolina Press, 1957.

Cox, Archibald: Constitutionalism in Change and Crises, in *Administration and Race Relations.* Washington, D.C., American Society for Public Admin., 1965.

Crackdown Coming on Future Rioters. USN&WR (Oct. 12, 1964), 80.

Crisis in Race Relations, USN&WR (Aug. 10, 1964), 23.

Cross, Granuilce J.: The Negro, Prejudice and Police, JCLC&PS, Vol.55, No.3 (Sept., 1964), 405.

Cross, Harold L.: *The People's Right to Know: Legal Access to Public Records and Proceedings.* New York, Columbia Univ. Press, 1953.

Curry, J. E., and King, Glen D.: *Race Tensions and the Police.* Springfield, Thomas, 1962.

Curtis, C. P.: *The Oppenheimer Case.* New York, Simon & Schuster, 1955.

Cushman, Robert E.: *Civil Liberties in the United States: a Guide to Current Problems and Experience.* Ithaca, Cornell Univ. Press, 1956.

Daly, Emmet: *A Guide to Race Relations for Peace Officers.* Sacramento, Calif. Dept. of Justice, 1952.

Darrow, C. S.: *The Story of My Life.* New York, Scribner, 1958.

Dash, Sam: *The Eavesdroppers.* New Brunswick, Rutgers Univ. Press, 1959.

Davidson, I. D., and Gehman, R.: *The Jury Is Still Out.* New York, Harper, 1959.

Davis, E.: *But We Were Born Free.* New York, Bobbs-Merrill, 1954.

DeGrazia, Alfred: *Human Relations in Public Administration: an Annotated Bibliography.* Chicago, Public Admin. Service, 1949.

Deutsch, A.: *The Trouble with Cops.* New York, Crown, 1955.

Diebold, John: *Automation: The Advent of the Automatic Factory.* New York, Van Nostrand, 1952.

Dienstein, W.: *Are You Guilty?* Springfield, Thomas, 1954.

Dixon, W. Macneile: *The Human Situation.* New York, Oxford Univ. Press, 1958.

Dobry, George: Wire Tapping and Eavesdropping: A Comparative Survey, JICJ, Vol.1 (Spring-Summer, 1958), 319-335.

Dohman, Joseph D.: *The Police and Minority Groups.* Chicago, Chicago Park Div., 1947.

Donnelly, Richard C.: Comments and Caveats on the Wire Tapping Controversy, YLJ, Vol.63 (Apr., 1954), 799-810.

Donner, Frank J.: *The Un-Americans.* New York, Ballantine, 1962.

Douglas, William O.: *The Right of the People.* New York, Pyramid Books, 1962.

Drake, Frances S., and Drake, Charles A.: *A Human Relations Case Book for Executives and Supervisors.* New York, McGraw-Hill, 1947.

Drake, Robert J.: Should Wiretapping Be Legalized? Cleveland Plain Dealer (Nov. 3, 1963), AA1.

Drinker, H. S.: *Some Observations on the Freedoms of the First Amendment,* Boston, Boston Univ. Press, 1957.

Dubin, Lawrence M.: Wiretapping: The Federalism Problem, JCLC&PS, Vol.51, No.6 (Mar.-Apr., 1960-61), 630.

Dubin, Robert: *Human Relations in Administration.* Englewood Cliffs, Prentice-Hall, 1961.

Duff, Charles: *A New Handbook on Hanging.* Chicago, Regenry, 1955.

Dumbuald, E.: *The Bill of Rights and What it Means Today.* Norman, Univ. of Oklahoma Press, 1957.

Ehrmann, H. B.: *The Untried Case: the Sacco-Vanzetti Case and the Morelli Gang,* Rev. Ed. New York, Vanguard, 1960.

Emerson, Thomas I., and Haber, David: *Politi-*

cal and Civil Rights in the United States, Rev. Ed. Buffalo, Dennis, 1956.

Ennis, Edward J.: Civil Rights, TPC, Vol.30 (Dec., 1963), 18.

————: Opportunity—Challenge, TPC, Vol.30, No.12 (Dec., 1963), 18-22.

————: Police Protection of Civil Rights—An Opportunity, and a Challenge, TPY (1964).

Ernest, Morris L.: *The First Freedom.* New York, Macmillan, 1946.

Fellman, David: *The Defendant's Rights.* New York, Rinehart, 1958.

Ferguson, Roosevelt: The Right to Demostrate, QRHEAN, Vol.28, No.238 (Oct., 1960).

Finley, William H., Sartain, A. Q., and Tate, Willis M.: *Human Behavior in Industry.* New York, McGraw-Hill, 1954.

Foley, John P., and Anastasi, Anne: *Human Relations and the Foreman.* National Foreman's Institute, New London, 1950.

Foster, Henry H., Jr.: Race Relations and American Law: JCLC&PS, Vol.51, No.2 (Mar.-Apr., 1960-61), 243.

Fox, Vernon, and Volakakis, Jo Ann: The Negro Offender in a Northern Industrial Area, JCLC&PS, Vol.46 (1955-56), 641-47.

Fraenkel, O. K.: *The Supreme Court and Civil Liberties.* Dobbs Ferry, Oceana, 1963.

Gallati, Robert R. J.: Operational Planning, TPC, Vol.30 (June, 1963), 51-57.

Gardner, Burleigh B., and Moore, David G.: *Human Relations in Industry,* 3rd Ed. Homewood, Irwin, 1955.

Garrison, H.: Local Problems Arising from the 1964 Act. TPC, Vol.31 (Sept., 1964), 22-25.

Gellhorn, Walter: *American Rights.* New York, Macmillan, 1960.

————: *Security, Loyalty and Science.* Ithaca, Cornell Univ. Press, 1950.

Germann, A. C.: Burden or Heritage, TPC, Vol.30, No.12 (Dec., 1963), 22-26.

————: Civil Rights, TPC, Vol.30 (Dec., 1963), 22.

————: Civil Rights—Unpleasant Police Burden or Proudly Guarded Heritage? POLICE, Vol.9, No.4 (Mar.-Apr., 1965), 84-88; TPY (1964).

Geron, Alexander R.: *Why Men Work.* Stanford, Stanford Univ. Press, 1948.

Gillmor, D.: *Fear and Accusor.* New York, Abelard-Schuman, 1954.

Ginger, R.: *Six Days or Forever? Tennessee vs. John Thomas Scopes.* Boston, Beacon, 1958.

Gittler, J. P.: *Understanding Minority Groups.* New York, Wiley & Sons, 1956.

Glover, John D., and Hower, Ralph M.: *The Administrator: Cases on Human Relations in Business.* Homewood, Irwin, 1952.

Grebstein, S. H. (ed.): *Monkey Trial: The State of Tennessee vs. John Thomas Scopes.* Boston, Houghton Mifflin, 1960.

Greenberg, J.: *Race Relations and American Law.* New York, Columbia Univ. Press, 1959.

Grimm, Victor E.: Wiretapping: The Federal Law, JCLC&PS, Vol.51, No.4 (Mar.-Apr., 1960-61), 441.

Griswold, E. N.: *The Fifth Amendment Today.* Cambridge, Harvard, 1955.

Guetzkow, Harold Steers: *Group Leadership and Men: Research in Human Relations.* New Brunswick, Rutgers Univ. Press, 1951.

A Guide to Race Relations for Police Officers. Sacramento, Dept. of Justice, 1946.

Haight, A. L.: *Banned Books,* New York, Bowker, 1956.

Hale, E. C.: The True Victims of Police Brutality Are the Police Themselves, TPC, Vol.30 (June, 1963), 30-32.

Hall, Clyde D., and Leich, Harold H.: The Human Touch in Civil Service Placement, PPR, Vol.12 (Summer, 1952), 178-80.

Handlin, Oscar: *The Newcomers.* Garden City, Anchor Books (Doubleday), 1959.

Haney, Robert W.: *Comstockery in America.* Boston, Beacon Press, 1960.

Hannah, John A.: *Equal Protection Under Law —Fact or Fiction.* Eighth Annual National Institute on Police and Community Relations Held at Michigan State Univ. May 21, 1962.

Hansson, Carl F.: On-the-scene Preventive Tactics, TPC, Vol.30 (June, 1963), 44-50.

Harding, A. L. (ed.): *Fundamental Law in Criminal Prosecutions.* Dallas, So. Methodist Univ., 1959.

Harlan, L. R.: *Separate and Unequal.* Chapel Hill, Univ. of North Carolina, 1958.

Harlem's Long Hot Summer Begins (Pictorial) LIFE, Vol.57, No.5 (July, 1964), 14.

Harlow, Rex F., and Black, Marvin M.: *Practical Public Relations.* New York, Harper, 1952.

Hebb, D. O.: *Organization of Behavior.* New York, Wiley, 1949.

Heller, F. H.: *The Sixth Amendment to the Constitution of the United States: a Study in Constitutional Development.* Lawrence, Univ. of Kansas, 1951.

Hofstadter, S. H.: *The Fifth Amendment.* New York, Fund for the Republic, 1955.

Hogan, Frank S.: Wiretapping, JCLC&PS, Vol.50, No.6 (Mar.-Apr., 1960), 575.

Holliday, Harold, and Whipple, David: Free Speech and the Right of Municipalities to Regulate the Use of Public Places, Vol.19, UKCLR (Apr.-June, 1951), 191-204.

Homans, George C.: *The Human Group.* New York, Harcourt, Brace, 1950.

Hopkins, V. C.: *Dred Scott's Case.* New York, Fordham, 1951.

Hoslett, Schuyler Dean (ed.): *Human Factors in Management.* New York, Harper, 1951.

How Far the Negro Has to Go and What it Will Take, USN&WR (June 21, 1965), 52-53.

HUMAN RELATIONS. Published quarterly by Tavistock Pub., Ltd., 68-74 Carter Lane, London, E.C. 4. U.S. Agent: Research Center for Group Dynamics, Univ. of Michigan, Ann Arbor, Mich.

Inbau, Fred E.: Individual vs. Society, TPC, Vol.29, No.1 (Jan., 1962), 29.

———: Public Safety vs. Individual Civil Liberties: The Prosecutor's Stand, JCLC&PS, Vol.53, No.1 (Mar.-May, 1962), 85.

———: More About Public Safety vs. Individual Right, JCLC&PS, Vol.53, No.3 (Sept.-Nov., 1962), 329.

———: *Self-incrimination.* Springfield, Thomas, 1950.

Inglish, Ruth A.: *Freedom of the Movies.* Chicago, Univ. of Chicago Press, 1947.

International Association of Chiefs of Police, Inc.: *The Police and the Civil Rights Act.* Washington, IACP, 1965. (A booklet designed to assist police executives in understanding the 1964 Civil Rights Act).

James, J. B.: *The Framing of the Fourteenth Amendment.* Urbana, Univ. of Illinois, 1956.

Janson, Donald, and Eismann, Bernard: *The Far Right.* New York, McGraw-Hill, 1963.

Javits, J. K.: *Discrimination—USA,* New York, Harcourt, Brace, 1960.

Jenkins, H. T.: Police Must Accept Change More Rapidly Than Other Community Groups, TPC (June, 1963), 18-24.

———: Utilizing Community Resources: A Report from Atlanta, TPC (Sept., 1964), 25-28.

Johnson, Robert W.: Human Relations in Modern Business, HBR (Sept., 1949), 521-541.

Joint Session of Congress: The Negro and the Vote—Here's L.B.J.'s Address to Congress, USN&WR, Vol.58, No.13 (Mar. 29, 1965).

Joughin, G. L., and Morgan, E. M.: *The Legacy of Sacco and Vanzetti.* New York, Harcourt, Brace, 1948.

Kamisar, Yale: Public Safety vs. Individual Liberties: Some Facts and Theories, JCLC&PS, Vol.53, No.2 (June-Aug., 1962), 171.

Kaplan, Benjamin, and Hall, Livingston (eds.): Judicial Administration and the Common Man, THE ANNALS, Vol.287 (May, 1953).

Katzenback, Nicholas deB.: *Administration and* Race Relations. Washington, D.C. American Society for Public Admin., 1965.

Kefauver, E.: *Crime in America.* New York, Doubleday, 1951.

Kelley, Douglas M.: The Area of Human Relations, TPY (1958).

Kenney, John P.: Police and Human Relations in Management, JCLC&PS, Vol.45 (July-Aug., 1954), 222-228.

Kephart, William M.: *Racial Factors and Urban Law Enforcement.* Philadelphia, Univ. of Pennsylvania Press, 1957.

Killian, Lewis, and Grigg, Charles: *Racial Crisis in America: Leadership in Conflict.* Englewood Cliffs, Prentice-Hall, 1965.

Kimble, Joseph P.: A Policeman Looks at Race Relations, POLICE, Vol.7, No.4 (Mar.-Apr., 1963), 79-81.

Kilpatrick, J. J.: *The Smut Peddlers.* New York, Doubleday, 1960.

King, Glenn D., and Curry, J. E.: *Race Tensions and the Police.* Springfield, Thomas, 1962.

Kluchesky, Joseph T.: *Police Action in Minority Problems.* New York, Freedom House, 1946.

Koestler, Arthur: *Reflections on Hanging.* New York, Macmillan, 1957.

Konvitz, M. R.: *Civil Rights in Immigration.* Ithaca, Cornell Univ. Press, 1953.

———: *Fundamental Liberties of a Free People.* Ithaca, Cornell Univ. Press, 1957.

———, & Leskes, J.: *A Century of Civil Rights.* New York, Columbia, 1961.

Kurland, Philip B.: *Religion and the Law.* London, Aldine, 1963.

Lahey, Edwin A.: Cops Unsung Heroes in Racial Tragedy, JCLC&PS, Vol.56, No.2 (June, 1965), 246.

Laponce, J. A.: *The Protection of Minorities.* Los Angeles, Univ. of Calif., 1960.

Lasswell, H. D.: *National Security and Individual Freedom.* New York, McGraw-Hill, 1950.

Lattimore, O.: *Ordeal by Slander.* Boston, Little, Brown, 1950.

Lee, George E.: Vandalism and Neglect Still the "Silent Voices" L&O, Vol.12 (June, 1964).

Lehman, J.: New Dimensions in Race Tension and Conflict, TPC, Vol.30 (July, 1963), 16.

Leighton, Alexander: *The Governing of Men.* Princeton, Princeton Univ. Press, 1945.

Lepold, N. F.: *Life Plus 99 Years.* New York, Doubleday, 1958.

Lincoln, E. E.: Black Muslims, TPC (June, 1963), 13-16.

Lindgren, Henry C.: *The Art of Human Relations.* New York, Hermitage House, 1953.

Lloyd, Bob: The Policeman Has Civil Rights Too, L&O, Vol. 12 (1964).

Lohman, Joseph D.: *Police and Minority Groups.* Chicago, Chicago Park Division.

Lomax, Louis: *The Negro Revolt.* New York, Harper, 1962.

Long, H. A.: The Dilemma: Crime and Constitutional Rights, TPC, Vol.32, No.6 (June, 1965), 14.

Looting—the High Cost of Race Violence, USN&WR (Sept., 1964), 36.

Louisville Conference on Racial Tension, TPC, Vol.30 (June, 1963), 60.

Louisville Division of Police, Committee on Police Training: *Principles of Police Work with Minority Groups.* Louisville, The Division, 1950.

Lowenstein, E. (ed.): *The Alien and the Immigration Law.* Dobbs Ferry, Oceana, 1958.

Lowenthal, M.: *The Federal Bureau of Investigation.* New York, Morrow, 1950.

Lustgarten, E.: *The Murder and the Trial.* New York, Scribner, 1958.

McCandless, David A.: Police Responsibility in Race Tension and Conflict, TPY (1964).

McCormick, Thomas C. T.: *Problems of the Postwar World.* New York, McGraw-Hill, 1945.

McEntire, D.: *Residence and Race.* Berkeley, Berkeley Univ. Press, 1960.

———, **& Powers, Robert B.:** *A Guide to Race Relations for Police Officers.* Sacramento, Calif. Dept. of Justice, 1946.

McGregor, Douglas: *The Human Side of Enterprise.* New York, McGraw-Hill, 1960.

McKenon, Richard, et al.: *The Freedom to Read.* New York, Bowker, 1957.

McKernan, M.: *The Amazing Crime and Trial of Leopold and Loeb.* New York, New American Library, 1958.

McManus, George: Human Relations Training for Police, JCLC&PS, Vol.46 (May-June, 1955), 105-111.

———: The Police and Human Relations, POLICE, Vol.1, No.2 (Nov.-Dec., 1956), 14-18.

MacIver, R. M.: *Academic Freedom in Our Time.* New York, Columbia Univ. Press, 1955.

Maguire, John: *Evidence of Guilt: Restrictions upon Its Discovery or Compulsory Disclosure.* Boston, Little, Brown, 1959.

Maier, Norman R. F.: *Principles of Human Relations.* New York, Wiley, 1952.

Martin, J. B.: *The Deep South Says Never.* New York, Ballentine, 1957.

Mayers, L.: *Shall We Amend the Fifth Amendment?* New York, Harper, 1959.

Mayo, Elton: *The Social Problems of an Industrial Civilization.* Boston, Harvard School of Business Administration, 1945.

Mays, Elton: *Human Problems of an Industrial Civilization.* Boston, Division of Research, Harvard Univ., 1946.

Medina, Harold R.: *The Anatomy of Freedom.* New York, Henry Holt, 1959.

Melnick, Norman: Crimebusters Like *Legal* Wiretapping, Cleveland Plain Dealer (Nov. 10, 1963), 7-A.

Mendelson, Wallace: *Discrimination.* Englewood Cliffs, Prentice-Hall, 1962.

Miller, M.: *The Judges and Judged.* New York, Doubleday, 1952.

Montgomery, R. H.: *Sacco-Vanzetti: the Murder and the Myth.* New York, Devin-Adair, 1960.

Moore, Charles E.: Anarchy on the Campus, TPC, Vol.32, No.4 (Apr., 1965), 10.

More, Harry W., Jr.: Federal Personnel Loyalty-Security Programs, POLICE, Vol.8, No.4 (Mar.-Apr., 1964), 20-23.

Morris, R. B.: *Fair Trial: Fourteen Who Stood Accused from Ann Hutchinson to Alger Hiss.* New York, Knopf, 1952.

Mulkggn, Wm. J.: Civil Rights Demonstrations, L&O, Vol.12 (May, 1964).

Murphy, Jay: Free Speech and the Interest in Local Law and Order, JPL, Vol.1 (Sept., 1952), 40-70.

Murphy, M. J.: Civil Disobedience, TPC (June, 1963), 58-59.

Newman, E. S. (ed.): *The Freedom Reader.* Dobbs Ferry, Oceana, 1958.

New York City Policy on Demonstrations, TPC, Vol.30 (July, 1963), 14.

Nyquist, Ewald B.: Your Public Servants Serve You Right, *Admin. & Race Relations.* Washinton, D.C., American Society for Public Administration, 1965.

O'Brian, J. L.: *National Security and Individual Freedom.* Cambridge, Harvard, 1955.

O'Brien, Thomas J.: Floaters and Unemployed Transients, TPY (1964).

O'Keefe, Jack A.: Migrant Laborers, TPY (1964).

———: *Criminal Procedure from Arrest to Appeal.* New York, New York Univ., 1947.

Orton, Dwayne: Human Relations in Technical Times, TPY (1956).

Overstreet, H. A., & B.: *What We Must Know About Communism.* New York, Norton, 1958.

Parker, Willard E., and Kleemeier, Robert W.: *Human Relations in Supervision.* New York, McGraw-Hill, 1951.

Parker, William H.: The Police Role in Civil Rights, TPY (1965).

Patterson, H.: *Scottsboro Boy.* New York, Doubleday, 1950.

Pfiffner, John M.: A Human Relations Reading List, PERSONNEL (Sept., 1949).

———: *The Supervision of Personnel: Human Relations in the Management of Men.* New York, Prentice-Hall, 1951.

Pollitt, Daniel H.: Dime Store Demonstrations: Events and Legal Problems of the First Sixty Days, DLJ, No.315 (Summer, 1960).

Pound, R.: *Criminal Justice in America.* New York, Holt, Rinehart & Winston, 1945.

———: *The Development of Constitutional Guarantees of Liberty.* New Haven, Yale Univ. Press, 1957.

Pritchett, C. H.: *Civil Liberties and the Vinson Court.* Chicago, Univ. of Chicago Press, 1954.

———: The Political Offender and the Warren Court, PULR, Vol.38, No.53 (Winter, 1958).

———, & Westin, Alan F. (eds.): *The Third Branch of Government.* New York, Harcourt, Brace, 1963.

The Public Order and the Rule of Law: A Workshop, *Administration and Race Relations,* Washington, D.C., American Society for Public Administration, 1965.

Purcell, P.: The Bill of Rights, TPC, Vol.30, No.12 (Dec., 1963), 26-27.

———: Civil Rights, TPC, Vol.30 (Dec., 1963), 26.

Purdy, E. Wilson: Meeting Current Problems Resulting from Racial Tension, TPC, Vol.30 (June, 1963), 41.

Putkammer, E. W.: *Administration of Criminal Law.* Chicago, Univ. of Chicago, 1953.

Race Relations and Personnel Management: A Panel, *Administration and Race Relations,* Washington, D.C., American Society for Public Administration, 1965.

Randel, William Pierce: *The Ku Klux Klan, a Century of Infamy.* Philadelphia, Chilton, 1965.

Record, W., and Record J. C. (eds.): *Little Rock, U.S.A.* San Francisco, Chandler, 1960.

Redding, J. S.: *The Lonesome Road: The Story of the Negro's Past in America.* New York, Doubleday, 1958.

———: *On Being Negro in America.* New York, Bobbs-Merrill, 1951.

Reik, T.: *The Compulsion to Confess.* New York, Farrar, 1950.

Reynolds, Q.: *Courtroom.* New York, Farrar, 1950.

Robin, E. F., and Hirsch, J. G.: *The Pursuit of Equality.* New York, Crown, 1957.

Rogge, O. J.: *The First and the Fifty.* New York, Nelson, 1960.

———: *Why Men Confess.* New York, Nelson, 1960.

Roncker, Robert: *The Southern Appalachian Migrant—a Social Study of His Attitudes, Customs and Environment.* Cincinnati, Division of Police, 1959.

Ronken, Harriet O., and Lawrence, Paul R.: *Administering Changes: A Case Study of Human Relations in a Factory.* Cambridge, Harvard Univ. Press, 1952.

Rose, A.: *The Negro in America.* Boston, Beacon, 1956.

Rossiter, Clinton: *Seedtime of the Republic: the Origin of the American Tradition of Civil Liberties.* New York, Harcourt, Brace, 1953.

Rudwick, Elliott M.: The Negro Policeman in the South, JCLC&PS, Vol.51, No.2 (Mar.-Apr., 1960-61), 273.

St. John-Stevas, N.: *Life, Death and the Law.* Bloomington, Indiana Univ. Press, 1961.

S.2813—Wire Tap Bill, TPC, Vol.29, No.6 (June, 1962), 36-41.

Sargent, S. Stansfeld, and Williamson, Robert C.: *Social Psychology—An Introduction to the Study of Human Relations.* New York, Ronald, 1958.

Scheiber, H. N.: *The Wilson Administration and Civil Liberties.* Ithaca, Cornell Univ. Press, 1960.

Schelb, Frank E.: The Sit-in Demonstration: Criminal Trespass or Constitutional Right? NYULR, Vol.36, No.779 (Apr., 1961).

Schrotel, Stanley R.: Crowd Control in a Period of Social Change. TPY (1965).

———: Civil Liberties for All, TPY (1964).

———: Rights for All, TPC, Vol.30, No.12 (Dec., 1963), 27-29.

Seagle, W.: *Acquitted—of Murder.* Chicago, Regnery, 1958.

Seldes, G.: *Freedom of the Press.* New York, Bobbs-Merrill, 1958.

———: *The People Don't Know.* Gaer Assoc., 1949.

Sellin, H. (ed.): *Practice and Procedure Under the Immigration and Nationality Act.* New York, New York Univ. Press, 1954.

Shannon, D. A.: *The Decline of American Communism: a History of the Communist Party of the U.S. Since 1945.* New York, Harcourt, Brace, 1959.

Shapiro, H. H.: *Federal Enforcement of the Criminal Civil Rights Statutes.* Newark, Rutgers, 1960.

Shaw, William: Secrecy System, L&O, Vol.10, No.2 (Feb., 1962), 56.

Shilis, E. A.: *The Torment of Secrecy: American Security Polices.* Glencoe, Free Press, 1956.

Siegel, Arthur I., Federman, Philip J., Schultz, Douglas G.: *Professional Police—Human*

Relations Training. Thomas, Springfield, 1963.

Silver, Edward S.: Law Enforcement and Wire Tapping, JCLC&PS, Vol.50, No.6 (Mar.-Apr., 1960), 576.

Simon, Herbert A.: *Models of Man.* New York, Wiley, 1957.

Skinner, Burnhus F.: *Science and Human Behavior.* New York, Macmillan, 1953.

Smith, B.: *Police Systems in the United States,* Rev. Ed. New York, Harper, 1949.

Smith, Henry C.: *Psychology of Human Relations.* New York, McGraw-Hill, 1955.

Snook, Russell A.: Your Stake in World Affairs, TPY (1962).

Sowle, Clyde R. (ed.): *Police Power and Individual Freedom.* Chicago, Aldine Pub., 1962.

Spates, Thomas G.: *Human Values Where People Work.* New York, Harper, 1960.

Spicer, Edward H.: *Human Problems in Technological Change.* New York, Russell Sage Foundation, 1952.

Stewart, James A.: Study of Desertion Cases, TPY (1957).

Stewart, G. R.: *The Year of the Oath: The Fight for Academic Freedom at the University of California.* New York, Doubleday, 1950.

Stewart, Richard: Public Speech and Public Order in Britain and the United States, VLR, Vol.12 (1960).

Stoffer, S. A.: *Communism, Conformity and Civil Liberties: a Cross-section of the Nation Speaks Its Mind.* New York, Doubleday, 1955.

Superintendent of Documents: *The Report of the U.S. Commission on Civil Rights.* 1959 & 1965.

Sutherland, Arthur: Establishment According to Engel, HLR, Vol.76, No.25 (Nov., 1962).

Swanson, Alan H.: Wiretapping: The State Law, JCLC&PS, Vol.51, No.5 (Mar.-Apr., 1960-61), 534.

Tamm, Quinn: Constitutional Law Enforcement, 66th Annual IACP Conference in New York City, Sept., 1959.

———: Police and the Civil Rights Act, TPC (Sept., 1964), 7.

———: Police Professionalism and Civil Rights, TPC (Sept., 1964), 28-32.

———: Police vs. Race Tension, TPC, Vol.30 (June, 1963), 7.

Titus, Charles H.: *The Process of Leadership: Human Relations in the Making.* Dubuque, Brown, 1950.

Tompkins, Dorothy C.: *Wiretapping.* Berkeley, Univ. of Calif., Bureau of Public Administration, 1955.

Tompson, Daniel C.: *Negro Leadership Class.* Englewood Cliffs, Prentice-Hall, 1965.

Towler, Juby E.: *The Police Role in Racial Conflicts.* Springfield, Thomas, 1964.

Tumin, Melvin, et al.: *Desegregation: Resistance and Readiness.* Princeton, Princeton Univ. Press, 1958.

Untereiner, Harry: Domestic Peace Corps, L&O, Vol.11, No.9 (Sept., 1963).

U.S. Commission on Civil Rights: 1961 REPORTS, Book 1-5, *Voting, Education, Housing, Justice & Employment.* Washington, U.S. Govt. Printing Office, 1961.

Wakefield, D.: *Revolt in the South.* New York, Grove, 1960.

Watson, Nelson A.: Developing Guidelines for Police Practices, TPC (Sept., 1964), 32-39.

———: Police and Group Behavior, TPC, Vol.21, No.3 (Mar., 1964), 16-42; Vol.30, No.11 (Nov., 1963), 8-44.

Way, H. Frank, Jr.: *Liberty in the Balance: Current Issues in Civil Liberties.* New York, McGraw-Hill, 1964.

Wechsler, J. A.: *The Age of Suspicion.* New York, Random House, 1953.

Weinberg, A.: *Attorney for the Damned.* New York, Simon & Schuster, 1957.

———: *Freedom and Protection the Bill of Rights.* San Francisco, Chandler, 1962.

Weinstein S., and Brown, H. S., Jr.: *Personnel Security Programs of the Federal Government.* Fund for the Republic, 1954.

Weintraub, R. G.: *How Secure These Rights.* New York, Doubleday, 1949.

Wertham, F.: *Seduction of the Innocent.* New York, Rinehart, 1954.

Weyl, N.: *The Battle Against Disloyalty.* New York, Crowell, 1951.

———: *Treason: the Story of Disloyalty and Betrayal in American History.* Washington, Public Affairs Printing, 1950.

Whitehead, D.: *The FBI Story: a Report to the People.* New York, Random, 1956.

Whitehall, Arthur M.: *Personnel Relations: the Human Aspects of Administration.* New York, McGraw-Hill, 1955.

Wilcox, C. (ed.): *Civil Liberties Under Attack.* Philadelphia, State College, Univ. of Penn. Press, 1952.

Wilkins, Roy, NAACP, TPC, Vol.30 (June, 1963), 12.

Williams, B.: *Due Process.* New York, Morrow, 1960.

Williams, Edward B.: *One Man's Freedom.* New York, Antheneum Pub., 1962.

Wilson, Charles M.: An Unusual Suicide, JCLC&PS, Vol.36, No.3 (1945-55), 220.

Wilson, H. H., and Glickman, H.: *The Problem of International Security in Great Britain, 1948-1953.* New York, Doubleday, 1954.

Wittenberg, P. (ed.): *The Lamont Case: History of a Congressional Investigation.* New York, Horizon, 1957.

Wood, Arthur Lewis: Minority-group Criminality and Cultural Integration, JCL&C, Vol.37, No.6 (Mar.-Apr., 1947), 498-510.

Wood, V.: *Due Process and the Law 1932-1949.* Baton Rouge, Louisiana State Univ., 1951.

Woodward, C. F.: *The Strange Race Progress:* the *Wavering Color Line.* Washington, Public Affairs Printing, 1957.

Younger, John: *Training in Human Relations.* Ann Arbor, Mich. Foundation for Research on Human Behavior, 1954.

Zanden, James W. Vander: *American Minority Relations—the Sociology of Race and Ethnic Groups.* New York, Ronald, 1963.

Zeichner, Irving B.: 1964 Civil Rights Act and the Police, L&O, Vol.12 (Sept., 1964).

————: The Right of Freedom, L&O, Vol.9 (Feb., 1961).

Zemi, Ferdinand J., Jr.: Wiretapping—The Right of Privacy vs. the Public Interest, JCL&C, Vol.40, No.4 (Nov.-Dec., 1949), 476.

Courts

Aaron, Thomas J.: The Dilemma of Judicial Review, POLICE, Vol.9, No.4 (Mar.-Apr., 1965), 35-37.

Admissibility of Hospital Record, JCLC&PS, Vol.46 (1955-56), 532.

American Bar Foundation: *Administration of Criminal Justice in the United States.* Amer. Bar Foundation, 1955.

Andrew, Carolyn J.: The Reluctant Witness for the Prosecution, JCLC&PS, Vol.55, No.1 (Mar., 1964), 1.

Annual Report of the Director of the United States Courts. A report prepared by the Administrative Office of the U.S. Courts, Washington, U.S. Govt. Printing Office, 1955.

Aspen, Marvin E.: The Investigative Function of the Prosecuting Attorney, JCLC&PS, Vol.48, No.5 (Jan.-Feb., 1955), 526.

Availability of Bail Pending Appeal, JCLC&PS, Vol.46 (1955-56), 80.

Barnes, Harry E.: Let's Reform the Jury System or Abolish It, CORONET, Vol.41 (Apr., 1957), 72-76.

Basta, Donald K.: Free Press—Fair Trial: How May a Defendant's Right to a Fair Trial Be Protected from Prejudicial Newspaper Publicity? JCLC&PS, Vol.50, No.4 (Nov.-Dec., 1959), 374.

Beaney, William M.: *The Right to Counsel in American Courts.* Ann Arbor, Univ. of Michigan Press, 1955.

Beckham, Walter H.: Helpful Practices in Juvenile Court Hearings, FP, Vol.13 (June, 1949), 10-14.

Bennett, James V.: Pilot Sentencing Institute, JCLC&PS, Vol.50, No.4 (Nov.-Dec., 1959), 385.

Berdan, George W.: Expert Witness Testimony, POLICE, Vol.9, No.2 (Nov.-Dec., 1964), 54-63.

Black, Charles L., Jr.: *The People and the Court: Judicial Review in a Democracy.* New York, Macmillan, 1960.

Braud, Jacob M.: "Boys" Court: Individualized Justice for the Youthful Offender, FP, Vol.12 (June, 1948), 9-14.

Brownell, Herbert: Too Many Judges Are Political Hacks, SATURDAY EVENING POST (Apr. 16, 1964), 10.

Burns, Kenneth J., Jr.: Conspiracy Prosecutions in the Federal Courts, JCL&C, Vol.40, No.6 (Mar.-Apr., 1950), 760.

Busch, Francis X.: The Jury System in America; Guarantees of Federal and State Constitutions, in *Law and Tactics in Jury Trials.* Indianapolis, Bobbs-Merrill, 1949.

Cahn, Edmond, (ed.): *Supreme Court and Supreme Law.* Bloomington, Univ. of Indiana Press, 1954.

Caldwell, Robert G.: Judicial Attitudes in Sentences, JCLC&PS, Vol.53, No.3 (Sept.-Nov., 1962), 360.

Campbell, William J.: Developing Systematic Sentencing Procedures, FP, Vol.18 (Sept., 1954), 45-50.

Carr, Lowell J.: Most Courts Have to Be Substandard, FP, Vol.13 (Sept., 1949), 29-33.

Chapman, Gerald: The Right of Counsel Today, JCL&C, Vol.39, No.3 (Mar.-Apr., 1948-49), 432-57.

Children's Bureau: *Courts Serving Children.* Washington, U.S. Govt. Printing Office, 1954.

Cohn, Edmond L.: Federal Constitutional Limitations on the Use of Coerced Confessions in State Courts, JCLC&PS, Vol.50, No.3 (Sept.-Oct., 1959), 265.

Coon, Thomas F.: Witness Testimony in the Area of Hearing, POLICE, Vol.8, No.1 (Sept.-Oct., 1963), 70-72.

Courts Crime Commission Expresses Indignation, TPC, Vol.31 (July, 1964), 39.

Dammann, Peter A.: Private Communications with Grand Juries, JCL&C, Vol.39, No.2 (Mar.-Apr., 1948-49), 72-89.

Devlin, Sir Patrick: *Trial by Jury*, Hamlyn Lectures, 8th Series. London, Stevens, 1956.

Donigan, Robert L.: Why Bail in Traffic Cases: An Indigent Defendant, TD&R (May, 1965), 4-7.

Edelstein, David N.: A Kind World for the Civil Jury, Vol.17, NACC LAW JOURNAL (May, 1956), 302.

Edwards, George: *Courts, Citizens and Police*. Michigan State Bar Journal, 1962.

Eliasberg, Waldimir: Psychiatric and Psychologic Opinions in Court, JCL&C, Vol.39, No.2 (Mar.-Apr., 1948-49), 152-58.

Fagan, Edward F.: Between Arrest and Trial, POLICE, Vol.4, No.6 (July-Aug., 1960), 75-77.

Fisher, Edward: *People's Court*. Evanston, Northwestern Univ. Traffic Institute, 1947.

Frank, Jerome: *Courts on Trial: Myth and Reality in American Justice*. Princeton, Princeton Univ. Press, 1950.

Frank, John P.: *Marble Palace: the Supreme Court in American Life*. New York, Knopf, 1958.

Freund, Paul A.: *The Supreme Court of the United States: Its Business, Purpose and Performance*. Cleveland, Meridian Books, 1961.

Gardner, Earle Stanley: *The Court of Last Resort*. New York, Pocket Books, 1954.

———: Need for New Concepts in the Administration of Criminal Justice, JCLC&PS, Vol.50, No.1 (1959-60), 20.

Gaynor, Malcolm: The Admission in Evidence of Statements Made in the Presence of the Defendant, JCLC&PS, Vol.48, No.2 (July-Aug., 1957), 193.

Gershenson, Alvin H.: *The Bench Is Warped*. Beverly Hills, Book Co. of America, 1964.

Glueck, S.: Further Comments on the Sentencing Problem. Washington, Administrative Office of the U.S. Courts in Cooperation with the Bureau of Prisons, 1957.

———: Pathways to Improved Sentencing. Address delivered before the American So-

ciety of Criminology, Denver, Colorado, Dec., 1961.

———: *The Sentencing Problem*. Address delivered at Judicial Conference of Third Circuit, U.S. Courts, Atlantic City, New Jersey, Sept., 1956; FP, Vol.20 (1957), 15.

———: Toward Improved Sentencing. In *Essays in Jurisprudence in Honor of Roscoe Pound*. Prepared by the American Society for Legal History, Ralph A. Newman, (ed.) Indianapolis, Bobbs-Merrill, 1962.

Hart, Henry M., and Wechsler, Herbert: *The Federal Courts and the Federal System*. New York, Foundation Press, 1953.

Heffron, Floyd N.: *The Officer in the Courtroom*. Springfield, Thomas, 1955.

Hill, Donald J.: Who's on Trial? L&O, Vol.12 (Oct., 1964).

Holbrook, James G.: Role of Juries in Judicial Administration, *A Survey of Metropolitan Trial Courts—Los Angeles* AREA, Los Angeles, Parker & Sons, 1956.

Holtzoff, Alexander (ed.): *Federal Rules of Criminal Procedure*. (With notes prepared under the direction of the Advisory Committee appointed by the U.S.). New York, N.Y. Univ. School of Law, 1946.

Houts, Marshall: *From Arrest to Release*. Springfield, Thomas, 1958.

How the Supreme Court Is Reshaping the Country, USN&WR (July 6, 1964), 31.

Hunt, Peter: *Oscar Slater: the Great Suspect*. New York, Collier Books, 1963.

Hyde, Laurance M.: The Missouri Plan for Selection and Tenure of Judges, JCL&C, Vol.39, No.3 (Mar.-Apr., 1948-49), 277-88.

Illinois Legislative Council: *Justices of the Peace*. Springfield, 1954.

Inbau, Fred E.: Short Course for Prosecuting Attorneys at Northwestern University School of Law, JCLC&PS, Vol.42 (1951-52), 625.

Instruction to Jury, JCLC&PS, Vol.46 (1955-56), 854.

Ireland, Gordon: Double Jeopardy and Conspiracy in the Federal Courts, JCL&C, Vol.40, No.4 (Nov.-Dec., 1949), 445.

Kahn, Alfred J.: *A Court for Children*. New York, Columbia Univ. Press, 1953.

Kalven, Harry, Jr.: Report on the Jury Project, *Conference on Aims and Methods of Legal Research*, Ann Arbor, Univ. of Michigan Law School, Nov. 5, 1955.

Kamisar, Yale: Some Reflections on Criticizing the Courts and Policing the Police, JCLC&PS, Vol.53, No.4 (Dec., 1962), 453.

Lawder, Lee E.: Evidence . . . The Key That Locks It Up, L&O, Vol.11, No.7 (July, 1963).

Lemert, Edwin: The Grand Jury as an Agency of Social Control, ASR, Vol.10 (Dec., 1945), 751-58.

Lenroot, Katharine F.: The Juvenile Court Today, FP, Vol.13, No.3 (Sept., 1949), 9-15.

Levin, Stanley H.: Cross-examination of Defendant's Character Witnesses, JCL&C, Vol.40, No.1 (May-June, 1949), 58.

Llevy, I. D., and Smolens, B. J.: *Court in Session.* New York, Crown Publishers, 1950.

McCloskey, Robert G.: *The American Supreme Court.* Chicago, Univ. of Chicago Press, 1960.

MacNamara, Donald E. J.: Death and the Supreme Court, JCLC&PS, Vol.53, No.1 (Mar.-May, 1962), 82.

Martin, W. S.: The Role of a Jury in a Civil Case, *Jury Trials.* Special Lectures of the Law Society of Upper Canada, Toronto, Boos, 1959.

Mendelson, Wallace: *The Constitution and the Supreme Court.* New York, Dodd, Mead, 1959.

Metropolitan Criminal Courts of First Instance, HLR, Vol.70 (Dec., 1956), 320-49.

Murphy, Walter F., and Pritchett, C. Herman: *Courts, Judges and Politics.* New York, Random House, 1961.

Nedrud, Duane R.: The Career Prosecutor—A Proposed Department of Criminal Justice Act, JCLC&PS, Vol.52, No.1 (May-June, 1961), 103.

Newman, Charles L.: Trial by Jury: An Outmoded Relic? JCLC&PS, Vol.46 (Nov.-Dec., 1955), 512-18.

Nims, Harry D.: Pre-trial. New York, Baker, Voorhis, 1950.

Nutter, Ralph H.: The Quality of Justice in Misdemeanor Arraignment Courts, JCLC&PS, Vol.53, No.2 (June-Aug., 1962), 215.

Oberer, Walter E.: Does Disqualification of Jurors for Scruples Against Capital Punishment Constitute Denial of Fair Trial on Issue of Guilt? TLR, Vol.39 (May, 1961), 545-67.

Ohio Legislative Service Commission: *Criminal Procedures in Municipal Courts,* Report No.11. Columbus, State House, 1955.

Orfield, Lester B.: *Criminal Procedure from Arrest to Appeal.* New York, N.Y. Univ. Press, 1947.

Ploscowe, Morris: The Court and the Correctional System in Paul W. Tappan (ed.), *Contemporary Correction.* New York, McGraw-Hill, 1951.

Poverty and the Administration of Federal Criminal Justice. Report of the Attorney General's Committee on Poverty and the Administration of Criminal Justice, Submitted on February 25, 1963.

Qualification of Witness: Question for Court to Decide Whether a Witness Is an Expert, SE&SCD, Vol.3, No.2 (1964).

Reed, George J.: The Federal Youth Corrections Act in Operation, FP, Vol.18 (Sept., 1954), 15-19.

Roche, Redmond: Law Enforcement and Courts, TPY (1962).

Scigliano, Robert: *The Courts.* Boston, Little, Brown, 1962.

Shalloo, J. P.: The Courts—Guilty or Not Guilty, PW, Vol.10 (May, 1948), 6-8.

Sharrel, Burke: Our Legal System and How It Operates, MLS, Ann Arbor, Univ. of Michigan Law School, 1951.

Simon, Carolyn: The Case for Trial by Jury, NEW YORK TIMES MAGAZINE (July 11, 1956).

Some Aspects of the California Grand Jury System, STAN.LR, Vol.8 (July, 1956), 631-54.

Spaniol, Joseph F.: *The United States Courts.* Washington, D.C., U.S. Govt. Printing Office, 1959.

Standards for Specialized Courts Dealing with Children. A report prepared by the U.S. Dept. of Health, Education, and Welfare, Children's Bureau Pub. No.346, Washington, D.C., 1954.

Sterns, Myron: The Scandal of Our Traffic Courts, HARPER'S, Vol. (1946), 274-78.

Sunderland, E. R.: Qualifications and Compensation of Minor Court Judges, JAJS, Vol.29 (Dec., 1945), 111-116.

Tamm, Quinn: A National Justice Foundation, TPC, Vol.32, No.2 (Feb., 1965), 6.

Vanderbilt, Arthur T.: *Judges and Jurors: Their Functions, Qualifications and Selection.* Boston, Boston Univ. Press, 1956.

———: Minimum Standards of Judicial Administration. New York, The Law Center of N.Y. Univ. for the National Conference of Judicial Councils, 1949.

Wall, Patrick: Judicial Admissions: Their Use in Criminal Trial, JCLC&PS, Vol.53, No.1 (Mar.-May, 1962), 15.

Wallack, Walter M.: Is the Indeterminate Sentence Practical? JCL&C, Vol.35, No.5 (Jan.-Feb., 1945), 341.

Westin, Alan F. (ed.): *The Supreme Court: Views from the Inside*. New York, Dodd, Mead, 1951.

Woodruff, Phillip: *Call the Next Witness*. New York, Harcourt, Brace, 1948.

Younger, Richard D.: The Grand Jury Under

Attack, JCLC&PS, Vol.46 (1955-56), 26-49, 214-225.

Zeichner, Irving B.: Right to Bail, L&O, Vol.9 (Jan., 1961).

Zeisel, Hans, Kalven, Harry, Jr., and Buchholz, Bernard: *Delays in the Court*. Boston, Little, Brown, 1959.

Criminal Law

Abraham, H. J.: *Courts and Judges: an Introduction to the Judicial Process*. New York, Oxford, 1959.

————: *The Judicial Process*. New York, Oxford, 1962. (An introductory analysis of the Courts of the U.S., England and France.)

Adams, J. Bodkin: Noted English Case Ends with Acquittal of Dr. J. Bodkin Adams, POLICE, Vol.3, No.3 (Jan.-Feb., 1959), 46-48.

Alexander, Franz, and Staub, Hugo: *The Criminal, the Judge and the Public*, Rev. Ed. Glencoe, Free Press, 1956.

Allen, C. K.: *Law in the Making*. Toronto, Oxford, 1957.

Allen, Francis: Criminal Justice, Legal Values and the Rehabilitative Ideal, JCLC&PS, Vol.50 (Sept.-Oct., 1959), 226-232.

American Bar Association: *Law and Courts in the News*. Chicago, the Association, 1960.

Andenaus, Joseph: Determinism and Criminal Law, JCLC&PS, Vol.47, No.4 (Nov.-Dec., 1956), 406.

Anderson, Ronald A.: *Wharton's Criminal Law and Procedure*. Rochester, Lawyers Cooperative, 1957.

Averbach, Carl A., *et al.*: *Legal Process*. San Francisco, Chandler, 1961.

Aumann, F. R.: *The Instrumentalities of Justice: Their Forms, Functions and Limitations*. Columbus, Ohio State Univ., 1956.

Bailey, R. Emmett: The Burden of Proving Self-defense in Homicide Cases, JCL&C, Vol.39, No.2 (Mar.-Apr., 1948-49), 189-93.

Ball, John C.: Sources of Our Liberties, JCLC&PS, Vol.51, No.1 (Mar.-Apr., 1960-61), 84.

Barrett, Edward L., Jr.: Personal Rights, Property Rights and the Fourth Amendment, *The Supreme Court Review*, 1960.

Barth, Alan: *The Price of Liberty*. New York, Viking, 1961.

Baskin, James D., Jr.: Admissibility and Use of Mechanically and Electronically Recorded Statements, POLICE, Vol.8, No.6 (July-Aug., 1964), 51-55.

Bastiat, Frederic: *The Law*. New York, Foundation for Economic Education, 1950.

Beaney, William M.: *The Right to Counsel in American Courts*. Ann Arbor, Univ. of Michigan Press, 1955.

Beili, Melvin M.: *Ready for the Plaintiff*. New York, Popular Library, 1965. (Stories behind the courtroom scenes of one of America's dynamic lawyers who also represented Jack Ruby in Dallas.)

Bennet, James V.: American Law Institute IV, After Sentence—What? JCLC&PS, Vol.45 (1954-55), 537-40.

Bensing, Robert C.: A Comparative Study of American Sex Statutes, JCLC&PS, Vol.42 (1951-52), 57.

Berman, Harold J.: *Nature and Functions of Law*. New York, Foundation Press, 1958.

Berry, F. P.: *Rights of the Accused in Criminal Procedure, USA and USSR: A Comparison*. Washington, IACP, 1964.

Black, Charles: *Perspectives in Constitutional Law*. Englewood Cliffs, Prentice-Hall, 1963.

Black, Henry: *Black's Law Dictionary*. St. Paul, West Publishing Co., 1951.

Blackinston, Don T.: The Judge, The Defendant, and Criminal Law Administration. Unpublished Ph.D. Dissertation Univ. of Chicago, 1952.

Blanco, Victor H.: The Expert Witness in Criminal Trials, JCLC&PS, Vol.52, No.3 (Sept.-Oct., 1961), 317.

Blaustein, Albert P., and Porter, Charles O.: *The American Lawyer*. Chicago, Univ. of Chicago Press, 1954.

Block, Robert C.: Conflicting State and Local Laws, JCL&C, Vol.38, No.1 (Mar.-Apr., 1947), 40-49.

Bloomfield, L. M.: 1957 European Convention on Extradition, TPY (1959).

Bodenheimer, Edgar: *Jurisprudence*. Cambridge, Harvard Univ. Press, 1962.

Boten, B.: *The Prosecutor*. New York, Simon & Schuster, 1956.

Botein, Bernard: *Trial Judge*. New York, Cornerstone, 1963.

Bowler, Manley J.: Oral Argument in Criminal Prosecution, JCLC&PS, Vol.52, No.2 (July-Aug., 1961), 203.

Bowman, G. A.: Defense Against Lawsuits, TPC, Vol.29, No.4 (Apr., 1962), 6.

Breckenridge, A. C.: The Constitutional Basis for Cooperative Crime Control, JCL&C, Vol.39, No.5 (Mar.-Apr., 1948-49), 565-681.

Brennan, William J., Jr.: Law and Psychiatry Must Join in Defending Mentally Ill Criminals, ABAJ (Mar., 1963).

Brown, C. G.: *You May Take the Witness.* Austin, Univ. of Texas, 1955.

Brown, Esther L.: *Lawyers, Law Schools and the Public Service.* New York, Russell Sage Foundation, 1948.

Brownell, Emory A.: *Legal Aid in the U.S.* Rochester, Lawyers Co-operative, 1951.

———: *Supplement to Legal Aid in the U.S.* Rochester, Lawyers Co-operative, 1961.

Bullard, Garry R.: Wiretapping and the Supreme Court, JCLC&PS, Vol.49, No.4 (1958-59), 342.

Buller, Arthur: Legal Remedies Against Corrupt Law Enforcement Officers, JCLC&PS, Vol.48, No.4 (Nov.-Dec., 1957), 414.

Bunn, C. W.: *A Brief Survey of the Jurisdiction and Practice of the Courts of the United States,* Rev. Ed. Minneapolis, West, 1949.

Busch, Francis X.: *Prisoners at the Bar.* New York, Signet, 1962.

Buzard, Donald S.: Jury Note Taking in Criminal Trials, JCLC&PS, Vol.42 (1951-52), 490.

Cahill, Thomas J.: Responsibility on your Shoulders, L&O, Vol.8, No.9 (1960).

Caldwell, Arthur B.: American Life Under the Rule of Law, POLICE (Jan.-Feb., 1963).

California Board of Equalization: *Rules and Regulations Issued in Pursuance of Section 22 of Beverage Control Act.* Sacramento, 1950.

California Dept. of Education; Bureau of Trade and Industrial Education: *Rules of Evidence.* Sacramento, 1949.

———: *Civil Process and Procedure.* Sacramento, 1949.

———: *Criminal Law Course, Student Officers' Work Outline Emphasizing Elements of Major Crime.* Sacramento, 1949.

———: *Criminal Law Outline.* Sacramento, 1949.

———: *Extradition and Rendition.* Sacramento, 1949.

California State Senate: *Constitution of the State of California and of the United States and Other Documents.* Sacramento, 1961.

California Youth Authority: *California Laws Relating to Youthful Offenders, Including Youth Authority Act, The Juvenile Court Law.* Sacramento, 1947.

Callagy, Martin V.: Legal Aid in Criminal Cases, JCLC&PS, Vol.42 (1951-52), 589.

Callison, I. P.: *Courts of Injustice.* New York, Twayne, 1956.

Canals, J. M.: Classicism, Positivism and Social Defense, JCLC&PS, Vol.50, No.6 (Mar.-Apr., 1960), 541.

Cardozo, Benjamin N.: Jurisprudence in *Selected Writings of Benjamin Cardozo.* New York, Fallon, 1947.

Carlin, Jerome: *Ethics and the Legal Profession.* New York, Columbia Univ., Bureau of Applied Research, Aug., 1963.

Castenholz, Fred E.: Judicial Rulings on Unions, TPC, Vol.29, No.4 (Apr., 1962), 38.

Cerny, Joe H.: Tips to Police Witnesses, PO-LICE, Vol.3, No.4 (Mar.-Apr., 1959), 39-43.

Chandler, H. P.: Making the Judicial Machinery Function Efficiently, NYULQR, Vol.22 (July, 1947), 445-456.

Chapple, Norman L.: Freedom of Assembly—Constitutional Right or Lynch Law, JCLC&PS, Vol.55, No.3 (Sept., 1964), 425.

Chell, Eugene P.: Sunday Blue Laws: An Analysis of Their Position in Our Society, TLR, Vol.12 (Spring, 1958), 505-21.

Chernak, John A.: Witness Not Entitled to Counsel in Hearing Before State Fire Marshall, JCLC&PS, Vol.46 (1955-56), 600.

Chessman, Caryl: *The Face of Justice.* Englewood Cliffs, Prentice-Hall, 1957.

Chidres, Robert: The Victims, HARPER'S, Vol.228, No.1367 (Apr., 1964), 159-163.

Chodorov, Stephan: *The Criminal Case.* New York, Collier, 1964.

Clark, George L.: *Cases on Criminal Law.* Indianapolis, Bobbs-Merrill, 1954.

Clark, and Marshall: *A Treatise on the Law of Crimes.* 6th Ed. Revised by Melvin Wigersky. Chicago, Callaghan, 1958.

Clayton, James E.: *The Making of Justice.* New York, Dutton, 1964.

Cleary, Edward: *Handbook of Illinois Evidence.* Boston, Little, Brown.

Coakley, J. Frank: A District Attorney's Experience with Extradition, TPY (1959).

Coben, Stanley: *A. Mitchell Palmer: Politician.* New York, Columbia Univ., 1963.

Cobin, Herbert L.: Citizen Action for Abolishment of Capital Punishment, JCLC&PS, Vol.52, No.1 (May-June, 1961), 90.

Cohen, Morris R.: *Reason and Law.* Glencoe, Free Press, 1950.

Cohen, George A.: Uniform Act to Secure the

Attendance of Out of State Witnesses in Criminal Cases, JCLC&PS, Vol.51, No.1 (Mar.-Apr., 1960-61), 72.

Cohen, Nathan: *Criminal Law Seminar.* Brooklyn, Central, 1961.

Combs, McFarland, Jr.: The Scope of Discovery Against the Prosecution in Criminal Cases— How Far Should It Be Widened?, JCLC&PS, Vol.42 (1951-52), 774.

Comisky, Marvin: *Basic Criminal Procedure.* Philadelphia, Committee on Continuing Legal Education, 1958.

Commission on Organization of the Executive Branch of the Government: *Legal Services and Procedure.* Washington, U.S. Govt. Printing Office, 1955.

Conwill, Allan F.: Suppression Prior to Indictment of Confessions Unconstitutionally Obtained, JCL&C, Vol.38, No.5 (Mar.-Apr., 1947-48), 509-17.

Cooper, Frank E.: *Administrative Agencies and the Court.* Ann Arbor, Univ. of Michigan Law School, 1951.

Corcoran, Charles W.: Federal Court Remedies Against State and Local Police Abuses (third degree practices enjoyed), JCL&C, Vol.39, No.4 (Mar.-Apr., 1948-49), 490-98.

Corroborating Evidence Must Connect Defendant Without Reference to Abortee's Testimony, JCLC&PS, Vol.46 (1955-56), 684.

Criminal Evidence: Admissibility of Doctor's Evidence as to Nature of the Instrument That Had Caused the Wound, SE&SCD, Vol.3, No.2 (1964).

Criminal Evidence: Admission of X-ray Photographs, SE&SCD, Vol.3, No.1 (1964).

Cushman, Robert E.: *Leading Constitutional Decisions.* New York, Appleton, 1963.

Dahl, Raymond A.: Importance of Observation in Law Enforcement, JCLC&PS, Vol.43, No.1 (May-June, 1952), 103.

Dammann, Peter A.: Criminal Liability of a Businessman for Conduct of His Employees, JCL&C, Vol.38, No.2 (Mar.-Apr., 1947-48), 132-151.

———: Recent Decisions on the Admissibility of Confessions, JCL&C, Vol.39, No.2 (Mar.-Apr., 1948-49), 202-08.

———: Recent Federal Court Decisions on Admissibility of Confessions, JCL&C, Vol.38, No.6 (Mar.-Apr., 1947-48), 627-629.

Daniel, Hawthorne: *Judge Medina.* New York, Funk, 1952.

Davis, Arthur A.: Limitations Upon the Prosecutor's Summation to the Jury, JCLC&PS, Vol.42 (1951-52), 73.

Davis, F. J., Foster, H. H., Jeffrey, C. R., and

Davis, E. E.: *Society and the Law.* New York, Free Press, 1962.

Davis, Kenneth C.: *Administrative Law.* Minneapolis, West, 1951.

Davitt, Thomas E.: *The Elements of Law.* Boston, Little, Brown, 1949.

Dawson, Robert O., and Ball, Harry: *Sentencing.* Boston, Little, Brown, 1965.

Day, Carl E.: *Handbook of California Evidence.* San Francisco, the Author, 1948.

Day, Frank D.: Criminal Law Enforcement and a Free Society, JCLC&PS, Vol.54, No.3 (1963), 360.

Denial of Right to Counsel Renders Conviction Void, JCLC&PS, Vol.46 (1955-56), 530.

Denning, Alfred: *The Road to Justice.* London, Stevens, 1955.

Dession, George H.: *Criminal Law Administration and Public Order.* Charlottesville, Michie Casebook, 1948.

Determination of Gestation Period in Bastardry Proceedings, JCLC&PS, Vol.46 (1955-56), 746.

Deutscher, Irwin: The Petty Defender: A Sociological Alien, JCL&C, Vol.44, No.5 (Jan.-Feb., 1954), 592-595.

Devlin, J. Daniel: *Criminal Courts and Procedure.* London, Butterworth, 1960.

Devlin, Patrick: *The Criminal Prosecution in England.* New Haven, Yale Univ. Press, 1958.

Dienstein, William: *Are You Guilty? An Introduction to the Administration of Criminal Justice in the United States.* Springfield, Thomas, 1954.

———: The Rights of the Subject in Lie-detector Interrogation, POLICE, Vol.1, No.2 (Nov.-Dec., 1956), 41-51.

Donigan, Robert L., and Fisher, Edward C.: Confessions: Warning of Rights, Part 1, TD&R (May, 1965), 20-24.

———, & ———: *Evidence Handbook.* Illinois, The Traffic Institute of Northwestern Univ., 1958.

———, & ———: *Know the Law.* Evanston, Traffic Institute of Northwestern Univ., 1958.

Dorf, Phillip: *The Constitution of the United States.* New York, Oxford, 1948.

Doud, Donald: Elements of Effective Testimony, JCL&C, Vol.44, No.4 (Nov.-Dec., 1953), 522-24.

Douglass, William O.: The Durham Rule: A Meeting Ground for Lawyers and Psychiatrists, ILR, Vol.41 (Summer, 1956), 485-95.

Doyle, Frederick: Marshalling of Proof in Homicide Cases, JCL&C, Vol.36, No.6 (1945-46), 473.

Drafts of the New Criminal Law Principles, CDSP, Vol.10 (Sept. 24, 1958), 3-8.

Drinkwater, John: A Three Hundred Fiftieth Anniversary: English Common Law in the United States, ABAJ (Sept., 1959).

Dubin, Lawrence M.: The Informer's Privilege vs. the Constitution, JCLC&PS, Vol.50, No.6 (Mar.-Apr., 1960), 554.

Edwards, J. L.: *Mens Rea in Statutory Offenses.* New York, St. Martin's, 1955.

Einhorn, Edward Martin: The Exclusionary Rule in Operation a Comparison of Illinois, California and Federal Law, JCLC&PS, Vol.50, No.2 (July-Aug., 1959), 144.

Eliasberg, W. G.: Wrong Sentences and Wrong Acquittals in Criminal Trials, JCLC&PS, Vol.51, No.1 (Mar.-Apr., 1960-61), 86.

———: Opposing Expert Testimony, JCL&C, Vol.36, No.4 (1945-46), 231.

———: To Examine Testamentary and Testimonial Capacity, JCL&C, Vol.44, No.3 (Sept.-Oct., 1953), 320-25.

Enforcement of Future Violations of Municipal Ordinance, JCLC&PS, Vol.46 (1955-56), 915.

Erisman, Fred: How a Defense Lawyer Hopes to Profit from the Testimony of an Officer, POLICE, Vol.4, No.2 (Nov.-Dec., 1959), 54-57.

Evan, William M. (ed.): *Law and Sociology.* New York, Free Press, 1962.

Eulau, Heinz, and Sprague, John D.: *Lawyers in Politics.* Indianapolis, Bobbs-Merrill, 1964.

Expert Witnesses: Contradiction of Expert Witnesses on a Collateral Issue, SE&SCD, Vol.2, No.6 (1964).

Fahr, Samuel M.: Why Lawyers Are Dissatisfied with the Social Sciences, WLR, Vol.1 (Spring, 1961), 161-75.

Failure to Provide Medical Care for Newborn Child: JCLC&PS, Vol.46 (1955-56), 80.

Fellman, David: *The Defendant's Rights.* New York, Holt, Rinehart, 1958.

Felony—Murder Rule Applied, JCLC&PS, Vol.46 (1955-56), 530.

Flynn, John L.: Indictment Sufficiency—The Latimore Case, JCLC&PS, Vol.45 (1954-55), 576-80.

———: The Right to a Public Trial vs. The Protection of Public Morals, JCLC&PS, Vol.45 (1945-55), 449-53.

Forrest Cool Law Review: *Criminal Law Evidence.* Woodland Hills, Forrest Cool.

Fowler, Gene: *The Great Mouthpiece.* New York, Bantam, 1962.

Fox, Sanford J.: Statutory Criminal Law: The

Neglected Part, JCLC&PS, Vol.52, No.4 (Nov.-Dec., 1961), 392.

Frank, Jerome: *Courts on Trial.* Princeton, Princeton Univ. Press, 1949.

———: *Law and the Modern Mind,* 6th Ed. New York, Coward-McCann, 1949.

———, **& Frank, Barbara:** *Not Guilty.* New York, Doubleday, 1957.

Frank, John P.: *Cases on the Constitution.* New York, McGraw-Hill, 1951.

Frankfurter, Felix: *The Case of Sacco and Vanzetti.* New York, Universal Library, 1961.

Freedman, Warren: *Society on Trial: Current Court Decisions and Social Change.* Springfield, Thomas, 1965.

Fremon, William J.: Private Communications with Grand Juries, JCL&C, Vol.38, No.1 (Mar.-Apr., 1947-48), 43-48.

Freund, Paul A.: *The Supreme Court of the United States.* Cleveland, Meridian, 1961.

Fricke, Charles W.: *Digest of California Criminal Decisions,* 1942-47. Los Angeles, Peace Officers' Civil Service Assn. 1947.

———, **& Alarcon, A. L.:** *California Criminal Evidence,* 5th Ed. Los Angeles, Legal Book Store, 1961.

———, **& ———:** *California Criminal Procedure.* Los Angeles, Legal Book Store, 1962.

Frood, Gerald S.: American Law Institute III, Sentencing Function of the Judge, JCLC&PS, Vol.45 (1954-55), 531-36.

Fundamentals of Soviet Criminal Legislation, the Judicial System and Criminal Court Procedure: Moscow, Foreign Languages Publ., 1960.

Galler, Gerald H.: Exclusion of Illegal State Evidence in Federal Courts, JCLC&PS, Vol.49, No.5 (1958-59), 455.

Ganong, C. K., and Pearce, R. W.: *Law and Society.* Homewood, Irwin, 1965.

Gardner, Erle Stanley: Need for New Concepts in the Administration of Criminal Justice, JCLC&PS, Vol.50, No.1 (May-June, 1959), 20.

Gehlbach, John R.: Res Judicata and Conspiracy, JCL&C, Vol.39, No.1 (Mar.-Apr., 1948-49), 58-65.

Gehr, Arthur C.: Enforcement of Constitutional Right to a Speedy Trial, JCL&C, Vol.39, No.2 (Mar.-Apr., 1948-49), 193-208.

George, B. J., Jr.: A New Approach to Criminal Law, HARPER'S, Vol.228, No.1367 (Apr., 1964), 183-86.

Georgia Laws for Weapons and Motor Vehicles, TPC, Vol.30 (Oct., 1963), 50.

Gerstein, Richard M.: A Prosecutor Looks at

Capital Punishment, JCLC&PS, Vol.51, No.2 (Mar.-Apr., 1960-61), 252.

———: Prosecution vs. Defense of Insanity, TPY (1959).

Giesler, Jerry: *Hollywood Lawyer: the Jerry Giesler Story.* New York, Permabook, 1962.

Ginsberg, Morris: *On Justice in Society.* Baltimore, Penguin, 1965.

Givskov, Carl Christian: The Danis "Purge Laws," JCL&C, Vol.39, No.4 (Mar.-Apr., 1948-49), 447-80.

Glueck, Sheldon: A Federal Act to Establish the Roscoe Pound Academy of Criminal Justice, HUJL, Vol.2 (1964).

———: Criminal Law, Criminology and Crime Causation, JJA, Vol.1 (1960).

———: *Law and Psychiatry.* Baltimore, Johns Hopkins, 1962.

———: Law and the Stuff of Life, HLSB, Vol.14, No.6 (1963).

———: The New Course in Criminal Law, HLSB, Vol.12 (1950).

———: On the Conduct of a Seminar in Administration of Criminal Justice, JLE, Vol.16, No.1 (1963).

———: Predictive Devices and the Individualization of Justice, LCP, Vol.23, (1958), 461-76.

———: *Roscoe Pound and Criminal Justice.* Dobbs Ferry, Oceana, 1965.

———, **and Livingston, Hall:** *Cases on Criminal Law and Its Enforcement,* 2nd Ed. St. Paul, West, 1958.

———, & ———: *Criminal Law.* Cambridge, Harvard Law School, 1950.

Golden, Milton M.: *Hollywood Lawyer.* New York, Signet, 1960.

Gourley, G. Douglas: Criminal Procedure and Civil Rights, JCLC&PS, Vol.50, No.1 (May-June, 1959), 71.

Grimshaw, Allen D.: Police Agencies and Prevention of Racial Violence, JCLC&PS, Vol.54, No.1 (1963), 110.

Green, Edward: *Judicial Attitudes in Sentencing.* London, Macmillan, 1961.

Guttmacher, M. S., and Weinhofen, H.: *Psychiatry and the Law.* New York, Norton, 1952.

Haley, Andrew G., *et al.: Law and Upper Space: A Symposium,* SLULJ, Vol.5 (Spring, 1958), 1-133.

Hall, Jerome: *Cases and Readings on Criminal Law and Procedure.* Indianapolis, Bobbs-Merrill, 1949.

———: *General Principles of Criminal Law.* Indianapolis, Bobbs-Merrill, 1960.

———: Science and Reform in Criminal Law, UPLR, Vol.100 (Apr., 1952), 787-804.

———: *Theft, Law and Society,* 2nd Ed. Indianapolis, Bobbs-Merrill, 1952.

Hand, Learned: *The Bill of Rights.* Cambridge, Harvard Univ. Press, 1958.

———: *The Spirit of Liberty.* Papers and addresses collected. With an Introduction and notes by Irving Dilliard, New York, Knopf, 1952.

Hansen, Kenneth H.: Waiver of Constitutional Right of Confrontation, JCL&C, Vol.39, No.1 (Mar.-Apr., 1948-49), 55-58.

Harding, A. L. (ed.): *The Administration of Justice in Retrospect.* Dallas, Southern Methodist Univ., 1957.

Harno, Albert J.: The American Law Institute Proceedings, May 20, 1954—I, Crime, and Punishment, JCLC&PS, Vol.45 (1954-55), 520-23.

———: *Legal Education in the U.S.* San Francisco, Bancroft-Whitney, 1953.

———: Some Significant Developments in Criminal Law and Procedure in the Last Century, JCLC&PS, Vol.42 (1951-52), 427.

Hart, H. L. A.: *The Concept of Law.* Oxford, Clarendon Press, 1961.

Hart, Henry M., Jr.: The Aims of the Criminal Law, L&CP (Summer, 1958).

Henson, Ray D. (ed.): *Landmarks of Law.* New York, Harper, 1960.

Hill, Warren P., and Watson, Daniel: Legislation Concerning Alibis, Perjury, Self-incrimination, Immunity, Official Conduct, and Grand Juries, JCL&C, Vol.39, No.5 (Mar.-Apr., 1948-49), 629-46.

Hilton, Ordway, Proof of an Unaltered Document, JCLC&PS, Vol.49, No.6 (1958-59), 601.

Hine, R. L.: *Confessions of an Un-common Attorney.* New York, Macmillan, 1945.

Hoebel, E. Adamson: *The Law of Primitive Man.* Cambridge, Harvard Univ. Press, 1954.

Holcomb, A. N.: *Our More Perfect Union: From 18th Century Principles to 20th Century Practice.* Cambridge, Harvard Univ. Press, 1950.

Holko, Ron: Small But: L&O, Vol.8, No.6 (June, 1960), 75.

Honig, Richard M.: Criminal Law Systematized, JCLC&PS, Vol.54, No.3 (1963), 273.

Hoover, J. Edgar: The Path of Democratic Justice, TPY (1961).

Houts, Marshall: *From Arrest to Release.* Springfield, Thomas, 1958.

———: *From Evidence to Proof.* Springfield, Thomas, 1956.

———: *The Rules of Evidence.* Springfield, Thomas, 1956.

Howard, Charles G., and Summers, Robert S.:

the Wind. New York, Bantam, 1960 (the Scopes Monkey Trial).

LeGrange, J. L.: Subpoena by Teletype, TPC, Vol.30 (Feb., 1963), 8.

Levi, Edward H.: *An Introduction to Legal Reasoning.* Chicago, Univ. of Chicago Press, 1949.

Levin, Kenneth: Habeas Corpus in Extradition Proceedings Involving Escaped Convicts, JCL&C, Vol.40, No.4 (Nov.-Dec., 1949), 484.

Levin, Theodore: Sentencing the Criminal Offender, FP, Vol.13 (Mar., 1949), 3-6.

Lewis, Anthony: *Gideon's Trumpet.* New York, Random, 1964.

Leyshon, Frank C.: *Leyshon's Briefs on Leading Ohio Cases.* Cincinnati, Anderson Co.

Liability for Failure to Protect Informer, JCLC&PS, Vol.46 (1955-56), 914.

Liability Respecting Non-existent Ordinance Violation, JCLC&PS, Vol.46 (1955-56), 153.

Libel, JCLC&PS, Vol.46 (1955-56), 914.

Linkon, Gordon: Proving Insanity Beyond a Reasonable Doubt: Leland vs. State of Oregon, JCLC&PS, Vol.43, No.4 (Nov.-Dec., 1952), 482.

Lipset, Seymour M., Trow, Martin A., and Coleman, James S.: *Union Democracy.* Glencoe, Free Press, 1956.

Llewellyn, K. N.: *The Bramble Bush: on Our Law and Its Study.* Dobbs Ferry, Oceana, 1957.

———: *Jurisprudence.* Chicago, Univ. of Chicago Press, 1962.

Lloyd, D. (ed.): *Introduction to Jurisprudence.* New York, Praeger, 1960.

Lockhart, William B., Kamisar, Yale, and Choper, Jesse H.: *The American Constitution Cases and Materials.* St. Paul, West, 1964.

———: *Constitutional Rights and Liberties.* St. Paul, West, 1964.

London, Ephraima (ed.): *The World of Law,* 2 Vols. New York, Simon & Schuster, 1960.

Lumbard, J. Edward: Mr. Justice Felix Frankfurter, JCLC&PS, Vol.56, No.2 (June, 1965), 138-42.

Lunden, Walter A.: Criminal Litigation in Iowa, 1935-1954, POLICE, Vol.3, No.3 (Jan.-Feb., 1959), 48-53.

McCart, Samuel W.: *Trial by Jury.* Philadelphia, Chilton, 1965.

McClaran, Joe W.: The Admissibility of an Accomplice's Confession Against a Non-confessing Defendant, JCL&C, Vol.39, No.4 (Mar.-Apr., 1948-49), 498.

McCloskey, Robert G.: *Essays in Constitutional Law.* New York, Vintage, 1957.

McCormick, Charles T.: *Cases and Materials on the Law of Evidence.* St. Paul, West.

———: *Evidence.* St. Paul, West.

———: *Handbook of the Law of Evidence.* St. Paul, West, 1954.

McGarr, Frank J.: The Exclusionary Rule: An Ill Conceived and Ineffective Remedy, JCLC&PS, Vol.52, No.3 (Sept.-Oct., 1961), 266.

McHargue, D.: *Appointments to the Supreme Court.* Unpublished, Ph.D. Dissertation, UCLA, 1949.

McKean, Dayton: *The Integrated Bar.* Boston, Houghton Mifflin, 1963.

McKinnon, H. R.: Hidden Power the Law, TPC, Vol.30 (Mar., 1963), 10.

McNaughton, John T.: The Privilege Against Self-incrimination—Its Constitutional Affection, Raison d'Etre and Miscellaneous Implications, JCLC&PS, Vol.51, No.2 (Mar.-Apr., 1960-61).

Maguire, Robert F.: How to Unpoison the Fruit—The Fourth Amendment and the Exclusionary Rule, JCLC&PS, Vol.55, No.3 (Sept., 1960), 307.

Mankiewicz, Don M.: *Trial.* New York, Harper, 1955.

Mannheim, Hermann: *Criminal Justice and Social Reconstruction.* New York, Oxford Univ. Press, 1946.

———: The Criminal Law and Mentally Abnormal Offenders, BJC, Vol.1 (Jan., 1961), 203-220.

———: The Criminal Law and Penology, Ginsberg, Morris (ed.), *Law and Opinion in 20th Century England.* Berkeley, Univ. of Calif. Press, 1959.

Mannaring, David R.: *Render Unto Caesar.* Chicago, Univ. of Chicago Press, 1962.

Mars, David: Legal Aid, Public Defenders and Criminal Justice, POLICE, Vol.1, No.3 (Jan.-Feb., 1957), 23-28.

———: Public Defenders, JCLC&PS, Vol.46 (1955-56), 199-210.

Mason, Alpheus T.: *Harlan Fiske Stone: Pillar of the Law.* New York, Viking Press, 1956.

———: *The Supreme Court from Taft to Warren.* New York, Norton, 1964.

———, **& Beaney, William M.:** *American Constitutional Law.* Englewood Cliffs, Prentice-Hall, 1959.

Mason, Paul: *Constitution of the State of California and the United States and Other Documents.* Sacramento, State Printing Office, 1949.

Mayer, Edward E.: Prefrontal Lobotomy in

Courts, JCL&C, Vol.38, No.6 (Mar.-Apr., 1947-48), 576-83.

Mayers, Lewis: *The American Legal Ssystem.* New York, Harper, 1963.

——: *The Machinery of Justice: an Introduction to Legal Structure and Process.* Englewood Cliffs, Prentice-Hall, 1963.

Melia, Aloysius J.: The Admissibility of Confessions in Evidence in Criminal Courts, POLICE, Vol.3, No.2 (Nov.-Dec., 1958), 12-15.

Meltzer, Bernard D.: Involuntary Confessions: The Allocation of Responsibility Between Judge and Jury, UCLR (Spring, 1954), Vol.29, No.3, 317-354.

Mendelson, Wallace: *The Constitution and the Supreme Court,* 2nd Ed. New York, Dodd, Mead, 1965.

Mental Incapacity to Stand Trial, JCLC&PS, Vol.46 (1955-56), 850.

Mentally Disabled and the Law. Chicago, American Bar Foundation, 1960.

Meyer, Lee W.: *Public Defenders.* New York, Institute of Judicial Administration, 1956.

Meyers, Thomas J.: The Riddle of Legal Insanity, JCL&C, Vol.44, No.3 (Sept.-Oct., 1953), 330-39.

Michie's Tenn. Code. Charlottesville, Va., Michie Co.

Michigan Police Law Manual. East Lansing, Michigan Association of Chiefs of Police, 1954.

Miller, Frank W.: *Prosecution.* Boston, Little, Brown, 1965.

Millspaugh, Martin: Trial by Mass Media, POQ, Vol.13 (1950), 554-558.

Minow, Newton: Some Legal Aspects of the Hiss Case, JCL&C, Vol.40, No.3 (Sept.-Oct., 1949), 344.

Modification of Sentence on Court's Own Motion, JCLC&PS, Vol.46 (1955-56), 529.

Montgomery, Robert H.: *Sacco-Vanzetti, the Murder and the Myth.* New York, Devin-Adair, 1960.

Mora, Ronald N.: The Right of an Accused to Obtain Pre-trial Inspection of His Confession, JCLC&PS, Vol.48, No.3 (Sept.-Oct., 1957), 305.

Moreland, C. C.: *Equal Justice Under Law.* Dobbs Ferry, Oceana, 1957.

Moreland, Roy: *Modern Criminal Procedure.* New York, Bobbs-Merrill, 1959.

Morgan, William G.: Expert Witness Fees, JCLC&PS, Vol.43, No.6 (Mar.-Apr., 1953), 777.

——: The Grand Jury Illinois, JCL&C, Vol.44, No.1 (May-June, 1953), 49-90.

Moreland, Roy: *Modern Criminal Procedure.* Indianapolis, Bobbs-Merrill, 1959.

——: *The Law of Homicide.* Indianapolis, Bobbs-Merrill, 1952.

Morris, Norval R.: Human Rights and Criminal Law: Progress in the United Nations, PO-LICE, Vol.6, No.6 (July-Aug., 1962), 23-25.

——, & Turner, Cynthia: The Lawyer and Criminological Research, VLR, Vol.44 (Feb., 1958), 163-83.

Mottla, Gabriel V.: *New York Evidence, Proof of Cases.* Rochester, The Lawyers Cooperative, 1954.

Mueller, Gerhard: Criminal Law and Its Administration, NYULR, Vol.34 (Jan., 1959), 82-115.

——: Tort, Crime and the Primitive, JCLC&PS, Vol.46 (1955-56), 303.

Mullen, James M.: *Let Justice Be Done.* Philadelphia, Dorrance, 1952.

Murphy, Glen R.: Court Decisions, TPC, Series appears in almost all editions.

Murphy W. F., and Pritchett, C. H. (eds.): *Courts, Judges and Politics.* New York, Random, 1961.

Musmanno, M. M.: *Verdict.* New York, Doubleday, 1958.

Nagel, Stuart S.: Judicial Background and Criminal Cases, JCLC&PS, Vol.53, No.3 (Sept.-Nov., 1962), 333.

Nedrud, Duane R.: The Career Prosecutor—Defects and Problems of the Present Prosecutor System, JCLC&PS, Vol.51, No.5 (Mar.-Apr., 1960-61), 557.

——: The Career Prosecutor—A Proposed Department of Criminal Justice Act, JCLC&PS, Vol.51, No.6 (Mar.-Apr., 1960-61), 649.

——: The Career Prosecutor—Prosecutors of Forty-Eight States, JCLC&PS, Vol.51, No.3 (Mar.-Apr., 1960-61), 343.

Negligence or Incompetency Not Ground for New Trial, JCLC&PS, Vol.46 (1955-56), 80.

Nellis, Joseph L.: Legal Aspects of the Kefauver Investigation, JCLC&PS, Vol.42 (1951), 163.

Nelson, Gerr: *Roulette Wheel Helps Village Enforce Laws.* Lansing, State Journal (Feb. 25, 1962).

New Federal Immunity Act Upheld, JCLC&PS, Vol.46 (1955-56), 79.

Newman, Donald J.: *Adjudication.* Boston, Little, Brown, 1965.

——: Pleading Guilty for Considerations: A Study of Bargain Justice, JCLC&PS, Vol.46 (Mar.-Apr., 1956), 780-90.

None Support Actions and the Uniform Reciprocal Enforcement Support Act, JCLC&PS, Vol.46 (1955-56), 519.

Notre Dame Lawyer (Symposium). The Role of the Supreme Court in the American Constitutional System, South Bend, Notre Dame Law School, 1959.

O'Donnell, Bernard: *Cavalcade of Justice.* New York, Macmillan, 1952.

Olney, Warren III: The American Bar Foundation's Survey of the Administration of Criminal Justice, POLICE, Vol.1, No.2 (Nov.-Dec., 1956), 52-57.

———: What the American Bar Foundation's Survey of Criminal Justice Means to Law Enforcement, TPY (1956).

Orfield, Lester B.: *Criminal Procedure From Arrest to Appeal.* New York, N.Y. Univ. Press, 1947.

———: Evidence of Guilt—Restrictions Upon Its Discovery or Compulsory Disclosure, JCLC&PS, Vol.51, No.3 (Mar.-Apr., 1960-61), 339.

Osterburg, James W.: Freedom of the Press vs. the Right to a Fair Trial, L&O, Vol.12 (Sept., 1964).

Overholser, Winfred: Psychiatric Expert Testimony in Criminal Cases Since McNaghton—A Review, JCLC&PS, Vol.42 (1951-52), 283.

———: *Psychiatrist and the Law.* New York, Harcourt, Brace, 1953.

Owen, John E.: A Quarter Century of Criminal Justice in Iowa, JCLC&PS, Vol.50, No.4 (Nov.-Dec., 1959), 387.

Ozmon, Nat P.: Defense Counsel Misconduct Resulting in Mistrial and Double Jeopardy, JCL&C, Vol.44, No.4 (Nov.-Dec., 1953), 468-471.

———: The Law Today on State Court Confession Admissibility, JLC&C, Vol.44, No.3 (Sept.-Oct., 1953), 342-43.

———: The Scope of Habeas Corpus Inquiry in Fugitive Extradition Cases, JCL&C, Vol.44, No.2 (July-Aug., 1953), 208-16.

Packard, Vance: *The Hidden Persuaders.* New York, McKay, 1957.

Palmer, Ben W.: An Imperishable System: What the World Owes to Roman Law, ABAJ (Nov., 1959).

Paulsen, Monrad G.: The Exclusionary Rule and Misconduct by the Police, JCLC&PS, Vol.52, No.3 (Sept.-Oct., 1962), 255.

———, **Kadish, Sanford H.:** *Criminal Law and Its Processes.* Boston, Little, Brown, 1962.

Peltason, Jack W.: *Federal Courts in the Political Process.* New York, Random House, 1955.

Pepper, Darrell L.: Some Factors Influencing Testimony, POLICE, Vol.3, No.5 (May-June, 1959), 65-69.

Perkins, Rollins: *Cases and Materials on Crim-*inal Law and Procedure. Brooklyn, Foundation Press, 1959.

———: *Criminal Law and Procedure.* Brooklyn, Foundation Press, 1959.

———: The Law of Homicide, JCL&C, Vol.36, No.6 (1945-46), 391.

———: *Perkins on Criminal Law.* Brooklyn, Foundation Press, 1957.

Peterson, Virgil W.: Case Dismissed the Unreasonable Leniency in American Justice, ATLANTIC MONTHLY, Vol.175 (Apr., 1945), 69-74.

Petrazycki, L. J.: *Law and Morality.* Cambridge, Harvard Univ. Press, 1955.

Physical Evidence—In Cases of Breaking and Entering, JCLC&PS, Vol.46 (1955-56), 911.

Pigeon, Helen: *Principles and Methods in Dealing with Offenders.* State College, Penn. Municipal Publ., 1948.

Police Manual of New Jersey Statutes. Newark, Gann Law Books. Pollock, Earl: Certiorari and Habeas Corpus: The Comity Comedy, JCLC&PS, Vol.42 (1951-52), 356.

———: Post-trial Remedies: The Illinois Merry-go-round Whirls On, JCLC&PS, Vol.42 (1951-52), 636.

Pollock, Frederick, and Maitland, Frederic W.: *The History of English Law,* 2nd Ed., 2 Vols. Washington, The Lawyer's Literary Club, 1959.

Post, C. Gordon: *An Introduction to the Law.* Englewood Cliffs, Prentice-Hall, 1963.

Pound, Roscoe: *Criminal Justice in America.* Cambridge, Harvard Univ. Press, 1945.

———: *An Introduction to the Philosophy of Law.* New Haven, Yale Univ. Press, 1954.

———: *Justice According to Law,* 3rd Ed. New Haven, Yale Univ. Press, 1958.

Prettyman, Barrett, Jr.: *Death and the Supreme Court.* New York, Harcourt, Brace, 1961.

The Proof of Guilt. London, Stevens & Sons, 1955.

Prosecutor's Use of "Rap Sheet" in Cross-examination, JCLC&PS, Vol.46 (1955-56), 852.

Public Trial: Discretion to Exclude Public and Press, JCLC&PS, Vol.46 (1955-56), 364.

Puttkammer, Ernst: *Administration of Criminal Law.* Chicago, Univ. of Chicago Press, 1953.

———: *Manual on Criminal Law Procedure.* Chicago, Chicago Crime Commission, 1946.

Radin, Max: *The Law and You.* New York, Mentor, 1955.

Radzinowicz, Leon, and Turner, J. W. C.: *The Modern Approach to Criminal Law,* 3 Vols.. London, Macmillan, 1948-53.

Reardon, Daniel P.: Criminal Law Enforcement and Personal Liberty, TPY (1963).

Reid, John: Understanding the New Hampshire

Doctrine of Criminal Insanity, YLJ, Vol.69 (Jan., 1960), 367-420.

Reversible Error to Admit Evidence, JCLC&PS, Vol.46 (1955-56), 745.

Reynolds, Quentin: *Courtroom.* New York, Popular, 1957.

Rheinstein, Max (ed.): *Max Weber on Law in Economy and Society.* Cambridge, Harvard Univ. Press, 1954.

Richardson, Wm.: *Law of Evidence,* 7th Ed. Boston, Little, Brown, 1948.

Rizer, Conrad: Mathematical Methods Used in a Manslaughter-by-Automobile Case, POLICE, Vol.1, No.2 (Nov.-Dec., 1956), 63-65.

Robin, Gerald D.: Justifiable Homicide by Peace Officer, JCLC&PS, Vol.54, No.2 (1963), 225.

Robinson, W. S.: Bias, Probability and Trial by Jury, ASR, Vol.15 (Feb., 1950), 73-78.

Rodell, Fred: *Woe Unto You, Lawyers!* New York, Pageant, 1957.

Roeburt, John: *Get Me Giesler.* New York, Belmont, 1962.

Rogers, William P.: Plea for a Public Defender, NEW YORK TIMES MAGAZINE (Apr. 21, 1957).

Rogge, John O.: *The First and Fifth with Some Excursions into Others.* New York, Thomas Nelson, 1960.

Rosenblum, Victor G.: *Law as a Political Instrument.* New York, Doubleday, 1955.

Rovers, Richard H.: *Howe & Hummel.* New York, Paperback, 1947.

Rubin, Philip: Collateral Relief from Convictions in Violation of Due Process in Illinois, JCL&C, Vol.38, No.2 (Mar.-Apr., 1947-48), 139-50.

Rubin, Sol.: *The Law of Criminal Correction.* St. Paul, West, 1963.

Rules, of Criminal Procedure for the U.S. District Courts. Washington, U.S. Govt. Printing Office, May 1, 1956. (Printed for the use of the Committee on the Judiciary House of Representatives.)

St. Johns, Adela Rogers: *Final Verdict.* Garden City, Doubleday, 1962.

Satterfield, John C.: The President's Page, ABAJ (July, 1962).

Savitz, Leonard D.: Capital Crimes as Defined in American Statutory Law, JCLC&PS, Vol.46 (Sept.-Oct., 1955), 355-63.

Schatkin, Sidney B.: Paternity Processings—A Changing Concept, JCLC&PS, Vol.42 (1951-52), 821.

Schigliano, R. G.: *The Michigan One-man Grand Jury.* East Lansing, Michigan State Univ. Press, 1957.

Schmidhauser, J. R.: *The Supreme Court: Its Politics, Personalities, and Procedures.* New York, Holt, Rinehart & Winston, 1960.

Schoepfer, Arthur E.: Legal Aid a Civic Responsibility, NPPAY (1948).

Schulman, Sidney: *Toward Judicial Reform in Pennsylvania.* Philadelphia, Univ. of Penn. Law School, 1962.

Schmideberg, Melitta: The Offender's Attitude Towards Punishment, JCLC&PS (Sept.-Oct., 1960).

Schultz, Fritz: *History of Roman Legal Science.* Oxford, Clarendon, 1946.

Schwartz, B.: *The Code Napoleon and the Common Law World.* New York, N.Y. Univ. Press, 1956.

Scott, Edgar E.: The Mallory Decision and the Vanishing Rights of Crime Victims, POLICE, Vol.4, No.5 (May-June, 1960), 61-64; No.6 (July-Aug., 1960), 28-30.

Schwartz, Bernard: *Supreme Court: Constitutional Revolution in Retrospect,* University of Chicago Press, 1960.

Seagle, William: *The History of Law.* New York, Tudor, 1946.

Sears, Roy W.: Illinois Double Jeopardy Act: An Empty Gesture, JCLC&PS, Vol.51, No.2 (Mar.-Apr., 1960-61), 236.

Sellers, Clark: Cross-examination from the Viewpoint of a Technical Witness, JCL&C, Vol.40, No.5 (Jan.-Feb., 1950), 654.

Selling, Lowell S.: The Role of the Court Clinic in the Administration of Justice, JCLIN.PSY. Vol.8 (Oct., 1946), 357-75.

Selzer, Melvin L.: Alcoholism and the Law: MIC.LR, Vol.56 (Dec., 1957), 237-48.

Shannon, Lyle W.: The Spatial Distribution of Criminal Defenses by States, JCLC&PS, Vol.45 (1954-55), 764-73.

Shuman, Samuel I.: *Legal Positivism.* Detroit, Wayne State Univ. Press, 1965.

Silving, Helen: Suicide and the Law, in Edwin S. Shneidman, and Norman L. Farberow, *Clues to Suicide.* New York, McGraw-Hill, 1957.

Shapiro, Irwin J.: Admissibility in Evidence of Statements Made in the Presence of the Defendant, JCL&C, Vol.38, No.5 (Mar.,-Apr., 1947-48), 514-17.

Slovenko, Ralph: *Sexual Behavior and the Law.* Springfield, Thomas, 1965.

Smigel, Erwin O.: *The Wall Street Lawyer.* New York, Free Press, 1964.

Smith, Emory: Unmasking the Pseudo-expert, SE&SCD, Vol.1, No.1 (1964).

Smith, Frederick: Extradition Requests—Some Practical Problems, TPY (1959).

Smith, Hiram M. J.: Implied Consent Law. TPC, Vol.29, No.8 (Aug., 1962), 6.

———: To Draw Blood, TPC, Vol.32, No.1 (Jan., 1965), 38-39.

Smith, J. M., and Murphy, P. L.: *Liberty and Justice.* New York, Knopf, 1958.

Snodgrasse, Richard M.: Crime and the Constitution Human: A Survey, JCLC&PS, Vol.42 (1951-52), 18.

Snyder, Orville C.: *An Introduction to Criminal Justice: Text and Cases.* Boston, Little, Brown, 1953.

Soberloff, Simon E.: Insanity and the Criminal Law, ABAJ, Vol.41 (Sept., 1955), 793-96.

Sowle, Claude R.: The Privilege Against Self-incrimination: Principles and Trends, JCLC&PS, Vol.51 No.2 (Mar.-Apr., 1960-61), 131.

Spaeth, Harold J.: *An Introduction to Supreme Court Decision Making.* San Francisco, Chandler, 1965.

Stannard, H.: *The Two Constitutions: a Comparative Study of British and American Constitutional Systems.* New York, Van Nostrand, 1959.

Stemm, Paul G.: Concepts in Modern Criminal Jurisprudence, JCLC&PS, Vol.49, No.3 (1958-59), 250.

Stibolt, Thomas B.: Exhaustion of State Remedies as Affecting Habeas Corpus Writs in Federal Courts, JCL&C, Vol.39, No.3 (Mar.-Apr., 1948-49), 357-59.

Strock, Faraday J.: Validity of the Admission Confession Distinction for Purposes of Admissibility, JCL&C, Vol.39, 743-50.

Sullivan, J. J.: *Criminal Procedures in Municipal, Justice and City Courts of California.* St. Paul, West, 1948.

Sullivan, Francis C.: Dying Declarations, PO-LICE, Vol.4, No.3 (Jan.-Feb., 1960), 46-47.

———: Public or Private Prosecution? POLICE, Vol.5, No.3 (Jan.-Feb., 1961), 31-32.

———: The Police and Criminal Procedures in Foreign Countries, POLICE, Vol.4, No.6 (July-Aug., 1960), 26-27.

———: The Res Gestae Exception to the Hearsay Rule, POLICE, Vol.4, No.4 (Mar.-Apr., 1960), 36-37.

———: The Hearsay Rule, POLICE, Vol.4, No.2 (Nov.-Dec., 1959), 37-39.

———: What about Extradition? POLICE, Vol.5, No.1 (Sept.-Oct., 1960), 50-51.

Sunderland, Edwon R.: *History of the American Bar Association.* 1953.

——— (ed.): *Government Under Law.* Cambridge, Harvard Univ. Press, 1956.

Swanson, Leland M.: A Cybernetic Law Information System of Los Angeles County. Unpublished doctoral dissertation, Univ. of Southern Calif., Los Angeles, 1963.

Symposium on the Right to Counsel, MLR (Apr., 1961).

Tamm, Quinn: Constitutional Law Enforcement, TPY (1960).

———: Law Enforcement in a Democracy, TPY (1959).

——— (ed.): Legal Status of Metal-studded Tires, TPC, Vol.32, No.2 (Feb., 1965), 35.

Testimony Insufficient to Sustain "Pig Larceny" Conviction, JCLC&PS, Vol.46 (1955-56), 364.

Thompson, Jim: Self-incrimination and the Two Sovereignties Rule, JCLC&PS, Vol.49, No.3 (1958-59), 240.

Tinnelly, Joseph T.: *Part-time Legal Education in the U.S.* Brooklyn, Foundation Press, 1957.

Traver, Robert: *Small Town D.A.* Greenwich, Fawcett, 1958.

Tremon, William J.: Private Communications with Grand Jury, JCL&C, Vol.38, No.1 (Mar.-Apr., 1947-48), 43-48.

Triska, Joseph F.: *Juvenile Laws in California,* 2nd Ed. Los Angeles, Smith, 1948.

Turner, J. W. Cecil (ed.): *Kenney's Outline of Criminal Law,* 17th Ed. Cambridge, Cambridge Univ. Press, 1958.

Tuttle, Harris B.: Mock Trial Highlights Camera Use in Courts, POLICE, Vol.4, No.5 (May-June, 1960), 74.

United Nations: *Second United Nations Congress on the Prevention of Crime and the Treatment of Offenders.* New York, Dept. of Economic and Social Affairs, 1960.

United States Bureau of the Census: *Annual Reports on Judicial Criminal Statistics,* 1932-45. Washington, D.C. U.S. Govt. Printing Office, 1934-47.

Use of Majority Verdicts in the United States, Vol.33, JAJS (Dec., 1949).

Vanderbilt, A. T.: *The Challenge of Law Reform.* Princeton, Princeton Univ. Press, 1955.

———: *The Doctrine of Separation of Powers and Its Present-day Significance.* Lincoln, Univ. of Nebraska, 1953.

———: *Judges and Jurors: Their Functions, Qualifications, and Selection.* Boston, Boston Univ., 1956.

———: *Men and Measures in the Law.* New York, Knopf, 1949.

———: *Minimum Standards of Judicial Administration.* New York, N.Y. Univ. Press, 1949.

Wagner, Wienczyslaw: Conspiracy in Civil Law Countries, JCLC&PS, Vol.42 (1951-52), 171.

———: *The Federal States and Their Judiciary: a Comparative Study.* New York, Humanities, 1959.

Wahlen, Howard: Defending Police Against Lawsuits, TPC, Vol.29, No.4 (Apr., 1962), 6.

Waite, John B.: *Criminal Law and Its Enforcement,* 3rd ed. Brooklyn, Foundation, 1947.

Walker, Daniel, and Hill, Warren P.: Legislation Concerning Alibis, Perjury, Self-incrimination, Immunity, Official Conduct and Grand Juries, JCL&C, Vol.39, No.5 (Mar.-Apr., 1948-49), 629-46.

Wang, Huai, Ming: Chinese and American Criminal Law—Some Comparisons, JCLC&PS, Vol.46 (1955-56), 796-832.

Ward, Francis M.: In-custody Interrogations, TPC, Vol.32, No.3 (Mar., 1965), 52-59.

Weeks, Robert P. (ed.): *Commonwealth vs. Sacco and Vanzetti.* Englewood Cliffs, Prentice-Hall, 1958.

Weinberg, Arthur: *Attorney for the Damned.* New York, Simon and Schuster, 1957.

Weshler, Herbert: American Law Institute. A Thoughtful Code of Substantive Law, JCLC&PS, Vol.45 (1954-55), 524-30.

Westin, Alan: *The Anatomy of a Constitutional Law Case.* New York, Macmillan, 1958. (The steel seizure case of 1952.)

————: *The Supreme Court: Views from Inside.* New York, Norton, 1961.

When Is a Trailer a Dwelling House, JCLC&PS, Vol.46 (1955-56), 744.

Wiard, Seth: The Cross-examination of Expert Witnesses, SE&SCD, Vol.2, No.6 (1964).

————: The Preparation and Presentation of Expert Testimony, SE&SCD, Vol.2, No.2 (1964).

Wigmore, John H.: *The Principles of Judicial Proof.* Boston, Little, Brown.

Wile, Ira A.: Francis Crowley vs. the People of the State of New York, SURVEY, Vol.68 (Feb., 1952), 476-578.

Williams, Francis Emmett: *The Lawyer and Law Notes.* Brooklyn, American Law Book, 1946.

Williams, Glanville L.: The Exclusionary Rule Under Foreign Law: England, JCLC&PS, Vol.52, No.5 (Sept.-Oct., 1961), 272-75.

————: Police Interrogation Privileges and Limitations Under Foreign Law: England, JCLC&PS, Vol.52, No.1 (Jan.-Feb., 1961), 50-57.

————: *The Sanctity of Life and the Criminal Law.* New York, Knopf, 1957.

Williams, J. B.: *Criminal Law Outline,* Rev. Ed. Sacramento, Calif. State Dept. of Education, 1954.

Winchell, John W.: Intent in Criminal Law: The Legal Tower of Babel, CULR, Vol.8 (Jan., 1958), 31-42.

Wingersky, Melvin F.: *A Treatise on the Law of Crime, Clark & Marshall,* 6th Ed. Chicago, Callaghan, 1958.

Wolff, Aaron S.: Prejudicial Evidence in Prosecution Under Habitual Criminal Acts, JCL&C, Vol.44, No.6 (Mar.-Apr., 1959), 759-766.

————: Validity of the Appointment of a Special Prosecutor in a Criminal Proceeding, JCL&C, Vol.44, No.5 (Jan.-Feb., 1954), 616-20.

Wolff, Hans Julius: *Roman Law: An Historical Introduction.* Norman, Univ. of Oklahoma Press, 1951.

Wolfgang, Marvin E.; Kelly, Arlene; and Nolde, Hans C.: Comparison of the Executed and the Commuted Among Admissions to Death Row, JCLC&PS, Vol.53, No.3 (Sept.-Nov., 1962), 301.

Wormser, Rene A.: *The Law.* New York, Simon and Schuster, 1949.

Wyman, Louis C.: A Common Sense View of the Fifth Amendment, JCLC&PS, Vol.51, No.2 (Mar.-Apr., 1960-61), 155.

Zeichner, Irving B.: Aiding and Abetting, L&O, Vol.11, No.11 (Nov., 1963). This and the following articles are from a feature "According to Law" appearing monthly.

————: Assemble or Congregate, L&O, Vol.11, No.1 (Jan., 1963).

————: Burden of Proof, L&O, Vol.9 (June, 1961).

————: Careless Driving, L&O, Vol.9 (Apr., 1961).

————: Confession, L&O, Vol.9 (Dec., 1961).

————: Conspiracy to Lie, L&O, Vol.9 (Mar., 1961).

————: Crime on Indian Reservation, L&O, Vol.9 (May, 1961).

————: Disturbing the Peace, L&O, Vol.13 (May, 1965).

————: Double Jeopardy, Entrapment, L&O, Vol.10 (Oct., 1962).

————: Drug at Trial, L&O, Vol.9 (Feb., 1961).

————: Entrapment, L&O, Vol.9 (Oct., 1961).

————: Equal Protection, L&O, Vol.11 (Oct., 1963).

————: Evidence of Another Crime, L&O, Vol.11 (Nov., 1963).

————: Eyewitness Arrest, L&O, Vol.11 (Jan., 1963).

————: Fraternization with Jurors, L&O, Vol.13 (May, 1965).

————: Game of Skill, L&O, Vol.11 (Apr., 1963).

————: Hotel Purposes, L&O, Vol.9 (Jan., 1961).

————: Intent, L&O, Vol.9 (Dec., 1961).

————: Involuntary Confessions, L&O, Vol.11 (Aug., 1963).

———: Jurisdiction of Crime, L&O, Vol.9 (Sept., 1961).

———: The Law and the Police, L&O, Vol.9 (Nov., 1961).

———: Lawful Confinement, L&O, Vol.11 (Sept., 1963).

———: Lawyer's Advice, L&O, Vol.11 (July, 1963).

———: Loitering, L&O, Vol.9 (Nov., 1961).

———: Loudspeaker, L&O, Vol.9 (July, 1961).

———: Mechanical Eavesdropping, L&O, Vol.9 (Sept., 1961).

———: Microphone in Cell, L&O, Vol.10 (Sept., 1962).

———: Misdemeanor vs. Felony, L&O, Vol.11 (Jan., 1963).

———: Order to Move On, L&O, Vol.9 (Dec., 1961).

———:Past Recollection Record, L&O, Vol.11 (July, 1963).

———: Peaceful Expression of Unpopular Views, L&O, Vol.11 (June, 1963).

———: Presence at Scene of Crime, L&O, Vol.9 (Nov., 1961).

———: Right to Confront Witnesses, Vol.13 (June, 1965).

———: Right to Counsel, L&O, Vol.9 (July, Aug., Sept., 1961).

———: Right to Defend, L&O, Vol.13 (June, 1965).

———: Sale of Contraceptives, L&O, Vol.11 (Oct., 1963).

———: Search of Companion, L&O, Vol.9 (May, 1961).

———: Search of Vehicle, L&O, Vol.9 (Jan., 1961).

———: Security at Trial, L&O, Vol.9 (Jan., 1961).

———: Self-incrimination, L&O, Vol.9 (Jan., 1961).

———: Service of Process, L&O, Vol.9 (Nov., 1961).

———: Stolen Property, L&O, Vol.9 (Oct., 1961).

———: Taking With Consent, L&O, Vol.11 Mar., 1963).

———: This Is the Law, L&O, Vol.9 (Aug., 1961).

———: Vagrancy, L&O, Vol.9 (Dec., 1961).

———: Value of Stolen Property, L&O, Vol.9 (Oct., 1961).

Zeisel, H., Klavern, H., Jr., and Buchholz, B.: *Delay in the Court.* Boston, Little, Brown, 1959.

Military Law and Police Administration

Aycock, William B., and Wurfel, S. W.: *Military Law Under the Uniform Code.* Chapel Hill, Univ. of North Carolina Press, 1955.

Boatner, Haydon L.: Role of the MP Corps in Your Modern Army, TPY (1959).

Boshes, Louis D., and Hermann, Phillip J.: Study of the Naval Delinquent by Questionnaire, JCL&C, Vol.38, No.3 (Mar.-Apr., 1947), 218-234.

Burnham, Robert F.: The Office of Special Investigations—United States Air Force, PO-LICE, Vol.8, No.5 (May-June, 1963), 65-67.

Butchers, Maj. Gen. R. J.: Military Police Public Relations, TPY (1963).

Cassel, Rusel N.: The Relation of Certain Factors to the Level of Aspiration and Social Distance for Forty-four Air Force Prisoners, JCL&C, Vol.44, No.5 (Jan.-Feb., 1954), 604-10.

Chappell, Richard A.: Treatment of Naval Offenders, War and Postwar, JCL&C, Vol.38, No.4 (Mar.-Apr., 1947-48), 342-351.

Chyatte, Conrad, and Fuchs, Edmond F.: On the Intelligence of Soldier Criminals, JCL&C, Vol.40, No.6 (Mar.-Apr., 1950), 753.

Colclough, O. S.: Naval Justice, JCL&C, Vol.38, No.3 (Mar.-Apr., 1947-48), 198-205.

East, Edmund R.: Postwar Military Training in Correctional Institutions, JCL&C, Vol.39, No.4 (Mar.-Apr., 1948-49), 441-447.

Eliasberg, W.: War Trials, JCL&C, Vol.36, No.2 (1945-46), 85.

Everett, Robinson O.: Criminal Investigation Under Military Law, JCLC&PS, Vol.46 (1955-56), 707-21, 892-904.

———: *Military Justice in the Armed Forces of the United States.* Harrisburg, Military Service Pub., 1956.

Franklin, Mitchell: Sources of International Law Relating to Sanctions Against War Criminals, JCL&C, Vol.36, No.3 (1945-46), 153.

Gault, P. F.: Prosecution of War Criminals, JCL&C, Vol.36, No.3 (1945-46), 180.

Glueck, S.: It's Allies' Duty and Right, as Victors, to Try and Punish Axis War Criminals, P.M. (Jan., 1945), 7.

———: Justice for War Criminals, THE AMERICAN MERCURY, Vol.60 (1945), 274-80.

———: The Nuremburg Trial and Aggressive War, HLR, Vol.59 (1946), 396-456.

————: *The Nuremberg Trial and Aggressive War.* New York, Knopf, 1946.

————: *Penologic Program for Axis War Criminals.* 1945.

————: War Criminals; Their Prosecution and Punishment, The Record of History, LAWYERS GUILD REVIEW, Vol.5 (1945), 1-10.

————, & Eleanor, *et al.:* Prediction of Behavior of Civilian Delinquents in the Armed Forces, MH, Vol.28, 456-75.

Goldberg, Herman L., and Hoefer, Frederick A. C.: The Army Parole System, JCL&C, Vol.40, No.2 (July-Aug., 1949), 158.

Karlem, Delmar: The Scope of Military Justice, JCLC&PS, Vol.43, No.3 (Sept.-Oct., 1952), 285.

Kenworthy, Charles C., Jr.: Fixed Military Installations, TPY (1962).

Leonard, V. A.: Youth and Postwar Military Training, JCL&C, Vol.35, No.5 (Jan.-Feb., 1945), 324.

Lunden, Walter A.: Military Service and Criminality, JCLC&PS, Vol.49 (1951-52), 766.

Luszki, Walter A.: Special Supervision for Military Offenders, JCLC&PS, Vol..49, No.5 (1958-59), 444.

Maglin, William H.: The Army's Correctional System, TPY (1956).

Manual for Courts Martial, United States. Washington, U.S. Govt. Printing Office, 1951.

Mudge, G. W.: Relationship with the Military, TPY (1962).

Pearl, Melvin E.: The Applicability of the Bill of Rights to a Court Martial Proceeding, JCLC&PS, Vol.50, No.6 (Mar.-Apr., 1960), 559.

Pepper, Louis H.: The Scope of Military Justice, JCLC&PS, Vol.43, No.3 (Sept.-Oct., 1952), 285.

Ramsey, Raymond R.: The Army's Correctional Program, JCLC&PS, Vol.50, No.3 (Sept.-Oct., 1959), 275.

Richardson, Robert E.: Salute to the Military Police, TPC (Sept., 1961), 10.

Rogers, C. R., and Wallen, J. L.: *Counseling with Returned Servicemen.* New York, McGraw-Hill, 1946.

Thomas, Henry G.: Armed Services Police, TPY (1958).

U.S. War Department: *The R.O.T.C. Manual.* Annapolis, National Service.

Riots

Adams, Thomas F.: Crowd and Riot Control, POLICE, Vol.8, No.4 (Mar.-Apr., 1964), 54-57.

Applegate, Rex: *Crowd and Riot Control.* Harrisburg, Stackpole, 1964.

————: Smoke vs. the Mob Cancer, TPC, Vol.30 (Oct., 1963), 20.

————: When "Riot Duty" Calls, L&O, Vol.12 (Jan.-Feb., 1964).

Barrett, James R.: Bomb Scares and Vandalism, TPY (1957).

Boolsen, Frank M.: *Panic Control and Prevention.* Sacramento, Calif. Office of Civil Defense, 1951.

Brown, William P.: The Police and Community Conflict, POLICE, Vol.8, No.5 (May-June, 1964), 51-59.

California Department of Justice, Governor's Peace Officers Committee on Civil Disturbances: *Report of Peace Officer' Committee on Civil Disturbances.* Sacramento, Calif. State Printing Office, 1945.

Cape, William H.: Insights Into Riot Readiness, POLICE, Vol.9, No.5 (May-June, 1965), 81.

————: Menace of "Riot Proneness" in a Community, L&O, Vol.13, No.4 (Apr., 1965), 68.

Carson, Dale G.: Emergency Mass Detention, POLICE, Vol.8, No.6 (July-Aug., 1964), 74-76.

Crowd Behavior—Operations and Techniques, TPC, Vol.30 (Jan., 1963), 38.

Davidson, George E.: Crowd Control, TPY (1965).

Diamond, Harry (ed.): Crowd Control and Riot Prevention, POLICE, Vol.9, No.4 (Mar.-Apr., 1965), 52-60.

———— (ed.): Handling Unusual Occurrences, POLICE, Vol.9, No.1 (Sept.-Oct., 1964), 38-39.

————: Police Duties and Responsibilities at the Scene of an Emergency or Disaster, POLICE, Vol.8, No.3 (Jan.-Feb., 1964), 50-57.

————: Police Duties and Responsibilities at the Scene of an Emergency or Disaster, POLICE, Vol.8 No.5 (May-June, 1964), 43-50.

Dillon, John D.: *Civil Disturbance Control.* Sacramento, Calif. State Department of Education, Bureau of Trade and Industrial Education, 1948.

Graney, Edward J.: Crowd Control Vehicles, L&O, Vol.10, No.11 (Nov., 1962), 22.

Huffman, Arthur V.: Violent Behavior—Possibilities of Prediction and Control, POLICE, Vol.8, No.5 (May-June, 1964), 13-16.

Jenkins, Herbert T.: Riot Control, TPY (1957).

Kay, Barbara A., Hartmen, Jeane, and Vedder, Clyde B.: The Bikini Patrol, POLICE, Vol.8, No.6 (July-Aug., 1963), 31-34.

Lee, Alfred, and Humphrey: *Race Riot.* New York, Dryden, 1959.

Martin, Julian A.: Handling Riots and Disasters, TPC, Vol.29, No.3 (Mar., 1962), 4.

McCandless, David A.: Considerations on Racial Tension, POLICE, Vol.9, No.1 (Sept.-Oct., 1964), 40-41.

McManus, George P.: Maintaining Order, TPY (1963).

——: Police Control of Riots and Mobs, FBILEB (Oct., 1962).

Moore, Charles E., and Fording, Addison H.: Anarchy on the Campus, TPC, Vol.32, No.4, 10. **(Must Reading.)**

O'Brien, Daniel J.: Crowd Control Barrier, L&O, Vol.8, No.6 (1960).

Oliver, Clyde W.: Crowd Control in Civil Disturbances, Pt. 2, MPJ (Mar.-Apr., 1965), 16.

Peterson, Philip L.: Psychological Factors in Mobs and Riots, POLICE, Vol.6, No.4 (May-June, 1962), 18-20.

——: Psychology and Riot Prevention, POLICE, Vol.6, No.6 (July-Aug., 1962), 42-44.

Piggins, Edward S.: Riot Control, TPY (1957).

Shaw, William: Electronics and Riot Control, L&O, Vol.12 (Dec., 1964).

Smellie, K.: Riots, ESS, Vol.13, 387.

Sweeney, Frank A.: Police Control of Disturbances in Small Communities, TPY (1957).

Tamm, Quinn: Democracy or Mobocracy, TPC, Vol.32, No.4, 6.

Wood, Sterling A.: *Riot Control by the National Guard.* Harrisburg, Military Service, 1946.

Training and Education

Adams, Thomas F.: *Training Officer's Handbook.* Springfield, Thomas, 1964.

Adkins, E. H., Jr.: An Idea for a Foreign Police Academy, POLICE, Vol.6, No.4 (Mar.-Apr., 1962), 62-65.

AID-IACP Training Contract Phased Out, TPC, Vol.30 (Apr., 1963), 34.

Alexander, Clarence: *The Law of Arrest.* New York, Dennis, 1949.

Allman, James J.: Training in Community Relations, TPY (1963).

The American National Red Cross: *First Aid Textbook.* Garden City, Doubleday, 1957.

American Prison Association: *In-service Training Standards for Prison Custodial Officers.* New York, American Prison Association, 1951.

Anderson, Stanley A.: Junior College and Police Professionalization, POLICE, Vol.6, No.3 (Jan.-Feb., 1962), 14-15.

Andrews, A. M.: Let's Stand Inspection, L&O, Vol.12 (Apr., 1964).

Anti-defamation League of B'nai B'rith and International Assoc. of Chiefs of Police: *With Justice for All—a Guide for Law Enforcement Officers.* A Report prepared by the Associations, 1963. **(Excellent.)**

Anti-defamation League of B'nai B'rith: Police and Free Choice, TPC, Vol.32, No.2 (Feb., 1965), 8-9.

Applegate, Rex: *Kill or Get Killed.* Harrisburg, Stackpole, 1961.

Armstrong, Henry C.: Development of Professionalism, TPY (1964).

Arthur, Richard O.: The Subversive in the Police Department, L&O, Vol.12 (July, 1964).

Ashenhust, Paul H.: The Goal: A Police Profession, JCLC&PS, Vol.49 (1958-59), 605.

Ashworth, Ray: Training and Research Program, TPY (1958).

Aubry, Arthur S.: Law Enforcement: Professional Status, POLICE, Vol.8, No.3 (Jan.-

Ayres, Loren: Standards of Police Conduct and Performance, L&O, Vol.12 (Apr., 1964).

Bagley, Gerald L.: Play Ball—The Value of a Feb., 1964), 15-19.

——: *The Officer in the Small Department.* Springfield, Thomas, 1960.

Sports Program, POLICE, Vol.8, No.3 (Jan.-Feb., 1964), 78-79.

Baril, Lawrence J.: Police Education in Michigan, L&O, Vol.10, No.2 (Feb., 1962), 28-29.

Barker, William: *A Survey of Law Enforcement Curriculums in California State Colleges.* Sacramento, Calif. State Dept. of Education, 1951.

Barry, A. G.: Selected List of References for Police School, SE&SCD, Vol.2, No.5 (1964).

Barthelemy, H., and Balthazard, V.: Course of Study at the University of Paris Institute of Criminology, SE&SCD, Vol.2, No.6 (1964).

Bates, Jerome E.: Notes on Recording, FOCUS (Mar., 1950), 56-57.

Bayle, Edmond: The Scientific Detective, SE&SCD, Vol.2, No.2 (1964).

Beckman, R. O.: *How to Train Supervisors,* 4th Ed. New York, Harper, 1952.

Bernays, Edward L. (ed.): *The Engineering of Consent.* Norman, Oklahoma Univ., 1956.

Betlach, Roy A.: Minimum Work Load System in Washington, TPY (1960).

Blum, Goggin, Whitmore, and Pomeroy: A

Further Study of Deputy Sheriff Selection Procedures, POLICE, Vol.6, No.4 (Mar.-Apr., 1962), 77-79.

Bond, Horatio (ed.): *NFPA Inspection Manual.* Boston, National Fire Protection Assoc., 1959.

Boolsen, Frank M. (ed.): *Directory of University and College Criminology Programs.* Fresno, Calif., Fresno State College, 1955.

Booth, Bates: Courses for Policemen at the Univ. of Southern Calif., SE&SCD, Vol.2, No.4 (1964).

Borkenstein, R. F.: Role of the University in Training Police Executives, TPC (1962).

————: Training for Effective Interrogation, TPY (1964).

————: Workshop: Progress in Police Training, TPY (1961).

Bourbon, Frank C.: Moral Aspects of Law Enforcement, TPC, Vol.32, No.1 (Jan., 1965), 35-37; No.2 (Feb., 1965), 32-35; No.3 (Mar., 1965), 47-51; No.4 (Apr., 1965), 62; No.5 (May, 1965), 45-58; No.6 (June, 1965), 51-54. (Series consisted of 6 sub-areas: Integrity, Courage, Responsibility, Sacrifice, Prejudice and Reputation.) **(Must Reading.)**

Bower, Marvin (ed.): *The Development of Executive Leadership.* Cambridge, Harvard, Univ. Press, 1949.

Boyn, Harry E.: The Buzz Technique in Training, PJ (June, 1952), 49-50.

Brandstatter, A. F.: Field Training in MSU's Program, TPC (May, 1962), 22.

————: Michigan's Answer to Its Law Enforcement Training Needs, TPY (1958).

————: Report of Committee on Education and Training, TPY (1957).

————: Report of Education and Training Committee, TPY (1959).

————: The School of Police Administration and Public Safety, Michigan State University, JCLC&PS, Vol.48, No.5 (Jan.-Feb., 1958), 564.

————: University Level Training for the Police Services, POLICE, Vol.3, No.3 (Jan.-Feb., 1959), 28-32.

————, & **Weaver, Leon:** Educating the Industrial Security Administrators of the Future, POLICE, Vol.6, No.6 (July-Aug., 1962), 63-65.

Brannon, Bernard C.: Need for Accelerated Progress in Training, TPY (1961).

————: The Set of the Sail, POLICE, Vol.11, No.1 (Sept.-Oct., 1957), 10-17.

Breitzmann, Albert L.: The Certification Program of the Academy for Scientific Interrogation, POLICE, Vol.1, No.3 (Jan.-Feb., 1957), 50-51; No.5 (May-June, 1957), 42-44.

Brereton, George H.: The Importance of Training and Education in the Professionalization of Law Enforcement, JCLC&PS, Vol.52, No.1 (May-June, 1961), 111.

————: Police Training in College and University, SE&SCD, Vol.3, No.1 (1964).

Bristow, Allen P.: A Matter of Professional Ethics, POLICE, Vol.5, No.1 (Sept.-Oct., 1960), 59-60.

————: Police College News, POLICE, Appears in every issue.

————: *Police Film Guide.* Walteria, Police Research, 1963.

————: Police Officer Shootings—A Tactical Evaluation, JCLC&PS, Vol.54, No.1 (1963), 93.

————, & **Gourley, Douglas:** *Patrol Administration.* Springfield, Thomas, 1961.

————, & **Throne, Dick:** An Institute for Marksmanship Instructors, POLICE, Vol.8, No.3 (Jan.-Feb., 1964), 25-27.

Broome, C. E.: Michigan's New Academy, TPC, Vol.29, No.5 (May, 1962), 20.

Brown, Albert N.: Human Relations Training, TPY (1962).

Brown, David L.: Apathy—It Can Kill You, L&O, Vol.13 (May, 1965), 10.

Brown, James W., Lewis, Richard B., and Harcleroad, Fred F.: *A-V Instruction Materials and Methods.* New York, McGraw-Hill, 1959.

Brown, Wesley, *Self Defense.* New York, Ronald, 1951.

Brown, William P.: The Police and the Academic World, TPC (May, 1965), 8-12.

————: Police—University Relations, TPY (1963).

————: Report of the Education and Training Committee, TPY (1962, 1963 & 1964).

————: Seminar: Developing the Police Executive, TPY (1962).

————: Seminar: State Sponsored Police Training, TPY (1962).

————: Training for Dignitary Protection: Seminar, TPY (1963).

————: Training to Meet the Sex Criminal: Seminar, TPY (1963).

Brunton, Robert L.: *A Manual for Municipal In-service Training.* Chicago, Int'l City Managers' Assoc., 1960.

Bundy, R. D.: *How to Teach a Job.* Deep River, National Foreman's Institute, 1946.

Bureau of Public Assistance: *Training for Service in Public Assistance.* Washington, Dept. of Health, Ed., and Welfare, 1961.

————: *The Policeman's Guide: Manual Study Construction.* New York, Harper, 1952.

Cahill, Thomas J.: Training in the Inter-racial Picture for 1963, TPY (1964).

Caldwell, Bernard R.: Northwestern University Pioneers Traffic Training and Research, POLICE, Vol.5, No.1 (Sept.-Oct., 1960), 27-30.

California State Department of Alcoholic Beverage Control: *A.B.C. Enforcement Manual: a Manual Prepared to Assist Peace Officers in the Conduct of Investigations of Violations of Alcoholic Beverage Control Act.* Sacramento, 1961.

California State Department of Education, Bureau of Trade and Industrial Education: *A Study Manual and Bibliography for Peace Officers.* Sacramento, 1950.

———: *Basic Course in Firearms.* Sacramento, 1949.

———: *Court Appearance and Testimony.* Sacramento, 1949.

———: *Self Defense.* Sacramento, 1949.

———: California Program for Peace Officers' Training, Sacramento, 1958.

———: *Procedures for Conducting Programs Under the California Plan for Trade and Industrial Education.* Bulletin C-3, Sacramento, 1955.

California State Department of Justice: *A Guide to Race Relations for Peace Officers.* Sacramento, 1946.

California State Office of Civil Defense: *Instructor's Manual and Teaching Outline: Panic Control and Prevention.* Sacramento, 1951.

California State Peace Officers' Training Series: *Beat Patrol and Observation,* No.65. Sacramento, Calif. State Dept. of Education, 1963.

———: *Court Appearance and Testimony,* No.10. Sacramento, Calif. State Dept. of Education, 1963.

———: *Elements of Interrogation,* No.23. Sacramento, Calif. State Department of Education, 1963.

———: *How to Investigate Assault Cases,* No.67. Sacramento, Calif. State Dept. of Education, 1964.

———: *Information: Sources and Uses for Investigators,* No.24. Sacramento, Calif. State Dept. of Education, 1963.

———: *The Law of Arrest, Search & Seizure,* No.1, Sacramento, Calif. State Dept. of Education, 1964.

———: *Mechanics of Arrest,* No.2. Sacramento, Calif. State Dept. of Education, 1964.

———: *Teacher Training Course.* Supplemental material numbers 4, 8, 10, 24, 27, 41 and 140. Sacramento, Calif. State Dept. of Education.

———: *Traffic Accident Investigation Procedure,* No.68. Sacramento, Calif. State Dept. of Education, 1964.

Canals, J. M.: Classicism, Positivism, and Social Defense, JCLC&PS, Vol.50, No.6 (1959-60), 541.

Canwell, Carl D.: Building Character Through Law Enforcement, TPY (1958).

Carlin, Vincent A.: Police Executive Development Course, POLICE, Vol.5, No.3 (Jan.-Feb., 1961), 62-65.

Chapman, Charles C.: Training to Meet Unusual Occurrences, POLICE, Vol.6, No.5 (May-June, 1962), 50-51.

Chapman, Samuel G., and Crockett, Thompson S.: Gunsight Dilemma: Police Firearms Policy, POLICE, Vol.7, No.5 (May-June, 1963), 51-56.

Chase, Stuart: *Power of Words.* New York, Harcourt, Brace, 1954.

Chenowith, James H.: Police Training Program Using Wax Bullets, JCLC&PS, Vol.52, No.3 (Sept.-Oct., 1961), 347.

———: Police Training Investigates the Fallibility of the Eye Witness, JCLC&PS, Vol.51, No.3 (Mar.-Apr., 1960-61), 378.

Chicago Park District: *The Police and Minority Groups: a Manual Prepared for Use in the Chicago Park District Police Training School.* Chicago, 1947.

Chicago Police Department: *Tear Gas Manual.* Washington, IACP, 1962.

———: *Uniform Drill Manual.* Chicago, Chicago Police Dept.

Children's Bureau: *Police Services for Juveniles,* Report of a Conference. Washington, D.C., U.S. Govt. Printing Office, 1954.

Chiotis, John C., and Pell, Joseph C.: *How to Become a Policeman.* New York, Funk, 1946.

Cincinnati Division of Police: *Manual of Rules and Regulations.* A Report prepared by the Cincinnati Div. of Police, Cincinnati, 1953.

Clark, Donald E.: The Role of the Individual Officer in Building Public Support for Law Enforcement. POLICE, Vol.8, No.6 (July-Aug., 1964), 77-79.

Clift, Raymond E.: *A Guide to Modern Police Thinking: a Panoramic View of Policing.* Cincinnati, Anderson, 1956.

———: Police Training, THE ANNALS, Vol.291 (Jan., 1954), 113-18.

Clowers, Norman L.: Prejudices and Discrimination in Law Enforcement, POLICE, Vol.8, No.3 (Jan.-Feb., 1964), 42-45.

Coe, Rodney M.: Relationship of Scores and Education to Adjustment, JCLC&PS, Vol.50, No.5 (1959-60), 460.

Cole, Warren H., and Puestow, Charles B.: *First Aid: Surgical and Medical.* New York, Appleton, 1954.

Command Officers' Training, 1951. E. Lansing, Michigan State Univ., Dept. of Police Admin., 1951.

Committee on Police Training, IACP: *The FBI and Law Enforcement Training.* A Report to the Annual Convention of the IACP, Colorado Springs, Oct., 7-12, 1950.

Conference Leadership. Washington, U.S. Int'l Cooperation Admin. Office of Industrial Resources, 1958. Reprinted by the U.S. Office of Education.

Connecticut Chiefs of Police Sponsor Supervisory Course, TPC, Vol.30 (Sept., 1963), 42.

Coolidge, Jeanne D.: Challenging Future, L&O, Vol.11, No.7 (July, 1963).

Coon, Thomas F.: Modern Report Writing, PO-LICE, Vol.6, No.3 (Jan.-Feb., 1962), 34-35.

Cooper, Alfred M.: *How to Conduct Conferences.* New York, McGraw-Hill, 1946.

Costa, Rudy: Sports for Policemen, L&O, Vol.7 (Mar., 1959).

Crawford, William: Notes for New Sergeants, L&O, Vol.9 (Oct.-Dec., 1961).

Crittenden, B. M.: California's Legislation for Police Training, TPY (1960).

Cross, Albert C.: The Problems of Marksmanship Training in the Smaller Police Dept., POLICE, Vol.5, No.2 (Nov.-Dec., 1960), 33-36.

Curtis, S. J.: Focus on the Future, POLICE, Vol.8, No.3 (Jan.-Feb., 1964), 20-24.

Dartnell Corporation: *Training Programs for Office Supervisors and Executives.* Chicago, The Dartnell Corp., 1951.

David, Henry (ed.): *Education and Manpower.* New York, Columbia Univ. Press, 1960.

Day, Frank D.: Police Administrative Training, JCLC&PS, Vol.47, No.2 (July-Aug., 1956), 253.

Dengler, Harry M.: Training of Prohibition Enforcement Officers in the United States, SE&SCD, Vol.2, No.1 (1964).

Department of Justice, State of Calif.: *A Guide to Race Relations for Police Officers.* Sacramento, 1946.

DePhillipp, Frank A., et al.: *Management of Training Programs.* Homewood, Irwin, 1960.

Diamond, Harry: Institute Planning, TPC, Vol.29, No.1 (Jan., 1962), 34.

———: Police Duties and Responsibilities at the Scene of an Emergency or Disaster, PO-LICE, Vol.8, No.1 (Sept.-Oct., 1963), 47-49.

Dienstein, William: Book Reviews, POLICE, Vol.9, No.4 (Mar.-Apr., 1965), 72-74.

———: *How to Write a Narrative Investigation Report.* Springfield, Thomas, 1964.

———: *Technics for the Crime Investigator.* Springfield, Thomas, 1959.

Donigan, Robert L., and Fisher, Edward C.: *The Evidence Handbook.* Evanston, Traffic Institute of Northwestern Univ., 1958.

Dooher, M. Joseph, and Marquis, Vivienne (eds.): *The Development of Executive Talent: a Handbook of Management Development Techniques and Case Studies.* New York, American Management Assoc., 1952.

Dudycha, George J.: *Psychology for Law Enforcement Officers.* Springfield, Thomas, 1960.

Dussia, Joseph: What a Police Officer Should Know About Handcuffs, Harrisburg, Penna. State Police, 1964 (unpublished).

Effective Writing. Sacramento, Personnel Management Series Report No.3, State Personnel Board, 1952.

Ellis, J. T.: The Birmingham City Police Training Center, TD&R (May, 1965), 10-14.

Ellsworth, L. L.: The Box Cars, L&O, Vol.11, No.5 (May, 1963), 31.

———: How About Me, L&O, Vol.12 (May, 1964), 12.

Emergency Hospitalization for the Mentally Ill. A Manual for Cleveland Police officers compiled by the Cleveland Mental Health Assn., Committee on Emergency Hospitalization, in cooperation with the Cleveland Police Dept., 2nd Ed., 1960.

Emerson, Lynn A.: *Industrial Education in a Changing Democratic Society,* Bulletin No.33, Ithaca, Cornell Univ., School of Ind. and Labor Relations, 1955.

Espie, D. A.: Discusses Statewide Training, TPC, Vol.29, No.3 (Mar., 1962), 30.

Fabian, Felix: International Association of Police Professors, TPC (May, 1965), 28-30.

Fagerstrom, Dorothy: Accent on Training Traffic Administrators, L&O, Vol.10, No.6 (June, 1962), 12.

Fall Course in Methods of Scientific Crime Detection, SE&SCD, Vol.2, No.3 (1964).

Farmer, M. S.: A Flash of Genius, POLICE, Vol.4, No.5 (May-June, 1960), 65-57.

Feary, Robert A.: Concept of Responsibility, JCLC&PS, Vol.45 (1954-55), 21-28.

Federal Bureau of Investigation: *Uniform Crime Reports.* A quarterly bulletin, Washington, D.C.

Fick, Samuel L.: *Procedures for Conducting Programs Under the California Plan for Trade and Industrial Education.* Bulletin

No. C-3. Sacramento, Calif. State Dept. of Education, 1947.

Fienberg, Robert L.: Massachusetts Chiefs Endorse . . . Something New in Old Boston, POLICE, Vol.7, No.3 (Jan.-Feb., 1963), 74-78.

Fifteenth Session of Boulder Crime School, TPC, Vol.30 (Aug., 1963), 22.

Flaugher, Paul: The Police Cadet, JCLC&PS, Vol.47, No.4 (Nov.-Dec., 1956), 500.

Fleming, Pierce J.: Need for Supervisory Training, TPY (1957).

Floherty, John J.: *Man Against Distance.* New York, Lippincott, 1954.

Follett, Mary Parker: *Freedom and Co-ordination: Lectures in Business Organization.* London, Management, 1949.

Fox, Vernon: Dilemmas in Law Enforcement, POLICE, Vol.9, No.1 (Sept.-Oct., 1964), 69-74.

Fricke, Charles W.: *California Peace Officers' Manual,* Rev. 7th Ed. Los Angeles, Smith, 1949.

———: *5000 Criminal Definitions, Terms and Phrases,* 2nd Ed. Los Angeles, Smith, 1949.

———: *1000 Police Questions and Answers for the California Peace Officer,* 4th Ed. Los Angeles, Smith, 1946.

———, **& Kolbiek:** *California Peace Officers' Manual.* Los Angeles, Legal Bookstore, 1964.

Friedman, Leonard M.: The Constitutional Cop, POLICE, Vol.9, No.2 (Nov.-Dec., 1964), 94-96.

Frost, Thomas M.: *A Forward Look in Police Education.* Springfield, Thomas, 1959.

———: Police Training Facilities and Training Personnel, JCLC&PS, Vol.47, No.4 (Nov.-Dec., 1956), 475.

Gabard, Caroline E.: More About Police Literature, JCLC&PS, Vol.50, No.1 (May-June, 1959), 89.

Gabard, Charles E., and Gabard, Caroline E.: The Present Status of Police Literature, JCLC&PS, Vol.48, No.6 (Mar.-Apr., 1958), 644.

———, **& Kenny, J.:** *Police Writing.* Springfield, Thomas, 1957.

Gallaghar, Walter W.: Hypnosis Crouse, TPC, Vol.29, No.1 (Jan., 1962), 16.

Gallati, Robert R.: A New Identification and Intelligence System Concept, L&O, Vol.12 (Dec., 1964).

———: Police Personnel Testing Experience of the New York City Police Department, POLICE, Vol.4, No.5 (May-June, 1960), 76-77; No.6 (July-Aug., 1960), 23-25.

———: Report of the Education and Training Committee, TPY (1961).

———: Where is 7 Hubert Street? POLICE, Vol.4, No.1 (Sept.-Oct., 1959), 19-26.

Gammage, Allen Z.: *Basic Police Report Writing.* Springfield, Thomas, 1960.

———: Sound Recordings as Police Training Aids, POLICE, Vol.6, No.5 (May-June, 1962), 35-38.

———: Still Projections in Police Training, POLICE, Vol.6, No.6 (July-Aug., 1962), 15-18.

———: The Third Dimension in Police Training, POLICE, Vol.6, No.4 (Mar.-Apr., 1962), 52-54.

Gault, Robert H.: Instructions in Police Science, JCL&C, Vol.36, No.3, 151.

Gebbard, Robert L.: Police Academy of Fort Wayne (Ind.). L&O, Vol.9, No.3 (Mar., 1963).

Geis, Gilbert: The Social Atmosphere of Policing, POLICE, Vol.9, No.1 (Sept.-Oct., 1964), 75-79.

Germann, A. C.: Hurdles to Professional Competence, POLICE, Vol.3, No.5 (May-June, 1959), 14-19; No.6 (July-Aug., 1959), 44-47.

———: Hurdles to Professional Police Competence, POLICE, Vol.8, No.3 (Jan.-Feb., 1964), 28-31.

———: Inadequate Discipline, POLICE, Vol.2, No.4 (Mar.-Apr., 1958), 51-53.

———: Scientific Training for Cops, JCLC&PS, Vol.50, No.2 (July-Aug., 1959), 206.

———, **Day, Frank D., and Gallati, R. J.:** *Introduction to Law Enforcement.* Springfield, Thomas, 1962.

Giachino, J. W., and Galington, Ralph O.: *Course Instruction in Industrial Arts and Vocational Education.* Chicago, American Technology Society, 1954.

Giardini, G. I.: Interviewing—A Two Way Process, *Bulwarks Against Crime.* NPPAY (1948).

Gilston, David H., and Podell, Lawrence: *The Practical Patrolman.* Springfield, Thomas, 1959.

Glaser, Robert: *Training, Research and Education.* New York, Wiley, 1965.

Glueck, Sheldon: A Federal Act to Establish the Roscoe Pound Academy of Criminal Justice, HJL, Vol.2 (1964).

Gocke, Blye W.: *Police Sergeants Manual.* Los Angeles, Legal Book Store, 4th Ed., 1960.

Golden, Olive H.: *Training Techniques—A Bibliographic Review.* Chicago, Industrial Relations Center, Univ. of Chicago.

Goldin, Hyman E., O'Leary, Frank, and Lipsius, Morris: Dictionary of American Underworld Lingo, NARCOTICS (1950).

Gourley, G. Douglas: An Experiment in the

Use of the Conference Method for Training Police Supervisors, JCL&C, Vol.39, No.3 (Mar.-Apr., 1948-49), 392-402.

———: In-service Training of Policemen by Universities and Colleges, JCLC&PS, Vol.44 (July-Aug., 1953), 229-238.

———: Police Service as a Profession, TPC (Feb., 1961), 18.

———: Programs for Educational Incentive, TPC (Dec., 1961), 14.

———: State Standards for Local Police Recruitment and Training, JCLC&PS, Vol.53, No.4 (Dec., 1962), 522.

———: Supervisory Institute Report, TPC (Jan., 1961), 30.

Government Printing Office: *Training for the Police Service*. Washington, a report prepared by the Vocational Division, U.S. Office of Education, Govt. Printing Office.

Grant, Charles E.: Police Science Programs in American Universities, Colleges and Junior Colleges, TPC (May, 1965), 32-42.

Gremel, Russell P.: When Can a Policeman Use His Gun? JCL&C, Vol.40, No.6 (Mar.-Apr., 1950), 756.

Griffin, John I.: The Police Science Program, POLICE, Vol.4, No.2 (Nov.-Dec., 1959), 50-54.

Gruzanski, Charles V.: Self Defense for Police Officers, POLICE, appears in every issue.

Haas, Kenneth, and Ewing, Claude: *Tested Training Techniques*. New York, Prentice-Hall, 1950.

Habbe, Stephen: *Company Programs of Executive Development*. New York, National Industrial Conference Board, 1950.

Halsey, George D.: *Supervising People*. New York, Harper, 1946.

Hankey, Richard O.: Education Fosters Informal Police Coordination, POLICE, Vol.5, No.3 (Jan.-Feb., 1961), 58-59.

Hanson, Carl F.: The Professional Policeman, TPY (1957).

Harney, Malachi L.: Watch Your Semantics! POLICE, Vol.4, No.6 (July-Aug., 1960), 40-42.

Harrison, Leonard H.: Use of the Training Film, POLICE, Vol.7, No.6 (July-Aug., 1963), 75-77.

Hartland, James R.: How Do You Spell It? L&O, Vol.12 (Nov. 1964).

Harvel, Paul: Policeman's Lot, TPC, Vol.29, No.4 (Apr., 1962), 44.

Harwood, Lt. Harry: Establishment and Operation of a Police Athletic League in a Police Dept., L&O, Vol.11, No.2, 4, & 8 (Feb., Apr., Aug., 1963).

Hawkins, Layton S.: *Development of Vocational Education*. Chicago, American Technical Society, 1945.

Hazelet, John C.: *Police Report Writing*. Springfield, Thomas, 1960.

Heffron, F. N.: *Evidence for the Patrolman*. Springfield, Thomas, 1958.

———: *The Officer in the Courtroom*. Springfield, Thomas, 1955.

Herbert, Charles: *Professionalization Through Ethics*. Oakland, Oakland Police Dept., 1960. (Police Training Program lesson plan.)

Hess, Fred: Police Training, JCLC&PS, Vol.49, No.1 (1958-59), 75.

———: Police Training in Small Communities, TPY (1958).

Hess, John J.: Checklist for Firearms Instructors, L&O, Vol.13, No.4 (Apr., 1965), 30.

Hewitt, William H.: *British Police Administration*. Springfield, Thomas, 1965.

———: The Objectives of a Formal Police Education, POLICE, Vol.11, No.2 (Nov.-Dec., 1964), 25-27.

———: Ohio Bill Draft on Training Standards, TPC, Vol.31 (Nov., 1964), 44.

———: Ohio Gets New College Course, TPC, Vol.30 (July, 1963), 14.

Heyel, Carl (ed.): *The Foreman's Handbook*, 2nd Ed. New York, McGraw-Hill, 1949.

Hilgard, Ernest R.: *Theories of Learning*. New York, Appleton, 1956.

Hilton, Ordway: Ethics of the Expert Witness, AL, Vol.17, No.4 (Oct., 1956), 419-25.

Hipskind, V. K.: The Departmental Safety Officer, POLICE, Vol.7, No.1 (Sept.-Oct., 1962), 66-70.

———: Training the Police Officer to Be a Safe Worker, POLICE, Vol.9, No.2 (Nov.-Dec., 1964), 71-72.

Holcomb, Richard L.: A Weakness in Police Training, TPY (1961).

———: Introduction to Law Enforcement, JCLC&PS, Vol.53, No.2 (June-Aug., 1962), 274.

———: Police Report Writing, JCLC&PS, Vol.51, No.5 (Mar.-Apr., 1960-61), 586.

———: The Practical Patrolman, JCLC&PS, Vol.51, No.2 (Mar.-Apr., 1960-61), 281.

———: Practical Police Knowledge, JCLC&PS, Vol.51, No.5 (Mar.-Apr., 1960-61), 585.

Hollingsworth, Dan: The Conference Method— A Stimulant for Police Management and Training, POLICE, Vol.11, No.1.

Holmes, Darrell F., Jr.: Knowing Isn't Enough, L&O, Vol.8, No.2 (1960).

Hutchinson, Lois I.: *Standard Handbook for Secretaries*, 7th Ed. New York, McGraw-Hill, 1956.

Igleheart, A. S., Spates, Thomas G., and Van-

Ark, G.: *The Job of General Management: A Case History of Executive Development*, General Management Series, No.138. New York, American Management Association, 1946.

Illinois State Police Physical Fitness Program, TPC, Vol.30 (July, 1963), 8.

Inbau, Fred E.: *Self Incrimination*. Springfield, Thomas, 1950.

Institute for Training in Municipal Administration: *Municipal Police Administration*. Chicago, International City Managers' Assoc., 1950.

IACP Course, D.C., Arlington, and Alexandria, TPC, Vol.30 (Feb., 1963), 34; (Apr., 1963), 38; (June, 1963), 59.

Int'l Assoc. of Chiefs of Police: *The Police Yearbook*. Washington, IACP, published annually.

Int'l City Managers' Association: *Municipal Personnel Administration*. Chicago, The Association, 1947.

————: *Municipal Police Administration*. Chicago, The Association, 1954.

Isaacson, Irving: *Manual for the Arresting Officer*. Lewiston, Legal Publications, 1964.

————: *Manual for the Conservation Officer*. Lewiston, Legal Publications, 1964.

Jeimlson, Samual Haig: Quo Vadimiss in Criminological Training, JCLC&PS, Vol.50, No.4 (1959-60), 358.

Jennings, E. E.: The Dynamics of Forced Leadership Training, JPA&IR (Apr., 1954), 110-18.

Jewell, K., and Spencer: Police Leadership—A Research Study, TPC, Vol.30 (Mar., 1963), 40.

Jones, Emmet L.: How's Your Team-work? TPC, Vol.32, No.2 (Feb., 1965), 10.

Jones, E. W.: *Police Pursuit Driving*, 4th Ed. Washington, IACP, 1963.

JOURNAL OF CRIMINAL LAW, CRIMINOLOGY AND POLICE SCIENCE. Baltimore, Williams and Wilkins Company, published bi-monthly.

Kammerer, Louis H.: ". . . It Was Very Good" L&O, Vol.11, No.6 (June, 1963), 55.

Keller, E. John: Train for Actual Combat Conditions, L&O, Vol.11, No.9 (Sept., 1963).

Kemeny, J. G., Snell, J. L., and Thompson, G. L.: *Introduction to Finite Mathematics*. Englewood Cliffs, Prentice-Hall, 1957.

Kennedy, Stephen P.: Law Enforcement as a Profession, TPY (1956).

Kenney, John P.: Police and Higher Education. Address delivered before a panel of the Annual Conference of the American So-

ciety for Public Administration, Detroit, Apr., 1963.

————: *Police Technical Assistance—an Evaluation of Training of Foreign Police Official in the United States*. Washington, Int'l Cooperation Admin., 1957.

————, & Gabard, Caroline E.: *Police Writing*. Springfield, Thomas, 1957.

————, & Pursuit, D.: *Police Work with Juveniles*. Springfield, Thomas, 1954. (**Must Reading.**)

Kennon, Leslie G.: The Student Police on the Campus, L&O, Vol.8, No.7 (1960).

Kephart, William M.: The Integration of Negroes into the Urban Police Forces, JCLC&PS, Vol.45 (1954-55), 325-33.

Kimble, Joseph P.: Police Training Today and the Challenge for Tomorrow, POLICE, Vol.9, No.1 (Sept.-Oct., 1964), 11-14.

King, Glen D.: *First-line Supervisor's Manual*. Springfield, Thomas, 1961.

Kirpatrick, A. M.: The Why and How of Discussion Groups, AJC (May-June, 1963), 19-22.

Knoles, George H., and Snyder, Rixford K.: *Readings in Western Civilization*. New York, Lippincott, 1954.

Kooken, Don L.: Ethics in Police Service—2, JCL&C, Vol.38, No.1 (May-June, 1947), 172-186, No.2 (July-Aug., 1947).

Kreml, Frank M.: *Evidence Handbook for Police*. Evanston, Traffic Institute, Northwestern Univ., 1948.

Krieger, Joseph L.: *Executive Development for Effective Executive Performance and Executive Success*. Unpublished doctoral dissertation, American Univ., 1956.

Krutza, William J.: Follow God's Law, Too, L&O, Vol.11, No.8 (Aug., 1963), 63.

Kuhn, Charles L.: *The Police Officer's Memorandum Book*. Springfield, Thomas, 1964.

Kuwashima, T. S., and Welch, A. R.: *Judo*. London, Putnam, 1957.

LaCouture, Ronald A.: Review of States Sponsored Police Training Programs, TPY (1962).

Liard, Donald A.: *The Techniques of Handling People*. New York, McGraw-Hill, 1947.

Laizure, C. J.: Using Student Cadets in a Small Department, L&O, Vol.9 (Dec., 1961).

Lambert, David T.: Unified Command, TPY (1962).

Lander, Bernard: *Towards an Understanding of Juvenile Delinquency*. New York, Columbia Univ. Press, 1954.

Lane, Marvin G.: New Police Academy for

Michigan, TPC, Vol.29, No.5 (May, 1962), 20.

Lardner, George, Jr.: Layton Urges His Policemen Toward a College Education, WASHINGTON POST (Feb. 10, 1965).

LAW AND ORDER. Published monthly by LAW AND ORDER MAGAZINE, 72 West 45th Street, New York 36, New York.

Lawder, Lee E.: It's a Push-button World, L&O, Vol.13, No.6 (June, 1965), 60.

————: Notes on the Investigator and His Credentials, L&O, Vol.8, No.8 (1960).

————: Police Training Films: Mob and Riot Control, L&O, Vol.12 (Sept., 1964).

————: Your Improvement Is Showing, L&O, Vol.11, No.6 (June, 1963).

Law Enforcement Code of Ethics, CPO, Vol.7 (Jan.-Feb., 1957), 8-9.

Lease, Richard J.: Future Developments in Combat Training, POLICE, Vol.7, No.2 (Nov.-Dec., 1962), 55-58.

————: The Highest and Most Difficult Hurdle in the Tedious Obstacle Course that Leads to Genuinely Successful Combat Marksmanship, POLICE, Vol.7, No.5 (May-June, 1963), 71-75.

————: Leading Policemen and Scientist Receives the Doctor of Science Degree, POLICE, Vol.8, No.1 (Sept.-Oct., 1963), 37-39.

————: Police Combat Skills and Related Skills as Living Assurance, POLICE, Vol.8, No.5 (May-June, 1964), 27-32.

————: Preparing for Combat Readiness, POLICE, Vol.7, No.4 (Mar.-Apr., 1963), 33-36.

Leonard, V. A.: August Vollmer, POLICE, Vol.1, No.1 (Sept.-Oct., 1956), 6-7.

————: New York State's Plan for Training Child Welfare Workers, JCL&C, Vol.35, No.5 (Jan.-Feb., 1945), 326.

Levin, Frank K.: *How to Read for Self-Improvement.* Chicago, American Technical Society, 1947.

Lindquist, E. F.: *Educational Measurements.* Washington, American Council on Education, 1951.

Lindquist, J. A.: *Current Practices in Police Training.* Sacramento, State Dept. of Education, 1956.

Linton, Calvin D.: *How to Write Reports.* New York, Harper, 1954.

Liu, Daniel S. C.: Professional Standards of the Police Service, TPY (1959).

Los Angeles Police Department: *Daily Training Bulletin.* Springfield, Thomas, 1958.

Los Angeles State College: The Los Angeles State College Dept. of Police Science and Administration, Unpublished paper, n.d.

Luellen, Elwood T.: Intensive Firearms Drill: Your Best Weapon! POLICE, Vol.9, No.4 (Mar.-Apr., 1965), 62-64.

McCandless, David A.: Advanced In-service Training, TPY (1961).

————: Police Training in Colleges and Universities, TPY (1956).

————: Report of the Committee on Education and Training, TPY (1965).

————: Southern Police Institute at the University of Louisville, JCLC&PS, Vol.42 (1951-52), 105.

————: The Southern Police Institute, POLICE, Vol.11, No.2 (Nov.-Dec., 1957), 18-25.

————: Statement of Objectives of SPI, TPC, Vol.30 (June, 1963), 10.

McKee, W. R.: Introduction to the Profession of Interviewing and Interrogation, POLICE, Vol.1, No.3 (Jan.-Feb., 1957), 46-49.

McLearney, William J.: *Management Training.* 3rd Ed. Homewood, Irwin.

McLellon, Howard: Shoot to Kill? A Note on the G-Men's Methods, HARPER'S, Vol.172.

MacIver, R. M.: The Social Significance of Professional Ethics, THE ANNALS, Vol.101 (Mar., 1952).

MacNamara, Donal E. J.: Higher Police Training at the University Level, JCL&C, Vol.40, No.5 (Jan.-Feb., 1950), 657.

————: Value of Technical Police Training in Prevention of Crime and Delinquency, JCLC&PS, Vol.42 (1951-52), 262.

Mace, Myles L.: *The Growth and Development of Executives.* Boston, Harvard School of Business Admin., 1950.

Mahler, Walter R.: Improving Coaching Skills, PA (Jan.-Feb., 1964), 28-33.

Martin, J. A.: Training in Louisiana, TPC, Vol.31 (Feb., 1964), 44.

Martin, T. F., and Priar, L. L.: Police Techniques in Gun Fights, JCLC&PS (Sept.-Oct., 1955).

Martone, John: *Handbook of Self Defense.* New York, Arco, 1961.

Maryland State Police Physical Fitness, TPC, Vol.30 (Nov., 1963), 41.

Mathews, Lloyd: The Austin (Texas) Police Aide Program, L&O, Vol.12 (Dec., 1964).

Matsuyama, F. A.: *How to Use the Yawara Stick.* Denver, Yawara School, 1948.

————: *Yawara Manual.* Denver, Yawara School, 1948.

Matt, A. Robert: Let's Start a Police Training Program, POLICE, Vol.4, No.5 (May-June, 1960), 36-38.

————: The Most Important Man, POLICE, Vol.4, No.3 (Jan.-Feb., 1960), 62-63.

———: Officer Continuation, POLICE, Vol.5, No.1 (Sept.-Oct., 1960), 6-9.

Matthues, Robert, and Rowland, Loyd: *How to Recognize and Handle Abnormal People: a Manual for the Police Officer.* New York, National Assoc. for Mental Health, 1954.

Maxwell, M. A.: Portland Police Tactical Platoon Gets Army Training, TPC, Vol.30 (May, 1963), 8.

Mayer, Morris Fritz: Training for Houseparents and Kindred Personnel in Institutions for Juvenile Delinquents, in *Training Personnel for Work with Juvenile Delinquents.* Washington, U.S. Dept. of Health, Education and Welfare, Children's Bureau Pub. No.348, 1954.

Mears, John A.: The Evolution of the Department of Police Administration at Indiana University, JCLC&PS, Vol.53, No.2 (June-Aug., 1962), 253.

Mears, Millard T.: How the Universities Can Help, TPY (1964).

Meehan, James B.: Police Participation in the College Training of Police, POLICE, Vol.8, No.4 (Mar.-Apr., 1964), 24-27.

Melchionne, Theresa M.: "Using Good Police Sense," L&O, Vol.11, No.8 (Aug., 1963); No.9 (Sept., 1963).

Merkeley, Donald K.: *The Investigations of Death.* Springfield, Thomas, 1957.

Michigan Assoc. of Chiefs of Police and the Traffic Division of the Int'l Assoc. of Chiefs of Police: *A Police Training Manual on the Apprehension of Speeders.* Lansing, Michigan State Safety Commission, 1948.

Michigan Chiefs Ask for Training Standards, TPC, Vol.30 (Oct., 1963), 39.

Michigan State College, Dept. of Police Admin.: *Command Officers Training.* 1951. East Lansing, Michigan State Press, 1951.

Miller, J. Guy: Whose Side Are We On? POLICE, Vol.8, No.5 (May-June, 1964), 75.

Minnesota Police Chiefs Institute, TPC, Vol.30 (Apr., 1963), 47.

MINNESOTA POLICE JOURNAL. Minnesota Police and Peace Officers Association, 1512 Hennepin Ave., Minneapolis 3, Minnesota.

Mirich, John J.: The Qualified Policeman—The Back Bone of Society, JCLC&PS, Vol.50, No.3 (Sept.-Oct., 1959), 315.

Missouri Training Standards Bill: TPC, Vol.30 (Nov., 1963), 39.

Moffett, Jack H.: The Art of Law Enforcement, POLICE, Vol.4, No.4 (Mar.-Apr., 1960), 6-10.

More, Harry W.: Law Enforcement Training in Institutions of Higher Learning, POLICE, Vol.5, No.3 (Jan.-Feb., 1961), 6-9.

——— (ed.): Professional Periodical Reviews, POLICE, Vol.9, No.4 (Mar.-Apr., 1965), 50-52.

Morris, W. B.: Minnesota Has Statewide Training Too. TPC, Vol.30 (May, 1963), 36.

Moynahan, James M., Jr.: Karate—The Arts of Self Defense, POLICE, Vol.7, No.2 (Nov.-Dec., 1962), 36-38.

———: *Police Ju Jitsu.* Springfield, Thomas, 1962.

Muelheisen, Gene: The California Standards and Training Program, TPY (1962).

———: Standardizing College Police Science Programs, TPY (1963).

Mulbar, H.: *Interrogation.* Springfield, Thomas, 1951.

Munshower, Elmer F.: Why It Is Necessary that State, Municipal, and Local Police Be Well-trained, POLICE, Vol.3, No.3 (Jan.-Feb., 1959), 18-21.

Murphy, Glen R.: Policies and Procedures for Action Programs, TPC, Vol.32, No.3 (Mar., 1965), 41-42.

Murphy, Lionel V.: A Selected Bibliography of Employee Training and Development, PA (Sept.-Oct., 1956), 62-68.

Murphy, Michael J.: Establishing a Police University Program, TPY (1963).

———: New York City's "Operation All-out," TPC, Vol.32, No.1 (Jan., 1965), 53.

Myren, Richard A.: A Core Curriculum for Undergraduate Academic Police Training, JCLC&PS, Vol.49, No.5 (1958-59), 507.

———: Police Training as Vocational Education, L&O, Vol.11, No.4 (Apr., 1963).

———: Teaching Law to Law Enforcers, POLICE, Vol.4, No.1 (Sept.-Oct., 1959), 32-35.

———: Teaching Law to Law Enforcers, POLICE, Vol.3, No.6 (July-Aug., 1959), 48-51.

National Rifle Assn.: *Guide to Selling the Police Marksmanship Program.* Washington, The Association, 1964.

Negley, James C.: Pre-service Training in California Junior Colleges, POLICE, Vol.7, No.3 (Jan.-Feb., 1963), 22-25.

Newton, Roy: *How to Improve Your Personality.* New York, McGraw-Hill, 1949.

Neyhart, A. E.: Police Drivers Also Need Training, TPC, Vol.30 (Jan., 1963), 34.

Northwestern Univ. Traffic Institute: *Accident Investigation Manual.* Evanston, a report prepared by the Northwestern Univ. Traffic Institute, 1948.

Oblinger, Walter L.: The Police Officer as a Witness, POLICE, Vol.1, No.4 (Mar.-Apr., 1957), 15-19.

O'Ballance, E.: The Qualities of a Good Patrolman, L&O, Vol.9 (Sept., 1961).

O'Connor, George W.: Advanced Information Systems for Law Enforcement: Needs, Concepts and Developments, TPY (1965).

———: Incentives for Learning, TPC (May, 1965), 24.

———: Making Experience a Better Teacher (Seminar), TPY (1965).

———: Mandatory Minimums for Professional Maximums (Seminar), TPY (1965).

O'Hara, Charles E.: *Fundamentals of Criminal Investigation.* Springfield, Thomas, 1956.

Ohio Learner's Manual Developed, TPC, Vol.30 (Jan., 1963), 64.

Ohio, State of: *Law Enforcement Officers' Manual.* Columbus, Enforcement Division, Ohio Department of Liquor Control, 1962.

Oklahoma Enacts Training Standards, TPC, Vol.30 (Dec., 1963), 47.

Organization. Washington, IACP Publications, 1963.

Osterburg, J. W., and Ziel, W. B.: Police Problems: Training, L&O, Vol.13, No.4 (Apr., 1965), 58.

Papanek, Ernst: The Training School: Its Program and Leadership, FP, Vol.17 (June, 1953), 16-22.

Parker, W. H.: *Los Angeles Police Daily Training Bulletin,* 2 Vols. Springfield, Thomas, 1958.

———: How Much Is Enough, TPY (1959).

Pasadena (City) Police Department: *Manual of Jail Operations.* Pasadena, General Order No.97, May 11, 1951.

Payton, George T.: Training Patrolmen to Dust for Latent Prints, POLICE, Vol.8, No.4 (Mar.-Apr., 1964), 41-45.

Peace Officers' Association of California: *California Peace Officer.* Sacramento, The Association, Vols.1-13.

———: *Proceedings of Annual Conferences.* Sacramento, The Association, 1922-1962 inclusive.

Peper, John: *Field Notetaking and Crime Scene Recording.* Sacramento, Calif. Peace Officers' Training Pub. No.73, Calif. State Dept. of Education, 1963.

———: Police Training in California, WCM, Vol.26 (Sept., 1950).

———: *Present Activities and Future Plans for Peace Officers Training,* Peace Officers' Assoc. of the State of Calif., 1948.

———: *A Recruit Asks Some Questions,* Springfield, Thomas, 1954.

Perkins, Rollin M.: *Police Examinations.* Brooklyn, Foundation, 1947.

Plavsic, Milan N.: Training Institute of Illinois, TPY (1962).

POLICE. Published Bimonthly by Charles C Thomas, Publisher, 301-327 East Lawrence Ave., Springfield, Illinois.

THE POLICE CHIEF. Published monthly by the International Association of Chiefs of Police, Washington, D.C.

POLICE MANAGEMENT REVIEW. Published monthly by the Planning Bureau of the NYCPD, 240 Centre Street, Room 117, New York, N.Y. 10013.

Police Pursuit Driving. Flint, Chevrolet Division, General Motors Corp., 1964.

Police Training Practices Relating to Juvenile Delinquency, TPC, Vol.30 (Jan., 1963), 29.

The Police Yearbook. Reports of the proceedings of the annual conferences of the International Association of Chiefs of Police. Washington, D.C.

Pomrenke, Norman E.: Florida Moves Progressively Forward in Law Enforcement, POLICE, Vol.8, No.6 (July-Aug., 1964), 6-9.

Price, Hugh G.: *California Public Junior Colleges.* Sacramento, bulletin of the Calif. State Dept. of Education, Vol.28, No.1, Calif. State Dept. of Education, 1958.

Problems of Physical Conditioning, TPC, Vol.30 (July, 1963), 8.

Psychology in Visual Observation Training Courses, FBILEB (Nov., 1959).

PUBLIC FINANCE: Published quarterly, Emmalaan 2, Haarlem, Netherlands.

Puddy, George H.: Operation P.O.S.T., POLICE, Vol.8, No.3 (Jan.-Feb., 1964), 80-82.

Purcell, Philip: Report of Committee on Education and Training, TPY (1960).

Purdy, Wilson E.: Administrative Action to Implement Selection and Training for Police Professionalization, TPC (May, 1965), 14-18.

———: Goals for Police Training Programs, TPY (1962).

———: 4-phase Program for Coping with Disorder, TPC, Vol.32, No.3 (Mar., 1965), 45-46.

Radelet, Louis A.: Police Community Programs: Nature and Purposes, TPC, Vol.32, No.3 (Mar., 1965), 38-40.

Radzinowicz, Leon, and Turner, J. W. C.: *The Journal of Criminal Science.* New York, Macmillan, 1948. (This book includes articles on Sexual Crime, Crime Detection, Training for the Work of a Probation Officer, Criminal Law Relating to Insanity, etc.)

Rafferty, Max: *A Study Manual and Bibliography for Peace Officers.* Sacramento, Calif.

State Peace Officers' Training Series, 1963.

Ralston, Lee, and Los Angeles Police Dept. Training Div.: *Instructional Techniques.* Unpublished outline. Los Angeles, The Police Dept., 1959.

Randall, Raymond L.: *An Evaluation of Selected Intensive Short-range Executive Development Programs for Government Officials.* Unpublished doctoral dissertation, Washington, American University, 1961.

———— (ed.): *Executive Development in Action: Patterns and Techniques,* Pamphlet No.9. Washington, Society for Personnel Admin., 1955.

Report of the Lectures Presented in the Peace Officers' Administrative Institutes for Law Enforcement Administrators of Calif. Conducted at Los Angeles and San Francisco, Calif. Sacramento, Calif. State Dept. of Education, 1956.

Rice, Charles Owen, Rev.: Untouchable—Humane, TPC, Vol.29, No.2 (Feb., 1962), 30.

Riegel, John W.: *Executive Development: Fifty American Corporations.* Report No.5, Ann Arbor, Univ. of Mich., 1952.

Rivo, Julian D.: Erie County Law Enforcement Academy, L&O, Vol.7 (Sept., 1959).

Rizer, Conrad: *Police Mathematics.* Springfield, Thomas, 1955.

Robin, Gerald D.: Police Slayings of Criminals, POLICE, Vol.8, No.6 (July-Aug., 1964), 32-35.

Roethlisberger, F. J., with the assistance of Lombard, George, F. F., and Ronken, Harriet O.: *Training for Human Relations.* Boston, Harvard School of Business Admin., 1954.

Rogers, Howard L.: Are You Planning a Police Recruit Training Program? POLICE, Vol.6, No.3 (Jan.-Feb., 1962), 46-48.

————: Determining Police Training Needs: Inservice, POLICE, Vol.6, No.4 (Mar.-Apr., 1962), 55-61.

Rogers, Jeptha S.: Role of the FBI in Police Training, TPY (1961), (1962).

Rutherford, J. W.: *The Feasibility of Instituting a Police Curriculum at the Junior College Level.* Washington, IACP, 1964.

Rychetnik, Joe: Cold Country Policing, L&O, Vol.11, No.6 (June, 1963).

Saul, Leon: *Emotional Maturity.* Chicago, Lippincott.

Savord, George H.: Significance of Badge, TPC, (Sept., 1961), 22.

Saxenian, Hrand: Readiness for Police Responsibility, POLICE, Vol.9, No.1 (Sept.-

Oct., 1964), 52-56; No.2 (Nov.-Dec., 1964), 73-77.

Schaich, J. F.: Illinois Police Training, TPC, Vol.29, No.1 (Jan., 1962), 49.

Schmidt, J. E.: Underworld English, POLICE, Vol.3, No.4 (Mar.-Apr., 1959), 33-34; No.5 (May-June, 1959), 19-20; No.6 (July-Aug., 1959), 47-48; Vol.4, No.1 (Sept.-Oct., 1959), 31-32; No.2 (Nov.-Dec., 1959), 47-48.

Schmidt, Willard E.: *Occupational Training for Law Enforcement in California State Colleges.* Sacramento, Calif. State Dept. of Education, 1950.

Schroeder, Oliver, Jr.: Police Education: A University Aids the Smaller Departments, PO-LICE, Vol.4, No.2 (Nov.-Dec., 1959), 15-19.

Schrotel, Stanley R.: Supervising the Use of Police Authority, JCLC&PS, Vol.47, No.5 (Jan.-Feb., 1957), 589.

Seares, Robert S.: The Police Cadet, THE ANNALS, Vol.291 (Jan., 1954), 107-12.

Sellers, Clark: Preparing to Testify, JCLC&PS, Vol.56, No.2 (June, 1965), 235-40.

Senn, Milton A.: *A Study of Police Training Programs in Minority Relations.* Los Angeles, Anti-defamation League of B'nai B'rith, 1950.

Shea, G. A.: Why Attend Police Conventions? TPC, Vol.30 (Aug., 1963), 50.

Shea, W. Joseph: Police Training Committee, TPC, (Apr., 1961), 45.

Sheehan, Robert: Northeastern University Police Training Program, TPC, (Apr., 1961), 45; (Oct., 1961), 37.

Shuptrine, Carl: Auxiliary Personnel and Special Skill Requirements, TPY (1962).

Sibiue, Mike: The Commando Squad, L&O, Vol.8, No.10 (1960).

Simon, Richard: Roll Call Training Program of the Los Angeles Police Department, JCL&C, Vol.40, No.4 (Nov.-Dec., 1949), 507.

Skehan, James J.: *Modern Police Work Including Detectives,* Rev. Ed. New York, Basuino, 1948.

Skousen, Cleon W.: Notes to a New Chief, L&O, Vol.10, No.8 (Aug., 1962), 10; No.10 (Oct., 1962), 26.

————: The Revival of Rigid Inspections, L&O, Vol.12 (Oct., 1964).

Sloane, Charles F.: State Academies for Police, JCLC&PS, Vol.45 (Mar.-Apr., 1955), 729-34.

Smith, Leo M.: A Dream Comes True, TPC, Vol.29, No.3 (Mar., 1962), 18.

Smyth and Murphy: *Evaluation and Employee Training.* New York, McGraw-Hill.

Soule, Rolland L.: Recognition Training in Law

Enforcement Work, JCLC&PS, Vol.49, No.6 (1958-59), 590.

——: Role Playing—A New Police Training Tool, POLICE, Vol.4, No.4 (Mar.-Apr., 1960), 19-22.

South, William E.: Law Enforcement Training in California, TPY (1958).

Sperhoff, B. J., and Heydrick, A. K.: The Incident Method, Its Use with Buzz Groups and Film Strips, PER.J (Oct., 1954), 171-178.

SPRING 3100. Published by the Police Department, City of New York, monthly, 400 Broome St., New York 13, N.Y.

Squires, Harry A.: *Guide to Police Report Writing.* Springfield, Thomas, 1964.

Struck, F. Theodore: *Vocational Education for a Changing World.* New York, Wiley, 1945.

Stewart, Ward: *Graduate Study in Public Administration.* Washington, U.S. Office of Education, 1961.

Stills. Washington, U.S. Treasury Dept., Pub. No.223 (Jan. 1, 1961). Part 196 of Title 26, Code of Federal Regulations.

Stinchcomb, James D.: Law Enforcement Education in the Tampa Bay Area Moves Ahead, POLICE, Vol.7, No.6 (July-Aug., 1963), 58-59.

——: The Police Chief Looks to His Community College, TPC, (May, 1965), 20-22.

——: The Student Internship in Law Enforcement Curricula, POLICE, Vol.7, No.2 (Nov.-Dec., 1962), 34-35.

Stoker, Mack: The Permissive Approach in Teaching, POLICE, Vol.4, No.2 (Nov.-Dec., 1959), 74-78.

Storm, Bill: Special "Ambush Squad" Training, L&O, Vol.12 (June, 1964).

Story of the FBI National Academy. Washington, Federal Bureau of Investigation.

Studt, Elliot, and Chernin, Milton: The Role of the School of Social Work in Educating and Training Personnel for Work with Juvenile Delinquents, *Training Personnel for Work with Juvenile Delinquents.* Washington, D.C., U.S. Dept. of Health, Education and Welfare, Children's Bureau, Pub. No.348, 1954.

SUPERVISION. Published monthly by the Supervision Publishing Company, Inc., 95 Madison Ave., New York, N.Y.

Sweeney, Daniel P. A., and Roos, Louis L.: Instructing Police Officers in the Criminal Law, JCL&C, Vol.35, No.5 (Jan.-Feb., 1945), 343.

Tamm, Quinn, (ed.): After College—What? TPC, Vol.32, No.2 (Feb., 1965), 46-47.

——: How Blue Is Blue? TPC, Vol.32, No.2 (Feb., 1965), 41.

——: Intermediate Course Added to New York State's Minimum Training Standards Program, TPC, Vol.32, No.2 (Feb., 1965), 40-41.

——: IACP—Highway to Leadership, TPC, Vol.30 (Apr., 1963), 7.

——: Training: An Expense, TPC, Vol.30 (Feb., 1963), 7.

Team Efforts in Training, TPC, Vol.30 (Apr., 1963), 38.

Tear Gas Training Manual. Saltsburg, Federal Laboratories, 15681, 1964.

Tegner, Bruce: *Aikido Self Defense.* Hollywood, Thor, 1964.

——: *Judo for Fun.* Hollywood, Thor, 1964.

——: *Judo, Karate for Law Officers.* Hollywood, Thor, 1962.

——: *Karate.* Hollywood, Thor, 1964.

——: *Karate,* Vol.2, Hollywood, Thor, 1964.

——: *Method of Self Defense.* Hollywood, Thor, 1964.

——: *Savate.* Hollywood, Thor, 1964.

——: *Self Defense for Women.* Hollywood, Thor, 1964.

——: *Stick Fighting for Self-Defense,* 1964.

——: *Teach Your Boy Self-Defense and Self-Confidence.* Hollywood, Thor, 1964.

Tentative Standards for Training Schools, 1954. Washington, a report prepared by the U.S. Dept. of Health, Education and Welfare, Children's Bureau Pub. No.351, 1954.

Thomas, Samuel F.: Baruch School's Experience, TPY (1963).

Totlen, James C.: Michigan State University Offers Course in Techniques for Investigators, L&O, Vol.7 (Aug., 1959).

Towler, Juby E.: Introduction to the Art of Leadership, POLICE, Vol. No.6 (July-Aug., 1962), 70-78.

——: *Practical Police Knowledge.* Springfield, Thomas, 1960.

Training, AID-IACP Training Program Ended, TPC, Vol.30 (Apr., 1963), 34.

Training Bulletin, 2 Vols. Los Angeles Police Dept., Springfield, Thomas, 1954.

Training for Railway Officials, TPC, Vol.30 (May, 1963), 50.

Training, IACP Supervisory Course, First for U.S. Park Police, TPC, Vol.30 (June, 1963), 59.

Training, IACP Supervisory Course, Lubbock, Texas, TPC, Vol.30 (Feb., 1963), 34.

Training, Southwest Institutes, TPC, Vol.30 (Apr., 1963), 44.

Training of Juvenile Court Probation Officers

and Related Workers Who Cannot Attend Graduate School, *Training Personnel for Work with Juvenile Delinquents.* Washington, U.S. Dept. of Health, Education and Welfare, Children's Bureau Pub. No.348, 1954.

Two New Courses, One in Police Training and One in Scientific Crime Detection, SE&SCD, Vol.2, No.6 (1964).

Union County, New Jersey Expands Training, TPC, Vol.30 (Oct., 1963), 45.

U.S. Air Force: *How to Instruct the Worker.* Training pamphlet No.50-2-16. Washington, U.S. Govt. Printing Office, 1955.

U.S. Civil Service Commission: *Assessing and Reporting Training Needs and Progress.* Washington, Personnel Methods Series No.3, 1956.

———: *How Federal Agencies Develop Executive Talent.* Washington, 1953.

———: *The Training of Federal Employees.* Washington, Personnel Methods Series No.7, 1958.

U.S. Office of Education: *Administration of Vocational Education.* Washington, Vocational Education Bulletin No.2, General Series No.1, Revised.

———: *The Operation of a Local Program of Trade and Industrial Education with Emphasis on Improving Instruction Through Supervision.* Washington, Vocational Education Bulletin No.250, Trade and Ind. Service, 1953.

———: *Public Vocational Education Programs.* Washington, 1956.

Vollmer, August: Outline of a Course in Police Organization and Administration, SE&SCD, Vol.2, No.1 (1964).

———: The Scientific Policeman, SE&SCD, Vol.1, No.1 (1964).

Watson, Nelson A.: Thoughts on Police Training, TPC, Vol.32, No.1 (Jan., 1965), 10-26.

Weston, Paul B.: The Case for Police Firearms Training, POLICE (Jan.-Feb., 1961).

———: *Combat Shooting for Police.* Springfield, Thomas, 1960.

———: Combat Shooting—Training for Combat Effectiveness, POLICE, Vol.3, No.4 (Mar.-Apr., 1959), 56-59.

———: The Role of College in Law Enforcement, Part 1, Vol.10, No.12 (Dec., 1962), 66; Part 2, Vol.11, No.1 (Jan., 1963).

What Are the Sources of the Curriculum?: A Symposium. Washington, Association for Supervision and Curriculum Development, NEA, 1962.

Wiard, Seth: The Army and the Policeman, SE&SCD, Vol.1, No.5 (1964).

Williams, Charles, and Hefforn, Floyd: *Court Appearance and Testimony.* Sacramento, Calif. Peace Officers' Training Pub. No.10, 1963.

Willis, Benjamin C.: Supplementary Education to Police Training, TPY (1957).

Wilson, O. W.: *Police Administration.* New York, McGraw-Hill, 1950.

Winters, Carl S.: The Policeman's Glory Road, TPY (1960).

York, Orrell A.: New York's State Sponsored Police Training, TPY (1962).

———: *Municipal Police Training in New York State.* Albany, Municipal Police Training Council, 1961.

Young, Carl B., Jr.: Acute Heart Emergencies, POLICE, Vol.11, No.2 (Nov.-Dec., 1957), 12-14.

———: *First Aid and Resuscitation.* Springfield, Thomas, 1954.

———: *Transportation of the Injured.* Springfield, Thomas, 1958.

Zink, Howard A.: *Report of Committee on Minimum Standards,* Peace Officers' Assoc. of the State of Calif., 1948.

Chapter Five

POLICE ADMINISTRATION*

CIVIL DEFENSE

American Municipal Association: *Emergency Ambulance and Hospital Service.* Chicago, American Municipal Assoc., 1949.

Beers, Barnet W.: Coordination of Civil and Military Functions in Civil Defense, TPY (1956).

Bennett, Wayne W.: Report of the Civil Defense Advisory Committee, TPY (1964); (1965).

Berry, Lewis E.: Civil Defense—Whose Real Responsibility, TPY (1960).

Blair, Edison T.: Knowledge of Nuclear Weapons Dispels Fears, TPC (Feb., 1961), 4.

Booth, Ralph M.: Relationships with other Disaster Services, TPY (1962).

Brannigan, F. L.: Accidents Involving Radioactive Material, TPY (1960).

———: Shipment of Radio-active Materials, TPY (1962).

Buckley, John L.: Security Officer's Notebook— Civil Defense Training and National Shelter Program, L&O, Vol.10, No.10 (Oct., 1962), 38.

California Department of Justice, State Disaster Council: *Minutes of Meeting.* Sacramento, Apr., 17, 1948. State Printing Office.

———: *California Disaster Office, Annual Report.* Sacramento, State Printing Office, 1961.

———: *Law Enforcement Mutual Aid Plan.* Sacramento, State Printing Office, 1961.

———: *Manual for Civil Defense in Govt. Buildings and Institutions.* Sacramento, State Printing Office, 1952.

Civil Defense ID Cards, TPC, Vol.30 (Apr., 1963), 46.

Clear, John W.: Nuclear Incidents in Transit, TPY (1959).

Cohn, Frank: Law and Order in Civil Defense: Some Aspects of Civil and Military Programs for the Maintenance of Law and Order in a Civil Defense Emergency. Unpublished

---

* This chapter includes: Civil Defense, Crime, Organized Crime, Police Administration, Police Buildings, Police-Fire Integration, Police Management & Supervision, Police Planning and Research, Public Administration, Public Relations, and Vice, which includes; Gambling, Prostitution, Liquor and Narcotics.

Master's Thesis, College Social Science, Michigan State Univ., 1963.

Conrad, Edward E.: Shipboard Reactor Plants, TPY (1962).

Crowe, Bazel E.: Disaster Government After Hurricane "Donna," POLICE, Vol.6, No.3 (Jan.-Feb., 1962), 22-24.

Department of the Army: *Civil Disturbances and Disasters.* Washington, U.S. Govt. Printing Office, 1958.

Diamond, Harry: Police Duties and Responsibilities at the Scene of an Emergency or Disaster, POLICE, Vol.8, No.2 (Nov.-Dec., 1963), 71-77.

———: Response to Disaster, POLICE, Vol.7, No.5 (May-June, 1963), 57-64; No.6 (July-Aug., 1963), 70-74.

Disaster Courses, TPC, Vol.31 (Sept., 1964), 51.

Eastman, George D.: Report of Civil Defense Committee, TPY (1959); (1960).

Ellis, Frank B.: Civil Defense Reorganization, TPC (Sept., 1961), 29.

———: Director, O.C.D.M., Guest Editorial, L&O, Vol.9 (June, 1961).

Fagerstrom, Dorothy: Police Disaster Information, L&O, Vol.7 (May, 1959).

Federal Civil Defense Administration: *Civil Defense in Industry and Institutions.* Washington, U.S. Govt. Printing Office, 1951.

Heck, H. N.: *Earthquake History of the United States.* U.S. Coast Geodetic Survey, Special Pub., No.49.

Holstrom, John D.: Report of Civil Defense Advisory Committee, TPY (1957); (1958).

———: Disasters—A Panel Discussion, TPY (1957).

James, Jesse R.: A Code of Ethics for Auxiliary Police, L&O (May, 1959).

Kimberling, A. E.: The Role of the Police in the H-bomb Era, TPY (1956).

King, Everett M.: *The Auxiliary Police Unit.* Springfield, Thomas, 1960.

Kirkman, H. N.: Viewpoint of a Police Executive, TPY (1965).

Landstreet, Barent F.: Police Problems in War-caused Emergency, TPY (1961).

Lawder, Lee E.: Reflections on a Disaster, L&O, Vol.11, No.12 (Dec., 1963).

Leonard, Donald S.: Catastrophe Control, PCN, Vol.16 (May, 1949).

Massey, E. E.: Control of Radioactive Material, TPY (1962).

McHugh, James E.: CONARC Training Program for Explosive Ordinance Reconnaissance, TPY (1958).

Mudge, G. W.: Police Role in Nuclear Accidents, TPY (1962).

National Security Resources Board: *United States Civil Defense.* Washington, U.S. Govt. Printing Office, 1950.

Office of Civil Defense and Mobilization: *The National Plan for Civil Defense and Defense Mobilization, Annex 16 Maintenance of Law and Order.* Washington, 1959.

Orientation to Civil Defense in California. Sacramento, Calif. Office of Civil Defense, 1951.

Orost, J., and Seckler, W. H.: A New Group— Alerting System, L&O, Vol.9 (Mar., 1961).

Penly, William J.: Nuclear Safety and Accident Response, TPY (1962).

Prior, J. Russell: The Federal Civil Defense Administration Rescue School, TPY (1956).

——: Government in Emergency, TPY (1959).

——: Nuclear Age Meets Your Job, L&O, Vol.9 (May, 1961).

——: Planning and Organizing for Traffic Control in National Defense, L&O, Vol.10, No.5 (May, 1962), 12.

Purdy, E. Wilson: Workshop: Mass Behavior and Governmental Breakdown in Major Disasters, TPY (1965).

Quarantelli, E. L.: Viewpoint of a Researcher, TPY, (1965).

Ratzloff, David: Preparedness, L&O, Vol.12 (Mar., 1964).

Rutter, Joseph D.: Emergency Activities in Large Scale Disasters, TPY (1962).

——: Report of the Civil Defense Advisory Committee, TPY (1962).

Safar, Porter, and McMahon, Martin C.: New Method of Artificial Respiration Gains

Recognition, POLICE, Vol.3, No.6 (July-Aug., 1959), 6-12.

Salvation Army, National Research Bureau, Disaster Emergency Committee: *The Salvation Army Disaster Emergency Service, Directives and Manual of Operation,* 1948.

Shaw, William: Civil Defense Communication, L&O, Vol.8, No.5 (1960).

——: Conelrad Alerting System—Past and Present, L&O, Vol.9 (Sept., 1961).

——: Emergency Power Plants, L&O, Vol.12 (June, 1964).

——: The Industrial Radiation Hazard, L&O, Vol.9 (Dec., 1961).

——: The National Emergency Alarm Repeater, L&O, Vol.10, No.3 (Mar., 1962), 44.

Skousen, W. Cleon: What About a Police Reserve Corps? L&O, Vol.9 (Sept., 1961).

Teasley, Harvey D.: 4168 Volunteer Hours Aid Police, L&O, Vol.7 (May, 1959).

Turner, Carl C.: Viewpoint of a Military Officer, TPY (1965).

U.S. Committee on Civilian Components: *Reserve Forces for National Security.* Washington, U.S. Govt. Printing Office, 1948.

U.S. Dept. of the Army: *Field Manual FM 21-76 —Survival.* Washington, 1957.

U.S. Dept. of Health, Education and Welfare: *An Outline Guide Concerning Sanitation Aspects of Mass Evacuations.* Washington, U.S. Govt. Printing Office, 1956.

U.S. Office of Civil Defense Planning: *Civil Defense for National Security.* Washington, U.S. Govt. Printing Office, 1949.

Ward, George: Radiation Hazards—A New Police Problem, L&O, Vol.9 (May, 1961).

Washburn, Burton: Disaster Preparedness Planning, *Peace Officers' Association of the State of California Proceedings.* Sacramento, 1948.

Weaver, Leon: The Role of Law Enforcement in Civil Defense, POLICE, Vol.5, No.5 (May-June, 1961), 55-56.

Weber, Donald J.: Movements of Nuclear Weapons, TPY (1962).

CRIME

Abrahamsen, David: *Crime and the Human Mind.* New York, Columbia Univ. Press, 1945.

——: *Who Are the Guilty? A Study of Education and Crime.* New York, Rinehart, 1952.

An Answer to the Rise in Crime and Violence, USN&WR (Nov. 9, 1964), 89.

Anderson, Clinton H.: *Beverly Hills Is My Beat.* New York, Popular, 1960.

Bell, Daniel: *Crime as an American Way of Life, The End of Ideology.* Glencoe, Free Press, 1960.

Bennett, James V.: A Cool Look at "The Crime Crisis," HARPER'S, Vol.228, No.1367 (Apr., 1964), 123-128.

Biederman, Ruth: A Specialized Approach to Crime, POLICE, Vol.1, No.3 (Jan.-Feb., 1957), 14-18.

Bloch, Herbert A. (ed.): *Crime in America*. New York, Philosophical, 1961.

———: Economic Depression as a Factor in Rural Crime, JCL&C, Vol.49 (Nov.-Dec., 1949), 458-70.

———, **& Geis, Gilbert:** *Man, Crime and Society*. New York, Random House, 1962.

Borre, Glen V.: Public Welfare Offenses: A New Approach, JCLC&PS, Vol.52, No.4 (Nov.-Dec., 1961), 418.

Brannon, Bernard C.: The Mana of the City, TPY (1959).

Brean, Herbert: Crooked, Cruel Traffic in Drugs, LIFE, Vol.48, No.3 (Jan. 24, 1960), 53-69. (Part 3 of a 4-part series on world crime.)

———: The Evil Domain of World Crime, LIFE, Vol.48, No.1 (Jan. 11, 1960), 18-90. (Part 1 of a 4-part series on world crime.)

———: Men of Mafia's Infamous Web, LIFE, Vol.48, No.4 (Jan. 31, 1960), 58-59. Part 4 of a 4-part series on world crime.)

———: Rich, Wild Racket: Smuggling, LIFE, Vol.48, No.2 (Jan. 17, 1960), 92-101. (Part 2 of a 4-part series on world crime.)

Britain's Great Train Robbery—A Mystery Unraveled, USN&WR, Vol.56, No.1 (Jan. 6, 1964), 46-49.

Brown, Lee P.: A Black Muslim and the Police, JCLC&PS, Vol.56, No.1 (Mar., 1965), 119-126.

Brown, William P.: Crime of National Significance, JCLC&PS, Vol.55, No.4 (Dec., 1964), 509.

Buckman, Charles: Criminal Responsibility, JCLC&PS, Vol.43, No.3 (Sept.-Oct., 1952), 335.

Cahill, Thomas J.: The Transient Professional Criminal, TPY (1964).

Campaign, The, TIME (July, 1964), 9.

Campion, Daniel J., and Sterns, Myron: *Crooks Are Human Too*. New York, Prentice-Hall, 1957.

Chessman, Caryl: *Cell 2455, Death Row*. New York, Perman, 1956.

Chicago Crime Commission Expressed Indignation, TPC, Vol.31 (July, 1964), 39.

Chute, C. L.: *Crime, Courts, and Probation*. New York, Macmillan, 1956.

Clinard, Marshall B.: *The Black Market*. New York, Rinehart, 1952.

Cosnow, Nat: Viewing the Crime Statistics, Chicago and Cook Country, 1948. CJ, Vol.77 (Jan., 1950), 27-28.

The Council of State Governments: *The Handbook of Interstate Crime Control*. Chicago, The Council of State Governments, 1949. (Reflecting states operating under Cooperative Uniform Crime Control Legislation or Compacts as of July 20, 1966).

Crime in the U.S.—Is It Getting Out of Hand? USN&WR (Aug. 26, 1963), 38.

Crime in Washington, USN&WR (Feb. 25, 1963), 98.

The Crime Problem in Canada—How the Mounties Handle It, USN&WR (June 29, 1963), 66-68. (Interview with Commissioner C. W. Harrison of the RCMP.)

Crime Rise: What the Records Show: USN&WR, (Mar. 19, 1965), 6.

Danforth, Harold R., and Horan, James D.: *Big City Crimes*. New York, Permabooks, 1960.

———, & ———: *The DA's Man*. New York, Permabooks, 1959.

Davis, F. J.: Crime News in Colorado Newspapers, AJS, Vol.58 (Jan., 1952), 325-330.

Dostoevsky, Fyodor: *Crime and Punishment*. New York, Bantam, 1959.

Dougherty, Richard: The Case for the Cop, HARPER'S, Vol.228, No.1367 (Apr., 1964), 129-133.

Drzazga, John: Muslim Terrorists, L&O, Vol.11, No.5 (May, 1963).

East, Norwood: *Society and the Criminal*. Springfield, Thomas, 1949.

Elliott, George F.: Controlling the Giant in Smallness, L&O, Vol.8, No.3 (1960), 39.

Elliott, Mabel A.: *Crime in Modern Society*. New York, Harper, 1952.

Eysenck, H. J.: *Crime and Personality*. Boston, Houghton, 1964.

Falk, Gerhard J.: The Influence of the Seasons on the Criminal Rate, JCLC&PS, Vol.43, No.2 (July-Aug., 1952), 199.

Fitzpatrick, Joseph P.: The Puerto Ricans, CATHOLIC MIND (May-June, 1960).

Florita, Giorgio: Enquiry into the Causes of Crime, JCL&C, Vol.44, No.1 (May-June, 1953), 1-17.

Frank, Aaron: Criminal Responsibility, JCLC&PS, Vol.43, No.3 (Sept.-Oct., 1952), 336.

Frank, Martin M.: *Diary of a D.A.* New York, Popular, 1961.

Fraser, Gordon S.: Impact of Modern Transportation on International Crime, TPY (1965).

Gardner, Erle Stanley: Fewer Criminals Make for Less Crime, POLICE, Vol.1, No.5 (May-June, 1957), 7-11.

Gault, Robert H.: Power and Morality, JCLC&PS, Vol.51, No.1 (Mar.-Apr., 1960-61), 85.

Gavzer, Bernard: Fear of Street Crime Grips New York, THE PLAIN DEALER, Cleveland, Ohio (May 9, 1965), 2AA.

Glueck, S.: Causal Bases, VLWDC, Vol.1 (1949), 16-18.

———: *Crime and Justice.* Cambridge, Harvard Univ. Press, 1945.

——— (ed.) Assisted by Edna Mahan: *Harvard Crime Survey: Handbook of Illustrative Cases.* Cambridge, Harvard Law School.

———: Prognosis of Recidivism, *Third International Congress on Criminology.* London, General Report, 1955.

——— (ed.): The Welfare State and the National Welfare, U.S.A. THE MAGAZINE OF AMERICAN AFFAIRS, Vol.2 (1952).

——— (ed.): *The Welfare State and the National Welfare: a Symposium on Some of the Threatening Tendencies of our Times.* Cambridge, Addison-Wesley, 1952.

Goldberg, N.: *Yevo Annual of Jewish Social Science,* Vol.5 (1950), 266-91.

Gollomb, Joseph: The War on Crime: SE&SCD, Vol.2, No.3 (1964).

A Government Lawyer Looks at the Crime Problem, USN&WR (Sept. 28, 1964), 74-76.

Graham, Billy, Rev.: Address, TPY (1965).

Grimm, Victor E.: Principals, Accessories and the Continuing Crime, JCLC&PS, Vol.51, No.1 (Mar.-Apr., 1960-61), 66.

Gustafson, Roy A.: Have We Created a Paradise for Criminals? SCLR, Vol.30 (Dec., 1956), 1-34.

Hall, Jerome: *Theft, Law and Society,* 2nd Ed. Indianapolis, Bobbs-Merrill, 1952.

Hartung, Frank E.: *Crime, Law and Society.* Detroit, Wayne State Univ. Press, 1965.

Hentig, Hans von: *Crime, Causes and Conditions.* New York, McGraw-Hill, 1949.

High Court: Its Growing Impact, USN&WR (June, 1964), 34.

Hoover, J. Edgar: Anti-crime Legislation, TPC (July, 1961), 20.

———: Crime: Community Responsibility, TPC (Mar., 1961), 4.

How One City Keeps Its Streets Safe, USN&WR (Sept. 28, 1964), 68-71. (Crime in Milwaukee and how it is fought.)

Hughes, Graham: Criminal Omissions, YLJ, Vol.67 (Fall, 1958), 590-637.

Hunter, David R.: *The Slums: Challenge and Response.* Glencoe, Free Press, 1964.

Illing, Hans A.: Zur Psychologie der Einzeldelikte, Vol.4: Die Expressung, JCLC&PS, Vol.51, No.2 (Mar.-Apr., 1960-61), 246. (Blackmail.)

Irey, Elmer L., and Slocum, William J.: *The Tax-dodger.* New York, Greenbert, 1948.

In the Nation's Capital—"Crisis in Crime," USN&WR (May 24, 1965), 58-60.

Is Crime in U.S. Out of Hand? Why LBJ Worries, USN&WR (Mar. 22, 1965), 38-42.

Is Crime Running Wild? USN&WR (Aug. 3, 1964), 19.

Is Nation's Capital Too Easy on Criminals? USN&WR (May 31, 1965), 11.

Jaffe, Carolyn: The Press and the Oppressed—A Study of Prejudicial News Reporting in Criminal Cases (Part 1), JCLC&PS, Vol.66, No.1 (Mar., 1965), 1-17.

Johnson, Malcom: *Crime on the Labor Front.* New York, McGraw-Hill, 1950.

Jones, Howard: *Crime in a Changing Society.* Baltimore, Pelican, 1965.

Kefauver, Estes: *Crime in America.* New York, Doubleday, 1951.

Kennedy, Robert F.: *The Enemy Within.* New York, Popular, 1960.

King, Daniel P.: Crime: A Perspective on the Problem, POLICE, Vol.9, No.1 (Sept.-Oct., 1964), 96-98.

Klein, Woody: *Let in the Sun.* New York, Macmillan, 1964.

Kraft, Joseph: Riot Squad for the New Frontier, HARPER'S (Aug., 1963), 69-75.

Lawrence, David: Good Behavior for Judges—Who Denies It, USN&WR (July 6, 1964), 92.

———: The Greatest Need—A Safe Society, USN&WR (Feb. 8, 1965), 108.

———: War Against Crime, USN&WR (June 29, 1964), 112.

Lee, Henry: The Courts, The Police, and The Public: Crime. THIS WEEK MAGAZINE, Cleveland Plain Dealer (May 16, 1965), 6-7.

Leonard, V. A.: The Moral Health of the Nation, POLICE, Vol.1, No.2 (Nov.-Dec., 1956), 58-61.

———: That Weekend, POLICE, Vol.1, No.1 (Sept.-Oct., 1956), 55.

Littlejohn, Frank N.: Causes of Crime, TPY (1957).

Liu, Daniel S. C.: Tourists and Conventioneers, TPY (1964).

Louchran, Robert: Now Its Bottles: The Feds Still Are Chasing Capone, AKRON BEACON JOURNAL (Mar. 3, 1963), 4G. (The Life of Ralph "Bottles" Capone, Al's brother.)

Lundern, Walter A.: Unemployment and Crime, POLICE, Vol.9, No.1 (Sept.-Oct., 1964), 6-10.

McKinnon, Harold R.: Terror in the Streets—Behind the Rise in U.S. Crime, USN&WR

(Dec. 24, 1962), Vol.53, No.26, 54-56. (An address before the San Francisco City Bar Association.)

Martienssen, Anthony: *Crime and the Police.* London, Secker, 1951.

Martin, John Bartlow: The Innocent and the Guilty, SATURDAY EVENING POST, Part 1 (July 20, 1960); Part 2 (Aug. 6, 1960); Part 3 (Aug. 13, 1960); Part 4 (Aug. 20, 1960); Conclusion (Aug. 27, 1960).

————: *My Life in Crime.* New York, Signet, 1953.

Mills, C. Wright: A Diagnosis of Our Moral Uneasiness, NEW YORK TIMES MAG. (Nov. 23, 1952), 10FF.

Miloslavich, Edward L.: Crushing Foot Injuries Due to External Violence from Below, JCLC&PS, Vol.43 (July-Aug., 1952), 257.

Mobers, David O.: Old Age and Crime: JCLC&PS, Vol.43, No.6 (Mar.-Apr., 1953), 764.

More Light on Crime in Nation's Capital, USN&WR (Nov. 4, 1963), 92.

Morris, Norval: *The Habitual Criminal.* Cambridge, Harvard Univ. Press, 1951.

Next: A National Police Force, USN&WR (Dec. 7, 1964), 44.

New Facts on the Rise of Crime and Communism: USN&WR (May 31, 1965), 10.

Ostrander, Mary Rita: Female Offender, L&O, Vol.11, Nos.11 & 12 (Nov. & Dec., 1963).

Parker, W. H.: The California Crime Rise: JCLC&PS, Vol.47, No.6 (Mar.-Apr., 1957), 721.

Petersen, Charles F.: Street Lighting Fights Crime, TPC, Vol.29, No.5 (May, 1962), 30.

Peterson, Virgil W.: *Barbarians in Our Midst: a History of Chicago Crime and Politics.* Boston, Little, Brown, 1952.

————: Citizens' Crime Commission, FP, Vol.17, No.1 (Mar., 1953), 9-15.

————: How to Form a Citizens Crime Commission, JCLC&PS, Vol.46 (1955-56), 485-99.

Pollack, Otto: *The Criminality of Women.* Philadelphia, Univ. of Penn. Press, 1950.

Porterfield, Austin L.: A Decade of Serious Crime in the United States: Some Trends and Hypotheses, ASR, Vol.13 (Feb., 1948), 44-54.

————, *et al.*: *Crime Suicide and Social Wellbeing in Your State and City.* Fort Worth, Potishman Foundation, 1948.

Ragen, Joseph E.: Today's Criminals—A New Species, POLICE, Vol.7, No.5 (May-June, 1963), 13-16.

Rauth, Joseph L., Jr.: Representation Before

Congressional Committee Hearings, JCLC&PS, Vol.50, No.3 (Sept.-Oct., 1959), 219.

Ray, Hoyt E.: Crime and Prohibition, JCL&C, Vol.38, No.2 (Mar.-Apr., 1947-48), 119-127.

Reckless, Walter C.: *The Crime Problem,* 3rd Ed. New York, Appleton, 1961.

Reifsnyder, Richard: Capital Crimes in the United States, JCLC&PS, Vol.45 (1945-55), 690-96.

Riempp, William F., Jr.: Itinerant Peddlers, Magazines Sales Teams, etc., TPY (1964).

Robert Kennedy Speaks His Mind: War on Crime, USN&WR (Jan. 28, 1963), 63-64.

Rogow, Arnold A., and Lasswell, Harold D.: *Poser, Corruption and Rectitude.* Englewood, Prentice-Hall, 1963.

Rosenberg, Bernard: Meet the Gang, JCL&C, Vol.36, No.2 (1945-46), 98.

Rosenthal, A. M.: *Thirty-eight Witnesses.* New York, McGraw-Hill, 1965.

Rovere, Richard H.: *Howe and Hummel: Their Tune and Scandalous History.* New York, Farrar, Straus, 1947.

Sattarfield, Val Beyer: Criminal Responsibility of Women, JCLC&PS, Vol.43, No.6 (Mar.-Apr., 1953), 756.

Schafer, Stephen: Restitution to Victims of Crime, TPC (June, 1961), 40.

Schur, Edwin M.: Common Sense About Crime & Punishment, JCLC&PS, Vol.53, No.2 (June-Aug., 1962), 235.

————: *Crimes Without Victims—Deviant Behavior and Public Police: Abortion, Homosexuality, Drug Addiction.* Englewood Cliffs, Prentice-Hall, 1965.

Scott, Harold: *Crime and Criminals.* New York, Hawthorn, 1961.

Short, James F., Jr.: A Note on Relief Programs and Crime During the Depression of the Thirties, ASR, Vol.17 (Apr., 1952), 226-229.

————: Social Aspect of the Business Cycle Reexamined: *Proceedings of the Pacific Sociological Society,* Vol.22, No.2, Research Studies of the State College of Washington (1952), 36-41.

Smith, Sandy: The Charmed Life of Tony Accardo: SATURDAY EVENING POST, Vol.235, No.42 (Nov. 24, 1962), 28-36. (How he makes crime pay.)

Speedier Justice in Britain: "We Reformed Our Laws in the 19th Century and U.S. Didn't," USN&WR (Mar. 22, 1965), 42-43. (An interview with Sir John Foster, A British authority on the Anglo-Saxon Legal System.)

Starnes, Richard: Crime: A Losing War—Violators Often Take Refuge in the Law, CLEVELAND PRESS (May 7, 1965), A21.

Starnes, Richard: Growth of Teen-age Crime Is Appalling, Says Hoover, CLEVELAND PRESS (May 14, 1965), B13.

State of California, Department of Justice: *Crime in California.* Sacramento, State Printing Office, 1954, 1962.

————: *Report of California Crime Study Commissions.* Sacramento, State Printing Office, 1949 & 1950.

Sutherland, Edwin H.: *The Crime Problem.* New York, Appleton, 1956.

Sykes, Gresham: *Crime and Society.* New York, Random House, 1956.

Tappan, Paul W.: Crime and the Criminal, FP, Vol.11, No.3 (July-Sept., 1947), 41-44.

Teeters, Negley K.: Can Society Reduce Crime and Criminals, JCL&C, Vol.35, No.6 (Mar.-Apr., 1945), 408.

Terror in the Streets—Behind the Rise in U.S. Crime, USN&WR (Dec. 24, 1962).

Toland, John: The Dillinger Days, LOOK, Vol.27, No.2 (Jan 29, 1963), 66-77.

Toland, John: The Last of Dillinger, LOOK, Vol.27, No.3 (Feb. 12, 1963), 79-90.

United States Senate: *Selected Committee on Improper Activities in the Labor or Management Field: Final Report.* Washington, U.S. Govt. Printing Office, 1951.

Vallow, Herbert Phillip: The Offense and the Offender, POLICE, Vol.9, No.1 (Sept.-Oct., 1964), 31-37.

Villela, Lavinia Costa: *Sex Ratio in Crime and Delinquency.* Unpublished Masters Thesis, Bloomington, Indiana Univ., 1946.

Voas, Robert G.: Why Do They Do It? TPY (1964).

Vold, George B.: Postwar Aviation and Crime, JCL&C, Vol.35, No.5 (Jan.-Feb., 1945), 297.

Vollmer, August: *The Criminal.* Brooklyn, Foundation, 1949.

Von Hentig, Hans: *Crime: Causes and Conditions.* New York, McGraw-Hill, 1947.

Waller, Stein, J. S., and Wyle, C. J.: Our Lawbreakers, PROBATION, Vol.25 (Mar.-Apr., 1947), 107-112.

Wertham, Fredric: *The Show of Violence.* New York, Doubleday, 1949.

Whitehead, Don: *Journey into Crime.* New York, Random House, 1960.

Whitman, Howard: Why Some Doctors Should Be in Jail, COLLIER'S (Oct. 30, 1953), 23-27.

Why So Much Crime in the Nation's Capital, USN&WR (Oct. 21, 1963), 92.

Will City Streets Ever Be Safe Again? USN&WR (Mar. 8, 1963), 80-83. (Interview with Stanley Schrotel, Chief of Police, Cincinnati, Ohio.)

Willbach, Harry: Recent Crimes and the Veterans, JCL&C, Vol.38, No.5 (Mar.-Apr., 1947-48), 501-08.

Williams, Jack Kenny: Catching the Criminal in Nineteenth Century South Carolina, JCLC&PS, Vol.46 (1955-56), 264-71.

————: *Vogues in Villainy.* Columbia, Univ. of South Carolina Press, 1959.

Winslow, Emma A.: Relationships Between Employment and Crime Fluctuations as Shown by Massachusetts Statistics.

Wylie, E. M., and Leary, R. V.: Hilarious Hunt for the Highwaymen, SATURDAY EVENING POST, Vol.236, No.14 (Mar. 13, 1963), 75-81.

You and the Law: KIWANIS INTERNATIONAL, 101 E. Erie St., Chicago, Ill., 1963.

ORGANIZED CRIME

Adams, Thomas F.: Organized Crime in America, POLICE, Vol.7, No.1 (Sept.-Oct., 1962), 37-38; No.2 (Nov.-Dec., 1962), 21-24; Vol.6, No.5 (May-June, 1962), 6-7; No.6 (July-Aug., 1962), 11-14.

Allen, Edward S.: The Mafia—and Salvafore Carnevale, POLICE, Vol.6, No.1 (Sept.-Oct., 1961), 26-29.

————: Mafia: Mediator and "Protector," POLICE, Vol.5, No.6 (July-Aug., 1961), 18-25.

————: Merchants of Menace: The Mafia, POLICE, Vol.5, No.4 (Mar.-Apr., 1961), 6-12; No.5 (June-July, 1961), 72-76.

————: Report of Committee on Organized Crime, TPY (1960).

————: Organized Crime, Workshop, TPY (1961).

Ambrose, Myles J.: The Roots of Organized Crime, TPY (1960).

American Academy of Political and Social Science. Combating Organized Crime (May, 1963). (Entire issue devoted to the subject.)

American Bar Association Commission on Organized Crime: *Organized Crime and Law Enforcement.* New York, Grosby, Vol.1, 1952; Vol.2, 1953.

Audett, Blackie: *Rap Sheet.* New York, Bantam, 1956.

Bean, Walton: *Boss Ruef's San Francisco.* Berkeley, Univ. of Calif. Press, 1952.

Bell, Daniel: *The End of Ideology.* Glencoe, Free Press, 1960.

Brennan, Bill: *The Frank Costello Story.* Derby, Monarch, 1962.

Burke, James: The Argot of the Racketeers, SE&SCD, Vol.2, No.5 (1964).

Burton, B. Turkus, and Feder, Sid: *Murder Inc.* New York, Farrar, 1951.

Busch, Francis X.: *Enemies of the State.* New York, Signet, 1962.

Cahill, Thomas J.: Report of the Committee on Organized Crime, TPY (1965).

California Special Crime Study Commission: *Final Report of the Special Crime Study Commission on Organized Crime.* Sacramento, State Printing Office, 1953.

California State Assembly: Interim Committee on Judiciary, Rackets—Organized Crime in California, *Assembly Interim Committee Reports.* Sacramento, State Printing Office, 1957-59, Vol.20, No.10.

Catton, Bruce: *The War Lords of Chicago.* New York, Harcourt, 1948.

Chandos, John (ed.): *To Deprave and Corrupt.* New York, Associated Press, 1962.

Coopers, Saul: *Dillinger.* New York, Hillman, 1959.

Crime: Kiss of Death, NEWSWEEK, Vol.62, No.15 (Oct. 7, 1963).

Dembitz, Nanette: The Appalachin "Conspiracy" RABCNY, Vol.16 (Jan., 1961), 47-58.

Dinneen, Joseph F.: *Underworld U.S.A.* New York, Permabooks, 1957.

Eighty-second Congress, 1st Session: Third Interim Report, *Special Committee to Investigate Organized Crime in Interstate Commerce.* Washington, U.S. Govt. Printing Office.

Eliasberg, Wladimir: Corruption and Bribery, JCLC&PS, Vol.42 (1951), 317.

Feder, Sid, and Joesten, Joachim: *The Luciano Story.* New York, Popular, 1960.

Final Report. Special Crime Study Commission on Organized Crime. Sacramento, Calif. 1953.

Fraley, Oscar: *4 Against the Mob.* New York, Popular Library, 1961.

Frasca, Dom: *Vito Genovese: King of Crime.* New York, Avon, 1959.

Fulton, E. D.: Organized Crime, TPY (1962).

Garmire, Bernard L.: The Enemy from Within, TPY (1961).

Gaylord, Otis H.: *The Rise and Fall of Legs Diamond.* New York, Bantam, 1960.

Giordano, Henry L.: Organized Crime, TPC, Vol.30 (Dec., 1963), 42.

————: Organized Crime in America, TPY (1964).

Grand Jury Report. Kansas City, May 4, 1961.

Grey, Harry: *The Hoods.* New York, Signet, 1956.

————: *Portrait of a Mobster.* New York, Signet, 1958.

Gurfein, Murray I.: Racketeering, ESS, New York, Macmillan.

Hamilton, Charles (ed.): *Men of the Underworld.* New York, Macmillan, 1952.

Hibbert, Christopher: *King Mob.* New York, Longmans, 1958.

Horan, James D.: *The Mob's Man.* New York, Crown, 1959.

Hynd, Alan: *The Giant Killers.* New York, McBridge, 1945.

Investigations: Killers in Prison, TIME, Vol.82, No.14 (Oct., 1963), 33.

Johnson, Earl: Organized Crime: Challenge to the American Legal System, Part 1, JCLC&PS, Vol.53, No.4 (Dec., 1962), 399; Part 2—The Legal Weapons: Their Actual and Potential Usefulness in Law Enforcement, Vol.54, No.1 (1963), 1; Part 3—Legal Antidotes for the Political Corruption Induced by Organized Crime, Vol.54, No.2 (1963), 127.

Johnson, Malcolm: *Crime on the Labor Front.* New York, McGraw-Hill, 1950.

Katcher, Leo: *The Big Bankroll.* New York, Pocket Books, 1960.

Keating, Kenneth B.: Organized Crime—What Can Congress Do About It? JCLC&PS, Vol.51, No.4 (Mar.-Apr., 1960-61), 458.

Kefauver, Estes: *Crime in America.* Garden City, Country Life, 1951.

Kennedy, Robert F.: The New Surge, NAT.B (May, 1959).

King, Rufus G.: The Control of Organized Crime in America, STAN.LR, Vol.4 (Dec., 1951), 52-67.

Lerner, Max: *America as a Civilization.* New York, Simon and Schuster, 1957.

Lever, Harry, and Young, Joseph: *Wartime Racketeers.* New York, Putnam, 1945.

Lyle, John H.: *The Dry and Lawless Years.* New York, Dell, 1961.

The Man Who Rocked the Boat. New York, Harper, 1956.

Martin, J. Bartlow: *Jimmy Hoffa's Hot.* Greenwich, Crest, 1959.

Martin, Raymond V.: *Revolt in the Mafia.* New York, Duell, Sloan & Pearce, 1963.

Mattei, Kenneth D.: Use of Taxation to Control Organized Crime, CAL.LR, Vol.39 (June, 1951), 225-234.

Miller, Herbert J., Jr.: Federal Approach to Organized Crime, TPC (Nov., 1961), 6.

———: A Federal Viewpoint of Combating Organized Crime, THE ANNALS, Vol.347 (May, 1963), 93.

Mullady, Frank, and Kofoed, William H.: *Meet the Mob.* New York, Belmont Books, 1961.

From the Statement of Federal Judge Irving R. Kaufman, THE NEW YORK TIMES (Jan. 14, 1960).

Organized Crime, TPC, Vol.30 (Dec., 1963), 10.

Perlmutter, Emanuel: Mafia Wields Sinister Power: Testimony by Valachi Points Up Strength of the Syndicate, THE NEW YORK TIMES (Sept. 29, 1963), E5.

Peterson, Virgil W.: *Barbarians in Our Midst.* Boston, Little, Brown, 1952.

———: Chicago: Shades of Capone, THE ANNALS, Vol.347 (May, 1963), 30.

———: The Myth of the Wide-open Town, JCL&C, Vol.39, No.3 (Mar.-Apr., 1948-49), 388-98.

———: Rackets in America, JCLC&PS, Vol.49, No.6 (1958-59), 583.

Ploscowe, Morris (ed.): *Organized Crime and Law Enforcement.* New York, Grosby, 1952.

Porter, Sylvia: On Wall Street, NEW YORK POST (Aug. 3-7, 1959).

Prager, Ted and Moberley, Leeds: *Hoodlums: New York.* New York, Retail Distributors, 1959.

Prall, Robert H., and Mockridge, Norton: *This Is Costello on the Spot.* Greenwich, Fawcett, 1957.

Preece, Harold: *The Dalton Gang.* New York, Signet, 1964.

Purvis, Melvin H.: *The Violent Years.* New York, Hillman, 1960.

Raymond, Allen: *Waterfront Priest.* New York, Holt, Rinehart, 1955.

Reid, Ed: *Mafia.* New York, Signet, 1954.

———, & Demaris, Ovid: *The Green Felt Jungle.* New York, Trident, 1963.

Roeburt, John: *The Mobster.* New York, Pyramid, 1960.

Roger, Touhy, and Brennan, Ray: *The Stolen Years.* Pennington Press.

Schlesinger, Arthur M.: *Paths to the Present.* New York, Macmillan.

Scotti, Alfred J.: Organized Crime and Racketeering, TPY (1960).

Sellin, Thorsten: Organized Crime. A Business Enterprise, THE ANNALS, Vol.347 (May, 1963), 12.

Shanley, J. F.: Objectives of the Police Intelligence Unit, TPC, Vol.31 (May, 1964), 10.

Shaw, Clifford R., McKay, Henry D., and McDonald, James F.: *Brothers in Crime.* Philadelphia, Saifer, 1952.

Shulman, Irving: *The Amboy Dukes.* New York, Bantam, 1961.

Siragusa, Charles: Its Label Is Mafia, TPY (1961).

Smith, Alson J.: *Syndicate City,* Chicago, Regnery, 1954.

Sondern, Frederic, Jr.: *Brotherhood of Evil: the Mafia.* New York, Bantam, 1960.

Strong, Dwight S.: New England: The Refined Yankee in Organized Crime. THE ANNALS, Vol.347 (May, 1963), 40.

Swanson, Warren L.: Legal Methods for the Suppression of Organized Crime, JCLC&PS, Vol.48 (Nov.-Dec., 1957), 415-30.

Taft, Philip: *Corruption and Racketeering in the Labor Movement.* Ithaca, N.Y. State School of Ind. & Labor Relations, 1958.

Thornton, Robert Y.: Organized Crime in the Field of Prostitution, JCLC&PS, Vol.46 (1955-56), 755-78.

Turkus, Burton B., and Feder, Sid: *Murder Inc.* New York, Bantam, 1960.

Tyler, Gus: The Big Fix, ADA WORLD (Sept., 1951).

——— (ed.): Combatting Organized Crime, THE ANNALS, Vol.346 (May, 1963).

———: *Organized Crime.* Ann Arbor, Univ. of Mich., 1962.

U.S. Attorney General's Conference on Organized Crime, Feb., 15, 1950, *Proceedings.* Washington, U.S. Dept. of Justice, U.S. Govt. Printing Office, 1950.

U.S. Congress, Senate Special Committee to Investigate Organized Crime in Interstate Commerce: *Third Interim Report.* 82nd Congress, First Session, Senate Report No.307, 1951. *Final Interim Report,* 82nd Congress, First Session, Senate Report, No.725, 1951. Washington, Government Printing Office, 1951.

U.S. Senate: *Final Report of the Select Committee on Improper Activities in the Labor or Management Field.* Washington, U.S. Govt. Printing Office, Mar. 28, 1960.

———: *Organized Crime and Illicit Traffic in Narcotics.* Hearing before the Permanent Subcommittee on Investigations of the Committee on Government Operations, U.S. Senate, 88th Congress. Washington, U.S. Govt. Printing Office, Sept. 25-Oct. 9, 1963. (Valachi Hearings.)

———: *Organized Crime and Illicit Traffic in*

Narcotics. Hearings before the Permanent Subcommittee on Investigations of the Committee on Government Operations, U.S. Senate, 88th Congress. Washington, U.S. Govt. Printing Office (Oct. 10-16, 1963). (Valachi Hearings.)

————: *Interim and Final Reports of the Special Committee to Investigate Organized Crime in Interstate Commerce.* Washington, Govt. Printing Office, 1951.

Walsh, Lawrence E.: Organized Crime, State Conference of Mayors. Los Angeles, July 15, 1959.

The Way Big Crime Operates in U.S.: Senators Learn About the Underworld, USN&WR (Oct. 7, 1963), 78-79.

Wendt, Lloyd, and Kogan, Herman: *Big Bill of Chicago.* Indianapolis, Bobbs-Merrill, 1953.

Wessel, Milton R.: The Appalachin Case: Its Significance, TPY (1961).

————: How We Bagged the Mafia, SATURDAY EVENING POST (July 16, 1964), 20; Part 2 (July 23, 1960), 19.

Weston, Paul B.: *Muscle on Broadway.* Evanston, Regency, 1962.

Woetzel, Robert K.: An Overview of Organized Crime: Mores Versus Morality, THE ANNALS, Vol.347 (May, 1963), 1.

Zumbrun, Alvin J. T.: Organized Crime, Gambling and Law Enforcement, POLICE, Vol.8, No.4 (Mar.-Apr., 1964), 58-63.

POLICE ADMINISTRATION

Adams, Thomas F.: Establishing a Juvenile Division for a Police Department Serving a City of 100,000, POLICE, Vol.7, No.3 (Jan.-Feb., 1963), 46-49.

Adrian, Charles R., and Press, Charles: *The American Political Process.* New York, McGraw-Hill, 1965.

Allen, Edward J.: Emerging Problems in a Changing Community, POLICE, Vol.7, No.3 (Jan.-Feb., 1963), 53-57.

————: The Police Chief of Tomorrow, TPC, Vol.25 (Mar., 1958), 8-10.

Allen, W. L.: Integration Viewpoints of Police Administration, TPC, Vol.30 (June, 1963), 24.

Alletto, William C.: Guidelines in Organization for Sheriffs' Departments of Large (Metropolitan) Counties, POLICE, Vol.7, No.4 (Mar., 1963), 73-76.

————: The State—The Administration of Justice and Law Enforcement, POLICE, Vol.8, No.4 (Mar.-Apr., 1964), 75-81.

Allman, James J.: Establishing a Police Community Relations Office Within a Police Department, TPC, Vol.32, No.3 (Mar., 1965), 11-14.

American Management Association: *Supervisory Practices and Organizational Structures as They Affect Employee Productivity and Morale.* Personnel Series No.120, New York, American Management Assoc., 1948.

Appleby, Paul H.: *Policy and Administration.* University, Univ. of Alabama Press, 1949.

Argyris, Cris: *Executive Leadership.* New York, Harper, 1953.

Arkin, Joseph: Tax Pointers for the Police Officer, L&O, Vol.7 (Feb., 1964).

Arm, Walter: "Cop Fighting," What Are Its Implications, TPC, Vol.29, No.4 (Apr., 1962), 10.

Arnwine, Henry B.: Development of Morale in the Police Department, POLICE, Vol.7, No.5 (May-June, 1963), 48-50; No.6 (July-Aug., 1963), 14-17; Vol.8, No.1 (Sept.-Oct., 1963), 40-44.

Arther, Richard O., and Phillips, Barbara J.: Words Make the Profession, L&O, Vol.11, No.2 (Feb., 1963).

Ashworth, Ray: The State Police Administration, TPY (1956).

Atherton, R. M.: Units Maintaining Liaison, TPC, Vol.31 (Nov., 1964), 31.

Aubry, Arthur S.: *The Officer in the Small Department.* Springfield, Thomas, 1961.

Baker, John C.: *Directors and Their Functions.* Cambridge, Harvard Univ. Press, 1945.

Bakke, E. Wight: *Organization and the Individual.* New Haven, Yale Univ. Press, 1952.

Barish, Norman N.: *Systems Analysis for Effective Administration.* New York, Funk & Wagnalls, 1951.

Barker, Ernest: *The Politics of Aristotle.* New York, Oxford Univ. Press, 1962. (An excellent treatise on the very early concepts of government.)

Barth, Alan: *Law Enforcement Versus the Law.* New York, Collier, 1963.

Bates, Billy Prior: I.S.Q.D., POLICE, Vol.8, No.2 (Nov.-Dec., 1963), 6-13.

Beasley, Kenneth A.: The Characteristics of a Good Police Department, THE CHIEFTAN, Vol.4 (Fall-Winter, 1957), 3-5, 8.

Beckman, R. O.: *How to Train Supervisors,* 3rd Ed. New York, Harpers, 1948.

Beckmann, John M.: Law Enforcement Is Big Business, L&O, Vol.8, No.10 (1960).

Beeley, Arthur L.: Utah Creates State Council on Criminal Justice Administration, JCLC&PS, Vol.52, No.2 (July-Aug., 1961), 190.

Bender, James F.: *Technique of Executive Leadership.* New York, McGraw-Hill, 1950.

Benson, James B.: Interdepartmental Relations, POLICE, Vol.7, No.5 (May-June, 1963), 80.

Beral, H., and Sisk, M.: Police Review Boards, TPC (Feb., 1964), 12-35.

Bernstein, Marver H.: *The Job of the Federal Executive.* Washington, Brookings Institution, 1958.

A Better Government for a Better City, a Study of Five Departments of the City of New York. The Citzens Budget Commission, Inc., 1948.

Black, Hil: *The Tarnished Badge.* New York, Crowell, 1965.

Blum, Richard H.: The Problems of Being a Police Officer, POLICE (Nov.-Dec., 1960) and (Jan.-Feb., 1961).

Bohardt, Paul H.: Training the Supervisor, TPY (1962).

Boston Police Survey—Blueprint for Modernization, TPC, Vol.30 (May, 1963) 28.

Bower, Marvin: *The Development of Executive Leadership.* Cambridge, Harvard Univ. Press, 1949.

Boyd, F. L.: Integration, Viewpoints of Police Administrators, TPC, Vol.30 (June, 1963), 26.

Bozett, W. C., Jr.: Three Steps to Eliminate a Problem, L&O, Vol.11, No.2 (Feb., 1963).

Bracken, Lawrence H., Msgr.: The Role of the Chaplain, TPY (1960).

Brandstatter, Arthur F.: Executive Development in Police Service, TPY (1962).

Brannon, Bernard C.: Administration: The Set of the Sail, TPY (1957).

————: Administration: Into Tomorrow, TPY (1958).

————: A Proposed Uniform Law Enforcement Examination Act, POLICE, Vol.4, No.2 (Nov.-Dec., 1959), 71-74.

————: Into Tomorrow, POLICE, Vol.3, No.3 (Jan.-Feb., 1959), 42-46.

————: Workshop: Police Legislation, TPY (1961).

Brereton, George H.: Law Enforcement—A Profession, POLICE, Vol.1, No.5 (May-June, 1957), 12-19.

Bristow, Allen P., and Gabard, E. C.: *Decision-making in Police Administration.* Springfield, Thomas, 1961.

————: *Police Decision Making.* Los Angeles, Univ. of Southern Calif., 1951.

———— (ed.): *Readings in Police Supervision.* Los Angeles, State College, Dept. of Police Admin.

Broaded, Charles H.: *Essentials of Management for Supervisors.* New York, Harper, 1947.

Bross, Irwin D. J.: *Design for Decision.* New York, Macmillan, 1953.

Brostron, C.: Use of Community Civic Groups in Strategic Planning, TPC, Vol.30 (June, 1963), 38.

Brown, Alvin: *Organization: a Formulation of Principle.* New York, Hibbert, 1945.

Brownrigg, William: *The Human Enterprise Process and Its Administration.* University, Univ. of Alabama Press, 1954.

Brunton, Robert L., and Carrell, Jeptha J.: *Management Practices for Smaller Cities.* Chicago, Int'l City Managers Association, 1959.

The Burglar Who Taught Cops How to Be Robbers, LIFE (Feb. 1, 1960), 20-21. (Chicago Police Scandal.)

Bursk, Edward C.: *How to Increase Executive Effectiveness.* Cambridge, Harvard Univ. Press, 1953.

Butchers, R. J.: Joint Civil and Military Responsibility in the Field of Nuclear Devices: Workshop, TPY (1962).

————: Military-Civil Police, TPC, Vol.29, No.11 (Nov., 1962), 22.

Cahill, Thomas J.: Challenges in Contemporary Law Enforcement, POLICE, Vol.9, No.1 (Sept.-Oct., 1964), 20-23.

Caldwell, Arthur B.: Efficient Police Administration of Law Enforcement as a Foundation of American Life Under the Rule of Law, POLICE, Vol.7, No.3 (Jan.-Feb., 1963), 79-82.

Caldwell, Bernard R.: Administration and Supervision of a State Police Organization, TPY (1956).

California State Dept. of Education: *Police Organization and Administration.* California Peace Officers Training Publication No.59, Sacramento, State Printing Office, 1951.

————: *Powers and Duties of the Sheriff and Other County Officers.* Sacramento, State Printing Office, 1949.

————: Reports of Lectures Presented in the Peace Officers' Administrative Institute for Law Enforcement Administrators, Sacramento, State Printing Office, 1956.

California State Dept. of Finance: *California State Government: a Guide to Its Organization and Functions.* Division of Organization and Cost Control. Sacramento, State Printing Office, 1958.

California State Printing Division: *California Blue Book—1961.* Sacramento, State Printing Office, 1961.

Callan, George D., and Stephenson, Richard: *Police Methods for Today and Tomorrow.* Newark, Duncan, 1939.

Carlson, Sune: *Executive Behavior: a Study of the Work Load and the Working Methods of Managing Directors.* Stockholm, Stromberg Aktielbolog, 1951.

Carrol, Joseph F.: Pulling Together, JCLC&PS, Vol.45 (1954-55), 597-604.

Carton, John E.: Police Problems at the National Level, TPY (1956).

Casper, Joseph J.: Obstacles Confronting a Vital Profession, TPY (1964).

Chapman, Brian: The Prefecture of Police, JCL&C, Vol.44, No.4 (Nov.-Dec., 1953), 505-21.

Chapman, Samuel G.: Pressing Matters, PO-LICE, Vol.7, No.3 (Jan.-Feb., 1963), 60-63; No.4 (Mar.-Apr., 1963), 70-72.

———, **& St. Johnston, T. Eric, C.B.E.:** *The Police Heritage in England and America.* East Lansing, Michigan State Univ. Press, 1962.

Charlesworth, James C.: *Governmental Administration.* New York, Harper, 1951.

Chastain, O. Jack: Self-pity, L&O, Vol.11, No.7 (July, 1963).

The Chicago Police: A Report of Progress. Chicago, Police Department, 1964.

Chicago Police Department: Policy Evaluation. Washington, Int'l Assn. of Chiefs of Police, The Institute for Police Management, 1964.

Cleeton, Glen U., and Mason, Charles W.: *Executive Ability, Its Discovery and Development.* Yellow Springs, Antioch, 1946.

Clift, Raymond E.: Change Your Pace in Police Work, L&O, Vol.7 (Jan., 1959).

Clift, Raymond E.: Communication—The Key to Good Supervision, POLICE, Vol.11, No.1 (Sept.-Oct., 1957), 7-9.

———: *A Guide to Modern Police Thinking.* Cincinnati, Anderson, 1956.

Columbia Round Table: *What Makes an Executive.* New York, Columbia Press, 1955.

Cooper, H. S.: The Role of Police Integrity, TPY (1962).

Cooperation Adds to Success of Monumental Event, THE CHIEFTAN, Vol.4 (Fall-Winter, 1957), 11, 36.

Cooperation: the Backbone of Effective Law Enforcement. Washington, Federal Bureau of Investigation.

Copeland, Melvin Thomas: *The Executive at Work.* Cambridge, Harvard Univ. Press, 1951.

Corson, John J.: *Executives for the Federal Service; a Program for Action in Time of Crisis.* New York, Columbia University Press, 1952.

Covell, Howard V.: Administrative Techniques: Utilization of Police Personnel, TPY (1959).

Craig, Marshall: Freeport, As I See It, THE CHIEFTAN, Vol.4 (Fall-Winter, 1957), 21, 22, 48.

Crawford, William: Police Salaries—A Critical View, L&O, Vol.11, No.9 (Sept., 1963).

Crouch, Winston W.: *California Government and Politics.* New York, Prentice-Hall, 1960.

Cushman, Charles H.: Relations Between the Commission and the Executive Officer, PPR, Vol.8 (Apr., 1947), 67-72.

Cushman, Frank, and Cushman, Robert W.: *Improving Supervision.* New York, Wiley, 1947.

Cutting Court Time of Personnel, TPC, Vol.30 (Feb., 1963), 8.

Dalton, John M.: Police—Citizen Responsibility in Freeport, THE CHIEFTAN, Vol.4 (Fall-Winter, 1957), 29-30, 48.

Davis, Tom W.: Administrative Techniques: Moderator's Comments on Techniques, TPY (1959).

Day, Frank D.: Criminal Law Enforcement and a Free Society, JCLC&PS (Sept., 1963).

Dayries, Provosty, L.: Administrative Techniques: Data Processing by Machine Records Units, TPY (1959).

———: What We Must Do to Attain a Truly Professional Status, TPC, Vol.25 (Apr., 1958), 20.

DeArmond, Fred: *Executive Thinking and Action.* Chicago, Wolfe, 1952.

Detroit Bureau of Governmental Research: *Police Precincts: How Many Precincts Are Necessary for Efficient and Economical Operations of the Police Department.* Report No.159. Detroit, 1945.

Dimock, Marshall E.: *The Executive in Action.* New York, Harper & Bros., 1945.

Donald, Howard C.: Use of the "H Units" by San Jose Police, POLICE, Vol.8, No.2 (Nov.-Dec., 1963), 35-36.

Dooher, M. Joseph, and Marquis, Vivienne (eds.): *The Supervisor's Management Guide.* New York, American Management Assoc., 1949.

Driver, Marvin D.: Restrictions on Law Enforcement, TPY (1961).

Drucker, Peter F.: *The Practice of Management.* New York, Harper & Row, 1954.

Durham, G. H.: What Can Be Done to Overcome Present Inadequacies in the American Public Service? THE ANNALS (Aug., 1963), 41-50.

Earl, Howard H.: *Contract Law Enforcement by the Los Angeles County Sheriff's Department.* Master's Thesis, Univ. of Southern Calif., 1960.

Eastman, George D.: So You Think You Are a Professional, L&O, Vol.9 (Aug., 1961).

Edwards, George: Detroit: A Lesson in Law Enforcement, THE ANNALS, Vol.347 (May, 1963), 67.

Egen, Frederick: *Plainclothesman.* New York, Greenberg, 1952.

Elam, Jerry: Close Ranks . . . March! L&O, Vol.10, No.2 (Feb., 1962), 6.

Emerson, R. A.: Police Work in Transportation, TPY (1965).

Fagerstrom, Dorothy: Accent on Training Traffic Administrators, L&O, Vol.10, No.6 (June, 1962), 12.

————: The Evolution of a Police Department, L&O, Vol.7 (Mar., 1959).

Fair, Ernest W.: Getting Willing Cooperation, L&O, Vol.8, No.10 (1960), 94.

Falzone, P. R.: *A Comparative Analysis of Executive's Role in Business and Law Enforcement.* Washington, IACP, 1965.

Farbell, Arthur M.: Political Intrusions in Police Service, TPY (1958).

Feaker, Fred: A Treatise on Internal Relations, L&O, Vol.12 (May, 1964), 64.

Ferguson, John H., and McHenry, Dean E.: *Elements of American Government,* 3rd Ed. New York, McGraw-Hill, 1958.

Ficklin, John R.: *Police Manpower Formula?* Formula for Determining a number of police officers for a City, Oct. 20, 1959.

Filley, Alan C.: Spotlighting on Moonlighting, PERSONNEL (Nov.-Dec., 1960), 45-49.

Findley, Paul: A Police Heroes Benefit Fund, TPC, Vol.31 (Nov., 1964), 58.

Fisher, Margaret: *Leadership and Intelligence.* New York, Columbia Univ., 1954.

Flanagan, William J.: What's Happening to Police Chiefs? L&O, Vol.12 (Oct., 1964).

Flynn, Edward J.: *You're the Boss.* New York, Viking, 1947.

Forbes, Russell: *Purchasing for Small Cities.* Chicago, Public Administration Service, 1951.

Franey, William H.: The Interstate System and the Police, TPY (1964).

Freeman, G. L., and Taylor E. K.: *How to Pick Leaders: Scientific Approach to Executive Selection.* New York, Funk and Wagnalls, 1950.

Fricke, Charles W.: *California Peace Officers' Manual.* Los Angeles, Smith, 1953.

Friedrich, Carl J.: *Man and His Government: an Empirical Theory of Politics.* New York, McGraw-Hill, 1963.

Frost, Thomas M.: *A Forward Look in Police Administration.* Springfield, Thomas, 1959.

Gabard, E. Caroline: *The Development of Law Enforcement in Early California.* Unpublished Master's Thesis, Univ. of Southern Calif., Los Angeles, 1960.

Gallati, R. R. J.: Operational Planning, TPC, Vol.30 (June, 1963), 51.

Garmire, Bernard L.: First-line Supervisor's Manual, JCLC&PS, Vol.53, No.1 (Mar.-May, 1962), 127.

Garrett, Bill, and Scott, Clifford L.: *Leadership for the Police Supervisor.* Springfield, Thomas, 1960.

Geis, Gilbert: *Municipal Law Enforcement in Oklahoma.* Oklahoma City, Oklahoma Crime Study Commission, 1955.

Gerletti, John D., and Black, Frank B.: *Successful Supervision.* Dubuque, Brown, 1956.

Germann, Albert C.: *The Executive Development of Police Administration by Agency and College.* Unpublished Master's Thesis, Univ. of So. Calif., Los Angeles, 1955.

————: Hurdles to Professional Police Competence, POLICE, Vol.8, No.1 (Sept.-Oct., 1963), 33-36; No.2 (Nov.-Dec., 1963), 55-57.

————, **Day, Frank D., and Gallati, Robert R. J.:** *Introduction to Law Enforcement.* Springfield, Thomas, 1963.

————: *Police Executive Development.* Springfield, Thomas, 1962.

————: *Police Personnel Management.* Springfield, Thomas, 1958.

————: Today and Tomorrow, L&O, Vol.11, No.6 (June, 1963).

Gladieux, Merla: The Command Officer, L&O, Vol.9 (Aug., 1961).

Gleason, John M.: Report on the Committee of Professional Standards, TPY (1945).

Gocke, B. W.: Morale in a Police Department, JCL&C, Vol.36, No.3 (1945-46), 215-19.

Goldstein, Joseph: Police Discretion Not to Invoke the Criminal Process: Low-visibility Decisions in the Administration of Criminal Justice, YLJ, Vol.69 (Mar., 1960), 543-94.

Goode, Cecil E.: Significant Research on Leadership, PERSONNEL (Mar., 1951), 342-49.

Gouldner, Alvin W.: *Studies in Leadership Leadership and Democratic Action.* New York, Harper, 1950.

Gourley, G. Douglas: Encouraging Compliance with Policies, POLICE, Vol.5, No.1 (Sept.

Oct., 1960), 61-64; No.2 (Nov.-Dec., 1960), 53-56.

————: Police Discipline, JCL&C, Vol.41 (May-June, 1950), 85-100.

————: Recognition and Status for Rank and File Policemen, JCL&C, Vol.40 (May-June, 1949), 75-84.

————, & Bristow, Allan P.: *Police Administration*. Springfield, Thomas, 1961.

Great Britain Royal Commission on the Police: *Interim Report*. (Command 1222, 1960), London, Her Majesty's Stationery Office, 1960.

Greening, J. A.: Report of the Committee on Professionalization, TPY (1945).

Griffin, John I.: Effective Statistical Presentation for Police Administration, JCLC&PS, Vol.48, No.4 (Nov.-Dec., 1957), 462.

————: *Statistics Essential for Police Efficiency*. Springfield, Thomas, 1958.

————: Statistics for Police Efficiency, POLICE, Vol.3, No.5 (May-June, 1959), 60-63; Vol.4, No.1 (Sept.-Oct., 1959), 62-79.

Groth, W. L.: Administrative Techniques Adopting Police Techniques to Changing Conditions, TPY (1959).

Hankey, Richard O.: Preparing for Supervision, POLICE, Vol.6, No.5 (May-June, 1962), 22-25.

Hawley, Cameron: *Executive Suite*. Boston, Houghton Mifflin, 1952.

Heady, Ferrel, and Klein, Bernard: The Quest for Quality in the Public Service, THE ANNALS (Aug., 1963), 179-96.

Hemphill, John K., *et al.:* *Leadership Acts*. Columbus, Ohio State Univ. Research Foundation, 1954.

Hewitt, William H.: *British Police Administration*. Springfield, Thomas, 1965.

Holden, Paul E., Fish, Lounsbary S., and Smith, Hubert L.: *Top Management Organization and Control*. New York, McGraw-Hill, 1951.

Hollady, Roy E.: The Police Administrator a Politician, JCLC&PS, Vol.53, No.4 (Dec., 1962), 526.

Holmgren, R. Bruce: *Primary Police Functions*. New York, Copp, 1960.

Hoover, J. Edgar: Youth and Police Careers, TPC (May, 1961), 28.

Hopkins, E. J.: *Our Lawless Police*. New York, Doubleday, 1951.

Hoyt, Dave: Peace Officers' Research Assoc. of the State of California: Its History and Accomplishments, 1953-62. An Address, Berkeley, Calif. Berkeley P.D., 1962.

Huberman, John: Discipline Without Punishment, HBR (July-Aug., 1964), 62-68.

Huntington, M. F.: Learning to Speechify, TPC, Vol.31 (Nov., 1964), 8.

Ingersoll, John E.: The Police Scandal Syndrome, TPC, Vol.30, No.5 (Aug., 1963), 10-49.

Institute for Training in Municipal Administration: *Municipal Police Administration*. Ann Arbor, Lithoprinted by Cushing-Mallory, Chicago, Int'l City Managers Assoc., 1961.

International Assoc. of Chiefs of Police: *Journal of American Insurance* (May-June, 1965), 12-15.

————, & U.S. Conference of Mayors: *Police— Community Relations, Police and Practices: a National Survey*. Washington, IACP, 1964.

International City Manager's Association: *Municipal Finance Administration*. Chicago, The Assoc., 1955.

————: *Municipal Police Administration*. Chicago, The Assoc., 1961.

————: *Municipal Public Works Administration*. Chicago, The Assoc., 1957.

————: *Municipal Year Book*. Published Annually. Chicago, The Assoc., 1313 E. 60th St., Chicago, Ill.

————: *Supervisory Methods in Municipal Administration*. Chicago, The Assoc., 1958.

————: *The Technique of Municipal Administration*. Chicago, The Assoc., 1958.

James, Charles S.: *A Frontier of Municipal Safety*. Chicago, Public Administration Service, 1955.

Janowitz, Morris, and Wright, Deil: The Prestige of Public Employment: 1929 and 1954, PAR (Winter, 1956), 15-22.

Jenkins, H. T.: Atlanta Accepts Challenge, TPC, Vol.29, No.3 (Mar., 1962), 8.

Jessup, Jacob A.: A Study of the Use of Police Reserves or Auxiliaries, POLICE, Vol.4, No.3 (Jan.-Feb., 1960), 26-29.

————: The Sunnyvale Public Safety Department: A Study of Integration, POLICE, Vol.1, No.2 (Nov.-Dec., 1956), 36-40.

Kahn, Robert L., and Katz, Daniel: *Leadership Practices in Relation to Productivity and Morale*. Ann Arbor, Univ. of Mich., Institute for Social Research, 1952.

Kalaidjian, Wm. G., Rev.: What Makes the Occupation of a Policeman a Profession, L&O, Vol.13, No.5 (May, 1965), 57.

Kenney, John P.: *Police Management Planning*. Springfield, Thomas, 1959.

————, & Williams, John B.: *Police Operations: Policies and Procedures*. Springfield, Thomas, 1960.

————: *Your Police Department*. Los Angeles, 1957 (Mimeographed.)

Kienzle, George J., and Dare, Edward H.:

Climbing the Executive Ladder. New York, McGraw-Hill, 1950.

King, Glen D.: *First-Line Supervisor's Manual.* Springfield, Thomas, 1961.

Kleinschmidt, H. E.: *How to Turn Ideas into Pictures.* New York, National Publicity Council, 1950.

Kooken, D. L.: Ethics in Police Service, JCL&C, Vol.38, No.1 (May-June, 1947); No.2 (July-Aug., 1947).

———: *Ethics in Police Service.* Springfield, Thomas, 1957.

Kreml, Franklin M.: The Role of the Transportation Center in Our Transportation System, TPY (1956).

Kynell, Kermit S.: The Role of the Police in a Democratic State, POLICE, Vol.3, No.3 (Jan.-Feb., 1959), 23-26.

LaCouture, Ron A.: One Answer to Professionalization, POLICE, Vol.7, No.3 (Jan.-Feb., 1963), 45.

Laird, D. A.: *Technique of Getting Things Done.* New York, McGraw-Hill, 1947.

Laizure, C. J.: Using Student Cadets in a Small Department, L&O, Vol.9 (Dec., 1961).

Langer, Susanne K.: *An Introduction to Symbolic Logic.* New York, Dover, 1953.

Lasser, Jacob Kay: *The Business Executive's Guide.* New York, McGraw-Hill, 1945.

Lawrence, Harry J.: Utilizing Available Resources, TPY (1961).

Lawrence, Leonard G.: Enforcement: Workshop, TPY (1963).

Learned, Edmund P., Ulrich, David N., and Booz, Donald R.: *Executive Action.* Boston, Division of Research, Harvard Univ., 1951.

Leighton, Alexander: *The Governing of Men.* Princeton, Princeton Univ. Press, 1945.

Leonard, V. A.: Police Administration in the Pacific Area, JCL&C, Vol.35, No.5 (Jan.-Feb., 1945), 328.

———: *The Police of the 20th Century.* New York, Foundation, 1964.

———: *Police Organization and Management.* New York, Foundation, 1964.

Lepawsky, Albert (ed.): *Administration: the Art and Science of Organization and Management.* New York, Knopf, 1949.

Lester, Ervis W.: Some Aspects of American Police Problems, JCL&C, Vol.40, No.6 (Mar.-Apr., 1950), 796.

Leys, Wayne A. R.: *Ethics for Policy Decisions: the Art of Asking Deliberative Questions.* New York, Prentice-Hall, 1952.

Lindgren, Henry C.: *Effective Leadership in Human Relations.* New York, Hermitage, 1954.

Liu, Daniel S. C.: A Philosophical View of Police Supervision, TPY (1962).

———: The President's Message, TPY (1965).

Livingston, Robert T.: *The Engineering of Organization and Management.* New York, McGraw-Hill, 1949.

Lohman, Joseph D.: Freeport, Missouri, Is Freeport, U.S.A., THE CHIEFTAN, Vol.4 (Fall-Winter, 1957), 33-36.

———: Upgrading Law Enforcement, POLICE, Vol.9, No.5 (May-June, 1965), 19.

Lombard, William: Increased Efficiency at Lower Cost, L&O, Vol.12 (Aug., 1964).

Luce, R. Duncan, and Raifa, Howard: *Games and Decisions.* New York, Wiley, 1958.

Ludwig, Donald J., and Brennan, Wm. T.: Appraising the Police Emergency Rescue Program, POLICE, Vol.8, No.4 (Mar.-Apr., 1964), 28-32.

Lunney, Thomas F.: Organization, Mission and Function of the Office of United States Marshal, POLICE, Vol.9, No.4 (Mar.-Apr., 1965), 88-90.

McCabe, Francis J.: Profile of the State and Provincial Section, TPY (1956).

McClellan, Geo. B.: Whose Side Are You On? TPC, Vol.32, No.6 (June, 1965), 30.

McGreevy, Thomas J.: Police Intelligence Operations, POLICE, Vol.8, No.4 (Mar.-Apr., 1964), 46-53.

McKinnon, D. A.: Internal Relations in Police Organizations, TPY (1957).

MacNamara, Donal E. J.: American Police Administration at Mid-Century, PAR, Vol.10, No.3 (Summer, 1950), 181-89.

———: *A Study and Survey of Municipal Police Departments of the State of New Jersey.* Trenton, New Jersey Law Enforcement Council, 1958.

Mace, Myles L.: *The Growth and Development of Executives.* Cambridge, Harvard Univ. Press, 1950.

Mackey, James P.: The Concept of Metropolitan Policing, TPY (1965).

Macy, J. W., Jr.: How Should We Implement a Program to Obtain an Adequate Public Service? THE ANNALS (Aug., 1963), 61-74.

———: A Perspective—Quest for Quality in the Public Service, THE ANNALS (Aug., 1963), 126-133.

Maddox, R. W., and Fuquay, R. F.: *State and Local Government.* Princeton, Nostrand, 1962.

Magruder, Clarice: The Police Executive Secretary, POLICE, Vol.7, No.3 (Jan.-Feb., 1963), 20-21.

Maier, Norman R. F., Solem, Allen R., and Maier, Ayesha A.: *Supervisory and Executive Development.* New York, Wiley, 1957.

Maloy, Patrick: What Really Happened? POLICE, Vol.8, No.6 (July-Aug., 1964), 39-40.

Maxim, George: Do You Want a Crime Laboratory, L&O, Vol.8, No.3 (1960).

Metcalf, Henry C., and Urwick, L.: *Dynamic Administration: The Collected Papers of Mary Parker Follet.* New York, Harper, 1947.

Metropolitan Life Insurance Company: *Stimulating and Maintaining Employee Morale.* New York, Metropolitan Life Ins. Co., 1945.

Michigan, Univ. of, Survey Research Center: *Productivity, Supervision and Employee Morale.* Ann Arbor, Human Relations Series No.1, Report 1.

Miles, Lester F.: *Brass Hat or Executive.* New York, Funk, 1949.

Miller, David W., and Starr, Martin K.: *Executive Decisions and Operations.* Englewood Cliffs, Prentice-Hall, 1960.

Milward, George E.: *Large-scale Organization.* London, The Institute of Public Administration, 1950.

Mirich, John J.: Certification of Law Enforcement, JCLC&PS, Vol.49, No.1 (1958-59), 92.

————, & **Voris, Eugene F.:** Recognition of Local Law Enforcement as a Profession: The Time Has Surely Come! POLICE, Vol.9, No.4 (Mar.-Apr., 1965), 42-44.

Misner, Gordon E.: Recent Developments in the Metropolitan Law Enforcement, JCLC&PS, Vol.50, No.5 (Jan.-Feb., 1960), 497; Vol.51, No.2 (Mar.-Apr., 1960-61), 265.

Model Department General Order, TPC, Vol.31 (July, 1964), 15.

Moffett, Jack H.: The Art of Law Enforcement, POLICE, Vol.4, No.5 (May-June, 1960), 9-12.

Mooney, James D.: *Principles of Organization.* New York, Harper, 1958.

Morris, William H.: State Police Supervision, TPY (1962).

Municipal Finance. Published quarterly, by the Municipal Finance Officers' Assoc. Also publishes a biweekly NEWS LETTER, 1313-E. 60th Street, Chicago, Ill.

Murdy, Ralph G.: Is There a Board in Your Future? TPC, Vol.32, No.6 (June, 1965), 10.

Murphy, Michael J.: Instant Manpower, TPY (1963).

————: Police and the Modern Community, TPC, Vol.29, No.3 (Mar., 1962), 9.

Newark, Police Dept.: *Written Orders and Memoranda.* Newark, Newark, N.J., Police Dept., 1961.

New Goals in Police Management, THE ANNALS (Jan., 1954).

Newman, William: *Administrative Action.* Englewood Cliffs, Prentice-Hall, 1959.

New York State Police Department Changes, TPC, Vol.30 (May, 1963), 32.

Nichols, Louis B.: Today's Challenges to Law Enforcement, TPY (1957).

Nott, William W.: Efficient Economy, TPC (Oct., 1961), 32.

Nugent, Francis, Father: Police Brutality, TPC, Vol.31 (Mar., 1964), 37.

Office of Strategic Services: *Assessment of Men.* New York, Rinehart, 1948.

On This We Stand. Chicago, Chicago Police Dept., 1964.

Pearson, C. C.: Police Statistics Are Coming of Age, TPC, Vol.30 (Apr., 1963), 36.

Peper, John P., and Vollmer, August: *Police Supervisory Control.* Sacramento, California Peace Officers Training Publication, No.71, Calif. State Dept. of Education, 1957.

Peterson, Virgil W.: An Examination of Chicago's Law Enforcement Agencies, CJ (Jan., 1950), 3-6.

————: Issues and Problems in Metropolitan Area Police Services, JCLC&PS, Vol.48, No.2 (July-Aug., 1957), 127.

Pettee, George S.: *The Future of American Secret Intelligence.* Washington, Infantry Journal Press, 1946.

Pfiffner, John M.: *Organization: The Study of Hierarchy.* Los Angeles, Univ. of Southern California, 1957.

————, & **Lane, S. Owen:** *A Manual for Administrative Analysis.* Dubuque, Brown, 1951.

Phelan, Joseph G.: Police Administration—Which Approach, Democratic, Authoritarian, or? POLICE, Vol.9 No.4 (Mar.-Apr., 1965), 32-35.

Phillips, Max D.: A Study of the Office of Law Enforcement Coordination, U.S. Treasury Department, JCLC&PS, Vol.54, No.3 (1963), 369.

Piggins, Edward S.: The Assignment and Distribution of Police Personnel for Most Effective Coverage, TPY (1956).

Pletcher, M. Waldorf: Cooperative Enforcement: The Lansing Plan, JCL&C, Vol.36, No.1 (1945-46), 61.

Police Legal Advisor Fellowship, TPC, Vol.31 (Sept. 1964), 62.

Police Review Boards, TPC, Vol.31 (Feb., 1964), 7-34.

The Policeman (Editorial), SATURDAY EVENING POST, No.5 (Mar. 13, 1965), 100.

Pomrenke, N. E.: *The Application of Accepted Organizational Principles as a Basis for Measuring the Internal Effectiveness of Selected Municipal Police Departments.* Washington, IACP, 1964.

Price, Carroll S.: Ethics and Professionalization in American Law Enforcement, POLICE, Vol.7, No.5 (May-June, 1963), 6-12.

Price, Paul J.: Utilizing Manpower, TPC (June, 1961), 16.

Rafferty, Max: California State Department of Education: *Police Supervisory Control*. Sacramento, Calif. State Peace Officers' Training Series, 1963.

Remington, Frank J.: The Role of Police in a Democratic Society, TPY (1965).

Report of Committee on Lawless Enforcement of Law, SE&SCD, Vol.1, No.6 (1964).

Reynolds, Quentin: *Headquarters*. New York, Harper, 1955.

Riegel, John W.: *Executive Development*. Ann Arbor, Michigan Univ. Press, 1952.

Roberts, Ernest F.: Paradoxes in Law Enforcement, JCLC&PS, Vol.52, No.2 (July-Aug., 1961), 224.

Roddenberry, E. W.: Achieving Professionalism, JCL&C, Vol.44, No.1 (May-June, 1953), 109-115.

Rules and Procedures. New York, N.Y. City Police Dept., 1965.

Rushing, Joe B.: Ethics and Law Enforcement: Let's Go Professional, L&O, Vol.13, No.4 (Apr., 1965), 52-56.

St. Louis Reduces Court Times for Officers, TPC, Vol.30 (Feb., 1964), 8.

Sanford, Fillmore H.: *Authoritarianism and Leadership: a Study of the Follower's Orientation to Authority*. Philadelphia, Institute for Research in Human Relations, 1950.

————: *The Technique of Executive Control*, 6th Ed. New York, McGraw-Hill, 1950.

Schrotel, Stanley R.: Supervising the Use of Police Authority, POLICE, Vol.11, No.2 (Nov.-Dec., 1957), 15-17.

Schulz, Ernst B.: *American City Government*. New York, Stackpole & Heck, 1949.

Schwerin, Kurt: Journal of Criminal Law, Criminology, and Police Science—1910-1960. A Brief Historical Note, JCLC&PS, Vol.51, No.1 (Mar.-Apr., 1960-61), 4.

Scott, Clifford L.: *Leadership for the Police Supervisor*. Springfield, Thomas, 1960.

————: Police Supervision and School Supervision a Comparison, POLICE, Vol.4, No.6 (July-Aug., 1960), 55-57; Vol.5, No.1 (Sept.-Oct., 1960), 41-43; No.2 (Nov.-Dec., 1960), 38-41.

Seckler, Cathryn Hudson: *Organization and Management: Theory and Practice*. Washington, The American Univ. Press, 1955.

Selznick, Philip: *Leadership in Administration*. New York, Harper & Row, 1957.

Shanks, Carrol M.: Organization, TPY (1959).

Sheehan, Thomas M.: Police Administration: A Note on Academic Problems, POLICE, Vol.9, No.5 (May-June, 1965), 13.

Sheehan, Robert: Lest We Forget, POLICE (Sept.-Oct., 1959), and (Nov.-Dec., 1959).

Sherrow, Dale Ellsworth: Dismissal of Police Officers for Exercising Privilege against Self Incrimination, JCL&C, Vol.38, No.6 (Mar.-Apr., 1947-48), 613-19.

Sherwood, Frank P., and Rest, Wallace H.: *Supervisory Methods in Municipal Administration*. Chicago, Int'l City Managers Assoc., 1958.

Sheeptrine, Carl L.: The Police and the Thief, TPY (1961).

Simon, Herbert A.: *Administrative Behavior*, 2nd Ed. New York, Macmillan, 1957.

Singleton, Robert: The Law's Strong Arm, SE&SCD, Vol.2, No.5 (1964).

Skehan, James J.: *Modern Police Work*. New York, Basuino, 1951.

Skousen, Cleon W.: Administrative Problems in a Big City Department, L&O, Vol.9 (Dec., 1961).

————: Building an Efficient Detective Division, L&O, Vol.11, No.6 (June, 1963), 12.

————: The Chief Takes a Look at the Vice Squad, L&O, Vol.11, No.8 (Aug., 1963).

————: Field Commanders—Latest Administrative Aid, L&O, Vol.8, No.12 (1960).

————: How to Handle a Scandal, L&O, Vol.10, No.1 (Jan., 1962), 22.

————: Professional Policies for a Vice Squad, L&O, Vol.11, No.9 (Sept., 1963).

————: Rehabilitating a Scandal-ridden Department, L&O, Vol.12 (Nov., 1964).

————: Running a Chief's Office, Part 2, L&O, Vol.11, No.1 (Jan., 1963).

————: Setting up a Chief's Office, L&O, Vol.10, No.11 (Nov., 1962), 26.

————: Suggestions for a Jail Manual, L&O, Vol.12 (July, 1964).

————: Trick in Making a Detective Bureau Click, L&O, Vol.11, No.7 (July, 1963).

————: What About Off Duty Jobs for Patrolmen, L&O, Vol.9 (Feb., 1961).

————: When the Chief Faces an Emergency, L&O, Vol.12 (Sept., 1964).

Sloane, Charles F.: Police Professionalization, JCLC&PS, Vol.45 (May-June, 1954), 77-79.

Smith, Bruce (ed.): New Goals in Police Management, THE ANNALS, Vol.219 (Jan., 1954).

————: *Police Systems in the United States*. New York, Harper & Bros., 1962.

Smith, E. E.: Ohio's Inventory Control Method, TPC (July, 1961), 32.

Smith, R. Dean: *Computer Applications in Police Manpower Distribution*. Washington, IACP, 1961. (Field Service Division.)

————: Inspection & Control, TPC, Vol.31 (July, 1964), 10.

————: Organization, TPC, Vol.29, No.6 (June, 1962), 10-44.

Smith, Ralph Lee: Cops as Robbers, POLICE, Vol.9 (May-June, 1965), 65.

Snyder, W. J.: The Association for Professional Law Enforcement, JCLC&PS, Vol.47, No.5 (Jan.-Feb., 1957), 601.

Sommers, William A.: The Birth of a Police Department, POLICE, Vol.5, No.2 (Nov.-Dec., 1960), 64-67.

South, W. E.: Importance of Channelling Inquiries, TPC, Vol.31 (Nov., 1964), 39.

Southwestern Law Enforcement Institute, The: *Police Management*. Springfield, Thomas, 1963.

Sowle, Claud R.: *Police Power and Individual Freedom*. Chicago, Aldine, 1962.

Spriegel, William R., Schulz, Edward, and Priegel, William B.: *Elements of Supervision*. New York, Wiley, 1957.

Stahl, O. Glenn: Do Present Public Servants Approach the Ideal? THE ANNALS (Aug., 1963), 25-40.

Stern, Mort: What Makes a Policeman Go Wrong, JCLC&PS, Vol.53, No.1 (Mar.-May, 1962), 97.

Sullivan, Robert E.: Qualities of Leadership, POLICE, Vol.8, No.3 (Jan.-Feb., 1963), 30-33.

Support Services for Police Administrators. Washington, IACP.

Sweeney, Frank A.: Enforcement: Workshop, TPY (1962).

————: International Objectives of IACP, TPY (1963).

Tamm, Quinn: Brutality or Smokescreen, TPC, Vol.30 (Dec., 1963), 7.

————: Cooperation and Integrity, TPC, Vol.30 (Jan., 1963), 7.

————: Price of Failure, TPC, Vol.19, No.4 (Apr., 1962), 4.

————: Rebuilding a Scandal-torn Police Force, TPC, Vol.29, No.2 (Feb., 1962).

————: A Richness and a Need, TPC, Vol.32, No.1 (Jan., 1965), 6.

————: A Time for Rededication, TPC, Vol.30 (May, 1963), 7.

Tannenbaum, Robert, Wechsler, Irving R., and Massarik, Fred: *Leadership and Organization: a Behavioral Science Approach*. New York, McGraw-Hill, 1961.

Tead, Ordway: *The Art of Administration*. New York, McGraw-Hill, 1951.

Teeters, Negley K.: Why Do We Not Adopt the Borstal System, JCL&C, Vol.35, No.6 (Mar.-Apr., 1945), 411.

They Spoke to the Mayors, TPC, Vol.30 (Aug., 1963), 18.

Thompson, Jim: Police Control Over Citizens Use of the Public Streets, JCLC&PS, Vol.49, No.6 (1958-59), 562.

Thompson, Victor A.: *Modern Organization*. New York, Knopf, 1961.

Toland, John: *The Dillinger Days*. New York, Random House, 1963.

Topping, C. W.: Can a National Police Force Serve a Municipality Effectively? POLICE, Vol.7, No.2 (Nov.-Dec., 1962), 6-10.

Toussaint, Maynard N.: Line—Staff Conflict; Its Causes and Cure, PERSONNEL (May-June, 1962), 18-20.

Tullock, Donald P.: Notes on the Matter of Police Salaries, L&O, Vol.8, No.5 (1960).

Urwick, L.: *Freedom and Coordination: Lectures in Business Organization by Mary Parker Follet*. London, Management, Publications, Ltd., 1949.

————: *Notes on the Theory of Organization*. New York, American Management Assoc., 1952.

Uris, Auren: *How to Be a Successful Leader*. New York, McGraw-Hill, 1953.

U.S. Civil Service Commission: *Basic Books on the Executive Function*. Washington, The Commission, 1960. (A selective annotated bibliography prepared by Franklin G. Connor.)

————: *Leadership and Supervision: A Survey of Research Findings*. Washington, Personnel Management Series No.9, The Assoc., 1955.

U.S. Federal Security Agency: *Do You Know What They Know?* Washington, Supervision and Management Series No. 6, U.S. Govt. Printing Office, 1948.

————: *One Way to Increase the Will-to-work*. Washington, Supervision and Management Series No.7, U.S. Govt. Printing Office, 1948.

————: *Their Fate Is in Your Hands*. Supervision and Management Series No.9. Washington, U.S. Govt. Printing Office, 1948.

————: *What's Going On up There*, Supervision and Management Series No.8, Washington, U.S. Govt. Printing Office, 1948.

Vernon, Wyman W.: Comments on the Reorganization of the Oakland Police Dept., POLICE, Vol.1, No.4 (Mar.-Apr., 1957), 37-43.

————: Oakland Appraises Its Manpower Distribution, POLICE (Mar.-Apr., 1957).

Viteles, Morris S.: *Motivation and Morale in Industry*. New York, Norton, 1953.

Vollmer, August: Bibliography on Police Organization and Administration, Criminal Identification and Investigation, SE&SCD, Vol.2, No.1 (1964).

———: *Police Organization and Administration.* Sacramento, Calif. Peace Officers' Training Pub. No.59, Calif. State Dept. of Education, 1951.

Waggoner, Hugh H.: Strengthening State and Provincial Organizations, TPY (1962).

Waldo, Dwight: *The Administrative State.* New York, Ronald, 1948.

———: *Perspectives on Administration.* University, Univ. of Alabama Press, 1956.

Walker, Harvey: *The Legislative Process.* New York, Ronald, 1948.

Wasserman, Paul, and Silander, Fred S.: *Decision-making: an Annotated Bibliography.* Ithaca, Cornell Univ. Press, 1958.

Watson, N. A.: Developing Guidelines for Police Practices, TPC, Vol.31 (Sept., 1964), 32.

———: Police & Group Behavior Leadership, TPC, Vol.31 (Aug., 1964), 12; (Nov., 1964), 12.

———: Probing Police Policy, POLICE, Vol.9, No.4 (Mar.-Apr., 1965), 78-82.

Wattenberg, William W.: Changing Attitudes Toward Authority, POLICE, Vol.7, No.3 (Jan.-Feb., 1963), 34-37.

Westley, William A.: Violence and the Police, AJS, Vol.56 (July, 1953), 34-41.

Weston, Paul B.: The Survey Analyst vs. the Police Chief, L&O, Vol.8, No.1 (1960).

What's Happening in Freeport? *The Chieftan,* Vol.4 (Fall-Winter, 1957), 25-27, 48.

Wheare, K. C.: *Federal Government.* New York, Oxford Univ. Press, 1964. (An excellent treatise on our U.S. government and how law enforcement and the courts function within this sphere.)

Whitehouse, Jack, E.: A Preliminary Inquiry into the Occupational Disadvantages of Law Enforcement Officers, POLICE, Vol.9, No.5 (May-June, 1965), 30.

Williams, Gerald O.: Political Police—Historical Origins and Development, POLICE, Vol.9, No.4 (Mar.-Apr., 1965), 22-28; Vol.9, No.5 (May-June, 1965), 52.

Williams, John B., and Kenney, John P.: *Police Operations.* Springfield, Thomas, 1960.

Wilson, O. W.: August Vollmer, JCL&C, Vol.44, No.1, (May-June, 1953), 91-103.

———: Can the State Help City Police Departments? JCLC&PS, Vol.45 (May-June, 1954).

———: How the Police Chief Sees It, HARPER'S, Vol.228, No.1367 (Apr., 1964), 140-44.

———, *et al.: Municipal Police Administration,* 5th Ed. Chicago, Int'l City Manager's Assoc., 1961.

——— (ed.): *Parker on Police.* Springfield, Thomas, 1957.

———: *Police Administration.* New York, McGraw-Hill, 1963.

———: *Police Planning.* Springfield, Thomas, 1952.

———: Police Brutality, TPC, Vol.30 (Nov., 1963), 40.

———: Progress in Police Administration, JCLC&PS, Vol.42 (1951-52), 141.

———: Reorganization in Chicago, TPY (1962).

Wilson, Woodrow: *Leaders of Men.* Princeton, Princeton Univ. Press, 1952.

Young, Bruce C.: *An Evaluation of the Royal Disciplinary Procedures of Three Metropolitan Police Departments: with a Recommended Procedure Guide.* Unpublished Master's Thesis, School of Police Admin. and Public Safety, Michigan State University, 1963.

Young, W. H.: *Ogg and Ray's Introduction to American Government: The National Government,* 11th ed. New York, Appleton, 1956.

Zemans, Eugene S.: *Held Without Bail: Physical Aspects of the Police Lock-ups of the City of Chicago, 1947-48.* Chicago, Howard Assoc., 1949.

Ziel, Walter B.: Police Problems, L&O, Vol.12 (Dec., 1964).

Zink, Howard A.: Report of Standards and Qualifications Committee, *Proceedings of the Twenty-ninth Annual Convention of the Peace Officer's Assoc. of the State of California.* Sacramento, State Printing Office, Oct., 1949.

Zumbrun, Alvin J. T.: Maryland: A Law Enforcement Dilemma, THE ANNALS, Vol.347 (May, 1963), 58.

POLICE BUILDINGS

Associations of Chiefs of Police: *Police Buildings.* A Report prepared by the Field Service Division. Washington, IACP, 1963.

Benethum, Harley M.: Shaker Heights, Ohio Police Department, L&O, Vol.7 (May, 1959).

Burke, D. P.: *The Functional Building.* Washington, IACP, 1961.

Crutcher, Tom: Police Court Building for Wyandotte, Michigan, L&O, Vol.9 (July, 1961).

Fanfare for a Public Safety Building, L&O, Vol.9 (July, 1961).

Lincke, Jack: Design a Police Station, But Don't Make It Look Like One, L&O, Vol.9 (July, 1961).

———: New Concept in Police Station Designing, L&O, Vol.7 (Feb., 1959).

Sommers, William A.: Franklin's Police Build Their Own Building, POLICE, Vol.7, No.3 (Jan.-Feb., 1963), 16-19.

Vogel, Joshua A.: *Police Stations: Planning and Specifications.* Seattle, Bureau of Governmental Research and Services, Univ. of Washington, 1954.

POLICE—FIRE INTEGRATION

A Decade of Public Safety. (Police—Fire Integration.) Sunnyvale (Calif.) Department of Public Safety.

Agres, Loren D.: Integration of Police and Fire Services, JCLC&PS, Vol.47, No.4 (Nov.-Dec., 1956), 490.

Allen, Edward J.: Panel Forum—Shall Policemen Be Firemen Also? TPY (1957).

———: Specialization Barriers in Police—Fire Integration, TPC (July, 1961), 5.

Bernitt, R. O.: *A Study of the Attitudes Held by Police Chiefs, Fire Chiefs, and City Managers Toward the Integration of Police and Fire Services.* Washington, IACP, 1962.

Byers, Kenneth, Montilla, Robert, and Williams, Elmer V.: *Elements of Position-classification in Local Government.* Chicago, Civil Service Assembly, 1955.

Combined Police and Fire Services for Medium-sized and Small Cities. Missouri Public Expenditure Survey, 1960.

Combining of Fire and Police Departments, *Special Bulletin,* No.300, New York, National Board of Fire Underwriters, 1953.

Holladay, R. E.: Police—Fire Integration Literature, TPC, Vol.29, No.9 (Sept., 1962), 38.

Holstrom, John D.: Fire—Police Integration—

Current Trends, POLICE, Vol.3, No.4 (Mar.-Apr., 1959), 43-46.

———: Trends in Police—Fire Integration, TPC (July, 1961), 6.

Integration of Fire and Police Services, JCLC&PS, Vol.46 (1955-56), 149.

International Association of Chiefs of Police: *Subject: Police—Fire Integration.* Reprinted from THE POLICE CHIEF (July, 1961), IACP, n.d.

James, Charles S.: Concepts of Fire—Police Integration, P.MGMT. (Sept., 1955), 194-98.

———: *Police and Fire Integration in the Small City.* Chicago, Public Admin. Service, 1955.

Kelsh, Hubert: Police—Fire Integration from Viewpoint of Experience, TPC (July, 1961), 9, 10.

Police—Fire Integration—A Survey. Cleveland, Cleveland Bureau of Governmental Research Inc., Nov., 1961.

Should Policemen & Firemen Get the Same Salaries? TPC, Vol.31 (Aug., 1964), 50.

Various Authors and Fire Departments: Fire Dept. Manuals—See for example, Greensboro, *N.C. Drill Manual,* 1950.

Waller, James I.: Police—Fire Integration from Viewpoint of Experience, TPC (July, 1961), 8.

POLICE MANAGEMENT AND SUPERVISION

American Management Association: *The American Management Association Handbook of Wage and Salary Administration.* New York, American Management Assoc., 1950.

———: *The Management Leader's Manual for Operating Executives, Supervisors, and Foremen.* New York, The Assoc., 1947.

———: *Personnel: Aptitude Testing, Training, and Employee Development.* New York, The Assoc., 1949.

———: Production: *How to Develop Competent Supervision.* New York, The Assoc., 1947.

———: *The Supervisor's Management Guide.* New York, The Assoc., 1949.

Anthony, Robert N.: *Management Controls in Industrial Research Organizations.* Boston, Harvard Univ. Division of Research, 1952.

Argyris, Chris: The Organization: What Makes It Healthy, HBR (Nov.-Dec., 1958).

———: *Personality and Organization.* New York, Harper, 1957.

———: T-groups for Organizational Effectiveness, HBR, 60-74.

———: *Understanding Organizational Behavior.* Homewood, Dorsey, 1960.

Avery, Robert S.: *Experiment in Management: Personnel Decentralization in the Tennessee Valley Authority.* Knoxville, Univ. of Tennessee, 1954.

Barnard, Chester I.: *Organization and Management: Selected Papers.* Cambridge, Harvard Univ. Press, 1948.

Beaumont, Richard A., and Tower, James W.: *Executive Retirement and Effective Management.* Ind. Rels. Monograph No.20, New York, Industrial Relations Counselors, Inc., 1961.

Benedict, H. G.: *Yardsticks for Management.* Los Angeles, Management Book Co., 1946.

Bethel, Lawrence L., et al.: *Essentials of Industrial Management.* New York, McGraw-Hill, 1955.

——, **Atwater, Franklin S., Smith, George H. E., and Stackman, Harvey A., Jr.:** *Industrial Organization and Management.* New York, McGraw-Hill, 1951.

Bittel, Lester R.: *What Every Supervisor Should Know.* New York, McGraw-Hill, 1950.

Bloch, Herbert A.: *Disorganization: Personal and Social.* New York, Knopf, 1952.

Boise, Robert J.: Management Notebook—Ford Motor Company, SW, Vol.1, No.3 (Nov.-Dec., 1964), 30-31.

Boyd, Bradford B.: The Man in Charge of Motivation, SM (Nov., 1963), 7-9.

Brandt, Allen D.: *Industrial Health Engineering.* New York, Wiley, 1947.

Brech, Edward F. L.: *Management: Its Nature and Significance.* London, Sir Isaac Pitman, 1953.

——: *The Principles and Practice of Management.* New York, Longmans, 1953.

Broaded, Charles H.: *Essentials of Management for Supervisors.* New York, Harper, 1949.

Brown, Wilfred: What Is Work? HBR (Sept.-Oct., 1962), 121-29.

Bursk, Edward C.: *The Management Team.* Cambridge, Harvard Univ. Press, 1955.

Buyniski, E. F.: Stress, Sickness and Supervision, PA (July-Aug., 1962), 38-42.

Buzby, Walter II: Management Notebook—Hotel Dennis, SW, Vol.2, No.2 (Mar.-Apr., 1965), 42-45.

Cameron, M. A.: *Principles of Management.* London, Harrap, 1948.

Cantor, Nathaniel: *The Learning Process for Managers.* New York, Harper, 1958.

Carpenter, William Seal: *The Unfinished Business of Civil Service Reform.* Princeton, Princeton Univ. Press, 1952.

Chapple, E. D., and Sayles L. R.: *The Measure of Management.* New York, Macmillan, 1961.

Close, Guy W., Jr.: *Work Improvement.* New York, Wiley, 1960.

Cruickshank, Henry M., and Davis, Keith: *Cases in Management.* Homewood, Irwin, 1954.

Dalton, Melville: *Men Who Manage.* New York, Wiley, 1950.

Davis, Ralph Currier: *The Fundamentals of Top Management.* New York, Harper & Bros., 1951.

DeSchweinitz, Dorothea: *Labor and Management in a Common Enterprise.* Cambridge, Harvard Univ. Press, 1949.

Dimock, Marshall E.: *Administrative Vitality.* New York, Harper, 1959.

——: *A Philosophy of Administration.* New York, Harper, 1958.

——: *The Executive in Action.* New York, Harper, 1945.

Dooher, Joseph M., and Marquis, Vivienne: *The Development of Executive Talent: a Handbook of Management Development Techniques and Case Studies.* New York, American Management Assoc., 1952.

Dreyfack, Raymond: You've Got the Ball—Now Run with It! SM (Feb., 1964), 22-25.

Drucker, Peter F.: *The Practice of Management.* New York, Harper, 1954.

Duvall, Sylvanus Milne: *The Art and Skill of Getting Along with People.* Englewood Cliffs, Prentice-Hall, 1961.

Elliott, Bill: Management Notebook—Bekins Van & Storage, SW, Vol.2, No.2 (Jan.-Feb., 1965), 27.

Ellis, James H.: Some Features of Moonlighting, TPC, Vol.32, No.1 (Jan., 1965), 32-34.

Etzinoni, Amitai: *Complex Organizations.* New York, Free Press, 1961.

Field, Oliver P.: *Civil Service Law.* Minneapolis, Univ. of Minnesota Press, 1949.

Fielden, John: What Do You Mean I Can't Write, HBR (May-June, 1964).

Filipetti, George: *Industrial Management in Transition.* Homewood, Irwin, 1953.

Gange, John: *The Secretarist Function: a Staff Aid for Executive Management.* Chicago, Public Administration Clearing House, 1953.

Gellerman, Saul W.: *Motivations and Productivity.* New York, American Management Association, 1963.

Gerfen, Richard C.: But That Isn't What I Meant! SM (Aug., 1963), 4-7.

German, A. C.: *Police Personnel Management.* Springfield, Thomas, 1958.

Gibbons, Charles C.: Putting New Ideas to Work, SM (June, 1963), 4-7.

Given, William B., Jr.: *Bottom-up Management:* Harper, 1949.

People Working Together. New York,
——: *Reaching Out in Management.* New York, Harper, 1953.

Godine, Morton R.: *The Labor Problem in Public Service.* Cambridge, Harvard Univ. Press, 1951.

Goldstein, Herman: Guidelines for Effective Use of Police Manpower, P.MGMT. (Oct., 1963), 218-222.

Gourley, Douglas G.: What Is Police Management, POLICE, Vol.3, No.5 (May-June, 1959), 34-38; No.6 (July-Aug., 1959), 60-63.

Gragg, Charles I.: Whose Fault Was It? HBR (Jan.-Feb., 1964), 107-110.

Grimshaw, Austin, and Hennessey, John W., Jr.: *Organizational Behavior: Cases and Readings.* New York, McGraw-Hill, 1960.

Haire, Mason: *Psychology in Management.* New York, McGraw-Hill, 1956.

Halsey, George D.: *Supervising People.* New York, Harper, 1953.

Hamblin, Robert L.: Punitive and Non-punitive Supervision, SP (Spring, 1964), 345-59.

Hankey, Richard L.: Personnel Management Practices at the Area Level in the California Highway Patrol, POLICE (July-Aug., 1962), 33-37.

Heron, Alexander, R.: *Sharing Information with Employees.* Palo Alto, Stanford Univ. Press, 1947.

Herrmann, Irvin A.: *Office Methods, Systems and Procedures.* New York, Ronald Press, 1950.

Hill, Lee T., and Hook, Charles R., Jr.: *Management at the Bargaining Table.* New York, McGraw-Hill, 1945.

Hill, Thomas M., and Gordon, Myron J.: *Accounting, a Management Approach.* Homewood, Irwin, 1959.

Holden, Paul E., Fish, Lounsbury S., and Smith, Hubert L.: *Top Management Organization and Control.* Palo Alto, Stanford Univ. Press, 1948.

———, **& Shallenberger, Frank K.:** *Selected Case Problems in Industrial Management.* New York, Prentice-Hall, 1953.

Hooper, Frederick C.: *Management Survey: the Significance of Management in the Modern Community.* London, Pitman, 1948.

Hoslett, Schuyler Dean: *Human Factors in Management: Integrated Readings.* Parkville, Park College Press, 1946.

———: *Human Factors in Management.* New York, Harper, 1951.

Huneryager, S. G.: Essentials of Effective Leadership, SUPERVISION (May, 1963), 4-6.

Jones, Dallas L.: The Supervisor and the Disciplinary Process in a Unionized Setting, PA (Jan.-Feb.), 42-48.

Jones, Manley Howe: *Executive Decision Making.* Homewood, Irwin, 1957.

Jucius, Michael J.: *Personnel Management.* Homewood, Irwin, 1955.

Juran, Joseph M.: *Management of Inspection and Quality Control.* New York, Harper & Bros., 1945.

Karman, Abraham K.: Selective Perception Among First Line Supervisors, PA (Sept.-Oct., 1963), 31-36.

Katz, Daniel, Maccoby, Nathan, and Morse, Nancy C.: *Productivity, Supervision and Morale in an Office Situation.* Ann Arbor, Institute for Social Research, Univ. of Mich., 1950.

Kay, Brian R., and Palmer, Stuart: *The Challenge of Supervision.* New York, McGraw-Hill, 1961.

Kenney, John P.: *Police Management Planning.* Springfield, Thomas, 1959.

Keuner, John J. W., and Haynes, B. R.: *Office Management: Principles and Practice.* Chicago, South-Western, 1953.

Kibbee, Joel M., et al.: *Management Games.* New York, Reinhold, 1961.

Kidney, E. B.: *Fringe Benefits for Salaried Employees in Government and Industry.* Chicago, Civil Service Assembly, 1954.

Kilpatrick, Franklin P., Cummings, Milton C., Jr., and Jennings, M. Kent: *The Image of the Federal Service.* Washington, Brookings Institution, 1964.

Kimball, D. S., and Kimball, D. S., Jr.: *Principles of Industrial Organization.* New York, McGraw-Hill, 1947.

Kindall, Alva F., and Gatza, James: A Positive Program for Performance Appraisal, HBR (Nov.-Dec., 1963), 153-156.

Knudson, Harry R., Jr.: *Human Elements of Administration.* New York, Holt, Rinehart & Winston, 1963.

Koontz, Harold, and O'Donnell, Cyrl: *Principles of Management.* New York, McGraw-Hill, 1955.

Koppers Company: *Organizational Manual.* Pittsburgh, Koppers Co., 1947.

Krah, Raymond: *Administrative Control of Sick Leave,* Report No.544. Chicago, Public Personnel Assoc., 1955.

Lasswell, Harold D., and Lerner, Daniel (eds.): *The Policy Sciences—Recent Developments in Scope and Methods.* Palo Alto, Stanford Univ., 1951.

Lateiner, Alfred R.: *The Techniques of Supervision.* New London, Conn., National Foreman's Institute, 1954.

Leffingwell, William H., and Robinson, Edward M.: *Textbook of Office Management.* New York, McGraw-Hill, 1950.

Leighton, Alexander H.: *The Governing of Men: General Principles and Recommendations Based on Experience at a Japanese Relocation Camp.* Princeton, Princeton Univ. Press., 1945.

Leonard, V. A.: *Police Organization and Management.* Brooklyn, Foundation, 1951.

Lepawsky, Albert: *Administration: the Art and*

Science of Organization and Management. New York, Knopf, 1949.

Likert, Rensis: *New Patterns of Management.* New York, McGraw-Hill, 1961.

———, **Zander, Alvin, Kahn, Robert L., and Schwab, Robert E.:** *Motivation: The Core of Management.* New York, American Management Assoc., 1953.

Long, Will, and Lewis, Gary A.: *Management Faces New Problems.* New York, Society for the Advancement of Management, 1954.

McCormick, Charles P.: *The Power of People: Multiple Management up to Date.* New York, Harper & Bros., 1949.

McLarney, William J.: *Management Training: Cases and Principles.* Homewood, Irwin, 1955.

McMurray, Robert N.: *McMurray's Management Clinic.* New York, Simon & Schuster, 1960.

Magee, John F.: Decision Trees for Decision Making, HBR (July-Aug., 1964), 126-135.

Maier, Norman R. F., et al.: *Supervisory and Executive Development.* New York, Wiley, 1957.

March, James G., and Simon, Herbert A.: *Organizations.* New York, Wiley, 1958.

Martindell, Jackson: *The Scientific Appraisal of Management.* New York, Harper, 1950.

Marvin, Philip R.: *Administrative Management.* Dayton, Research Press, Inc., 1954.

Mechanic, David: The Power to Resist Change Among Low-ranking Personnel, PA (July-Aug., 1963), 5-11.

Mental Measurements Yearbooks, 4th Ed. New Jersey, Gryphon, 1953.

Merrihue, Willard V.: *Managing by Communication.* New York, McGraw-Hill, 1960.

Millett, John D.: *Management in the Public Service: the Quest for Effective Performance.* New York, McGraw-Hill, 1954.

Milward, George E.: *An Approach to Management.* Cambridge, Harvard Univ. Press, 1948.

Miner, John B.: *The Management of Ineffective Performance.* New York, McGraw-Hill, 1963.

Montgomery, Bernard Law: *The Path to Leadership.* New York, Putnam's, 1961.

Mooney, James D.: *The Principles of Organization.* New York, Harper & Bros., 1947.

Mueller, Robert K.: *Effective Management Through Probability Controls: How to Calculate Managerial Risks.* New York, Funk, 1950.

Newcomb, Robert, and Sammons, Marg: *Speak up, Management.* New York, Funk & Wagnalls, 1951.

Newman, William H.: *Administrative Action:* the Techniques of Organization and Management. New York, Prentice-Hall, 1951.

———: *Business Polices and Management.* Cincinnati, South-Western, 1953.

———, **& Summer, Charles E., Jr.:** *The Process of Management.* Englewood Cliffs, Prentice-Hall, 1961.

Niles, Mary Cushing: *The Essence of Management.* Bombay, Orient Longmans, 1956.

———: *Middle Management: the Job of Junior Administrator.* New York, Harper & Bros., 1954.

Nissen, Hartwig: *Some Human Aspects of Administration.* Brussels, International Institute of Admin. Services, 1952.

Performance Reports: an Information Manual for Supervisors. Beverly Hills, Civil Service Commission, 1955.

Pffifner, John: *Supervision of Personnel.* Los Angeles, Univ. of Southern Calif., 1949.

———: *The Supervision of Personnel.* Englewood Cliffs, Prentice-Hall, Inc., 1964.

———, **& Sherwood, Frank P.:** *Administrative Organization.* Englewood Cliffs, Prentice-Hall, 1960.

Pigors, Paul: Of Giving Orders and Getting Results, PERSONNEL (Mar.-Apr., 1960), 47-54.

Planty, Earl G., and Freeston, J. Thomas: *Developing Management Ability.* New York, Ronald Press, 1954.

Plummer, Norman: *Advanced Management* (Sept., 1960), 21-24.

Pollock, James K.: The Michigan Civil Service: An Action Program, GG, Vol.72 (Jan.-Feb., 1955), 7-9.

Powell, Norman J.: *Personnel Administration in Government.* Englewood Cliffs, Prentice-Hall, 1956.

Randall, Raymond L.: *Developing Management Potential Through Appraisal Panels.* Personnel Management Series No.8, Washington, U.S. Civil Service Commission, 1955.

Raub, Edwin S.: Requisite of Effective Management Development, PERSONNEL (Sept.-Oct., 1963), 62-68.

Raudsepp, Eugene: How to Boost Idea Power, NAT.B. (Jan., 1961), 74-80.

Redfield, Charles E.: *Communication in Management: a Guide to Administrative Communication.* Chicago, Univ. of Chicago, 1953.

Rose, T. G.: *Higher Control on Management.* London, Pitman, 1945.

Ross, Murray G., and Hendry, Charles E.: *New Understandings of Leadership.* New York, Associated Press, 1957.

Rowland, Virgil: *Managerial Performance Stan-*

dards. New York, American Management Assoc., 1960.

Rytten, Jack Edward: Principles of Effective Leadership, POLICE, Vol.4, No.5 (May-June, 1960), 70-73.

Schaffer, A. J.: The Attitude Survey as a Management Tool, PA, Vol.26 (Nov.-Dec., 1963), 36-39.

Schell, Erwin Haskell: *Technique of Administration: Administrative Proficiency in Business.* New York, McGraw-Hill, 1951.

Schrotel, Stanley R.: Supervision of Personnel: Workshop, TPY (1962).

————: Use of Staff Personnel, TPY (1957).

Scott, Walter D., et al.: *Personnel Management.* New York, McGraw-Hill, 1954.

Scott, Jerome F., and Lynton, R. P.: *Three Studies in Management.* London, British Institute of Management, 1952.

Seckler-Hudson, Catheryn: *Organization and Management: Theory and Practice.* Washington, The American University Press, 1955.

————: *Process of Organization and Management.* Washington, Public Affairs Press, 1948.

Seward, William: *Teamwork in Industry: a Tested Program for Worker—Management Cooperation.* New York, Funk & Wagnalls, 1949.

Sherwood, Frank P., and Best, Wallace H.: *Supervisory Methods in Municipal Administration.* Chicago, Int'l City Managers Assoc., 1958.

Shuman, Ronald B.: *The Management of Men.* Norman, Univ. of Oklahoma Press, 1948.

Simon, Herbert A.: *Administrative Behavior.* New York, Institute of Public Administration, 1952.

————: The Decision Maker as Innovator in *Concepts and Issues in Administrative Behavior,* edited by **Sidney Mailick,** Englewood Cliffs, Prentice-Hall, 1962.

Simpson, Robert G.: *Case Studies in Management Development: Theory and Practice in Selected Companies.* New York, American Management Assoc., 1954.

Singer, Harry A.: The Management of Stress, A.MGMT. (Sept., 1960), 11-13.

Shartle, Carroll I.: *Executive Performance and Leadership.* Englewood Cliffs, Prentice-Hall, 1956.

Spriegel, William R.: *Industrial Management.* New York, Wiley, 1955.

————, & **Davies, Ernest C.:** *Principles of Business Organization and Operation.* New York, Prentice-Hall, 1952.

Stryker, Perrin: *A Guide to Modern Management Methods.* New York, McGraw-Hill, 1954.

Sutton, X. F., and Tyler, Allen H.: *The Foreman's Training Job.* New London, National Foreman's Institute, 1950.

Tannenbaum, Robert, et al.: *Leadership and Organization.* New York, McGraw-Hill, 1961.

Taylor, Fredrick W.: *Scientific Management.* New York, Harper & Bros., 1947.

Tayol, Henri: *General and Industrial Management.* London, Pitman, 1949.

Terry, George R.: *Office Management and Control.* Homewood, Irwin, 1953.

————: *Principles of Management.* Homewood, Irwin, 1953.

Thompson, C. E.: *Personnel Management for Supervisors.* New York, Prentice-Hall, 1948.

Torpe, William G.: *Public Personnel Management.* New York, Nostrand, 1953.

Trice, Jarrison M.: *The Problem Drinker on the Job—Bulletin No.40.* Ithaca, New York State School of Industrial and Labor Relations, Cornell Univ., 1959.

Turfboer, Robert: Alcoholism: Management's Problem, A.MGMT. (Sept., 1960), 14-15, 28.

U.S. Civil Service Commission: *Salary and Wage Administration in the Public Service: a Select List of References.* Washington, U.S. Govt. Printing Office, 1947.

U.S. Federal Security Agency, Division of Personnel Management, Staff Development Branch: *Staff Development: the Supervisor's Job.* Washington, U.S. Govt. Printing Office, 1948.

Urwick, L.: *The Elements of Administration.* London, Pitman, 1947.

————: *Management Education in American Business.* New York, American Management Assoc., 1954.

————: *Short Survey of Industrial Management.* London, British Institute of Mgmt.

Valentine, Raymond F.: The Seven Deadly Sins of Supervision, SM (Feb., 1963), 4-8.

Villalon, Luis J. A.: *Management, Men and Their Methods: Thirty-three Studies in Executive Techniques.* New York, Funk & Wagnalls, 1949.

Villers, Raymond: *The Dynamics of Industrial Management.* New York, Funk & Wagnalls, 1954.

Walker, Nigel: *Morale in the Civil Service.* London, Edinburgh Univ. Press, 1961.

Watkins, Gordon S., et al.: *The Management of Personnel and Labor Relations.* New York, McGraw-Hill, 1950.

Weston, Paul B.: The Role of the Patrol Sergeant, L&O (Sept., 1959), 31-34.
———: *Supervision in the Administration of Justice.* Springfield, Thomas, 1965.
White, Leonard D.: *The Federalists: a Study in Administrative History.* New York, Macmillan, 1948.
———: *The Jeffersonians: a Study in Administrative History, 1801-1829.* New York, Macmillan, 1951.
———: *The Jacksonians: a Study in Administrative History, 1829-1861.* New York, Macmillan, 1954.
———: Strikes in the Public Service, PPR, Vol.10 (Jan., 1949), 3-10.
Whitin, Thomas M.: *Theory of Inventory Management.* Princeton, Princeton Univ. Press, 1953.

Whyte, William H., Jr.: *The Organization Man.* Garden City, Doubleday, 1956.
Worthy, James C.: *Big Business and Free Men.* New York, Harper, 1959.
Wright, J. Handly, and Christian, Byron H.: *Public Relations in Management.* New York, McGraw-Hill, 1949.
Yoder, Dale: *Personnel Principles and Policies: Modern Manpower Management.* New York, Prentice-Hall, 1952.
Younger, John: *Management for Supervisors.* Washington, Federal Aviation Agency.
———: *The Supervisor's Management Guild.* New York, American Management Assoc., 1949.
Zalensnik, Abraham: The Human Dilemma of Leadership, HBR (July-Aug., 1963), 49-55.

POLICE PLANNING AND RESEARCH

Abruzzi, Adam: *Work Measurement: New Principles and Procedures.* New York, Columbia Univ. Press, 1952.
Ackerman, A. A.: *The Construction of a Procedural Model for Decision-Making and Its Comparison with the Practices Used by Police Administrators.* Washington, IACP, 1964.
Ahlberg, Clark D., and Honey, John C.: *Some Administrative Problems in Governmental Research.* Washington, Research Office, 1951.
AMERICAN INSTITUTE OF PLANNERS JOURNAL. Published quarterly by the American Institute of Planners, Institute Headquarters, 77 Massachusetts Ave., Cambridge, Mass.
American Management Association: *Personnel: Supervisory Practices and Organizational Structures as They Affect Employee Productivity and Morale.* New York, American Management Assoc., 1948.
———: *Rating Employee and Supervisory Performance: a Manual of Merit Rating Techniques.* New York, American Management Assoc., 1952.
———: *Research: Planning and Developing the Company Organizational Structure.* New York, American Management Assoc., 1952.
Barnes, Ralph M.: *Motion and Time Study.* New York, Wiley, 1949.
———: *Motion and Time Study Applications.* New York, Wiley, 1949.
———: *Motion and Time Study Problems and Projects.* New York, Wiley, 1949.
———: *Work Measurement Manual.* Dubuque, Brown, 1951.
———: *Work Sampling.* New York, Wiley, 1957.

Beall, William P., Jr.: *Survey and Reorganization of the Police Department of Medford, Oregon,* 1951.
Beck, George N.: Municipal Police Performance Rating, JCLC&PS, Vol.51, No.5 (Mar.-Apr., 1960-61), 567.
Bedford, James H.: *Your Future Job.* Los Angeles, Society for Occupational Research, 1950.
Beer, Stafford: *Cybernetics and Management.* New York, Wiley, 1959.
Belcher, David, and Hereman, Herbert G.: *How to Make a Wage Survey.* Minneapolis, Ind. Relations Center, Univ. of Minnesota Press, 1948.
Black, Russell Van Nest: *Planning for the Small American City.* Chicago, Public Administration Service, 1944.
Brandstatter, A. F.: New Frontiers for the Police, POLICE, Vol.7, No.2 (Nov.-Dec., 1962).
Bristow, Allen P.: *Decision Making in Police Administration.* Springfield, Thomas, 1961.
———: Prospectus-Police Armament Research Project, POLICE, Vol.7, No.1 (Sept.-Oct., 1962), 78-80.
Brown, Albert N.: Operation Spanish in Philadelphia, TPC Vol.29, No.4 (Apr., 1962), 20.
Brown, Richard E.: *A Review of Employee Evaluation System, Personnel Report No.634.* Chicago, Public Personnel Assoc., 1963.
Brown, William P.: Planning & Research, Seminar, TPY (1963).
Bruce, Robert T., Chaudruc, Jean, and Hornbruch, Frederick W., Jr.: *Practical Planning and Scheduling.* New London, National Foreman's Institute, 1950.
Bush, George P.: *Bibliography on Research Ad-*

ministration: Annotated. Washington, University Press of Washington, D.C., 1954.

———: *Scientific Research: Its Administration and Organization*. Washington, Univ. Press of Washington D.C., 1950.

———, & Hattery, Lowell H.: *Teamwork in Research*. Washington, The American Univ. Press, 1953.

California Youth Authority: *The Youth Authority Organization and Program*. Sacramento, Calif. Printing Office, 1945.

Carroll, Phil: *How to Chart Timestudy Data*. New York, McGraw-Hill, 1950.

Cartwright, Dorwin, and Zander, Alvin: *Group Dynamics: Research and Theory*. Evanston, Pow, Peterson, 1953.

Case Institute of Technology Operations Research Group: *A Comprehensive Bibliography on Operations Research*. New York, Wiley, 1958.

THE CENTER. Published quarterly by the IACP, 1319-18th St., N.W., Washington, D.C. 20036, for law enforcement research information. First issue published in 1965.

Center for Law Enforcement Research Information, TPC, Vol.31 (Aug., 1964), 54.

Chase, Stuart: *Men at Work*. New York, Harcourt, Brace, 1945.

Churchman, C. W., Ackoff, R. A., and Arnoff, E. L.: *Introduction to Operations Research*. New York, Wiley, 1957.

Colliton, Patrick: *The Evaluation of the Research-planning Function in the American Police Service*. A Master's Thesis, Washington State Univ., 1962.

Colvin, Hugh F.: *Controls for Research & Development*. Mgmt. Series, No.176. New York, American Management Assoc., 1955.

Crooke, William M.: An Information Center, POLICE, Vol.6, No.4 (Mar.-Apr., 1962), 39-40.

Crouch, Winston W.: *Metropolitan Services: Studies of Allocation in a Federated Organization, Part II, the Police Function*. Los Angeles, Bureau of Governmental Research, Univ. of Calif. at Los Angeles, 1962.

Crutchfield, Carroll: Familiarity Breeds Respect, L&O, Vol.13, No.6 (June, 1965), 50.

Curtis, S. J.: Focus on the Future, POLICE, Vol.8, No.1 (Sept.-Oct., 1963), 26-29; No.2 (Nov.-Dec., 1963), 25-27.

Dale, Ernest: *Planning and Developing the Company Organization Structure*. New York, American Management Assoc., 1952.

DeLatil, Pierre: *Thinking by Machine, a Study of Cybernetics*. Boston, Houghton Mifflin, 1957.

Dewhurst, H. S.: *Departmental Organization of*

the Railroad Police, POLICE, Vol.1, No.1 (Sept.-Oct., 1956), 29-36.

Diamond, Harry: Factors in Planning & Evaluating In-Service Training Programs, JCLC&PS, Vol.53, No.4 (Dec., 1962), 503.

Dimock, Marshal C.: *The Executive Action*. New York, Ronald, 1953.

Donnelly, Hugh A.: Planning: A Summary, TPY (1963).

Enrick, Norbert L.: *Quality Control*. New York, Industrial Press, 1954.

Feigenbaum, Armand V.: *Quality Control, Principles, Practice, and Administration: an Industrial Management Tool for Improving Product Quality and Design and for Reducing Operating Costs and Losses*. New York, McGraw-Hill, 1951.

Foster, Harvey: Administrative Techniques: Bank Robberies, TPY (1959).

Frankel, Hyman: The New National Research and Information Center, POLICE, Vol.6, No.3 (Jan.-Feb., 1962), 49-51.

Gallati, Robert R. J.: Report of the Research Committee, TPY (1964); (1965).

Germann, A. C.: Planning and Research, POLICE, Vol.6, No.3 (Jan.-Feb., 1962), 36-39.

Gill, William A.: *A Performance Analysis System*. Brussels, International Institute of Administrative Sciences, 1953.

Goetz, Billy Early: *Management Planning and Control: a Managerial Approach to Industrial Accounting*. New York, McGraw-Hill, 1949.

Griffin, John I.: What Electronic Data Processing May Do for the Police Chief in the Future, POLICE, Vol.4, No.3 (Jan.-Feb., 1960), 68-71.

Grupp, Stanley E.: Work Release in the United States, JCLC&PS, Vol.54, No.3 (1963), 267.

Hankey, Richard O.: Personnel Management Practices at the Area Level in the Dept. of the Calif. Highway Patrol, POLICE, Vol.7, No.1 (Sept.-Oct., 1962), 27-31.

Hempel, Edward H.: *Top Management Planning*. New York, Harper, 1945.

Hollday, Roy E., and Sheehan, Robert: How Do You Rate? POLICE, Vol.6, No.6 (July-Aug., 1962), 59-62.

International City Managers' Association: *Local Planning Administration*. Chicago, the Int'l City Managers' Assn., 1948.

———: *Municipal Police Administration*. Chicago, The Association, 1961.

Issacs, Norman E.: The Crime of Present Day Crime Reporting, JCLC&PS, Vol.52, No.4 (Nov.-Dec., 1961), 405.

Jaffe, A. J., and Stewart, Charles D.: *Manpower Resources and Utilization: Principles of*

Working Force Analysis. New York, Wiley, 1951.

Juran, Joseph M.: *Quality Control Handbook*. New York, McGraw-Hill, 1951.

Kenney, John P.: A Master Plan for Reorganization of the Police Department, City and County of Denver, POLICE, Vol.7, No.4 (Mar.-Apr., 1963), 66-69.

———: *Police Management Planning*. Springfield, Thomas, 1959.

———, & Williams, John: *Police Operations*. Springfield, Thomas, 1960.

Koepke, Charles A.: *Plant Production Control*. New York, Wiley, 1949.

Landy, Thomas M.: *Production Planning and Control*. New York, McGraw-Hill, 1950.

Lane, Jean R.: Maui County Police Department Time Expenditure Analysis, POLICE, Vol.6, No.6 (July-Aug., 1960), 18-22.

Leonard, A. Everett: Workshop: Exploring IACP Field Service Division Management Surveys, TPY (1965).

Levin, J. L.: *How Cities Control Juvenile Delinquency*. Chicago, American Municipal Assoc., 1957.

Lloyd, David D.: *Spend and Survive*. Indianapolis, Bobbs-Merrill, 1960.

Lombard, William M.: Survey in Rochester, New York, TPY (1965).

Lytle, Charles Walter: *Job Evaluation Methods*. New York, Ronald, 1954.

McCloskey, J. F., and Trefethen, F. N. (eds.): *Operations Research for Management*, Vol.1. Baltimore, Hopkins Press, 1955.

——— *Operations Research for Management*, Vol.2. Baltimore, Hopkins Press, 1956.

McCormick, Thomas C., and Francis, Roy G.: *Methods of Research and the Behavioral Sciences*. New York, Harper, 1958.

McDonald, Hugh C.: New Concept in Operational Filing, L&O, Vol.11, No.1 (July, 1963).

McDonell, R. E.: Planning and Research, TPC, Vol.29, No.9 (Sept., 1962), 4.

McKean, Rolan N.: *Efficiency in Government through Systems Analysis*. New York, Wiley, 1958.

McNally, George E.: Survey in Mobile, Alabama, TPY (1965).

Mac Niece, E. H.: *Production Forecasting, Planning, and Control*. New York, Wiley, 1951.

Magee, John F.: *Production Planning and Inventory Control*. New York, McGraw-Hill, 1958.

Mees, C. E. Kenneth, and Leermakers, John A.: *The Organization of Industrial Scientific Research*. New York, McGraw-Hill, 1950.

Millderbrandt, T. H.: *A Preliminary Study of the Issuance of the Written Warning by State Law Enforcement Agencies in Certain Violations of Traffic Laws*. Washington, IACP, 1964.

Moore, Franklin G.: *Production Control*. New York, McGraw-Hill, 1951.

Mundel, Marvin Everett: *Motion and Time Study: Principles and Practice*. New York, Prentice-Hall, 1959.

Murphy, Glen R.: Application of Planning Procedures, TPY (1963).

Murphy, Wm. A.: Specialization of Police, TPC, Vol.29, No.10 (Oct., 1962), 18.

Murray, Robert V.: The Promise of Police Research, TPY (1961).

Myers, George E.: *Planning Your Future*. New York, McGraw-Hill, 1953.

National Industrial Conference Board: *Appraisal of Job Performance*. New York, National Industrial Conference Board, 1951.

Niebel, Benjamin W.: *Motion and Time Study*. Homewood, Irwin, 1955.

O'Connell, J. J.: Have Police Kept Pace? TPC, Vol.31 (Nov., 1964), 41.

O'Donnell, Paul D.: *Production Control*. New York, Prentice-Hall, 1952.

OFFICE MANAGEMENT. Published monthly by the National Research Bureau, 415 North Dearborn St., Chicago.

Olson, Bruce: A Center for Police Planning and Research, a Proposal, JCLC&PS, Vol.50, No.3 (Sept.-Oct., 1959), 296.

Operational Manual for Disasters. New York City Police Department, 1962.

Organization and Function of Police Planning and Research Units. Washington, IACP, 1963.

Patton, John A., and Smith, Reynold S.: *Job Evaluation*. Homewood, Irwin, 1950.

Payne, Dorothy E.: New Dimension in Police Service, L&O, Vol.11, No.5 (May, 1963).

Petit, Jose A. H.: *A Work Simplification Method*. Brussels International Institute of Administrative Science, 1953.

Program for the Control and Operation of Bicycles. Prepared by the Berkeley P.D. Washington, IACP, 1949.

Randolph, Ross V.: A Method of Developing University Research Programs in Correctional Institutions, JCLC&PS, Vol.52, No.1 (May-June, 1961), 90.

Remington, Frank J.: Criminal Justice Research, JCLC&PS, Vol.51, No.1 (Mar.-Apr., 1960-61), 7.

Ritchie, William E.: *Production and Inventory Control*. New York, Ronald, 1951.

Roscoe, E. Scott: *Organization for Production.* Homewood, Irwin, 1955.

Rowland, Floyd H.: *Business Planning and Control.* New York, Harper & Bros., 1947.

Rules and Regulations. Chicago, Chicago Police Department, maintained annually.

Rules and Regulations. Multnomah County Sheriff's Office. Portland, Oregon, maintained annually.

Rutherford, John G.: *Quality Control in Industry.* London, Pitman, 1948.

Saaty, Thomas L.: *Mathematical Methods of Operations Research.* New York, McGraw-Hill, 1959.

Sasieni, M., Yaspan, A., and Friedman, L.: *Operations Research, Methods and Problems.* New York, Wiley, 1959.

Savord, George H.: How Many Men? POLICE, Vol.6, No.6 (July-Aug., 1962), 66-69.

Seckler-Hudson, Catheryn: *Budgeting: an Instrument of Planning and Management.* Washington, American University Press, 1944-1946.

Seiveno, Virgil H.: Reducing an Officer's Paper Work, L&O, Vol.12 (Dec., 1964).

Shaw, William: Greater Efficiency in Law Enforcement Work Is Up to You, L&O, Vol.11, No.5 (May, 1963).

Simon, Richard: Planning & Research Division of the Los Angeles Police Dept., JCLC&PS, Vol.44, No.3 (Sept.-Oct., 1953).

Skousen, Cleon W.: Should the Small Department Have a Juvenile Officer, L&O, Vol.9 (Oct., 1961).

Smith, Bruce: *The New Orleans Police Survey.* New Orleans, Bureau of Governmental Research, Inc., 1946.

————: *The New York Police Survey.* New York, Institute of Public Admin., 1952.

Smith, R. D.: *Computer Applications in Police Manpower Distribution.* Washington, IACP, 1961.

Sonne, Hans Christian: *Democratic Planning in Action.* New York, Sanders, 1946.

Staley, John D., and Dellaff, Irving A.: How to Make a Work Distribution Analysis, SM (May, 1964), 24-28.

Stewart, Irvin: *Organizing Scientific Research for War.* Boston, Little, Brown, 1948.

Strecher, Victor G.: Interaction of Planning, Research and Training, TPY (1963).

Suranyi-Unger, Theo: *Private Enterprise and Governmental Planning: an Integration.* New York, McGraw-Hill, 1950.

Tamm, Quinn: Discipline & Performance Appraisal, TPC, Vol.29, No.9 (Sept., 1962), 6.

————: Rebuilding a Scandal Torn Police Force, TPC, Vol.29, No.2 (Feb., 1962), 4.

Temple University: *Survey of Federal Reorganization.* Philadelphia, Temple Univ., 1953.

University of Michigan: *Publications of the Institute for Social Research.* Ann Arbor, 1960.

U.S. Executive Office of the President, Bureau of the Budget: *Techniques for the Development of a Work Measurement System.* Management Bulletin, 1950, Washington.

Williams, D. L.: Real-time Computer Systems for the Police Dept., L&O, Vol.12 (July, 1964).

Wilson, O. W.: *Police Administration.* New York, McGraw-Hill, 1963.

————: *Police Planning.* Springfield, Thomas, 1958.

Wiltberger, William R.: The Police System of Thinking, POLICE, Vol.5, No.2 (Nov.-Dec., 1960), 45-47.

Woodson, Charles W., Jr.: Report of Research Committee, TPY (1963).

Wooton, Barbara: *Freedom under Planning.* Chapel Hill, Univ. of North Carolina Press, 1945.

Younger, John: *Work Routing, Scheduling and Dispatching.* New York, Ronald Press, 1947.

POLICE UNIONS

Anderson, Arvid: Labor Relations in the Public Service, LLJ (Nov., 1961).

Andrews, Louis C.: What's the Law—Police Labor Unions, MMR (Dec., 1961).

Bakke, E. Wright: *Mutual Survival: the Goal of Unions and Management.* New Haven, Yale Univ. Press, 1946.

Berger, Harriett F.: The Grievance Process in the Philadelphia Public Service, ILRR (July, 1960).

Bernstein, Irving: The Growth of American Unions, AER (June, 1954), 303-18.

Brownlow, Lewis: *A Passion for Anonymity.* Chicago, Univ. of Chicago Press, 1958.

Carpenter, William Seal: *The Unfinished Business of Civil Service Reform.* Princeton, Princeton Univ. Press, 1952.

Castenholz, Fred E.: City Employees and Unionizations, TPC (Aug., 1959).

————: Lower Court Rules for Police Unions, TPC (Apr., 1962).

Davidson, Apos and Sol: Structure of A.F. of L. Union, LLR (May, 1959), Bureau of National Affairs.

Dishman, Robert B.: *The State of the Union.* New York, Scribner's, 1965.

Donigan, Robert L.: The Police Service as a Profession, TPC (Apr., 1956).

Fitchm, J. A.: On the Labor—Management Front, SURVEY (Nov., 1951).

Ford, Fred L.: Law Enforcement and Unionization, TPY (1958).

———: Violates Oath—Divides Loyalty, TPC (Nov., 1957).

Givens, Royce L.: The American Police Problems and Progress, TPC (June, 1957).

Godine, Morton Robert: *The Labor Problem in the Public Service: a Study in Political Pluralism.* Cambridge, Harvard Univ. Press, 1951.

Goldberg, Arthur: *AFL-CIO Labor United.* New York, McGraw-Hill, 1956.

Heutis, Carl E.: Best Interest Not Served by Unions, TPC (Nov., 1957).

———: Police Unions, JCLC&PS, Vol.48, No.6 (Mar.-Apr., 1958), 643, TPY (1958).

Hogan, John D., and Inni, Francis: *American Social Legislation.* New York, Harper & Bros., 1956.

Holladay, Roy E.: Police Unions, TPC, Vol.30, No.8 (Aug., 1963), 30-34.

———: Police Unions—Programs of Negation, POLICE (Nov.-Dec., 1961).

International City Managers' Association: *Municipal Year Book.* Chicago, Published annually.

Kaplan, H. Eliot: *The Law of Civil Service.* New York, Matthew Bender, 1958.

Kennedy, S. P.: No Union for the New York City Police, AC (Oct., 1958).

Killingsworth, Charles S.: Grievance Adjudication in Public Employment, TAJ (Jan., 1958).

Kramer, Leo: *Labor's Paradox.* Wiley, 1962.

Lahne, Herbert: The Intermediate Body in Collective Bargaining, ILRR (Jan., 1953).

Lahne and Kovner: Shop Society and the Union, ILRR (Oct., 1953).

Leonard, V. A.: *Police Organization and Management.* Brooklyn, Foundation, 1951.

Lester, Richard A.: *As Unions Mature,* Princeton, Princeton Univ. Press, 1958.

Lindbom, Charles E.: *Unions and Capitalism.* New Haven, Yale Univ. Press, 1949.

McGinty, A. B., and Kling, S.: Forum: Have Public Employees the Right to Strike? FORUM (May, 1947).

Meyers, James, and Laidler, Harry: *What Do You Know about Labor.* New York, Day, 1956.

Murray, E. P.: Should the Police Unionize, NATION (June, 1959).

Nichols, Marion C.: North Carolina Bans Union Membership, TPC (July, 1959).

———: Police Unions are a Threat to Needed Discipline, TPC (Apr., 1962).

———: Police Unions in the News, TPC (Oct., 1958).

Perlman, Selig: *A Theory of the Labor Movement.* Kelly Pub., 1949.

Police Unions. Washington, IACP, 1958.

Proham, Mark: *Labor Union Theories in America.* Evanston, Row, Peterson, 1958.

Reile, A. S.: Why the Unionization of Police Forces Is in the Public Interest, TPY (1958).

Rhyne, Charles S.: *Labor Unions and Municipal Employee Law.* Washington, National Institute of Municipal Law Officers, 1946.

Roskin, A. H.: Do Police Strikes Violate Public Trust, NEW YORK TIMES MAGAZINE (Jan., 1961).

Ross, Arthur M.: *Trade Union Wage Policy.* Berkeley, Univ. of Calif., 1950.

Schweppe, Emma: *The Fireman's and Patrolman's Unions in the City of New York.* New York, Columbia Univ., 1948.

Selakman, Ben M.: Trade Unions—Romance and Reality, HBR (May-June, 1958).

Sheehan, Robert: Lest We Forget, POLICE, Vol.4, No.1 (Sept.-Oct., 1959), 14-19; No.2 (Nov.-Dec., 1959), 8-15.

Smith, Bruce: *Police Systems in the United States.* New York, Harper & Bros., 1960.

Spero, Sterling D.: *Government as Employer.* New York, Remson, 1948.

Stephensky, Ben: The Structure of the American Labor Movement, *Interpreting the Labor Movement, Industrial Relations Research Association,* Madison, 1956.

Strong, M. K.: Unionization of Government Employees, FORUM (Aug., 1946).

Summers, Clyde: Disciplinary Powers of Unions, ILRR, Vol.3; and Vol.4 (1950).

Taft, Philip: *The Structure and Government as Employer.* Cambridge, Harvard Univ. Press, 1954.

Ulman, Lloyd: *The Rise of the National Trade Union.* Cambridge, Harvard Univ. Press, 1955.

Wike, Leroy E.: Police Unions, *Bulletins on Police Problems.* Prepared by the IACP, Washington, Aug., 1958.

Zeichner, Irving B.: Police Unions, L&O, Vol.7 (Apr., 1959).

PUBLIC ADMINISTRATION

Achieving Excellence in Public Service, THE ANNALS (Aug., 1963), 209.

Adrian, Charles R.: *Governing Urban America.* New York, McGraw-Hill, 1961. (A text on community development and services.)

Ahlberg, Clark D., and Honey, John C.: *Attitudes of Scientists and Engineers about Their Government Employment.* Syracuse, Maxwell School of Citizenship & Public Affairs, 1950.

Alderfer, Harold: *American Local Government and Administration.* New York, Macmillan, 1956.

Allen, Robert S.: *Our Fair City.* New York, Vanguard, 1947.

AMERICAN ARCHIVIST. Published quarterly by the Society of American Archivists, Treasurer, 8917 Seneca Lane, Bethesda, Maryland.

American Assembly, Sixth: *The Federal Government Service: Its Character, Prestige, and Problems.* New York, Columbia Univ., 1954.

AMERICAN MUNICIPAL NEWS. Published monthly. Current municipal developments and practices.

Anderson, Hurst R.: Ethical Values in Administration, PA (Jan., 1954).

Anderson, William, Penniman, Clara, and Weidner, Edward W.: *Government in the Fifty States.* New York, Holt, Rinehart & Winston, 1962.

Appleby, Paul H.: *Big Democracy.* New York, Knopf, 1945.

———: *Morality and Administration in Democratic Government.* Baton Rouge, Louisiana State Univ. Press, 1952.

———: *Policy and Administration.* University, Univ. of Alabama Press, 1949.

Argyris, Chris: *Personality and Organization.* New York, Harper & Row, 1957.

Association of the Bar of the City of New York: *Conflict of Interest and Federal Service: Report of the Special Committee on Federal Conflicts of Interest Laws.* Cambridge, Harvard Univ. Press, 1960.

Aumann, Franics R., and Walker, Harvey: *The Government and Administration of Ohio.* New York, Crowell, 1956.

Babcock, Robert S.: *State and Local Government and Politics.* New York, Random, 1956.

Baker, Benjamin: *Urban Government.* New York, Nostrand, 1957.

Bartholomew, Paul C.: *Public Administration.* Paterson, Littlefield, Adams, 1959.

Beard, Charles A.: *American Government and Politics,* 10th Ed. New York, Macmillan, 1949.

Bernstein, Marver H.: *The Job of the Federal Executive.* Washington, The Brookings Institution, 1958.

Bigger, Richard, and Kitchen, James D.: *How the Cities Grew.* Los Angeles, Hayness Foundation, 1952.

Bishop, Hillman, and Hendel, Samuel: *Basic Issues of American Democracy,* 3rd Ed. New York, Appleton, 1956.

Blackwood, George: Boston Politics and Boston Politicians, in Murray B. Levin, *The Alienated Voter: Politics in Boston.* New York, Holt, Rinehart & Winston, 1960.

Blundred, R. H., and Hanks, D. W.: *Federal Services to Cities and Towns.* Chicago, American Municipal Assoc., 1950.

Bock, Edwin A., and Campbell, Alan K.: *Case Studies in American Government.* Englewood Cliffs, Prentice-Hall, 1963.

Bollens, John C.: *The Problem of Government in the San Francisco Bay Region.* Berkeley, Bureau of Public Administration, Univ. of Calif., 1949.

———: *Special District Governments in the United States.* Los Angeles, Univ. of Calif. Press, 1957.

———: *The States and the Metropolitan Problem.* Chicago, Council of State Governments, 1956.

Bone, Hugh A.: *American Politics and the Party System.* New York, McGraw-Hill, 1955.

BRITISH MANAGEMENT REVIEW. Published quarterly by the British Institute of Management, Management House, 8 Hill St., London, W.1.

Brogan, D. W.: *Politics in America.* New York, Harper & Bros., 1954.

Bromage, Arthur W.: *A Councilman Speaks.* Ann Arbor, George Wahr, 1951.

———: *Councilman at Work.* Ann Arbor, Wahr, 1954.

———: *Managed Plan Abandoments.* New York, National Municipal League, 1954.

———: *On the City Council.* Ann Arbor, Wahr, 1950.

Brownlow, Louis: *A Passion for Politics.* Chicago, Univ. of Chicago Press, 1955.

———: *The President and the Presidency.* Chicago, Public Administration Service, 1949.

Burkhead, Jesse: *Government of Budgeting.* New York, Wiley, 1956.

Byron, William F.: Population Problems, JCL&C, Vol.35, No.5 (Jan.-Feb., 1945), 331.

Caldwell, Lynton K.: *Comparative Public Administration: an Outline of Topics and Readings.* Albany, Graduate Program in Public Administration, 1953.

———: *The Government and Administration of New York.* New York, Crowell, 1957.

California State Department of Justice: *Report of the Department of Justice for 1958-1960.* Sacramento, Calif. State Printing Office, 1960.

Callard, Keith: On the Ethics of Civil Servants in Great Britain and North America, PP, Vol.4 (1953), 133-156.

Campbell, Clyde M.: *Practical Application of Democratic Administration.* New York, Harper, 1952.

Carrell, Jeptha: *Interjurisdictional Agreements in the Philadelphia Metropolitan Area.* Ph.D. Dissertation, Philadelphia, Univ. of Penna., 1953.

Celebrezze, Anthony J.: Change and Challenge in Public Administration, THE ANNALS (Aug., 1963), 75-90.

Challenge for a Machine, LIFE (Feb. 21, 1955), 53.

Charlesworth, James C.: *Governmental Administration.* New York, Harper & Bros., 1951.

Childs, Richard S.: *Civic Victories.* New York, Harper & Bros., 1952.

Cipolla, Carlo: *The Economic History of World Population.* Baltimore, Penguin Books, 1962.

CITY MANAGERS' NEWSLETTER. Published biweekly by the International City Managers' Assoc., 1313 E. 60th Street, Chicago, Ill.

Clapp, Gordon R.: A Credo for the Public Servant, PPR (Jan., 1951).

———: Ethical Standards and Professional Conduct, THE ANNALS (Jan., 1955).

Cole, Taylor: *Canadian Bureaucracy.* Durham, Duke Univ. Press, 1949.

———: *European Political Systems,* 2nd Ed. New York, Knopf, 1961.

Colm, Gerhard, and Nicol, Henel O.: *Essays in Public Finance and Fiscal Policy.* New York, Oxford Univ. Press, 1955.

Commager, Henry Steele: *Documents of American History,* 5th Ed. New York, Appleton, 1949.

Commission on Intergovernmental Relations: *A Report to the President for Transmittal to Congress.* A Report prepared by the Intergovernmental Relations Commission. Washington, Government Printing Office, 1955.

Constitution of the United States and of the State of California as Last Amended, November 6, 1962, and Other Documents. Sacramento, Calif. Legislature (Assembly, Nov., 1962).

Cooper, Weldon: *Metropolitan County: A Study of Government in the Birmingham Area.* University, Bureau of Public Admin. Univ. of Alabama, 1949.

Corson, John J.: *Executives for the Federal Service.* New York, Columbia Univ. Press, 1952.

———, **& Harris, Joseph P.:** *Public Administration in Modern Society.* New York, McGraw-Hill, 1963.

Corwin, Edward S.: *The President: Office and Powers, 1787-1948: History and Analysis of Practice and Opinion.* New York, N.Y. Univ. Press, 1948.

Cottrell, E. A., and Jones, Helen: *Characteristics of the Metropolis.* Los Angeles, Haynes Foundation, 1954.

Council of Economic Advisers: *The American Economy in 1961: Problems and Policies a Statement Before the Joint Economic Committee of the U.S. Congress, Mar. 6, 1961.*

Council of State Governments: *Book of the States, 1962-1963.* Chicago, The Council, Vol.15, 1962.

———: *State—Local Relations.* Chicago, Council of State Govts., 1946.

Crouch, William: *The Initiative and Referendum in California,* 3rd. Ed. Los Angeles, Haynes Foundation, 1950.

———: *Intergovernmental Relations.* Los Angeles, Haynes Foundation, 1955.

Crumlish, Joseph D.: *A City Finds Itself: the Philadelphia Home Rule Chapter Movement.* Detroit, Wayne State Univ., 1959.

David, Paul T., and Pollock, Ross: *Executives for Government.* Washington, Brookings Institution, 1957.

Dean, Joel: *Managerial Economics.* New York, Prentice-Hall, 1951.

Dimock, Marshall Edward, and Dimock, Ogden: *Public Administration,* New York, Rinehart, 1953.

———: *A Philosophy of Administration.* New York, Harper & Bros., 1958.

———, **Dimock, Gladys O., and Koenig, Louis W.:** *Public Administration,* Rev. Ed. New York, Holt, Rinehart & Winston, 1958.

Dolan, Paul: *The Government and Administration of Delaware.* New York, Crowell, 1956.

Douglas, Paul H.: *Ethics in Government.* Cambridge, Harvard Univ. Press, 1952.

Douglas, William O.: *America Challenged.* New York, Avon, 1960.

Doyle, Wilson K., McLaird, Angus, and Weiss, C. Sherman: *The Governmental Administration of Florida.* New York, Crowell, 1954.

Duncan, Otis, and Reiss, Albert J., Jr.: *Social Characteristics of Urban and Rural Communities.* New York, Wiley, 1956.

Eliot, Thomas H.: *Governing America.* New York, Dodd, Mead, 1960.

Emmerick, Herbert: *Essays on Federal Reorganization.* University, Univ. of Alabama Press, 1950.

Ewing, Cortez A. M.: *Primary Elections in the South: a Study in Uniparty Politics.* Norman, Univ. of Oklahoma Press, 1953.

Fesler, James W.: *Area and Administration.* University, Univ. of Alabama Press, 1949.

FINANCE. Published monthly by the Finance Publishing Corp., 20 North Wacker Drive, Chicago, Ill.

Finer, Herman: *The Theory and Practice of Modern Government.* New York, Holt, 1949.

Fisher, Robert M. (ed.): *The Metropolis in Modern Life.* Garden City, Doubleday, 1955.

Fisher, Webb S.: *Master of the Metropolis.* Englewood Cliffs, Prentice-Hall, 1963.

Flynn, Edward J.: *You're the Boss.* New York, Viking, 1947.

Follett, Mary Parker: *Dynamic Administration.* New York, Harper & Bros., 1947.

Fordham, Jefferson B.: *A Larger Concept of Community.* Baton Rouge, Univ. of Louisiana Press, 1956.

————: *Local Government Law.* Brooklyn, Foundation Press, 1949.

Forthal, Sonya: *Cogwheels of Democracy: a Study of the Precinct Captain.* New York.

Friedrich, Carl J., and Galbraith, J. K.: *Public Policy: A Yearbook of the Graduate School of Business Administration, Harvard University.* Cambridge, Harvard Univ., Vols.3 & 4, 1953; Vol.5, 1954.

Galloway, George B.: *Reform of the Federal Budget. Washington, U.S. Library of Congress, Legislative Reference Service,* Public Affairs Bulletin No.80, 1950.

————, *et al.:* *The Reorganization of Congress.* Washington, Public Affairs Press, 1945.

Gaus, John Merriman: *Reflections on Public Administration.* University, Univ. of Alabama Press, 1947.

Gervasi, Frank: *Big Government: The Meaning and Purpose of The Hoover Commission Report.* New York, Whitlesey House, McGraw-Hill, 1949.

Gillespie, John: *Government in Metropolitan Austin.* Austin, Institute of Public Affairs, Univ. of Texas, 1956.

Gladden, Edgar N.: *The Essentials of Public Administration.* London, Staples, 1953.

GOOD GOVERNMENT. Published bimonthly by the National Civil Service League, 120 East 29th Street, New York, New York.

Goode, Cecil E.: *The Federal Career Service: a Look Ahead.* Washington, Society for Personnel Administration, 1954.

Goodman, William: *The Two-party System in the United States.* Princeton, Nostrand, 1956.

Gordon, Mitchell: *Sick Cities: Psychology and Pathology of American Urban Life.* Baltimore, Penguin, 1963.

Gosnell, Cullen B., and Anderson, C. David: *The Government and Administration of Georgia.* New York, Crowell, 1956.

GOVERNMENT NEWS. Published quarterly by Governmental News, 925 North 12th St., Milwaukee, Wisconsin.

GOVERNMENT PUBLICATIONS MONTHLY LIST. Published by Her Majesty's Stationery Office, London, U.S. Agent: British Information Services, 30 Rockefeller Plaza, New York.

Graham, George A.: *Morality in American Politics.* New York, Random, 1952.

Grant, Daniel R., and Nixon, H. C.: *State and Local Government in America.* Boston, Allyn and Bacon, 1965.

Graves, W. Brooke: *Public Administration in a Democratic Society.* Boston, Heath, 1950.

Greer, Scott: *Metropolitics.* New York, Wiley, 1963.

Gross, Bertram M.: *The Legislative Struggle: a Study of Social Combat.* New York, McGraw-Hill, 1953.

Gulick, Luther: *Administrative Reflections From World War II.* University, Univ. of Alabama Press, 1948.

Gundaker, G.: *Rotarian Campaign for Ethical Standards,* THE ANNALS, Vol.101 (Mar., 1952).

Gunther, John: *Inside U.S.A.* New York, Harper & Bros., 1947.

Haire, Mason (ed.): *Modern Organization Theory.* New York, Wiley, 1959.

Hardwick, Clyde T., and Landuyt, Bernard F.: *Administrative Strategy.* New York, Simons-Boardman, 1961.

Harris, Joseph P.: *A Model Primary Elections System.* New York, National Municipal League, 1957.

HARVARD BUSINESS REVIEW. Published bimonthly by the Harvard University Graduate School of Business Administration, Gallatin House, Soldiers Field, Boston, Mass.

Heady, Ferrell, and Stokes, Sybil L.: *Compara-*

tive Public Administration: a Selective An-notated Bibliography, 2nd Ed. Ann Arbor, Univ. of Michigan Institute of Public Admin., 1960.

Heckert, J. Brooks, and Willson, James D.: *Business Budgeting and Control.* New York, Ronald, 1955.

———: *Public Administration and the Public Interest.* New York, McGraw-Hill, 1956.

Hewitt, William H.: *British Police Administration.* Springfield, Thomas, 1965.

Highsaw, Robert B., and Fortenberry, Charles N.: *The Government and Administration of Mississippi.* New York, Tho. Crowell, 1956.

———, **& Mullican, Carl D., Jr.:** *The Units of Government in Mississippi.* University, Univ. of Mississippi, Bureau of Public Administration, 1949.

Hobbs, Edward H.: *Behind the President: A Study of Executive Office Agencies.* Washingington, Public Affairs Press, 1954.

Holland, L. M.: *The Direct Primary in Georgia.* Urbana, Univ. of Illinois Press, 1949.

Hoover, Institute Studies: *Revolution and the Development of International Relations.* Palo Alto, Stanford Univ. Press, 1951.

Huntington, Samuel P.: *The Common Defense: Strategic Programs in National Politics.* New York, Columbia Univ. Press, 1961.

Hyneman, Charles S.: *Bureaucracy in a Democracy.* New York, Harper & Bros., 1950.

Hyman, Sidney: *The American President.* New York, Harper & Bros., 1954.

The International City Managers' Association: *Municipal Finance Administration.* Chicago, The Assoc., 1962.

———: *Municipal Fire Administration.* Chicago, The Assoc., 1956.

———: *Municipal Personnel Administration.* Chicago, The Assoc., 1950.

———: *Municipal Police Administration.* Chicago, The Assoc., 1961.

———: *Municipal Public Works Administration.* Chicago, The Assoc., 1950.

———: *Municipal Recreation Administration.* Chicago, The Assoc., 1948.

———: *Municipal Year Book.* Chicago, The Assoc. Published Annually.

———: *Planning for Postwar Municipal Services.* Chicago, The Assoc., 1945.

———: *Technique of Municipal Administration.* Chicago, The Assoc., 1947.

Jacob, Herbert, and Vines, Kenneth N. (eds.): *Politics in the American States.* Boston, Little, 1965.

Janosik, G. Edward, and Cooke, Edward F.: *Guide to Pennsylvania Politics, 1957.* New York, Holt, 1957.

Johnson, C. O., et al.: *American State and Local Government.* Binghamton, Vail-Ballou, 1965.

JOURNAL OF FINANCE. Published quarterly by the American Finance Association, 5750 Ellis Ave., Chicago, Ill.

JOURNAL OF PUBLIC ADMINISTRATION. Published semi-annually by the New Zealand Institute of Public Administration, T. R. Smith, Editor, Education Dept., Wellington, New Zealand.

Kefauver, Estes: Past and Present Standards of Public Ethics in America, THE ANNALS, Vol.101 (Mar., 1952).

Key, V. O., Jr.: *Politics, Parties and Pressure Groups,* 4th Ed. New York, Crowell, 1958.

Kingdom, Thomas D.: *Improvement of Organization and Management in Public Administration: A Comparative Study.* Brussels, Belgium, International Institute of Administrative Sciences, Administrative Practices Office, 1951.

Klaus, Ida: Collective Bargaining by Government Employees, in Emanuel Stein (ed.) *Proceedings of New York University Twelfth Annual Conference on Labor.* New York, 1959.

Kneier, Charles M.: *City Government in the United States,* Rev. Ed. New York, Harper & Bros., 1947.

———, **& Fox, Guy:** *Readings in Municipal Government and Administration.* New York, Rinehart, 1953.

Kurtzman, David G.: *Methods of Controlling Votes in Philadelphia.* Ph.D. Thesis, Philadelphia, Univ. of Pennsylvania Press, 1955.

Lancaster, Lane W.: *Government of Rural America,* 2nd Ed. New York, Nostrand, 1952.

Landis, James M.: *Report on Regulatory Agencies to the President-elect.* Printed for the use of the Committee on the Judiciary, U.S. Senate, Washington, 1960.

LaPalombara, J. G.: *A Study of Initiative Referendum in Oregon, 1938-1948.* Corvallis, Oregon State College, 1950.

Latham, Earl: *The Group Basis of Politics.* Ithaca, Cornell Univ. Press, 1952.

Lepawsky, Albert: *Administration: the Art and Science of Organization and Management.* New York, Knopf, 1949.

Lev, J.: Validating Selection Procedures for Interviewers and Claims Adjusters, PPR, Vol.18 (1957), 232.

Leys, Wayne A. R.: *Ethics for Policy Decisions.* New York, Prentice-Hall, 1952.

Liebling, A. J.: *Chicago: the Second City.* New York, Knopf, 1952.

Lippmann, Walter: *The Public Philosophy.* Boston, Little, Brown, 1955.

Lipson, Leslie: *The Democratic Civilization.* New York, Oxford Univ. Press, 1964.

———: *The Great Issues of Politics.* Englewood Cliffs, Prentice-Hall, 1954.

London's Answer to "Big City Sprawl"—Pattern for U.S.? USN&WR (June 21, 1965), 61-62.

Lorwin, Lewis L.: Time for Planning: *a Social—Economic Theory and Program for the Twentieth Century.* New York, Harper & Bros., 1945.

McCamy, James L.: *The Administration of American Foreign Affairs.* New York, Knopf, 1950.

———: *Government Publications for the Citizen.* New York, Columbia Univ. Press, 1949.

McCormic, Richard P.: *The History of Voting in New Jersey: A Study of the Development of Election Machinery, 1644-1911.* New Brunswick, Rutgers Univ. Press, 1953.

McKean, D. D.: *Party and Pressure Politics.* Boston, Houghton Mifflin, 1949.

McKean, Roland N.: *Efficiency in Government Through Systems Analysis.* New York, Wiley, 1958.

McQuillen, Eugene: *The Law of Municipal Corporations,* 3rd Ed. Chicago, Callaghan, 1949.

MacDonald, Austin F.: *American City Government and Administration,* 4th Ed. New York, Crowell, 1947.

———: *American State Government and Administration,* 3rd Ed. New York, Crowell, 1948.

MacIver, Robert M.: *Democracy and the Economic Challenge.* New York, Knopf, 1952.

———: The Social Significance of Professional Ethics, THE ANNALS, Vol.101 (Mar., 1952).

———: *The Web of Government.* New York, Macmillan, 1947.

Magnusson, Leifur: *Government and Union—Employer Relations: an Analysis of Statutes and Administrative Regulations.* Chicago, Public Admin. Service, 1945.

Magruder, F. A.: *American Government.* Boston, Allyn & Bacon, 1946.

Mailey, Hugo V.: *The Italian Vote in Philadelphia, 1928-1946.* Ph.D. Dissertation, Philadelphia, Univ. of Penna., 1950.

Mair, Lucy: *Primitive Government.* Baltimore, Penguin, 1962.

March, James G., and Simin, Herbert A.: *Organizations.* New York, Wiley, 1958.

Martin, J. B.: Who Really Runs Chicago? THE SATURDAY EVENING POST (Nov. 19, and Nov, 26, 1955).

Merton, Robert K., Gray, Ailsa P., Hockey, Barbara, and Selvin, Hanan C.: *Reader in Bureaucracy.* Glencoe, Free Press, 1952.

Metcalf, Henry C., and Urwick, L.: *Dynamic Administration: the Collected Papers of Mary Parker Follett.* New York, Harper & Bros., 1947.

Meyerson, Martin, and Banfield, E. C.: *Politics, Planning and the Public Interest.* Glencoe, Free Press, 1955.

Millett, John D.: *Government and Public Administration.* New York, McGraw-Hill, 1959.

———: *Management in the Public Service.* New York, McGraw-Hill, 1954.

———: *The Process and Organization of Government Planning.* New York, Columbia Univ. Press, 1947.

———: Will Our Governmental System Get Bigger and More Pervasive? THE ANNALS (Aug., 1963), 1-14.

Milligan, M. M.: *Missouri Waltz: the Inside Story of the Pendergast Machine by the Man Who Smashed It.* New York, Scribner's, 1948.

Mire, Joseph: Collective Bargaining in the Public Service, *Papers and Proceedings of the 58th Annual Meeting of the American Economic Association,* 1946.

Morlan, Robert L.: *Capital, Courthouse and City Hall.* Boston, Houghton Mifflin Co., 1954.

Morstein, Marx Fritz: *The Bureau of the Budget: Its Evolution and Present Role,* reprinted from THE AMERICAN POLITICAL SCIENCE REVIEW, Vol.39, Nos.4 & 5 (Aug. & Oct., 1945).

———: *Elements of Public Administration,* 2nd Ed. New York, Prentice-Hall, 1959.

———: *The President and His Staff Services.* Chicago, Public Administration Service, 1947.

Mosher, Frederick C.: *Program Budgeting: Theory and Practice, with Particular Reference to the U.S. Department of the Army.* Chicago, Public Admin. Service, 1954.

Mosher, William E., Kingsley, J. Donald, and Stahl, O. Glenn: *Public Personnel Administration.* New York, Harper & Bros., 1950.

Mott, Rodney: *Home Rule for America's Cities.* Chicago, American Municipal Assoc., 1949.

MUNICIPAL FINANCE. Published quarterly by the Municipal Finance Officers' Assoc. of the United States and Canada, 1313 East 60th St., Chicago, Ill.

Municipal Finance Officers' Assoc.: Committee

on Public Employee Retirement Admin. *Retirement Plans for Public Employees.* Chicago, The Assoc., 1946.

Municipal Police Administration, 5th Ed. International Assoc. of City Managers, Chicago, 1961.

The Municipal Yearbook. Published annually, by the International City Managers' Association, 1313 East 60th St., Chicago, Ill.

Munro, William Bennett: *Personality in Politics.* New York, Macmillan, 1934.

Murphy, Michael J.: Sterocracy vs. Democracy, TPC, Vol.29, No.2 (Feb., 1962), 36.

Nash, Bradley D., and Lynde, Cornelius: *A Hook in Leviathan: A Critical Interpretation of the Hoover Commission Report.* New York, Macmillan, 1950.

National Civil Service League, Employee Organizations in Government, GG (Nov., 1960).

National Municipal League: *The Citizen Association: How to Organize and Run It.* New York, the League, 1953.

————: *The County Manager Plan.* New York, The League, 1950.

————: *Model County Charter.* New York, The League, 1956.

————: *Model State Constitution,* 5th Ed. New York, The League, 1948.

NATIONAL TAX JOURNAL. Published quarterly by the National Tax Association. Features information on municipal taxation.

Neustadt, Richard E.: *Presidential Power.* New York, Wiley, 1960.

NEWSLETTER. Published monthly by the American Society of Planning Officials.

New York State Coordination Commission: *Staff Report on Public Authorities.* A report prepared by the N.Y. State Coordinating Commission, Albany, Williams Press, 1956.

NEW YORK TIMES. Published daily, Reports important political and administrative developments throughout the country of general interest. New York.

Nigro, Felix: *Public Administration.* New York, Ronald, 1953.

———— (ed.): *Public Administration Readings and Documents.* New York, Rinehart, 1951.

————: *Public Personnel Administration.* New York, Holt, 1959.

Nutting, Charles B.: Legislative Implications of the Reapportionment Decision, ABAJ (June, 1962).

Odegard, Peter H., and Helms, E. Allen: *American Politics, a Study in Political Dynamics.* New York, Harper & Bros., 1947.

Owen, Wilfred: *The Metropolitan Transporta-*

tion Problem. Washington, Brookings Institution, 1957.

Pate, James E.: *Local Government and Administration.* New York, American, 1954.

Penniman, Howard R.: *Sait's American Parties and Elections,* 5th Ed. New York, Appleton, 1952.

Perkins, John A.: State Responsibility and Home Rule, *State Government* (Feb., 1949).

Petersen, Elmore, and Plowman, E. Grosvenor: *Business Organization and Management.* Homewood, Irwin, 1953.

Pfiffner, John M., and Presthus, Vance R.: *Public Administration,* 4th Ed. New York, Ronald, 1960.

Phillips, Jewell Cass: *Municipal Government and Administration in America.* New York, Macmillan, 1960.

President's Commission on National Goals: *Report of the . . . Commission . . .* and Chapters Submitted for the Consideration of the Commission, published together in *Goals for Americans.* New York, Columbia Univ. Press, 1960.

Prestus, Robert: *The Organizational Society.* New York, Knopf, 1962.

Price, Don K.: *Government and Science: Their Dynamic Relation in American Democracy.* New York, N.Y. Univ. Press, 1954.

Pritchett, C. Herman: *The American Constitutional System.* New York, McGraw-Hill, 1965.

Public Administration Clearing House: *Public Administration Organizations.* Chicago, 1954.

PUBLIC ADMINISTRATION. Published quarterly by the Institute of Public Administration, Haldane House, 76A New Cavendish St., London, W.1.

PUBLIC ADMINISTRATION REVIEW. Published quarterly by the American Society for Public Administration.

Public Administration Service: *The Government of Metropolitan Miami.* Chicago, PAS, 1954.

————: *Work Simplification: as Exemplified by the Work Simplification Program of the U.S. Bureau of the Budget.* Chicago, Public Admin. Service, 1945.

PUBLIC EMPLOYEE. Published monthly by the American Federation of State, County and Municipal Employees.

PUBLIC MANAGEMENT. Published monthly by International City Managers' Association, 1313 East 60th St., Chicago, Ill.

PUBLIC OPINION QUARTERLY. Published quarterly by the Princeton Univ. Press, Princeton, N.J.

Pusey, Merlo J.: *Big Government: Can We Control It?* New York, Harper, 1945.

Rankin, Robert S.: *The Government and Administration of North Carolina.* New York, Crowell, 1957.

RECREATION. Published monthly by the National Recreation Assoc.

Redding, W. M.: *Tom's Town: Kansas City and the Pendergast Legend.* Philadelphia, Lippincott, 1957.

Reichley, James: *The Art of Government: Reform and Organization Politics in Philadelphia.* New York, The Fund for the Republic, 1959.

Revue Internationale des Sciences Administratives. Published quarterly by the Institute International des Sciences Administratives, Residence Belliard, 205 rue Belliard, Bruxelles, Belgium.

Rhyne, Charles: *Municipal Law.* Washington, National Institute of Municipal Law Officers, 1957.

Rich, Bennett M.: *The Government and Administration of New Jersey.* New York, Crowell, 1957.

Roberts, Samual M.: The Management Aspects of Budgeting, *Municipal Finance.* Chicago, Municipal Finance Officers Assoc., 1949.

Robsen, W. A. (ed.): *Great Cities of the World.* New York, Macmillan, 1955.

Rossiter, Clinton: *The American Presidency.* New York, American Library of World Literature, 1956.

Rowat, Donald C. (ed.): *Basic Issues in Public Administration.* New York, Macmillan, 1961.

Rowland, Floyd H., and Harr, William H.: *Budgeting for Management Control.* New York, Harper & Bros., 1945.

Ruhl, Eleanor S.: *Public Relations for Government Employees: an Action Program.* Chicago, Civil Service Assembly, 1952.

Rutherford, Geddes W.: *Administrative Problems in a Metropolitan Area: the National Capital Region.* Chicago, Public Admin. Service, 1952.

Saye, Albert B., Pound, Merritt B., and Allums, John F.: *Principles of American Government.* Englewood Cliffs, Prentice-Hall, 1962.

Sayer, Wallace S., and Kaufman, Herbert: *Governing New York City.* New York, Russell Sage Foundation, 1960.

Seckler-Hudson, Catheryn: *Bibliography on Public Administration—Annotated.* Washington, American University Press, 1953.

Segrest, Earl C., and Misner, Arthur J.: *The Impact of Federal Grants-in-aid on California.* Berkeley, Bureau of Public Admin., Univ. of Calif., 1954.

Silva, Ruth C.: Apportionment in New York, FLR, Vol.30 (1962), 591.

Simon, Herbert A.: *Public Administration.* New York, Knopf, 1950.

Smith, George Albert, Jr., and Christensen, C. Roland: *Policy Formulation and Administration: a Case Book of Top-management Problems in Business.* Homewood, Irwin, 1955.

Smith, Harold D.: *The Management of Your Government.* New York, McGraw-Hill, 1955.

Smithies, Arthur: *The Budgetary Process in the United States.* New York, McGraw-Hill, 1955.

Snider, Clyde F.: *Local Government in Rural America.* New York, Appleton, 1957.

Snyder, Richard C., and Wilson, H. Hubert: *Roots of Political Behavior.* New York, American Book Co., 1949.

Spero, Sterling D.: *Government as Employer.* Brooklyn, Remsen Press, 1949.

Stahl, O. Glenn: The Network of Authority, PAR (Winter, 1960).

————: What A Bureaucrat Thinks About Executives, JSI (Dec., 1945).

STATE GOVERNMENT (Chicago, 1926). Published monthly by the Council of State Governments. Contains articles of general political and administrative interest.

Steffens, Lincoln: *Autobiography of Lincoln Steffens.* New York, Harcourt, Brace, 1960.

Stein, Harold: *Public Administration and Policy Development: a Case Book.* New York, Harcourt, Brace, 1952.

Steiner, George A.: *Government's Role in Economic Life.* New York, McGraw-Hill, 1953.

Strong, Donald S.: *Registration of Voters in Alabama.* University, Bureau of Public Admin., Univ. of Alabama, 1956.

Swarthout, John M., and Bartley, Ernest R.: *Principles and Problems of State and Local Government.* New York, Oxford Univ., 1958.

Sweeney, Stephan B., and Blairleds, George S.: *Metropolitan Analysis.* Philadelphia,, Univ. of Penn., Press, 1958.

Tableman, Betty: *Governmental Organization in Metropolitan Areas.* Ann Arbor, Univ. of Michigan Press, 1951.

THE TAX DIGEST. Published monthly by California Taxpayers Assoc., but with items of nationwide interest.

TAXES—THE TAX MAGAZINE. Published monthly by Commerce Clearing House. Reports on local developments.

Taylor, Telford: The Ethics of Public Office,

SATURDAY EVENING POST (Apr., 16, 1960).

Tead, Ordway: *Democratic Administration.* New York, Association, 1945.

Tennessee Valley Authority: *The Employee Relationship Policy.* Knoxville, 1945.

Terhune, George A.: *An Administrative Case Study of Performance Budgeting in the City of Los Angeles, California.* Chicago, Municipal Finance, 1954.

Torpey, William G.: *Public Personnel Management.* Princeton, Nostrand, 1952.

Trachsel, Herman H., and Wade, Ralph M.: *The Government and Administration of Wyoming.* New York, Crowell, 1953.

Truman, David B.: *The Governmental Process.* New York, Knopf, 1953.

Ulmer, Sidney (ed.): *Introductory Readings in Political Behavior. Chicago, Rand McNally,* 1961.

United Nations: *A Handbook of Public Administration.* Dept. of Economic and Social Affairs, New York, United Nations, 1961.

———: *Training in Public Administration.* Technical Assistance Admin. New York, United Nations, 1958.

U.S. Congress, Senate Committee on Labor and Public Welfare, Subcommittee on Ethical Standards: *Ethical Standards in Government.* 82nd Cong., 1st Sess., Washington, 1951.

U.S. Dept. of Commerce, Bureau of the Census: *Compendium of City Government Finances in 1958.* Washington, 1959.

UNITED STATES MUNICIPAL NEWS. Published monthly by U.S. Conference of Mayors.

University of Alabama Press: *New Horizons in Public Administration: a Symposium.* University, Univ. of Alabama Press, 1945.

Upson, Lent D.: *Letters on Public Administration.* Detroit, Citizens Research Council of Michigan, 1954.

Wagner, Paul (ed.): *Country Government Across the Nation.* Chapel Hill, Univ. of North Carolina Press, 1950.

Walby, H. O.: *The Patronage System in Oklahoma.* Norman, Univ. of Oklahoma Press, 1950.

Waldo, Dwight: *The Administrative State: a Study of the Political Theory of American Public Administration.* New York, Ronald, 1948.

———: *Ideas and Issues in Public Administration—a Book of Readings.* New York, McGraw-Hill, 1953.

———: *The Study of Public Administration.* Garden City, Doubleday, 1955.

Walker, Robert A.: *The Planning Function in Urban Government.* Chicago, Univ. of Chicago Press, 1950.

WALL STREET JOURNAL. Published daily, Chicago and New York. Frequent articles on municipal finance and other developments.

Wallace, Schuylor: *State Administrative Supervision over Cities in the United States.* New York, Columbia Univ. Press, 1958.

Warner, Richard: *The Principles of Public Administration.* London, Pitman, 1947.

Warner, W. Lloyd: The Careers of American Business and Government Executives: A Comparative Analysis, in George B. Strother (ed.): *Social Science Approaches to Business Behavior.* Homewood, Dorsey, 1962.

Webb, James E.: What Kinds of People Are Needed for an Adequate Government of the Future? THE ANNALS (Aug., 1963), 15-24.

Webster, Donald H.: *Urban Planning and Municipal Public Policy.* New York, Harper & Bros., 1958.

White, Leonard: *Introduction to the Study of Public Administration,* 4th Ed. New York, Macmillan, 1955.

———: Strikes in the Public Service, PPR (Jan., 1949).

White, Max R.: *Units of Local Government in Connecticut.* Storrs, Univ. of Conn., Institute of Public Service, 1953.

Wilson, O. W.: *Parker on Police.* Springfield, Thomas, 1956.

———: POLICE ADMINISTRATION, 2nd Ed. New York, McGraw-Hill, 1963.

Wingersky, Melvin F.: A Freeman and His Peers, JCLC&PS, Vol.46 (1955-56), 1-3.

Woodbury, Coleman (ed.): *The Future of Cities and Urban Redevelopment.* Chicago, Univ. of Chicago Press, 1953.

Woodrow Wilson Foundation: *United States Foreign Policy: Its Organization and Control.* New York, Columbia Univ. Press, 1952.

Woodson, C. W., Jr.: Mayor's Conference, TPC, Vol.30 (Aug., 1963), 18.

Wooten, Barbara: *Testament for Social Science.* New York, Norton, 1951.

Zink, Harold: *Government of Cities in the United States.* New York, Macmillan, 1948.

PUBLIC RELATIONS

Adlow, Elijah: *Policemen and the Public.* Boston, Rochfort, 1947.

Allen, Riley H.: Police, Politics and Public Interest, TPY, 1958.

Allman, James J.: Establishing a Police-Community Relations Office Within a Police Department, TPC, Vol.32, No.3 (Mar., 1965), 11-14.

——: Public Attitude Toward Police, TPC, Vol.30 (Jan., 1963), 8.

Altes, M.: What Is Your Congressman's Record, TPC, Vol.31 (Jan., 1964), 44.

Anderson, Clinton H.: Report of the Radio, Television and Motion Pictures Committee, TPY (1965).

Arm, Walter: Not Words, But Deeds, TPY (1962).

Ashenhust, Paul H.: Crashing the Barrier, POLICE, Vol.11, No.1 (Sept.-Oct., 1957), 39-43.

——: *Police and the People.* Springfield, Thomas, 1956.

——: Police Public Relations, POLICE, Vol.2, No.4 (Mar.-Apr., 1958), 7-12; Vol.3, No.1 (Sept.-Oct., 1958), 30-33; Vol.3, No.2 (Nov.-Dec., 1958), 50-54.

Baker, Helen Cody, and Routzahn, Mary Swain: *How to Interpret Social Welfare.* New York, Russell Sage Foundation, 1947.

Bantey, Bill: The Press and the Police, TPY (1962).

Baus, Herbert M.: *Publicity in Action.* New York, Harper, 1954.

Beasley, Wallace D., and Jonas, L. K.: The Eleventh Commandment, L&O, Vol.10, No.3 (Mar., 1962), 12.

Bernays, Edward L.: *Public Relations.* Norman, Oklahoma Press, 1952.

Bishop, L. K.: Building Cooperation Between the Citizen and the Policeman, THE CHIEFTAN, Vol.4 (Spring, 1957), 13-14.

Blackmore, John R.: Eliminating the PR Vacuum, TPY (1961).

——: The Law Enforcement Image: A Partnership With the Community, TPY (1964).

——: Public Relations as Related to the Youth of the Community, TPY (1965).

Blinick, M.: The Police Chief—Integrated or Insulated? TPC, Vol.31 (Jan., 1964), 36.

Blum, Richard H.: The Problems of Being a Police Officer, POLICE, Vol.5, No.2 (Nov.-Dec., 1960), 10-13.

Booth, Willis, D., Jr.: Public Relations as Related to Other Law Enforcement Agencies, TPY (1965).

Brandstatter, A. F.: New Frontiers for the Police, POLICE, Vol.7, No.2 (Nov.-Dec., 1962), 13-20.

Brashear, Ernest: *Municipal Public Relations Techniques.* Chicago, Int'l City Managers' Assoc., 1961.

Breckinridge, A. C.: Wanted: Uniform Law Enforcement, JCLC&PS, Vol.45 (1954-55), 170-75.

Brennan, James J.: Public Relations in Police Work with Delinquents, POLICE, Vol.9, No.4 (Mar.-Apr., 1965), 14-17.

Bright, Sallie E.: *Public Relations Programs— How to Plan Them.* New York, National Publicity Council for Health & Welfare, 1950.

Brostron, Curtis: The Role of the Community Relations Officer, TPY (1962).

Brown, Albert N.: Police—Community Relations, TPY (1963).

Brown, James B.: The See, Hear and Read Public Relations Program, L&O, Vol.10, No.5 (May, 1962), 63.

Brown, T. F.: Types of Assistance Available, TPC (Nov., 1964), 33.

Brown, William P.: The Police and Community Conflict, POLICE (May-June, 1964), 51-59.

Burgess, Ernest W., and Locke, Harvey J.: *The Family.* New York, American, 1945.

Busichio, Sal, Rev.: Power to Rule, L&O, Vol.11, No.1 (Jan., 1963).

Caldwell, A. B.: Needed Areas of Cooperation— Federal and Local, TPC, Vol.30 (Jan., 1963), 34.

Calhoun, Paul B.: How to Counteract an Unfavorable Public Image Which May Result from Racial Tension Situation, TPY (1964).

——: Public and Community Relations, TPY (1963).

California Dept. of Education; Bureau of Trade and Industrial Education: *Public Relations.* Sacramento, State Printing Office, 1949.

——: *Public Speaking.* Sacramento, State Printing Office, 1949.

Campbell, Lyle J.: Good Public Relations From Top to Bottom, TPY (1962).

Campbell, Robert A.: The Story of Kiddie Car Safety at the Illinois State Fair, POLICE, Vol.4, No.1 (Sept.-Oct., 1959), 72-74.

Canlis, Michael N.: Public Relations and Community Relations, TPY (1963).

Capp, William C.: "Big Story" vs. Caution, L&O, Vol.11, No.12 (Dec., 1963).

Carmack, William R.: Practical Communication Tools for Group Involvement in Police Community Programs, TPC, Vol.32, No.3 (Mar., 1965), 34-36.

Carp, Bernard: *Your Annual Meeting.* New York, National Publicity Council for Health & Welfare, 1955.

Castenholz, Fred E.: Local Government and Split Channels, TPY (1961).

Cawthorne, Dennis: Police Public Relations and

Summer Visitor, L&O, Vol.11, No.3 (Mar., 1963).

Chapman, Samuel G.: Press Periscope, POLICE, Vol.7, No.5 (May-June, 1963), 76-79; No.6 (July-Aug., 1963), 38-41; Vol.8, No.2 (Nov.-Dec., 1963), 68-70; No.3 (Jan.-Feb., 1964), 63-66; No.4 (Mar.-Apr., 1964), 66-68; No.6 (July-Aug., 1964), 56-59; Vol.9, No.2 (Nov.-Dec., 1964), 88-90.

Chicago Park District: *Police and Minority Groups.* Chicago, The District, 1958.

Civil Service Assembly: *Public Relations for Government Employees: an Action Program.* Chicago, The Assembly, 1952.

Civil Support for Professionalization, TPC, Vol.30 (Aug., 1963), 26.

Clift, Raymond E.: Police, Press and Public Relations, JCL&C, Vol.39, No.5 (Mar.-Apr., 1948-49), 667-81.

Code of Personal Commitment, TPC, Vol.31 (Feb., 1964), 46.

Coe, Rodney M., and Duke, Austin B.: Public Attitudes Toward the Police, POLICE, Vol.8, No.1 (Sept.-Oct., 1963), 73-76.

Collins, LeRoy: The Federal Community Relations Service, TPC, Vol.31 (Sept., 1964), 18.

Community Relations & Police Institute, TPC, Vol.31 (Apr., 1964), 47; (July, 1964), 47.

Connally, J. E.: Texas Citizens Honor Lawmen, POLICE, Vol.3, No.4 (Mar.-Apr., 1959), 23-26.

Cookson, Arthur G.: Police and the Public Mind, TPY (1962).

Coon, Thomas F.: The Friendly Cop, POLICE, Vol.7, No.3 (Jan.-Feb., 1963), 58-59.

————: How Are Your Public Relations? POLICE, Vol.5, No.4 (Mar.-Apr., 1961), 76-77.

————: The New Jersey Sheriff—Restoration of an Old Image, POLICE, Vol.7, No.4 (Mar.-Apr., 1963), 37-39.

————: Police Public Relations, TPC (Mar., 1961), 30.

Cormack, J.: Program to Build Public Relations and Public Morale, TPC, Vol.30 (Oct., 1963), 12.

Craven, Joseph D.: Law Enforcement and Public Opinion, JCLC&PS, Vol.49, No.4 (1958-59), 377.

Cutlip, Scott M., and Center, Allen H.: *Effective Public Relations.* New York, Prentice-Hall, 1952.

Davis, William J.: Manufacturers' Cooperative Efforts, TPY (1961).

Dearmont, Russell L.: Law Enforcement, The Community and Industry, TPY (1963).

Dodson, Dan W.: Human Understanding and Police—Community Relations, THE CHIEFTAN, Vol.4 (Spring, 1957), 25, 26-28.

Dolan, Marguerite M.: New Image for the Police Officer, L&O, Vol.12 (Apr., 1964).

Dunne, Joseph A., Msgr.: "Thank You, Officer," L&O, Vol.11, No.2 (Feb., 1963).

Dyment, Robert: Continuing Safety Program Is the Answer in Jamestown, N.Y., L&O, Vol.10, No.2 (Feb., 1962), 78.

Earle, Howard H.: More on Police Rapport with the Press and the Public, POLICE, Vol.7, No.4 (Mar.-Apr., 1963), 47-49.

————: The Supervisor and the Press, POLICE, Vol.6, No.3 (Jan.-Feb., 1962), 6-9.

Engle, Karl E.: Public Relations Program Aids Florida Chiefs Counteract Burglary, L&O, Vol.8, No.6 (1960).

Eno, David L.: Tips on Public Relations, TPC (Sept., 1961), 26.

Fagerstrom, Dorothy: A Police Department Holds Open House, L&O, Vol.8, No.10 (1960).

————: Public Understanding—A Challenge to the Imagination, L&O, Vol.11, No.3 (Mar., 1963).

Fairly, Kenneth W.: The Tale of the One-armed Trusty and "His" Hound Dog, POLICE, Vol.8, No.5 (May-June, 1964), 68-69.

Fanfare for a Public Safety Building, L&O, Vol.9 (July, 1961).

Feledick, Winifred Mertens: Personal Touch, L&O, Vol.11, No.5 (May, 1963).

Ferguson, John P.: Answers to Criticism, TPY (1963).

Fitzgerald, Stephen E.: *Communicating Ideas to the Public.* New York, Funk & Wagnalls, 1950.

Fleishman, Alfred: Community Relations—Public Relations: Some Differences and Some Similarities, TPC, Vol.32, No.3 (Mar., 1965), 36-37.

Flesh, Rudolph: *The Art of Plain Talk.* New York, Harper & Bros., 1946.

Ford, Russel W.: The Traffic Officer and the Public Relations Program, L&O, Vol.10, No.6 (June, 1962), 8.

Frankel, Hyman: Coordination of Community Agencies, TPY (1963).

Garrison, Homer, Jr.: Internal—External Police Public Relations, TPY (1964).

————: Police Public Relations, TPY (1961).

————: Public Relations as Related to the Laboring Element and Lower Economic Groups, TPY (1965).

Golden, Hal, and Hanson, Kitty: *Working with the Working Press.* Dobbs Ferry, Oceana, 1962.

Good Dog Neighbor, TPC, Vol.30 (Mar., 1963), 46.

Goodman, J. C.: Police-press Relations, POLICE, Vol.9, No.5 (May-June, 1965), 87.

Gourley, C. Douglas: *Public Relations and the Police.* Springfield, Thomas, 1953.

Griswold, Glenn, and Griswold, Denny: *Your Public Relations.* New York, Funk & Wagnalls, 1948.

Guide to Community Relations for Peace Officers. Sacramento, California Dept. of Justice, 1958.

Hall, Jerome: Police Law in a Democratic Society, ILJ, Vol.28 (Winter, 1953), 133-177.

Handlin, Oscar: Community Organization as a Solution to Police-Community Problems, TPC, Vol.32, No.3 (Mar., 1965), 16-22.

Harlow, Rex F.: *Social Science in Public Relations.* New York, Prentice-Hall, 1952.

Harral, Stewart: *Patterns of Publicity Copy.* Norman, Univ. of Oklahoma Press, 1950.

Hayes, Marshall: Printed Word Aids Community Relations, L&O, Vol.12 (Mar., 1964).

Headley, Walter E., Jr.: Courtesy in Public Relations, TPY (1961).

Higgins, Louis L.: Local, National and International Effort, TPY (1961).

Hobes, Charles W., Sr., Rev.: Take the Offensive, L&O, Vol.12 (Sept., 1964).

Holcomb, Richard L.: *The Police and the Public.* Springfield, Thomas, 1957.

Hollingsworth, Dan.: *Rocks in the Roadway: a Treatise on Police Public Relations.* Chicago, Stromberg-Allen, 1954.

Holsborg, Arthur M.: The Teachers of Safety Recognition Program in Yonkers, N.Y., L&O, Vol.10, No.3 (Mar., 1962), 62.

Howard, John P.: Integrating Public Relations Training for Police Officers, POLICE, Vol.7, No.1 (Sept.-Oct., 1962), 57-58.

How Does Your Department Rate in Courtesy, FBILEB (May, 1965), 8-12.

Humphreys, Ray: One Way of Doing It, L&O, Vol.7 (Aug., 1959).

Hunger, John, and Schten, Edward V.: Training the Public Administrator in Public Relations, TDJ (Jan., 1964), 37-40.

Independence Day Observation, TPC, Vol.30 (Jan., 1963), 64.

Isaacs, Norman E.: The Crime of Crime Reporting, C&D (Oct., 1961), 312-320.

Isaacs, Julius: Let Us Plan for People, JCLC&PS, Vol.43, No.2 (July-Aug., 1952), 144.

Jefferson, Walter L.: The Changing Image, TPY (1964).

Jenkins, Herbert T.: Developing Public Relations: Workshop, TPY (1962).

———: Report of the Public Relations Committee, TPY (1960); (1961).

———: Utilizing Community Resources, TPC, Vol.31 (Sept., 1964), 25.

Johanns, Chuck: Lite-a-bike, TPC, Vol.32, No.3 (Mar., 1965), 61.

Johnson, Bert W.: Do Our Public Relations Really Concern Us? POLICE, Vol.2, No.3 (Jan.-Feb., 1958), 32-33.

Kennedy, Stephen P.: Prosecutors and Police, JCLC&PS, Vol.49, No.4 (1958-59), 367.

———: Symposium: Teamwork in Law Enforcement, TPY (1960).

Kettmann, August G.: Police Community Relations: A Critical Problem, TPY (1964).

King, Everett H.: *The Officer Speaks in Public.* Springfield, Thomas, 1958.

Kinsey, Barry A.: The Police and Public Opinion, POLICE, Vol.4 No.2 (Nov.-Dec., 1959), 78-81.

Kooken, Don L.: *Ethics in Police Service.* Springfield, Thomas, 1957.

Knowles, D.: Civic Support for Professionalization, TPC, Vol.30 (Aug., 1963), 26.

LaCoe, Mickey: Maintain Public Interest, L&O, Vol.7 (Mar., 1959).

LaCouture, R. A.: Changing Public Attitude, TPY (1961).

———: The Police, the Press and Public Relations, POLICE, Vol.5, No.5 (May-June, 1961), 48-50; No.6 (July-Aug., 1961), 38-40; Vol.6, No.1 (Sept.-Oct., 1961), 44-46.

———: Public Relations as an Operating Concept, TPY (1962).

LaFata, Peter A.: Make the Public Speedometer Conscious, L&O, Vol.7 (June, 1959).

Lawder, Lee E.: Blueprint for an Open House, L&O, Vol.10, No.3 (Mar., 1962), 6.

———: Public Relations and Your Camera, L&O, Vol.9 (Apr., 1961).

LeGrande, J. L.: The Patrol Division: Proving Ground for Police-Community Relations, TPC, Vol.32, No. 1 (Jan., 1965), 40.

Lesly, Phillip (ed.): *Public Relations Handbook.* New York, Prentice-Hall, 1950.

Liu, Daniel S. C.: A Proper Concept in Police Service, POLICE, Vol.2, No.3 (Jan.-Feb., 1958), 29-31.

———: Toward Total Cooperation in Law Enforcement, TPY (1961).

Lohman, Joseph D.: *The Police and Minority Groups.* Chicago, Chicago Park District Police Training School, 1946.

Lumbard, J. Edward: The Citizen's Role in Law Enforcement, JCLC&PS, Vol.56, No.1 (Mar., 1965).

Lunden, Walter A.: The Police and the Public,

POLICE, Vol.9, No.5 (May-June, 1965), 24.

McCall, Frances: Cooperation—Keynote to Good Public Relations, L&O, Vol.11, No.4 (Apr., 1963).

McClung, Troy E.: Public Relations in Small Police Department, TPY (1963).

McKnight, Felix R.: Cooperation Between Chiefs and Editors, TPY (1957).

McMillen, Wayne: *Community Organization for Social Welfare*. Chicago, Univ. of Chicago Press, 1945.

MacCormick, Austin H.: The Community and the Corrective Process, FOCUS (May, 1948), 65-69.

Maglin, William H.: The Service Man and American Society, TPY (1957).

Make Friends with Your Telephone, *The Sacramentan*, Vol.22 (June, 1955), 24-25.

Minanovich, Clement S.: Programming for Citizen Participation in Police Action Programs, LE (Mar.-Apr., 1965), 31; TPC, Vol.32, No.3 (Mar.-1965), 27-31.

Mingle, George: Report of the Committee on Committee on Federal, State and Local Cooperation, TPY (1956).

Moore, C. E.: Making Police Week Work for You, TPC, Vol.30 (Mar.-1963), 14.

Morris, George F.: Open House—The Gateway to Improved Public Relations, POLICE, Vol.1, No.5 (May-June, 1957), 20-23.

Murphy, Glenn R.: Policies and Procedures for Action Programs, TPC, Vol.32, No.3 (Mar., 1965), 41-42.

Murphy, Michael J.: Improving the Law Enforcement Image, JCLC&PS, Vol.56, No.1 (Mar., 1965), 105-108.

Murray, Robert V.: Guideposts to Good Public Relations, TPY (1958).

O'Keefe, Jack: Responsibility to Community, TPC, Vol.29, No.5 (May, 1962), 12.

O'Neill, James F.: First Line of Defense, L&O, Vol.11, No.2 (Feb., 1963).

Orton, Dwayne: Human Relations in Technical Times, TPY (1956).

Oswald, Russell G.: Parole's Cooperative Role in Law Enforcement, TPY (1964).

Pantaleoni, Mrs. G., Jr.: Policeman a Child's Best Friend, TPC, Vol.31 (Sept., 1964), 45.

Parker, W. H.: The Police Role in Community Relations, JCLC&PS, Vol.47, No.3 (Sept.-Oct., 1956), 368.

Pay for Crime Victims: Second Nation Adopts Plan, USN&WR, No.12 (Apr. 6, 1964).

Peck, Leo G.: Developing a Precinct or District Committee, TPC, Vol.32, No.3 (Mar., 1965), 24-27.

Peper, John P.: *Public Relations for the Law Enforcement Officer*. Sacramento, Bureau of Ind. Education, Calif. State Dept. of Education, 1963.

Petry, A. G.: So Who Needs a Cop? TPC, Vol.31 (Apr., 1964), 8.

Piggins, Edward S.: Report of the Public Relations Committee, TPY (1959).

Pimlott, J. A. R.: *Public Relations in American Democracy*. Princeton, Princeton Univ. Press, 1951.

Pitchess, Peter J.: "Selling" Law Enforcement, TPY (1962).

Plackard, Dwight H., and Blackman, Clifton: *Blueprint for Public Relations*. New York, McGraw-Hill, 1947.

Police Chief Talks of Police Brutality, USN&WR (Aug. 10, 1964), 33.

Pritchett, Laurie: How to Counteract the Unfavorable Public Image Which May Result from Racial Tension Situation, TPY (1964).

————: Public Relations as Related to News Media, TPY (1965).

PUBLIC RELATIONS JOURNAL. Published monthly by the Public Relations Society of America, 2 West 46th St., New York, N.Y.

Puncke, Martin M.: Role of Police in Community, TPC (Feb., 1961), 28.

Quigley, Martin: Some Salient Points on Public Relations, TPY (1963).

Radelet, Louis A.: The Development of Police Leadership in Community Relations, TPY (1964).

————: Police & Community Relations on the National Scene, TPC, Vol.31 (Sept., 1964), 40.

————: Police Community Programs: Nature and Purpose, TPC, Vol.32, No.3 (Mar., 1965), 38-40.

Robbins, David W.: Importance of Good Public Relations, TPY (1962).

Roden, John A.: Community Understanding, L&O, Vol.11, No.9 (Sept., 1963).

Rose, Jesse T.: The Role of the Small Department, TPY (1962).

Ross, Victor: Win Public Support with Audio-visual Techniques, L&O, Vol.9 (Aug., 1961).

Ruby, D. W.: Civic Organization Can Help Police, TPC, Vol.31 (July, 1964), 18.

Ruhl, Eleanor S.: *Public Relations for Government Employees: an Action Program*. Personnel Report No.524. Chicago, Public Personnel Assoc., 1952.

Sagalyn, Arnold: Role of Local Police, TPY (1963).

Scafers, Ted: Public Relations, TPY (1963).

Schoephoester, Lloyd: Public Relations Via Radio Aids in Accident Prevention, L&O, Vol.12 (July, 1964).

Schudlich, Gerald, Rev.: "Power of the Law," L&O, Vol.11, No.9 (Sept., 1963).

Shimota, Kenneth L.: A Study of Police Services & Children in a Rural Wisconsin County, JCLC&PS, Vol.56, No.2 (June, 1965), 275.

Simon, Clifford E., Jr.: The Suppression of Radio and Newspaper Comment on Pending Criminal Trials, JCL&C, Vol.40, No.1 (May-June, 1949), 50.

Skousen, Cleon W.: The Police and the Press, L&O, Vol.10, No.3 (Mar., 1962), 18.

———: What About the Chief's Son? L&O, Vol.12 (Dec., 1964).

Slayton, J. E.: City vs. Dogs, TPC, Vol.30 (Sept., 1963), 12.

Smyth, Lou: Report of the Public Relations Committee, TPY (1956); (1957).

Stetler, Roy H., Jr.: Show Perfect Courtesy, L&O, Vol.11, No.3 (Mar., 1963).

Struthers, James R., Rev.: Consider the Police Officer, L&O, Vol.8, No.12 (1960).

Sullivan, Daniel V.: Cooperation Between District Attorney and Police, TPY (1960).

Tamm, Quinn: The Invisible Wall, TPC, Vol.32, No.3 (Mar., 1965), 6.

———: Police and the Community: Relationship and Responsibilities, TPC, Vol.32, No.3 (Mar., 1965), 10.

Toothman, Edward M.: Advertising Safety, L&O, Vol.10, No.3 (Mar., 1962), 67.

To Protect & To Serve, TPC, Vol.31 (Apr., 1964), 50.

VanDyck, L. B.: Name Tags—An Aid in Public Relations, L&O, Vol.12 (Mar., 1964).

Vannatter, Dale O.: Police Training and Your Public Relations, L&O, Vol.10, No.8 (Aug., 1962), 55.

Vedder, Clyde B., and Keller, Oliver J., Jr.: The Police and Middle Class Conflicts, POLICE, Vol.9, No.5 (May-June, 1965), 6.

Wallace, Anthony E.: Public Relations and the Police Officer, L&O, Vol.12 (Mar., 1964).

Watson, N. A.: Police and Group Behavior, TPC, Vol.30 (Nov., 1963), 8.

———: Probing Police Policy, TPY (1964).

Westley, William A.: Violence and the Police, AJS (July, 1953), 34-41.

Wheeler, Pan Dodd: Police Public Relations— The Public of the Police Unit, POLICE, Vol.1, No.4 (Mar.-Apr., 1957), 7-11; Vol.2, No.3 (Jan.-Feb., 1958), 24-28.

Williams, Gerald O.: Crime News and Its Relation to Police Press Policies, POLICE, Vol.8, No.4 (Mar.-Apr., 1964), 10-16; No.5 (May-June, 1964), 60-67; No.6 (July-Aug., 1964), 63-69; Vol.9, No.1 (Sept.-Oct., 1964), 57-65.

Wilson, O. W. (ed.): *Parker on Police.* Springfield, Thomas, 1956.

Wirths, Claudine Givson: The Development of Attitudes Toward Law Enforcement, POLICE, Vol.3, No.2 (Nov.-Dec., 1958), 50-52.

Woodson, Charles W., Jr.: Report of the Committee on Federal State and Local Cooperation, TPY (1957); (1958).

Wright, Handley, and Byron, Christian H.: *Public Relations in Management.* New York, McGraw-Hill, 1949.

Wynn, Ed R.: Building Interprofessional Cooperation Between Police and Community Agencies, POLICE, Vol.9, No.5 (May-June, 1965), 15.

Your Public Relations. Washington, American Vocational Assoc., Committee and Research & Publications, 1954.

Zeichner, Irving B.: The People and the Police, L&O, Vol.7 (Sept., 1959).

———: Police Image, L&O, Vol.11, No.8 (Aug., 1963).

Zumbrun, Alvin J. T.: Problems & Rewards in Organizing and Directing a Citizen's Committee, POLICE, Vol.6, No.5 (May-June, 1962), 39-41.

VICE

The Abuse of Barbiturates in the United Kingdom, United Nations, BN, Vol.14, No.2 (Apr.-June, 1962), 19-38.

Adams, James Truslow: *The Epic of America.* Boston, Little, Brown.

Adams, T. F.: Narcotics. Santa Ana Police Dept. Training Bulletin, Santa Ana.

Adler, Polly: *A House Is Not a Home.* New York, Popular, 1955.

Agoston, Tibor: Some Psychological Aspects of Prostitution, IJP, Vol.26 (1945), 62-67.

Aikman, Duncan (ed.): *Taming of the Frontier.* New York, Minton, Balch, 1947.

Alden, Robert: "Beatnik" Police Seize 96 in Narcotic Raid, THE NEW YORK TIMES (Nov. 9, 1959).

Aldrich, Ann (ed.): *Carol in a Thousand Cities.* Greenwich, Fawcett, 1960.

Allen, Edward J.: *Merchants of Menace.* Springfield, Thomas, 1962.

Allen, Forrest: *City Gamblers Join Nevada Ring.* CLEVELAND PRESS (Feb., 11, 1950).

Allen, Robert S. (ed.): *Our Fair City.* New York, Vanguard, 1947.

————: *Our Sovereign State.* New York, Vanguard, 1949.

Allsop, Kenneth: *The Bootleggers and Their Era.* New York, Doubleday, 1961.

Altrocchi, Julia Cooley: *The Spectacular San Franciscans.* New York, Dutton, 1949.

American Academy of Political and Social Science: Gambling, THE ANNALS, Vol.269 (May, 1950), 1-149.

American Bar Association and the American Medical Association on Narcotics Drugs: *Drug Addiction: Crime or Disease.* Interim and Final Reports of Joint Committee of American Bar Assoc., and American Medical Assoc., on Narcotic Drugs. Bloomington: Indiana Univ. Press, 1961.

————: Interim Report of the Joint Committee on Narcotic Drugs: Comments on Narcotic Drugs, Washington, U.S. Treasury Dept., Bureau of Narcotics.

American Medical Association, Council on Mental Health: Report on Narcotic Addiction, JAMA, Vol.165 (Nov. 30, 1957), 1707-1713; (Dec. 7, 1957), 1834-1841; (Dec., 14, 1957), 1968-1974.

American Racing Manual, The: New York, Triangle Publ., 1949.

Anonymous: *The Laws of the Town of San Francisco, 1847.* San Marino, Huntington Library, 1947.

Ansley, Norman: International Efforts to Control Narcotics, JCLC&PS, Vol.50, No.2 (1959-60), 105.

Anslinger, H. J.: British Narcotic System, JAMA (Oct. 23, 1954).

————: Drug Addiction, ENCYCLOPAEDIA BRITANNICA, 14th Ed., Vol.7, 679.

————, & **Oursler, Will:** *The Murderers.* New York, Farrar, Straus, 1961.

————, & **Tompkins, W. F.:** *The Traffic in Narcotics.* New York, Funk & Wagnalls, 1953.

Application of Federal Gambling Tax Law, DPLR, Vol.8 (Summer, 1959), 362-68.

Audett, Blackie: *Rap Sheet.* New York, Slone, 1954.

Ausubel, D. P.: *Drug Addiction: Physiological, Psychological and Sociological Aspects.* New York, Random, 1958.

————: *Controversial Issues in the Management of Drug Addiction: Legalization, Ambulatory Treatment, and the British System.*

Papers read at the Convention of the American Psychological Assoc., Sept. 4, 1959.

Avalos, Jibaja Carols: Consultative Group on Coca Leaf Problems, United Nations, BN, Vol.16, No.3 (July-Sept., 1964), 25-37.

Bachelder, W. K.: The Suppression of Bookie Gambling by a Denial of Telephone and Telegraph Facilities, JCLC&PS, Vol.40, No.2 (July-Aug., 1959), 176.

Ball, John C.: Two Patterns of Narcotic Drug Addiction in the United States, JCLC&PS, Vol.56, No.2 (June, 1965), 203-11.

Barona, Juan: Some Aspects of Narcotics Control in Mexico, United Nations, BN, Vol.16, No.3 (July-Sept., 1964), 1-5.

Battergay, R.: Comparative Investigations of the Genesis of Alcoholism and Drug Addiction, United Nations, BN, Vol.13, No.2 (Apr.-June, 1961), 7-17.

Bazzell, Kenneth: *Drug Addiction in the Medical Profession,* Los Angeles, L.A. State College, 1960.

Bean, Walton: *Boss Ruef's San Francisco.* Berkeley, Univ. of Calif. Press, 1952.

Becker, Howard S.: *Outsiders: Studies in the Sociology of Deviance.* New York, Free Press, 1963.

Beebe, Lucius, and Clegg, Charles: *The American West.* New York, Dutton, 1955.

————, & ————: *Legends of the Comstock Lode.* Stanford, Stanford Univ. Press, 1956.

Bellizzi, John J.: The Narcotics Addict: A Reappraisal, RD:STJAM, Vol.11, No.1 (Winter, 1962-63), 14-25.

Benham, W. Gurney: *Playing Cards.* London, Spring Books.

Benjamin, Harry, and Masters, R. E. L.: *A Definitive Report on the Prostitute in Contemporary Society and an Analysis of the Causes and Effects of the Suppression of Prostitution.* New York, Julian, 1964.

Berger, Herbert: The Richmond County Medical Society's Plan for the Control of Narcotic Addiction, NYSJM, Vol.56 (Mar. 15, 1956), 888-94.

Bergler, Edmund: *The Psychology of Gambling.* New York, Hill & Wang, 1957.

Berrey, Lester V., and Van Den Bark, Melvin: The American Thesaurus of Slang, NARCOTICS.

Bertschinger, J. P., Weiss, Gnadinger, and Durrer, A.: Narcotics Control in Switzerland. United Nations, BN, Vol.16, No.2 (Apr.-June, 1964), 1-16.

Bilek, Arthur J., and Gonz, Olon S.: The B-girl Problem—a Proposed Ordinance, JCLC&PS, Vol.56, No.1 (Mar., 1965), 39-44.

Blanch, Lesley (ed.): *The Game of Hearts: Harriette Wilson's Memoirs.* New York, Simon & Schuster, 1955.

Blesh, Rudi, and Janis, Harriet: *They All Played Ragtime.* New York, Knopf, 1950.

Bloch, Herbert A.: The Dilemma of American Gambling, JCLC&PS, Vol.50, No.2 (1959-60), 162.

——: The Sociology of Gambling, AJS, Vol.57 (Nov., 1951), 215-221.

Blomquist, Edward: Operations Narcotics, MT, Vol.85 (Mar., 1957), 349-353.

Bloom, Sol: *The Autobiography of Sol Bloom.* New York, Putnam's, 1948.

Bobbitt, Joseph M.: The Drug Addiction Problem, NYSJM, Vol.14 (May, 1953), 538-39.

Bouquet, J.: Bulletin on Narcotics, NARCOTICS, Vol.3 (Jan., 1951), 22.

Bromberg, Walter, and Rogers, Terry C.: Marihuana and Aggressive Crime, AJPSY, Vol.102, No.6 (May, 1946), 825-27.

Brown, Edmund G.: Letter to National Association of Attorney Generals (by Deputy Attorney General Raymond M. Momboisse), Sept., 1958.

Brown, Ted: Oakland Police Dept., BNSCP (Dec., 1958).

——: Peyote: Narcotic or Not? POLICE, Vol.6, No.1 (Sept.-Oct., 1961), 6-10.

——: Three Years of Nalline, POLICE, Vol.5, No.3 (Mar.-Apr., 1961), 49-52; Vol.5, No.5 (May-June, 1961), 6-10.

Brown, Thorvald T.: *The Enigma of Drug Addiction.* Springfield, Thomas, 1963.

Buck, Fred S.: *Horse Racing Betting.* New York, Greenberg, 1946.

Buckley, Thomas: State Giving Narcotics to Addicts in Test, THE NEW YORK TIMES (Mar. 9, 1964), 1.

Bundschu, Barbara: *UPI News Story.* Dateline, New York, 1959.

Burnett, Stan, and Seeger, Alan: *Prostitution Around the World.* Derby, Monarch, 1963.

Bushnell, Robert T.: *Public Document Number 12.* A report prepared by the Attorney General, Mass., Jan. 10, 1945.

Cahen, Herb: *Only in San Francisco.* Garden City, Doubleday, 1960.

Cahen, Raymond: The Pharmacology of Pholcodine, United Nations, BN, Vol.13, No.2 (Apr.-June, 1961), 19-36.

California Citizen's Advisory Committee to the Attorney General on Crime Prevention: *Narcotic Addiction Report to Attorney General Edmond G. Brown.* California, Mar. 26, 1954. Sacramento, State Printing Office, 1954.

California Department of Education, Bureau of Trade and Industrial Education: *Investigation of Prostitution.* Sacramento, State Printing Office, 1949.

——: *Narcotic Investigation and Narcotic Enforcement.* Sacramento, State Printing Office, 1949.

California Special Study Commission on Narcotics: *Final Report.* Sacramento, State Printing Office, June, 1961.

——: *Interim Report.* Los Angeles, Dec. 9, 1960.

California State Board of Corrections: *Narcotics in California: Usage, Trends and Recommendations for Controls.* Feb. 19, 1959, Sacramento, State Printing Office, 1959.

——: *California Narcotics Addict Control and Rehabilitation Program.* Sacramento, State Printing Office, 1961.

California State Department of Justice, Division of Criminal Statistics: *Narcotics Arrest in California. July 1, 1959-June 30, 1960.* Report prepared by the Dept. of Justice. Sacramento, State Printing Office, Dec. 5, 1960.

——: *Summary Narcotic Statistics for California: 1954-1959.* Report prepared by Dept. of Justice, State of Calif. Sacramento, State Printing Office, Feb. 10, 1961.

California State Dept. of Public Health: *California Pure Drugs Act.* Sacramento, State Printing Office, 1959.

——: *Recommended Procedure for the Nalorphine Test—a Guide to Physicians.* Sacramento, State Printing Office, 1958.

California State Assembly Interim Committee Reports: *Reports of the Subcommittee on Narcotics and Dangerous Drugs.* Sacramento, State Printing Office, Mar., 1959.

California State Narcotic Act, 1959. Sacramento, Calif. State Printing Office, 6260, 1959.

California State Report of the Senate Interim Committee on Narcotics, June 1959. Sacramento, State Printing Office, 1959.

Call, Harvey: *The Sun.* New York, 1949.

Cannabis Problem, The: A Note on the Problem and the History of International Action, United Nations, BN, Vol.14, No.4 (Oct.-Dec., 1962), 27-32.

Canton, Donald J.: The Criminal Law and the Narcotics Problem, JCLC&PS, Vol.51 (Jan.-Feb., 1961), 516-519. A good survey of state laws.

Cantor, Donald J.: The Criminal Law and the Narcotics Problem, JCLC&PS, Vol.51, No.5 (Mar.-Apr., 1960-61), 512.

Caputo, Rudolph R.: Narcotics—Legalization or Enforcement, L&O, Vol.8, No.3 (1960).

Carlisle, Norman and Madelyn: The Big Slot-Machine Swindle, COLLIER'S (Feb. 19, 1949).

Chapman, K. W.: Drug Addiction: The General Problem, FP (Sept., 1956).

————: Management and Treatment of Drug Addiction, JCD, Vol.9 (Mar., 1959), 315-26.

Chein, Isidor, *et al.*: *The Road to H: Narcotics, Delinquency and Social Policy.* New York, Basic, 1964.

Chicago Police Department, Detective Division, Narcotic Section: *A Special Report in Summation of Narcotics Problem to Be Used with the Annual Report of the Narcotics Section for the Year 1959.* Unpublished memo to the Superintendent of Police, Apr. 15, 1960.

Ciliberti, Benjamin J., Shroff, Phyllis, and Eddy, Nathan B.: Pre-anaesthetic Medication, Phenazocine and Levophenacylmorphan Compared with Morphine, Pethidine and a Placebo, United Nations, BN, Vol.16, No.2 (Apr.-June, 1964), 41-51.

Clappe, Louis A. K. S.: *The Shirley Letters from the California Mines in 1851-52.* New York, Knopf, 1949.

Clark, Alfred E.: Erickson's Records of Gambling Bare Underworld Links, THE NEW YORK TIMES (May 18, 1950).

Clausen, John: Social and Psychological Factors in Narcotics Addiction: L&CP, Vol.22 (Winter, 1957), 34-51.

Cohane, Tim: The Gambler's Fix Menaces Sports, LOOK (Apr. 20, 1947).

Comment: Narcotics Regulation, YLJ, Vol.62 (Apr., 1953), 751-87.

Conrad, Edwin C.: The Admissibility of the Nalline Test as Evidence of the Presence of Narcotics, JCLC&PS, Vol.50, No.2 (July-Aug., 1959), 187.

Control and Treatment of Drug Addicts in Israel, United Nations, BN, Vol.14, No.2 (Apr.-June, 1962), 11-18.

Cookle, J. Frank, and Hederman, A. E., Jr.: California District Attorney's Office, Alameda County, *The Nalline Test and Its Use in the City of Oakland.* 1958.

Coon, Thomas F.: Gambling Investigations, PO-LICE, Vol.6, No.4 (May-June, 1962), 16-17.

————: Whither Goest Gambling? POLICE, Vol.9, No.5 (May-June, 1965), 36.

Coons, John E.: The Federal Gambling Tax and the Constitution, JCLC&PS, Vol.43, No.5 (Jan.-Feb., 1953), 637.

Cowdry, E. V., Jr., and Gottschalk, L. A.: The Language of the Narcotic Addict, NAR-COTICS (1948).

Creighton, Walter R.: *Narcotic Investigation and Narcotic Law Enforcement.* Sacramento, Calif. Peace Officers Training Bulletin, No.33.

————: *Narcotics: Their Legitimate and Illicit Use.* 1955.

Cross, John C., and Harney, Malachi: *The Informer in Law Enforcement.* Springfield, Thomas, 1959.

Crowley, William F.: A New Weapon Against Confidence Games, JCLC&PS, Vol.50, No.3 (Sept.-Oct., 1959), 233.

Daley, Arthur: Menace to All Sports—The Fix, NEW YORK TIMES MAGAZINE (Jan. 5, 1947).

Davis, Rex D.: The Traffic in Illicit Liquor, POLICE, Vol.8, No.4 (Mar.-Apr.), 6-9.

Day, John I.: Horse Racing and the Pari-Mutuel, THE ANNALS, Vol.269 (May, 1950), 55-61.

DeQuille, Dan: *The Big Bonanza.* New York, Knopf, 1947.

Deutsch, Albert: *What We Can Do About the Drug Menace,* 3rd Ed. New York, Public Affairs Commission, 1958.

Devereux, Edward: *Gambling and the Social Structure.* Ph.D. Dissertation, Cambridge, Harvard Univ., 1950.

Dillon, Richard H.: *The Hatchetman.* New York, Coward-McCann, 1962.

————: *Shanghaiing Days.* New York, Coward-McCann, 1961.

Dingwall, Eric John: *The American Woman: An Historical Study.* New York, Rinehart, 1957.

Diskind, Meyer H., Hallinan, Robert F., and Stanton, John M.: *An Experiment in the Supervision of Paroled Offenders Addicted to Narcotic Drugs.* Final Report of the Special Project, N.Y. State Division of Parole, New York, 1960.

    Part 1. Specialized Supervision of Parolees Having a History of Narcotic Addiction by Meyer H. Diskind and Robert F. Hallinan.

    Part 2. An Empirical Study of the Results of the Special Narcotic Project, by John M. Stanton.

Dobie, Charles Caldwell: *San Francisco's Chinatown.* New York, Appleton, 1936.

Dobro, Murray S., and Kusafuka, Satoru: The Application of Paper Chromatography to the Analysis of Narcotics, JCL&C, Vol.43, No.2 (July-Aug., 1953), 247-57.

Drake, St. Clair, and Cayton, Horce R.: *Black Metropolis.* New York, Harcourt, Brace, 1945.

Drug Identification: A Problem and a Solution, Identification Laboratory, Smith Kline & French Lab., 1500 Spring Garden St., Philadelphia 1, Penn. (A Chart in color, with descriptions for police officers showing the most common amphetamines and barbiturates.)

The Drug Takers. New York, Times, Inc., 1965.

Drzazga, John: Bennies + Gasoline = Death, POLICE, Vol.6, No.4 (Mar.-Apr., 1962), 66-68.

———: Gambling and the Law, JCLC&PS, Vol.42, No.4 (Nov.-Dec., 1951-52), 543; Vol.43, No.1 (May-June, 1952), 114 (Slot machines); No.3 (Sept.-Oct., 1952), 405 (Dice); No.5 (Jan.-Feb., 1953), 695 (Cards); Vol.44, No.5 (Jan.-Feb., 1954), (Policy).

———: A Lottery Loophole, L&O, Vol.9, No.6 (June, 1961).

———: Recent Additions to the Foreign Lottery Family, POLICE, Vol.1, No.6 (July-Aug., 1957), 51-53.

———: *Wheels of Fortune.* Springfield, Thomas, 1963.

Egen, Frederick W.: *A Handbook of Vice and Gambling Investigation.* New York, Arco, 1952.

———: *Plainclothesman: A Handbook of Vice and Gambling Investigation.* New York, Arco, 1959.

Ehardt, H.: Drug Addiction in the Medical and Allied Professions in Germany, United Nations, BN, Vol.11 (Jan.-Mar., 1959), 18-25.

Eighteenth Session of the Commission on Narcotic Drugs and Thirty-Sixth Session of the Economic and Social Council, United Nations, BN, Vol.15, No. 3-4 (July-Dec., 1963), 39-42.

Eldridge, William Butler: *Narcotics and the Law: A Critique of the American Experiment in Narcotic Drug Control.* New York, N.Y. Univ. Press, 1962.

Encyclopaedia Britannica: *The Opium.* New York, 1952.

Estimated World Requirements of Narcotics Drugs in 1961, United Nations, BN, Vol.13, No.2 (Apr.-June, 1961), 42-43.

Estimated World Requirements of Narcotic Drugs in 1962, United Nations, BN, Vol.14, No.1 (Jan.-Mar., 1962), 47-48.

Ezell, John: *Fortune's Merry Wheel: the Lottery in America.* Cambridge, Harvard Univ. Press, 1960.

Federal Bureau of Narcotics, Treasury Department: *Graphic Results of Mandatory Penalties Against Peddlers.* Washington, U.S. Treasury Dept., 1958.

Fiddle, Seymour: The Addict Culture and Movement Into and Out of Hospitals as reprinted in U.S. Senate, Committee on the Judiciary, Subcommittee to Investigate Juvenile Delinquency, Washington, D.C.

Finestone, Harold: Narcotics and Criminality, L&CP, Vol.22 (Winter, 1957), 69-85.

Fisher, Sethard: The Rehabilitative Effectiveness of a Community Correctional Residence for Narcotics Users, JCLC&PS, Vol.56, No.2 (June, 1965), 190-96.

Frank, Stanley: Basketball's Big Wheel, SATURDAY EVENING POST (Jan. 15, 1949).

Fraser, H. F., Jones, B. E., Rosenberg, D. E., and Thompson, A. K.: Effect of a Cycle of Addiction to Intravenous Heroin on Certain Physiological Measurements, United Nations, BN, Vol.16, No.3 (July-Sept., 1964), 17-23.

———, **VanHorn, G. D., and Harris, Isbell:** Studies on N-Allylnormorphine in Man: Antagonism to Morphine and Heroin and Effects of Mixtures of N-Allylnormorphine and Morphine. AJMS, Vol.231, No.1 (Jan. 1956).

Freedman, Alfred M.: Treatment of Drug Addicts in a Community General Hospital, CP, Vol.4 (June, 1963), 199.

Fry, Monroe: *Sex Vice and Business.* New York, Ballantine, 1959. Gambling, THE ANNALS, Vol.269 (May, 1950).

Gasque, C. Aubrey: Senate Committee on the Judiciary Rejects Plan for Legal Distribution of Narcotics to Drug Addicts, POLICE, Vol.2, No.5 (May-June, 1958), 26-28.

Geiss, Gilbert: Narcotic Treatment Programs in California. Paper presented at Conference sponsored by Mass. Health Research Institute and U.S. Public Health Service, Chatham, Mass., Sept., 1963.

Gentry, Curt: *The Madams of San Francisco.* New York, Signet, 1964.

Giarrusso, Joseph I.: Narcotic Addiction Among Juveniles, TPY (1963).

Gilbert, Rodney: Why Dope Clinics Won't Work, AMERICAN MERCURY (May, 1957).

Goldberger, Isodore Harry, and Hallock, Grace T.: *Understanding Health.* Boston, Ginn, 1955.

Granier-Doyeux, Marcel: Some Sociological Aspects of the Problem of Cocainism, United Nations, BN, Vol.14, No.4 (Oct.-Dec., 1962), 1-16.

Greenwald, Harold: *The Call Girl.* New York, Ballantine, 1958.

———: Psychoanalysis of the Prostitute,

JCLC&PS, Vol.53, No.2 (June-Aug., 1962), 240.

———, & Krich, Aron (eds.): *The Prostitute in Literature*. New York, Ballantine, 1960.

Grennan, Arthur M.: The Policeman's Viewpoint in Wm. C. Bier (ed.) PROBLEMS IN ADDICTION. New York, Fordham Univ. Press, 1962.

Grlic, Ljubisa: A Comparative Study on Some Chemical and Biological Characteristics of Various Samples of Cannabis Resin, United Nations, BN, Vol.14, No.3 (July-Sept., 1962), 37-46.

———: A Simple and Rapid Method for Distinguishing Opium of Mexican Orgin from Other Types of Opium, JCLC&PS, Vol.52, No.2 (July-Aug., 1961), 229.

Gundaku, G.: Rotarian Campaign for Ethical Standards, THE ANNALS, Vol.101 (Mar., 1952).

Haenni, M., and Feldmann, H.: Features of Drug Addiction in Geneva, United Nations, BN, Vol.16, No.3 (July-Sept., 1964), 7-16.

Hall, William A., and McFarland, Robert L.: A Survey of One Hundred Suspected Drug Addicts, JCL&C, Vol.44, No.3 (Sept.-Oct., 1953), 308-319.

Harney, Malachi L.: Current Provisions and Practices in the United States of America Relating to the Commitment of Opiate Addicts, United Nations, BN, Vol.14, No.3 (July-Sept., 1962), 11-23.

———, & Cross, John C.: *The Informer in Law Enforcement*. Springfield, Thomas, 1959.

———: The "New Look" at Narcotics Is Just the Same Old Sack, POLICE, Vol.3, No.4 Mar.-Apr., 1959), 28-30; No.5 (May-June, 1959), 31-34.

———: Trial and Failure of the Ambulatory Treatment of (Opiate) Drug Addiction in the United States, United Nations, BN, Vol.16, No.2 (Apr.-June, 1964), 29-40.

———, & Cross, J. C.: *The Narcotic Officer's Notebook*. Springfield, Thomas, 1961.

Harris, Sara: *Nobody Cries for Me*. New York, Signet, 1959.

———: They Sell Sex. Greenwich, Fawcett, 1960.

Hederman, Albert E., Jr., and Coakley, J. Frank: *The Nalline Test and Its Use in the City of Oakland*. Oakland Police Dept., 1958.

Hesse, Erich: *Narcotics and Drug Addiction*. New York, Philosophical, 1946.

Higgins, Lois L.: The Public and Liquor Law Enforcement, L&O, Vol.12 (Apr., 1964).

Hoch, P. H., and Zubin, J. (eds.): *Problems of Addiction and Habituation*. New York, Grune & Stratton, 1958.

Hong Kong Government: *The Problem of Narcotic Drugs in Hong Kong*. Hong Kong, The Government Press, 1959.

Horan, James D.: *Desperate Women*. New York, Putnam's, 1952.

Howe, Hubert S.: A Physician's Blueprint for the Management and Prevention of Narcotic Addiction, NYSJM, Vol.55 (Feb.1, 1955), 341-49.

———: *Narcotics and Youth*. West Orange, Brook Foundation, 1953.

Hughes, Helen M. (ed.): *The Fantastic Lodge: the Autobiography of a Girl Drug Addict*. Boston, Houghton Mifflin, 1961.

Human Pharmacology and Addictiveness of Certain Dextroisomers of Synthetic Analgesics, United Nations, BN, Vol.14, No.3 (July-Sept., 1962), 25-35.

Huvanandana, Malai: The Centre for Treatment and Rehabilitation of Opium Addicts, Rangsit, Thailand (Cont'd), United Nations, BN, Vol.14, No.4 (Oct.-Dec., 1962), 17-24.

Hynd, Alan: Coster-Musica: Man Who Doped Drug Houses, in *Murder, Mayhem and Mystery*. New York, Barnes, 1958.

Illing, Hans: Die Prostitution Als Psychologisches Problem, JCLC&PS, Vol.51, No.6 (Mar.-Apr., 1960-61), 647.

———: Some Aspects of Treatment in the Case of a Drug Addict, JCLC&PS, Vol.50, No.3 (Sept.-Oct., 1959), 277.

Illinois Narcotics and Dangerous Drug Investigation Commission: *A Report in the Interest of the Health and Safety of the People of the State of Illinois*. Danville, State of Illinois, 2nd report, 1959; 3rd report, 1961.

Interdepartmental Committee on Narcotics: *Report of the Interdepartmental Committee on Narcotics to the President of the U.S.* Washington, U.S. Govt. Printing Office, 1961.

Isbell, H.: Medical Clinics of North America, NARCOTICS, Vol.34, No.2 (Mar., 1950).

———: *Meeting a Growing Menace—Drug Addiction, the Merck Report*. Rakway, Merck, 1951.

———: Opium Poisoning, Cocaine Poisoning and Chronic Amphetamine Poisoning, NARCOTICS (1951).

———: Rapid Diagnosis of Addiction to Morphine, JAMA, Vol.154, No.5 (Jan.30, 1954), 414.

———: *What to Know about Drug Addiction*. (Public Health Service Publication No.94.) Washington, U.S. Govt. Printing Office, 1951, Revised May, 1958.

———, & Fraser, H. F.: Addiction to Analgesics and Barbiturates, PHARMACOL. REV. Vol.2 (1950), 355-97.

Jackman, Norman, O'Toole, Richard, and Geis, Gilbert: The Self-image of the Prostitute, Norman, Univ. of Oklahoma, 1958.

Joachimoglu, G., and Miras, C.: Study of the Pharmacology of Hashish, United Nations, BN, Vol.15, No.3-5 (July-Dec., 1963), 7-8.

Joesten, Joachim: *Dope, Inc.* New York, Avon, 1953.

Joint Committee of the American Bar Assn., and American Medical Assn.: *Drug Addiction: Crime or Disease?* Bloomington, Indiana Univ. Press, 1961.

Joint Legislative Committee on Professional Boxing, N.Y.: *Report on Professional Boxing.* Washington, IACP, 1963.

Kefauver, Estes: Past and Present Standards of Public Ethics in America, THE ANNALS, Vol.101 (Mar., 1952).

King, Alexander: *Mine Enemy Grows Older.* New York, Simon & Schuster, 1958.

King, Daniel P.: Narcotics and the Nalline Test, L&O, Vol.12 (June, 1964).

King, Rufus G.: The Narcotics Bureau and the Harrison Act: Jailing the Healers and the Sick, YLJ, Vol.62 (Apr., 1953).

———: Narcotic Drug Laws and Enforcement Policies, L&CP, Vol.22 (Winter, 1951), 113-131.

———: The Rise and Decline of Coin Machine Gambling, JCLC&PS, Vol.55, No.2 (June, 1964), 199.

King, William: The Packaging of Narcotics in Evidence, POLICE, Vol.4, No.3 (Jan.-Feb., 1960), 20-22.

———: Spoon Cases: A Quick Method of Identifying Heroin, POLICE, Vol.5, No.1 (Sept.-Oct., 1960), 73.

Koestler, Arthur: *Reflections on Hanging.* New York, Macmillan, 1957.

Kogan, Herman: Dope and Chicago's Children, THE CHICAGO SUN TIMES, 1950.

Kolb, Lawrence: *Drug Addiction.* Springfield, Thomas, 1962.

———: Drug Addiction Muddle, POLICE, Vol.1, No.3 (Jan.-Feb., 1957), 57-62.

———: Let's Stop this Narcotics Hysteria, SATURDAY EVENING POST. Vol.229 (July 28, 1956), 19, 50, 54, 55.

Krishnamoorthy, E. S.: Comparative Analysis of the Permanent Central Opium Board and Drug Supervisory Body and Their Functions, on the One Hand, and of the Future International Control Board and Its Functions, on the Other, United Nations, BN, Vol.14, No.3 (July-Sept., 1962), 1-9.

Kuh, Richard H.: Dealing with Narcotics Addiction, NYLJ, Vol.143, No.4 (June 8, 9 & 10, 1960).

———: A Prosecutor's Thoughts Concerning Addiction, JCLC&PS, Vol.52, No.3 (Sept.-Oct., 1961).

Kussner, Willi: Poppy Straw: A Problem of International Narcotics Control, United Nations, BN, Vol.13, No.2 (Apr.-June, 1961), 1-6.

Larimore, G. W., and Brill, H.: The British Narcotic System: Report of Study, NYJM, Vol.60 (1960), 107-15.

———, & ———: *Report to Governor Nelson A. Rockefeller of an on the Site Study of the British Narcotic System.* Unpublished Report, Mar. 3, 1959. (Mimeo.)

Larrick, George P.: Misuse of Restricted Drugs— A Dangerous Problem, POLICE, Vol.8, No.6 (July-Aug., 1964), 10-13.

Law and Contemporary Problems, NARCOTICS, Vol.22, No.1 (Winter, 1957), 1-154.

Lawrence, Louis: Bookmaking, THE ANNALS, Vol.269 (May, 1950), 46-54.

Lewis, Oscar: *Sea Routes to the Gold Fields.* New York, Knopf, 1949.

———: *Silver Kings.* New York, Knopf, 1947.

Lindesmith, Alfred R.: Addiction: Beginnings of Wisdom, THE NATION (Jan. 19, 1963), 49.

———: The British System of Narcotics Control, L&CP, Vol.22 (Winter, 1957), 138-54.

———: Federal Law and Drug Addiction, SP, Vol.1 (Summer, 1959), 48-57.

———: *Opiate Addiction.* Bloomington, Principia Press, 1947.

———: Traffic in Dope: Medical Problem, THE NATION, Vol.182 (Apr. 21, 1956), 337-339.

Lipsyte, Robert M.: Cops in the World of "Junk," NEW YORK TIMES MAGAZINE (Oct. 14, 1962), 63.

Living Death: the Truth about Drug Addiction. Washington, U.S. Treasury Dept., Bureau of Narcotics, 1952.

Lomax, Alan: *Mister Jelly Roll.* New York, Grove Press, 1950.

Lord Denning's Report: *The Profumo—Christine Keeler Affair.* New York, Popular Library, 1963.

Los Angeles Police Department: Youth and Narcotics. Los Angeles, L.A. Police Dept., 1953.

Lowry, James V.: Hospital Treatment of the Narcotic Addict, FP, Vol.20 (Dec., 1956), 42-51.

———, & **Simrell, Earle V.:** Medicine and Law in the Treatment of Drug Addiction, United Nations, BN, Vol.15, No.3-4 (July-Dec., 1963), 9-16.

Lyman, George D.: *The Saga of the Comstock Lode.* New York, Scribner's, 1957.

McAllister, Robert, and Miller, Floyd: *The Kind of Guy I Am.* New York, McGraw-Hill, 1957.

McConnell, T. W., Farmilo, Charles G., and Genest, Klaus: Analysis of an Impure Heroin Seizure, United Nations, BN, Vol.14, No.3 (July-Sept., 1962), 47-57.

McDonald, Joseph F.: Gambling in Nevada, THE ANNALS, Vol.269 (May, 1950), 33.

McLaughlin, Glen H.: Traveling Thieves, PO-LICE, Vol.6, No.4 (Mar.-Apr., 1962), 28-31.

McManus, Virginia: *Not for Love.* New York, Dell, 1961.

McNickle, Roman K.: Drug Addiction, ERR, Vol.1 (Mar. 28, 1951), 221-37.

MacDougall, Michael: *Don't Be a Sucker.* New York, Malba, 1945.

Manes, Hugh R.: Gambling and the Law, JCLC&PS Vol.42 (1951-52), 205.

Martin, L. K., Genest, J. A., Cloutier, R., and Farmilo, Charles: Physico-chemical Methods for the Identification of Narcotics (Cont'd). Part VI—Common Physical Constants, UV, IR and X-ray Data for 12 Narcotics and Related Compounds, United Nations, BN, Vol.15, No.3-4 (July-Dec., 1963), 17-38.

Marx, Herbert L. (ed.): *Gambling in America.* New York, Wilson, 1952.

Maurer, David W.: The Argot of the Criminal Narcotic Addict, NARCOTICS (Apr. 25, 1952).

——: Reflections of the Behavior Pattern in the Argot of Underworld Narcotic Addicts, NARCOTICS (Dec. 29, 1952).

——, & Vogel, Victor H.: *Narcotics and Narcotic Addiction.* Springfield, Thomas, 1962.

May, Geoffrey: Prostitution, ESS, Vol.12, 553.

Meisler, Stanley: Federal Narcotics Czar, THE NATION, Vol.190 (Feb., 1960), 159-62.

Meyer, Alan S.: *Social and Psychological Factors in Opiate Addiction.* New York, Columbia, 1952.

Milligan, Maurice M.: *The Inside Story of the Pendergast Machine by the Man Who Smashed It.* New York, Scribner's, 1948.

Mills, James: I Told Them Not to Go Home, LIFE (Part 2 of 2 parts), Vol.58, No.9 Mar. 4, 1965), 92B-114.

——: We Are Animals in a World No One Knows, LIFE (Part 1 of 2 parts), Vol.58, No.8 (Feb. 26, 1965), 66B-92.

Ministry of Health, Interdepartmental Committee on Drug Addiction: *Report.* London, Her Majesty's Stationery Office, 1961.

Morris, Lloyd: *Incredible New York.* New York, Random, 1951.

Morse, Mary: *The Unattached.* Baltimore, Penguin, 1965.

Murtagh, John M., and Harris, Sara: *Cast the First Stone.* New York, Pocket Books, 1958.

——, & ——: *Who Live in Shadow.* New York, Ballantine, 1959.

Narcotic Clinics in the United States. A pamphlet. Washington, U.S. Government Printing Office, 354483, 1955.

Narcotic Educational Foundation of America, Suite 5, 1645 North La Brea Ave., Los Angeles, Calif. (Display board containing Hypnotic and Stimulant Drugs in tablet and capsule forms.)

The Narcotic Problem, UCLALR, Vol.1, No.4 (June, 1954), 405-46.

Narcotics Addiction and Nalline. A Pamphlet. Oakland, Oakland Police Dept., 1959.

Narcotics Regulation: A Study in Irresolution, TLQ, Vol.34 (Spring, 1961), 310, 22.

Narcotics: Slum to Suburb, NEWSWEEK (Feb. 22, 1965), 68A-68C.

National Parole Institutes: *The Control and Treatment of Narcotic Use.* Washington, IACP, 1964.

New Jersey Commission on Narcotic Control: *Report of Study and Recommendations.* Trenton, State of N.J., 1st Rep., Feb. 21, 1955; 2nd, Mar. 1, 1956; 3rd, Mar. 15, 1957; 4th, Mar. 15, 1958; 5th, Apr. 15, 1959; 6th, Apr. 15, 1960.

New York Academy of Medicine, Committee on Public Health, Subcommittee on Drug Addiction: Report on Drug Addiction, BNYAM, Vol.31 (Aug. 1955), 592-607.

New York (City) Board of Education: *What Secondary Schools Can Do about Narcotics Addiction.* New York, Curriculum Bulletin, 1956-57, No.3.

New York (City) Police Department: *Use of Narcotics by Children and Adolescents.* New York, N.Y. Police Dept., 1951.

New York City Youth Board, In-service Training Department: *Report of Three Day Conference on Narcotic Addiction and the Teenager.* New York, N.Y. City Youth Board, Oct., 1959.

New York State Division of Parole: *An Experiment in the Supervision of Paroled Offenders Addicted to Narcotic Drugs: Final Report of the Special Narcotic Project.* Albany, State of New York, 1959.

New York State: *Report of the State of New York Joint Legislative Committee on Narcotic Study.* Legislative Document No.7, Albany, State Capitol, 1959.

No Author: *I Am a Marked Woman.* New York, Avon, 1954.

Noble, John Wesley, and Averbuch, Bernard: *Never Plead Guilty: the Story of Jake Erlich.* New York, Farrar, Straus, 1955.

Note—An Experiment in the Supervision of Paroled Offenders Addicted to Narcotic Drugs, United Nations, BN, Vol.14, No.2 (Apr.-June, 1962), 39-40.

Note—Report of the Interdepartmental Committee on Drug Addiction, United Kingdom, United Nations, BN, Vol.14, No.2 (Apr.-June, 1962), 41.

Nyswander, Marie: *The Drug Addict as a Patient.* New York, Grune & Stratton, 1956.

————, **et al.:** The Treatment of the Drug Addicts as Voluntary Outpatients: A Progress Report, AJO, Vol.28 (Oct. 1958), 704-27.

O'Briene, Robert: *California Called Them.* New York, McGraw-Hill, 1951.

O'Carroll, Patrick: The Narcotic Case: Initiation and Development, TPC, Vol.29, No.7 (July, 1962), 6-10.

O'Connor, Richard: *High Jinks on the Klondike.* Indianapolis, Bobbs-Merrill, 1954.

Oliff, Jay: Equitable Devices of Controlling Organized Vice, JCLC&PS, Vol.48, No.6 (Mar.-Apr., 1958), 623.

Opium and Coca Leaves, Regulations No.2 Relating to the Importation and Transshipment of. Washington, U.S. Treasury Dept., Bureau of Narcotics, 1960.

Parker, Dan: *The ABC of Horse Racing.* New York, Random House, 1947.

Patri, Angelo: Children Should Be Protected Against Gambling Habit, CHICAGO DAILY NEWS (Nov.6, 1945).

Pearl, Cyril: *The Girl with the Swansdown Seat.* Indianapolis, Bobbs-Merrill, 1956.

Pennsylvania Chiefs Adopt Resolution on Narcotics, TPC, Vol.31 (Sept., 1964), 62.

Pescor, Michael J.: The Problem of Narcotic Drug Addiction, JCLC&PS, Vol.43, No.4 (Nov.-Dec., 1952), 471-81.

Peterson, Virgil W.: *Gambling—Should It Be Legalized?* Springfield, Thomas, 1951.

————: Gambling—Should It Be Legalized? JCL&C, Vol.40, No.3 (Sept.-Oct., 1949), 259.

————: Vitalizing Liquor Control, JCL&C, Vol.40, No.2 (July-Aug., 1949), 119.

Pfeffer, Arnold Z.: Narcotic Addiction, JCLC&PS, Vol.43, No.3 (Sept.-Oct., 1952), 382.

Photography Used in Identifying Narcotic Traffickers, L&O, Vol.9 (Apr., 1961).

Pincus, William: Police Problems in Social Change, TPY (1965).

The Plenipotentiary Conference for the Adoption of a Single Convention on Narcotic Drugs, United Nations, BN, Vol.14, No.1 (Jan.-Mar., 1962), 40-43.

Poston, Ted: The Numbers Racket, NEW YORK POST (Feb. 20-Mar. 10, 1960).

Prevention and Control of Narcotic Addiction. Washington, Bureau of Narcotics, U.S. Treasury Dept.

Proceedings of the White House Conference on Narcotic and Drug Abuse. Washington, U.S. Govt. Printing Office, 1962.

Pruner, Giuseppe: Pocket Kit for the Detection of the Commonest Narcotic Drugs, United Nations, BN, Vol.14, No.4 (Oct.-Dec., 1962), 25-26.

Radner, Sidney H.: *Roulette and Other Casino Games.* Key Publ., 1958.

Rajeswaran, Ponnusamy, and Kirk, Paul L.: Tranquillizing and Related Drugs: Properties for Their Identification (Part III), United Nations, Vol.14, No.1 (Jan.-Mar., 1962), 19-33.

Rasor, Robert W.: Narcotic Addiction as a Health Problem, POLICE, Vol.9, No.2 (Nov.-Dec., 1964), 64-66.

Rathbone, Josephine L.: *Tobacco, Alcohol and Narcotics.* New York, Oxford, 1952.

Ray, Marsh: The Cycle of Abstinence and Relapse Among Heroin Addicts, SP, Vol.9 (Fall, 1961), 132-40.

Reichard, J. D.: Federal Probation, NARCOTICS, Vol.9 (Oct.-Dec., 1946), 15.

Report of the Interdepartmental Committee on Narcotics to the President of the United States, January, 1961, United Nations, BN, Vol.14, No.1 (Jan.-Mar., 1962), 37-39.

Riccio, Vincent, and Slocum, Bill: *All the Way Down.* New York, Ballantine, 1962.

Rice, Thurman Brooks, and Harger, Rolla N.: *Effect of Alcoholic Drinks, Tobacco, Sedatives, Narcotics.* Chicago, Wheeler, 1958.

Roberts, W. Adolphe: *The American Lake Series.* Indianapolis, Bobbs-Merrill, 1946.

Roebuck, Julian B.: The Negro Drug Addict as an Offender Type, JCLC&PS, Vol.53, No.1 (Mar.-May, 1962), 36.

Rosenthal, Vin: Narcotic Addicts, JCLC&PS, Vol.49, No.2 (1958-59), 140.

Ross, Barney, and Abramson, Martin: *No Man Stands Alone.* Philadelphia, Lippincott, 1957.

Rutherford, James W.: Who Needs Heroin? L&O, Vol.12 (Aug., 1964).

St. Charles, Alwyn J.: *The Narcotic Menace.* Los Angeles, Borden, 1952.

Scarne, John: *Scarne on Cards.* New York, Crown, 1949.

———, & **Rowson, Clayton:** *Scarne on Dice.* Harrisburg, Military Service Publ. Co., 1945.

Schiaui, Sam J.: Where Are Your Narcotic Addicts? L&O, Vol.9 (July, 1961).

Schmidt, Jacob Edward: *Narcotics Lingo and Lore.* Springfield, Thomas, 1959.

Schur, Edwin M.: Attitudes Toward Addicts: Some General Observations and Comparative Findings, AJO, Vol.34 (Jan., 1964), 80-90.

———: British Narcotics Policies, JCLC&PS, Vol.51 (Mar.-Apr., 1961), 619-29.

———: *Narcotic Addiction in Britain and America.* Bloomington, Indiana Univ. Press, 1962.

Seventeenth Session of the Commission on Narcotic Drugs and Thirty-fourth Session of the Economic and Social Council, United Nations, BN, Vol.14, No.4 (Oct.-Dec., 1962), 33-36.

Shelley, Joseph: Role of Probation in Narcotics Addiction, JCLC&PS, Vol.43, No.3 (Sept.-Oct., 1952), 331.

Sherman, Gene: *Mexican Monkey on Our Back.* Reprinted from LOS ANGELES TIMES (July, 1959).

Silver, Edward S.: Organized Gambling and Law Enforcement, JCLC&PS, Vol.50, No.4 (Nov.-Dec., 1959), 397.

Sinclair, Andrew: *Prohibition: the Era of Excess.* Boston, Little, Brown, 1962.

Skousen, W. Cleon: Challenging the Gambling Syndicate, L&O, Vol.11, No.11 (Nov., 1963).

———: How to Beat the "Call Girl" Racket, L&O, Vol.12 (Jan., 1964).

———: How to Beat the Narcotics Racket, L&O, Vol.12 (Apr., 1964).

———: Latest Trends in Narcotics Control, L&O, Vol.9 (Nov., 1961).

———: A New Approach to Vice Supervision, L&O, Vol.9 (Jan., 1961).

———: Professional Policies for a Vice Squad, L&O, Vol.11, No.9 (Sept., 1963), 14-23.

———: Psychology of Narcotics Addiction, L&O, Vol.12 (Mar., 1964).

———: Sex Racketeers, L&O, Vol.11, No.12 (Dec., 1963), 12-17.

———: Should the Chief Speak Out Against Gambling, L&O, Vol.11, No.10 (Oct., 1963).

———: What About Legalizing Narcotics for Addicts, L&O, Vol.10, No.4 (Apr., 1962), 32.

———: What Every Chief Should Know about Narcotics, L&O, Vol.12 (Feb., 1964).

Skranz, Alice A.: Who Needs Heroin? L&O, Vol.12 (Aug., 1964).

Smith, Austin E.: Drug Habit, *World Book Encyclopedia,* 1961 Ed. IV, 289.

———: Narcotic, *World Book Encyclopedia,* 1961 Ed., XIII, 20.

Smith, Stanley S.: Lotteries—2, JCL&C, Vol.38, No.6 (Mar.-Apr., 1947-48), 659-69.

Smyrna, Chandler Lee: Harmful Drugs, L&O, Vol.10, No.9 (Sept., 1962), 13.

The Social Evil in Chicago: A Study of Existing Conditions with Recommendations by the Vice Commission of Chicago. Chicago, Gunthorp-Warren Printing Co.

Speer, W. L.: Narcotic Addiction, TPY (1959).

Stanley, Eugene: Marihuana as a Developer of Criminals, SE&SCD, Vol.2, No. 3 (1964).

State of California: *Second Progress Report of the Special Crime Study Commission on Organized Crime.* Sacramento (Mar. 7, 1949).

Steigleman, Walter: *Horseracing.* New York, Prentice-Hall, 1947.

Stern, Richard Martin: *The Bright Road to Fear.* New York, Ballantine, 1958.

Sternberg, David: Synanon House—a Consideration of Its Implications for American Correction, JCLC&PS, Vol.54 (Dec., 1963), 447-55.

Stevens, Alden: Make Dope Legal, HARPERS, Vol.155 (Nov., 1952), 40-47.

Swados, Harvey: *Years of Conscience—the Muckrakers.* Cleveland, Meridian, 1962.

Tallant, Robert: *The Romantic New Orleanians.* New York, Dutton, 1950.

Taylor, Bayard: *Eldorado, or Adventures in the Party of Empire.* New York, Knopf, 1949 (Reprinted from 1850 edition).

Taylor, G. Rattray: *Sex in History.* New York, Ballantine, 1954.

Taylor, N.: Flight from Reality, NARCOTICS (1949).

Ten Years of the Coca Monopoly in Peru, United Nations, BU, Vol.14, No.1 (Jan.-Mar., 1962), 9-17.

Terrot, Charles: *Traffic in Innocents.* New York, Bantam, 1961.

Terry, J. G.: *Santa Rita Rehabilitation Clinic Ten Year Report,* 1949-1959. Alameda County, Alameda Co. Sheriff's Dept., 1960.

———: *Remarks California Narcotic Officers' Association,* Second Conference, Sept., 1965.

———, & **Braumoeller, Fred:** Nalline: An Aid in Detecting Narcotics Users, reprinted from CALIFORNIA MEDICINE, Vol.85 (Nov., 1956), 229-301.

Thomason, Donald O.: Nalline as an Aid in Probationary Supervision of Narcotics Offenders: Three Years' Retrospect, a pamphlet. Alameda, Alameda Co. Probation Dept., 1959.

Thornton, Robert Y.: Organized Crime in the Field of Prostitution, JCL&C, Vol.46 (Mar.-Apr., 1956), 775-79.

Traffic in Narcotic Drugs in Canada. (The Senate of Canada.) Ottawa, Queen's Printer and Controller of Stationery, 1955.

Uhr, L., and Miller, J. G. (eds.): *Drugs and Behavior.* New York, Wiley, 1960.

United Nations, Division of Narcotic Drugs, BN, Vol.13, No.2 (Apr.-June, 1961), Geneva; Vol.14, No.1 (Jan.-Mar., 1962); No.2 (Apr.-June, 1962; No.3 (July-Sept., 1962); No.4 Oct.-Dec., 1962); Vol.15, No.3-4 (July-Sept., 1963); Vol.16, No.2 (Apr.-June, 1964); No.3 (July-Sept., 1964).

United Nations Expert Committee on Drugs Liable to Produce Addiction, Report 6-7. New York, World Health Organization Technical Report Series No.21, 1950.

United Nations: *Model Guide for the Application of the Protocol for Limiting and Regulating the Cultivation of the Poppy Plant, the Production of, International and Wholesale Trade in, and Use of Opium.* New York, United Nations, 1955.

———: *Report to the United Nations: Her Majesty's Government in the United Kingdom of Great Britain and Northern Ireland on the Working of the International Treaties on Narcotic Drugs for 1957.* Geneva, 1958.

———: *Single Convention on Narcotic Drugs, 1961.* New York, United Nations, 1961.

———: *Survey of Available Information on Synthetic and Other New Narcotic Drugs.* New York, United Nations, 1957, Report No.E/CN.7; 319.

———: *The United Nations and Narcotic Drugs.* New York, United Nations, 1959.

U.S. Advisory Committee to the Federal Bureau of Narcotics: *Comments on Narcotic Drugs.* Washington, Bureau of Federal Narcotics, 1959.

U.S. Bureau of Narcotics: *Living Death, the Truth About Drug Addiction.* Washington, Govt. Printing Office, 1956.

———: *Prescribing and Dispensing of Narcotics Under Harrison Narcotic Law,* pamphlet No.56. Washington, U.S. Bureau of Narcotics, U.S. Govt. Printing Office, 1956.

U.S. Congress, Committee on Appropriations: *Hearings on Treasury and Post Office Departments Appropriations for 1961 Before the Subcommittee of the Committee on Appropriations,* Jan. 26, 1960. Washington,

U.S. Govt. Printing Office. (86th Cong., 2nd Session, 1960.)

———: *Control of Narcotics, Marihuana and Barbiturates, Subcommittee on Ways and Means, Houses of Representatives.* Washington, U.S. Govt. Printing Office, 1951, 82nd Congress.

———: *Illicit Narcotics Travel.* Washington, U.S. Govt. Printing Office, 1956, 84th Cong., 2nd Session, Report No. 1440.

———: *Treatment and Rehabilitation of Narcotics Addicts.* Washington, U.S. Govt. Printing Office, 1956, 84th Cong., 2nd Session, Report No.1850.

U.S. Dept. of Health, Education & Welfare: *Report of Survey, Riverside Hospital.* Washington, Public Health Service, 1956.

U.S. House of Representatives: *Traffic in, and Control of, Narcotics, Barbiturates and Amphetamines.* Washington, U.S. Govt. Printing Office, 1956.

U.S. Interdepartmental Committee on Narcotics: *Report to the President.* Washington, U.S. Govt. Printing Office, 1956.

U.S. NEWS & WORLD REPORT. Another Problem for the Big Cities (Apr., 6, 1959).

U.S. Senate: *The Illicit Narcotics Traffic.* Report of the Committee on the Judiciary. Washington, U.S. Govt. Printing Office, 1956.

———, **Subcommittee on Juvenile Delinquency, Part 7:** *Enforcement of Federal Narcotic Laws.* Washington, U.S. Govt. Printing Office, 1960.

———, **Subcommittee on Juvenile Delinquency:** *Treatment and Rehabilitation of Juvenile Drug Addicts.* Washington, U.S. Govt. Printing Office, 1957; 1956.

———: *Third Interim Report of Special Committee to Investigate Crime in Interstate Commerce, Senate Report No.307.* Washington, U.S. Govt. Printing Office.

U.S. Treasury Department, Bureau of Narcotics Advisory Committee: *Comments on Narcotic Drugs—Interim Report of the Joint Committee of the A.B.A. and the A.M.A. on Narcotic Drugs.* Washington, U.S. Govt. Printing Office, 1959.

———: *Control and Rehabilitation of the Narcotic Addict: a Symposium.* Washington, U.S. Govt. Printing Office, 1961.

———: *Graphic Results of Mandatory Penalties Against Peddlers—Narcotic Control Act of 1965.* Washington, U.S. Govt. Printing Office, 1958.

———: *Prescribing and Dispensing of Narcotics*

Under the Harrison Narcotic Law. Washington, U.S. Govt. Printing Office, 1946.

————: *Prevention and Control of Narcotic Addiction.* Washington, U.S. Govt. Printing Office, 1960.

————: *Reported Number of Addicts, 1959.* Washington, U.S. Govt. Printing Office, 1959.

————: *Traffic in Opium and Other Dangerous Drugs—for Year Ending December 31, 1959.* Washington, U.S. Govt. Printing Office, 1960.

U.S. Treasury Department: *Opium, Coca Leaves, Isonipecaine or Opiates.* IRS Pub. No.428. Washington, U.S. Govt. Printing Office, 1959.

Vaille, C.: The Use of Diamorphine (Heroin) in Therapeutics, United Nations, BN, Vol.15, No.3-4 (July-Dec., 1963), 1-5.

Vernon, Wyman W.: The Nalline Test as a Means of Controlling Narcotics Traffic, POLICE, Vol.11, No.2 (Nov.-Dec., 1957), 7-11.

Vetter, Ernest G.: *Fabulous Frenchtown.* Washington, D.C., Coronet Press.

————, & **Vogel, V. E.:** *Facts About Narcotics.* Chicago, Science Research Assoc., 57 W. Grand Ave., 1951.

————, & **Harris, Isbell:** Medical Aspects of Addiction to Analgesic Drugs, United Nations, BN, Vol.111, No.4 (Oct., 1950).

————, ————, & **Chapman, K. W.:** Present Status of Narcotic Addiction, NARCOTICS, (1948).

————, **Whitman H., and White, G. H.:** Town Hall, NARCOTICS (1951).

Wakefield, Dan (ed.): *The Addict.* Greenwich, Fawcett, 1963.

Walsh, L. M.: *Directive Issued to Teachers . . .* California State Board of Pharmacy. (n.d.)

Weston, Paul B. (ed.): *Narcotics U.S.A.* New York, Greenberg, 1956.

Winkler, Abraham: *Opiate Addiction.* Springfield, Thomas, 1953.

————: Psychodynamic Study of a Patient During Self-Regulated Addiction to Morphine, NARCOTICS, Vol.26 (Apr., 1952), 270.

————, **Fraser, A. F., and Harris, I.:** N-Allylnormorphine: Effects of Single Doses and Precipitation of Acute Abstinence Syndromes During Addiction to Morphine, Methodome or Heroin in Man, JPET, Vol.109 (1953), 8-20.

————, & **Rasor, Robert W.:** Psychiatric Aspects of Drug Addiction, AJM, Vol.14 (May, 1953), 566-70.

Williams, Jesse Feiring: *Narcotics, the Study of a Modern Problem.* Sacramento, Calif. State Dept. of Education, 1952.

Williams, John B.: *Narcotics.* Dubuque, Brown, 1963.

Winick, Charles: The Drug Addict and His Treatment, in *Legal and Criminal Psychology.* New York, Holt-Rinehart, 1961.

————: Maturing Out of Narcotic Addiction, United Nations, BN, Vol.14, No.1 (Jan.-Mar., 1962), 1-7.

————: *The Narcotic Addiction Problem.* New York, The American Social Health Assn., 1962.

————: Narcotics Addiction and Its Treatment, L&CP, Vol.22 (Winter, 1957), 9-33.

————: Physician Narcotic Addicts, SP, Vol.9, No.2 (Fall, 1961), 174-86.

————: The Use of Drugs by Jazz Musicians, SP, Vol.7, No.3 (Winter, 1959-60), 240-53.

Wolff, P. O.: Bulletin of the Health Organization of the League of Nations, NARCOTICS, Vol.12 (1945-46), 455.

————: Marihuana in Latin America, The Threat It Constitutes, NARCOTICS (1949).

The Work of the Permanent Central Opium Board in 1960, United Nations, BN, Vol.13, No.2 (Apr.-June, 1961), 39-41.

The Work of the Permanent Central Opium Board in 1961, United Nations, BN, Vol.14, No.1 (Jan.-Mar., 1962), 44-46.

World Health Organization: Expert Committee on Addiction-producing Drugs, *Seventh Report.* Washington, World Health Organization Technical Report Series No.116.

————: Expert Committee on Addiction-producing Drugs, Eleventh Report. United Nations, BN, Vol.13, No.2 (Apr.-June, 1961), 44-45.

————: Expert Committee on Addiction-producing Drugs, Twelfth Report, United Nations, BN, Vol.14, No.2 (Apr.-June, 1962), 42-43.

————: Expert Committee on Addiction-producing Drugs, Thirteenth Report, United Nations, BN, Vol.16, No.2 (Apr.-June, 1964), 53-55.

————: U.N. Expert Committee on Drugs Liable to Produce Addiction, *Report*, 6-7, No.21. New York, United Nations, 1950.

————: WHO Expert Committee on Addiction-producing Drugs, *Thirteenth Report*, No.273. Geneva, United Nations, 1964.

Yablonsky, Lewis: *The Violent Gang.* New York, Macmillan, 1962.

Yost, Orin Ross: *The Bane of Drug Addiction.* New York, Macmillan, 1954.

Zumbrun, Alvin J. T.: An Honest Look at Gambling, POLICE, Vol.6, No.3 (Jan.-Feb., 1962), 73-75.

Chapter Six

POLICE TECHNICAL SERVICES ADMINISTRATION*

EQUIPMENT

Aaron, Thomas J.: The Uniform: A Neglected Police Tool, L&O, Vol.12 (Nov., 1964).

Applegate, Rex: New Police Shock-baton, L&O, Vol.11, No.10 (1963).

———: Tear Gas . . . CN and CS, L&O, Vol.12 (July, 1964).

Balcom, Lois: When Light Gets in Your Eyes, L&O, Vol.8, No.9 (1960), 39.

Baumann, W. H.: Vermont Symposium: Electronic Tools, TPC, Vol.30 (Jan., 1963), 36.

Braden, Larry: Helmet for General Duty, L&O, Vol.11, No.2 (Feb., 1963).

Brown, Arthur F.: It's Happening Right Under Your Feet, L&O, Vol.7 (Aug., 1959).

Carlson, Charles E.: Make the Mark Tell, L&O, Vol.9 (June, 1961).

Colangelo, Felix J.: Permanent Crease for Uniforms, L&O, Vol.11, No.8 (Aug., 1963).

Dana, Homer J., and Barnett, Claude C.: The Emotional Stress Meter, POLICE, Vol.1, No.3 (Jan.-Feb., 1957), 52-56.

Darton, R. E.: The Tape Recorder, A Police Tool, TPC, Vol.31 (June, 1964), 10.

Doyle, Richard: Another "Tool" for the Police Officer, L&O, Vol.12 (Jan., 1964).

East, F. D.: Internal Tire Service Facility for Police, TPC, Vol.30 (Oct., 1963), 32.

Fagerstrom, Dorothy: The "Bristleless" Brush, L&O, Vol.9 (Oct., 1961).

———: Designed for Good Looks, L&O, Vol.8, No.8 (1960), 28.

———: From Wool to Woolens, L&O, Vol.8, No.2 (1960), 2.

———: Information—When You Want It, L&O, Vol..9 (July, 1961).

Finegan, Robert F.: Sun Glasses or Glare Glasses, L&O, Vol.9 (Aug., 1961).

Gilbertson, Virgil C.: When Electric Power Fails at Police Headquarters, L&O, Vol.11, No.5 (May, 1963).

Hildebrand, Norbert A.: Panic Stops—Test Tires for Stopping Ability, POLICE, Vol.3, No.3 (Jan.-Feb., 1959), 26-28.

———

* This Chapter includes: Equipment, Police Records & Communication.

Holkes, W. H.: Lightweight Winter Uniform Fabrics, L&O, Vol.7 (Aug., 1959).

Hopfer, Westly M.: From Badges to Collectors' Items, POLICE, Vol.9, No.4 (Mar.-Apr., 1965), 60-62.

Jones, Phillip R.: Colorful Revolution in Police Badges, L&O, Vol.9, Feb., 1961.

Kamen, Ima: Coded TV—A New PD Weapon, POLICE, Vol.7, No.1 (Sept.-Oct., 1962). 17-20.

Keller, John A.: Survey on Police Uniforms, L&O, Vol.9 (Aug., 1961).

Kirwan, Wm. E., and Hart, A. B.: Water-tank Bullet Recovery, POLICE, Vol.1, No.6 (July-Aug., 1957), 9-11.

Laverenz, Harold: Points to Remember When Buying Police Shoes, L&O, Vol.7 (Feb., 1959).

Lawder, Lee E.: No Tubes, No Glass, No Roller or Mess, L&O, Vol.11, No.8 (Aug., 1963).

———: Notes on Your Uniform, L&O, Vol.9 (Feb., 1961).

Leonard, V. A.: It's New (High Powered Portable Loudspeaker Developed), POLICE, Vol.1, No.2 (Nov., Dec., 1956), 57.

———: It's New (New Secret Recorder Completely Hidden in Briefcase Operates Anywhere on Dry-Cell Batteries), POLICE, Vol.1, No.1 (Sept.-Oct., 1956), 65-66.

———: Stoelting MPH Speed Timer), POLICE, Vol.1, No.1 (Sept.-Oct., 1956), 65-66.

Lincke, Jack: Facilities Must Be Tailored for the Job, L&O, Vol.8, No.9 (1960).

McComb, Russell R.: Facts and Figures in an Electronic World, L&O, Vol.7 (Oct., 1964).

Mahoney, Bill: Electronic Eyes, L&O, Vol.9 (Nov., 1961).

Miller, Ted, and Hobbs, P. V., Jr.: Your Number Is Up, L&O, Vol.9 (Mar., 1961).

Millimaki, Robert: Notes on Locks, L&O, Vol.9 (Dec., 1961).

Morse, Philip M.: *Queues, Inventories and Maintenance.* New York, Wiley, 1958.

Office Copying System in the Boston (Mass.) Police Department, L&O, Vol.9 (July, 1961).

Patrick, L. M.: Don't Lose Your Head (Head

179

Covering), L&O, Vol.13, No.5 (May, 1955), 66.

Perone, Ralph A.: Trained Officers Get DWI, Convictions (Breathalyzer), L&O, Vol.13, No.5 (May, 1965), 70.

Rogers, William H.: Reflective Braids Aids Safety, L&O, Vol.7 (Jan., 1959).

Roller, J. H.: The Use of Color Movie Film in Law Enforcement, POLICE, Vol.3, No.1 (Sept.-Oct., 1958), 61.

Rotta, Frank: Miniature Radios Help St. Louis Police Capture Thugs, POLICE, Vol.8, No.1 (Sept.-Oct., 1963), 82-84.

Schneider, Russel J.: Electric Vulcanization Tire Repairs Prove Economical, L&O, Vol.11, No.11 (Nov., 1963).

Shaw, William: Are Electronic Kits Applicable to Police Work, L&O, Vol.11, No.6 (June, 1963).

———: 1960-63, A Quick Review, L&O, Vol.11, No.8 (Aug., 1963), 46. (Electronics.)

———: "Class D" Citizens Band Revisted, L&O, Vol.12 (Oct., 1964).

———: Effects of Variable Body Resistance, L&O, Vol.8, No.12 (1960), 12.

———: Sound Recorder Applications, L&O, Vol.10, No.4 (Apr., 1962), 40.

Silvarman, A.: Building and Use of a Mobile Surveillance Unit, L&O, Vol.13, No.4 (Apr., 1965), 76.

Stratton, James E.: Alternator—Solution for Heavy Drain on the Electrical System, L&O, Vol.11, No.11 (Nov., 1963).

UNIFORMS AND EQUIPMENT. Daily Training Bulletins, Volume 11, Bulletin 30, Sept. 10-17, 1962.

Warner, Selma W.: A Tradition of Quality, L&O, Vol.8, No.6 (1960), 41.

Weinart, C. R.: Proper Use of Tear Gas and Police Weapon, TPC (Jan., 1961), 16.

Young, Carl B., Jr.: First Aid Equipment for the Emergency Ambulance, POLICE, Vol.3, No.6 (July-Aug., 1959), 21-24.

———: Proper Equipment for an Emergency Ambulance, POLICE, Vol.1, No.1 (Sept.-Oct., 1956), 21-22.

RECORDS AND COMMUNICATION

Adams, Thomas F.: Police Radio Procedure, POLICE, Vol.7, No.5 (May-June, 1963), 35-38.

Allen, Francis A.: Report of the Commission of Inquiry on Capital Punishment, JCLC&PS, Vol.51, No.4 (Mar.-Apr., 1960-61), 451.

Albert, Harry: National Series on State Judicial Criminal Statistics Discontinued, JCL&C, Vol.39, No.2 (Mar.-Apr., 1948-49), 181-89.

Anderson, C. H.: Report of the Committee on Motion Picture, Radio and Television, TPY (1964).

Associated Police Communications Officers Inc.: *The National Police Communications Network Directory*. Detroit, 6th Ed., 1951.

Beattie, Ronald: California Bureau of Criminal Statistics, Sacramento, Calif. State Dept. of Justice, Apr. 29, 1960.

———: Criminal Statistics in the United States, JCLC&PS, Vol.51, No.1 (Mar.-Apr., 1960), 49.

———: *Manual of Criminal Statistics*. New York, American Prison Assoc., 1950.

———: Problems of Criminal Statistics in the United States, JCLC&PS, Vol.46 (1955-56), 178-86.

Bellman, Richard E.: *Dynamic Programming*. Princeton, Princeton Univ. Press, 1957.

Bird, Diademma F.: Nerve Center of the Police Department, L&O, Vol.10, No.2 (Feb., 1962), 77.

———: Weather Teletype Writer, L&O, Vol.12 (Mar., 1964).

Black, Stephan: From the Lay of the PB-2, L&O, Vol.10, No.6 (June, 1962), 44.

Bramley, Frank: Some Factors to Be Considered in the Selection of a Large Area Radio System, JCL&C, Vol.36, No.1 (1945-46), 49.

Braxton, Harold M.: Police Radio 1961, L&O, Vol.9 (Jan., 1961).

Brereton, George H.: Integrated California Law Enforcement Records and Communications System, the State's Role. Paper presented to the Working Group on Integrated Calif. Law Enforcement Records and Communications, a seminar co-sponsored by the Univ. of Southern Calif. and Systems Development Corporation, Santa Monica, Jan. 14, 1963.

Brooks, Philip C.: *Public Records Management*. Chicago, Public Admin. Service, 1949.

Burck, Gilbert, et al.: *The Computer Age*. New York, The Academy Library, Harper Torchbooks, 1965.

Bureau of the Census: *Statistical Abstract of the United States*. Washington, U.S. Govt. Printing Office, 1948.

Campbell, Frank D.: The Indianapolis Police Communication System, POLICE, Vol.3, No.6 (July-Aug., 1959), 24-26.

Carmack, William R.: Practical Communication Tools for Group Involvement in Police

Community Programs, TPC, Vol.32, No.3 (Mar., 1965), 34-36.

Carpenter, M. R.: Play Back the Call, L&O, Vol.10, No.10 (Oct., 1962), 64.

California Department of Education: *Police Records.* Sacramento, Bureau of Trade and Industrial Ed., 1949.

————: *Traffic Accident Records and Analysis.* Sacramento, Bureau of Trade and Industrial Ed., 1949.

————: *Use of Records.* Sacramento, Bureau of Trade and Industrial Education, 1949.

California Department of Justice: *Modus Operandi and Crime Reporting.* Sacramento, Division of Criminal Investigation, 1947.

California Special Crime Study Commission: *Final Report of the Special Crime Study Commission on Criminal Law and Procedure.* Sacramento, State Printing Office, 1949.

————: *Final Report of the Special Crime Study Commission on Juvenile Justice.* Sacramento, State Printing Office, 1949.

California State Dept. of Justice: *Manual of Practices and Procedures for the California Department of Justice Teletypewriter System: Relay and Message Centers.* Sacramento, State Printing Office, 1954, 1959, 1960.

Call Diverter, TPC, Vol.31 (July, 1964), 47.

Castenholz, Fred E.: Communications, TPY (1963).

————: Report of the Communications Committee, TPY (1963).

Catching Thieves by Telephone, JCLC&PS, Vol.46 (1955-56), 908.

Cherry, Colin: *On Human Communication.* Boston, Mass. Institute of Technology Press, 1957.

Chicago Police Department: *The 13-period System: Direct Comparability of Crime Statistics.* A report prepared by the Management Analysis Division of the Chicago Police Department for O. W. Wilson, Chicago, Chicago Police Dept., 1963.

Chicago—13 Month Year for Crime Reporting, TPC, Vol.31 (Jan., 1964), 30.

Christman, Glen: Reporting on Offenses in Police Department, JCL&C, Vol.39, No.1 (Mar.-Apr., 1948-49), 118.

————: *Uniform Crime Reporting.* New York, IACP, 1929.

Communications—S.E. Police TW New Operative, TPC, Vol.31 (Mar., 1964), 44.

Coon, Thomas F.: Intelligence Files, POLICE, Vol.6, No.4 (Mar.-Apr., 1962), 26-27.

Creel, R. K.: Dial "O" for Officer, L&O, Vol.11, No.1 (Jan., 1963).

Crittenden, B. M.: Federal Intervention Warning Signals, TPC, Vol.30 (Sept., 1963), 14.

Crooke, Wm. M.: Property Control, POLICE, Vol.8, No.3 (Jan.-Feb., 1964), 46-49.

Cuelenalre Al: Secret Communications, JCLC&PS, Vol.50, No.3 (1959-60), 307.

Cunningham, D. K., and Graves, Fred J.: Simplified Report Writing, POLICE, Vol.6, No.4 (Mar.-Apr., 1962), 72-73.

Daunt, Jerome J.: Police Records, TPY (1963).

————: Role of the Contributor in the UCR Program, TPY (1961).

Demby, Ben: Communications the Pulse of a City, L&O, Vol.9 (Jan., 1961).

————: Emergency Communications System in Miami, TPY (1961).

Design and Operations of Police Communications Systems. Washington, IACP Publications, 1964.

Diebold, William: Coded Message for Small Departments, L&O, Vol.10, No.4 (Apr., 1962).

Dillon, Martin F.: International Teletype System, TPY (1961).

Economics, James P.: State Reporting of Convictions, TPY (1958).

Elam, Gerald: The Tattoo File, L&O, Vol.8, No.5 (1960).

Elliott, George F.: Pacific Northwest Officers Create Clearing House for Crime Information, L&O, Vol.9 (June, 1961).

————: The Printed Word as a Tool, L&O, Vol.8, No.10 (1960).

Ellis, James H.: Notes on Police Report Writing, L&O, Vol.7 (Oct., 1959).

Elsworth, L. L.: Surveillance with Radio, L&O, Vol.10, No.1 (Jan., 1962).

Emergency-city-wide Police Phone Number, TPC, Vol.31 (Dec., 1964), 47.

Federal Bureau of Investigation: *Manual of Police Records.* Washington, The Bureau, 1965.

————: *Uniform Crime Reports for the United States and Its Possessions.* Washington, U.S. Govt. Printing Office. Printed annually.

————: *Uniform Crime Reporting Handbook.* Washington, The Bureau, 1960.

Ferracuti, Franco, Hernandez, Rosita Perez, and Wolfgang, Marvin E.: A Study of Police Errors in Crime Classification, JCLC&PS, Vol.53, No.1 (Mar.-May, 1962).

Field, Annita Tolivar: Single Hand Classification and Filing, POLICE, Vol.6, No.3 (Jan.-Feb., 1962), 25-33.

Field Reporting Manual. Chicago, Chicago Police Dept., 1964. (A complete guide of crime reporting for the street patrolman.)

Fischer, A.: New Advances in Mobile Radio Equipment, L&O, Vol.12 (Feb., 1964).

Foley, R. J.: Tubes or Transistors for Your Next Mobile Radios? L&O, Vol.10, No.1 (Jan., 1962).

Forysth, Julie: *Communication—from Cave Writings to Television.* New York, Harcourt, Brace, 1953.

Freeman, Craig: A Radio System for Wildlife Conservation Officers, L&O, Vol.8, No.12 (1960).

Gallagher, Ray P.: Report of Radio and Television Committee, TPY (1957).

Gallien, Shelby W.: Statistics Essential for Police Efficiency, JCLC&PS, Vol.51, No.1 (Mar.-Apr., 1960-61), 127.

General Information Manual: an Introduction to IBM Punched Card Data Processing. White Plains, IBM Technical Publications Dept.

General Information Manual: St. Louis Metro Police Department Accounting. White Plains, IBM Technical Publ. Dept.

Gilmore, G. R., and Gain, Anthony J.: The Los Angeles Police Communication System, POLICE, Vol.3, No.5 (May-June, 1959), 38-44.

Goldman, Stanford: *Information Theory.* New York, Prentice-Hall, 1953.

Griffin, John I.: Better Charts for Police Reports, POLICE, Vol.5, No.1 (Sept.-Oct., 1960), 38-40.

———: The Big Count—1960. POLICE, Vol.4, No.4 (Mar.-Apr., 1960), 43-46.

———: The Criminal Statistics Program in New York State, POLICE, Vol.4, No.2 (Nov.-Dec., 1959), 48-50.

———: Current Issues in Uniform Crime Reporting, POLICE, Vol.3, No.3 (Jan.-Feb., 1959), 71-73.

———: The Future of Police Statistics, POLICE, Vol.5, No.2 (Nov.-Dec., 1960), 68-71.

———: How to Estimate on the Basis of Samples, POLICE, Vol.4, No.6 (July-Aug., 1960), 47-49.

———: How to Sample, POLICE, Vol.4, No.5 (May-June, 1960), 57-59.

———: New Perspective in Police Statistics, JCLC&PS, Vol.46 (1955-56), 879-881.

———: Reporting of the Consultant Committee on Uniform Crime Reporting, POLICE, Vol.3, No.4 (Mar.-Apr., 1959), 59-62.

———: *Statistics Essential for Police Efficiency.* Springfield, Thomas, 1958.

———: What Electronic Data Processing May Do for the Police Chief in the Future, POLICE, Vol.4, No.3 (Jan.-Feb., 1960), 68-71.

Haukedahl, Stanley: State Teletype Network Links Midwest Law Enforcement Agencies, L&O, Vol.10, No.1 (Jan., 1962).

Hearle, Edward F. R.: Can Electronic Data Processing Be Applied to All Police Agencies? Logistics Department, the Rand Corp., TPC (Feb., 1962).

———: Electronic Data Processing, TPC, Vol.29, No.2 (Feb., 1962).

Hegele, Martin G.: Teletypewriter Net, TPY (1961).

Hilliard, A. M.: Personalized Belt Radio for Police, L&O, Vol.7 (Jan., 1959).

Hipskind, V. K.: Police Personnel Accident Reports and Records, POLICE, Vol.9, No.4 (Mar.-Apr., 1965), 74-78.

Hunter, T. P.: Records Systems in Small Police Departments, POLICE, Vol.6, No.3 (Jan.-Feb., 1962), 52-56.

IPM Progress Report, TPC, Vol.30 (Jan., 1963), 28.

Important FCC Action, TPC, Vol.30 (Apr., 1963), 49.

Kamen, Ira: Headquarters to Precinct Via Video, L&O, Vol.10, No.7 (July, 1962), 12.

Kenney, John P.: Internal Police Communications, JCLC&PS, Vol.46 (1955-56), 547-53.

Kentucky State Police: *Radio Communications System Procedure and Training Manual.* Frankfort, Kentucky State Police.

Lain, Frank: Population Explosion Places New Demands on Police Communications, L&O, Vol.10, No.1 (Jan., 1962).

Lampke, Ken.: Portable Radios Aid Police Operations, L&O, Vol.12 (Jan., 1964).

Lejins, Peter: Cooperation in Uniform Crime Reporting, TPY (1961).

Lenike, Jack: Status System Console of Burbank (Calif.), L&O, Vol.10, No.9 (Sept., 1962.)

Leonard, Donald S.: Report of the Committee on Legislation, TPY, 1960, 1961, 1963.

Los Angeles and Long Beach Police Streamline Report Processing, POLICE, Vol.8, No.5 (May-June, 1964), 72-74.

Los Angeles Radio Unit in New Division, TPC, Vol.30 (Aug., 1963), 41.

Lunden, Walter A.: Crime Down Under: In Tasmania, 1934-56, POLICE, Vol.4, No.3 (Jan.-Feb., 1960), 6-10.

Lyddy, John A.: Communications—Progress and Problems, TPY (1960).

———: Report of Committee on Motion Pictures, Radio and Television, TPY (1963).

———: Report of Communications Committee, TPY, 1956; 1957; 1958; 1959.

———: Report of the Television Committee, TPY 1958.

McCue, John: FCC Rules and Regulations, TPY (1961).

McNamara, Edmund L.: Discussion of Implementation of IACP Survey Recommendations, TPY (1964).

Mahoney, Bill: Second Look at Chicago's Communication System, L&O, Vol.11, No.1 (Jan., 1963).

————: Sign Control by Radio, L&O, Vol.10, No.6 (June, 1962), 21.

Marks, Milton S.: A Commentary on the System of Permanently Retaining Criminal Records, JCL&C, Vol.36, No.1 (1945-46), 17.

Marshall, Joseph T.: Point to Point Communications, TPY (1961).

————: Report of the Communications Committee, TPY (1965).

Martin, Milton R.: Plan Ahead for Your Radio Installation, L&O, Vol.8, No.1 (1960).

Mason, Robert A.: A Brief History of Police Communications, POLICE, Vol.3, No.4 (Mar.-Apr., 1959), 50-53.

————: The Police Communications System, POLICE, Vol.4, No.1 (Sept.-Oct., 1959), 43-46.

Matt, A. Robert: PTO—Communicate! POLICE, Vol.5, No.4 (Mar.-Apr., 1961), 23-27.

Modus Operandi and Crime Reporting. Sacramento, Calif. Dept. of Justice, 1961.

Murphy, William E.: Single Channel Monitor Records Twenty-four Hours, L&O, Vol.11, No.1 (Jan., 1963).

Newcomb, Robert, and Samons, Marg: *Employee Communications in Action.* New York, Harper, 1961.

Nolting, Orin F.: *Public Emergency Communications Systems.* Chicago, Int'l City Managers' Assoc., 1956.

Norris, Fred F.: Accepting Crime Statistics, POLICE, Vol.6, No.6 (July-Aug., 1962), 40-41.

O'Connell, Jeremiah: Report of Uniform Crime Records Committee, TPY (1958).

Odell, Margaret K.: *Records Management and Filing Operations.* New York, McGraw-Hill, 1947.

Page, Richard A.: Full-time Dispatch Service for CD Operations, L&O, Vol.11, No.5 (May, 1963).

————: Simultaneous Monitoring Radio System, L&O, Vol.11, No.1 (Jan., 1963).

————: Testing Transistorized Mobile Radios, L&O, Vol.12 (Jan., 1964).

Patterson, Sandy: New Radio System Gives Complete Protection, L&O, Vol.9 (Jan., 1961).

Perry, Greg: Recording for Efficiency, L&O, Vol.13, No.6 (June, 1965), 64.

Pigors, Paul: *Effective Communication in Industry.* New York, National Assoc. of Manufacturers, 1949.

Poli, Joseph G.: Development and Trend of Police Radio Communications, JCL&C, Vol.33, No.2, 193-97.

Price, Carroll S.: Sources of Information, POLICE, Vol.4, No.3 (Jan.-Feb., 1960), 30-35.

Redfield, Charles E.: *Communications in Management: a Guide to Administrative Communication.* Chicago, Univ. of Chicago, 1953.

Reed, Judith L.: Magnetic Traffic Viz-u-lizer, L&O, Vol.8, No.6 (1960).

Reinke, Roger W.: Design and Operation of Police Communications Systems—Part I, TPC, Vol.32, No.6 (June, 1965), 40.

Ridley, Clarence E., and Nolting, Orin F.: *The Municipal Year Book.* Chicago, Int'l City Managers' Assoc., 1950.

Ross, Victor: The Parking Meter Enforcement Program of New York City, L&O, Vol.8, No.11 (1960).

Rotta, Frank: Police Radio Technicians Benefit from Training Institute, L&O, Vol.10, No.1 (Jan., 1962).

St. John, William L.: Mechanical Record Keeping in Nashville, TPC (June, 1961), 28.

Schlaifer, Robert: *Probability and Statistics for Business Decisions.* New York, McGraw-Hill, 1959.

Schmeig, A. L., Sr.: Total Communications, TPC, Vol.31 (Nov., 1964), 46.

Schnur, Alfred C.: Fact or Fiction, JCLC&PS, Vol.49, No.4 (1958-59), 331.

Schrotel, Stanley R.: Report of Uniform Crime Records Committee, TPY (1959).

————: Uniform Crime Committee Report, TPY, 1960; 1962; 1963.

————: Workshop: Uniform Crime Reporting, TPY, 1961.

Sellin, Thorsten: The Significance of Records of Crime, LQR, Vol.67 (Oct., 1951), 489-504.

————: The Uniform Criminal Statistics Act, JCL&C, Vol.40, No.6 (Mar.-Apr., 1950), 679-700.

Shannon, C. E., and Weaver, W.: *The Mathematical Theory of Communications.* Urbana, Univ. of Illinois Press, 1949.

Shaw, William: An Introduction to Law Enforcement Electronics and Communications, L&O, Vol.13, No.4 (Apr., 1965), 44-48; No.6 (June, 1965), 30.

————: Automatic Location of Mobiles by Radio, L&O, Vol.10, No.8 (Aug., 1962).

————: Automatic Location of Radio Transmitters, L&O, Vol.12, (Feb., 1964).

———: The Citizens Band Radio, L&O, Vol.8, No.10 (1960).

———: The Departmental Radio Shop, L&O, Vol.8, No.8 (1960).

———: FCC Rules Nov. 1, 1963, L&O, Vol.10, No.12 (Dec., 1962), 66.

———: Federal Communications Commission Rule Changes Affecting Law Enforcement, L&O, Vol.12 (Sept., 1964).

———: Handling the TV Interference Complaint at the Police Desk, L&O, Vol.11, No.4 (Apr., 1963), 34.

———: High Frequency Reception Mobile, L&O, Vol.8, No.9 (1960).

———: The Leased Telephone Line and Radio Applied to Alarms, L&O, Vol.12 (Apr., 1964).

———: Long Distance Communications by Sky Wave, L&O, Vol.9 (Oct., 1961).

———: Teletype—Past, Present and Future, L&O, Vol.11, No.9, 10, 12 (Sept., Oct., Dec., 1963).

———: Pre-installation Planning Does Pay Off, L&O, Vol.9 (Jan., 1961).

———: R.F.1. (Radio Frequency Interference), L&O, Vol.10 (June, 1962), 44.

———: Sky Hook, L&O, Vol.9 (Feb., 1961).

———: Some of the Merits of Low Power Two Way Communications, L&O, Vol.9 (May, 1961).

———: Urgent! Final Call, L&O, Vol.9, No.7 (July, 1963).

———: The Vanishing Radio Spectrum, L&O, Vol.9 (Nov., 1961).

———: The Very Near Future in Police Electronics, L&O, Vol.8, No.6 (1960).

Simpson, Charles E.: Report of the Committee on Communications, TPY (1964).

Skousen, W. Cleon: Police Reports in Less than One Hour, L&O, Vol.8, No.9 (1960).

———: Report Writing Under the Gun, L&O, Vol.12 (Aug., 1964).

Slavin, James M.: Report of the Committee on Uniform Crime Records, TPY (1964).

———: UCRs—An Administrative Tool, TPY (1961).

Smalley, Alfred T.: Report of Legislative Committee, TPY (1958; 1959).

———: *Teletype System, 1958-1960.* Sacramento, Dept. of Justice, State Printing Office, 1960.

Stibitz, G. R., and Larrivee, J. A.: *Mathematics and Computers.* New York, McGraw-Hill, 1957.

Strecker, Sherry: Notes on Keeping Records, L&O, Vol.7 (Mar., 1959).

Swanson, C. O., Jr.: *A Comparative Study of a Civilian and a Military Police Records System.* Washington, IACP, 1961.

Toothman, Edward M.: Report of the Committee on Uniform Crime Records, TPY (1965).

Uniform Crime Reporting—A Complete Manual for Police Records. Washington, FBI, 1965.

Uniform Crime Reporting Manual. Committee on Uniform Crime Records, International Association of Chiefs of Police, Washington.

U.S. Dept. of Justice: *FBI Uniform Crime Reports.* Washington, U.S. Govt. Printing Office, printed semi-annually.

Updike, Everett C.: National Teletype Network, TPY (1957).

Vajda, S.: *The Theory of Games and Linear Programming.* New York, Wiley, 1956.

Vazsonyi, Andrew: *Scientific Programming in Business and Industry.* New York, Wiley, 1958.

Waller, James I.: Uniform Crime Reporting, TPY (1962).

Walton, Eugene: A Study of Organizational Communication Systems, PA (May-June, 1963), 46-49.

Wedding, Lee: Pocket-sized Radio Inaugurated in National Capitol, L&O, Vol.10, No.1 (Jan., 1962).

Wilcox, Thomas C.: The Detroit Police Department Radio System, SE&SCD, Vol.1, No.5 (1964).

Winner, Lewis: The Epic Progress of Police Radio, L&O, Vol.8, No.2 (1960).

———: New Frontiers in Two-way Communications, L&O, Vol.7 (Apr., 1959).

———: The New Look in Electronic Communications, L&O, Vol.7 (May, 1959).

———: Split Channel Communications (Equipment Requirement), L&O, Vol.8, No.1 (1960).

———: Transistor Terminology, L&O, Vol.8, No.3 (1960).

———: Transistorized Communications, L&O, Vol.8, No.1 (1960).

———: Two-way Radio, L&O, Vol.7, (Mar., 1959).

Wolfgang, Marvin E.: Uniform Crime Reports: A Critical Appraisal, UPLR, Vol.708 (1963).

Wood, Norton: Meeting Communication Needs in a Diversified Area, L&O, Vol.11, No.1 (Jan., 1963).

Chapter Seven

TRAFFIC*

TRAFFIC

A Plan to Save Lives. Chicago, The Assoc. of Western Railways, 105 W. Adams St., 1965.

Accident Investigator's Manual Revised, TPC, Vol.30 (May, 1963), 47.

Addams, Stanton: Driving Under the Influence, POLICE, Vol.7, No.6 (July-Aug., 1963), 27-30.

Allen, Edward J.: Acquiescence to Manslaughter, POLICE, Vol.4, No.3 (Jan.-Feb., 1960), 23-15.

Allen, Robert J.: In Case You're Traffic Minded, POLICE, Vol.4, No.1 (Sept.-Oct., 1959), 64-69.

Annett, Robert B.: Police Services on Controlled Access Highways, TPC (Jan., 1961), 8.

Alvarez, K. C.: The Uniform Traffic Ticket and Complaint, POLICE, Vol.7, No. 2 (Nov.-Dec., 1962), 32-33.

American Automobile Association: *Adult School Crossing Guards.* Washington, Amer. Auto. Assoc., Traffic Engineering & Safety Dept.

———: *Policies and Practices for School Safety Patrols.* Washington, 20036, National Education Assoc., 1201-16th St.

———: *Sportsmanlike Driving.* Washington, The Assoc., 1947.

American Bar Association: *Judge and Prosecutor in Traffic Court.* Evanston, Traffic Institute, Northwestern Univ. 1951 (out of print).

American Optometric Association: Vision and Driving Hazards, POLICE, Vol.1, No.1 (Sept.-Oct., 1956), 58-64.

Ammerman, Mort: Public Apathy in Traffic Law Enforcement, L&O, Vol.12 (Mar., 1964).

Ashworth, Ray: Annual Report of Traffic Division, TPY (1956).

———: Report of the IACP Traffic Division, TPY (1957); (1958); (1959).

———: Vehicle Needs Study—A Progress Report, TPY (1960).

Association of Casualty and Surety Companies: *Man and the Motor Car.* New York, A report prepared by the Accident Prevention Department, Association of Casualty and Surety Companies, 60 John St., New York 7, N.Y.

———: *Manual of Traffic Engineering Studies,* 2nd Ed. New York, The Association, 1953.

Avery, Angelyn: Revocation of Drivers' Licenses for Out-of-State Violations, JCL&C, Vol.39, No.1 (Mar.-Apr., 1948-49), 52-55.

Backstrand, L. M.: Legislative Support for Safety and Efficient Highway Transportation, TPC, Vol.31 (July, 1964), 8.

Bailey, Harold J.: In Case You're Traffic Minded How a Good Vision Test Should Be Conducted, POLICE, Vol.1, No.3 (Jan.-Feb., 1957), 38-45.

Baker, James Stannard: Analysis of Accident Data: TPY (1957).

———: New Accident Report Form, TPY (1957).

———: Reconstructing a Traffic Accident, TPY (1956).

———: *Traffic Accident Investigator's Manual for Police.* Evanston, Northwestern Traffic Institute, 1963.

Baran, Stephen: Protecting the Fellow On Foot, L&O, Vol.13, No.6 (June, 1965), 6-7.

Barnes, Henry A.: *The Man with Red and Green Eyes: the Autobiography of Henry A. Barnes, Traffic Commissioner, New York City.* New York, Dutton, 1965.

Barnes, James A.: Idea for an On the Spot Safety Campaign, L&O, Vol.9 (Aug., 1961).

Barton-Aschman Associates: *A Parking Program for Chicago's Central Area: A Study.* Chicago, Chicago Central Area Committee (Feb., 1965).

Bassett, James E.: The Need for Traffic Safety Legislation, POLICE, Vol.9, No.5 (May-June, 1965), 38.

Baumann, William H.: Symposium on Electronic Systems, L&O, Vol.11, No.2 (Feb., 1963).

Beddoe, Harold L.: Hit Run Murders, JCLC&PS, Vol.49, No.3 (1958-59), 280.

Beier, L. E.: Assignment of Officers to Interstate Highway Systems, TPY (1962).

———: Clock Speeders Accurately, TPC, Vol.31 (Jan., 1964), 8.

Bergman, Roy J.: A Case for Traffic Law Enforcement, POLICE, Vol.1, No.6 (July-Aug., 1957), 45-49.

---

* This Chapter includes: Traffic and Alcohol.

Berry, James R.: New Traffic Consultant, TPC (Nov., 1961), 59.

Birdsong, T. B.: Cuts Down Mississippi Highway Patrol Services, TPC (Aug., 1961), 30.

Blanchard, Don: The Question of Motor Vehicle Safety Seat Belts, POLICE, Vol.1, No.2 (Nov.-Dec., 1956), 30-33.

Bloomer, R. H.: Programmed Driver Instruction, TPC, Vol.29, No.9 (Sept., 1962), 14.

———, & **Schlesinger, Lawrence:** A Portable Low-cost Clinic for Traffic Violators, PO-LICE, Vol.7, No.4 (Mar.-Apr., 1963), 53-58.

Borkenstein, Robert F.: The Role of Alcohol in The Traffic Safety Problem, POLICE, Vol.4, No.2 (Nov.-Dec., 1958), 48-49.

Bowren, Patrilia W.: Measuring Wheels Aids Accident Investigation, L&O, Vol.12 (June, 1964).

Bramson, Bernard: New York Experiments with the Traffic Court School for Traffic Violators, POLICE, Vol.3, No.4 (Mar.-Apr., 1959), 62-67.

Bremer, Roger E.: Safe and Efficient Movement of Traffic, TPY (1965).

Brody, Leon, and Stack, Herman J.: *Highway Safety and Driver Education.* New York, Prentice-Hall, 1954.

Brown, Russell I.: Insurance Institute Program for Highway Safety, TPY (1960).

———: Traffic Report: Heavy but Moving, TPY (1963).

Budenz, Rudolph: Use of Television for Traffic Control, TPC (Sept., 1961), 6.

Burd, David Q., and Green, Roger S.: Headlight Glass as Evidence, JCL&C, Vol.40, No.1 (May-June, 1949), 85.

Buschnell, Veto A.: Police Safety Precautions During Accident Investigation, L&O, Vol.9 (Mar., 1961).

Caldwell, Bernard R.: Annual Report of the Traffic Committee, TPY (1956).

———: Northwestern University Pioneers Traffic Training and Research, POLICE, Vol.5, No.1 (Sept.-Oct., 1960), 27-30.

———: Police Traffic Supervision as an Aid to Drivers, POLICE, Vol.8, No.4 (Mar.-Apr., 1964), 64-65.

———: Report of the Traffic Committee, TPY (1957); (1958); (1959).

California Dept. of Education: *Drunk Driver Testing—Use of Chemical Tests for Intoxication.* Sacramento, Bureau of Trade and Industrial Education, 1949.

———: *Traffic Accident Investigation.* Sacramento, Bureau of Trade and Industrial Education, 1949.

———: *Traffic Accident Record and Analysis.* Sacramento, Bureau of Trade and Industrial Education, 1949.

California Department of Motor Vehicles: *1964 California Driver Record Study, PT.II—Accidents, Traffic Citations and Negligent Operator Count by Sex.* Sacramento, The Dept., 1965.

———: *California Vehicle Code Summary.* Sacramento, Highway Transportation Agency, 1962.

———: *California Blue Book*, 1961 Ed. Sacramento, Dept. of Motor Vehicles, Summary of Organization and Function, 1961.

———: *Financial Responsibility Information Manual.* Sacramento, Division of Drivers Licenses, 1962.

California State Department of Highway Patrol: *California Highway Patrol.* Sacramento, The Department.

Campbell, B. J.: Automotive Crash Injury Research, TPY (1965).

Campbell, Robert A.: Illinois Breaks New Ground in Highway Safety, POLICE, Vol.7, No.3 (Jan.-Feb., 1963), 40-44.

Carmichael, Glenn V.: Can Traffic Administration Overtake the Traffic Explosion, TEXAS P. J. (Apr., 1965), 11.

———: Can Traffic Administration Overtake the Traffic Explosion? TPY (1965).

Carpentier, Charles F.: Driver License Control and Traffic Safety, POLICE, Vol.7, No.1 (Sept.-Oct., 1962), 39-41.

Chaudoin, L. E.: Pedestrian Enforcement Saves Lives, JCL&C, Vol. 39, No.2 (Mar.-Apr., 1948-49), 265.

Cheualier, Neil: The Warning Ticket of Sayreville, N.J., L&O, Vol.7 (Nov., 1959).

City of Cincinnati, Ohio: *Cincinnati Traffic Code.* A report prepared by the City of Cincinnati. Cincinnati, Ohio.

Clark, Tom C.: The District Attorney and the Traffic Problem, JCLC&PS, Vol.51, No.2 (Mar.-Apr., 1960-61), 249.

Classification List of Traffic Law Violaters, TPC, Vol.31 (Dec., 1964), 48, TPY (1965), 298.

Cleary, William J.: Slow Down Your Traffic Deaths, L&O, Vol.8, No.8 (1960).

Cleveland, Donald E.: *Manual of Traffic Engineering Studies.* Washington, Institute of Traffic Engineers, 1964.

Conger, John J.: Research Trends in Traffic Safety, POLICE, Vol.5, No.6 (July-Aug., 1961), 44-47.

Coppin, R. S., Ferdun, G. S., and Peck, R. C.: *Teen-aged Driver: An Evaluation of Age, Maturity, Driving Exposure and Driver Training as They Relate to the Driving*

Record. Sacramento, Calif. Dept. of Motor Vehicles, 1965.

———, **Marsh, W. C., and Bibl, R. C.:** *Re-evaluation of Group Driver Improvement Meetings.* Sacramento, Calif. Dept. of Motor Vehicles, 1965.

———, **& Oldenbeck, G. Van:** *Driving Under Suspension and Revocation: a Study of Suspended and Revoked Drivers Classified as Negligent Operators.* Sacramento, Calif. Dept. of Motor Vehicles, 1965.

Cox, E. F.: Safety Program—Aimed at Speeders, L&O, Vol.11, No.6 (June, 1963).

Crittenden, Bradford M.: State Police Viewpoint, TPY (1964).

———: State Traffic Law Enforcement, TPY (1962).

———: Traffic Law Enforcement, TPY (1963).

Curry, Manfred: The Relationship of Weather Conditions, Facial Characteristics and Crime, JCL&C, Vol.39, No.2 (Mar.-Apr., 1948-49), 253.

Daley, Robert: Driver Selection, Driver Training, TRUCKING NEWS (Apr., 1965), 16-18.

Damon, Norman C.: ASF Objectives in Highway Safety, TPY (1962).

———: Future Program: Automotive Safety Foundation, TPY (1960).

Daniel, Ralph W.: A Juvenile Jury for Young Traffic Offenders, FOCUS (Jan., 1950), 23-26.

Davin, Frank: The Traffic Violations Point System in Illinois, POLICE, Vol.3, No.5 (May-June, 1959), 53-56.

Davis, Charles A.: Notes on Physical Evidence in Pedestrian Hit and Run Accidents, JCLC&PS, Vol.50, No.3 (1959), 302.

DeSilva, Harry R.: *Why We Have Auto Accidents.* New York, Wiley.

Desrosiers, Richard D.: Moving Picture Technique for Highway Signing Studies; an Investigation of Its Applicability, PUBLIC ROADS (Apr., 1965), 143-47.

Donaldson, Clyde: The Traffic Violator's Own Word's, L&O, Vol.10, No.10 (Oct., 1962), 80.

Donigan, Robert L.: Enforcement in Traffic Collision Cases, TPY (1959).

———: Important Revisions in the Uniform Vehicle Code, TPY (1963).

Driver Limitation, Kentucky Pioneers Plan, TPC, Vol.31 (Feb., 1964), 45.

Drunken Drivers Laws, TPC, Vol.30 (Aug., 1963), 44.

Drymalski, Raymond P.: Traffic Law Enforcement and American Justice, TPY (1956).

Drzazga, John: Bennies + Gasoline = Death, POLICE, Vol.7, No.4 (Mar.-Apr., 1962), 66-68.

Dunn, Henry: New Traffic Ticket Aids Public Relations, L&O, Vol.7 (June, 1959).

Dyment, Robert: Road Blockade Plan, L&O, Vol.11, No.9 (Sept., 1963).

Economos, James P.: A Guide to Assist Traffic Judges in Court and Police Aspects in the Use of Uniform Traffic Complaint with the Rules Governing Procedure in Traffic Cases, Lansing, Weger Governmental Systems, 117 W. Shiawassee St., 1958.

Eliot, William G.: Interstate Highway Signs Get Research Attention, POLICE, Vol.3, No.2 (Nov.-Dec., 1958), 22-23.

Ellisor, H. L.: City Police Viewpoint, TPY (1964).

Ellsworth, L. I.: Control of Traffic by Radio, L&O, Vol.9 (Jan., 1961).

Emergency-aid & Transportation Course, TPC, Vol.31 (Apr., 1964), 33.

Espie, David A.: Report of the Committee on Highway Safety, TPY (1964); (1965).

———: Some Special Problems, TPY (1964).

Evans, Henry K.: *Traffic Engineering Handbook.* New Haven, Institute of Traffic Engineers, 1950.

———, **& Kreml, Franklin M.:** *Traffic Engineering and the Police.* Evanston, National Conservation Bureau and Int'l Assoc. of Chiefs of Police, 1947 (out of print).

Fagerstrom, Dorothy: Accent on Training Traffic Administration, L&O, Vol.10, No.6 (June, 1962), 12.

———: Notes on Pavement Markings, L&O, Vol.7 (June, 1959).

———: The Drinking Driver a National Problem, L&O, Vol.9 (June, 1961; Sept., 1961).

Fannin, Paul: Report of Committee on Roads and Highway Safety, TPC, Vol.30 (Sept., 1963), 30.

Faustman, Jackson: *Traffic Engineering.* Sacramento, Calif. Dept. of Ed., Bureau of Trade and Ind. Ed., 1948.

Finesilver, Sherman G.: Deaf Driver Symposium, TPC, Vol.29, No.4 (Apr., 1962), 42.

Fisher, Edward C.: Modern Traffic Law Enforcement, THE CHIEFTAN (Fall-Winter, 1956).

———: *Right of Way in Traffic Law Enforcement.* St. Louis, Thomas Law Book Co., 1956.

———: *Traffic Officer in Court.* Evanston, Traffic Institute of Northwestern Univ., 1960.

Floch, Maurice: Attitude Toward the Grave Traffic Offense, JCLC&PS, Vol.42 (1951-52), 399.

———: Speed Law Enforcement in Metropolitan Areas, JCLC&PS, Vol.42 (1951-52), 833.

Flohr, Milton: Identification of Parking and Turn Signal Lenses, JCLC&PS, Vol.51, No.1 (Mar.-Apr., 1960-61), 99.

Fong, Wilkaan: Identification of Parking and Turn Signal Lenses, JCLC&PS, Vol.51, No.1 (Mar.-Apr., 1960-61), 99.

Forbes, T. W.: Effect of "Keep Right" Signs on the Arroyo-Seco Parkway, Research Report No.9-3. Institute of Transportation and Traffic Engineering, Univ. of Calif., 1951.

Forrester, Glenn: *Chemical Tests for Alcohol in Traffic Enforcement.* Springfield, Thomas, 1961.

Franey, W. H.: IACP Position Statement on Police Traffic Management, TPC, Vol.31 (Jan., 1964), 12.

Fredericks, Robert: Crash and Live, TPY (1956).

Friedlander, P. P., Jr.: Standards for Retreading Tires, TPC, Vol.31 (Mar., 1964), 12.

Furman, David D.: New Jersey's Traffic Legislation, TPY (1960).

Gardner, Harold J.: Traffic Contacts in Law Enforcement, POLICE, Vol.2, No.6 (July-Aug., 1958), 46-48.

Garmire, Bernard L.: Traffic, TPY (1963).

———: Traffic: Workshop, TPY (1962).

———: Report of the Traffic Committee, TPY (1961); (1962); (1963).

———: Traffic Control and Enforcement—Tattooing the Bubble, TPY (1961).

Garrison, Homer, Jr.: Traffic Inventory, TPY (1962).

Giarrusso, Joseph I.: The Inroads of Decadency, TPY (1961).

Gibbens, Murray E.: Prevention of Automobile Casualties, POLICE, Vol.3, No.6 (July-Aug., 1959), 12-17.

Gissane, William: The Prevention of Inquiry and Death from Road Traffic Accidents, POLICE, Vol.5, No.3 (Jan.-Feb., 1961), 51-54.

Gleason, John M.: Youth on Wheels, TPC (Mar., 1961), 33.

Governor's Conference Adopts Guide for Highway Safety, TPC, Vol.30 (Sept., 1963), 28.

Griselle, Sherman W.: Parking Related to Residential Development, URBAN LAND (Apr., 1961), 7-8.

Gunn, Herman N.: Suicide in a Moving Automobile on a Highly Traveled Highway, JCLC&PS, Vol.43, No.6 (Mar.-Apr., 1953), 827.

Halsey, Maxwell: Accident Prevention vs. Accident Cause, JCL&C, Vol.36 (1945-46), 349.

———: *Let's Drive Right.* Chicago, Scott, Foresman, 1954.

———: *Traffic Accidents and Congestion.* New York, Wiley, 1948.

Hammond, Harold F.: *Traffic Engineering Handbook.* Washington, Institute of Traffic Engineers, 1950.

Hankey, Richard O., Moorman, Robert R., Kennedy, Phyliss, and Heywood, Harold L.: TVA Selection System and State Traffic Officer Job Performance, POLICE, Vol.9, No.4 (Mar.-Apr., 1965), 10-14.

Harno, Albert J.: Legal and Implied Duties of the Traffic Judge, POLICE, Vol.6, No.6 (July-Aug., 1962), 47-50.

Harper, William W.: Prevention and Reduction of Injuries in Traffic Collisions, JCLC&PS, Vol.43, No.4 (Nov.-Dec., 1952), 515.

Harvey, Robert O., and Clark, W. A. V.: The Nature and Economics of Urban Sprawl, LAND ECONOMICS (Feb., 1965), 1-9.

Hathaway, G. O.: Arizona's Traffic Ticket and Complaint, TPC, Vol.32, No.6 (June, 1965), 59.

Hausman, Robert: Dead Men Tell No Tales, But Chemists Make Them Talk, POLICE, Vol.3, No.5 (May-June, 1959), 69-73.

Headey, Walter E.: Miami Safety Plan, TPC, Vol.29, No.7 (July, 1962), 28.

Hearst, William R., Jr.: The Traffic Accident Problem and the U.S. President's Committee for Traffic Safety, JCLC&PS, Vol.51, No.1 (May-Apr., 1960-61), 90.

Henderson, Harold: Sigmund Freud—Back Seat Driver, SAFETY EDUCATION (Apr., 1965), 17-19.

Henson, H. P.: What Our Community Is Doing About Speeding, L&O, Vol.11, No.6 (June, 1963).

Hewitt, William H.: Directing Traffic at Night, L&O, Vol.9 (Feb., 1961).

Highway Capacity Manual. Washington, Committee on Highway Capacity, Dept. of Traffic & Operations Research Board, U.S. Govt. Printing Office, 1950.

Highway Safety and Traffic Control, THE ANNALS (Nov., 1958).

Highway Safety—Chemical Tests Institute, TPC, Vol.31 (July, 1964), 48.

Highway Safety—Classification List of Traffic Law Violations, TPC, Vol.31 (Dec., 1964), 48.

Highway Safety—May Days, TPC, Vol.31 (July, 1964), 48.

Hill, Paul F.: Annual Inventory of Traffic Safety Activities, TPY (1957).

Hilton, Ordway: *The Action Program.* President's Committee for Safety, a report to the

President prepared by the Committee. Washington, Sept., 1964.

Hockaday, E. I.: Motor Fleet Operation, JCLC&PS, Vol.51, No.4 (Mar.-Apr., 1960-61), 476.

———: The Police Traffic Control Function, JCLC&PS, Vol.51, No.4 (Mar.-Apr., 1960-61), 492.

Hollingsworth, Dan: *Rocks in the Roadway.* Chicago, Stronberg Allen, 1954.

Horton, Thomas R. (ed.): *Traffic Control Theory and Instrumentation.* New York, Plenum Press, 1965.

Hrunek, Jack: Bicycle Riders Get Tickets Too, L&O, Vol.13, No.5 (May, 1965), 62.

Hulbert, S. F., and Mathewson, J. H.: The Driving Stimulator, POLICE, Vol.3, No.2 (Nov.-Dec., 1958), 44-47.

Hurd, C. E., and Frederick, W.: Yale University Addresses Its Attention to the Traffic Problem, POLICE, Vol.3, No.6 (July-Aug., 1959), 29-32.

IACP and National Safety Council: *State Traffic Law Enforcement.* Chicago, a report prepared by IACP and National Safety Council.

IACP Traffic Committee Makes Plans, TPC Vol.30 (Apr., 1963), 44.

Ingraham, Joseph C.: *Modern Traffic Control.* New York, Funk & Wagnalls, 1954.

Institute of Traffic Engineers: *A Program for School Crossing Protection.* Washington, Institute of Traffic Engineers.

Institute of Traffic Engineers: *Traffic Engineering Handbook.* New Haven, Yale University.

International Association of Chiefs of Police: *Definitions and Enforcement Rates.* Evanston, Traffic Institute of Northwestern University, 1950.

———: *Guide to a School Pedestrian Safety Program.* Washington, IACP, 1965.

———: *Hit and Run Investigation.* A report prepared by Field Service Division, IACP. Training Key No.7, Washington, 1964.

Isaacson, Irving: *Legal Driving.* Lewiston, Legal Publ., 1964.

———: *Manual for the Traffic Officer.* Lewiston, Legal, 1964.

Jacobson, William T.: Limitations on Municipal Use of Parking Meters, JCL&C, Vol.40, No.5 (Jan.-Feb., 1950), 601.

Jaycees Push for Uniform Traffic Laws, TPC, Vol.30 (May, 1963), 44.

Johanns, Chuck: Lite-a-bike, TPC, Vol.32, No.3, (Mar., 1965), 61.

Joint Committee of American Association of State Highway Officials, American Public

Works Association and Institute of Traffic Engineers: *Traffic Engineering: Functions and Administration.* Chicago, Public Admin. Service, 1948, reprinted, 1953.

Keefer, Louis E.: City Traffic Engineer and Urban Transportation Study, TRAFFIC ENGINEERING (Apr., 1965), 10-12.

Kennedy, Stephen P.: New York Police Stiffen Attack on Traffic Deaths and Injuries, POLICE, Vol.2, No.3 (Jan.-Feb., 1958), 45-48.

Kennelly, Martin M.: Chicago Tackles a Tough Problem, PUBLIC SAFETY (Jan., 1948).

Kostka, Ronald W.: Pennsylvania State Police Fight Fires on Turnpike, L&O, Vol.7 (Oct., 1959).

Kowalsky, Robert E.: Accident Investigation, L&O, Vol.9 (Nov., 1961).

Kraft, Merwyn A.: Coping with Driver Failure, POLICE, Vol.8, No.6 (July-Aug., 1964), 36-37.

Kreml, Franklin M.: A Look into the Future in Traffic Policing, TPY (1956).

———: Training Traffic Court Judges and Prosecutors, JCL&C, Vol.38, No.2 (Mar.-Apr., 1947-48), 161-64.

———, & Evans, Henry K.: *Traffic Engineering and the Police.* Washington, National Conservation Bureau and IACP, 1946.

Kulowski, Jacob: Motor Vehicle Safety in the Age of Speed and Power, POLICE, Vol.2, No.5 (May-June, 1958), 33-36; No.6 (July-Aug., 1958), 14-18.

Kummer, Jerome M.: What Makes Drivers Tick: POLICE, Vol.6, No.1 (Sept.-Oct., 1961), 59-61.

Kusaila, Joseph: The New York D.W.I. Seminars, L&O, Vol.13, No.6 (June, 1965), 16.

Ladd, Walter D.: *Organizing for Traffic Safety in Your Community.* Springfield, Thomas, 1959.

LaFata, Peter A.: Make the Public Speedometer Conscious, L&O, Vol.7 (June, 1959).

Lange, Walter W.: Officer Violator Contacts in Traffic Enforcement Actions, L&O, Vol.9 (June, 1961).

Larsen, George: Application of Management Principles to Police Traffic Supervision, TPY (1958).

Larson, John C.: On Rehabilitating of Chronic Traffic Offenders, JCLC&PS, Vol.47, No.1 (May-June, 1956), 46.

Latchaw, James: Cure for the Sloppy Driver, TPC (June, 1961), 12.

Lauer, A. R.: A Study of Driving Efficiency. Unpublished report, Driving Research Laboratory, Iowa State College, Iowa City, 1951.

———: Basic Factors of Safe Automobile Driving, POLICE, Vol.4, No.3 (Jan.-Feb., 1960), 57-59; No.4 (Mar.-Apr., 1960), 60.

———: Certain Structural Components of Letters for Improving the Efficiency of STOP Signs, HRBP, Vol.27 (1947), 360-71.

———: Driving Refresher Course for Firemen, Police and Public Transportation Drivers, POLICE, Vol.5, No.2 (Nov.-Dec., 1960), 57-58.

———: Improvement of the Drivers' Licensing Program, POLICE, Vol.11, No.1 (Sept., Oct., 1957), 45-54.

———: Psychological Factors in Effective Traffic Control Devices, TQ, Vol.5 (1951), 186-95.

———: Psychological Factors in Highway Traffic and Traffic Control, POLICE, Vol.1, No.4 (Mar.-Apr., 1957), 53-59, Pt.1; No.5 (May-June, 1957), 32-39, Pt.2.

———: Sharpening the Attack, POLICE, Vol.2, No.4 (Mar.-Apr., 1958), 43-45.

Lawder, Lee E.: Police Car Round-up, L&O, Vol.11, No.11 (Nov., 1963).

Leahey, Arthur J.: Observations on the Problems of Traffic Control, JCL&C, Vol.38, No.6 (Mar.-Apr., 1947-48), 654-58.

Leonard, V. A. (ed.): Action on Many Fronts to Stem Rising Traffic Toll, POLICE, Vol.1, No.2 (Nov.-Dec., 1956), 35.

———: In Case You're Traffic Minded, POLICE, Vol.1, No.1 (Sept.-Oct., 1956), 58; No.2 (Sept.-Oct., 1956), 58.

———: Sleepy Driver Guilty of Reckless Homicide, POLICE, Vol.1, No.2 (Nov.-Dec., 1956), 34.

———: That Weekend, POLICE, Vol.1, No.1 (Sept.-Oct., 1956), 55.

Library—The Transportation Center: *Current Literature in Traffic and Transportation.* Evanston, Northwestern Univ., 1965.

Littleton, J. T.: Transportation of the Acutely Injured—a Neglected "Disease" with a "Cure," POLICE, Vol.9, No.2 (Nov.-Dec., 1964), 16-21.

Littmann, Gerhard: The Traffic Situation in Western Germany, TPY (1956).

———: Use of Television in Traffic Control, TPC (Sept., 1961), 31.

Lofgren, Nils A.: Highway Safety and the Great Society, TPC, Vol.32, No.1 (Jan., 1965), 54.

Long, W. A.: Eliminate the Negative Approach to a Traffic Problem, L&O, Vol.12 (Oct., 1964).

———: Murder Is Murder, TPC (Sept., 1961), 34.

McEnnis, L. J., Jr.: The Background and Development of the Traffic Institute of North-western University, JCLC&PS, Vol.42 (1951-52), 663.

MacDonald, John M.: Deliberate Death on the Highways, POLICE, Vol.9, No.4 (Mar.-Apr., 1965), 30-32.

Mahoney, William: Using Television to Control Traffic, L&O, Vol.11, No.6 (June, 1963).

Malfetti, J. L.: *Traffic Safety: The Driver and Electronics.* Washington, IACP, 1965.

Mann, Guy: Why Business Must Support Traffic Safety, TPY (1959).

Manual of Traffic Engineering Studies. New York, The Accident Prevention Dept. of the Assoc., of Casualty and Surety Companies, 1953.

Martz, Paul R.: Traffic Enforcement and Its Relationship to Accident Prevention, TPY (1957).

Marx, Barbara: Programmed Driver Instruction, TPC, Vol.29, No.9 (Sept., 1962), 14.

Matson, Theodore M., Smith, Wilbur S., Hurd, Frederick W.: *Traffic Engineering.* New York, McGraw-Hill, 1955.

Matthews, Paul W.: Pursuit Driving, HIGH-WAY USER, Mar., 1965), 19-20.

Menninger, Karl: Accident Proneness, TPC (Feb., 1961), 35.

Michigan State College: *What Can the Colleges Do About the Traffic Problem?* East Lansing, Michigan, Michigan State College, 1953.

Milldebrandt, T. H.: Workshop: Policing Controlled Access Highways, TPY (1964).

Miller, H. B.: Calling All Police, Vol.2, No.6 (July-Aug., 1958), 28-30.

Miller, Seward E.: The Effects of Alcohol on Driving, POLICE, Vol.5, No.5 (May-June, 1961), 22-24.

Model Traffic Ordinance. Washington, National Committee on Uniform Traffic Laws and Ordinances, 1319-18th St., N.W., 1962. (A companion document to the CODE, generally serving the same purpose for municipalities as the CODE serves the State.)

Montgomery, Robert, Jr.: Uniform Traffic Code, TPC, Vol.29, No.10 (Oct., 1962), 28.

Moore, John O.: Crash Injury Research, TPY (1958; 1959).

———: Scientific Approach to Controlling Highway Accidents, TPY (1960).

———: Something You Can Do About It, L&O, Vol.8, No.11 (1960), 30.

Moore, K. K.: Committee Develops Guide for Preparing Paint Specs, TE (Apr., 1965), 15-17.

Morris, Robert L.: The Motor Vehicle and Megalopolis, U.S.A., L&O, Vol.13, No.6 (June, 1965), 32.

Moskowitz, Karl: Research and the Engineer, TE (Apr., 1965), 13-14.

Motorcycle Operation, Publication, TPC, Vol.31 (Sept., 1964), 61.

Moynihan, Daniel P.: Public Health and Traffic Safety, JCLC&PS, Vol.51, No.1 (Mar.-Apr., 1960-61), 93.

Mulligan, R. M.: Safety Circus, TPC, Vol.31 (June, 1964), 38.

Murray, John J.: Municipal Traffic Law Enforcement, TPY (1962).

Myren, Richard A.: Evaluation of the Measurement of Motor Vehicle Ground Speed from Aircraft, JCLC&PS, Vol.52, No.2 (July-Aug., 1961), 213.

National Committee on Uniform Laws and Ordinances: *Model Traffic Ordinance.* Washington, The Committee, 1956.

————: *Uniform Vehicle Code.* Washington, National Committee on Uniform Traffic Laws and Ordinances, 1319-18th St., N.W., 1964.

National Conference on Uniform Traffic Accident Statistics: *Uniform Definitions of Motor Vehicle Accidents.* Washington, U.S. Govt. Printing Office, 1954.

National Joint Committee on Uniform Control Devices et al.: *Manual on Uniform Traffic Control Devices for Streets and Highways.* Washington, U.S. Govt. Printing Office.

National Safety Council: *Accident Facts.* A report prepared by the National Safety Council Annual Publication, Chicago.

Nelson, A. T., and Smith, H. E.: *Car Clouting.* Springfield, Thomas, 1958.

Nichol, Ridley T.: The Mooresville Plan, PO-LICE, Vol.3, No.1 (Sept.-Oct., 1958), 23-28.

Noffsinger, Forest R.: Traffic Institute's Training Option Teaches Relationship to Management, POLICE, Vol.9, No.5 (May-June, 1965), 93.

Non-resident Violator Compact, TPC, Vol.31 (Jan., 1964), 14.

Northwestern University Traffic Institute: *Accident Investigation Manual.* A report prepared by Northwestern Univ. Traffic Institute, Evanston.

O'Connor, Timothy J.: Chicago's Traffic Problem, TPY (1959).

Office of the Governor: *Governor's Traffic Safety Conference, in Cooperation with the California Traffic Safety Foundation: Summary.* Sacramento, Assembly Chamber, State Capitol, Nov. 30, 1960.

Patterson, Sandy: Greater Efficiency in Traffic Control, L&O, Vol.9 (Oct., 1961).

Pearie, Leon: Serving Speeding Summons, by Mail, L&O, Vol.8, No.6 (1960).

Pedestrian Safety Awards Presented to Missouri Cities by AAA, THE CHIEFTAN, Vol.4 (Fall-Winter, 1957), 46-47.

Peet, Creighton: Solution to a Parking Problem, L&O, Vol.12 (June, 1964).

Penn, Hugh S.: *Accident Characteristics of Four Types of Passenger Automobiles.* Sacramento, a report prepared for the Calif. Highway Patrol, 1964.

————: *Causes and Characteristics of Single Car Accidents.* Sacramento, a report prepared for the Dept. of Calif. Highway Patrol, 1963.

Pennsylvania State College: *Driver Training Reduces Traffic Accidents One Half.* Washington, American Automobile Assoc., 1945.

Perone, Ralph: Accident Investigations, L&O, Vol.12 (June, 1964).

————: Hit and Run Accident Investigation, L&O, Vol.11, No.6 (June, 1963).

Petry, Arthur G.: Mass Communications in Traffic Safety, TPY (1964).

Petterson, Sandy: Greater Efficiency in Traffic Control, L&O, Vol.9 (Oct., 1961).

Phelps, Arthur: Policing Turnpikes and Limited Access Road, TPY (1957).

Planned Pedestrian Program. Washington, American Automobile Assoc., Foundation for Traffic Safety, 1958.

Policies and Practices for Driver and Traffic Safety Education, *National Commission on Safety Education.* Washington, National Education Assn., 1201-16th St., N.W. 10036. (Contains charts, tables, etc.)

Public Administration Service: *Traffic Engineering Functions and Administration.* Chicago, PAS, 1948.

Purdy, E. Wilson: Modern Traffic Investigation Units, TPC (Feb., 1961), 12.

Pyle, Howard A.: National Safety Council and the Action Program for Highway Safety, TPY (1964).

Qualifications of Expert Witness on Harger Breath-o-meter, JCLC&PS, Vol.46 (1955-56), 915.

Radar Evidence Held to Be Admissable, JCLC&PS, Vol.46 (1955-56), 601.

Ray, James C.: Two Lane Left Turns Studied at Signalized Intersections, TE (Apr., 1965), 17-19.

Reardon, J. M.: Safety to Life Committee, TPC, Vol.29, No.5 (May, 1962), 45.

Regan, C. G.: Reorganization of the Chicago Police Department Traffic Bureau, JCL&C, Vol.39, No.6 (Mar.-Apr., 1948-49), 790.

Reid, Roger: National Jaycee Safe Driving Road-e-o Reaches Half Million Teen-agers, POLICE, Vol.4, No.6 (July-Aug., 1960), 65-67.

Rizer, Conrad: Mathematical Methods Used in a Manslaughter by Automobile Case, PO-LICE, Vol.1, No.2 (Nov.-Dec., 1956), 63-65.

Robinson, Ivan A.: *Traffic Accident Investigation.* Sacramento, Calif. State Dept. of Education, Bureau of Trade and Ind. Ed., 1947.

————: *Traffic Accident Records and Analysis.* Sacramento, Calif. State Dept. of Education, Bureau of Trade and Ind. Ed., 1947.

————: *Traffic (Selective) Enforcement.* Sacramento, Calif. State Dept. of Education, Bureau of Trade and Ind. Ed., 1947.

Roche, George: Identification of Parking and Turn Signal Lenses, JCLC&PS, Vol.51, No.1 (Mar.-Apr., 1960-61), 99.

Rockey, H. C.: The Problem of the Slow Driver, TPC, Vol.30 (Mar., 1963), 8.

Rogers, Emmett V.: Silent Partner in Highway Safety, TPC (Apr., 1961), 30.

Rosenau, Louis: Operation Spot Check, L&O, Vol.9 (Jan., 1961).

Royster, Paul F.: The Interstate Highway System, TPY (1959).

Russell, V. & G.: World's Cheapest Parking, L&O, Vol.8, No.6 (1960).

Rutter, Joseph D.: A Panel Presentation—Traffic Programs of National Organizations, TPY (1960).

————: Report of the Traffic Committee, TPY (1960).

Safety Education. Chicago, National Safety Council.

Schlesinger, L. E.: Programmed Driver Instruction, TPC, Vol.29, No.9 (Sept., 1962), 14.

Schrum, Donald J.: Building Safety Into the Automobile, POLICE, Vol.3, No.2 (Nov.-Dec., 1958), 29-38.

Scott, Clifford L.: The Universal Language, PO-LICE, Vol.4, No.5 (May-June, 1960), 6-8.

Shaw, William: Beam Directed Energy Weapons, L&O, Vol.11, No.2 (Feb., 1963).

————: Electronics Training, L&O, Vol.10, No.10 (Oct., 1962), 30.

————: The Radar Speed Control Detector and How to Limit Its Effectiveness, L&O, Vol.10, No.1 (Jan., 1962), 36.

————: What Happens to the Electronic Highway? L&O, Vol.10, No.5 (May, 1962), 42.

————: What Is Your PEQ? (Police Electronic Quotient), L&O, Vol.11, No.1 (Jan., 1963).

Sheehe, Gordon H.: Factors Influencing Driver Attitudes, Skill and Performance, POLICE, Vol.9, No.2 (Nov.-Dec., 1964), 81-85.

————: Light Treatment of Fatal Drivers, TPC (Apr., 1961), 38.

Shoemaker, N. E.: *A Study of Human Kine-matics in a Rolled-over Automobile.* Washington, IACP, 1959.

Siegle, A. B.: Emergency Highway Traffic Regulation, TPC, Vol.31 (Apr., 1964), 12.

Sio, Arnold A.: *Parking—What Cities Are Doing.* Chicago, American Municipal Assoc., 1949.

Skousen, Cleon W.: Facing Up to the Trials and Tribulations of Traffic Control, L&O, Vol.11, No.4 (Apr., 1963).

Slavin, James M.: Emergency Traffic Control, TPY (1962).

Smith, Hiram M., Jr.: To Draw Blood, TPC, Vol.32, No.1 (Jan., 1965), 38-39.

————: Who's on the Road? TPC, Vol.29, No.1 (Jan., 1962), 26.

Smith, R. Dean: Enforcement & Driving Behavior, TPC, Vol.29, No.12 (Dec., 1962), 8.

————: Some Critical Policing Problems Arising from Controlled Access Roadways, TPY (1964).

Smith, Wilbur S.: New Developments: Traffic Control Equipment, TE (Apr., 1965), 20-23.

The Southwestern Law Enforcement Institute: *Traffic Law Enforcement.* Springfield, Thomas, 1963.

Spiker, Edward E.: Ounce of Prevention, An, L&O, Vol.11, No.10 (Oct., 1963).

Spitler, William L., and Trubitt, Hillard: Report of an Experiment Demonstrating the Effects of Alcohol on Driving Skills, PO-LICE, Vol.6, No.2 (Nov.-Dec., 1961), 25-31.

Spitz, Louis P.: Juvenile Traffic Problems and Preventive Measures, POLICE, Vol.11, No.2 (Nov.-Dec., 1957), 38-43.

State Department of California Highway Patrol: *Organization of the Department of the California Highway Patrol.* Sacramento, 1961.

State Highway Department: *Traffic Control Device Manuals* for Individual States. Available from State Highway Dept.

Stinson, Palmer: A Case of De-specialization of Traffic Operations, JCLC&PS, Vol.51, No.5 (Mar.-Apr., 1960-61), 561.

Supervisory Management. New York, American Management Assoc.

Swinson, James D.: Integrity in Law Enforcement, FBILEB (May, 1965), 17-19.

Tamm, Quinn: America's Traffic Toll Call, TPC, Vol.30 (Mar., 1963), 7.

————: Let's Clip the DWI's Wings, TPC, Vol.30 (Sept., 1963), 7.

————: Temporary Licenses for Iowa Drivers, TPC, Vol.32, No.2 (Feb., 1965), 45.

————: Traffic Facts, TPC, Vol.32, No.2 (Feb., 1965), 48-49.

————: The Traffic Inventory, Its Relationship to the State Law Enforcement, TPC, Vol.31 (May, 1964), 26.

———: Unmarked Patrol Car, TPC, Vol.32, No.1 (Jan., 1965), 53.

Teasley, Harvey D.: Shreveport Corrects Mystic Maze, L&O, Vol.13, No.4 (Apr., 1965), 60-62.

———: Traffic Engineering Reduces Accidents, L&O, Vol.12 (June, 1964).

Texas Police Journal. Dallas, Texas Police Association, 1508 Kirby Bldg.

Thompson, Philip A.: Reserved for Handicapped, TPC, Vol.29, No.1 (Jan., 1962), 39.

Thorndike, Robert L.: Human Factors in Accidents, Washington, School of Aviation Medicine, Air Univ., USAF, American Institute of Research, Oct., 1950.

Tobin, Thomas W.: Children on Bicycles, L&O, Vol.12 (June, 1964).

Tocchio, O. J.: Traffic Accidents, Not Crime, Nation's Greatest Killer, POLICE, Vol.7, No.6 (July-Aug., 1963), 23-26.

Traffic, Accident Investigator's Manual Revised, TPC, Vol.30 (May, 1963), 47.

Traffic Deaths Less on Turnpikes, Thruways, TPC, Vol.30 (Feb., 1963), 32.

Traffic Digest and Review. Traffic Institute, Northwestern Univ., 1804 Hinman, Evanston, Ill. 60204.

Traffic Enforcement Forums, THE CHIEFTAN, Vol.4 (Fall-Winter, 1957), 13-14.

Traffic Engineering. Washington, Institute of Traffic Engineers, Suite 506, 1725 De Sales St., 20006.

Traffic Facts, TPC, Vol.30 (May, 1963, 46; June, 1963, 62; July, 1963, 40; Aug., 1963, 48; Sept., 1963, 48; Oct., 1963, 42; Nov., 1963, 42).

Traffic Fatalities High in 1962, TPC, Vol.30 (Feb., 1963), 46.

Traffic Institute of Northwestern Univ.: *Adult Guards for School Crossings.* Evanston, Northwestern Univ., 1965.

———: *Traffic Accident Investigator's Manual for Police.* Evanston, Traffic Inst., of Northwestern, Univ., 1957.

———: *Traffic Law Enforcement Series.* Evanston, Univ. of Northwestern, list available from Traffic Institute, 1804 Hinman Ave., Evanston.

Traffic Laws Annual. Washington, National Committee on Uniform Traffic Laws and Ordinances, 1319-18th St., N.W., published annually.

Traffic—5 Reasons Why the 41,000, TPC, Vol.30 (Mar., 1963), 12.

Traffic Resolutions Adopted, TPC, Vol.30 (Dec., 1963), 38.

TRAFFIC SAFETY. Published monthly by the National Safety Council, 425 N. Michigan Ave., Chicago, Ill. 60611.

Traffic Statistics for 1962, TPC, Vol.30 (Feb., 1963), 46.

Traffic—Winter Driving Kits, TPC, Vol.30 (Dec., 1963), 37.

Traffic World. 825 Washington Bldg., Washington, D.C. 20005.

Truett, John T.: Some Observations on Parking and Enforcement, L&O, Vol.7 (June, 1959).

Turner, C. C.: The Psychological Testing of Traffic Police, TPC, Vol.31 (May, 1964), 12.

Tuttle, Harris B.: Drunken Driver Movies Save Taxpayers $100,000, L&O, Vol.12 (May, 1964).

Tyan, John J.: Computers Help Connecticut Cut Down Auto Violations, L&O, Vol.13, No.6 (June, 1965), 40.

Uniform Vehicle Code, Proposed Changes, TPC, Vol.31 (Dec., 1964), 38.

Uniform Vehicle Code. Washington, National Committee on Uniform Traffic Laws and Ordinances, 1319-18th St., N.W., 1962. (A specimen set of motor vehicle laws providing the necessary guidelines for the development of sound, uniform state traffic laws.)

United for Uniformity. Washington, National Committee on Uniform Traffic Laws and Ordinances, 1319-18th St., N.W., 1961. (An introductory brochure outlining the purpose, scope and function of the National Committee.)

U.S. Bureau Roads, Dept. of Commerce: *Highway Capacity Manual.* Washington, Dept. of Commerce, 1950.

U.S. Federal Bureau of Investigation: *Traffic Control and Accident Investigation.* Chapel Hill, Univ. of North Carolina, Institute of Government, 1947.

U.S. President's Highway Safety Conference: *Report of Committee on Enforcement.* Washington, U.S. Govt. Printing Office, 1949.

Urban Freeway Development in Twenty Major Cities: *System Planning, Design Concept, Progress.* Washington, Automotive Safety Foundation, 200 Ring Bldg.

Use of Radar Not a Speed Trap, JCLC&PS, Vol.46 (1955-56), 287.

Vickery, R. E.: We Have Parking Problems Too! L&O, Vol.7 (June, 1959).

Victoria, Vesta: Los Angeles Cures "Freeway Fallout," L&O, Vol.8, No.6 (1960), 63-64.

Villian, John: Physical Evidence in Hit and Run Traffic Deaths, JCLC&PS, Vol.50, No.1 (1956-60), 80.

Walters, Nydia: Spokane Police Eliminate Meter Looting, L&O, Vol.9 (June, 1961).

Webster, Richard F.: Protect Youngsters from Crippling Injuries, THE CHIEFTAN, Vol.4 (Spring, 1957), 27-28.

Weston, Paul B.: Homicide on the Highways, L&O, Vol.7 (June, 1959).

——: *The Police Traffic Control Function.* Springfield, Thomas, 1960.

Wilcox, R. G.: A Valuable Police Role in Safe Winter Driving, TPC, Vol.31 (Sept., 1964), 55.

Williams, Charles: *Traffic Accidents.* Springfield, Thomas, 1954.

——, *et al.: Traffic Accident Investigation.* Sacramento, Calif. Dept. of Ed., 1949.

Williams, Don: The Pedestrian Program in Rochester, N.Y., L&O, Vol.13, No.6 (June, 1965), 8.

Williams, James K.: New Dimension in Highway Safety, TPY (1963).

Winner, Lewis: Electronic Traffic Controls—A Progress Report, L&O, Vol.7 (Dec., 1959).

——: Electronic Traffic Control in Washington, D.C., L&O, Vol.7 (Nov., 1959).

——: Highways Go Electronic, L&O, Vol.7 (June, 1959).

——: Quiet Please! L&O, Vol.7 (Oct., 1959).

Woodson, Charles W., Jr.: The Traffic Program in Virginia, TPY (1958).

——: A Panel Discussion: Controlled-access Highway Use Problems, TPY (1960).

Woodward, Fletcher D.: An Apology to Those Who Are About to Die, POLICE, Vol.5, No.4 (Mar.-Apr., 1961), 35-38.

Yost, Light B.: Objectives of the President's Committee for Traffic Safety, TPY (1958).

Youell, J. A.: Pedestrian Signals for School Crossings, TPY, (1959).

Young, Carl B., Jr.: Resuscitation, POLICE, Vol.1, No.6 (July-Aug., 1957), 7-8.

——: Traffic Accidents First Aid, and the Police Officer, POLICE, Vol.1, No.3 (Jan.-Feb., 1957), 33-37.

Zeichner, Irving B.: Operation of Vehicle, L&O, Vol.11, No.3 (Mar., 1963).

ALCOHOL

Adams, Donald L.: An Adaption of the Beckman "B" Spectrophotometer to the Shupe and Dubowski Method of Alcohol Determination in Body Fluids, JCLC&PS, Vol.45 (1954-55), 621-24.

Alcohol Breath Tests, JCLC&PS, Vol.46 (1955-56), 149.

Alcohol in Post Mortem Specimens, JCLC&PS, Vol.46 (1955-56), 430.

Alcoholic Anonymous: the Story of How Many Thousands of Men and Women Have Recovered from Alcoholism. New York, Works, 1946.

Anonymous: *Alcoholics Anonymous.* New York, Works, 1948.

American Optometric Association: Vision and Driving Hazards, POLICE, Vol.1, No.1 (Sept.-Oct., 1956), 58-64.

Armstrong, Wayne K.: Blacklisting Drunks from Public Bars, L&O, Vol.8, No.5 (1960), 81-82.

Association of Casualty and Surety Companies: Alcohol Education, POLICE, Vol.3, No.3 (Jan.-Feb., 1959), 21-23.

Bacon, Sheldon D.: Alcohol and Complex Society, *Alcohol, Science and Society.* New Haven, Jrnl. of Studies on Alcohol, Inc., 1945.

Barron, Milton L.: Alcoholism in the Cantonese of New York City, Oskar Diethelm (ed). *Etiology of Chronic Alcoholism.* Ithaca, Cornell Univ. Press, 1955.

Borkenstein, R. L.: Chemical Tests to Determine Intoxication, TPY (1959).

California State Board of Equalization: *California Alcoholic Beverage Control Act and Related Constitutional Provisions.* Sacramento, State Printing Office, 1949.

Chafetz, Morris E., and Demone, Harold W., Jr.: *Alcoholism and Society.* New York, Oxford Univ. Press, 1962.

Chastin, J. D., Strauss, H. J., and Maupin, C. W.: A Correlation Study of Blood Alcohol Levels as Determined by Alcometer, Brethalyzer and Direct Blood Analysis Including Blood-Urine Alcohol Ratio, POLICE, Vol.2, No.6 (July-Aug., 1958), 50.

Chemical Tests for Intoxication, JCLC&PS, Vol.46 (1955-56), 430.

Derome, Wilfred: Quantitave Determination of Alcohol in the Human Organism, SE&SCD, Vol.1, No.5 (1964).

Donigan, Robert L.: Chemical Tests to Determine Alcoholic Influence in Their Use and Misuse, TPY (1958).

Dubowski, Kurt M.: Some Major Developments Related to Chemical Tests for Intoxication, POLICE, Vol.2, No.2 (Nov.-Dec., 1957), 54-56.

Dughi, Louis J.: The Role of County and Prosecuting Attorneys with Respect to Alcoholism, JCLC&PS, Vol.49, No.4 (1958-59), 370.

Earle, C. J.: *How to Help an Alcoholic.* Philadelphia, Westminster, 1952.

Ellis, Harry D. and Fielding, Hal E.: An Evaluation of the Alcotest, POLICE, Vol.4, No.2 (Nov.-Dec., 1959), 63-65.

Fagerstrom, Dorothy: Drinking Driver—A National Problem, L&O, Vol.9, (June, 1961; Sept., 1961), 2 parts.

Forrester, Glen C.: *Use of Chemical Tests for Alcohol in Traffic Law Enforcement.* Springfield, Thomas, 1950.

Haggard, H. W., and Jellinek, E. M.: *Alcohol Explored.* New York, Doubleday, 1960.

Harger, R. N.: Debunking the Drunkometer, JCL&C, Vol.40, No.4 (Nov.-Dec., 1949), 497.

Harris, Sara: *Skid Row, U.S.A.* New York, Doubleday, 1956.

Harvison, Clifford W.: Facts Established in Tests, on Effects of Alcohol on Drivers, TPY (1956).

Heise, H. A.: *How Experts Measure Drunkenness.* Washington, American Medical Assoc., 1953.

Hirsh, J.: *The Problem Drinker.* New York, Duell, Sloan, 1949.

Jellinek, E. M.: *The Disease Concept of Alcoholism.* New Haven, Hillhouse Press, 1960.

———: Notes of the First Half Year's Experience at the Yale Plan Clinics, QJSA, Vol.5 (1944-45), 279-302.

Kant, Fritz: *Treatment of the Alcoholic.* Springfield, Thomas, 1954.

Kelly, Harold F.: The Police Approach to the Alcoholic Problem, TPY, 1959.

Kessel, Joseph: The Road Back Report on Alcoholics Anonymous, L&O, Vol.10, No.7 (July, 1962), 48.

Leonard, Donald S.: Tests for Intoxication, JCL&C, Vol.38, No.5 (Mar.-Apr., 1947-48), 533-541.

Leven, Rals, and Vardre, Vincent: A Calif. Study of Relationships Between Drinking and Crime, POLICE, Vol.6, No.1 (Sept.-Oct., 1961), 18-21.

Mamet, Bernard M.: Constitutionality of Compulsory Chemical Tests to Determine Alcoholic Intoxication, JCL&C, Vol.36, No.2 (1945-46), 132.

Mann, M.: *Primer on Alcoholism.* New York, Rinehart, 1950.

McCarthy, R. G., and Douglas, E. M.: *Alcohol and Social Responsibility.* New York, Crowell, 1949.

Miller, Dudley P., and Brown, Paul R.: Can Drugs Prevent Alcoholism? PW, Vol.11 (May-June, 1949), 23, 30-31.

Miller, Seward E.: The Effects of Alcohol on Driving, POLICE, Vol.5, No.5 (May-June, 1961), 22-24.

Monnier, Denys: The Breathalyzer, POLICE, Vol.2, No.3 (Jan.-Feb., 1958), 7-9.

Muehlberger, C. W.: The Scientific Estimation of Alcoholic Intoxication, SE&SCD, Vol.1, No.2 (1964).

National Forum: *The Alcohol Problem.* Chicago, National Forum, 1948.

National Safety Council: *Committee on Tests for Intoxication—1953 Report.* Chicago, a report prepared by the National Safety Council of Chicago.

New Method for Blood Alcohol Determination, JCLC&PS, Vol.46 (1955-56), 909.

Pittman, David J., and Snyder, Charles R. (eds.): *Society, Culture, and Drinking Patterns.* New York, Wiley, 1962.

Puri, Dewan K. S.: A Liquor Drop Helps in Crime Detection, POLICE, Vol.8, No.5 (May-June, 1964), 70-71.

Qualification of Witnesses: As to Familiarity with the Odor of Alcoholic Liquor, SE&SCD, Vol.2, No.6 (1964).

Qualification of Witnesses: Telling Intoxicating Liquor by Its Odor, SE&SCD, Vol.3, No.1 (1964).

Roth, Lillian: *I'll Cry Tomorrow.* New York, Popular Library, 1955.

Rothman, David B.: Alcoholism and Crime, FP, Vol.11 (Sept., 1947), 31-33.

Russel, James F.: A Comparative Study of Police Handling of the Alcoholic Offender, Unpublished Master's Thesis, School of Police Admin. and Public Safety, Michigan State Univ. E. Lansing, 1964.

Seliger, Robert V.: Alcohol and Crime, JCL&C, Vol.34, No.4 (Nov.-Dec., 1953), 438-441.

———: Alcohol and the Wheel, JCL&C, Vol.34, No.3 (Sept.-Oct., 1953), 402-05.

———: Medical—Psychological Aspects of Contemporary Alcoholism, JCL&C, Vol.39, No.4 (Mar.-Apr., 1948-49), 452-41.

Shupe, Lloyd M.: Alcohol and Crime, JCL&C, Vol.34, No.5 (Jan.-Feb., 1954), 661-64.

Stephenson, William H.: Tests for the Drinking Driver, L&O, Vol.7, No.4 (Apr., 1959), 34-54.

Ullman, Albert D.: Sociocultural Backgrounds of Alcoholism, THE ANNALS, Vol.315 (Jan., 1958), 48-54.

Use of Vandic Acid in Determining Alcohol Content, JCLC&PS, Vol.46 (1955-56), 595.

Weinstein, Jack B.: Statute Compelling Submission to a Chemical Test for Intoxication, JCL&PS, Vol.45 (1954-55), 541-58.

Whittemore, Dick: Don't Punish the Alcoholic, L&O, Vol.7, No.5 (May, 1959), 46-77.

———: Half-way House Operation for Skid-Row Homeless Alcoholics, L&O, Vol.11, No.10 (Oct., 1963).

Williams, Roger J.: Identifying and Treating Potential Alcoholics, JCLC&PS, Vol.49, No.3 (1958-59), 218.

Zeichner, Irving B.: According to Law: Breath Tests, L&O, Vol.9 (Feb., 1961), 46-48.

———: Drunken Driving, L&O, Vol.9 (Apr., 1961), 38.

Chapter Eight

INDUSTRIAL AND BUSINESS SECURITY*

COMMUNISM, ESPIONAGE, SABOTAGE AND SUBVERSION

Alsop, Stewart: CIA: The Battle for Secret Power, SATURDAY EVENING POST (July 27, 1963), 17-21.

———, & **Braden, Thomas:** *Sub Rosa: the OSS and American Espionage.* New York, Reynal & Hetchcock, 1946.

Arkin, Joseph: Taxability of Private Industry Wages While Doing Undercover Work, L&O, Vol.8, No.4 (1960).

Aubry, Arthur S., Jr.: Law Enforcement and Communism, POLICE, Vol.6, No.6 (July-Aug., 1962), 30-32.

Bakeless, John: *Turncoats, Traitors and Heroes.* Philadelphia, Lippincott, 1959.

Basseches, N.: *Stalin.* New York, Dutton, 1952.

Blodgett, Ralph H.: *Comparative Economic Systems.* New York, Macmillan, 1949.

Blodgett, Ralph H.: *Comparative Economic Systems.* New York, Macmillan, 1949.

Brogan, Colm: Britain's Scandalous Spy Case, NATIONAL REVIEW (Mar. 12, 1963), Vol.14, No.10, 195-210.

Buckley, W. F., Jr.: The End of Whittaker Chambers, ESQUIRE (Sept., 1962), 1-6.

———: Quiet—Conspiracy at Work, NATIONAL REVIEW (Mar. 12, 1963), Vol.14, No.10, 188.

Bullock, John, and Miller, Henry: *Spy Ring: a Story of the Naval Secrets Case.* London, Seckler & Warburg, 1961.

Burnham, James: *The Web of Subversion.* New York, Day, 1954.

Byrnes, James: *Speaking Frankly.* New York, Harpers, 1947.

Cabell, C. P.: Foreign Police Forces—A Main Target of International Communism, TPY (1957).

Callaghan, James: Spying for Freedom Can Be Frustrating, AKRON BEACON JOURNAL (Mar. 3, 1963), 5G.

Carre, John Lee: *The Spy Who Came in from the Cold.* New York, Coward-McCann, 1963.

Cater, Douglass: *The Fourth Branch of Government.* Boston, Houghton Mifflin, 1959 and New York Vintage, 1965.

Chambers, Whittaker: *Witness.* New York, Random, 1952.

Chapman, Samuel G.: *Security Checks.* Police Services in Whitefish Bay, Wisconsin, Nov. 10, 1961 and Police Services in East Providence, Rhode Island, Oct. 26, 1960.

Chase, Harold W.: Communism and the First Amendment: The Membership Clause of the Smith Act, NULR, No.527 (1957).

———: *The Libertarian Case for Making It a Crime to Be a Communist,* TLQ, No.121 (Winter, 1956).

———: *Security and Liberty: the Problem of Native Communists 1945-55.* New York, Doubleday & Co., 1955.

Chao, L. W.: The Struggle Between Police of Free China and the Chinese Communists, TPY (1958).

Cogley, John: *Report on Blacklisting.* New York, Fund for the Republic, 1956.

Committee on Un-American Activities, House of Representatives: *Communist Penetration of Radio Facilities (Conelrad Communications Part 1).* Washington: 86th Congress, Sec. Session, U.S. Govt. Printing Office, 1960.

———: *Communist Target—Youth: Communist Infiltration and Agitation Tactics.* Washington, 86th Congress, U.S. Govt. Printing Office, 1960.

———: *Guide to Subversive Organizations and Publications (an Appendix).* Washington, U.S. Govt. Printing Office, 1957.

———: *How the Chinese Reds Hoodwink Visiting Foreigners.* Washington, 86th Congress, Second Session, U.S. Govt. Printing Office, 1960.

———: *The Ideology of Freedom vs. The Ideology of Communism.* Washington, 85th Congress, Second Session, U.S. Govt. Printing Office, 1958.

———: *International Communism (the Communist Mind).* Washington, 85th Congress, First Session, U.S. Govt. Printing Office, 1957.

———: *The Kremlin's Espionage and Terror Organizations.* Washington, 86th Congress,

---

* This chapter includes: Communism, Espionage, Sabotage, Subversion, Industrial Security, and Retail Security.

First Session, U.S. Govt. Printing Office, 1959. (Testimony of Peter S. Deriabin, Former Officer of the USSR's Committee of State Security [KGB].)

————: *Soviet "Justice" "Showplace" Prisons vs. Real Slave Labor Camps.* Washington, 86th Congress, Second Session, U.S. Govt. Printing Office, 1960.

Communist Psychological Warfare: Brainwashing. Washington, 85th Congress, 2nd Session, Mar. 13, 1958. (Consultation with Edward Hunter.)

Crankshaw, Edward: *Khrushchev's Russia.* Baltimore, Penguin, 1959.

Dallin, David J.: *Soviet Espionage.* New Haven, Yale Univ. Press, 1956.

Dash, S., Schwarts, R., and Knowlton, R. E.: *The Eavesdroppers.* Newark, Rutgers, 1959.

Decker, Stanley D.: Report of Security Committee: *Peace Officers' Association of the State of California, Proceedings, 1947 & 1948.*

Deriabin, Peter, and Gibney, Frank: *The Secret World,* Garden City, Doubleday, 1959.

Diamond, Harry: Operation Security, POLICE, Vol.7, No.1 (Sept.-Oct., 1962), 59-61.

Draper, Theodore: *The Roots of American Communism.* New York, Viking, 1957.

Drzazga, John: Police Departments: Targets for Communism, L&O (Feb., 1962), 66-67.

Dulles, Allen: *The Craft of Intelligence.* New York, Harper, 1963.

————: What Makes a Spy? THIS WEEK MAGAZINE (Dec. 1, 1963), 6-9.

Ebenstein, William: *Today's Isms.* Englewood Cliffs, Prentice-Hall, 1964.

Ellsworth, L. L.: The Washington Reward, L&O, Vol.8, No.6 (1960).

Federal Bureau of Investigation, U.S. Dept. of Justice: EXPOSÉ OF SOVIET ESPIONAGE, May 1960, Washington, Committee on the Judiciary, U.S. Senate, 86th Congress, Second Session, U.S. Govt. Printing Office, 1960.

Ferguson, Harry: CIA Outspent, Outmaned by Soviet Spy Arm, AKRON BEACON JOURNAL (Mar. 5, 1963), 20.

————: CIA Successes Secret, Failures Aren't AKRON BEACON JOURNAL (Mar. 6, 1963), 15.

————: Without Secrecy CIA Would Not Exist a Month, AKRON BEACON JOURNAL (Mar. 4, 1963), 4.

Foote, Alexander: *Handbook for Spies.* Garden City, Doubleday, 1949.

Fosselman, David H.: The Man Up Front, L&O, Vol.7 (Aug., 1959).

Francis Gary Powers. Washington, U.S. Govt. Printing Office, 1962. (Hearing Before the Committee on Armed Services, U.S. Senate, 87th Congress, 2nd Session, Mar. 6, 1962.)

From J. Edgar Hoover: A Report on Campus Reds, USN&WR (May, 31, 1965), 84.

Gellhorn, Walter (ed.): *The States and Subversion.* Ithaca, Cornell Univ. Press, 1952.

Germann, A. C.: Two Sides to Every Coin, POLICE, Vol.6, No.4 (Mar.-Apr., 1962), 31-38.

Ginzburg, Benjamin: *Rededication to Freedom.* New York, Simon and Schuster, 1959.

Gouzenko, Igor: *The Iron Curtain.* New York, Dutton, 1948.

Griffith, Samuel B.: *Sun Tzu, the Art of War.* Oxford, Clarendon, 1963.

Halm, George N.: *Economic Systems.* New York, Rinehart, 1951.

Helms, Richard: The Security Implications of World Communism in 1957. TPY (1958).

Hoover, J. Edgar: America—Soviet Espionage Target No.1, IS (Apr., 1964).

————: *Masters of Deceit.* New York, Holt, 1958.

————: *A Study of Communism.* New York, Holt, 1962.

House of Representatives: *Facts on Communism,* Vol.1, The Communist Ideology, No.336, 86th Congress, 2nd Session. Washington, U.S. Govt. Printing Office, 1960.

Howe, I., and Coser, L.: *The American Communist Party: A Critical History 1919-1957,* Rev. Ed. New York, Praeger, 1962.

Hunt, R. N. C. (ed.): *Books on Communism.* Princeton, Ampersand, 1959.

Hydo, E. J., Rev.: The Moral and Legal Aspects of the U-2. RMSJUAM, Vol.11, No.1 (Winter, 1962-63), 10-13.

Ison, Jack E.: Research and Information Centers on Subversive Activities, L&O, Vol.9 (June, 1961).

J. Edgar Hoover Tells How U.S. Reds Use "Pseudo Liberals" as a Front, USN&WR (Apr.13, 1956), 138-39.

Jordan, George Racey: *From Major Jordan's Diaries.* New York, Harcourt, Brace, 1952.

Kaznacheev, Aleksandr: *Inside a Soviet Embassy.* Philadelphia, Lippincott, 1962.

Keenan, George F.: *Russia and the West Under Lenin and Stalin.* Boston, Little, Brown, 1961.

Kent, Sherman: *Strategic Intelligence for American World Policy.* Princeton, Princeton Univ. Press, 1949.

Kirkpatrick, L. B.: Expose of Communism's Tactics to Negate Police Action, TPC (Dec., 1961), 35.

———: Free World Police; The Target, TPY (1961).

Knepper, Alvin: The Most Important Single Menace, L&O, Vol.9 (Sept., 1961).

Korbel, Josef: *The Communist Subversion of Czechoslovakia, 1938-1948.* Princeton, Princeton Univ. Press, 1959.

Kurt, Singer (ed.): *Spies Who Changed History.* New York, Ace, 1960.

Kurzman, Dan: *Subversion of the Innocents.* New York, Random, 1963.

La Pira, Giorgio: *The Philosophy of Communism.* New York, Fordham Univ. Press, 1952.

Latham, Sid: Secrets of Security, POLICE, Vol.1, No.4 (Mar.-Apr., 1957), 20-21.

Laws Relating to Espionage, Sabotage, etc. Washington, U.S. Govt. Printing Office, 1958. (Compiled by Gilman G. Udell.)

Lefkowitz, Louis J.: New York: Criminal Infiltration of the Securities Industry, THE ANNALS, Vol.347 (May, 1963), 51.

Lovell, Stanley P.: *Of Spies and Stratagems.* Englewood Cliffs, Prentice-Hall, 1963.

McClosky, Herbert, and Turner, John E.: *The Soviet Dictatorship.* New York, McGraw-Hill, 1960. **(Must Reading.)**

McGarvey, Francis S.: The Role of Intelligence Units, TPY (1961).

McGovern, William M.: *Strategic Intelligence and the Shape of Tomorrow.* Chicago, Regnery, 1961.

McNeal, Robert H.: *Bolshevik Tradition: Lenin, Stalin, Khrushchev,* Englewood Cliffs, Prentice-Hall, 1965.

———: *Lenin, Stalin, Khrushchev: Voices of Bolshevism.* Englewood Cliffs, Prentice-Hall, 1965.

Messick, Harry J.: Transportation of Government Equipment Under Arms, TPY (1963).

Monat, Powel: *Spy in the U.S.* New York, Harper, 1961.

Montagu, Ewen (ed.): *The Man Who Never Was.* Philadelphia, Lippincott, 1954.

Moorehead, Alan: *The Traitors.* New York, Harper, 1963.

Morros, Boris: *My Ten Years as a Counterspy.* New York, Dell, 1959.

National Industrial Conference Board, Inc.: Ind. Security I. *Combatting Subversion and Sabotage.* New York, The Board, 1952.

NBC News: *Profile on Communism.* New York, National Broadcasting Company, 1963.

The New Drive Against the Anti-communist Program, 87th Congress, 1st session, July 11, 1961. Washington, U.S. Govt. Printing Office, 1961. (Hearing Before the Subcommittee to Investigate the Administration of the Internal Security Act and other Internal Security Laws of the Committee on the Judiciary.)

No Author: *Outline History of the U.S.S.R.* Moscow: Foreign Languages Publishing House, 1960.

Orlov, Alexander: *Handbook of Intelligence and Guerrilla Warfare.* Ann Arbor, Univ. of Michigan Press, 1963.

Overstreet, Harry and Bonaro: *What We Must Know about Communism.* New York, Pocket Book, 1963. (Excellent Reading.)

Packer, Herbert L.: *Ex-communist Witnesses.* Stanford, Stanford, Univ. Press, 1962.

Passports for Communists, TIME (July 3, 1964), 51.

Petersen, William (ed.): *Realities of World Communism.* Englewood Cliffs, Prentice-Hall, 1965.

Petrov, Valdimir and Evdokia: *Empire of Fear.* New York, Praeger, 1957.

Ponomaryor, B. N., et al.: *History of Communist Party of the Soviet Union.* Moscow, Foreign Languages Pub. 1960.

Post, C. Gordon: *An Introduction to the Law.* Englewood Cliffs, Prentice-Hall, 1965.

Przazza, John: Police Departments Target for Communism, L&O, Vol.10, No.2 (Feb., 1962), 60.

Qualter, Terence H.: *Propaganda and Psychological Warfare.* New York, Random, 1962.

Ransom, Harry H.: *Central Intelligence and National Security.* Cambridge, Harvard Univ. Press, 1958.

Report of the Royal Commission. Ottawa, Edmond Cloutier, 1946.

Research and Information Centers on Subversive Activity, L&O, Vol.9 (June, 1961).

Schick, Franz B.: Crimes Against Peace, JCL&C, Vol.38, No.5 (Mar.-Apr., 1947-48), 445-65.

Seth, Ronald: *Anatomy of Spying.* New York, Dutton, 1963.

Seton-Watson, Hugh: *From Lenin to Malenkov.* New York, Praeger, 1953.

Shannon, David A.: *The Decline of American Communism.* New York, Harcourt, Brace, 1959.

Shaw, William: Alerting the Protection, L&O, Vol.8, No.7 (1960).

Skousen, Cleon W.: *The Naked Communist.* Salt Lake City, Ensign, 1960.

———: Scientific Mobocracy—A New Communist Technique, L&O, Vol.10, No.5 (May, 1962), 8.

Slusser, Robert M., and Wolin, Simon: *The*

Soviet Secret Police. New York, Praeger, 1957.

Stuart, John L.: *Fifty Years in China.* New York, Random, 1955.

Subcommittee to Investigate the Administration of the Internal Security Act and Other Internal Security Laws of the Committee on the Judiciary, U.S. Senate: *The Communist Party of the United States of America: What It Is—How It Works—a Handbook for Americans.* Washington, U.S. Govt. Printing Office, 1956.

————: *The Revival of the Communist International and Its Significance for the United States.* Washington, U.S. Govt. Printing Office, 1959.

Subversive Activities Control Board: *Report of the Subversive Activities Control Board.* Washington, A report prepared by the Subversive Activities Control Board, Apr. 20, 1953.

Suh, Chun Hak: Communism the Enemy of Freedom, TPY (1958).

Sullivan, William C.: The Challenges of Communism, TPY (1962).

————: FBI Challenges of Communism, TPC (Nov., 1961), 10.

Sutherland, A. E.: *Two Reference Volumes on Communism in the United States.* Cambridge, Harvard Univ. Press. 1956.

Toledano, Ralph De, and Lasky, Victor: *Seeds of Treason.* Chicago, Regnery, 1962.

The Trial of the U-2. Chicago, Translation World Publishers, 1960.

Tully, Andrew: *CIA: The Inside Story.* Greenwich, Fawcett, 1963.

U.S. Spying: How Good? USN&WR (Oct. 21, 1963), 100.

Urban, George R. (ed.): *Scaling the Wall: Talking to Eastern Europe.* Detroit, Wayne State Univ. Press, 1965.

Van Deusen, Charles: The Spies Take Over, THIS WEEK MAGAZINE, CLEVELAND PLAIN DEALER (June 13, 1965), 4-5.

Wade, W.: *U.N. Today.* New York, Wilson, 1954.

Werth, Alexander: *Russia under Khrushchev.* Greenwich, Fawcett, 1962.

West, Rebecca: *The New Meaning of Treason.* New York, Viking, 1964.

Who Is Spying and Why: A Look Behind the Charges, USN&WR (Aug. 8, 1960), 57-59.

Who's Spying for Whom? World Puzzle and a Shake-Up, USN&WR (July 29, 1963), 54-55.

Williams, James H.: Trade Secrets—Too Easy to Steal, SW, Vol.1, No.3 (Nov.-Dec., 1964), 18-21.

Wilson, Edmund: *To the Finland Station.* New York, Doubleday, 1953.

Wise, David, and Ross, Thomas B.: *The U-2 Affair.* New York, Bantam, 1962.

Zeichner, Irving B.: The Swastika Writhes Again, L&O, Vol.8, No.5 (1960).

INDUSTRIAL SECURITY

Ahern, John J.: Workshop: Liaison Between Police and Industrial Security Officers, TPY (1964).

Akerman, S. B.: *Insurance.* New York, Ronald, 1948.

American District Telegraph: *The Watchman's Handbook,* 3rd Ed. New York, American District Telegraph, 1949.

American Society for Industrial Security, L&O, Vol.9 (Sept., 1961).

Arm, Walter: Operation Security, TPC (Mar., 1961), 8.

Armstrong, T. O., Blake, Roland P., Boulet, C. B., Gimbel, M. A., Homan, S. W., and Keefer, W. Dean: *Industrial Safety,* 2nd Ed. New York, Prentice-Hall, 1953.

Arthur, Calvert: Watch Those Wiretaps, SW, Vol.2, No.2 (Mar.-Apr., 1965), 38-41.

ASIS Seminar, L&O, Vol.9 (Jan., 1961).

Astor, Saul D.: More Shortages—Discount Dilemma, SW, Vol.2, No.1 (Jan.-Feb., 1965), 28-33 & 35.

Bennett, Leonard E.: Entertaining with Safety, L&O, Vol.8, No.9 (1960).

Berman, H. H. and McCrone H. W.: *Applied Safety Engineering.* New York, McGraw-Hill.

Berry, Alfred B. and Buckley, John L. (ed.): Security Officer's Notebook, Industrial Security and Law Enforcement, L&O, Vol.10, No.12 (Dec., 1962), 60.

Birmingham, Michael G.: Field Operations for Security, TPY (1963).

Blake, Roland P.: *Industrial Safety,* 2nd Ed. New York, Prentice-Hall, 1953.

Bond, Horatio (ed.): *NFPA Inspection Manual.* Boston, National Fire Protection Assoc., 1950.

————: *Research on Fire.* Boston, National Fire Protection Assoc., 1957.

————, **Nolting, Orin S. (eds.):** *Municipal Fire Administration,* 5th Ed. Chicago, International City Managers' Assoc., 1950.

Bontecou, Eleanor: *The Federal Loyalty—Se-*

curity Program. Ithaca, Cornell Univ. Press, 1953.

Brandt, Allen D.: *Industrial Health Engineering.* New York, Wiley, 1947.

Brostron, Curtis: A Full Circuit Relationship, TPY (1964).

———: Liaison Between Police and Industrial Security Officers, POLICE, Vol.8, No.6 (July-Aug., 1964), 60-62.

Brown, Ralph S.: *Loyalty and Security.* New Haven, Yale Univ. Press, 1958.

Buckley, F. S.: New Methods Make an Exact Science of Anti-Intrusion Protection, L&O, Vol.7 (Mar., 1964).

Buckley, John L.: A New Look at Industrial Security, L&O, Vol.13, No.5 (May, 1965), 54; No.6 (June, 1965), 34.

———: Law Enforcement in the Space Age, L&O, Vol.13, No.4 (Apr., 1965), 50-51.

———: Security Officer's Notebook, L&O, Vol.10, No.2 (Feb., 1962), 36; No.3 (Mar., 1962), 24—How Big Can a See Jog Get; No.4 (Apr., 1962), 58—The Sheriff's Dept. and Plant Security; No.5 (May, 1962), The Navy "Cog" Officer; No.6 (June, 1962), 28; No.8 (Aug., 1962), Industrial Security as a Career Field; No.9 (Sept., 1962), 30; No.10 (Oct., 1962), 38; No.11 (Nov., 1962), 32—Investigation in Industry.

Bureau of Labor Standards, U.S. Dept. of Labor: *Safety Subjects.* Washington, Bulletin No.67, Rev. Ed., U.S. Govt. Printing Office, 1953.

Burstein, Harvey: The M.I.T. Security Guards, L&O, Vol.7 (June, 1959).

Caffey, J. J.: Protection by Electronic Watchmen, L&O, Vol.11, No.12 (Dec., 1963).

Case for Security Classifications, L&O, Vol.9 (Dec., 1961).

Colling, Russell L.: Hospital Security Problems, POLICE, Vol.6, No.5 (May-June, 1962), 69-71.

Collins, William P.: Trends in Planning Plant Security, TPC (Oct., 1961), 14.

Editor: Color Returns Dividends in Operation Safety and Appearance, THE PLANT. Plant Pub. Co., Aug., 1955.

Commission on Government Security: Federal Civilian Loyalty Program, *Report of the Commission on Government Security.* Washington, 1957.

Coon, Thomas F.: Basic Minimums of Plant Security Blended with Proper Leadership, POLICE, Vol.9, No.4 (Mar.-Apr., 1965), 92-94.

———: The Railroad Police—The World's Largest Privately Supported Police System, POLICE, Vol.9, No.2 (Nov.-Dec., 1964), 91-93.

Courtney, Jeremiah: Section 605 and You, SW, Vol.1., No.1 (July-Aug., 1964), 16-21 & 57-60; No.2 (Sept.-Oct., 1964), 34-38 & 46.

Crichton, Whitcomb: *Practical Course in Modern Locksmithing.* Chicago, Nelson Hall, 1957.

Crosby-Fiske-Forster: *NFPA Handbook of Fire Protection,* 10th Ed. Boston, National Fire Prevention Assoc., 1948.

Curran, Charles: *Handbook of Radio and TV Technique.* New York, Pelligrin & Cudahy, 1953.

Curtis, S. J.: The Psychology of Security Training, POLICE, Vol.4, No.5 (May-June, 1960), 47-50.

———: Security Hely for the Smaller Store, POLICE, Vol.6, No.3 (Jan.-Feb., 1962), 43-45; No.4 (Mar.-Apr., 1962), 41-44.

Dalla, Valle, J. M.: *The Industrial Environment and Its Control.* New York, Pitman, 1948.

Davis, John R.: Contract vs. Company Guard Service, POLICE, Vol.9 No.5 (May-June, 1965), 75.

———: *Industrial Plant Protection.* Springfield, Thomas, 1957.

———: Legal Aspects of Industrial Security, POLICE, Vol.4, No.3 (Jan.-Feb., 1960), 48-51.

DeKay, R. C.: Safety at the Sidewalk, L&O, Vol.8, No.11 (1960).

Department of the Army: *Physical Security of Military and Industrial Installations.* Washington, FM 19-30, U.S. Govt. Printing Office, 1952.

Dewhurst, H. S.: *The Railroad Police.* Springfield, Thomas, 1955.

Diamond, Harry: Operation Security, POLICE, Vol.7, No.2 (Nov. Dec., 1962), 51-54.

Dorian, George: Airport Security at Los Angeles International, SW, Vol.2, No.3 (May, 1965), 40.

Drucker, Peter F.: The Way to Industrial Peace: Citizenship in the Plant, HARPERS (Dec., 1946).

Dublin, Louis I., and Lotka, A. J.: *The Money Value of Man.* New York, Ronald, 1946.

Dunlap, Leighton C., Jr.: It's a Two-way Street,, TPY (1963).

Dyment, Robert: Continuing Safety Program Is the Answer in Jamestown, N.Y., L&O, Vol.2 (Feb., 1962).

Editor: How to Stop Stealing in Your Plant, FACTORY MANAGEMENT AND MAINTENANCE. New York, McGraw-Hill, 1954.

Einreinhof, Emrey L.: Anti-robbery Program for Bank Employees, L&O, Vol.11, No.3 (Mar., 1963).

Fleming, George: Security Police at Picatinny, L&O, Vol.12 (Sept., 1964).

General Services Administration: *Handbook for Guards.* Washington U.S. Govt. Printing Office, 1952.

Ghiselli, E. E., and Brown, C. W.: *Personnel and Industrial Psychology,* New York, Mc-Graw-Hill, 1955.

Gocke, B. W.: Aspects of Security Protection for Business and Industry, JCLC&PS, Vol.48, No.2 (July-Aug., 1957), 224.

————: *Personnel Aspects of Industrial Plant Security,* POLICE, Vol.2, No.5 (May-June, 1958), 40-43.

————: *Practical Plant Protection and Policing.* Springfield, Thomas, 1957.

Goddard, R. J.: Company & Law Enforcement Relationships, TPC, Vol.31 (July, 1964), 33.

Good Industrial Security Does Not Cost—It Pays, Industrial Security, L&O, Vol.9 (July, 1961).

Gordis, Philip: *Property and Casualty Insurance.* Indianapolis, Rough Notes, 1953.

Government Checks Can Bounce, SW, Vol.1, No.2 (Sept.-Oct., 1964), 31.

Graman, H. R.: *A Good Mechanic Seldom Gets Hurt.* Chicago, American Technical Society.

Gregg, James R.: Visual Needs of Policeman: L&O, Vol.7 (Oct., 1959).

Hale, I. B.: Cooperative Efforts of Police and Industrial Security Officers, TPY (1964).

Harkness, Richard, and Harkness, Gladys: How About Those Security Cases? READER'S DIGEST (Sept., 1955), and (Nov., 1955).

Hata, Bill: Demonstration Halts Employee In-plant Stealing, L&O, Vol.12 (Oct., 1964).

Hayden, Douglas: Industrial Security, L&O, Vol.9 (July, 1961).

Healy, Richard J.: A Coordinated System in Industrial Security, SW, Vol.1, No.2 (Sept.-Oct., 1964), 16-21.

————: *Facility Planning,* SW, Vol.1., No.1 (July-Aug., 1964), 12-15.

Heinrich, H. W.: *Industrial Accident Prevention,* 3rd Ed. New York, McGraw-Hill, 1953.

Hemeon, W. C. L.: *Plant and Process Ventilations.* New York, Industrial Press, 1955.

Hess, Gaylord R.: *Medical Service in Industry and Workmen's Compensation Laws.* Chicago, American College of Surgeons, 1946.

Hyman, Harold M.: *To Try Men's Souls: Loyalty Tests in American History.* Berkeley, Univ. of Calif. Press, 1959.

Industrial Security Activities at the Ford Motor Company's San Jose Assembly Plant, L&O, Vol.9 (Sept., 1961).

Industrial Security in the Space Age, L&O, Vol.9 (Mar., 1961).

INDUSTRIAL SECURITY. Published quarterly by the American Society for Industrial Security, 431 Investment Building, Washington, 5, D.C.

Industrial Security Seminar in San Francisco, TPC, Vol.30 (Aug., 1963), 22.

Industrial Union Department, AFL-CIO: *Handbook on the Industrial Security Program of the Department of Defense.* 1955.

Investigative Services, L&O, Vol.9 (May, 1961).

The Illinois Licensing Law, SW, Vol.1, No.2 (Sept.-Oct., 1964), 28.

Johnson, Howard O.: Snow Safety Measures, TPC, Vol.19, No.3. (Mar., 1962), 24.

Jones, Charles L.: *Safety in Lacquer Plants.* Wilmington, Hercules Powder Co.

JOURNAL OF THE AMERICAN SOCIETY OF SAFETY ENGINEERS. Published monthly by the Society, 5 North Wabash Ave., Chicago, Ill., 60602.

Karn, H. W. and Gilmer, B.: *Readings in Industrial and Business Psychology.* New York, McGraw-Hill, 1952.

Kissel, Gary: Fire Safety in Los Angeles. SW, Vol.1, No.2 (Sept.-Oct., 1964), 22-25.

————: *The Girls in 629,* SW, Vol.2, No.2 (Mar.-Apr., 1965), 43.

Klinger, Keith E.: Fire Security Is Vital, SW, Vol.1, No.1 (July-Aug., 1964), 4-11.

Knight, Paul E., and Richardson, Alan M.: *The Scope and Limitations of Industrial Security.* Springfield, Thomas, 1963.

LaForge, Charles P.: The Leak in the Dike: The Petty Larceny of Ideas, SW, Vol.2, No.3 (May, 1965), 34.

Lang, Frank: *Workmen's Compensation Insurance.* Homewood, Irwin, 1947.

Laing, Philip P.: Hidden Crime, POLICE, Vol.4, No.1 (Sept.-Oct., 1959), 58-61.

Lawshe, C. H., *et al.:* *Psychology of Industrial Relations.* New York, McGraw-Hill, 1953.

Lewe, William T.: Your Warehouse—Sitting Duck or Ft. Knox? SW, Vol.1, No.3 (Nov.-Dec., 1964), 22-29.

Levin, M.: Industrial Security of Intellectual Property, TPC, Vol.32, No.6 (June, 1965), 34.

Lippert, Frederick G.: *Accident Prevention Administration.* New York, McGraw-Hill, 1947.

Love, Robert C.: The Security Officer's Note-book, L&O, Vol.9 (Jan., & Apr., 1961).

Lowell, Leonard S.: Employee Theft: We Create Our Own Problems, SW, Vol.2, No.3 (May, 1965), 48.

McCartney, Fred G.: Industrial Police, TPY (1963).

Mahoney, Bill: Electronic Eyes, L&O, Vol.9 (Nov., 1961).

———: Protecting Life and Property with TV, L&O, Vol.12 (May, 1964).

Maier, Norman R. F.: *Psychology in Industry,* 2nd Ed. New York, Houghton Mifflin, 1955.

Matthias, A. J., Jr.: *How to Install and Design Plumbing.* Chicago, American Technical Society, 1953.

Meagher, Walter: Supermarket Fire Security, SW, Vol.1, No.3 (Nov.-Dec., 1964), 44-46.

Meyer, Edward J.: Hospital Fire Safety Program, SW, Vol.1, No.1 (July-Aug., 1964), 47-49.

Mich, Daniel, and Eberman, Edwin: *The Technique of the Picture Story.* New York, McGraw-Hill, 1945.

Miller, Delbert C., and Form, William: *Industrial Sociology.* New York, Harper, 1951.

Miller, Jos. G.: Infrared Burglar Alarms, TPC, Vol.29, No.3 (Mar., 1962), 22.

Morris, Howard B.: *Elements of Successful Plant Protection.* Louisville, Industrial Training Associates, 1953.

Moses, F. J.: Security Coordination, TPY (1963).

Moulton, Robert S. (Ed.): *Handbook of Fire Protection,* 10th Ed. Boston, National Fire Protection Association, 1948.

Munitions Board, Dept. of Defense: *Industrial Security Manual for Safeguarding Classified Security Information.* Washington, U.S. Govt. Printing Office, 1951.

———: *Principles of Plant Protection.* Washington, U.S. Govt. Printing Office, 1951.

———: *Standards for Plant Protection.* Washington, U.S. Govt. Printing Office, 1952.

Murphy, John T.: Between Patience and Fortitude, POLICE, Vol.5, No.2 (Nov.-Dec., 1960), 26-28.

Murphy, Michael J.: Law Enforcement and "Operation Security," L&O, Vol.12 (Oct., 1964).

National Board of Fire Underwriters: *Care and Maintenance of Sprinkler Systems:* New York, NBFU, 1954.

———: *Fire Prevention Code.* New York, NBFU, 1956.

———: *First Aid Fire Appliances.* New York, NBFU, 1950.

———: *Private Fire Brigades.* New York, NBFU, 1949.

National Fire Protection Association: *Employee Organization for Fire Safety.* Boston, NFPA, 1951.

———: *Handbook of Fire Protection,* 11th Ed. Boston, NFPA, 1954.

———: *Volunteer Fire Departments.* Boston, NFPA, 1952.

National Industrial Conference Board, Inc.: Industrial Security III, *Theft Control Procedures.* New York, NICB, 1954.

———: Industrial Security II, *Plant Guard Handbook.* New York, NICB, 1953.

———: *Studies in Business Policy: Industrial Security— I. Combating Subversion and Sabatoge, 1952; II. Plant Guard Handbook, 1953; III. Theft Control Procedures, 1954.* New York, NICB.

National Safety Council: *Accident Prevention Manual for Industrial Operations,* 3rd Ed. Chicago, National Safety Council, 1955.

———: *Accidents in the Meat Packing Industry.* Chicago, National Safety Council, 1953.

NATIONAL SAFETY NEWS. Published monthly by National Safety Council, 425 N. Michigan Ave., Chicago, Ill. 60611.

Nieman, R.: Industrial Security as Seen Through the Eyes of the Cognizant Security Officer, L&O, Vol.12 (Oct., 1964).

OCCUPATIONAL HAZARDS. Published monthly by the Industrial Pub. Co., 812 Huron Road, Cleveland, Ohio, 44115.

Office of the State Fire Marshal: *Excerpts from Laws Relating to the Office of State Fire Marshal.* Sacramento, State Printing Office, 1961.

Ohio Legislative Service Commission: *Industrial Safety Enforcement in Ohio,* Report No.36. Columbus, State House, 1959.

Otterbourg, Robert K.: Efficient & Accurate Tape Monitor Aids Public Safety, L&O, Vol.7 (Oct., 1959).

Owsley, Roy H.: *City Plans for Promoting Industrial Peace.* Chicago, American Municipal Assoc., 1947.

Pakalik, Michael J.: Security and Protection in the Museum, POLICE, Vol.3, No.1 (Sept.-Oct., 1958), 26-29.

Parker, W. H.: A Chief of Police Views Industrial Security, TPY (1964).

Play Ball-Security at Dodger Stadium, SW, Vol.2, No.2 (Mar.-Apr., 1965), 12-15.

Port Security at Matson Terminals, Inc., L&O, Vol.9 (Apr., 1961).

Problems Confronting Small Business in Classified Defense Work, L&O, Vol.9 (Oct., 1961).

Proetz, William F.: Safety Devices Demonstrated During University Seminar, L&O, Vol.8, No.7 (1960).

Professional Industrial Security Manager, L&O, Vol.9 (Nov., 1961).

———: *Industrial Protection Training Series.* Lafayette, Purdue Univ. Press (Organization of Protection Units, Plant Geography, Rules and Regulations for Plant Police, Patrol Problems, Personnel Investigation, Safety Rules and Regulations, Safety Inspections, Legal Problems, Panic Control, Sabotage, Bombs and Explosives, Training Guide, Practical Training Methods).

Reigeluth, R. J.: *Safety and Economy in Heavy Construction.* New York, McGraw-Hill.

Rose, Richard P.: $$$ and Sense of Precaution, Part I to V, SW, Vol.1 & Vol.2, No.3; No.1, 2, 3 (1965).

Rosenagel, W. E.: *Handbook of Rigging.* New York, McGraw-Hill.

Rubenstein, Sidney: Your Safe Can Save Your Company, SW, Vol.2, No.1 (Jan.-Feb., 1965), 10-14; No.2 (Mar.-Apr., 1965), 16-20.

Rudolphs, Willem (ed.): *Industrial Wastes—Disposal and Treatment.* New York, Ronald, 1953.

Ryan, T. A.: *Work and Effort.* New York, Ronald, 1947.

Safeguarding Records After the Fire, SW, Vol.2, No.1 (Jan.-Feb., 1965), 11.

Saunders, George W.: Classifying Physical Security Equipment, TPY (1965).

Scruton, Robert A.: University Security: The City Campus, SW, Vol.2, No.4 (June, 1965), 12.

Security of Classified Material Shipments, TPC, Vol.30 (May, 1963), 34.

Standards for Physical Security of Industrial and Governmental Facilities. Washington, Office of Civil Defense, Dept. of Defense, 1962.

The Strucinski Case, L&O, Vol.9 (Feb., 1961).

Taylor, L. B., Jr.: Guardians of the Space Frontier, L&O, Vol.9 (Dec., 1961).

Thorpe, Harold R.: The Tools Are Available, L&O, Vol.12 (June, 1964).

Thorsen, Roger: Button, Button, Who's Got the Button? POLICE, Vol.4, No.2 (Nov.-Dec., 1959), 29-31.

Tiffin, Joseph, and McCormick, Ernest J.: *Industrial Psychology,* 4th Ed. Englewood Cliffs, Prentice-Hall, 1959.

Tryon, George H. (ed.): *Fire Protection Handbook.* Boston, NFPA, 1962.

U.S. Congress, Subcommittee of the Senate Committee on Post Office and Civil Service: *Adminstration of the Federal Employees' Security Program,* Report No. 2750, 84th Cong., 2nd Session. Washington, U.S. Govt. Printing Office, 1956.

U.S. Dept. of the Army: FM 19-20: *Criminal Investigation.* Washington, U.S. Govt. Printing Office, 1951.

————: FM 19-30: *Physical Security of Military and Industrial Installations.* Washington, U.S. Govt. Printing Office, 1952.

U.S. Dept. of Commerce: *Emergency and Disaster Planning for Chemical and Allied Industries.* Washington, U.S. Govt. Printing Office, 1953.

U.S. Dept. of Defense: *Armed Forces Industrial Defense Regulations.* Washington, U.S. Govt. Printing Office, 1955.

————: *Industrial Security Manual for Safeguarding Classified Information.* Washington, U.S. Govt. Printing Office, 1956.

————: *Industry Guide to Planning for Restoration of Production.* Washington, U.S. Govt. Printing Office, 1954.

————: *Principles of Plant Protection.* Washington, U.S. Govt. Printing Office, 1950.

————: *Standards for Plant Protection.* Washington, U.S. Govt. Printing Office, 1952.

U.S. Dept. of State: *Foreign Service Security Regulations.* Washington, U.S. Govt. Printing Office, 1955.

U.S. Office of Defense Mobilization: *Standards for Physical Security of Industrial and Government Facilities.* Washington, U.S. Govt. Printing Office, 1958.

Van Pelt, H. C.: Law Enforcement and Industrial Security Interface, TPC, Vol.31 (Nov., 1964), 30.

Video Aids in Industrial Security, TPC, Vol.30 (May, 1963), 44.

————: *Motivation and Morale in Industry.* New York, Norton, 1953.

Von Haller, Gilmer B.: *Industrial Psychology.* New York, McGraw-Hill, 1961.

Walsh, Timothy J.: Law Enforcement Controls in Labor Disturbances, POLICE, Vol.8, No.6 (July-Aug., 1964), 25-31.

Weaver, Leon H. (ed.): *Industrial Personnel Security.* Springfield, Thomas, 1964.

Westinghouse Electric Corp., Lighting Division: *Light for Plant Safety and Security.* Cleveland, Westinghouse, 1951.

Whyte, William H., Jr.: *Is Anybody Listening?* New York, Simon & Schuster, 1952.

Wilson, Thomas J.: The Fingertip Alarm System, L&O, Vol.8, No.8 (1960).

Wright, Karl F.: Railroad Police, TPY (1962).

Yarmolinsky, Adam (ed.): *Case Studies in Personnel Security.* Washington, Bureau of National Affairs, Aug., 1955.

Young, Carl B.: *First-aid and Resuscitation-emergency Procedures for Rescue Squads, Ambulance Crews, Interns and Industrial Nurses.* Springfield, Thomas, 1954.

RETAIL SECURITY

Abrahamson, E. M.: *Body and Mind and Sugar.* New York, Holt.

Angelino, Henry: Shoplifting: A Critical Review, MS, Vols.1-5 (Spring, 1953), 17-22.

Arieff, Alex J., and Bowie, Carol G.: Some Psychiatric Aspects of Shoplifting, J.CLIN.PSY. Vol.8 (Jan., 1947), 565-576.

Ashby, W. R.: *Design for a Brain.* New York, Wiley, 1952.

Bleeker, Philip: Controlling Internal Theft, CHAIN STORE AGE, June, 1960.

Calif. Dept. of Education: *Investigation of Fictitious Checks.* Sacramento, Bureau of Trade and Industrial Education, 1949.

Cameron, Mary Owen: *The Booster and the Snitch.* New York, Free Press, 1964.

————: *Department Store Shoplifting.* Ph.D. Dissertation, Indiana University, 1953.

Controlling Shortages and Improving Protection. New York, National Retail Dry Goods Assoc., 1953.

Coping with Shoplifting. Los Angeles, Rogers & Assoc., 1954.

Counterfeit Currency, SW, Vol.1, No.3 (Nov.-Dec., 1964), 47.

Curtis, S. J.: *Modern Retail Security.* Springfield, Thomas, 1960.

Davis, John Richelieu: Packaging Can Curb Pilferage, POLICE, Vol.7, No.4 (Mar.-Apr., 1963), 44-46.

Debo, Charles: The Key to Shoplifting Control, SW, Vol.1, No.1 (July-Aug., 1964), 44-46.

The Doors of Perceptions. New York, Harper, 1954.

Edwards, Loren E.: The Challenge of Store Security, POLICE, Vol.3, No.4 (Mar.-Apr., 1959), 34-39.

————: *Shoplifting and Shrinkage Protection for Stores.* Springfield, Thomas, 1958.

Fisher, Jacob: *Art of Detection.* Newark, Rutgers Univ. Press.

Freud, A.: *The Ego and the Mechanisms of Defense.* New York, International Univ. Press, 1946.

Griffin, R. K.: Shoplifting in Supermarkets, TPC, Vol.31 (July, 1964), 37.

Hodgson, Tom: *You Can Do Something About Shoplifting.* Minneapolis, Minnesota Retail Federation.

Inbau, Fred E.: *Manual for Store Protection.* Chicago, Retail Special Service, 1951.

————: *Self Incrimination.* Springfield, Thomas, 1950.

Industrial Security III: Theft Control Proce-

dures. New York, National Industrial Conference Board, 1954.

Keating, James H.: Paper Bandits, SW, Vol.1, No.2 (Sept.-Oct., 1964), 30-33.

Kellett, William: Check Recovery: a Cooperative Solution, SW, Vol.2, No.2 (Mar.-Apr., 1965), 34-35.

Landis, John C.: The First-time Shoplifters, SW, Vol.1, No.1 (July-Aug., 1964), 23 & 61-62.

Lawder, Lee E.: Shoplifting—A Growing Occupation, L&O, Vol.12 (July, 1964).

Legal Aspects of Shoplifting, STLJ, Vol.3 (Summer-Fall, 1958), 353-83.

Lindner, Robert: *Must You Conform.* New York, Rinehart.

Machen, Ernest W., Jr.: *Search and Seizure.* Chapel Hill, Institute of Government.

Maier, Norman R. F.: *Psychology in Industry.* Boston, Houghton Mifflin.

May, Rollo: *Man's Search for Himself.* New York, Morton.

Morgan, Patrick: *Successful Handling of Casualty Claims.* New York, Prentice-Hall.

Morris, Howard B.: *Elements of Successful Plant Protection.* 231 W. Breckenridge, Louisville 3, Kentucky.

National Retail Dry Goods Assoc.: *Controlling Shortages and Improving Protection.* A report prepared by the National Retail Dry Goods Assoc., 1953.

Ordway, John A.: "Successful" Court Treatment of Shoplifters, JCLC&PS, Vol.53, No.3 (Sept.-Nov., 1962), 344.

Pollack, Jack H.: The War on Shoplifters, THIS WEEK (Oct., 30, 1949), 4.

Robin, Gerald D.: The American Customer: Shopper or Shoplifter? POLICE, Vol.8, No.3 (Jan.-Feb., 1964), 6-14.

Robinson and Bresco: *Store Organization and Operation.* New York, Harper.

Rogers, Keith and Whitam, W. G.: *Coping with Shoplifting.* Los Angeles, Rogers & Assoc.

Rouke, Fabian L.: Psychology of the Retail Criminal, POLICE, Vol.4, No.4 (Mar.-Apr., 1960), 28-32.

————: Shoplifting: Its Symbolic Motivation, NPPA JOURNAL, Vol.3 (Jan., 1957), 54-58.

Savord, George H.: Teaching Clerks to Look at Checks, TPC (Jan., 1961), 6.

Sears, Roebuck & Co.: *Retail Security Manual.* Chicago, Sears, Roebuck & Co., 1963.

Shoplifting Racket—Tricks of the Trade, 1953. American Stores, Inc., 1953.

Shortage Control Manual. Detroit, J. L. Hudson Co. Stealing Is a Symptom, PARENTS (Jan., 1952).

Sterling, Stewart: Stop the Shoplifter, SATURDAY EVENING POST (Oct. 22, 1949).

Sternitsky, Julius L.: *Forgery and Fictitious Checks.* Springfield, Thomas, 1955.

Stock Shortage Control Manual. New York, Controller Congress, NRMA, 1951.

Stock Shortages. New York, National Retail Merchants Assoc., 1959.

Store Protection. Boston, Retail Trade Board, Greater Boston Chamber of Commerce, 1954.

Stores Mutual Protection Assoc.: *Manual for Store Security.* New York, 1954.

Swift, S. K.: *The Cardinal's Story.* New York, Macmillan, 1949.

Tocchio, O. J.: Counterfeiting: Another Merchants' Dilemma, POLICE, Vol.8, No.2 (Nov.-Dec., 1963), 44-47.

————: Shoplifting—The Scourge of Mercantile Establishments, POLICE, Vol.6, No.5 (May-June, 1962), 8-15; Vol.7, No.1 (Sept.-Oct., 1962), 53-56; No.2 (Nov.-Dec., 1962), 28-31.

Trading Dollars for Worthless Checks, AMERICAN STORES, 1953.

Waltz, John R.: Shoplifting and the Law of Arrest, YLJ, Vol.62 (Apr., 1953), 788-805.

Watch Out for That Thief. New York, Store Management Group, NRMA.

Wendell, Roy: Shoplifting a Growing Menace, KIWANIS MAGAZINE (Feb., 1953).

Why Boys Steal, ATLANTIC (Oct., 1951).

Why Shoplifters Get Caught, CORONET (Aug., 1950).

You Can Do Something About Shoplifting. Minneapolis, Minnesota Retail Federation, Inc., 1955.

Chapter Nine

MISCELLANEOUS SUBJECTS*

CRIMINOLOGY

Abrahamsen, David: Family Tension Basic Cause of Criminal Behavior, JCL&C, Vol.40, No.3 (Sept.-Oct., 1949), 330.

Alexander, Franz, and Healy, William: *Roots of Crime: Psychoanalytic Studies.* New York, Knopf, 1954.

———, **& Staub, Hugo:** *The Criminal, The Judge and the Public.* Glencoe, Free Press, 1956.

Allen, Francis A.: Raffaele Gadford (1852-1934), JCLC&PS Vol.45 (1954-55), 373-90.

Alter, Julius: *Crimes of Puerto Ricans in Brooklyn.* Master's Thesis, Brooklyn College, 1958.

Ball, John C.: The Deterence Concept on Criminology and Law JCLC&PS, Vol.46 (1955-56), 347-54.

Barnes, Harry E., and Teeters, Negley K.: *New Horizons in Criminology,* 3rd Ed. New York, Prentice-Hall, 1959.

Barry, John Vincent: Alexander Macanochie, JCLC&PS, Vol.47, No.2 (July-Aug., 1956), 145.

Bianchi, Hermanus: *Position and Subject-matter of Criminology.* Amsterdam, North Holland Publishing, 1956.

Bloch, Herbert A.: They Are Not Born Criminals, FP, Vol.22 (Sept., 1958), 15-20.

———, **& Geis, Gilbert:** Man, Crime and Society, THE ANNALS, Vol.347 (May, 1963), 169.

Bradford, Lowell W.: The California Association of Criminalists, JCLC&PS, Vol.53, No.2 (Sept.-Nov., 1962), 375.

Branham, Vernon C., and Kutash, Samuel B.: *Encyclopedia of Criminology.* New York, Philosophical Library, 1949.

Brasol, Boris: Institute of Scientific Criminology, SE&SCD, Vol.1, No.1 (1964).

Bressler, Marvin: Criminological Research Bulletin, JCL&C, Vol.34, No.2 (July-Aug., 1953), 185-203.

Bromberg, Walter: American Achievements in Criminology (1938-50), JCL&C, Vol.44, No.2 (July-Aug., 1953), 156-70.

———: *Crime and the Mind: an Outline of Psychiatric Criminology.* Philadelphia, Lippincott, 1948.

Caldwell, Morris G.: Case Analysis Method for the Personality Study of Defenders, JCLC&PS, Vol.45 (1954-55), 291-98.

Caldwell, Rogert G.: *Criminology,* 2nd Ed. New York, Ronald, 1965.

California Special Crime Study Commission: *Final Report of the Special Crime Study Commission on Social and Economic Causes of Crime and Delinquency.* Sacramento, State Printing Office, 1949.

Caputo, Rudolph R.: Women—Better Liars than Men? L&O, Vol.11, No.10 (Oct., 1963).

Cavan, Ruth Shonel: *Criminology,* 3rd Ed. New York, Harper & Bros., 1962.

Cavanagh, John R.: The Comics War, JCL&C, Vol.40, No.1 (May-June, 1949), 28.

Chwast, Jacob: The Malevolent Transformation, JCLC&PS, Vol.54, No.1 (1963), 42.

Clinard, Marshall B.: A Cross Cultural Replication of the Relationship of Urbanism to Criminal Behavior, ASR, Vol.25 (Apr., 1960), 253-67.

———: Criminological Theories of Violations of Wartime Regulations, ASR, Vol.11, No.3 (June, 1946), 258-70.

Cressey, Donald R.: Differential Association Theory and Compulsive Crimes, JCL&C, Vol.45 (May-June, 1954), 29-40.

———: Epidemiology and Individual Conduct: A Case from Criminology, PSR, Vol.3 (1960), 47-58.

Crittenden, B. M.: Problems in the Field of Legislation, TPY (1961).

Culbert, Sidney S.: Systematic Error in the Estimation of Short Time Intervals, JCL&C, Vol.44, No.5 (Jan.-Feb., 1954), 684-88.

Dauticourt, Joseph Y.: Crime Against Humanity —European Views on Its Concept and Its Future, JCL&C, Vol.40, No.2 (July-Aug., 1949), 170.

Driver, Edwin D.: Charles Buckman Goring (Pioneers in Criminology), JCLC&PS, Vol.47, No.5 (Jan.-Feb., 1957), 515.

East, W. Norwood: Physical Factors and Criminal Behavior, JCLIN.PSY.

---

* This Chapter includes: Criminology, International Police, Law Enforcement Agencies, Sociology and Psychology of Crime.

Eliasberg, Waldimir: Urge and Motivation in Criminology, JCLC&PS, Vol.43, No.3 (Sept.-Oct., 1952), 319.

Eliot, Thomas D.: A Criminological Approach to the Social Control of International Aggressions, AJS, Vol.58 (Mar., 1953), 513-18.

Evans, Jean: *Three Men.* New York, Knopf, 1954.

Floch, Maurice: The Concept of Temporary Insanity Viewed by a Criminologist, JCLC&PS, Vol.45 (1954-55), 685-89.

Forcible Taking Under Honest Claim Does Not Constitute Robbery, JCLC&PS, Vol.46 (1955-56), 239.

Gardiner, Gordon A., Khanna, L. Jaswatt, and Pratt, Steve: Attitudes of Psychiatric Aides Toward Criminally Insane Patients, JCLC&PS, Vol.53, No.1 (Mar.-May, 1962), 55.

Garrity, Donald L., and Gibbons, Don C.: Definition and Analysis of Certain Criminal Types, JCLC&PS, Vol.53, No.1 (Mar.-May, 1962), 27.

Gault, Robert H.: Character Development and Criminology, JCLC&PS, Vol.43, No.3 (Sept.-Oct., 1952), 346.

———: Criminologists in a Pan American Congress, JCL&C, Vol.38, No.2 (Mar.-Apr., 1947-48), 93-94.

———: Criminology in Northwestern Univ., JCLC&PS, Vol.42 (1951-52), 2.

———: The International Society of Criminology, JCL&C, Vol.40, No.1 (May-June, 1949), 1.

Geis, Gilbert: In Search of Criminology, JCLC&PS, Vol.53, No.3 (Sept.-Nov., 1962), 359.

———: Jeremy Bentham (Pioneers in Criminology), JCLC&PS, Vol.46 (1955-56), 159-71.

Gibbons, Don C. and Garrity, Donald L.: Definition and Analysis of Certain Criminal Types, JCLC&PS, Vol.53, No.1 (Mar., 1962), 27-35.

———, & ———: Some Suggestions for the Definition of Etiological and Treatment Theory in Criminology, SF, Vol.38 (Oct., 1959), 51-57.

Gibbs, Jack P.: Needed: Analytical Typologies in Criminology, SSSQ, Vol.40 (Mar.), 321-29.

Gillin, John L.: *Criminology and Penology.* New York, Appleton, 1945.

Glover, Edward: Psychoanalysis and Criminology: a Political Survey, IJP, Vol.37 (1956), 311-17.

Glueck, S.: Theory and Fact in Criminology, BJD, Vol.7 (1956), 92-109.

———: Two International Criminologic Congress: a Panorama, MH, Vol.40 (1956), 384-599.

———, & Glueck, Eleanor: A Decade of Research in Criminology: Stock-taking and a Forward Look, ECRIM, Vol.3, No.5 (1963).

———, & ———: Progress Report to Members of Fourth International Congress of Criminology, The Hague, Issued by the Secretariat to the Congress, 1960.

Grafton, Samuel: What Has Happened to Law and Order in the United States, LOOK (July 3, 1962).

Grassberger, Roland: Hans Gross (Pioneers in Criminology), JCLC&PS, Vol.47, No.4 (Nov.-Dec., 1956), 397.

Gutman, Daniel: The Criminal Gets the Breaks, TPC, Vol.32, No.2 (Feb., 1965), 36-40.

Hall, Jerome: Criminology, in Georges Gruvitch and Wilbert E. Moore, *Twentieth Century Sociology,* New York, Philosophical Library, 1945, 342-365.

———: *Studies in Jurisprudence and Criminal Theory.* New York, Oceana, 1958.

Hayner, N. S.: Criminologenic Zones in Mexico City, ASR, Vol.11 (Aug., 1946), 428-38.

Helldoerfer, Heinrich: A New Copy Pencil, JCLC&PS, Vol.43, No.6 (Mar.-Apr., 1953), 834.

Hobsbawm, E. J.: *Social Bandits and Primitive Rebels.* Glencoe, Free Press, 1959.

Hoebel, Edward A.: *The Law of Primitive Man.* Cambridge, Harvard Univ. Press, 1954.

Horowitz, Milton W.: The Psychology of Confession, JCLC&PS, Vol.47, No.2 (July-Aug., 1956), 197.

House, Robert E.: The Use of Scopolamine in Criminology, SE&SCD, Vol.2, No.4 (1964).

Hurwitz, Stephan: *Criminology.* London, George Allen & Unwin, 1952.

IACP Seeks Information on Legislation, TPC, Vol.30 (May, 1963), 44.

Iane, Robert E.: Why Business Men Violate the Law, JCL&C, Vol.44, No.2 (July-Aug., 1953), 151-65.

Inbau, Fred E.: *Self-Incrimination.* Springfield, Thomas, 1950.

Jameson, Samuel: Haig-Quo Vadimus in Criminological Training, JCLC&PS, Vol.50, No.4 (Nov.-Dec., 1959), 358.

Jeffery, C. Ray: Criminology and Penology, JCLC&PS, Vol.51, No.1 (Mar.-Apr., 1960-61), 82.

———: Pioneers in Criminology: Historical Development of Criminal Justice, JCLC&PS (May-June, 1959).

———: The Structure of American Criminological Thinking, JCLC&PS, Vol.46 (1955-56), 658-72.

Johnson, Elmer Hubert: *Crime, Correction, and Society.* Homewood, Dorsey, 1964.

Johnston, Norman B.: V. John Haviland (1792-1852), JCLC&PS, Vol.45 (1954-55), 509-19.

Kenison, Frank R.: Charles Dow (Pioneers in Criminology), JCLC&PS, Vol.47, No.3 (Sept.-Oct., 1956), 277.

Kinsey, Barry A.: A Study of Adverse Community Reaction to the Starkweather Case, PO-LICE, Vol.4, No.4 (Mar.-Apr., 1960), 62-64.

Kirk, Paul L.: Standardization of Criminological Nomenclature, JCL&C, Vol.38, No.2 (Mar.-Apr., 1947-48), 165-67.

Korn, Richard R., and McCorkle, Lloyd W.: *Criminology and Penology.* New York, Holt, 1959.

Larson, Cedric: Harry Soderman of Stockholm: Master Criminologist, JCLC&PS, Vol.43, No.1 (May-June, 1952), 95.

Lilienthal, David E.: *This I Do Believe.* New York, Harper, 1949.

Lindesmith, Alfred R.: Pioneers in Criminology, JCLC&PS, Vol.53, No.1 (Mar.-May, 1962), 79.

Lipton, Harry R.: An Analysis of 31 Individuals Examined While Awaiting Trial in Federal Court, JCL&C, Vol.38, No.6 (May-Apr., 1947-48), 595-612.

Lopez-Rey, Manuel: Pedro Dorada Montero (Pioneers in Criminology), JCLC&PS, Vol.46 (1955-56), 605-11.

Lunden, Walter A.: Pioneers in Criminology, JCLC&PS, Vol.49, No.1 (1958-59), 2.

McCormick, C. T.: Deception Tests and the Law of Evidence, SE&SCD, Vol.2, No.5 (1964).

McKeown, James E.: Poverty, Race and Crime, JCL&C, Vol.39, No.4 (Mar.-Apr., 1948-49), 480-85.

Mann, Arthur: Group Therapy-irradiation, JCLC&PS, Vol.46 (1955-56), 50-66.

Mannheim, Hermann: *Pioneers in Criminology.* Chicago, Quadrangle Books, 1960.

Martin, John Barlow: *Why Did They Kill?* New York, Ballatine, 1953.

Menninger, Karl, and Statten, Joseph: The Development of a Psychiatric Criminology, BMC, Vol.25 (July, 1961), 164-172.

Monachesi, Elio: Cesare Beccaria (Pioneers in Criminology), JCLC&PS, Vol.46 (1955-56), 439-49.

Mandel, Nathan G.: Recidivism Studies and Defined, JCLC&PS, Vol.56, No.1 (Mar., 1964), 59-66.

Morris, Albert: The Comprehensive Classification of Adult Offenders, JCLC&PS, Vol.56, No.2 (June, 1965), 197-202.

Morris, Terence: *The Criminal Area: a Study in Social Ecology.* London, Routledge & Kegan, Paul, 1958.

Moses, Earl R.: Differentials in Crime Rates Between Negroes and Whites on Comparisons of Four Socio-economically Equated Areas, ASR, Vol.12 (Aug., 1947), 411-20.

Mouledous, Joseph C.: Pioneers in Criminology: Edward Livingston, JCLC&PS, Vol.54, No.3 (1963), 288.

Overholster, Winfred: Issac Ray, M.D., JCLC&PS, Vol.45 (1954-55), 249-63.

Peterson, Virgil W.: Why Honest People Steal, JCL&C, Vol.38, No.2 (Mar.-Apr., 1947-48), 94-103.

Poddlsky, Edward: The Chemical Brew of Criminal Behavior, JCLC&PS, Vol.45 (1954-55), 675-78.

Pollak, Otto: Criminological Research Bulletin —New Series No.1, JCL&C, Vol.40, No.6 (Mar.-Apr., 1950), 701.

Radzinowicz, Leon: Criminology Goes on Par with Other Sciences, L&O, Vol.7 (Sept., 1959).

Rasch, Philip and Von Hentig, Hans: Red Hair and Outlawry, JCL&C, Vol.38, No.4 (Mar.-Apr., 1947-48), 352-57.

Reitzes, Dietrich C.: The Effect of Social Environment Upon Former Felons, JCLC&PS, Vol.46 (1955-56), 226-31.

Ribman, Ronald B., and Ribman, Samuel M.: The Poor Man in the Scales, HARPER'S, Vol.228, No.1367 (Apr., 1964), 150-58.

Robin, Gerald D.: Pioneers in Criminology, JCLC&PS, Vol.55, No.1 (Mar., 1964), 59.

Roebuck, Julian B.: The Negro Numbers Man as a Criminal Type: The Construction and Application of a Typology, JCLC&PS, Vol.54, No.1 (1963), 48.

Savitz, Leonard D.: Capital Crimes As Defined in American Statutory Law, JCLC&PS, Vol.46 (1955-56), 355-63.

Schiller, Andrew: People in Trouble, HARPER'S, Vol.228, No.1367 (Apr., 1964), 145-49.

Schmideberg, Melitta: The Offender's Attitude Toward Punishment, JCLC&PS, Vol.51, No.3 (Mar.-Apr., 1960-61), 328.

Scott, Peter: Hendy Maudsley (Pioneer in Criminology), JCLC&PS, Vol.46 (1955-56), 753-69.

Sellin, Thornsten: The Philadelphia Gibbet Iron, JCLC&PS, Vol.46 (1955-56), 11-25.

Shaw, Van B.: Relationship Between Crime Rates and Certain Population Characteristics in Minnesota Counties, JCL&C, Vol.49, No.1 (May-June, 1949), 43.

Shoham, Shlomo: The Application of the Culture Conflict, Hypothesis of the Criminality of Immigrants in Israel, JCLC&PS, Vol.53, No.2 (June-Aug., 1962), 207.

Shulman, Harry M.: Cultural Aspects of Criminal Responsibility, JCLC&PS, Vol.43, No.3 (Sept.-Oct., 1952), 323.

Slovenko, Ralph: Are Women More Law-abiding Than Men? POLICE, Vol.8, No.6 (July-Aug., 1964), 17-24.

Sorenson, Robert C.: U.S. Vs. Hiss: Its Significance for Criminology, JCLC&PS, Vol.43, No.3 (Sept.-Oct., 1952), 299.

Stewart, James W.: Legislative Problems, TPY (1961).

Sutherland, Edwin H., & **Cressey, Donald:** *Principles of Criminology*, 6th ed. Philadelphia, Lippincott, 1960.

Sykes, Gresham: Review of Criminology and Penology, ASR, Vol.25 (Apr., 1960), 304.

Taft, Donald R.: *Criminology*, rev. ed. New York, Macmillan, 1950.

————: Implication of the Glueck Methodology for Criminological Research, JCLC&PS, Vol.42 (1951-52), 300.

Tappan, Paul W.: *Crime, Justice and Correction*. New York, McGraw-Hill, 1960.

————: Florida's Enquiry into the Causes of Crime, JCL&C, Vol.44, No.1 (May-June, 1953), 17-21.

————: Who Is the Criminal, ASR, Vol.12, No.1 (Feb., 1947), 96-102.

Taylor, Telford: *Grand Inquest*. New York, Ballantine, 1961.

Turk, Austin T.: Prospects for Theories of Criminal Behavior, JCLC&PS, Vol.55, No.4 (Dec., 1964), 452.

VanBemmelen, J. M.: Willem Adriaan Bonger (Pioneers in Criminology), JCLC&PS, Vol.46 (1955-56), 293-302.

Vanderbosch, C. G.: Before the Lights Go Out, TPC,, Vol.31 (Jan., 1964), 32.

Vedder, Clyde B. Koenig, Samuel, and Clark, Robert E. (eds.): *Criminology: a Book of Readings*. New York, Dryden, 1953.

Vold, George B.: Criminology at the Cross-Roads, JCLC&PS, Vol.42 (July-Aug., 1951), 155-62.

————: Some Basic Problems in Criminological Research, FP, Vol.17 (Mar., 1953), 37-42.

————: *Theoretical Criminology*. New York, Oxford Univ. Press, 1958.

Vollmer, August: *The Criminal*. New York, Foundation Press (out of print).

Von Hentig, Hans: Gustav Aschaffenburg (1866-1944), JCLC&PS, Vol.45 (1954-55), 117-22.

Weihofen, Henry: *Mental Disorder as a Criminal Defense*. Buffalo, Dennis, 1954.

Weinber, S. Kirson: Theories of Criminality and Problems of Prediction, JCLC&PS, Vol.45 (1954-55), 412-24.

Whyte, William Foote: *Street Corner Society*. Chicago, Univ. of Chicago, 1958.

Wilber, G. L.: The Scientific Adequacy of Criminology Concepts, SF, Vol.28 (Dec., 1949), 165-174.

Wilson, Margaret S.: Gabiel Tarde, JCLC&PS, Vol.45 (1954-55), 3-11.

Wilson, O. W.: Bruce Smith, JCLC&PS, Vol.47, No.2 (July-Aug., 1956), 235.

Wolfgang, Marvin E.: Criminology and the Criminologist, JCLC&PS, Vol.54, No.2 (1963), 155.

————: Pioneers in Criminology: Cesare Lombroso (1835-1909), JCLC&PS, Vol.52, No.4 (Nov.-Dec., 1961), 361.

————: Socio-economic Factors Related to Crime and Punishment in Renaissance Florence, JCLC&PS, Vol.47, No.3 (Sept.-Oct., 1956), 311.

INTERNATIONAL POLICE

Abe, Harau: Criminal Justice in Japan, ABAJ, Vol.47 (June, 1961), 555-559.

————: Criminal Procedure in Japan, JCLC&PS, Vol.48, No.4 (Nov.-Dec., 1957), 359.

————: The Exclusionary Rule Under Foreign Law, JCLC&PS, Vol.52, No.3 (Sept.-Oct., 1961), 284.

————: Police Detention and Arrest Under Foreign Law, JCLC&PS, Vol.51, No.4 (Mar.-Apr., 1960-61), 429.

————: Police Interrogation Privileges and Limitations Under Foreign Law, JCLC&PS, Vol.52, No.1 (May-June, 1961), 67.

————: The Privilege Against Self-Incrimination Under Foreign Law, JCLC&PS, Vol.51, No.2 (Mar.-Apr., 1960-61), 178.

————: Self-Incrimination—Japan and the U.S., JCLC&PS, Vol.46 (1955-56), 613-31.

Adkins, E. H., Jr.: Malaya Controls Its Criminal Societies, POLICE, Vol.7, No.2 (Nov.-Dec., 1962), 63-71.

Allen, C. K.: *The Queen's Peace*. London, Stevens, 1953.

Amory, Robert, Jr.: Law Enforcement in Soviet Russia, TPY (1960).

Anthony, M. F. E.: Police Training in Canada, TPY (1962).

Archer, P.: *Queen's Courts*. Baltimore, Penguin, 1956.

Asratyan, E. A.: *Pavlov, His Life and Work*. Moscow, Foreign Language, 1953.

Asuni, T.: Socio-psychiatric Problems of Cannabis in Nigeria, United Nations, BN, Vol.16, No.2 (Apr.-June, 1964), 17-28.

Babkin: *B. P. Pavlov, A Biography.* London, Gollancz, 1951.

Barr, R.: *The Scotland Yard Story.* London, Hodder, 1962.

Batson, W. C.: The London River Police, ICPR, No.74 (Jan., 1954), 3-11.

Battaglini, Giulio: The Exclusion of the Concourse of Causes in Italian Criminal Law, JCLC&PS, Vol.43, No.4 (Nov.-Dec., 1952), 441.

Baumann, W. H.: Report of the Committee on International Relations, TPY (1962); (1963); (1964).

Beck, F., and Godin, W.: *Russian Purge and the Extraction of Confession.* New York, Viking, 1950.

Beg, Sherullas: Pakistani Official Visits European Police, TPC (Oct., 1961), 28.

Berman, H. J.: *Justice in Russia: an Interpretation of Soviet Law.* Cambridge, Harvard, 1950.

Bernaut, Elsa, and Ruggles, Melville J.: *Collective Leadership and the Political Police in the Soviet Union.* Santa Monica, Rand Corp, 1956.

Bernstein, Victor H.: *Final Judgment: the Story of Nuremberg.* New York, Boni & Gaer, 1947.

Bischoff, P.: The Institute of Police Science at the University of Lausanne (Switzerland), SE&SCD, Vol.1, No.5 (1964).

Bonifacio, Rizalina S.: Philippine Policewoman Visits U.S., TPC (Mar., 1961), 26.

Books for the Philippine Constabulatory, TPC, Vol.30 (Oct., 1963), 30.

Bovell, Kerr, Sir: Police of Nigeria, TPC, Vol.29, No.10 (Oct., 1962), 12.

Boynton, Lindsay: The Tudor Provost-Marshal, EHR, Vol.77 (Jan., 1962), 437-55.

Brandsted, Ernest K.: *Dictatorship and Political Police: the Technique of Control by Fear.* Oxford, Oxford Univ. Press, 1945.

Bratholm, Anders: The Exclusionary Rule Under Foreign Law, JCLC&PS, Vol.52, No.3 (Sept.-Oct., 1961), 287.

———: Police Detention and Arrest Privilege Under Foreign Law (Norway), JCLC&PS, Vol.51, No.4 (Mar.-Apr., 1960-61), 437.

———: Police Interrogation Privileges and Limitations Under Foreign Law, JCLC&PS, Vol.52, No.1 (May-June, 1961), 72.

———: The Privilege Against Self-incrimination Under Foreign Law (Norway), JCLC&PS, Vol.51, No.2 (Mar.-Apr., 1960-61), 186.

Browne, Douglas G.: *The Rise of Scotland Yard:*

A History of the Metropolitan Police. London, Harrap, 1956.

Bull, Henry H.: The Carrer Prosecutor of Canada, JCLC&PS, Vol.53, No.1 (Mar.-May, 1962), 89.

Butchers, R. J.: International Police Public Relations, TPY (1964).

Byron, William F.: Canadian Penal Institutions, JCL&C, Vol.35, No.5 (Jan.-Feb., 1945), 330.

Calvert, Fred: *The Constable's Pocket Guide to Powers of Arrest and Charges,* 3rd Ed. London, Butterworth, 1962.

Career in Scarlet: Ottawa, Royal Canadian Mounted Police, 1964.

Castberg, F.: *Freedom of Speech in the West.* Dobbs Ferry, Oceana, 1960.

Caughley, J. G., and Taylor, A. J. W.: New Methods in the Promotion of Constables to Sergeants in the New Zealand Police Force, JCLC&PS, Vol.48, No.2 (July-Aug., 1957), 207.

Cavan, Ruth Schonle: International Review of Criminal Policy, JCLC&PS, Vol.51, No.2 (Mar.-Apr., 1960-61), 245.

Central Office of Information: *The Police in Britain,* Central Office of Information, London, 1954.

Chapman, Samuel G.: Rural Police Patrol in England and Wales, JCLC&PS, Vol.45, No.4 (Nov.-Dec., 1954), 499-501.

———: Urban Police Patrol in England and Wales, JCLC&PS, Vol.45 (1954-55), 349-58.

———, & St. Johnston, T. Eric, Col.: *The Police Heritage in England and America.* East Lansing, Michigan State Univ., 1962.

Chi-Yu, Cheng: The Chinese Theory of Criminal Law, JCL&C, Vol.39, No.4 (Mar.-Apr., 1948-49), 461-80.

Chu, Kwang-Shee: The Chinese Central Police College, JCL&C, Vol.36, No.4 (1945-46), 290.

Clemens, Walter R.: The Exclusionary Rule Under Foreign Law, JCLC&PS, Vol.52, No.3 (Sept.-Oct., 1961), 277.

———: Police Detention and Arrest Privileges Under Foreign Law, JCLC&PS, Vol.51, No.4 (Mar.-Apr., 1960-61), 421.

———: Police Interrogation Privileges and Limitations Under Foreign Law, JCLC&PS, Vol.52, No.1 (May-June, 1961), 59.

———: The Privilege Against Self-incrimination Under Foreign Law (Germany), JCLC&PS, Vol.51, No.2 (Mar.-Apr., 1960-61), 172.

Coatman, J.: *Police.* London, Oxford Univ. Press, 1959.

Cohn, Haim H.: The Exclusionary Rule Under

Foreign Law (Israel), JCLC&PS, Vol.52, No.3 (Sept.-Oct., 1961), 282.

———: Police Detention and Arrest Privileges Under Foreign Law (Israel), JCLC&PS, Vol.51, No.4 (Mar.-Apr., 1960-61), 426.

———: Police Interrogation Privileges and Limitations Under Foreign Law (Israel), JCLC&PS, Vol.52, No.1 (May-June, 1961), 63.

———: The Privilege Against Self-Incrimination Under Foreign Law (Israel), JCLC&PS, Vol.51, No.2 (Mar.-Apr., 1960-61), 175.

Common, Wellis B.: The Administration of Criminal Justice in Canada, JCLC&PS, Vol.43, No.1 (May-June, 1952).

Conacher, J. B.: Peel and the Peelites, 1846-1850, EHR, Vol.73, 431-52 (Jan., 1958), 431-52.

Conlin, J.: *Elements of Local and Central Government for the Police Officer.* London, Cox & Wyman, Ltd., 1962.

Contract Police Service, RCMP, TPC, Vol.31 (June, 1964), 50.

Cowen, Z.: *Federal Jurisdiction in Australia.* New York, Oxford Univ. Press, 1959.

Cristoph, James B.: Capital Punishment and British Policies, THE ANNALS, Vol.347 (May, 1963), 167.

Dahlberg, Gunnar: A New Method of Crime Statistics Applied to the Population of Sweden, JCL&C, Vol.39, No.3 (Mar.-Apr., 1948-49), 327-54.

Dangerous Drugs Act, Great Britain, 1951, 1953. London, Her Majesty's Stationery Office.

Darwish, Abdel Karim I.: Vendetta in Upper Egypt, L&O, Vol.8, No.9 (1960).

David, R., and De Vries, H. P.: *The French Legal System: an Introduction to Civil Law Systems.* Dobbs Ferry, Oceana, 1958.

Derome, Wilfrid: The Laboratory of Legal Medicine and Technical Police of Montreal, SE&SCD, Vol.1, No.2 (1964).

Devlin, J. Daniel: *Moriarty's Questions and Answers on Police Subjects,* 2nd Ed. London, Butterworth, 1961.

———: *The Criminal Prosecution in England.* New Haven, Yale Univ. Press, 1958.

Dicey, A. V.: *Law and Public Opinion in England During the 19th Century.* New York, Torch, 1958.

Dues, IACP Members Outside the U.S., TPC, Vol.30 (May, 1963), 50.

Dunner, Gene: The Police of Venice, TPC, Vol.28, No.9 (Sept., 1961).

Eaton, Joseph W.: *Prisons in Israel: a Study of Policy Innovations.* Pittsburgh, Univ. of Pittsburgh Press, 1964.

Emerson, Donald: *The Police System of Joseph*

II. Unpublished Master Thesis, Univ. of Washington, Pullman, 1950.

Falkenstam, Curt: 1965 Reorganization in Sweden, TPC, Vol.31 (Feb., 1964), 41.

Feldbrugge, F. J.: Soviet Criminal Law—The Last Six Years, JCLC&PS, Vol.54, No.3 (1963), 249.

Ferenez, Benjamin B.: Nuremberg Trial Procedure and the Rights of the Accused, JCL&C, Vol.39, No.2 (Mar.-Apr., 1948-49), 144-52.

Fraser, Gordon: Australian International Airline Security, POLICE, Vol.8, No.1 (Sept.-Oct., 1963), 30-32.

———: Letter from Australia, TPC, Vol.29, No.5 (May, 1962), 43.

Fujiki, Hideo: Recent Trends of Juvenile Crime in Japan, JCLC&PS, Vol.53, No.2 (June-Aug., 1962), 219.

Gallagher, Richard F.: *Nuremberg: The Third Reich on Trial.* New York, Avon, 1961.

Gelinas, Paul-Marcel: Special Seminar Conducted by Canadian Mental Health Association, TPY (1962).

Gilbert, G. M.: *Nuremberg Diary.* New York, Signet, 1961.

Giles, F. T.: *The Criminal Law.* New York, Penguin, 1955.

Glyde: Localities of Crime in Suffolk, JSSL, Vol.19 (1956).

Goddard, Calvin: Scientific Crime Detection Laboratories in Europe, SE&SCD, Vol.1, No.1; Vol.1, No.2 (1964).

Goedhard, Neil: Organization and Administration of the Police in West Germany, 1945-50. Unpublished Master's Thesis, Los Angeles, Univ. of So. Calif., 1954.

Goldenbert, H. Carl: *Report of the Royal Commission on Metropolitan Toronto.* Ontario, Frederich H. Finnis, MBE, Secretary and Research Director, 1965.

Goefer, Frederick: The Nazi Penal System, JCL&C, Vol.35, No.6 (Mar.-Apr., 1945), 385.

Gosovsky, V., and Grzybowski, K. (eds.): *Government, Law and the Courts in the Soviet Union and Eastern Europe.* New York, Praeger, 1960.

Hanbury, H. G.: *English Courts of Law,* 2nd Ed. New York, Oxford, 1953.

Hardesty, M. Norton: International Technical Cooperation, TPY, 1956.

Harris, John S.: Central Inspection of Local Police Services in Britain, JCLC&PS, Vol.45 (1954-55), 85-95.

Harris, R. E.: New Police College Opened in Britain, JCL&C, Vol.40, No.2 (July-Aug., 1949), 217.

————: The Police Federation in Britain, JCL&C, Vol.36, No.2 (1945-46), 121.

Hart, J. M.: *The British Police*. London, Allen & Unwin, 1951.

————: Reform of the Borough Police, 1835-56, EHR, Vol.70 (Jan., 1955), 411-27.

Harvey, S.: *London Policewoman*. London, Angus & Robertson, 1958.

Hasanat, Abul: The CID in East Pakistan, JCLC&PS, Vol.48, No.4 (Nov.-Dec., 1957), 447.

Hazard, John N.: *Law and Social Change in the USSR*. London, Stevens, 1953.

Helot, Henry: The Laboratory of Legal Medicine and Crime Detection of Algiers, SE&SCD, Vol.2, No.2 (1964).

Hewitt, William H.: *British Police Administration*. Springfield, Thomas, 1965.

Higgins, Lois L.: Bombay and a Lovely Police Woman, L&O, Vol.12 (July, 1964).

His Majesty's Stationery Office: *Criminal Statistics, England and Wales*. London, HMSO, Published Annually.

Holdsworth, William, Sir: *A History of English Law*, Vol.1, 7th Ed., London, Methusen, 1956.

Holt, J. C.: The Making of Magna Carta, EHR, Vol.72 (Jan., 1957), 401-22.

Home Office: *Higher Training for the Police Service in England and Wales*. London, Her Majesty's Stationery Office, 1960.

————: *Memorandum on the Design and Construction of Police Stations*. London, Her Majesty's Stationery Office, 1955.

————: *Metropolitan Police: Manual of Metropolitan Police*. London, Her Majesty's Stationery Office, 1960.

————: *The Police Ace*, 1919. London, Her Majesty's Stationery Office, 1963.

————: *Police Counties and Boroughs, England and Wales*. London, Her Majesty's Stationery Office, 1960.

————: *Police of the Metropolis*. London, Her Majesty's Stationery Office, 1960.

————: *Police Pensions: Report of the Working Party of the Police Council*. London, Her Majesty's Stationery Office, 1952.

————: *The Police Regulations, 1952*. London, Her Majesty's Stationery Office, 1952.

————: *Report of the Commissioner of Police of the Metropolis for the Year 1960*. London, Her Majesty's Stationery Office, 1960.

————: *Report of the Committee of the Police Council on Police Representative Organisations and Negotiation Machinery*. London, Her Majesty's Stationery Office, 1952.

————: *Report of the Committee on Police Extraneous Duties*. London, Her Majesty's Stationery Office, 1953.

————: *Report of the Police Council on the Standardisation of the Promotion Examinations*. London, Her Majesty's Stationery Office, 1951.

————: *The Report of Working Group on Crime Prevention Methods*. London, Her Majesty's Stationery Office, 1956.

————: *Royal Commission of the Police: Interim Report*. London, Her Majesty's Stationery Office, 1960.

————: *Royal Commission of the Police: Selection of Further Evidence Submitted Which Was Not Made the Basis of Oral Examination in Public*. London, Her Majesty's Stationery Office, 1962.

————: *Royal Commission of the Police*. London, Her Majesty's Stationery Office, 1962.

Howard, G.: *Guardians of the Queen's Peace*. London, Odhams, 1953.

Illing, Hans A.: Ich Beantrage Freispruch, JCLC&PS, Vol.51, No.3 (Mar.-Apr., 1960-61), 341.

Influence of the Royal Canadian Mounted Police in the Building of Canada. Ottawa, Royal Canadian Mounted Police, 1964.

International Congress of Criminology, JCLC&PS, Vol.46 (1955-56), 857.

Interpretation of Changes in Crimes in Japan, JCLC&PS, Vol.46 (1955-56), 243.

Jackson, R. M.: *The Machinery of Justice in England*, 3rd Ed. Cambridge, Cambridge Univ., 1960.

Jackson, Robert H.: *The Nuremberg Case*. New York, Knopf, 1947.

Jeffrey, Clarence R.: The Development of Crime in Early English Society, JCLC&PS, Vol.47 (Nov.-Dec., 1957), 647-666.

Jewell, Donald P.: Mexico's Tres Marias Penal Colony, JCLC&PS, Vol.48, No.4 (Nov.-Dec., 1957), 410.

Jones, A. H.: *Studies in Roman Government and Law*. New York, Praeger, 1960.

Jones, Sherbert B.: Customs Police of Germany, TPC, Vol.29, No.9 (Sept., 1962), 43.

Kaganice, Henry J.: Lie-tests and "Freedom of the Will" in Germany, JCLC&PS, Vol.47, No.5 (Jan.-Feb., 1957), 570.

Kawai, Hisato: The Japanese Police, TPY (1956).

Kelson, H.: *The Communist Theory of Law*. New York, Praeger, 1960.

Kempner, Robert M. W.: The German National Registration System as a Means of Police Control Over Population, JCL&C, Vol.36, No.5 (1947), 326.

Kershaw, Alister: *Murder in France.* London, Constable, 1955.

Kienle, Otto: Police of Baden-Wurttemberg, TPC, Vol.29, No.1 (Jan., 1962), 42.

Kinberg, Olof: The Swedish Organization of Forensic Psychiatry, JCL&C, Vol.34, No.2 (July-Aug., 1953), 135-50.

Kiralfy, A. K.: *The English Legal System.* London, Sweet & Maxwell, 1960.

Kirwan, William E.: Escape Tactics of German War Prisoners, JCL&C, Vol.35, No.5 (Jan.-Feb., 1945), 357.

Kittrie, Nicholas N.: A Post Mortem of the Eichmann Case—The Lessons for International Law, JCLC&PS, Vol.55, No.1 (Mar., 1964), 16.

Koessler, Maximilian: Euthanasia in the Hadamar Sanitarium and International Law, JCLC&PS, Vol.43, No.6 (Mar.-Apr., 1953), 735.

Kroger, Wilhelm: The Meeting of Two Police Ideas—Anglo-German Experiments in West Germany, JCLC&PS, Vol.51, No.2 (Mar.-Apr., 1960-61), 257.

Lambert, Leon: The International Police Picture Today, TPY (1956).

——: Report of the International Relations Committee, TPY (1957); (1958); (1959); (1960); (1961).

Langham, James: London's "Old Bailey," JCL&C, Vol.39, No.6 (Mar.-Apr., 1948-49), 778-82.

Lawrence, L. G.: Ontario Chief's Seminar, TPC, Vol.29, No.7 (July, 1962), 24.

Lee, Don-Ho: Taiwan Police Progress, TPY (1956).

Lo, Kivan: Police in Free China, TPY (1956).

Lord Denning's Report. London, Her Majesty's Stationery Office, 1963.

Louwage, F. E.: Belgian Police Official's Impressions from His Travels in the USA, JCLC&PS, Vol.42 (1951-52), 237.

Lucus, Paul: Blackstone and the Reform of the Legal Profession, EHR, Vol.77 (Jan., 1962), 456-489.

Lukban, Joseph: International Policing and Global Peace, POLICE, Vol.9, No.4 (Mar.-Apr., 1965), 90-92.

Lunden, Walter A.: Crime Down Under: In Tasmania, 1934-56, POLICE, Vol.4, No.3 (Jan.-Feb., 1960), 6-10.

——: The Increase of Criminality in Underdeveloped Countries, POLICE, Vol.6, No.5 (May-June, 1962), 30-34.

——: Murders, Infanticides and Criminal Justice in England and Wales, 1925-1955, POLICE, Vol.4, No.4 (Mar.-Apr., 1960), 74-77.

——: U.S. Army Supervision of Civil Prisons in Bavaria, JCL&C, Vol.38, No.4 (Mar.-Apr., 1947-48), 358-68.

Lyman, J. L.: The Metropolitan Police Act of 1829: An Analysis of Certain Events Influencing the Passage and Character of the Metropolitan Police Act in England, JCLC&PS, Vol.55, No.1 (Mar., 1964).

McClellan, George B.: Royal Canadian Mounted Police, TPY (1963).

McWhinney, E. (ed.): *Canadian Jurisprudence: the Civil Law and the Common Law in Canada.* Toronto, Toronto Press, 1958.

——: *Judicial Review in the English-speaking World,* 2nd Ed. Toronto, Toronto Press, 1961.

The Machinery of Justice in England, 2nd Ed. London, Cambridge Univ. Press, 1953.

Macmahon, Arthur W.: *Administration in Foreign Affairs.* University, Univ. of Alabama Press, 1953.

Mannheim, Hermann: Crime and Its Treatment in Postwar England, FP, Vol.11 (Oct., 1947), 3-7.

——: Developments in Criminal Law and Criminology in Postwar Britain, JCLC&PS, Vol.51, No.6 (Mar.-Apr., 1960-61), 587.

Martin, G. Arthur: The Exclusionary Rule Under Foreign Law (Canada), JCLC&PS, Vol.52, No.3 (Sept.-Oct., 1961), 271.

——: Police Detention and Arrest Privileges Under Foreign Law (Canada), JCLC&PS, Vol.51, No.4 (Mar.-Apr., 1960-61), 409.

——: Police Interrogation Privileges and Limitations Under Foreign Law (Canada), JCLC&PS, Vol.52, No.1 (May-June, 1961), 47.

——: The Privilege Against Self-incrimination Under Foreign Law (Canada), JCLC&PS, Vol.51, No.2 (Mar.-Apr., 1960-61), 161.

Mandukananda, Chamras: The Police of Thailand, TPC, Vol.28, No.6 (June, 1961), 8-10, 44.

Mann, Abby: *Judgment at Nuremberg.* New York, Signet, 1961.

Mei, Ko-wang: University Police Training in the Orient, POLICE, Vol.5, No.1 (Sept.-Oct., 1960), 65-67.

Meyjes, P.: Scientific Criminal Investigation Techniques Under Dutch Law, JCLC&PS, Vol.51, No.6 (Mar.-Apr., 1960-61), 653.

Moriarty, C. C. H.: Police Law, 16th Ed. London, Butterworth, 1961.

——, & **William, W. J.:** *Police Procedure and Administration,* 6th Ed. London, Butterworth, 1962.

Moynahan, John: The Police of Jamaica, TPC, Vol.28, No.9 (Sept., 1961), 9-61.

Mueller, G. O. W. (ed.): *The French Penal Code.* South Hackensack, Rothman, 1960.

————: The Meeting of Two Police Ideas—Anglo-German Experiments in West Germany, JCLC&PS, Vol.51, No.2 (Mar.-Apr., 1960-61), 257.

————: Resocialization of the Young Adult Offender in Switzerland, JCLC&PS, Vol.43 No.5 (Jan.-Feb., 1953), 578.

————: Typical Accident Causes in German Road Traffic, JCLC&PS, Vol.51, No.6 (Mar.-Apr., 1960-61), 675.

————: Typische Unfallursachen im Deutschen Strassenverkehr (Typical Accident Causes in German Road Traffic), JCLC&PS, Vol.52, No.3 (Sept.-Oct., 1961), 359.

Nakahara, Hidenori: The Japanese Police, JCLC&PS, Vol.46 (1955-56), 583-94.

Nelson, Elmer K.: A New Approach to Graduate Training in Criminology at the University of British Columbia, JCL&C, Vol.34, No.4 (Nov.-Dec., 1953), 433-37.

Nott-Bower, John, Sir: Growth and Ideals of the British Police, TPY (1960).

Ontario Sponsors Training Course, TPC, Vol.30 (Oct., 1963), 45.

Osborough, Nial: Police Discretion Not to Prosecute Students: A British Problem, JCLC&PS, Vol.56, No.2 (June, 1965), 241-45.

Owen, John E.: Crime in Pakistan, JCLC&PS, Vol.50, No.6 (1959-60), 568.

————: International Review of Criminal Policy, No.14—United Nations, JCLC&PS, Vol.51, No.1 (Mar.-Apr., 1960-61), 83.

Paterson, Ales J., Chief Constable: The Results of Team Policing in Salford, Extract from the *Report of the Chief Constable on the (Salford) Police Establishment for the Year Ended December 31, 1951.*

————: The Salford Method of Team Policing, A Report and Study Prepared for the Home Office, by Chief Constable Paterson, B.E.M., M.A., B.L., Nov. 13, 1950.

Payne, Howard C.: A Day's Work of the Press Police During the Second Empire in France, POLICE, Vol.1., No.3 (Jan.-Feb., 1957), 19-22.

————: An Early Concept of the Modern Police State in France, JCLC&PS, Vol.43, No.3 (Sept.-Oct., 1952), 377.

————: The French Commissaire of Police in the Mid-Nineteenth Century, POLICE, Vol.5, No.1 (Sept.-Oct., 1960), 34-37; No.2 (Nov.-Dec., 1960), 21-23.

Petty, Edward A.: Directed Change and Cul-ture Adhesion: A Study of Functional Integration in Police Administration of Japan, Unpublished Doctoral Dissertation, Los Angeles, Univ. of Calif, 1961.

Pihl Blad, C. Terence: The Juvenile Offender in Norway, JCLC&PS, Vol.46 (1955-56), 500-511.

Pringle, P.: *Hue and Cry: the Birth of the British Police.* London, Museum Press, 1955.

Radzinowicz, Leon: *A History of English Criminal Law*, 3 Vols. London, Macmillan, 1948-53.

Reifen, David: Observations on the Juvenile Court in Israel, SSR, Vol.26 (June, 1952), 202-214.

Reith, Charles: *The Blind Eye of History.* London, England, Faber & Faber, 1952.

————: *A New Study of Police History.* London, Oliver & Boyd, 1956.

————: *A Short History of the British Police.* London, Oxford, 1948.

Reorganization Scheme—Redistribution of Manpower in Accordance with Formula Based on Weighted Mileage. London, Metropolitan Police, R.U.F./1,M.P. 30—17282/200.

Report of the Working Party Set Up to Consider the Aberdeen System of Policing. An Integral Part of the *Report of the Committee on Police Conditions of Service, Part II*, 1949, Cmnd. 7831 (The Oaksey Report). London, Her Majesty's Stationery Office.

Richardson, R. E.: Germany's Civil Defense in Wary, TPC, Vol.29, No.2 (Feb., 1962), 18.

Risku, Artturi M.: Traffic Problems in Finland, L&O, Vol.8, No.9 (1960).

Rivard, Antoine: Internationally Speaking, TPY (1957).

Rizkallah, Elias, Maj.: The Police of Lebanon, TPC, Vol.28, No.6 (June, 1961), 6-61.

Roig, Salvador T.: Puerto Rico's Unique Position for Development of Police Programs for Central and South America, TPY (1959).

Rolph, C. H.: *Police and the Public.* London, Heinemann, 1962.

Romashkin, P. S. (ed.): *Fundamentals of Soviet Law.* Moscow, Foreign Languages Publishing House.

Rosen, S. McKee: *The Combined Boards of the Second World War: An Experiment in International Administration.* New York, Columbia Univ. Press, 1951.

Royal Canadian Mounted Police: *Law and Order in Canadian Democracy.* Ottawa, Edmond Cloutier, 1952.

Royal Commission Report on the Reorganization of the British Police. Her Majesty's Stationery Office, 1962.

Rudd, G. R.: *English Legal System.* London, Butterworth, 1962.

Ryu, Paul K.: The New Korean Criminal Code of October 3, 1953, JCLC&PS, Vol.48, No.3 (Sept.-Oct., 1957), 275.

St. John-Stevas, N.: *Life, Death, and the Law: Law and Christian Morals in England and the U.S.* Bloomington, Indiana Univ. Press, 1961.

St. Johnston, T. E.: The Legal Limitation of the Interrogation of Suspects and Prisoners in England and Wales, JCL&C, Vol.39, No.1 (Mar.-Apr., 1948-49), 89-99.

————: Royal Commission of Police of Great Britain, TPY (1962).

Sampson, Richard A., Jr.: The Police of the Republic of China, TPC, Vol.28, No.9 (Sept.- 1961), 4.

Schlesinger, R.: *Comparative Law,* 2nd Ed. Brooklyn, Foundation Press, 1959.

————: *Soviet Legal Theory.* New York, Humanities, 1951.

Schur, Edwin M.: British Narcotics Policies, JCLC&PS, Vol.51, No.6 (Mar.-Apr., 1960-61), 619.

Schwerin, Kurt: Foreign Language Periodicals and Articles of Interest in the Field of Criminal Law and Criminology, JCLC&PS, Vol.51, No.5 (Mar.-Apr., 1960-61), 555; No.6 (Mar.-Apr., 1960-61), 673.

Scott, Harold, Sir: Policewomen in Great Britain, ICPR (May, 1953).

Shaw, William: *Evidence and Procedure in Magistrates' Courts.* 2nd Ed. London, Butterworth, 1946.

Shimasue, Tatsujiro: The Maritime Safety Board (Coast Guard of Japan), TPY (1958).

Shohan, Shlomo: Sentencing Policy of Courts in Israel, JCLC&PS Vol.50, No.4 (1959-60), 415.

————: The Two Sides of the Barricade, PO-LICE, Vol.9, No.2 (Nov.-Dec., 1964), 28-35 (Israel).

Shook, Russel A.: International Police Training —The Challenge and the Opportunity, TPY (1956).

————: Progress in International Relations, TPY (1963).

Soemarsono, Major: Human Relations in the Indonesian Police, TPY (1956).

South Africa and the Rule of Law. Geneva, International Commission of Jurists, 1960.

Spencer, R.: *A.B.C. of the British Police.* London, Ian Allan, 1956.

Stevenson, Adlai E.: The American Tradition and Its Implications for International Law, POLICE, Vol.7, No.4 (Mar.-Apr., 1963), 14-17.

Stevenson, Edward H.: Training in the Royal Canadian Mounted Police, TPY (1962).

Stockholm Police: *The Organization of the Swedish Police.* A Report Published in the SVENSK POLIS by Curt Kalkenstam, Released by an Information Service Survey.

Stokes, Joseph M.: International Cooperation in Police Administration, TPY (1957).

Sullivan, Francis C.: Wire Tapping in England, POLICE, Vol.5, No.2 (Nov.-Dec., 1960), 42-44.

Tegel, Heinrich F.: New Problems for the Police Within the European Art Business, JCLC&PS, Vol.53, No.1 (Mar.-May, 1962), 105.

Tenny, Frank S.: Law Enforcement in the Far East, POLICE, Vol.8, No.1 (Sept.-Oct., 1963), 46.

Themis on the Rack in Indonesia, JCLC&PS, Vol.46 (1955-56), 370.

Thomas, J. L., Supt.: *Police Organisation and Administration,* 4th Ed. London, Police Review Publishing Co., 1952.

Thomas, M. Ladd: Philippine Police Systems, JCLC&PS, Vol.46 (1955-56), 116-121.

Timasheff, N. S.: The Dutch Prison System, JCLC&PS, Vol.48, No.6 (Mar.-Apr., 1958), 608.

Totten, James C.: African Police Chief Visits America, L&O, Vol.8 No.3 (1960).

Turner, John Peter: *The North-west Mounted Police,* 1873-1893. Ottawa, Edmond Cloutier, CMG., B.A., L.Ph. King's Printer & Controller of Stationery 1950. 2 Vols.

Turner, Carl C.: The Police of Bavaria, TPC, Vol.30, No.8 (Aug., 1963), 36-40.

————: Police of Japan, TPC, Vol.30 (Feb., 1963), 42.

————: The Police of the Republic of South Africa, TPC, Vol.29, No.7 (July, 1962), 16-20.

————: Police of Southern Rhodesia, TPC, Vol.30 (Apr., 1963), 40.

————: School Safety Patrols of Europe, TPC, Vol.29, No.8 (Aug., 1962), 31.

Van der Walt, Piet J.: University Teaching of Criminology in the Republic of South Africa, JCLC&PS, Vol.52, No.2 (July-Aug., 1961), 191.

Vishinsky, Andrei: *The Law of the Soviet State.* New York, Macmillan, 1948.

Van Knieriem, August: *The Nuremberg Trials.* Chicago, Regnery, 1959.

Vouin, Robert: The Exclusionary Rule Under Foreign Law (France), JCLC&PS, Vol.52, No.3 (Sept.-Oct., 1961), 275.

————: Police Detention and Arrest Privileges

Under Foreign Law (France), JCLC&PS, Vol.51, No.4 (Mar.-Apr., 1960-61), 419.

———: Police Interrogation Privileges and Limitations Under Foreign Law (France), JCLC&PS, Vol.52, No.3 (Sept.-Oct., 1961), 57.

———: The Privilege Against Self-Incrimination Under Foreign Law (France), JCLC&PS, Vol.51, No.2, (Mar.-Apr., 1960-61), 169.

Walker, D. M.: *The Scottish Legal System.* Glasgow, Green, 1959.

Wang, Tai-Hsuing: Police Progress in Free China, TPY (1957).

Wildes, Harry E.: The Post War Japanese, JCLC&PS, Vol.43, No.5 (Jan.-Feb., 1953), 655.

Williams, Glanville L.: The Exclusionary Rule Under Foreign Law (England), JCLC&PS, Vol.52, No.3 (Sept.-Oct., 1961), 272.

———: Police Detention and Arrest Privileges Under Foreign Law (England), JCLC&PS, Vol.51, No.4 (Mar.-Apr., 1960-61), 413.

———: Police Interrogation Privileges and Limitations Under Foreign Law (England), JCLC&PS, Vol.52, No.1 (May-June, 1951), 50.

———: The Privilege Against Self-incrimination Under Foreign Law (England), JCLC&PS, Vol.51, No.2 (Mar.-Apr., 1960-61), 166.

Wilson, O. W.: The British Police, JCLC&PS, Vol.50, No.5 (May, 1949), 637-50.

Wolfgang, Marvin E.: Political Crimes and Punishments in Renaissance Florence, JCL&C, Vol.44, No.5 (Jan.-Feb., 1954).

———: Travel Notes on Italian Prisoners, JCLC&PS, Vol.45 (1954-55), 133-50.

Yee, Frank S. H.: Chinese Communist Police and Courts, JCLC&PS, Vol.48, No.1 (May-June, 1957), 83.

Zagorin, Perez: The Court and the Country: A Note on Political Terminology in the Earlier 17th Century, EHR, Vol.77 (Jan., 1962), 306-11.

Zelitch, Judah: *Soviet Administration of Criminal Laws.* Philadelphia, Lippincott.

Zubryn, Emil: New Regulations for Mexico's Drivers, L&O, Vol.8, No.7 (1960).

LAW ENFORCEMENT AGENCIES

Ansley, Norman: The United States Secret Service, JCLC&PS, Vol.47, No.1 (May-June, 1956), 93.

Baughman, U. E., and Robinson, Leonard Wallace: *Secret Service Chief.* New York, Popular, 1960.

Bavin, Clark R., and Studholme, Allen T.: Wildlife Law Enforcement at the Federal Level, POLICE, Vol.9, No.1 (Sept.-Oct., 1964), 26-30.

Bower, Walter S., and Edward, Harry: *The United States Secret Service.* Philadelphia, Chilton, 1960.

Brandt, A. P.: Rural Police Problems, in Alaska, TPY (1959).

California State Department of Fish & Game: *Forty-sixth Biennial Report, 1958-60, California Dept. of Fish & Game.* Sacramento State Printing Office, 1960.

Chernin, Milton: *State Police.* Berkeley, Univ. of Calif., Bureau of Public Admin.

Clede, Bill: The Conservation Officer in Action, L&O, Vol.7, No.8 (Aug., 1959), 78-81.

Collins, Frederick L.: *The FBI in Peace and War.* New York, Ace, 1962.

Consentine, Joseph P.: The Secret Service Chief, RMSJUAM, Vol.11, No.1 (Winter, 1962-63), 1-10.

Cook, Fred J.: *The FBI Nobody Knows.* New York, Macmillan, 1964.

Coon, Thomas F.: The Immigration and Naturalization Service, POLICE, Vol.8, No.6 (July-Aug., 1964), 80-82.

———: Waterfront Commission Investigator, POLICE, Vol.7, No.1 (Sept.-Oct., 1962), 42-47.

———, & Sabatino, Nicholas S.: U.S. Customs Performing at the World's Busiest Port, POLICE, Vol.8, No.2 (Nov.-Dec., 1963), 19-24.

Editors of Look: *The Story of the FBI.* New York, Dutton, 1947.

Ellis, James H.: The Connecticut Resident State Police System, POLICE (Sept.-Oct., 1960).

Fagerstrom, Dorothy: Masters of Diplomacy—The White House Police, L&O, Vol.8, No.9 (1960).

Farley, William T.: Functions of the Railroad Police, JCLC&PS, Vol.42 (1951-52), 385.

Federal Bureau of Investigation: *The Story of the FBI National Academy.* Washington, D.C.

Flag of NYCPD, TPC, Vol.30 (Aug., 1963), 22.

Hall, Theo E.: The Public Safety Program of IACP, TPY (1959).

Hamilton, James, LEIU—Its Objectives and Operations, TPY (1961).

Hamilton, Ontario Rates Training Firsts, TPC, Vol.30 (May, 1963), 26.

Harrison, Richard: *Scotland Yard.* New York, Ziff-Davis, 1949.

———: *The CID and the FBI.* London, Muller, 1956.

Hartman, Jerry, and Chapman, Samuel G.: Conservation Law Enforcement in Michigan, JCLC&PS, Vol.53, No.3 (Sept.-Nov., 1962), 384.

Hicks, Sam: The Avenging Angels—The First in their Field, POLICE, Vol.4, No.4 (Mar.-Apr., 1960), 56-59.

Jessup, Jacob A.: A Study of the Use of Police Reserves or Auxiliaries, POLICE (Jan.-Feb., 1960).

Johnson, Francis W.: Minnesota State Game Wardens Have Many Jobs, FBILEB (Nov., 1960).

Jones, Ken: *The FBI in Action.* New York, Signet, 1957.

Kelly, John C.: Connecticut's Resident State Police System, TPY (1958).

King, Everett M.: *The Auxiliary Police Unit.* Springfield, Thomas, 1960.

Kuhfeld, Albert M.: The NATO Status of Forces Agreement, TPY (1958).

Liu, Daniel S. C.: A Cosmopolitan Metropolis Policed by Honolulu's Finest, POLICE, Vol.11, No.1 (Sept.-Oct., 1957), 29-33.

Lloyd, Bob: The Navajo Police Department, L&O, Vol.8, No.6 (1960), 6-14.

McCartney, Frank G., Commissioner, The Pennsylvania State Police, L&O, Vol.8, No.11 (1960), 60-61.

Martin, J. A.: The California Highway Patrol, L&O, Vol.7, No.11 (Nov. 1959), 92-94.

Matt, A. Robert: Law Enforcement Officers of the Sea; L&O, Vol.8, No.2 (1960), 5-10.

Misner, Gordon E.: The St. Louis County Department of Police, JCLC&PS, Vol.48, No.6 (Mar.-Apr., 1958), 652.

Murdy, Ralph G.: A Follow-up Study of FBI Service, POLICE, Vol.7, No.3 (Jan.-Feb., 1963), 50-52.

Harper, James C.: *North Carolina Sheriff's Manual: A Guidebook for Sheriffs and Their Deputies.* Chapel Hill, Univ. of North Carolina, Institute of Govt., June, 1964.

O'Reiley, Patrick: San Diego Establishes Police Cadet Program, POLICE, Vol.5, No.2 (Nov.-Dec., 1960), 6-9.

Packer, William M.: The Hundred Club, TPY (1965).

Peterson, Virgil: An Examination of Chicago's Law Enforcement Agencies, CJ, (Jan., 1950), 3-6.

Renner, Tom: A New County Police Force, L&O, Vol.8, No.12 (1960), 22-26.

Reynolds, Quentin: *Headquarters.* New York, Popular, 1956.

Richardson, Robert E.: A Salute to the Military Police, TPC, Vol.28, No.9 (Sept., 1961), 6-61.

Roark, Garland: *The Coin of Contraband.* Garden City, Doubleday, 1965. (Story of U.S. Customs Service.)

Rowley, James J.: United States Secret Service, TPY (1963).

Services of the FBI. Washington, Federal Bureau of Investigation.

Shepperd, John Ben: Citizens Improve Law Enforcement in Texas, POLICE, Vol.2, No.4 (Mar.-Apr., 1958), 17-21.

Smalley, Alfred T.: History and Purpose of the IACP, TPY (1959).

Smith, Bruce: *Police Systems in the U.S.* New York, Harper, 1949.

Stewart, Harold F.: U.S. Park Police, L&O, Vol.8, No.9 (1960). 41-67.

Story of the FBI. Washington, Federal Bureau of Investigation.

Tamm, Quinn: Ohio Highway Patrol Academy, TPC, Vol.32, No.1 (Jan., 1965), 23.

Taylor, L. B., Jr.: Space Age Police Force, L&O, Vol.8, No.5 (1960), 6-11.

Tully, Andrew: *Treasury Agent.* New York, Simon & Schuster, 1958.

United States Dept. of Justice: Training in Law Enforcement and Criminal Investigation for Treasury Agents, POLICE, Vol.9, No.4 (Mar.-Apr., 1965), 94-97.

Walters, Nydia: Spokane Police Eliminate Meter Looting, L&O, Vol. 9 (June, 1961).

Washington State Patrol Performance Evaluation, TPC, Vol.30 (Feb., 1963), 16.

Whitehead, Don: *Border Guard.* New York, Avon, 1963.

———: *The FBI Story.* New York, Pocket, 1958.

Wike, Leroy E.: IACP Conference Through the Years, TPY (1959).

SOCIOLOGY & PSYCHOLOGY OF CRIME

Abrahamsen, David: *The Psychology of Crime.* New York, Wiley, 1964.

Adler, Martin D.: The Applications of Discretion in Enforcement of the Law in Mental Health Situations, POLICE, Vol.9, No.2 (Nov.-Dec., 1964).

Alexander, Leo: Destructive and Self-Destructive Trends in Criminal Society; a Study of Totalitarianism, JCL&C, Vol.39, No.5 (Mar.-Apr., 1948-49), 553-65.

———: War Crimes and Their Motivation the Socio-Psychological Structure of the SS and the Criminalization of a Society, JCL&C, Vol.39, No.3 (Mar.-Apr., 1948-49), 298-327.

Allen, Francis A.: Criminal Justice, Legal Values and the Rehabilitative Ideal, JCLC&PS, Vol.50, No.3 (Sept.-Oct., 1959), 226.

Allen, Robert M., Haines, William H., and Kennedy, Foster: Discussion on the "Psychiatric Study of William Heirens," JCL&C, Vol.39, No.1 (Mar.-Apr., 1948-49), 49-52.

Allport, G., and Postman, L.: *The Psychology of Rumor*. New York, Henry Holt, 1947.

Anderson, J. E.: *The Psychology of Development and Personal Adjustment*. New York, Holt, 1949.

Arieff, Alex J., and Rotman, David B.: Psychopathic Personality; Some Social and Psychiatric Aspects, JCL&C, Vol.39, No.2 (Mar.-Apr., 1948-49), 158-167.

Arons, Harry: Areas of Application, Contraindications, Legal and Ethical Considerations in Hypnosis, POLICE, Vol.9, No.2 (Nov.-Dec., 1964), 11-15.

Aubry, Arthur S.: The Criminal Psychopath in Law Enforcement, POLICE, Vol.8, No.1 (Sept.-Oct., 1963), 18-22.

Balogh, Joseph K.: A Validation of the Kvaraceus KD Verbal Proneness Scale with Matched White Male Subjects, JCLC&PS, Vol.52, No.3 (Sept.-Oct., 1961), 305.

Bates, Jerome E.: Abrahamsen's Theory of the Etiology of Criminal Acts, JCL&C, Vol.40, No.4 (Nov.-Dec., 1949), 471.

Berg, Charles: The Psychology of Punishment, BJMP, Vol.20 (Oct., 1945), 295-313.

Bergel, Egon E.: *Urban Sociology*. New York, McGraw-Hill, 1955.

Berlien, Ivan C.: Rehabilitation Centers: Psychiatry and Group Therapy, JCL&C, Vol.36, No.4 (1945-46), 249.

Berliner, Arthur K.: Some Aspects of Mental Abnormality in Relation to Crime, JCLC&PS, Vol.46 (1955-56), 67-72.

Bielinski, Brunon: Importance to Psychiatrist of First on Scene Officer's Observation, POLICE, Vol.6, No.5 (May-June, 1962), 26-29.

Biggs, John, Jr.: *The Guilty Mind*. New York, Harcourt, Brace, 1955.

Bondy, Curt: A Psychological Interpretation of Waywardness, JCL&C, Vol.36, No.1 (1945-46), 3.

Bowlby, John: *Maternal Care and Mental Health*. Geneva, World Health Organization Monograph No.2, 1951.

Bovet, L.: *Psychiatric Aspects of Juvenile Delinquency*. Geneva, World Health Organization Monograph No.1, 1951.

Britt, S.: *Social Psychology of Modern Life*. New York, Rinehart, 1949.

Bromberg, Walter: *Crime and the Mind: the Outline of Psychiatric Criminology*. Philadelphia, Lippincott, 1948.

Burton, A.: Functions of Clinical Psychological Service in California Juvenile and Adult Courts, AJP, Vol.22 (July, 1946), 93-96.

Cameron, N.: *The Psychology of Behavior Disorders*. New York, Houghton Mifflin, 1947.

———, **& Margaret, A.**: *Behavior Pathology*. New York, Houghton Mifflin, 1951.

Cleckley, H.: *The Mask of Sanity*. St. Louis, Mosby, 1950.

Clinard, Marshal B.: *Sociology of Deviant Behavior*. New York, Holt, Rinehart & Winston, 1963.

Cressey, Donald R.: Application and Verification of the Differential Association Theory, JCLC&PS, Vol.43, No.1 (May-June, 1952), 43.

Davidson, Henry A.: Psychiatrists in Administration of Criminal Justice, JCLC&PS, Vol.45 (1954-55), 12-20.

Demone, Harold W., Jr., Ullman, Albert D., Sterns, A. Warren, and Washburne, Norman F.: Some Social Characteristics of Misdemeants, JCLC&PS, Vol.48, No.1 (May-June, 1957), 44.

Doob, L.: *Social Psychology*. New York, Holt, 1952.

Donahue, Vincent J.: Psychiatry vs. Law Enforcement, TPY (1958).

Durkheim, Emile: *Suicide: A Study of Sociology*. Glencoe, Free Press, 1951.

Edmunds, Simeon: Hypnotism and Crime, POLICE, Vol.7, No.1 (Sept.-Oct., 1962), 11-16.

Esselotyn, T. C.: The Social Role of the County Sheriff, JCL&C, Vol.44, No.2 (July-Aug., 1953), 177-84.

Eysenck, H. J.: *Dimensions of Personality*. London, Routledge, 1947.

———: *The Structure of Personality*. New York, Wiley, 1953.

Falstein, Eugene I.: The Psychodynamics of Male Adolescent Delinquency, AJO, Vol.28 (1958), 613-26.

Fenichel, O.: *The Psychoanalytic Theory of Neurosis*. New York, Norton, 1945.

Ferenczi, S.: States in the Development of the Sense of Reality, in *An Outline of Psychoanalysis*. New York, Modern, 1952.

Ferentz, Edward J.: Mental Deficiency Related to Crime, JCLC&PS, Vol.45 (1954-55), 299-307.

Fink, Arthur E.: *The Field of Social Work*. New York, Holt, 1949.

Fox, Vernon: The Influence of Personality on Social Non-conformity, JCLC&PS, Vol.42 (1951-52), 746.

Foxe, Arthur N.: Heredity and Crime, JCL&C, Vol.36, No.1 (1945-46), 11.

Friedlander, Kate: *The Psycho-analytical Approach to Juvenile Delinquency.* New York, International Univ. Press, 1947.

Gagnieur, J. P.: The Judicial Use of Psychonarcosis in France, JCL&C, Vol.39, No.5 (Mar.-Apr., 1948-49), 663-67.

———: Judicial Use of Psychonarcosis in France, JCL&C, Vol.40, No.3 (1949), 370.

Gautier, Maurice: The Psychology of the Compulsive Forger, CJC, Vol.1 (July, 1959), 62-69.

Geis, Gilbert: Sociology and Crime in Joseph S. Roucek (ed.): The Sociology of Crime. New York, Philosophical, 1960.

Glueck, Bernard C.: Changing Concepts in Forensic Psychiatry, JCLC&PS, Vol.45 (1954-55), 123-32.

Glueck, Sheldon: Mental Illness and Criminal Responsibility, JST, Vol.2 (Third Quarter, 1956), 134-57.

Graham, James J.: What to Do with the Psychopath, JCLC&PS, Vol.53, No.4 (Dec., 1962), 446.

Haines, William H., Kennedy, Foster, and Hoffman, Harry R.: Psychiatric Study of William Heirens, JCL&C, Vol.38, No.4 (Mar.-Apr., 1947-48), 311-41.

Hakeem, Michael: A Critique of the Psychiatric Approach to Crime and Correction, L&CP, Vol.33 (Autumn, 1958), 650-82.

Hartung, Frank E.: Methodical Assumption in a Socio-psychological Theory of Criminality, JCLC&PS, Vol.45 (1954-55), 652-61.

Hentig, Hans Von: The Suspect: A Study in the Psychopathology of Social Standards, JCL&C, Vol.39, No.1 (Mar.-Apr., 1948-49), 19-34.

Hovland, Carl I., Janis, Irving L., and Kelley, Harold H.: *Communication and Persuasion: Psychological Studies of Opinion Change.* New Haven, Yale Univ. Press, 1953.

Hunter, E.: *Brain-washing in Red China, the Calculated Destruction of Men's Minds.* New York, Vanguard, 1951.

Illing, Hans A.: Group Psychotherapy and Group Work in Authoritarian Settings, JCLC&PS, Vol.48, No.4 (Nov.-Dec., 1957), 387.

———: Social Work Yearbook, JCLC&PS, Vol.51, No.4 (Mar.-Apr., 1960-61), 456.

———: The Psychology of Crime, JCLC&PS, Vol.51, No.5 (Mar.-Apr., 1960-61), 554.

———: The Sociological Imagination, JCLC&PS, Vol.51, No.1 (Mar.-Apr., 1960-61), 87.

Jeffery, Clarence R.: An Integrated Theory of Crime and Criminal Behavior, JCLC&PS, Vol.49, No.6 (1958-59), 533.

Johnson, Elmer H.: Sociology of Confinement: Assimilation and the Prison Rat, JCLC&PS, Vol.51, No.5 (Mar.-Apr., 1960-61), 528.

Johnston, Norman, Savitz, Leonard, and Wolfgang, Marvin E. (eds.): *The Sociology of Punishment and Correction.* New York, Wiley, 1962.

Karpman, Benjamin: An Attempt at a Re-evaluation of Some Concepts of Law and Psychiatry, JCL&C, Vol.38, No.3 (Mar.-Apr., 1947-48), 206-17.

———: Criminality, Insanity and the Law, JCL&C, Vol.39, No.5 (Mar.-Apr., 1948-49), 584-606.

———: Emotional Background of White Slavery: Toward Psychogenesis of So-called Psychopathic Behavior, JCL&C, Vol.39, No.1 (Mar.-Apr., 1948-49), 1-19.

———: Lying, A Minor Inquiry into the Ethics of Neurotic and Psychopathic Behavior, JCL&C, Vol.40, No.2 (July-Aug., 1949), 135.

———: On Reducing Tensions and Bridging Gaps Between Psychiatry and the Law, JCLC&PS, Vol.48, No.2 (July-Aug., 1957), 164.

———: The Psychogenesis of So-called Psychopathic Behavior, JCL&C, Vol.36, No.5 (1945-46), 305.

Kennedy, Foster, Allen, Robert M., and Haines, William H.: Discussion on the Psychiatric Study of William Heirens, JCL&C, Vol.39, No.1 (Mar.-Apr., 1948-49), 49-52; Vol.38, No.4 (Mar.-Apr., 1947-48), 311-41.

Kinberg, Olof: Forensic Psychiatry Without Metaphysics, JCL&C, Vol. 40, No.5 (Jan.-Feb., 1950), 555.

Kinsey, Alfred C.: *Sexual Behavior in the Human Male.* Philadelphia, Saunders, 1948.

Krafft-Ebing, Richard: *Aberrations of Sexual Life, after the Psychopathia Sexualis.* London, Staples, 1959.

Krech, D., and Crutchfield R.: *Theory and Problems of Social Psychology.* New York, McGraw-Hill, 1948.

LaPiere, Richard T.: *A Theory of Social Control.* New York, McGraw-Hill, 1954.

———, **& Farnsworth, P.:** *Social Psychology,* 3rd Ed. New York, McGraw-Hill, 1949.

Lanzer, Irving: Forensic Social Case Work: An Analytic Survey, JCL&C, Vol.39, No.1 (Mar.-Apr., 1948-49), 34-49.

Leet, Alfred McClung (ed.): *Readings in Sociology.* New York, Barnes & Noble, 1960.

Leonard, V. A.: Sexual Psychopath Laws Upheld, JCL&C, Vol.35, No.6 (Mar.-Apr., 1945), 396.

Linder, Robert: *The Fifty-minute Hour.* New York, Bantam, 1956.

———, **& Seliger, R. V.:** *Handbook of Correc-*

tional Psychology. New York, Philosophical, 1947.

Linton, Ralph: *Culture and Mental Disorders.* Springfield, Thomas, 1954.

Lipton, Harry R.: The Psychopath, JCL&C, Vol.40, No.5 (Jan.-Feb., 1950), 584.

Lukas, Edwin J.: Rebel Without a Cause: the Hypnoanalysis of a Criminal Psychopath, JCL&C, Vol.35, No.5 (Jan.-Feb., 1945), 333.

Lunden, Walter A.: Captivity Psychoses Among Prisoners of War, JCL&C, Vol.39, No.6 (Mar.-Apr., 1948-49), 721-34.

McConahy, Malcolm W.: The Role of the Police in Mental Health, POLICE, Vol.6, No.3 (Jan.-Feb., 1962), 16.

MacDonald, John M.: The Teaching of Psychology in Law Schools, JCLC&PS, Vol.49, No.4 (1958-59), 310.

MacDonald R., St. J. (ed.): *Current Law and Social Problems.* Toronto, Univ. of Toronto Press, 1960.

Machtinger, S. J.: Psychiatric Testimony for the Impeachment of Witnesses in Sex Cases, JCL&C, Vol.39, No.6 (Mar.-Apr., 1948-49), 750-71.

Mannheim, Hermann: *Criminal Justice and Social Reconstruction.* New York, Oxford Univ. Press, 1946.

Maslow, A. H., and Mittelmann, Bela: *Principles of Abnormal Psychology.* New York, Harper, 1951.

Mead, Margaret: *Male and Female.* New York, Morrow, 1949.

Meerloo, J. A. M.: *The Rape of the Mind.* New York, World Publishing, 1956.

Megers, Thomas J.: Psychiatric Examination of the Sexual Psychopath, JCLC&PS, Vol.56, No.1 (Mar., 1965), 27-31.

Meiers, Joseph I.: *Origins and Development of Group Psychotherapy,* Psychodrama Monographs, No.17, New York, Beacon House, 1946.

Menninger, Karl: The Psychiatric View of the Police, Their Function, Their Personalities and Their Employers, TPY (1957).

Merton, Robert K.: *Social Theory and Social Structure.* Glencoe, The Free Press, 1957.

Meyers, Thomas J.: The Psychiatric Examination, JCLC&PS, Vol.54, No.4 (1963), 431.

Monachesi, Elio D.: Personality Characteristics and Socio-Economic Status of Delinquents and Non-Delinquents, JCL&C, Vol.40, No.5 (Jan.-Feb., 1950), 570.

———: Some Personality Characteristics of Delinquents and Non-delinquents, JCL&C, Vol.38, No.5 (Mar.-Apr., 1947-48), 487-500.

Munn, N. L.: *Psychology, the Fundamentals of Human Adjustment,* 2nd Ed. New York, Houghton Mifflin, 1951.

Neustatter, W. Lindesay: *Psychological Disorder and Crime.* London, Johnson, 1953.

Overstreet, H. A.: *The Mature Mind.* New York, Norton, 1949.

Page, J. P.: *Abnormal Psychology.* New York, McGraw-Hill, 1947.

Palmer, Stuart: Frustration and Murder, JCLC&PS, Vol.50, No.3 (Sept.-Oct., 1959), 276.

Parlour, Richard R., and Lbanex, Richard A.: Psychiatric Contributions to the Processes of the Law: POLICE, Vol.8, No.2 (Nov.-Dec., 1963), 58-62.

Patients in Mental Institutions, 1946. A report prepared by the U.S. Dept. of Commerce, Bureau of the Census, Washington, D.C., 1949.

Porterfield, Austin L.: *Crime, Suicide and Social Well-being in Your State and City.* Fort Worth, Leo Potishman Foundation, Texas Christian Univ., 1946.

Pospisil, Leopold: *Kapauku Papuans and Their Law.* New Haven, Yale Univ. Press, 1954.

Radzinowicz, L., and Turner, J. W. C. (eds.): *Mental Abnormality and Crime.* English Studies in Criminal Science, Vol.II, London, Macmillan, 1949.

Rankin, James H.: Preventive Psychiatry in the Los Angeles Police Department, POLICE (July-Aug., 1957).

Redl, Fritz: The Psychology of Gang Formation and the Treatment of Juvenile Delinquents in *The Psychoanalytic Study of the Child.* New York, International Univ. Press, 1945.

Redmount, Robert S.: The Psychological Basis of Evidence Practices; Memory, JCLC&PS, Vol.50, No.3 (Sept.-Oct., 1959), 249.

Reiss, Albert, Jr.: The Accuracy, Efficiency and Validity of a Prediction Instrument, AJS, Vol.56 (May, 1951), 552-61.

Roche, Philip Q.: Psychiatry and the McNaughten Rule, JCLC&PS, Vol.50, No.2 (1959-60), 160.

Rotman, David B., and Arieff, Alex J.: Psychopathic Personality: Some Social and Psychiatric Aspects, JCL&C, Vol.39, No.2 (Mar.-Apr., 1948-49), 158-67.

Rud, F.: The Social Psychopathology of Schizophrenic States, JCLEP, Vol.12 (1951).

Schuessler, Karl F., and Cressey, Donald R.: Personality Characteristics of Criminals, AJS, Vol.55, No.5 (Mar., 1950), 476-84.

Segal, H. A.: Initial Psychiatric Findings of Recently Repatriated Prisoners of War, AJPSY, Vol.3 (1954).

Selling, Lowell S.: Case Studies in the Psychopathology of Crime, JCL&C, Vol.35, No.6 (Mar.-Apr., 1945), 405.

———: Forensic Psychiatry, JCL&C, Vol.39, No.5 (Mar.-Apr., 1948-49), 606-18.

———: Mental Abnormality and Crime, JCL&C, Vol.35, No.6 (Mar.-Apr., 1945), 406.

Sells, S. B.: *Essentials of Psychology.* New York, Ronald, 1962.

Selznick, Philip: *TVA and the Grass Roots: A Study in the Sociology of Formal Organization.* Berkeley, Univ. of Calif. Press, 1949.

Shaw, William: Day Dreaming, L&O, Vol.8, No.11 (1960).

Siegal, Lewis J.: Inability to Remember Its Analysis in Medicolegal Orientation, JCLC&PS, Vol.45 (1954-55), 151-56.

Siegel, William L.: A Study of Law and Psychiatry, JCL&C, Vol.34, No.3 (Sept.-Oct., 1953), 338-41.

Silving, Helen: Psychoanalysis and Criminal Law, JCLC&PS, Vol.51, No.1 (Mar.-Apr., 1960-61), 19.

Skousen, W. Cleon: Law Enforcement Looks at Mental Health, L&O, Vol.9 (Mar., 1961).

Smith, Phillip M.: Organized Religion and Criminal Behavior, S&SR, Vol.33 (May, 1949), 262-67.

Sperling, G. E.: The Interpretation of the Trauma as a Command, PQ, Vol.19 (1950).

Stagner, R., and Karwoski, T.: *Psychology.* New York, McGraw-Hill, 1952.

Stouffer, Samuel: *The American Soldier, Vol.I; Adjustment During Army Life,* Vol.2, *Combat and Its Aftermath.* Princeton, Princeton Univ., 1949.

Sullivan, Harry Stack: *Modern Conceptions of Psychiatry.* Washington, William Allanson White Psychiatric Foundation, 1945.

Super, Donald E.: *The Psychology of Careers.* New York, Harper, 1957.

Syngg, D., and Combs, A. W.: *Individual Behavior,* New York, Harper & Bros., 1949.

Tarjan, George: The Psychopathic Delinquent and Custodian: Discussion of the Therapeutic Attitudes, AJMD, Vol.53 (Jan., 1949), 477-85.

Tasher, Dean C.: The Criminal Psychotic in an Institutional Setting, JCLC&PS, Vol.50, No.2 (July-Aug., 1959), 163.

Thorpe, Louis P.: *The Psychology of Abnormal Behavior.* New York, Ronald, 1948.

———, & Katz, B.: *The Psychology of Behavior.* New York, Ronald, 1948.

Trice, Harrison M.: Sociological Factors in Association with A.A., JCLC&PS, Vol.48, No.4 (Nov.-Dec., 1957), 378.

Uallinga, Jack: The Probation Officers Role in Psychiatric Cases, JCLC&PS, Vol.50, No.4 (1959-60), 364.

Walker, R. K.: *Psychological Control.* New Haven, Yale Univ. Press, 1955.

Wertham, Frederic: A Psychiatrist Looks at Psychiatry and the Law, BLR, Vol.41, No.3 (1953).

———: *Show of Violence.* New York, Doubleday, 1949.

Whyte, Wm. F.: *Street Corner Society.* Chicago, Univ. of Chicago Press, 1945.

Winokur, G.: Brainwashing a Social Phenomenon of Our Time, HO, Vol.13 (1955).

Wolfgang, Marvin E., Savitz, Leonard, and Johnson, Norman (eds.): *The Sociology of Crime and Delinquency.* New York, Wiley, 1962.

Wortis, J.: Some Recent Developments in Soviet Psychiatry, AJPSY, Vol.109 (1953).

Zeichner, Irving B.: Hypnosis, L&O, Vol.9 (July, 1961).

Zunno, Frank A.: A Police Officer Discusses Some Social Problems, POLICE, Vol.8, No.2 (Nov.-Dec., 1963), 16-18.

PERIODICALS

AA	Applied Anthropology
ABAJ	American Bar Association Journal
AC	American City
ACJ	Alabama Correctional Journal
ACSR	American Catholic Sociological Review
AER	American Economic Review
AHR	The American Historical Review
AJC	American Journal of Correction
AJMD	American Journal of Mental Deficiency
AJMS	The American Journal of the Medical Sciences
AJO	American Journal of Orthopsychiatry
AJP	American Journal of Psychology
AJPHAR	American Journal of Pharmacy
AJPSY	American Journal of Psychiatry
AJS	American Journal of Sociology
AKD	Alpha Kappa Delton
AL	Alabama Lawyer
AM	Atlantic Monthly
AMGMT	Advanced Management
AMJ	Alabama Municipal Journal
AP	Archives of Psychology
APSR	American Political Science Review
AR	American Review
ASR	American Sociological Review
ASS	Alcohol, Science & Society
BJD	British Journal on Delinquency
BJMP	British Journal on Medical Psychology
BLR	Buffalo Law Review
BMC	Bulletin of the Menninger Clinic
BN	Bulletin on Narcotics
BNASSP	The Bulletin, National Assoc. of Secondary School Principals
BNSCP	The British Narcotic System and the Clinic Plan
BNYAM	Bulletin of the New York Academy of Medicine

BULR	Boston University Law Review
CAL.LR	California Law Review
CBBMR	Conference Board Business Management Record
CBJ & CONNBJ	Connecticut Bar Journal
CC	Contemporary Correction
C&C	Case & Comment
CD	Child Development
C&D	Crime and Delinquency
CDSP	Current Digest of the Soviet Press
CE	Correctional Education
CHICAGO DAILY NEWS	Chicago Daily News
CHILDREN	Children
CJ	Criminal Justice
CJC	Canadian Journal of Corrections
CJCP	California Journal of Clinical Psychology
CL	Country Life
CLEVELAND PLAIN DEALER	The Plain Dealer (Cleveland)
CLQ	Cornell Law Quarterly
CLR	Criminal Law Review
CLT	Current Legal Thought
CM	California Medical
COL.LR	Columbia Law Review
COMMENTARY	Commentary
CONNLR	Connecticut Law Review
CORRECTION	Correction
COSMOPOLITAN	Cosmopolitan
CP	Comprehensive Psychiatry
CPM	Comparative Psychology Monographs
CPO	California Peace Officer
CPR	Criminal Police Review
CR	Correctional Review
CS	Child Study
CULR	Catholic University Law Review
CYAQ	California Youth Authority Quarterly
DELINQUENCY	Delinquency
DETROIT NEWS	Detroit News
DIC	Dogs in Canada
DLJ	Duke Law Journal
DPLR	DePaul Law Review
EC	Exceptional Child

ECONOMIST	Economist
ECRIM	Excerpta Criminologica
EHR	English Historical Review
ERB	Educational Research Bulletin
ERR	Editorial Research Reports
ESJ	Elementary School Journal
ESS	Encylopedia of the Social Sciences
FBILEB	FBI Law Enforcement Bulletin
FD	Family Development
FLR	Fordham Law Review
FOCUS	Focus
FORTUNE	Fortune
FP	Federal Probation
FP&IM	Finger Print & Identification Magazine
FSH	Family Service Highlights
FSSSB	Friend's Social Service Series Bulletin
FW	Family Weekly
GALAXY	Galaxy Magazine
GG	Good Government
HAB	Harvard Alumni Bulletin
HARPER'S	Harper's Magazine
HB	Human Biology
HBR	Harvard Business Review
HER	Harvard Educational Review
HJL	Harvard Journal on Legislation
HLR	Harvard Law Review
HLSB	Harvard Law School Bulletin
HO	Human Organization
HR	Human Relations
HRBP	Highway Research Board Proceedings
HSJ	High School Journal
IAC	International Annals of Criminology
IAVE	Industrial Arts and Vocational Education
ICPR	International Criminal Police Review
IE	Illinois Education
IJE	International Journal of Ethics
IJP	International Journal of Psychoanalysis
IJSP	International Journal of Social Psychology
ILJ	Indiana Law Journal
ILRR	Industrial & Labor Relations Review
IRCP	International Review of Criminal Policy

IS	Industrial Security
JAJ	Jail Association Journal
JAJS	Journal of the American Judicature Society
JAMA	Journal of the American Medical Association
JAP	Journal of Abnormal Psychology
JASA	Journal of American Statistical Association
JA&SP	Journal of Abnormal & Social Psychology
JCD	Journal of Chronic Diseases
JCE	Journal of Correctional Education
JCEP	Journal of Clinical & Experimental Psychopathology
JCL&C	Journal of Criminal Law and Criminology
JCLC&PS	Journal of Criminal Law, Criminology and Police Science
JCLIN.PSY	Journal of Clinical Psychopathology
JCP	Journal of Consulting Psychology
JCRI.PSY	Journal of Criminal Psychology
JE	Journal of Education
JES	Journal of Educational Society
JFS	Journal of Forensic Science
JGP	Journal of Genetic Psychology
JICJ	Journal of the International Committee of Jurists
JJA	Journal of Jurisprudence Association
JJR	Journal of Juvenile Research
JLE	Journal of Legal Education
JMAG	Journal of the Medical Association of Georgia
JNE	Journal of Negro Education
JN&MD	Journal of Nervous & Mental Disease
JP	Journal of Psychology
JPA&IR	Journal of Personnel Administration & Industrial Relations
JPE	Journal of Political Economy
JPET	Journal of Pharmacology & Experimental Theory
J.PHIL	Journal of Philosophy
JPL	Journal of Public Law
JRSS	Journal of the Royal Statistical Society
JSH	Journal of Social Hygiene
JSI	Journal of Social Issues
JSP	Journal of Social Psychology

JSSL	Journal of the Statistical Society of London
JST	Journal of Social Therapy
KLJ	Kentucky Law Journal
KYOTO LAW REVIEW	Kyoto Law Review
LAR	Legal Aid Review
L&CP	Law & Contemporary Problems
LD	Literary Digest
LE	Law Enforcement
LIFE	Life
LLJ	Labor Law Journal
LLR	Labor Relations Reporter
L&O	Law and Order
LOOK	Look
LQR	Law Quarterly Review
MASSLQ	Massachusetts Law Quarterly
MC CALLS	Mc Calls
M&FL	Marriage & Family Living
MH	Mental Hygiene
MICHLR	Michigan Law Review
MLQ	Miami Law Quarterly
MLR	Minnesota Law Review
MLS	Michigan Law Studies
MMFQ	Milbank Memorial Fund Quarterly
MMR	Michigan Municipal Review
MOLR	Monthly Labor Review
MOPJ	Missouri Police Journal
MPJ	Michigan Police Journal
MS	Midwest Sociologist
MT	Medical Times
NAR	North American Review
NARCOTICS	Narcotics
NATB	Nations Business
NB	News Bulletin
NEWSWEEK	Newsweek
NEW YORK TIMES MAGAZINE	New York Times Magazine
NGM	National Geographic Magazine
NMR	National Monthly Review
NPPAJ	National Probation & Parole Association Journal
NPPAY	National Probation & Parole Association Yearbook

NC	Nervous Child
NCSW	National Conference Social Work
NR	New Republic
NS	New Statesmen
NSSEY	National Society for Study of Education Yearbook
NULR	Northwestern University Law Review
NY	New Yorker
NULJ	New York Law Journal
NYSJM	New York State Journal of Medicine
NYULR	New York University Law Review
ODS	Official Detective Stories
OG	On Guard
OH&LS	Oxford Historical & Literary Studies
OWV	Ohio Women Voter
PA	Personnel Administration
PAJ	Photo Art Journal
PAN	Policeman's Association News
PAPA	Proceedings of the American Prison Association
PAR	Public Administration Review
PASANS	Publication of the American Statistical Association, New Series
PB	Psychological Bulletin
PCN	Police Chiefs News
PDK	Phi Delta Kappan
PERJ	Personnel Journal
PERSONNEL	Personnel
P&GJ	Personnel & Guidance Journal
PHM	Public Health Monograph
PJ	Prison Journal
PM	Psychological Monograph
PMEC	Popular Mechanics
PMGMT	Public Management
PMR	Police Management Review
POLICE	Police
POQ	Public Opinion Quarterly
POST.M	Postgraduate Medicine
PP	Public Policy
PPR	Public Personnel Review
PROBATION	Probation

PQ	Psychoanalytic Quarterly
PR	Psychological Review
PRISON	Prison
PS	Popular Science Monthly
PSQ	Political Science Quarterly
PSR	Pacific Social Review
PSYCHIATRY	Psychiatry
PSY.Q	Psychiatric Quarterly
PSY.R	Psychoanalytic Review
PW	Prison World
QJSA	Quarterly Journal of Studies on Alcohol
QRHEAN	Quarterly Review of Higher Education Among Negroes
RABCNY	Record of the Association of the Bar of the City of New York
RBNEA	Research Bulletin of the National Education Association
RE	Religious Education
READER'S DIGEST	Reader's Digest
RLR	Rutgers Law Review
RMLR	Rocky Mountain Law Review
RMSUJAM	Red Man: St. John's University Alumni Magazine
ROR	Review of Reviews
RS	Rural Sociology
SA	Social Action
SAS	The Scientific American Supplement
SATURDAY EVENING POST	Saturday Evening Post
SATURDAY REVIEW OF LITERATURE	Saturday Review
SC	Social Casework
SCI.A	Scientific American
SCLR	Southern California Law Review
SCSSW	Smith College Studies in Social Work
SEC.W	Security World
SE&SCD	Scientific Evidence & Scientific Crime Detection—Wm. S. Hein Co., Buffalo, N.Y.
SF	Social Forces
SG	Survey Graphic
SLJ	Southwestern Law Journal
SLR	Syracuse Law Review

SLULJ	St. Louis University Law Journal
SM	Supervisory Management
SOC.R	Sociological Review
SP	Social Problems
SR	Soviet Review
S&S	School & Society
S&SR	Sociology & Social Research
SSR	Social Service Review
SSREV	Social Science Review
SSSQ	Southwestern Social Science Quarterly
STAN.LR	Stanford Law Review
STATISTICAL BULLETIN	Statistical Bulletin
STLJ	South Texas Law Journal
SURVEY	Survey
SW	Social Work
SWY	Social Work Yearbook
TAC	The American City
TAJ	The Arbitration Journal
TBJPA	The British Journal Photographic Almanac
TC	The Child
TCAM	The Camera
TCM	The Century Magazine
TDJ	Training Directors Journal
TDR	Traffic Digest Review
TE	Traffic Engineering
TEXASPJ	Texas Police Journal
TF	The Family
TH	Today's Health
THE ANNALS	The Annals of the American Academy of Political and Social Science
THE ILLUSTRATED LONDON NEWS	The Illustrated London News
THE SHERIFF	The Sheriff
TLQ	Temple Law Quarterly
TLR	Tulane Law Review
TM	Travel Magazine
TMUN	The Municipality
TN	The Nation
TNE	The New Era
TPC	The Police Chief
TPJ	The Police Journal (England)

TPQ	The Political Quarterly
TPY	The Police Yearbook (IACP ANNUAL)
TQ	Traffic Quarterly
TRUE	True
TTLG	The Trial Lawyer's Guide
TULQ	Temple University Law Quarterly
UCLALR	U.C.L.A. Law Review
UKCLR	University of Kansas City Law Review
ULR	Utah Law Review
UPLR	University of Pennsylvania Law Review
USN&WR	U.S. News & World Report
VALR	Virginia Law Review
VLR	Vanderbilt Law Review
VSD	Vital Speeches of the Day
VLWDC	Virginia Law Weekly Dicta Compilation
WASHINGTON POST	Washington Post
WCM	Western City Magazine
WHC	Woman's Home Companion
WLR	Washburn Law Review
WMH	World Mental Health
WRLR	Western Reserve Law Review
YLJ	Yale Law Journal
YLR	Yale Law Review
YR	Yale Review

PUBLISHERS

Abelard-Schuman Ltd.
6 W. 57th St.
New York, New York

Ace Books, Inc.
1120 Avenue of the Americas
New York, New York

Alabama University
University, Alabama

Aldine Publishing Co.
64 E. Van Buren St.
Chicago, Illinois

Alicat Bookshop Press
287 S. Broadway
Yonkers, New York

Ian Allan, Ltd.
London, England

The Wm. Allanson White
Psychiatric Foundation
Washington, D.C.

Allen, George and Unwin, Ltd.
Museum St.
London, England

Allyn & Bacon, Inc.
150 Tremont St.
Boston, Massachusetts

American Academy of Political
    & Social Science
3937 Chestnut St.
Philadelphia, Pennsylvania

American Bar Foundation
1155 E. 60th St.
Chicago, Illinois

American College of Surgeons
40 E. Eric St.
Chicago, Illinois

American Correctional Assoc.
135 E. 15th St.
New York, New York

The American Council on Education
1785 Massachusetts Ave., N.W.
Washington, D.C.

American Law Book Co.
272 Flatbush Ave., E. Brooklyn
Brooklyn, New York

American Law Institute
101 N. 33rd St.
Philadelphia, Pennsylvania

American Management Assoc., Inc.
135 W. 50th St.
New York, New York

American Medical Assoc.
535 N. Dearborn St.
Chicago, Illinois

The American Press Publication, Inc.
282 7th Ave.
New York, New York

The American Prison Assoc., Central Office
135 E. 15th St.
New York, New York

The American Social Health Assoc., Inc.
1790 Broadway
New York, New York

American Technical Society
850 E. 58th St.
Chicago, Illinois

The American University Press
Washington, D.C.

Ames and Rollinson
50 Church St.
New York, New York

Ampersand Press, Inc.
135 E. 56th St.
New York, New York

Amphoto
(American Photographic Book Publishing
    Co., Inc.)
915 Broadway
New York, New York

Anchor Books
Garden City, New York

The W. H. Anderson Co.
646 Main St.
Cincinnati, Ohio

Angus and Robertson Ltd.
London, England

The Antioch Press
Yellow Springs, Ohio

Appleton-Century-Crofts
440 Park Ave. S.
New York, New York

Arco Publishing Co., Inc.
219 Park Avenue S.
New York, New York

The Associated Press
50 Rockefeller Plaza
New York, New York

Association Press
291 Broadway
New York, New York

Atheneum Publishers
162 E. 38th St.
New York, New York

Avon Books
959 8th Ave.
New York, New York

Baker, Voorhis and Co., Inc.
30 Smith Ave.
Mount Kisco, New York

Ballantine Books, Inc.
101 5th Ave.
New York, New York

Bancroft-Whitney Co.
301 Brannan St.
San Francisco, California

Banks and Co.
205 E. 42nd St.
New York, New York

Bantam Books, Inc.
271 Madison Ave.
New York, New York

Barnes and Noble, Inc.
105 5th Ave.
New York, New York

Basic Books, Inc., Publishers
404 Park Ave. S.
New York, New York

Beacon Press
25 Beacon St.
Boston, Massachusetts

Belmont Books
66 Leonard St.
New York, New York

Berkley Publishing Corp.
15 E. 26th St.
New York, New York

A. and C. Black, Ltd.
London, England

The Blakiston Co.
1012 Walnut St.
Philadelphia, Pennsylvania

W. Blackwood and Sons
London, England

Blue Ribbon Printing Corp.
21 Hudson
New York, New York

Clark Boardman Co., Ltd.
22 Park Place
New York, New York

The Bobbs-Merrill Co., Inc.
4300 W. 62nd St.
Indianapolis, Indiana

The Book Co., Ltd.
Calcutta, India

R. R. Bowker Co.
1180 Avenue of the Americas
New York, New York

Boyd Printing Co., Inc.
372 Broadway
Albany, New York

Bradford Printing Service, Inc.
8 E. 12th St.
New York, New York

Brentano's Inc.
586 5th Ave.
New York, New York

British Institute of Management
London, England

The Brookings Institution
1775 Massachusetts Ave., N.W.
Washington, D.C.

Brown and Ferguson, Ltd.
Glasgow, Scotland

William C. Brown Co., Publishers
135 S. Locust St.
Dubuque, Iowa

The Bruce Publishing Co.
400 N. Broadway
Milwaukee, Wisconsin

Bureau of National Affairs (BNA, Inc.)
1231 24th St. N.W.
Washington, D.C.

Burns, Oates and Washburn
London, England

Butterworths Publishing Co., Ltd.
88 Kingsway
London, W.C. 2, England

Cadillac Publishing Co.
220 5th Ave.
New York, New York

California State Department of Corrections
Sacramento, California

California State Printing Office
Sacramento, California

Callaghan and Co.
6141 N. Cicero Ave.
Chicago, Illinois

Carnegie Foundation for the Advancement
    of Teaching
589 5th Ave.
New York, New York

The Carswell Co., Ltd.
145 Adelaide St. W.
Toronto, Canada

Cassell and Co., Ltd.
London, England

Castle Books Publishers
352 Park Ave. S.
New York, New York

The Catholic University of America Press
620 Michigan Ave., N.E.
Washington, D.C.

Census Bureau
Washington, D.C.

Chandler Publishing Co.
124 Spear St.
San Francisco, California

Chapman and Hall, Ltd.
37 Essex St.
London, W.C. 2, England

Charter Books
 (Bobbs-Merrill Co., Inc.)
4300 W. 62nd St.
Indianapolis, Indiana

Chatto and Windus
London, England

Chilton Books
525 Locust St.
Philadelphia, Pennsylvania

J. and A. Churchill, Ltd.
104 Gloucester Place
London, W. 1, England

Citadel Press
222 Park Ave. S.
New York, New York

Civil Service Commission
Chicago, Illinois

Civil Service Publishing Corp.
132 Livingston St.
Brooklyn, New York

Clarendon Press
Oxford, England

Clark University
Worcester, Massachusetts

Edmond Cloutier, Co.
Ottawa, Canada

Collier Books
60 5th Ave.
New York, New York

Columbia University Press
2960 Broadway
New York, New York

The Commercial Press Ltd.
Shanghai, China

The Commonwealth Fund
1 E. 57th St.
New York, New York

Comstock Publishing Associates
124 Roberts Place
Ithaca, New York

T. G. Cooke
1920 Sunnyside Ave.
Chicago, Illinois

Wm. Copp Publishers
72 W. 45th St.
New York, New York

Cornell University Press
124 Roberts Place
Ithaca, New York

Cornerstone Library, Inc.
630 5th Ave.
New York, New York

The Council of State Governments
1313 E. 60th St.
Chicago, Illinois

Coward-McCann, Inc.
2 W. 45th St.
New York, New York

Crest and Premier Books
67 W. 44th St.
New York, New York

Thomas Y. Crowell and Co.
201 Park Ave. S.
New York, New York

Crown Publishers, Inc.
419 Park Ave. S.
New York, New York

F. A. Davis Co.
1914-16 Cherry St.
Philadelphia, Pennsylvania

The John Day Co., Inc.
62 W. 45th St.
New York, New York

Dell Publishing Co., Inc.
750 3rd Ave.
New York, New York

Dennis and Co.
251 Main St.
Buffalo, New York

Department of Correction
100 Centre
New York, New York

The Detroit News
615 Lafayette Blvd.
Detroit, Michigan

Devin-Adair Co.
23 E. 26th St.
New York, New York

Dial Press, Inc.
750 3rd Ave.
New York, New York

Dodd Mead and Co.
432 Park Ave. S.
New York, New York

Dorsey Press
Homewood, Illinois

Doubleday and Co., Inc.
Garden City, New York

Dover Publications, Inc.
180 Varick St.
New York, New York

Duckworth and Co.
London, England

Duell, Sloan & Pearce
60 E. 42nd St.
New York, New York

Duke University Press
Box 6697, College Station
Durham, North Carolina

E. P. Dutton and Co., Inc.
201 Park Ave. S.
New York, New York

Eastman Kodak Co.
Rochester, New York

Edinburgh University Press
London, England

Elliott Service Co.
30 McOuston Parkway N.
Mt. Vernon, New York

The Essex Press
Newark, New Jersey

Faber & Faber
London, England

Fallon Press, Inc.
245 7th Ave.
New York, New York

Farrar, Straus and Giroux, Inc.
19 Union Sq. W.
New York, New York

Fawcett World Library: Crest,
    Goldmedal and Premier Books
67 W. 44th St.
New York, New York

Federal Bureau of Investigation
U.S. Department of Justice
Washington 25, D.C.

Federal Bureau of Prisons
Washington, D.C.

Federal Prisons Ind. Inc. Press
Leavenworth, Kansas

Fordham University Press
441 E. Fordham Rd.
Bronx, New York

Foreign Language Publishing House
Moscow, U.S.S.R.

The Foundation for Economic Education, Inc.
30 S. Broadway, Irvington
New York, New York

Foundation for Research on Human Behavior
Ann Arbor, Michigan

The Foundation Press, Inc.
268 Flatbush Ave. Ext.
Brooklyn, New York

Free Press of Glencoe, Inc.
60 5th Ave.
New York, New York

Freedom House, Inc.
20 W. 40th St.
New York, New York

Friendship Press
475 Riverside Dr.
New York, New York

Fund for the Republic, Inc.
133 E. 54th St.
New York, New York

Funk & Wagnalls Co., Inc.
360 Lexington Ave.
New York, New York

Wilfred Funk Inc., Publishers
360 Lexington Ave.
New York, New York

Galaxy Publishing Corp.
421 Hudson
New York, New York

Ginn and Co.
Statler Bldg., Back Bay
P.O. Box 191
Boston, Massachusetts

G.E.C. Gods
Copenhagen, Denmark
Gollancz
London, England

W. Green Publishers, Ltd.
Glasgow, Scotland

Gresham Publishing Co.
London, England

Greystone Corp.
100 Avenue of the Americas
New York, New York

Griffin, Charles and Co. Ltd.
42 Drury Lane
London, W.C. 2, England

Grosset and Dunlap, Inc.
51 Madison Ave.
New York, New York

Grove Press, Inc.
80 University Place
New York, New York

Grune and Stratton, Inc.
381 Park Ave. S.
New York, New York

The Gun Digest Co.
Chicago, Illinois

Harcourt, Brace and World, Inc.
757 3rd Ave.
New York, New York

Harper and Row Publishers
49 E. 33rd St.
New York, New York

Harrar Press, Ltd.
London, England

L. S. Hart, State Printer
Harrisburg, Pennsylvania

Harvard University Press
79 Garden St.
Cambridge, Massachusetts

The Haynes Foundation
Los Angeles, California

D. C. Heath and Co.
285 Columbus Ave.
Boston, Massachusetts

Heinemann, Ltd.
London, England

Helicon Press, Inc.
1120 N. Calvert St.
Baltimore, Maryland

Hibbert Printing Co.
271 Madison Ave.
New York, New York

Hill and Wang, Inc.
141 5th Ave.
New York, New York

Sidney Hillman Foundation, Inc.
15 Union Sq.
New York, New York

Her Majesty's Stationery Office
Director of Publications
421 Oxford St.
London, England

Hodge Press, Ltd.
London, England

Paul B. Hoeber, Inc., Publishers
49 E. 33rd St.
New York, New York

Henry Holt and Co., Publishers
383 Madison Ave.
New York, New York

Holt, Rinehart and Winston, Inc.
383 Madison Ave.
New York, New York

The Johns Hopkins Press
Baltimore, Maryland

Horizon Press
156 5th Ave.
New York, New York

Houghton Mifflin Co.
2 Park St.
Boston, Massachusetts

John Howard Association
Chicago, Illinois

Howell Book House, Inc.
845 3rd Ave.
New York, New York

B. W. Huebsch, Publishers
625 Madison Ave.
New York, New York

Humanities Press
303 Park Ave. S.
New York, New York

Illinois Assoc. for Criminal Justice
Chicago, Illinois

Industrial Press
93 Worth St.
New York, New York

Industrial Relations Center
University of Chicago
Chicago, Illinois

Infantry Journal Press
1115 17th St., N.W.
Washington 6, D.C.

Institute of Judicial Administration
40 Washington Sq. S.
New York, New York

Institute of Public Administration
55 W. 44th St.
New York, New York

Institute of Traffic Engineers
National Conservation Bureau
Washington, D.C.

International Association of Chiefs of Police
1319 18th St., N.W.
Washington, D.C.

International City Managers' Assoc.
1313 E. 60th St.
Chicago, Illinois

International Institute of Administrative Sciences
Brussels, Belgium

International Publishers Co., Inc.
381 Park Ave. S.
New York, New York

International Universities Press, Inc.
227 W. 13th St.
New York, New York

Interscience Publishers, Inc.
605 3rd Ave.
New York, New York

Richard D. Irwin, Inc.
1818 Ridge Rd.
Homewood, Illinois

Johnson, Ltd.
London, England

Julian Press, Inc.
119 5th Ave.
New York, New York

Kegan, Paul, Trench, Trubner and Co., Ltd.
London, England

Key Publishing Co.
817 Broadway
New York, New York

Alfred A. Knopf, Inc.
501 Madison Ave.
New York, New York

John Lane Co.
London, England

Lawyer's Co-operative Publishing Co., The
Aqueduct Bldg.
Rochester, New York

Lea and Febiger
600 S. Washington Sq.
Philadelphia, Pennsylvania

Legal Book Store
1220 S. Broadway
Los Angeles, California

Levin and Munkogaard
Copenhagen, Denmark

The Linacre Press, Inc.
1708 Massachusetts Ave., N.W.
Washington 6, D.C.

Lincoln Williams and Co., Ltd.
London, England

J. B. Lippincott Co.
E. Washington Sq.
Philadelphia, Pennsylvania

Little, Brown and Co.
34 Beacon St.
Boston, Massachusetts

Littlefield, Adams & Co.
81 Adams Dr.
Totowa, New Jersey

Liveright Publishing Corp.
386 Park Ave.
New York, New York

London University Press,
London, England

J. B. Lyon
(Williams Press Inc.)
1 Park Ave.
New York, New York

McGraw-Hill Book Co.,
330 W. 42nd St.
New York, New York

David McKay Co., Inc.
750 3rd Ave.
New York, New York

McKnight & McKnight Publishing Co.
U.S. Rte. 66 at Towanda Ave.
Bloomington, Illinois

The Macaulay Publishers
352 Park Ave. S.
New York, New York

Macfadden Publications, Inc.
205 E. 42nd St.
New York, New York

The Macmillan Co.
60 5th Ave.
New York, New York

Management Pub. Trust, Ltd.
London, England

Marquette University Press
1131 W. Wisconsin Ave.
Milwaukee, Wisconsin

Matthew Bender & Co., Inc.
205 E. 42nd St.
New York, New York

Chas. Mendel Publishing Co.
Paris, France

Meridian Books
119 W. 57th St.
New York, New York

Chas. E. Merrill Books, Inc.
1300 Alum Creek Dr.
Columbus, Ohio

Methuen and Co., Ltd.
36 Essex St., Strand
London, W.C. 2, England

Michie Casebook Corp.
Charlottesville, Virginia

Michigan State University Press
Box 550
East Lansing, Michigan

The Military Service Publishing Co.
Telegraph Press Building
Harrisburg, Pennsylvania

Minton, Balch and Co., Publishers
200 Madison Ave.
New York, New York

Monarch Press, Inc.
387 Park Ave. S.
New York, New York

Wm. Morrow Co., Inc.
425 Park Ave. S.
New York, New York

The C. V. Mosby Co.
3207 Washington Blvd.
St. Louis, Missouri

J. Murray Co., Ltd.
London, England

National Automobile Theft Bureau
1107 Mercantile Bldg.
Dallas, Texas

National Foremen's Institute
Bureau of Business Practice
(Formerly National Foremen's Institute)
24 Rope Ferry Rd.
Waterford, Conn.

National Industrial Conference Board
845 3rd Ave.
New York, New York

The National Municipal League
47 E. 68th St.
New York, New York

National Probation Association
Washington, D.C.

Thomas Nelson and Sons
18 E. 41st St.
New York, New York

New American Library of World Literature, Inc.
301 Avenue of the Americas
New York, New York

New York City Youth Board
79 Madison Ave.
New York, New York

New York University of Law
Washington Sq.
New York, New York

Nordisk—Rotogravyr
Stockholm, Sweden

North Holland Publishing Co.
Amsterdam, Holland

The Northwestern University Traffic Institute
1735 Benson
Evanston, Illinois

W. W. Norton and Co., Inc.
55 5th Ave.
New York, New York

Oceana Publications, Inc.
40 Cedar St.
Dobbs Ferry, New York

Odhams and Co., Ltd.
London, England

Odyssey Press, Inc.
55 5th Ave.
New York, New York

Oliver and Boyd, Ltd.
London, England

Orient Longmans
Bombay, India

Albert S. Osborn
233 Broadway
New York, New York

Outlet Book Co.
419 Park S.
New York, New York

Oxford University Press, Inc.
417 5th Ave.
New York, New York

Pacific Books
Box 558
Palo Alto, California

Pageant Press, Inc.
101 5th Ave.
New York, New York

Park College Press
Parkville, Missouri

Parsons Co.
London, England

Stanley Paul
London, England

Pelican Publishing Co.
Baltimore, Maryland

Penguin Publishing Co.
3300 Clipper Mill Rd.
Baltimore, Maryland

Penns Valley Publishers, Inc.
State College, Pennsylvania

Pennsylvania Prison Assoc.
Philadelphia, Pennsylvania

Philosophical Library, Inc.
15 E. 40th St.
New York, New York

Sir Isaac Pitman, Ltd.
Toronto, Ont., Canada

The Plain Dealer
1801 Superior Ave.
Cleveland, Ohio

Plenum Press
227 W. 17th St.
New York, New York

Pocket Books, Inc.
630 5th Ave.
New York, New York

The Police Chronicle
53 Fleet St.
London, E.C. 4, England

Police Science Press
Cocoa Beach, Florida

Popular Library, Inc.
355 Lexington Ave.
New York, New York

Frederick A. Praeger, Inc.
111 4th St.
New York, New York

Prentice-Hall, Inc.
Englewood Cliffs, New Jersey

Princeton University Press
Princeton, New Jersey

The Psychological Corp.
304 E. 45th St.
New York, New York

Public Administration Service
1313 E. 60th St.
Chicago, Illinois

Public Affairs Printing Office
Washington, D.C.

G. P. Putnam's Sons
200 Madison Ave.
New York, New York

Pyramid Publications, Inc.
444 Madison Ave.
New York, New York

Random House, Inc.
457 Madison Ave.
New York, New York

Receiver for the Metropolitan Police District
New Scotland Yard
London, S.W. 1, England

Henry Regnery Co.
114 W. Illinois St.
Chicago, Illinois

Reinhold Publishing Corp.
430 Park Ave.
New York, New York

Remsen Press
212 5th Ave.
New York, New York

Retail Distributors Council
229 Park Ave. S.
New York, New York

Reynal and Co., Inc.
221 E. 49th St.
New York, New York

Riverside Press
Cambridge, Massachusetts

Riviere Press
Paris, France

The Ronald Press Co.
15th E. 26th St.
New York, New York

Rough Notes Co., Inc.
1142 N. Meridian St.
Indianapolis, Indiana

George Routledge and Sons, Ltd.
Broadway House
68-74 Carter Lane
London, E.C., England

Row, Peterson and Co.
1911 Ridge Ave.
Evanston, Illinois

Roxburghe Press
London, England

Russell Sage Foundation
230 Park Ave.
New York, New York

Rutgers University Press
30 College Ave.
New Brunswick, New Jersey

Rutledge Books
17 E. 45th St.
New York, New York

Ryerson Press
299 Queen St., W.
Toronto 2 B., Canada

St. Martin's Press, Inc.
175 5th Ave.
New York, New York

W. B. Saunders Co.
W. Washington Sq.
Philadelphia, Pennsylvania

Science Editions, Inc.
605 3rd Ave.
New York, New York

Scientific American, Inc.
415 Madison Ave.
New York, New York

Scott, Foresman and Co.
433 E. Erie St.
Chicago, Illinois

Charles Scribner's Sons
597 5th Ave.
New York, New York

The Seabury Press, Inc.
815 2nd Ave.
New York, New York

Seeley and Co., Ltd.
London, England

Sheed and Ward
64 University Place
New York, New York

Signet Books Publishers
501 Madison Ave.
New York, New York

Simmons-Boardman Publishing Corp.
30 Church St.
New York, New York

Simon and Schuster, Inc.
630 5th Ave.
Rockefeller Center
New York, New York

Skeffington and Son, Ltd.
London, England

Small Arms Technical Publishing Co.
Plantersville, South Carolina

Smith, Elder and Co.
London, England

Turner E. Smith and Co.
680 Forrest Rd., N.E.
Atlanta, Georgia

Sociological Press
Hanover, Maine

South-Western Publishing Co.
5101 Madison Rd.
Cincinnati, Ohio

Spring Books
London, England

Stackpole Books
The Stackpole Co.
Cameron and Kelker Sts.
Harrisburg, Pennsylvania

Stanford University Press
Stanford, California

State of Illinois Printing Office
Springfield, Illinois

State Publishing House
Moscow, U.S.S.R.

Sterling Publishing Co., Inc.
419 Park Ave. S.
New York, New York

Steven's Publishing Co., Ltd.
London, England

Stoeger Arms Corp.
55 Ruta Court
S. Hackensack, New Jersey

Stromberg Aktielbolg
Stockholm, Sweden

Sweet and Maxwell
11 New Fetter Lane
London, E.C. 4, England

The Tax Foundation, Inc.
50 Rockefeller Plaza
New York, New York

Charles C Thomas, Publisher
301-327 E. Lawrence Ave.
Springfield, Illinois

Thomas Law Book Co.
1909 Washington Ave.
St. Louis, Missouri

Thor Publishing Co.
Box 27608
Los Angeles, California

Torchstream Publishing Ltd.
London, England

Triangle Press
9 Murray
New York, New York

Trident Press, Inc.
630 5th Ave.
New York, New York

Tudor Publishing Co.
221 Park Ave. S.
New York, New York

Twayne Publishers, Inc.
31 Union Sq.
New York, New York

T. Union Co.
London, England

U.N. Department of Economics and Social Affairs
New York, New York

U.S. Bureau of Prisons
Washington, D.C.

U.S. Government Printing Office
N. Capitol & H St., N.W.
Washington, D.C.

University of California Press
Bureau of Public Administration
Berkeley, California

University of Chicago Press
5720 Ellis Ave.
Chicago, Illinois

University of Cincinnati
Cincinnati, Ohio

University of Georgia Press
Athens, Georgia

University of Iowa Press
Iowa City, Iowa

The University Press
Cambridge, England

Vanguard Press, Inc.
424 Madison Ave.
New York, New York

D. Van Nostrand Co., Inc.
120 Alexander St.
Princeton, New Jersey

The Viking Press, Inc.
625 Madison Ave.
New York, New York

Vintage Books
33 W. 60th St.
New York, New York

Harr Wagner Publishing Co.
609 Mission St.
San Francisco, California

University of Kentucky Press
McVey Hall, University of Kentucky
Lexington, Kentucky

The University of Michigan Press
Ann Arbor, Michigan

University of Oklahoma Press
Norman, Oklahoma

University of Pennsylvania Press
3729 Spruce St.
Philadelphia, Pennsylvania

University of Texas Press
Box 7819
University Station
Austin, Texas

University Tutorial Press
London, England

University of Wisconsin Press
Box 1379
Madison, Wisconsin

Ives Washburn, Inc.
750 3rd Ave.
New York, New York

Watt Publishing Co.
850 3rd Ave.
New York, New York

West Publishing Co.
50 W. Kellogg Blvd.
St. Paul, Minnesota

The Westminster Press
Witherspoon Bldg.
Philadelphia, Pennsylvania

Whitman Publishing Co.
1220 Mound Ave.
Racine, Wisconsin

Whittlesey House
330 W. 42nd St.
New York, New York

John Wiley and Sons, Inc.
605 3rd Ave.
New York, New York

William-Frederick Press
55 E. 86th St.
New York, New York

The Williams and Wilkins Co.
428 E. Preston St.
Baltimore, Maryland

H. W. Wilson Co.
950 University Ave.
Bronx, New York

Yale University Press
149 York St.
New Haven, Connecticut

Ziff-Davis Publishing Co.
1 Park Ave.
New York, New York